PREVIOUS YEARS' SOLVED PAPERS

LAW

For UGC-NET/JRF

Paper I, II and III

Atlantic Research Division

PUBLISHERS & DISTRIBUTORS (P) LTD

Published by
ATLANTIC
PUBLISHERS & DISTRIBUTORS (P) LTD
7/22, Ansari Road, Darya Ganj,
New Delhi-110002
Phones : +91-11-40775252, 23273880, 23275880, 23280451
Fax : +91-11-23285873
Web : www.atlanticbooks.com
E-mail : orders@atlanticbooks.com

Branch Office
5, Nallathambi Street, Wallajah Road,
Chennai-600002
Phones : +91-44-64611085, 32413319
E-mail : chennai@atlanticbooks.com

Printed in India at Nice Printing Press, A-33/3A, Site-IV,
Industrial Area, Sahibabad, Ghaziabad, U.P.

Preface

The University Grants Commission (UGC) conducts National Eligibility Test (NET) on various subjects twice every year, once each in June and December, to determine eligibility for college and university level lectureship and for award of Junior Research Fellowship (JRF), for Indian nationals in order to ensure minimum standards for the entrants in the teaching profession and research.

The book contains previous years' solved papers (objective type questions) on the subject of Law, from June 2005 to December 2015. It covers all three papers (Paper I, II and III). In Paper I (General Paper on Teaching and Research Aptitude), solved papers have been included from December 2005, while in Paper II (Elective), solved papers have been included from June 2005. In Paper III (Core and Elective), solved papers of objective type questions have been included from June 2012, conforming to the existing UGC-NET pattern. In addition, two sets of Mock Tests for Paper I, II and III have been included in the book under Practice Papers. Answers have been given at the end of each set for self-check.

It will be useful for those preparing for UGC-NET/JRF in the subject of Law. It will give them a feel of the type of questions asked in NET in this subject, i.e. Multiple-choice, Matching type, True/False, Assertion-Reasoning type, etc. The papers included in this book will enable the students to judge their own level of competence besides adding to their knowledge. It will also help them revise the important questions in the entire syllabus and enhance their self-confidence. Suggestions for further improvement of the book are, however, welcome.

Atlantic Research Division

Contents

DECEMBER–2005

Note: This paper contains fifty (50) objective type questions, each question carrying two (2) marks. All questions are compulsory.

PAPER–I

1. Team teaching has the potential to develop:
   (a) Competitive spirit
   (b) Cooperation
   (c) The habit of supplementing the teaching of each other
   (d) Highlighting the gaps in each other's teaching

2. Which of the following is the most important characteristic of Open Book Examination system?
   (a) Students become serious.
   (b) It improves attendance in the classroom.
   (c) It reduces examination anxiety amongst students.
   (d) It compels students to think.

3. Which of the following methods of teaching encourages the use of maximum senses?
   (a) Problem-solving method
   (b) Laboratory method
   (c) Self-study method
   (d) Team teaching method

4. Which of the following statements is correct?
   (a) Communicator should have fine senses
   (b) Communicator should have tolerance power
   (c) Communicator should be soft spoken
   (d) Communicator should have good personality

5. An effective teacher is one who can:
   (a) control the class
   (b) give more information in less time
   (c) motivate students to learn
   (d) correct the assignments carefully

6. One of the following is not a quality of researcher:
   (a) Unison with that of which he is in search
   (b) He must be of alert mind
   (c) Keenness in enquiry
   (d) His assertion to outstrip the evidence

7. A satisfactory statistical quantitative method should not possess one of the following qualities:
   (a) Appropriateness (b) Measurability
   (c) Comparability (d) Flexibility

8. Books and records are the primary sources of data in:
   (a) historical research
   (b) participatory research
   (c) clinical research
   (d) laboratory research

9. Which of the following statements is correct?
   (a) Objectives should be pin-pointed
   (b) Objectives can be written in statement or question form
   (c) Another word for problem is variable
   (d) All of the above

10. The important pre-requisites of a researcher in sciences, social sciences and humanities are:

(a) laboratory skills, records, supervisor, topic
(b) Supervisor, topic, critical analysis, patience
(c) archives, supervisor, topic, flexibility in thinking
(d) topic, supervisor, good temperament, pre-conceived notions

Read the following passage and answer the questions 11 to 15:

Knowledge creation in many cases requires creativity and idea generation. This is especially important in generating alternative decision support solutions. Some people believe that an individual's creative ability stems primarily from personality traits such as inventiveness, independence, individuality, enthusiasm, and flexibility. However, several studies have found that creativity is not so much a function of individual traits as was once believed, and that individual creativity can be learned and improved. This understanding has led innovative companies to recognise that the key to fostering creativity may be the development of an idea-nurturing work environment. Idea-generation methods and techniques, to be used by individuals or in groups, are consequently being developed. Manual methods for supporting idea generation, such as brainstorming in a group, can be very successful in certain situations. However, in other situations, such an approach is either not economically feasible or not possible. For example, manual methods in group creativity sessions will not work or will not be effective when : (1) there is no time to conduct a proper idea-generation session; (2) there is a poor facilitator (or no facilitator at all); (3) it is too expensive to conduct an idea-generation session; (4) the subject matter is too sensitive for a face-to-face session; or (5) there are not enough participants, the mix of participants is not optimal, or there is no climate for idea generation. In such cases, computerised idea-generation methods have been tried, with frequent success.

Idea-generation software is designed to help stimulate a single user or a group to produce new ideas, options and choices. The user does all the work, but the software encourages and pushes, something like a personal trainer. Although idea-generation software is still relatively new, there are several packages on the market. Various approaches are used by idea-generating software to increase the flow of ideas to the user. Idea Fisher, for example, has an associate lexicon of the English language that cross-references words and phrases. These associative links, based on analogies and metaphors, make it easy for the user to be fed words related to a given theme. Some software packages use questions to prompt the user towards new, unexplored patterns of thought. This helps users to break out of cyclical thinking patterns, conquer mental blocks, or deal with bouts of procrastination.

11. The author, in this passage has focussed on
(a) knowledge creation
(b) idea-generation
(c) creativity
(d) individual traits

12. Fostering creativity needs an environment of
(a) decision support systems
(b) idea-nurturing
(c) decision support solutions
(d) alternative individual factors

13. Manual methods for the support of idea-generation, in certain occasions,
(a) are alternatively effective
(b) can be less expensive
(c) do not need a facilitator
(d) require a mix of optimal participants

14. Idea-generation software works as if it is a:
(a) stimulant
(b) knowledge package
(c) user-friendly trainer
(d) climate creator

15. Mental blocks, bouts of procrastination and cyclical thinking patterns can be won when:
(a) innovative companies employ electronic thinking methods
(b) idea-generation software prompts questions
(c) manual methods are removed
(d) individuals acquire a neutral attitude towards the software

16. Level C of the effectiveness of communication is defined as:
(a) channel noise
(b) semantic noise
(c) psychological noise
(d) source noise

17. Recording a television programme on a VCR is an example of:
(a) time-shifting
(b) content reference
(c) mechanical clarity
(d) media synchronisation

18. A good communicator is the one who offers to his audience:
(a) plentiful of information
(b) a good amount of statistics
(c) concise proof
(d) repetition of facts

19. The largest number of newspapers in India is published from the state of:
(a) Kerala (b) Maharashtra
(c) West Bengal (d) Uttar Pradesh

20. Insert the missing number:
8 24 12 ? 18 54
(a) 26 (b) 24
(c) 36 (d) 32

21. January 1, 1995 was Sunday. What day of the week lies on January 1, 1996?
(a) Sunday (b) Monday
(c) Saturday (d) None of these

22. The sum of a positive number and its reciprocal is twice the difference of the number and its reciprocal. The number is:
(a) $\sqrt{2}$ (b) $\frac{1}{\sqrt{2}}$
(c) $\sqrt{3}$ (d) $\frac{1}{\sqrt{3}}$

23. In a certain code, ROUNDS is written as RONUDS. How will PLEASE will be written in the same code:
(a) LPAESE (b) PLAESE
(c) LPAEES (d) PLASEE

24. At what time between 5.30 and 6.00 will the hands of a clock be at right angles?
(a) $43\frac{5}{11}$ min. past 5
(b) $43\frac{7}{11}$ min. past 5
(c) 40 min. past 5
(d) 45 min past 5

25. **Statements:** I All students are ambitious
II All ambitious persons are hard working
Conclusions: (i) All students are hard working
(ii) All hardly working people are not ambitious
Which of the following is correct?
(a) Only (i) is correct
(b) Only (ii) is correct
(c) Both (i) and (ii) are correct
(d) Neither (i) nor (ii) is correct

26. **Statement:** Most students are intelligent
Conclusions: (i) Some students are intelligent
(ii) All students are not intelligent

Which of the following is implied?
(a) Only (i) is implied
(b) Only (ii) is implied
(c) Both (i) and (ii) are implied
(d) Neither (i) nor (ii) is implied

27. **Statement:** Most labourers are poor
Conclusions: (i) Some labourers are poor
(ii) All labourers are not poor

Which of the following is implied?
(a) Only (i) is implied
(b) Only (ii) is implied
(c) Both (i) and (ii) are implied
(d) Neither (i) nor (ii) is implied

28. Line access and avoidance of collision are the main functions of:
(a) the CPU
(b) the monitor
(c) network protocols
(d) wide area networks

29. In the hypermedia database, information bits are stored in the form of:
(a) Signals (b) Cubes
(c) Nodes (d) Symbols

30. Communications bandwidth that has the highest capacity and is used by microwave, cable and fibre optics lines is known as:
(a) Hyper-link (b) Broadband
(c) Bus width (d) Carrier wave

31. An electronic bill board that has a short text or graphical advertising message is referred to as:
(a) Bulletin (b) Strap
(c) Bridge line (d) Banner

32. Which of the following is not the characteristic of a computer?
(a) Computer is an electrical machine
(b) Computer cannot think of its own
(c) Computer processes information error free
(d) Computer can hold data for any length of time

33. Bitumen is obtained from:
(a) Forests and plants
(b) Kerosene oil
(c) Crude oil
(d) Underground mines

34. Malaria is caused by:
(a) bacterial infection
(b) viral infection
(c) parasitic infection
(d) fungal infection

35. The cloudy nights are warmer compared to clear nights (without clouds) during winter days. This is because:
(a) clouds radiate heat towards the earth
(b) clouds prevent cold wave from the sky, descend on earth
(c) clouds prevent escaping of the heat radiation from the earth
(d) clouds being at great heights from earth absorb heat from the sun and send towards the earth

36. Largest soil group of India is:
(a) Red soil (b) Black soil
(c) Sandy soil (d) Mountain soil

37. Main pollutant of the Indian coastal water is:
(a) oil spill
(b) municipal sewage
(c) industrial effluents
(d) aerosols

38. Human ear is most sensitive to noise in the following frequency ranges:
(a) 1-2 kHz (b) 100-500 Hz
(c) 10-12 kHz (d) None of these

39. Which species of chromium is toxic in water:

(a) Cr + 2 (b) Cr + 3
(c) Cr + 6 (d) Cr is non-toxic element

40. Match List I (Dams) with List II (Rivers) in the following:

List I (Dams)	List II (Rivers)
(A) Bhakra	(i) Krishna
(B) Nagarjunasagar	(ii) Damodar
(C) Panchet	(iii) Sutlej
(D) Hirakud	(iv) Bhagirathi
(E) Tehri	(v) Mahanadi

Codes:	A	B	C	D	E
(a)	v	iii	iv	ii	i
(b)	iii	i	ii	v	iv
(c)	i	ii	iv	iii	v
(d)	ii	iii	iv	i	v

41. A negative reaction to a mediated communication is described as:
(a) flak
(b) fragmented feedback
(c) passive response
(d) non-conformity

42. The launch of satellite channel by IGNOU on 26th January 2003 for technological education for the growth and development of distance education is:
(a) Eklavya channel
(b) Gyandarshan channel
(c) Rajrishi channel
(d) None of these

43. Match List I with List II and select the correct answer from the code given below:

List I (Institutions)
(A) The Indian Council of Historical Reasearch (ICHR)
(B) The Indian Institute of Advanced Studies (IIAS)
(C) The Indian Council of Philosophical Research (ICPR)
(D) The Central Institute of Coastal Engineering for fisheries

List II (Locations)
(i) Shimla (ii) New Delhi
(iii) Bangalore (iv) Lucknow

Codes:	A	B	C	D
(a)	ii	i	iv	iii
(b)	i	ii	iii	iv
(c)	ii	iv	i	iii
(d)	iv	iii	ii	i

44. Which of the following is not a Fundamental Right?
(a) Right to equality
(b) Right against exploitation
(c) Right to freedom of speech and expression
(d) Right of free compulsory education of all children upto the age of 14

45. The Lok Sabha can be dissolved before the expiry of its normal five year term by:
(a) The Prime Minister
(b) The Speaker of Lok Sabha
(c) The President on the recommendation of the Prime Minister
(d) None of the above

Study the following graph carefully and answer Q.No. 46 to 50 given below it:

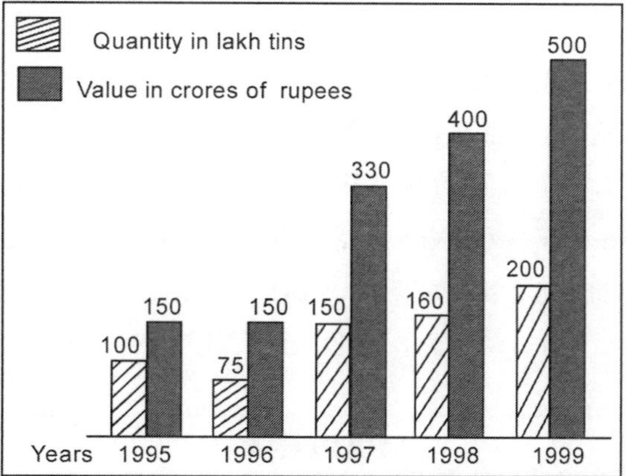

46. In which year the value per tin was minimum?
(a) 1995 (b) 1996
(c) 1998 (d) 1999

47. What was the difference between the tins exported in 1997 and 1998?

(a) 10 (b) 1000
(c) 100000 (d) 1000000

48. What was the approximate percentage increase in export value from 1995 to 1999?
(a) 350 (b) 330.3
(c) 433.3 (d) None of these

49. What was the percentage drop in export quantity from 1995 to 1996?
(a) 75 (b) 50
(c) 25 (d) None of these

50. If in 1998, the tins were exported at the same rate per tin as that in 1997, what would be the value (in crores of rupees) of export in 1998?
(a) 400 (b) 375
(c) 352 (d) 330

ANSWERS

1. (c)	2. (d)	3. (b)	4. (a)	5. (c)
6. (d)	7. (d)	8. (a)	9. (a)	10. (b)
11. (a)	12. (b)	13. (a)	14. (a)	15. (b)
16. (a)	17. (d)	18. (a)	19. (d)	20. (c)
21. (b)	22. (d)	23. (b)	24. (b)	25. (c)
26. (b)	27. (b)	28. (c)	29. (a)	30. (b)
31. (b)	32. (a)	33. (d)	34. (c)	35. (c)
36. (a)	37. (c)	38. (d)	39. (c)	40. (b)
41. (c)	42. (a)	43. (a)	44. (d)	45. (c)
46. (a)	47. (a)	48. (d)	49. (c)	50. (c)

PAPER–II

Note: This paper contains fifty (50) objective type questions, each question carrying two (2) marks. All questions are compulsory.

1. In which of the following cases the Supreme Court held that allowing medical examination of women to prove her virginity amounts to violation of her right to privacy guaranteed under Article 21 of the Constitution?
(a) Prabha Dutt V. Union of India
(b) Surjeet Singh Thind V. Kanwaljit Kaur
(c) Kamla Devi V. State of Punjab
(d) P. Nulla Thampi V. Union of India

2. Reservation for the promotion of Scheduled Castes and Scheduled Tribes are valid as it is provided in:
(a) The Constitution [Seventy-Seventh Amendment] Act
(b) The Constitution [Eighty-First Amendment] Act
(c) The Constitution [Eighty-Fifth Amendment] Act
(d) The Constitution [Eighty-Seventh Amendment] Act

Direction for question 3 and 4

The following items consist of two statements one labelled the 'Assertion (A)' and the other labelled the 'Reason (R)'. You are to examine these statements and decide if the Assertion (A) and the Reason (R) are individually true and if so whether the Reason is a correct explanation of the Assertion. Select your answer to these items using the codes given below:

Codes:
(a) Both (A) and (R) are true and (R) is the correct explanation of (A)
(b) Both (A) and (R) are true and (R) is not a correct explanation of (A)
(c) (A) is true but (R) is false
(d) (A) is false but (R) is true

3. **Assertion (A):** A proclamation of emergency can be issued by the President if there is imminent danger of war or external aggression or armed rebellion.

Reason (R): The President can suspend the enforcement of all Fundamental Rights during the period of emergency.

4. **Assertion (A):** It is legal and constitutional duty of the State to provide legal aid to the poor.
   Reason (R): No one shall be denied Justice by reason of his poverty.

5. Match List I with List II and select the correct answer using the codes given below the list:
   List I
   (A) Freedom of Press
   (B) Minority Rights
   (C) Just, fair and reasonable
   (D) Special Courts
   List II
   (i) State of West Bengal V. Anwar Ali
   (ii) Brij Bhushan V. State of U.P.
   (iii) Ajiz Basha V. Union of India
   (iv) Maneka Gandhi V. Union of India

Codes:	A	B	C	D
(a)	(i)	(iii)	(iv)	(ii)
(b)	(ii)	(iv)	(iii)	(i)
(c)	(i)	(iv)	(iii)	(ii)
(d)	(ii)	(iii)	(iv)	(i)

6. Match List I with List II and select the correct answer using the codes given below the list:
   List I
   (A) Writ of Habeas Corpus
   (B) Writ of Mandamus
   (C) Writ of Quo-warranto
   (D) Writ of Certiovari
   List II
   (i) Unlawful occupation of public office
   (ii) Superior Court's direction to subordinate Courts
   (iii) Unlawful Detention
   (iv) Non-performance of public duties

Codes:	A	B	C	D
(a)	(ii)	(i)	(iv)	(iii)
(b)	(iii)	(iv)	(i)	(ii)
(c)	(ii)	(iv)	(i)	(iii)
(d)	(iii)	(i)	(iv)	(ii)

7. '*Nemo debut vis Vexari*' principle is related to:
   (a) Self-incriminatory
   (b) Ex-post facto law
   (c) Retrospective operation
   (d) Double Jeopardy

8. "Law is no doubt a remedy for greater evils yet it brings evils of its own" was said by:
   (a) Lord Devlin (b) Lord Atkin
   (c) Chipman Grey (d) Salmond

9. "Custom is the sign of positive law" was expounded by:
   (a) Hegal (b) Marx
   (c) Austin (d) Savigny

10. *Ubi civitas ibi lex* means:
    (a) Where there is state there will not be anarchy
    (b) Where there is society there is law
    (c) State is necessary evil
    (d) Both (a) and (c)

11. The correlative of liberty is:
    (a) Right (b) No right
    (c) Power (d) Duty

12. "A right to retain the possession of a property until the due amount is paid" is known as:
    (a) Lease (b) Licence
    (c) Lien (d) Mortgage

13. The application of physical force of the State for the enforcement of law is:
    (a) Punishment (b) Liability
    (c) Direction (d) Sanction

14. Emmanuel Kant is the exponent of:
    (a) Retributive theory of punishment
    (b) Reformative theory of punishment
    (c) Deterrent theory of punishment
    (d) Preventive theory of punishment

15. Human Rights are operative against:

(a) Humans (b) Enemies
(c) State (d) Immorality

16. International disputes are settled by:
   (a) Supreme Court
   (b) United Nations
   (c) International Court of Justice
   (d) Panchayats

17. Two statements are given below, one is labelled as Assertion (A), and the other is labelled as Reason (R):
   Assertion (A): International Law is pure law.
   Reason (R): International Law is made by a national legislature.
   Give the correct answer from the following codes:
   (a) (A) is true, but (R) is false
   (b) (A) is false, but (R) is true
   (c) Both (A) and (R) are true
   (d) Both (A) and (R) are false

18. Match the following words with their correct Article from codes given below:
   List I
   (A) Freedom of association
   (B) Right of reservation
   (C) Right of livelihood
   (D) Right of habeas corpus
   List II
   (i) Article 14 (ii) Article 21
   (iii) Article 19 (iv) Article 22

Codes:	A	B	C	D
(a)	(i)	(ii)	(iii)	(iv)
(b)	(i)	(iii)	(ii)	(iv)
(c)	(iii)	(i)	(ii)	(iv)
(d)	(iv)	(ii)	(iii)	(i)

19. Source of International Law is:
   (a) Lok Sabha
   (b) Rajya Sabha
   (c) Supreme Court of India
   (d) None of above

20. International disputes are settled by:
   (a) Panchayats (b) Municipalities
   (c) Land tribunals (d) None of above

21. Read the two statements. One is Assertion (A) and the other is Reason (R).
   Assertion (A): A having a wife alive marries another wife. The marriage is void.
   Reason (R): Monogamy is the rule. Give correct answer from the following codes.
   (a) Both (A) and (R) are true
   (b) Both (A) and (R) are false
   (c) (A) is true but (R) is false
   (d) (A) is false but (R) is true

22. Which of the following is not condition for a marriage under Section 5 of the Hindu Marriage Act, 1955?
   (a) Neither should have a spouse living
   (b) If the bride is below 18, consent of her guardian has been obtained
   (c) They are not within prohibited degrees of relationship
   (d) Neither should be subject to recurrent attack of ephilepsy

23. Where no form of marriage was gone through under Section 7 of the Hindu Marriage Act, the marriage is:
   (a) Valid (b) Voidable
   (c) Void (d) Ineffective

24. Under Section 19 of the Hindu Marriage Act, 1955 a petition in a matrimonial case has to be filed in the place:
   (a) Where the marriage was solemnised
   (b) Where the Respondent was residing at the time of the presention of petition
   (c) The parties last resided together
   (d) All of the above

25. A Muslim wife may sue for divorce under the Dissolution of Muslim Marriage Act, 1939 if the husband has been insane for a period of:
   (a) 1 year (b) 2 years
   (c) 3 years (d) 5 years

26. In which of the case the Question of Constitutional validity of section 9 of the Hindu Marriage Act, 1955 came for consideration for the first time?
   (a) Digvijay Singh V. Pratap Kumari
   (b) T. Sareeth V. T. Venkat Subbiaiah
   (c) Yamunabai Adhav V. Anantrao Shivram Adhav
   (d) Saroj Rani V. Sudarshan Kumar

27. Agreement is meeting of:
   (a) Brains (b) Minds
   (c) Hands (d) Documents

28. An offer cannot be accepted unless and until it has been brought to the knowledge of the person:
   (a) who made the offer
   (b) who asked for the offer
   (c) who made invitation to offer
   (d) for whom it is made

29. To convert a proposal into a promise, the acceptance must be:
   (a) qualified
   (b) unqualified
   (c) general
   (d) absolute and unqualified

30. In which of the following statements "undue influence" does not exist?
   (a) When dominating party holds real or apparent authority
   (b) When a person's mental capacity is affected because of bodily distress
   (c) When a party threatens another to commit suicide
   (d) When the party holds fiduciary relationship

31. Consideration must be of some value, but need not be:
   (a) Inadequate (b) Minimum
   (c) Adequate (d) Maximum

32. Damage actually caused by a breach of contract where special circumstances have been brought to the knowledge of the promisee is recoverable provided that when the contract was made such damages:
   (a) are excessive
   (b) are reasonable
   (c) arise due to the fault of promisee
   (d) were reasonably forseeable

33. In which of the following cases the plea of volenti non fit Injuria can be taken?
   (a) Rescue cases
   (b) Plaintiff has knowledge of the risk
   (c) Plaintiff is employed in the job involving risk
   (d) Plaintiff had knowledge and volunteered to take the risk

34. Which one of the following pairs is correctly matched in the maxim "Injuria sine damno" in the code?
   (A) Actionable per se
   (B) Not actionable
   (C) Actionable on proof of damage
   (D) Actionable on violation of legal right

   Codes:
   (a) A B (b) C B
   (c) C D (d) A D

35. Write the correct sequence or chronological order of the concept of absolute liability with the help of the code below:
   i. Liability for dangerous substances arises on negligence
   ii. Strict liability rule has various exceptions
   iii. Strict liability arises without negligence
   iv. Liability for dangerous substances is absolute in India

   Codes
   (a) i, iii, ii, iv (b) i, ii, iii, iv
   (c) iv, i, ii, iii (d) i, iv, iii, ii

36. Match the following List I with List II and point out the correct code:

List I
(A) Vis Major
(B) Res Ipsa Loquitur
(C) Actionable per se
(D) Volenti non fit Injuria

List II
(i) Trespass
(ii) Act of God
(iii) Negligence
(iv) Scienti non fit Injuria

Codes:	A	B	C	D
(A)	(ii)	(iii)	(i)	(iv)
(B)	(iii)	(ii)	(iv)	(i)
(C)	(ii)	(i)	(iii)	(iv)
(D)	(iv)	(ii)	(iii)	(i)

37. Mark the correct answer:
(a) Tort is a statutory remedy
(b) Tort is a criminal wrong
(c) Tort is a civil wrong
(d) Tort is a contractual wrong

38. Direction
The following items consist of two statements, one labelled as Assertion (A) and the other is labelled as Reason (R). You are to examine these statements and decide if the Assertion (A) and the Reason (R) are individually true and if so whether the Reason is a correct explanation of the Assertion. Select your answer to these items using the codes given below.
Assertion (A): When you invite somebody to your house, you cannot sue him for trespass.
Reason (R): One cannot enforce a right which one has voluntarily waiued or abandoned.
Codes:
(a) Both (A) and (R) are true but (R) is not the correct explanation
(b) Both (A) and (R) are true and (R) is the correct explanation
(c) (A) is true and (R) is false
(d) (A) is false but (R) is true

39. Which one of the following is not essential of an offence?
(a) intention (b) motive
(c) act (d) punishment

40. Which one of the following jurists opined that crime is an act or omission in violation of public rights?
(a) Pollock (b) Austin
(c) Blackburn (d) William Glanvillo

41. x abets y to commit murder of z. y commits murder of z. x is liable under:
(a) Sec. 109 of the Indian Penal Code
(b) Sec. 120 B of the Indian Penal Code
(c) Sec. 302 of the Indian Penal Code
(d) Sec. 115 of the Indian Penal Code

42. Two lovers not allowed by their parents to marry agreed to commit suicide but later on gave up the idea of suicide. Decide the liability of the lovers:
(a) They are guilty U/S 120 B of the Indian Penal Code
(b) They are not guilty U/S 120 B of the Indian Penal Code
(c) They are guilty U/S 34 of the Indian Penal Code
(d) They are guilty U/S 309 of the Indian Penal Code

43. x, a girl of 16 years old was sleeping on her cot in the evening. y seeing here alone falls upon her and pulls her lower clothes. Y is liable:
(a) U/S 375/511 of the Indian Penal Code
(b) U/S 354 of the Indian Penal Code
(c) U/S 509 of the Indian Penal Code
(d) U/S 352 of the Indian Penal Code

44. Under which one of the following circumstance x cannot cause death of y in exercise of his right of private defence of body U/S 100 of the Indian Penal Code, even if y has created an apprehension of imminent danger to his life:

(a) of causing death
(b) of causing robbery
(c) of causing rape or unnatural lust
(d) of causing grievous hurt

45. Lock-out is:
(a) antithesis of strike
(b) anti-strike
(c) equal to strike
(d) none of the above

46. Closure means:
(a) Permanent closing down of place of employment
(b) Temporary closing down of place of employment
(c) Both of the above
(d) None of the above

47. The Trade Union Act, 1926 applies to:
(a) Registered trade union only
(b) Un-registered trade union only
(c) Both of the above
(d) None of the above

48. An employer is liable to pay compensation to his workman under the Workmen's Compensation Act 1923 for:
(a) injury caused
(b) injury caused by accident
(c) injury caused in course of employment
(d) injury caused by accident in course of employment and out of employment

49. An industrial dispute may be brought before the Labour Court:
(a) by an aggrieved party
(b) by both the parties
(c) by both parties with prior permission from the Government
(d) by reference by the appropriate Government

50. The Trade Union can contribute to a political party:
(a) From its common fund
(b) From its common fund with consent of its members
(c) By raising a fund for this purpose from voluntary subscriptions by its members
(d) None of the above

ANSWERS

1. (d)	2. (b)	3. (b)	4. (a)	5. (d)
6. (b)	7. (c)	8. (b)	9. (c)	10. (d)
11. (b)	12. (d)	13. (b)	14. (a)	15. (d)
16. (c)	17. (c)	18. (c)	19. (d)	20. (d)
21. (a)	22. (b)	23. (b)	24. (d)	25. (b)
26. (d)	27. (b)	28. (a)	29. (d)	30. (d)
31. (a)	32. (d)	33. (d)	34. (d)	35. (c)
36. (a)	37. (c)	38. (a)	39. (d)	40. (b)
41. (a)	42. (d)	43. (b)	44. (b)	45. (a)
46. (a)	47. (a)	48. (c)	49. (d)	50. (b)

JUNE–2005

Note: This paper contains fifty (50) objective type questions, each question carrying two (2) marks. All questions are compulsory.

PAPER–II

1. Mere possibility of abuse or misuse of P 0 T A cannot be a ground to declare it unconstitutional..... Need of P 0 T A is a matter of policy of the government and it cannot be examined by the court. The Supreme Court of India so held in:
   (a) Peoples Union for Civil liberties V. Union of India
   (b) Narendra Kumar V. Union of India
   (c) K.S. Bhoir V. State of Maharashtra
   (d) A.K. Sen V. Union of India

2. In which of the constitutional Amendments it has been laid down that the total number of ministers including Prime Minister in the union council of Ministers shall not exceed 15% of the total members of the House of People?
   (a) The Constitution [Ninety-First Amendment] Act
   (b) The Constitution [Ninety-Third Amendment] Act
   (c) The Counstitution [Eighty-Eighth Amendment] Act
   (d) The Counstitution [Eighty-Ninth Amendment] Act

Direction for questions 3 and 4

The following items consist of two statements one labelled the 'Assertion (A)' and other lablled the 'Reason (R)': You are to examine these statements and decide if the 'Assertion (A)' and the 'Reason (R)' are individually true and if so whether the Reason is a correct explanation of the Assertion. Select your answer to these items using the codes given below:

Codes:
(a) Both (A) and (R) are true and (R) is the correct explanation of (A)
(b) Both (A) and (R) are true and (R) is not a correct explanation of (A)
(c) (A) is true but (R) is false
(d) (A) is false but (R) is true

3. **Assertion (A):** There is a division of powers between the centre and the states in a federalism.
   Reason (R): A lagislation is not invalid merely because it incidentally encroaches on matters which have been assigned to another legislature.

4. **Assertion (A):** The Supreme Court is a Court of Record.
   Reason (R): Once a court is made a Court of Record its power to punish for its contempt necessarily follows from that position.

5. Match List I with List II and select the correct answer using the codes given below the lists:
   List I
   (A) K.C. Vasanth Kumar V. State of Karnataka
   (B) Parmanand Kotari V. Union of India
   (C) A.S. Narayana V. State of Andhara Pradesh
   (D) Kihota V. Zachilhu

List II

(1) Doctrine of Severability
(2) Religious Freedom
(3) Fundamental right to life and personal liberty
(4) Reservation for Backward Classes

Codes:	**A**	**B**	**C**	**D**
(a)	4	1	2	3
(b)	2	3	4	1
(c)	4	3	2	1
(d)	2	1	4	3

6. Which of the following Articles of the constitution of India provide for circumstances under which parliament has power to make a law on any subject enumerated in the state list?
   (a) 249, 250, 252 and 253
   (b) 248, 249, 250 and 252
   (c) 249, 250, 251 and 252
   (d) 245, 246, 248 and 249

7. Justice J.S. Verma's Committee Report relates to:
   (a) Effectuation of Fundamental Duties
   (b) Duty to vote in election
   (c) Freedom of Religion
   (d) National Judicial Commission

8. According to Savigny law is the product of
   (a) Volkgeist
   (b) National spirit or genius of the people
   (c) Custom and tradition
   (d) (a) and (b) only

9. Hans Kelsen regards law a:
   (a) Natural science
   (b) Positive science
   (c) Normative science
   (d) Physical science

10. "Constitution is both a matter of fact and a matter of law". Who is the author of it?
    (a) A.V. Dicey (b) John Austin
    (c) Salmund (d) Hans Kelsen

11. Right to divorce is
    (a) Right in Stricto senso
    (b) Liberty
    (c) Power
    (d) Privilege

12. The maxim necessitatis non habet legem means
    (a) Necessity is the mother of invention
    (b) Necessity knows no law
    (c) Injury to the legal right
    (d) Injury to the moral right

13. The concept of exemplary punishment comes under which one of the following theories of punishment?
    (a) Deterrent (b) Preventive
    (c) Reformative (d) Retributive

14. "Jurisprudance is lawyer's extraversion". Who is the exponent of this thesis?
    (a) Jermy Bentham (b) Stuart Mill
    (c) Julius Stone (d) Roscol pound

15. International law and municipal law are
    (a) Same
    (b) Different
    (c) Mutually exclusive
    (d) Interdependent

16. Which one of the following statement is correct?
    (a) Source of Public International Law is writings of jurists.
    (b) Sources of Public International Law are treaties.
    (c) Source of Public International Law is treatise.
    (d) Sources of Public International Law are judicial precedents.

17. Given below are two statements one labelled as Assertion (A) and the other labelled as Reason (R) Match the correct

    Assertion (A): International law is not a law.

    Reason (R): States do not accept international law.

(a) Both (A) and (R) are true
(b) Both (A) and (R) are false
(c) (A) is true, but (R) is false
(d) (A) is false, but (R) is true

18. Given below are two statements one labelled as Assertion (A) and the other labelled as Reason (R) Match the correct:
Assertion (A): Settlement of international disputes is done by United Nations.
Reason (R): United Nations is a court.
Give correct answer form the following codes:
(a) Both (A) and (R) are true
(b) (A) is true, but (R) is wrong
(c) (A) is wrong, but (R) is true
(d) Both (A) and (R) are false

19. Match List I with List II and indicate the correct answer using the codes given below:
List I
(A) Right to human dignity
(B) Freedom of religion
(C) Protective discrimination
(D) Preventive detention
List II
(i) Article 22
(ii) The Preamble to Indian Constitution
(iii) Article 14
(iv) Article 25

Codes:	**A**	**B**	**C**	**D**
(a)	(i)	(iii)	(iv)	(ii)
(b)	(ii)	(iv)	(iii)	(i)
(c)	(i)	(ii)	(iii)	(iv)
(d)	(iv)	(iii)	(ii)	(i)

20. United Nations Organisation was established in
(a) 1947 (b) 1956
(c) 1945 (d) 1946

21. Given below are two statements, one labelled as Assertion (A) and then the other labelled as Reason (R). With the help of codes given below, point out the correct explanation:
Assertion (A): Marriage under Hindu Law was indissoluble.
Reason (R): Marriage was regarded assacrament.
(a) Both (A) and (R) are true
(b) Both (A) and (R) false
(c) (A) is true but (R) is false
(d) (A) is false but (R) is true

22. Marriage of a girl below the age of 18 is:
(a) Void
(b) Voidable
(c) Valid
(d) Valid but punishable

23. Which of the following is not essential for divorce by mutual consent?
(a) They have been living separately for one year
(b) They have not been able to live together
(c) The wife has not received any maintenance
(d) They have mutually agreed that the marriage should be dissolved

24. A clear proof of usage will outweigh the written text of law. It was observed in
(a) Appovier V Rama Subba Aiyar
(b) Collector of Madura V Mootoo Ramalinga
(c) Atmaram V Bajirao
(d) Arunachala Mudaliar V Murugantha

25. Sources of Muslim law are:
(A) The Koran (B) The Ijmaa
(C) The Hadis (D) The Kiyas
Indicate their correct sequence
(a) (A) (B) (D) and (C)
(b) (A) (C) (B) and (D)
(c) (A) (D) (C) and (B)
(d) None of the above

26. Marriage between a Muslim male and a Christian female under Muslim Law is
(a) Void (b) Voidable
(c) Irregular (d) Valid

27. Illegal objcet makes an agreement
(a) Void (b) Voidable
(c) Void ab initio (d) a contact

28. Offer must be
(a) General
(b) Specific
(c) Incapable of Communication
(d) Possible

29. A contract arising out of natural love and affection
(a) Consideration is not necessary
(b) Insufficient Consideration is sufficient
(c) Sufficient Consideration is insufficient
(d) Consideration must be naturally lovely and affectionate

30. Supply of necessaries to a minor is
(a) Contract (b) Quasi Contract
(c) Tort (d) Legal contract

31. Under which one of the following sections of the Indian Contract Act, 1872, remedies for breach of contract are available?
(a) Sec. 72 (b) Sec. 73
(c) Sec. 74 (d) Sec. 32

32. Contract is frustrated due to frustration of
(a) Subject matter of contract
(b) Change of one party's desire
(c) Consideration of Contract
(d) Capacity to contract

33. Which of the following pairs is correctly matched in the code
(A) Strict liabilty means no-fault liability
(B) Rylands V Fletcher lays down the rule of trespass ab initio
(C) Vis major is a good defence in absolute liability
(D) Supreme Court has overruled strict liability by absolute liability

Codes:
(a) (A) and (B) (b) (B) and (C)
(c) (C) and (D) (d) (A) and (D)

34. In which of the following cases the plea of sovereign immunity can be taken
(a) Army truck injuring a pedestrian
(b) Police constable firing at a religious gathering
(c) Chief of Army Staff ordering war action
(d) An M.P. making a defamatory statement in a press-meet

35. Write the correct sequence or chronological order of the items of tort of contributory negligence in the given codes
(A) The last opportunity rule
(B) The law Reform (contributory negligence) Act, 1945
(C) Damages are apportioned according to the fault of the plaintiff and defendent
(D) Damage should rest where it lies

Codes:
(a) A B C D (b) B C D A
(c) D A B C (d) C A B D

36. After matching List I and List II point out the correct code

List I
(A) Mersey Dock's V Protor
(B) Metropolitan Asylum District V Hill
(C) Nichols V Marsland
(D) Holmes V Mather

List II
(1) Statutory Authority
(2) Vicarious liability
(3) Inevitable Accident
(4) Act of God

Codes:	A	B	C	D
(a)	2	1	4	3
(b)	3	2	1	4
(c)	1	2	3	4
(d)	4	1	2	3

37. Mark the correct answer for the statement "When consequences of wrongful action are forseen".

(a) Liabilty for damage is not too remote
(b) Liability is too remote
(c) There is no liabilty
(d) Lialiblity for consequences does not arise

38. Direction: The following items consist of two statements one labelled as Assertion (A) and the other as Reason (R). You are to examine these statements and decide if the Assertion (A) and the Reason (R) are individually true and if so whether the Reason is a correct explanation of the Assertion. Select your answer in these items using the codes given below:
Assertion (A): Immunity under statutory authority is not only for the harm which is obvious but also for that harm which is incidental.
Reason (R): When an act is done under the authority of an Act, it is a complete defence.
Codes:
(a) Both (A) and (R) are true and (R) is the correct explanation
(b) Both (A) and (R) are true but (R) is not the correct answer
(c) (A) is false but (R) is true
(d) (A) is true but (R) is false

39. X abets Y to beat Z. While Y was beating Z at the residence of Z, X reaches there with three of his friends. Y still continues to beat him. Point out the correct answer.
(a) X is liable U/s 109 of the Indian Penal Code
(b) X is liable U/s 323/34 of the Indian Penal Code
(c) X is liable U/s 120-B of the Indian Penal Code
(d) X is liable U/s 114 of the Indian Penal Code

40. In which of the following cases a clear difference between common intention and similar intention was well discussed?
(a) Barendra Kumar Ghose vs Emperor
(b) Mahboob Shah vs King Emperor
(c) Amjad Khan vs State of MP
(d) Sheraz vs De Rutzen

41. X, a married woman of 40 years old with her own free will leaves her husband's house and began to live with her paramour Y as husband and wife. The husband of the wife files a criminal case against Y. Point out the correct answer.
(a) Y is liable for keeping the woman as wife
(b) Y is not liable because the woman has left her husband's house by her own free will
(c) Y is not liable because neither she has been kidnapped nor abducted
(d) Y is liable for bigamy

42. In which of the following circumstances X cannot cause death of Y while exercising his right of private defence of property U/s 103 of the Indian Penal code if
(a) Y is committing dacoity
(b) Y is likely to cause death of X
(c) Y is committing house breaking by night with dangerous weapon
(d) Y is committing robbery

43. A shoots at a bird in B's house in order to steal it but accidentally kills B. Point out the correct answer:
(a) A is liable for murder of B
(b) A is not liable for murder of B
(c) A is liable for culpable homicide of B
(d) A is not liable becasue it was an accident U/s 80 of the Indian Penal Code

44. A ran away with B's watch A weak later B saw A wearing his watch. B forthwith seized A and recovered his watch using

necessary force which resulted is some injuries to A. Point out the correct answer.
(a) B is not liable to any injury caused to A
(b) B is liable for causing injuries to A
(c) B has full rights to recover his watch even by using necessary force here
(d) B's right to recover his watch continues unitl it is recovered

45. Industrial dispute does not mean and include
(a) Dispute between employer and employees
(b) Dispute between employer and employer
(c) Dispute between a workman and his employer
(d) Dispute between employees and employees

46. Lay-off means
(a) Dismissing a workman
(b) Removing a workman
(c) Retirement of a workman
(d) Inability of employer to provide work to workman

47. Strike is the legitimate weapon in the hands of
(a) The workmen
(b) The employer
(c) Both employers and workmen
(d) None of the above

48. An employer is not liable to pay compensation to a workman for the injury caused
(a) by accident
(b) by negligence of his co-workman
(c) when the workman was under the influence of drink or drugs
(d) The workman had given consent to the risk of injury

49. The verdict of the labour court in industrial dispute is described as
(a) Judgement (b) Decree
(c) Award (d) Relief

50. The trade union cannot spend its common fund on
(a) Payment of salary to its office-bearers
(b) Education of children of its members
(c) Litigation
(d) Funding of a political parly

ANSWERS

1. (a)	2. (a)	3. (b)	4. (a)	5. (c)
6. (d)	7. (a)	8. (a)	9. (c)	10. (a)
11. (a)	12. (b)	13. (a)	14. (c)	15. (d)
16. (a)	17. (c)	18. (d)	19. (b)	20. (c)
21. (d)	22. (b)	23. (c)	24. (c)	25. (a)
26. (d)	27. (a)	28. (b)	29. (a)	30. (b)
31. (b)	32. (a)	33. (b)	34. (a)	35. (d)
36. (a)	37. (a)	38. (a)	39. (c)	40. (a)
41. (b)	42. (b)	43. (b)	44. (d)	45. (a)
46. (d)	47. (a)	48. (c)	49. (c)	50. (a)

DECEMBER–2006

Note: This paper contains fifty (50) multiple-choice questions, each question carrying two (2) marks. Attempt all of them.

PAPER–I

1. Which of the following is not instructional material?
   (a) Over Head Projector
   (b) Audio Casset
   (c) Printed Material
   (d) Transparency

2. Which of the following statement is not correct?
   (a) Lecture Method can develop reasoning
   (b) Lecture Method can develop knowledge
   (c) Lecture Method is one-way process
   (d) During Lecture Method students are passive

3. The main objective of teaching at Higher Education Level is:
   (a) To prepare students to pass examination
   (b) To develop the capacity to take decisions
   (c) To give new information
   (d) To motivate students to ask questions during lecture

4. Which of the following statements is correct?
   (a) Reliability ensures validity
   (b) Validity ensures reliability
   (c) Reliability and validity are independent of each other
   (d) Reliability does not depend on objectivity

5. Which of the following indicates evaluation?
   (a) Ram got 45 marks out of 200
   (b) Mohan got 38 percent marks in English
   (c) Shyam got First Division in final examination
   (d) All of the above

6. Research can be conducted by a person who:
   (a) has studied research methodology
   (b) holds a postgraduate degree
   (c) possesses thinking and reasoning ability
   (d) is a hard worker

7. Which of the following statements is correct?
   (a) Objectives of research are stated in first chapter of the thesis
   (b) Researcher must possess analytical ability
   (c) Variability is the source of problem
   (d) All of the above

8. Which of the following is not the Method of Research?
   (a) Observation (b) Historical
   (c) Survey (d) Philosophical

9. Research can be classified as:
   (a) Basic, Applied and Action Research
   (b) Quantitative and Qualitative Research
   (c) Philosophical, Historical, Survey and Experimental Research
   (d) All of the above

10. The first step of research is:
    (a) Selecting a problem
    (b) Searching a problem
    (c) Finding a problem
    (d) Identifying a problem

Read the following passage and answer the question nos. 11 to 15:

After almost three decades of contemplating Swarovski-encrusted navels on increasing flat abs, the Mumbai film industry is on a discovery of India and itself. With budgets of over 30 crore each, four soon to be released movies by premier directors are exploring the idea of who we are and redefining who the other is. It is a fundamental question which the bling-bling, glam-sham and disham-disham tends to avoid. It is also a question which binds an audience when the lights go dim and the projector rolls : as a nation, who are we? As a people, where are we going?

The Germans coined a word for it, zeitgeist, which perhaps Yash Chopra would not care to pronounce. But at 72, he remains the person who can best capture it. After being the first to project the diasporic Indian on screen in *Lamhe* in 1991, he has returned to his roots in a new movie. *Veer Zaara*, set in 1986, where Pakistan, the traditional other, the part that got away, is the lover and the saviour. In Subhas Ghai's *Kisna*, set in 1947, the other is the English woman. She is not a memsahib, but a mehbooba. In Ketan Mehta's *The Rising*, the East India Englishman is not the evil oppressor of countless cardboard characterisations, which span the spectrum from *Jewel in the Crown* to *Kranti*, but an honourable friend.

This is Manoj Kumar's *Desh Ki Dharti* with a difference : there is culture, not contentious politics; balle balle, not bombs : no dooriyan (distance), only nazdeekiyan (closeness).

All four films are heralding a new hero and heroine. The new hero is fallible and vulnerable, committed to his dharma, but also not afraid of failure—less of a boy and more of a man. He even has a grown up name : Veer Pratap Singh in *Veer Zaara* and Mohan Bhargav in *Swades*. The new heroine is not a babe, but often a bebe, dressed in traditional Punjabi clothes, often with the stereotypical body type as well, as in *Bride and Prejudice* of Gurinder Chadha.

11. Which word Yash Chopra would not be able to pronounce?
    (a) Bling + bling (b) Zeitgeist
    (c) Montaz (d) Dooriyan

12. Who made *Lamhe* in 1991?
    (a) Subhash Ghai (b) Yash Chopra
    (c) Aditya Chopra (d) Sakti Samanta

13. Which movie is associated with Manoj Kumar?
    (a) *Jewel in the Crown*
    (b) *Kisna*
    (c) *Zaara*
    (d) *Desh Ki Dharti*

14. Which is the latest film by Yash Chopra?
    (a) *Deewar*
    (b) *Kabhi Kabhi*
    (c) *Dilwale Dulhaniya Le Jayenge*
    (d) *Veer Zaara*

15. Which is the dress of the heroine in *Veer Zaara*?
    (a) Traditional Gujarati Clothes
    (b) Traditional Bengali Clothes
    (c) Traditional Punjabi Clothes
    (d) Traditional Madrasi Clothes

16. Which one of the following can be termed as verbal communication?
    (a) Prof. Sharma delivered the lecture in the classroom.
    (b) Signal at the cross-road changed from green to orange.

(c) The child was crying to attract the attention of the mother.
(d) Dipak wrote a letter for leave application.

17. Which is the 24 hours English Business news channel in India?
(a) Zee News (b) NDTV 24×7
(c) CNBC (d) India News

18. Consider the following statements in communication:
(i) Hema Malini is the Chairperson of the Children's Film Society, India.
(ii) Yash Chopra is the Chairman of the Central Board of Film Certification of India.
(iii) Sharmila Tagore is the Chairperson of National Film Development Corporation.
(iv) Dilip Kumar, Raj Kapoor and Preeti Zinta have all been recipients of Dada Saheb Phalke Award.
Which of the statements given above is/are correct?
(a) (i) and (iii) (b) (ii) and (iii)
(c) (iv) only (d) (iii) only

19. Which of the following pair is *not* correctly matched?
(a) N. Ram : The Hindu
(b) Barkha Dutt : Zee News
(c) Pranay Roy : NDTV 24×7
(d) Prabhu Chawla : Aajtak

20. "Because you deserve to know" is the punchline used by:
(a) The Times of India
(b) The Hindu
(c) Indian Express
(d) Hindustan Times

21. In the sequence of numbers 8, 24, 12, X, 18, 54 the missing number X is:
(a) 26 (b) 24
(c) 36 (d) 32

22. If A stands for 5, B for 6, C for 7, D for 8 and so on, then the following numbers stand for 17, 19, 20, 9 and 8:
(a) PLANE (b) MOPED
(c) MOTOR (d) TONGA

23. The letters in the first set have certain relationship. On the basis of this relationship what is the right choice for the second set?
AST : BRU : : NQV : ?
(a) ORW (b) MPU
(c) MRW (d) OPW

24. In a certain code, PAN is written as 31 and PAR as 35. In this code PAT is written as:
(a) 30 (b) 37
(c) 38 (d) 39

25. The sides of a triangle are in the ratio of $\frac{1}{2}:\frac{1}{3}:\frac{1}{4}$. If its perimeter is 52 cm, the length of the smallest side is:
(a) 9 cm (b) 10 cm
(c) 11 cm (d) 12 cm

26. Which one of the following statements is completely non-sensical?
(a) He was a bachelor, but he married recently.
(b) He is a bachelor, but he married recently.
(c) When he married, he was not a bachelor.
(d) When he was a bachelor, he was not married.

27. Which of the following statements are mutually contradictory?
(i) All flowers are not fragrant.
(ii) Most flowers are not fragrant.
(iii) None of the flowers is fragrant.
(iv) Most flowers are fragrant.
Choose the correct answer from the code given below:
Codes:
(a) (i) and (ii) (b) (i) and (iii)
(c) (ii) and (iii) (d) (iii) and (iv)

28. Which of the following statements say the same thing?
   (i) "I am a teacher" (said by Arvind)
   (ii) "I am a teacher" (said by Binod)
   (iii) "My son is a teacher" (said by Binod's father)
   (iv) "My brother is a teacher" (said by Binod's sister)
   (v) "My brother is a teacher" (said by Binod's only sister)
   (vi) "My sole enemy is a teacher" (said by Binod's only enemy)

   Choose the correct answer from the code given below:

   Codes:
   (a) (i) and (ii)
   (b) (ii), (iii), (iv) and (v)
   (c) (ii) and (vi)
   (d) (v) and (vi)

29. Which of the following are correct ways of arguing?
   (i) There can be no second husband without a second wife.
   (ii) Anil is a friend of Bob, Bob is a friend of Raj, hence Anil is a friend of Raj.
   (iii) A is equal to B, B is equal to C, hence A is equal to C.
   (iv) If everyone is a liar, then we cannot prove it.

   Choose the correct answer from the code given below:

   Codes:
   (a) (iii) and (iv)
   (b) (i), (iii) and (iv)
   (c) (ii), (iii) and (iv)
   (d) (i), (ii), (iii) and (iv)

30. Which of the following statement/s are always false?
   (i) The sun will not rise in the East some day.
   (ii) A wooden table is not a table.
   (iii) Delhi city will be drowned under water.
   (iv) Cars run on water as fuel.

   Choose the correct answer from the code given below:

   Codes:
   (a) (i), (iii) and (iv) (b) Only (iii)
   (c) (i), (ii) and (iii) (d) (ii) alone

Study the following graph and answer question numbers 31 to 33:

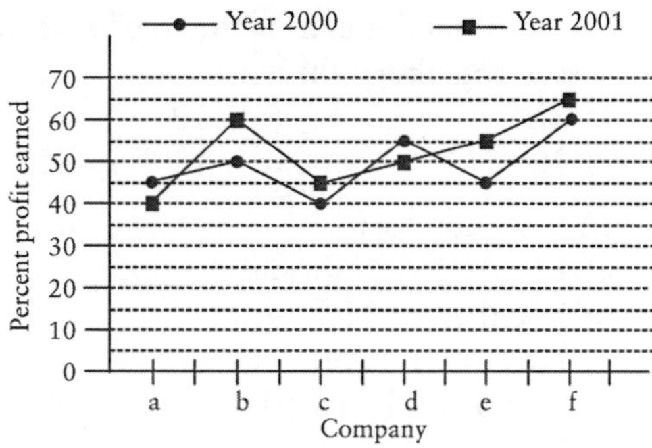

31. In the year 2000, which of the following Companies earned maximum percent profit?
   (a) a (b) b
   (c) d (d) f

32. In the year 2001, which of the following Companies earned minimum percent profit?
   (a) a (b) c
   (c) d (d) e

33. In the years 2000 and 2001, which of the following Companies earned maximum average percent profit?
   (a) f (b) e
   (c) d (d) b

34. Human Development Report for 'each' of the year at global level has been published by:
   (a) UNDP (b) WTO
   (c) IMF (d) World Bank

35. The number of students in four classes A, B, C, D and their respective mean marks obtained by each of the class are given below:

	Class A	Class B	Class C	Class D
Number of students	10	40	30	20
Arithmetic mean	20	30	50	15

The combined mean of the marks of four classes together will be:
(a) 32 (b) 50
(c) 20 (d) 15

36. LAN stands for:
(a) Local And National
(b) Local Area Network
(c) Large Area Network
(d) Live Area Network

37. Which of the following statements is correct?
(a) Modem is a software
(b) Modem helps in stabilizing the voltage
(c) Modem is the operating system
(d) Modem converts the analog signal into digital signal and vice-versa

38. Which of the following is the appropriate definition of a computer?
(a) Computer is a machine that can process information.
(b) Computer is an electronic device that can store, retrieve and process both qualitative and quantitative data quickly and accurately.
(c) Computer is an electronic device that can store, retrieve and quickly process only quantitative data.
(d) Computer is a machine that can store, retrieve and process quickly and accurately only qualitative information.

39. Information and Communication Technology includes:
(a) On line learning
(b) Learning through the use of EDUSAT
(c) Web Based Learning
(d) All the above

40. Which of the following is the appropriate format of URL of e-mail?
(a) www_mail.com
(b) www@mail.com
(c) WWW@mail.com
(d) www.mail.com

41. The most significant impact of volcanic eruption has been felt in the form of:
(a) change in weather
(b) sinking of islands
(c) loss of vegetation
(d) extinction of animals

42. With absorption and decomposition of CO_2 in ocean water beyond desired level, there will be:
(a) decrease in temperature
(b) increase in salinity
(c) growth of phyto plankton
(d) rise in sea level

43. Arrange column II in proper sequence so as to match it with column I and choose the correct answer from the code given below:

Column I Water Quality	Column II pH Value
(A) Neutral	(i) 5
(B) Moderately acidic	(ii) 7
(C) Alkaline	(iii) 4
(D) Injurious	(iv) 8

Codes:	(A)	(B)	(C)	(D)
(a)	(ii)	(iii)	(i)	(iv)
(b)	(i)	(iii)	(ii)	(iv)
(c)	(ii)	(i)	(iv)	(iii)
(d)	(iv)	(ii)	(iii)	(i)

44. The maximum emission of pollutants from fuel sources in India is caused by:
(a) Coal
(b) Firewood
(c) Refuse burning
(d) Vegetable waste product

45. The urbanisation process accounts for the wind in the urban centres during nights to remain:
(a) faster than that in rural areas
(b) slower than that in rural areas
(c) the same as that in rural areas
(d) cooler than that in rural areas

46. The University Grants Commission was constituted on the recommendation of:
(a) Dr. Sarvapalli Radhakrishnan Commission
(b) Mudaliar Commission
(c) Sargent Commission
(d) Kothari Commission

47. Which one of the following Articles of the Constitution of India safeguards the rights of Minorities to establish and run educational institutions of their own liking?
(a) Article 19 (b) Article 29
(c) Article 30 (d) Article 31

48. Match List I (Institutions) with List II (Functions) and select the correct answer by using the code given below:
List I (Institutions)
(A) Parliament
(B) C.&A.G.
(C) Ministry of Finance
(D) Executing Departments
List II (Functions)
(i) Formulation of Budget
(ii) Enactment of Budget
(iii) Implementation of Budget
(iv) Legality of expenditure
(v) Justification of Income

Codes:	**(A)**	**(B)**	**(C)**	**(D)**
(a)	(iii)	(iv)	(ii)	(i)
(b)	(ii)	(iv)	(i)	(iii)
(c)	(v)	(iii)	(iv)	(ii)
(d)	(iv)	(ii)	(iii)	(v)

49. Foundation training to the newly recruited IAS (Probationers) is imparted by:
(a) Indian Institute of Public Administration
(b) Administrative Staff College of India
(c) L.B.S. National Academy of Administration
(d) Centre for Advanced Studies

50. Electoral disputes arising out of Presidential and Vice-Presidential Elections are settled by:
(a) Election Commission of India
(b) Joint Committee of Parliament
(c) Supreme Court of India
(d) Central Election Tribunal

ANSWERS

1. (d)	2. (a)	3. (b)	4. (b)	5. (d)
6. (c)	7. (d)	8. (b)	9. (d)	10. (b)
11. (b)	12. (b)	13. (d)	14. (d)	15. (c)
16. (c)	17. (c)	18. (d)	19. (b)	20. (d)
21. (c)	22. (b)	23. (d)	24. (b)	25. (d)
26. (b)	27. (b)	28. (b)	29. (a)	30. (d)
31. (d)	32. (a)	33. (a)	34. (a)	35. (a)
36. (b)	37. (d)	38. (b)	39. (d)	40. (b)
41. (a)	42. (c)	43. (c)	44. (c)	45. (b)
46. (a)	47. (c)	48. (b)	49. (c)	50. (c)

PAPER–II

Note: This paper contains fifty (50) objective type questions, each question carrying two (2) marks. All questions are compulsory.

1. Which one of the following statements is correct?
(a) Directive Principles of State Policy are part and parcel of Fundamental Rights

(b) Directive Principles of State Policy override Fundamental Rights
(c) Fundamental Rights override Directive Principles of State Policy
(d) Neither override each other

2. Point out the correct answer:
Right to education by the 86th Amendment of the Constitution has provided:
(a) education upto any level
(b) free and compulsory education upto 14 years
(c) education subject to financial capacity of the state
(d) education without considering the financial capacity of the state

3. A member of a House is disqualified if:
(a) he resigns from his party
(b) he becomes a Speaker of the House
(c) he is expelled from his party
(d) all the above grounds are correct

4. A constitutional amendment requires:
(a) a majority of the total membership of the House
(b) not less than two-third majority of members present and voting
(c) a simple majority of the total members present and voting
(d) both (a) and (b)

5. The harmony between Fundamental Rights and Directive Principles was laid down by the Supreme Court in:
(a) The A.K. Gopalan's case
(b) The Golaknath case
(c) The Minerva Mills case
(d) The Champakam Dorairajan case

6. In the Islamic Academy of Education case guidelines were laid down for:
(a) Fixing fees by private educational institutions
(b) State Government Committee to conduct admission test
(c) Admissions by minority professional institutions to admit students of their own community
(d) All of the above

7. To strive towards excellence in all spheres of individual and collective activity is a part of:
(a) GATT
(b) ICCPR
(c) Directive Principles of State Policy
(d) Fundamental Rights

8. Which one of the following Articles is not suspended during enforcement of Article 356 of the Constitution?
(a) Article 20 (b) Article 21
(c) Articles 20 and 21 (d) Article 32

9. Who of the following jurists said that law is a Command of Sovereign?
(a) Salmond (b) Julius Stone
(c) Hans Kelson (d) Austin

10. Who of the following has made distinction between distributive justice and corrective justice?
(a) Plato (b) Aristotle
(c) John Stuart (d) John Austin

11. Who of the following jurists propounded volksgiest theory?
(a) Salmond (b) Savigny
(c) Ihering (d) Ehrlich

12. Hypothesis of Grundnorm was propounded by:
(a) Austin (b) Diguit
(c) Hart (d) Kelson

13. Adverse possession may lead to loss of:
(a) Possession (b) Ownership
(c) Power (d) Liberty

14. The purpose of punishment is:
(a) Recreative (b) Refreshing
(c) Reformative (d) None of these

15. Monism and dualism theories are:

(a) Complementary to each other
(b) Different from each other
(c) Similar to each other
(d) None of above

16. Law making treaties perform the same function in the international field as the state does by:
(a) Custom (b) Public opinion
(c) Legislation (d) Delegated legislation

17. Through recognition, a political community acquires:
(a) international personality
(b) corporate personality
(c) political entity
(d) political personality

18. United Nations was established in the year:
(a) 1941 (b) 1945
(c) 1944 (d) 1946

19. The Naulilaa Incident relates to:
(a) Obstruction of ships
(b) Reprisals
(c) Retorsion
(d) Embargo

20. Article 22 of the Universal Declaration of Human Rights corresponds to which one of the following Articles of the Constitution of India:
(a) Article 21 (b) Article 22
(c) Article 25 (d) Article 29(1)

21. The European Social Charter came into being in the year:
(a) 1962 (b) 1961
(c) 1963 (d) 1964

22. Main reason to include Human Rights in the UDHR was:
(a) French Revolution
(b) English occupation of North America
(c) Moral principles
(d) Bitter experience of mankind during the first and second world wars

23. In which of the following cases, the Court held that "Dower is a sale price of women"?
(a) Humara Begum Case
(b) Subrunnissan Case
(c) Shah Bano Case
(d) Abdul Kadir Case

24. In which of the following cases, the Supreme Court held that "The three talaq would be treated as a single talaq and not a valid talaq"?
(a) Shamim Ara v. State of U.P., AIR 2002 SCW 4162
(b) Mohammad Ahmad Khan v. Shah Bano, AIR 1985 SC 365
(c) Bai Tahira v. Ali Hussain, AIR 1979 SC 362
(d) None of the above

25. If a husband compare his wife with his real sister, this form of divorce is called:
(a) Zihar (b) Khula
(c) Illa (d) Mubarrah

26. A marriage under Hindu Marriage Act, 1955 between persons within Sapinda relationship is:
(a) Valid (b) Voidable
(c) Void (d) Irregular

27. Muta marriage is recognised by:
(a) Hanafi School
(b) Maliki School
(c) Ithna Ashari School
(d) Hanbali School

28. Match List I with List II and indicate the correct answer using the codes given below:

List I
(A) Ashok Hura v. Rupa Hura case
(B) Bipin Chandra v. Prabhavati
(C) Sarla Mudugal v. Union of India
(D) T. Sareetha v. State of A.P.

List II
(i) Restitution of Conjugal-Rights
(ii) Uniform Civil Code

(iii) Dessertion
(iv) Divorce by Mutual Consent

Codes:	A	B	C	D
(a)	(i)	(ii)	(iii)	(iv)
(b)	(iv)	(iii)	(ii)	(i)
(c)	(ii)	(iii)	(i)	(iv)
(d)	(iv)	(iii)	(i)	(ii)

29. Arrange the sequence of the following concepts in which they appear in a contract, using the code:
   (i) Communication of acceptance
   (ii) Deceit
   (iii) Invitation to offer
   (iv) Damages

   Codes:
   (a) (iii), (ii), (i), (iv) (b) (iii), (iv), (ii), (i)
   (c) (iii), (i), (ii), (iv) (d) (iii), (ii), (i), (iv)

30. Point out the correct explanation from the following Assertion and Reason:
   Assertion (A): Consideration must be market price of offer.
   Reason (R): Offerer must get equitable price for his offer. Codes:
   (a) Assertion and Reason are wrong
   (b) Assertion and Reason are right
   (c) Assertion is right, but Reason is wrong
   (d) Assertion is wrong, but Reason is right

31. In the Nash v. Inman case, the issue was:
   (a) minor's liability
   (b) frustration
   (c) fraud
   (d) misrepresentation

32. Contractual remedies are provided by the Indian Contract Act, Section:
   (a) 56 (b) 65
   (c) 73 (d) 37

33. Some, all or none of the following statements are right. Answer using the codes:
   (i) A minor's liability for necessaries depends on his consent to supply the necessaries to him.
   (ii) An infant is capable of making a contract of purchase of necessaries.
   (iii) A minor has to pay agreed price for necessaries.
   (iv) In Peter v. Fleming, (1840) 6 M and W 92, the court took judicial notice that it was Prima Facie unreasonable that an undergraduate at a college should have a watch and a watch chain.

   Codes:
   (a) All are right
   (b) All are wrong
   (c) Only (i), (ii), (iii) are right
   (d) Only (ii) is right

34. Some, all or none of the following statements are right. Answer using the codes.
   (i) A help given or promised to a dancing girl is not tainted with immorality.
   (ii) Public policy is an unruly ass.
   (iii) A wife who is entitled to maintenance can give up her right in consideration of a lump sum payment, but the surrender of the right to claim revision of the amount in the context of rising prices would not be opposed to public policy.
   (iv) A contract for sale of goods whose tenor shows that the price was intended to be paid out of black money is opposed to public policy.

   Codes:
   (a) All are right
   (b) All are wrong
   (c) Only (i), (ii), (iv) are right
   (d) Only (iv) is right

35. Which of the following is the correct statement?

   Vicarious liability means:
   (a) Liability without fault
   (b) Servant's liability for the wrong of the master

(c) Master's liability for the wrong of the servant
(d) Damage which could not be prevented

36. The tort involved in Hurst v. Picture Theatre Ltd. case is:
(a) Defamation (b) Nuisance
(c) Negligence (d) Trespass

37. Res Ipsa loquitur means:
(a) as you sow, you reap
(b) guilty shall be punished
(c) the thing speaks for itself
(d) the guilty speaks lies

38. *Damnum Sine injuria* means:
(a) an objective right
(b) suffering of loss without violation of legal right
(c) violation of legal right and suffering of loss
(d) violation of legal right

39. This item consists of two statements. One labelled as Assertion (A) and the other as Reason (R). Examine these statements and decide if the Assertion (A) and the Reason (R) are true or false. Select your answer using the code:
Assertion (A): Law cannot take account of everything that follows a wrongful act.
Reason (R): Causes of causes or consequences of consequences are outside the scope of liability.
(a) Both (A) and (R) are true
(b) Both (A) and (R) are false
(c) (A) is true, but (R) is false
(d) (A) is false, but (R) is true

40. Mark the correct answer in the following statements:
(a) Dangerous goods arise on proof of negligence
(b) Strict liability arises only when the thing causing harm escapes
(c) Liability for dangerous goods in India is absolute
(d) Liability for dangerous goods in India is strict

41. Defence of insanity under Section 84 of the Indian Penal Code requires:
(a) unsoundness of mind of any kind
(b) legal insanity
(c) medical insanity
(d) moral insanity

42. In which set of sections of the Indian Penal Code even death can be caused in exercise of right to private defence of person and property.
(a) Sections 100 and 101
(b) Sections 100 and 102
(c) Sections 100 and 103
(d) Sections 102 and 105

43. Point out the correct answer:
'A' instigates 'B' to instigate 'C' to kill 'D'. Inpursuance of that instigation B writes a letter to C to kill D. C does not read the letter. Therefore:
(a) 'A' and 'B' are liable for abetment of murder.
(b) 'A' is liable for abetment of murder but 'B' is not liable for abetment of murder.
(c) 'A' is liable for abetment of murder but 'B' is liable for attempt to abetment of murder.
(d) None of the above is correct.

44. Point out the correct statement.
Crime is:
(a) an illegal act
(b) an immoral act
(c) an illegal or immoral act
(d) an illegal and immoral act

45. Point out the correct statement:
A and B went to cause murder of C. A was with a spear and B was with a stick.

B caught C and beat C with stick. A did nothing while B was beating. When C fell down and became unconscious A took him to a nearby hospital for care where he died.
(a) A and B both are liable under Sections 302 and 34 of Indian Penal Code.
(b) A is liable under Section 302 of the Indian Penal Code but B is liable for nothing.
(c) B is liable for murder and A is liable for abetment of murder.
(d) None of the above.

46. In which of the following cases, the Supreme Court held that "the members of non-recognised union cannot be represented in collective bargaining proceedings or individual grievances of its members".
(a) Chairman, Bank of India v. All Orissa State Bank Officers Association (2003) 3 ILJ 751 (S.C.)
(b) W. Willard Wirtz v. Hotel and Club Employee's Union, AIR 1969 SC 25
(c) Indian Oxygen Ltd. v. Their Workmen, AIR 1969 SC 306
(d) None of the above

47. The Supreme Court has awarded twenty lacs rupees as a compensation in the case of "Bandh" calls given by political party/ parties. Select the correct one from among the following:
(a) Communist Party of India
(b) BJP
(c) Both (a) and (b)
(d) Congress Party

48. The Indian Trade Union laws is a replica of the Model prevailing in:
(a) England (b) France
(c) America (d) Australia

49. Lay-off means:
(a) removing a workman
(b) retirement of a workman
(c) dismissing a workman
(d) inability of employer to provide work to a workman

50. Retrenchment means:
(a) Voluntary retirement
(b) Dismissal
(c) Discharge of surplus labour
(d) None of the above

ANSWERS

1. (c)	2. (b)	3. (d)	4. (b)	5. (b)
6. (a)	7. (c)	8. (d)	9. (d)	10. (b)
11. (b)	12. (d)	13. (b)	14. (c)	15. (b)
16. (c)	17. (c)	18. (b)	19. (c)	20. (a)
21. (b)	22. (c)	23. (b)	24. (b)	25. (a)
26. (c)	27. (c)	28. (b)	29. (c)	30. (b)
31. (a)	32. (c)	33. (c)	34. (a)	35. (c)
36. (c)	37. (c)	38. (b)	39. (a)	40. (b)
41. (a)	42. (c)	43. (c)	44. (d)	45. (b)
46. (a)	47. (b)	48. (a)	49. (a)	50. (a)

JUNE–2006

Note: This paper contains fifty (50) objective type questions, each question carrying two (2) marks. All questions are compulsory.

PAPER–I

1. Which of the following comprise teaching skill:
   (a) Black Board writing
   (b) Questioning
   (c) Explaining
   (d) All of the above

2. Which of the following statements is most appropriate?
   (a) Teachers can teach.
   (b) Teachers help can create in a student a desire to learn.
   (c) Lecture Method can be used for developing thinking.
   (d) Teachers are born.

3. The first Indian chronicler of Indian history was:
   (a) Megasthanese (b) Fahiyan
   (c) Huan Tsang (d) Kalhan

4. Which of the following statements is correct?
   (a) Syllabus is a part of curriculum.
   (b) Syllabus is an annexure to curriculum.
   (c) Curriculum is the same in all educational institutions affiliated to a particular university.
   (d) Syllabus is not the same in all educational institutions affiliated to a particular university.

5. Which of the two given options is of the level of understanding?
   (I) Define noun.
   (II) Define noun in your own words.
   (a) Only I (b) Only II
   (c) Both I and II (d) Neither I nor II

6. Which of the following options are the main tasks of research in modern society?
   (I) to keep pace with the advancement in knowledge.
   (II) to discover new things.
   (III) to write a critique on the earlier writings.
   (IV) to systematically examine and critically analyse the investigations/sources with objectivity.
   (a) IV, II and I (b) I, II and III
   (c) I and III (d) II, III and IV

7. Match List I (Interviews) with List II (Meaning) and select the correct answer from the code given below:
   List I (Interviews)
   (A) Structured interviews
   (B) Unstructured interviews
   (C) Focussed interviews
   (D) Clinical interviews
   List II (Meanings)
   (i) greater flexibility approach
   (ii) attention on the questions to be answered
   (iii) individual life experience
   (iv) Pre determined question
   (v) non-directive

Codes:	A	B	C	D
(a)	(iv)	(i)	(ii)	(iii)
(b)	(ii)	(iv)	(i)	(iii)
(c)	(v)	(ii)	(iv)	(i)
(d)	(i)	(iii)	(v)	(iv)

8. What do you consider as the main aim of inter-disciplinary research?
   (a) To bring out holistic approach to research.
   (b) To reduce the emphasis of single subject in research domain.
   (c) To over simplify the problem of research.
   (d) To create a new trend in research methodology.
9. One of the aims of the scientific method in research is to:
   (a) improve data interpretation
   (b) eliminate spurious relations
   (c) confirm triangulation
   (d) introduce new variables
10. The depth of any research can be judged by:
   (a) title of the research.
   (b) objectives of the research.
   (c) total expenditure on the research.
   (d) duration of the research.

Read the following passage and answer the questions 11 to 15:

The superintendence, direction and control of preparation of electoral rolls for, and the conduct of, elections to Parliament and State Legislatures and elections to the offices of the President and the Vice-President of India are vested in the Election Commission of India. It is an independent constitutional authority.

Independence of the Election Commission and its insulation from executive interference is ensured by a specific provision under Article 324(5) of the Constitution that the chief Election Commissioner shall not be removed from his office except in like manner and on like grounds as a Judge of the Supreme Court and conditions of his service shall not be varied to his disadvantage after his appointment.

In C.W.P. No. 4912 of 1998 (Kushra Bharat Vs. Union of India and others), the Delhi High Court directed that information relating to Government dues owed by the candidates to the departments dealing with Government accommodation, electricity, water, telephone and transport etc. and any other dues should be furnished by the candidates and this information should be published by the election authorities under the commission.

11. The text of the passage reflects or raises certain questions:
   (a) The authority of the commission can not be challenged.
   (b) This would help in stopping the criminalization of Indian politics.
   (c) This would reduce substantially the number of contesting candidates.
   (d) This would ensure fair and free elections.
12. According to the passage, the Election Commission is an independent constitutional authority. This is under Article No.:
   (a) 324 (b) 356
   (c) 246 (d) 161
13. Independence of the Commission means:
   (a) have a constitutional status.
   (b) have legislative powers.
   (c) have judicial powers.
   (d) have political powers.
14. Fair and free election means:
   (a) transparency
   (b) to maintain law and order
   (c) regional considerations
   (d) role for pressure groups
15. The Chief Election Commissioner can be removed from his office under Article:
   (a) 125 (b) 352
   (c) 226 (d) 324
16. The function of mass communication of supplying information regarding the

processes, issues, events and societal developments is known as:
(a) Content supply (b) Surveillance
(c) Gratification (d) Correlation

17. The science of the study of feedback systems in humans, animals and machines is known as:
(a) cybernetics
(b) reverse communication
(c) selectivity study
(d) response analysis

18. Networked media exist in inter-connected:
(a) social environments
(b) economic environments
(c) political environments
(d) technological environments

19. The combination of computing, telecommunications and media in a digital atmosphere is referred to as:
(a) online communication
(b) integrated media
(c) digital combine
(d) convergence

20. A dialogue between a human being and a computer programme that occurs simultaneously in various forms is described as:
(a) man-machine speak
(b) binary chat
(c) digital talk
(d) interactivity

21. Insert the missing number:

$\frac{16}{32}, \frac{15}{33}, \frac{17}{31}, \frac{14}{34}, ?$

(a) $\frac{19}{35}$ (b) $\frac{19}{30}$
(c) $\frac{18}{35}$ (d) $\frac{18}{30}$

22. Monday falls on 20th March 1995. What was the day on 3rd November 1994?
(a) Thursday (b) Sunday
(c) Tuesday (d) Saturday

23. The average of four consecutive even numbers is 27. The largest of these numbers is
(a) 36 (b) 32
(c) 30 (d) 28

24. In a certain code, FHQK means GIRL. How will WOMEN be written in the same code?
(a) VNLDM (b) FHQKN
(c) XPNFO (d) VLNDM

25. At what time between 4 and 5 O'clock will the hands of a watch point in opposite directions?
(a) 45 min. past 4
(b) 40 min. past 4
(c) $50\frac{4}{11}$ min. past 4
(d) $54\frac{6}{11}$ min. past 4

26. Which of the following conclusions is logically valid based on statement given below?
Statement: Most teachers are hard working.
Conclusions: (I) Some teachers are hard working.
(II) Some teachers are not hard working.
(a) Only (I) is implied
(b) Only (II) is implied
(c) Both (I) and (II) are implied
(d) Neither (I) nor (II) is implied

27. Who among the following can be asked to make a statement in Indian Parliament?
(a) Any MLA
(b) Chief of Army Staff
(c) Solicitor General of India
(d) Mayor of Delhi

28. Which of the following conclusions is logically valid based on statement given below?

Statement: Most of the Indian States existed before independence.

Conclusions: (I) Some Indian States existed before independence.

(II) All Indian States did not exist before independence.

(a) Only (I) is implied
(b) Only (II) is implied
(c) Both (I) and (II) are implied
(d) Neither (I) nor (II) is implied

29. Water is always involved with landslides. This is because it:
(a) reduces the shear strength of rocks
(b) increases the weight of the overburden
(c) enhances chemical weathering
(d) is a universal solvent

30. Direction for this question:
Given below are two statements (A) and (B) followed by two conclusions (i) and (ii). Considering the statements to be true, indicate which of the following conclusions logically follow from the given statements by selecting one of the four response alternatives given below the conclusion:

Statements: (A) All businessmen are wealthy.

(B) All wealthy people are hard working.

Conclusions: (i) All businessmen are hard working.

(ii) All hardly working people are not wealthy.

(a) Only (i) follows
(b) Only (ii) follows
(c) Both (i) and (ii) follow
(d) Neither (i) nor (ii) follows

31. Using websites to pour out one's grievances is called:
(a) Cyberventing (b) Cyber ranting
(c) Web hate (d) Web plea

32. In web search, finding a large number of documents with very little relevant information is termed:
(a) poor recall
(b) web crawl
(c) poor precision rate
(d) poor web response

33. The concept of connect intelligence is derived from:
(a) virtual reality
(b) fuzzy logic
(c) bluetooth technology
(d) value added networks

34. Use of an ordinary telephone as an Internet applicance is called:
(a) Voice net (b) Voice telephone
(c) Voice line (d) Voice portal

35. Video transmission over the Internet that looks like delayed livecasting is called:
(a) virtual video
(b) direct broadcast
(c) video shift
(d) real-time video

36. Which is the smallest North-east State in India?
(a) Tripura (b) Meghalaya
(c) Mizoram (d) Manipur

37. Tamil Nadu coastal belt has drinking water shortage due to:
(a) high evaporation
(b) sea water flooding due to tsunami
(c) over exploitation of ground water by tubewells
(d) seepage of sea water

38. While all rivers of Peninsular India flow into the Bay of Bengal, Narmada and Tapti flow into the Arabian Sea because these two rivers:

(a) Follow the slope of these rift valleys
(b) The general slope of the Indian peninsula is from east to west
(c) The Indian peninsula north of the Satpura ranges, is tilted towards the west
(d) The Indian peninsula south of the Satpura ranges is tilted towards east

39. Soils in the Mahanadi delta are less fertile than those in the Godavari delta because of:
(a) erosion of top soils by annual floods
(b) inundation of land by sea water
(c) traditional agriculture practices
(d) the derivation of alluvial soil from red-soil hinterland

40. Which of the following institutions in the field of education is set up by the MHRD Government of India?
(a) Indian council of world Affair, New Delhi
(b) Mythic Society, Bangalore
(c) National Bal Bhawn, New Delhi
(d) India International Centre, New Delhi

41. **Assertion (A):** Aerosols have potential for modifying climate.

Reason (R): Aerosols interact with both short waves and radiation.
(a) Both (A) and (R) are true, and (R) is the correct explanation of (A)
(b) Both (A) and (R) are true, but (R) is not the correct explanation of (A)
(c) (A) is true, but (R) is false
(d) (A) is false, but (R) is true

42. 'SITE' stands for:
(a) System for International technology and Engineering
(b) Satellite Instructional Television Experiment
(c) South Indian Trade Estate
(d) State Institute of Technology and Engineering

43. What is the name of the Research station established by the Indian Government for 'Conducting Research at Antarctic?
(a) Dakshin Gangotri
(b) Yamunotri
(c) Uttari Gangotri
(d) None of the above

44. Ministry of Human Resource Development (HRD) includes:
(a) Department of Elementary Education and Literacy
(b) Department of Secondary Education and Higher Education
(c) Department of Women and Child Development
(d) All of the above

45. Parliament can legislate on matters listed in the State list:
(a) With the prior permission of the President.
(b) Only after the Constitution is amended suitably.
(c) In case of inconsistency among State legislatures.
(d) At the request of two or more States.

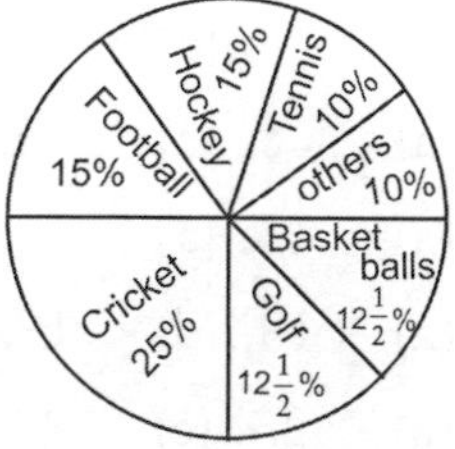

The above pie chart indicates the expenditure of a country on various sports during a particular year. Study the pie chart and answer Question Numbers 46 to 50.

46. The ratio of the total expenditure on football to that of expenditure on hockey is:

(a) 1 : 15 (b) 1 : 1
(c) 15 : 1 (d) 3 : 20

47. If the total expenditure on sports during the year was ₹ 1,20,000,00 how much was spent on basket ball?
(a) ₹ 9,50,000 (b) ₹ 10,00,000
(c) ₹ 12,00,000 (d) ₹ 15,00,000

48. The chart shows that the most popular game of the country is:
(a) Hockey (b) Football
(c) Cricket (d) Tennis

49. Out of the following country's expenditure is the same on:
(a) Hockey and Tennis
(b) Golf and Basketball
(c) Cricket and Football
(d) Hockey and Golf

50. If the total expenditure on sport during the year was ₹ 1,50,00,000 the expenditure on cricket and hockey together was:
(a) ₹ 60,00,000 (b) ₹ 50,00,000
(c) ₹ 37,50,000 (d) ₹ 25,00,000

ANSWERS

1. (d)	2. (b)	3. (d)	4. (a)	5. (b)
6. (a)	7. (a)	8. (a)	9. (b)	10. (b)
11. (d)	12. (a)	13. (a)	14. (b)	15. (d)
16. (a)	17. (a)	18. (d)	19. (d)	20. (d)
21. (d)	22. (a)	23. (c)	24. (c)	25. (d)
26. (c)	27. (c)	28. (b)	29. (b)	30. (a)
31. (a)	32. (a)	33. (d)	34. (c)	35. (d)
36. (c)	37. (d)	38. (a)	39. (a)	40. (c)
41. (a)	42. (b)	43. (a)	44. (d)	45. (d)
46. (b)	47. (a)	48. (c)	49. (b)	50. (a)

PAPER–II

Note: This paper contains fifty (50) objective type questions, each question carrying two (2) marks. All questions are compulsory.

1. Which among the following is not a fundamental right?
(a) Right to Privacy
(b) Right to Speedy Trial
(c) Right to Clean Environment
(d) Right to Property

2. The president shall revoke a proclamation of emergency if the house of people passes a resolution disapproving the proclamation of emergency by a:
(a) Majority of total membership of the house.
(b) Majority of not less than two-third of the house present and voting
(c) Simple Majority
(d) Both (a) and (b)

3. Decision in D.K. Baru's case relates to:
(a) Dowry Death
(b) Murder
(c) Sexual harassment at work place
(d) Arrest

4. The Supreme Court is a court of record means:
(a) It has the powers of a court to punish for contempt of itself
(b) Its judgements are binding on all courts
(c) It has got powers to pass orders for enforcement of its own judgements
(d) Full faith and credit shall be given to all its judgements

5. Original jurisdiction of the Supreme Court means that it has got jurisdiction in any dispute:

(a) between the Government of India and one or more states
(b) between states on inter-state river water
(c) between two or more states
(d) both (a) and (c)

6. In Maneka Gandhi's case the Supreme Court held that the procedure established by law must be:
(a) fair and reasonable
(b) fair, just and reasonable
(c) fair, just and equitable
(d) duly enacted by legislature

7. In which case the Supreme Court held that secularism is part of the basic structure of the Constitution of India.
(a) Minerva Mills Case
(b) S.R. Bommai's Case
(c) S.P. Gupta's Case
(d) M.C. Mehta's Case

8. In the matter of appointment of High Court judges, the CJI is required to consult:
(a) Two senior most judges of the Supreme Court
(b) Two senior most judges of the concerned High Court
(c) The chief justice of the concerned High Court
(d) Governor of the state

9. Fiction theory is related to which one of the following concepts:
(a) Legal Personality (b) Ownership
(c) Liability (d) Justice

10. Jurisprudence is:
(a) the systematic study of nature
(b) lawyer's extroversion
(c) study of government's behaviour
(d) None of the above

11. Right and duties exist:
(a) together
(b) separately
(c) opposite to each other
(d) complementary to each other

12. "Liberty is without independent jural significance" was propounded by:
(a) Hans Kelsen (b) Duguit
(c) Rosquo Pound (d) Mill

13. "A legal system is only the sum total of laws and that one only needs to identify a law" was propounded by:
(a) Bentham (b) Austin
(c) Salmond (d) Ihring

14. The difference between judicial and legislative creativity has been that "The creative power of the court is limited by existing legal material at their command. They find the material and shape it. The legislature may manufacture entirely new material" was stated by:
(a) Ehrlich (b) Rosquo Pound
(c) Kelson (d) Savigny

15. International law is:
(a) Collection of legislations of various countries.
(b) Body of rules and principles of action which are binding upon civilized states in their relation with each other.
(c) Collection of customs of various countries.
(d) A legal instrument in service of domestic policy.

16. International treaties are the most important source of:
(a) Environmental law
(b) Cyber Law
(c) International law
(d) None of the above

17. Estrada doctrine is related to
(a) Mexico (b) Spain
(c) Portugal (d) Grenada

18. "Uniting for Peace Resolution" came into being in the year
(a) 1949 (b) 1950
(c) 1951 (d) 1952

19. The Savarkar (1911) case is related to:
    (a) Rights of revolutionaries
    (b) International obligation of fighters for independence
    (c) Terms and conditions of sea law
    (d) Terms and conditions of the extradition treaties

20. Article 23(1) of the UDHR corresponds with which article of the Indian constitution?
    (a) Art. 41 (b) Art 39(d)
    (c) Art. 43 (d) Art. 38

21. Section 19 of the Protection of Human Rights Act, 1993 provides protection to
    (a) Police (b) Army
    (c) Navy (d) All of above

22. The convention on the right of child came into being in the year
    (a) 1988 (b) 1989
    (c) 1990 (d) 1991

23. Marriage under the Hindu law after the Hindu marriage (Amendment) Act, 1976 is:
    (a) Purely a contract (b) Sacrament
    (c) Sacrosent (d) None of these

24. Single 'act of adultery' is a ground for:
    (a) Judicial separation
    (b) Divorce
    (d) Both (a) and (b)
    (d) None of the above

25. A and B petitioned for divorce by mutual consent. After the expiry of 18 months B withdrew her consent and refused to appear before the court. Choose the correct legal position.
    (a) B has a right to withdraw her consent
    (b) B does not have the right to withdraw her consent
    (c) Divorce is complete
    (d) None of the above

26. Given below are two statements, one labelled as Assertion (A) and the other labelled as Reason (R), with the help of codes given below, point out the correct explanation.
    Assertion (A): Marriage under the Hindu Marriage Act, 1955 is dissoluble.
    Reason (R): Marriage is a sacrosant Union.
    (a) Both (A) and (R) are true
    (b) Both (A) and (R) are false
    (d) (A) is true but (R) is false
    (d) (A) is false but (R) is true

27. Match items in List I with items in List II using the code:

    List I
    (a) Marriage during Iddat period is
    (b) Marriage with an impotent person is
    (c) Marriage below the age of 18 years is
    (d) Marriage with a person of unsound mind is

    List II
    (i) Voidable (ii) Valid
    (iii) Voidable (iv) Voidable

Codes:	A	B	C	D
(a)	(i)	(ii)	(iii)	(iv)
(b)	(i)	(iii)	(iv)	(ii)
(c)	(i)	(iii)	(ii)	(iv)
(d)	(iii)	(ii)	(i)	(iv)

28. In which of the following cases, the High Court held that "the presence of Qazi is not necessary at the time of marriage ceremony under the Muslim law"?
    (a) Qazi Mohd. Najmuddin Husain V State of A.P.
    (b) Mohd. Yunus V Malooki
    (c) Shamim Ara V state of U.P.
    (d) Bai Tahira V Ali Hussain

29. In the case of Mc Gregor V Mc Gregor, (1888) 21 Q. B.D. 424, the wife withdrew her complaints as the husband entered into an agreement with her on the condition that if she withdrew her

complaints and refrained from pledging his credit, he will pay her an allowance.

(a) The agreement is a social agreement and is not binding
(b) The agreement is a family agreement and is not a contract
(c) The agreement is based on love and affection and is binding
(d) Parties had the intention to have a binding contract between them

30. Some, all or none of the following statements are correct, answer using the code:
(a) Consideration is the recompense given by the party contracting with the other
(b) If the promised act has been done before the agreement is made, it is past consideration and past consideration is no consideration.
(c) Consideration should be something which has some value in law
(d) Consideration may not be adequate

31. An infant who obtains loan by falsely misrepresenting his age can be made to repay the amount:
(a) As if he never entered into the void contract
(b) The contract is void so he is not liable to repay
(c) He is liable because of the fraud
(d) The contract is valid

32. Mistake of both the parties about subject matter renders an agreement:
(a) Voidable (b) Unavoidable
(c) Void (d) Valid

33. Arrange the sequence of following concepts in a contract. Use the code given below:
(i) Damage
(ii) Damages
(iii) Undue influence
(iv) Invitation to offer

Codes:

(a)	(i)	(ii)	(iii)	(iv)
(b)	(iv)	(iii)	(ii)	(i)
(c)	(iv)	(iii)	(i)	(ii)
(d)	(iv)	(i)	(iii)	(ii)

34. Principle of law in Hadley V Baxendate related to:
(a) Quasi-Contract
(b) Fraud
(c) Special Damages
(d) Unjust Enrichment

35. A hazardous or inherently dangerous activity can be tolerated only on the condition that it indemnifies all those who suffer because of the dangerous activity. The above statement pertains to:
(a) the principle of strict liability
(b) vicarions liability
(c) absolute liability
(d) principle of negligence

36. In contributory negligence plaintiff is injured because of the wrong of:
(a) The plaintiff
(b) Plaintiff as well as the defendant
(c) Defendant
(d) None of the above

37. Choose the correct statement out the following "volenti non fit injuria" means
(a) A specific tort
(b) Is a good defence if injury to risk is consented
(c) Is a good defence if there is knowledge of the risk
(d) Is a good defence in cases of rescue

38. Select the correct code for the following statement:

To protect himself and his property
(a) Law recognises the right of self-defence
(b) Law does not allow any such right

(c) One should go to the police station
(d) Use of force for whatever object is not allowed

39. The principle of Novus actus interveniens applies to determine:
(a) Vicarious liability
(b) Remoteness of damage
(c) Strict liability
(d) Act of God

40. For the negligence of skillful and qualified persons such as doctors or engineers an employer is liable even though they are not under his control. The above statement is in reference to the tort of :
(a) Strict liability
(b) Negligence
(c) Vicarious liability
(d) Damnum sine injuria

41. A entered a house to commit theft. Old lady living in the house saw the thief and shouted for help. Neighbours collected near the house and caught hold of the thief who was trying to escape. The neighbours gave the thief beatings with fists and lathis. The neighbours are liable for:
(a) Similar intention
(b) Common intention
(c) Unlawful assembly
(d) Conspiracy

42. Which one of the following statements is correct?
(a) Abetment of an offence is an incomplete offence
(b) Abetment of an offence is a continuing offence
(c) Abetment of an offence is a complete offence
(d) Abetment of an offence is an offence depending upon circumstances of the case

43. A village Vaidya used to successfully operate wounds with shaving blade. Victim who was suffering from piles was operated with shaving blade by the Vaidya. Due to profound bleeding, the victim died and the Vaidya was prosecuted for causing death of the victim. If you are a defence counsel under which of the following sections of the Indian Penal Code you can defend the Vaidya.
(a) Section 87 (b) Section 88
(c) Section 92 (d) None of these

44. During the murder trial it was proved that the murder was committed by six persons.
Out of the six accused persons, identity of two accused persons could not be verified. Hence the two accused persons were acquitted. Rest of the four accused persons claimed acquittal. Point out the correct answer in determining liability of the four accused persons.
(a) Shall be liable u/s 302/149 of the Indian Penal Code
(b) Shall be liable u/s 302/34 of the Indian Penal Code
(c) Liable for negligence
(d) Shall not be liable for murder

45. The maxim "actus non facit reum nisi mens sit rea" means
(a) Prohibited act constitutes an offence
(b) Guilty intention of the accused constitutes an offence
(c) Neither guilty intention alone nor the prohibited act alone constitutes an offence
(d) Prohibited act followed by guilty intention constitutes an offence

46. In which one of the following cases, the Supreme Court had held 'Bandh' to be unconstitutional:
(a) L. Chandra V Union of India
(b) Prabhat Kumar V State of Kerala
(c) Raudher Kumar V Union of India
(d) None of the above

47. Right to education is a fundamental right under Article:
    (a) 21 (b) 20
    (c) 21A (d) 19

48. In which of the following cases the Supreme Court recognised the theory of "Hire and Fire" in labour law?
    (a) The steel Authority workers' Corporation case
    (b) The Air India Authority Corporation case
    (c) Mohini Jain case
    (d) The Gujrat Electricity Workers' case

49. Strike is a legitimate right in the hands of:
    (a) The employer (b) Workmen
    (c) Both (a) and (b) (d) None of these

50. Lock-out to is:
    (a) anti-thesis of strike
    (b) anti-strike
    (c) equal to strike
    (d) none of the above

ANSWERS

1. (d)	2. (b)	3. (d)	4. (a)	5. (d)
6. (b)	7. (b)	8. (a)	9. (a)	10. (b)
11. (d)	12. (c)	13. (b)	14. (c)	15. (b)
16. (c)	17. (a)	18. (b)	19. (d)	20. (a)
21. (b)	22. (b)	23. (b)	24. (c)	25. (a)
26. (a)	27. (a)	28. (b)	29. (a)	30. (d)
31. (c)	32. (c)	33. (d)	34. (c)	35. (a)
36. (a)	37. (c)	38. (a)	39. (b)	40. (c)
41. (c)	42. (b)	43. (a)	44. (b)	45. (d)
46. (d)	47. (c)	48. (b)	49. (d)	50. (a)

DECEMBER–2007

Note: This paper contains fifty (50) objective type questions, each question carrying two (2) marks. All questions are compulsory.

PAPER–I

1. Verbal guidance is least effective in the learning of
   (a) Aptitudes (b) Skills
   (c) Attitudes (d) Relationship
2. Which is the most important aspect of the teacher's role in learning?
   (a) The development of insight into what consititutes an adequate performance
   (b) The development of insight into what consititutes the pitfalls and dangers to be avoided
   (c) The provision of encouragement and moral support
   (d) The provision of continuous diagnostic and remedial help
3. The most appropriate purpose of learning is
   (a) personal adjustment
   (b) modification of behaviour
   (c) social and political awarness
   (d) preparing oneself for employment
4. The students who keep on asking questions in the class should be
   (a) encouraged to find answer independently
   (b) advised to meet the teacher after the class
   (c) encouraged to continue questioning
   (d) advised not to disturb during the lecture
5. Maximum participation of students is possible in teaching through
   (a) discussion method
   (b) lecture method
   (c) audio-visual aids
   (d) textbook method
6. Generalised conclusion on the basis of a sample is technically known as
   (a) Data analysis and interpretation
   (b) Parameter inference
   (c) Statistical inference
   (d) All of the above
7. The experimental study is based on
   (a) The manipulation of variables
   (b) Conceptual parameters
   (c) Replication of research
   (d) Survey of literature
8. The main characteristic of scientific research is
   (a) Empirical (b) Theoretical
   (c) Experimental (d) All of the above
9. Authenticity of a research finding is its
   (a) Originality (b) Validity
   (c) Objectivity (d) All of the above
10. Which technique is generally followed when the population is finite?
    (a) Area Sampling Technique
    (b) Purposive Sampling Technique
    (c) Systematic Sampling Technique
    (d) None of the above

Read the following passage and answer the questions 11 to 15:

Gandhi's overall social and environmental philosophy is based on what human beings need rather than what they want. His early introduction to the teachings of Jains, Theosophists, Christian sermons, Ruskin and Tolstoy, and most significantly the *Bhagavad Gita*, were to have profound impact on the development of Gandhi's holistic thinking on humanity, nature and their ecological interrelation. His deep concern for the disadvantaged, the poor and rural population created an ambience for an alternative social thinking that was at once far-sighted, local and immediate. For Gandhi was acutely aware that the demands generated by the need to feed and sustain human life, compounded by the growing industrialisation of India, far outstripped the finite resources of nature. This might nowadays appear naive or commonplace, but such pronouncements were as rare as they were heretical a century ago. Gandhi was also concerned about the destruction, under colonial and modernist designs, of the existing infrastructures which had more potential for keeping a community flourishing within ecologically-sensitive traditional patterns of subsistence, especially in the rural areas, than did the incoming Western alternatives based on nature-blind technology and the enslavement of human spirit and energies.

Perhaps the moral principle for which Gandhi is best known is that of active non-violence, derived from the traditional moral restraint of not injuring another being. The most refined expression of this value is in the great epic of the *Mahabharata* (c. 100 BCE to 200 CE), where moral development proceeds through placing constraints on the liberties, desires and acquisitiveness endemic to human life. One's action is judged in terms of consequences and the impact it is likely to have on another. Jainas had generalised this principle to include all sentient creatures and biocommunities alike. Advanced Jaina monks and nuns will sweep their path to avoid harming insects and even bacteria. Non-injury is a non-negotiable universal prescription.

11. Which one of the following have a profound impact on the development of Gandhi's holistic thinking on humanity, nature and their ecological interrelations?
    (a) Jain teachings
    (b) Christian sermons
    (c) *Bhagavad Gita*
    (d) Ruskin and Tolstoy

12. Gandhi's overall social and environmental philosophy is based on human beings'
    (a) Need (b) Desire
    (c) Wealth (d) Welfare

13. Gandhiji's deep concern for the disadvantaged, the poor and rural population created an ambience for an alternative
    (a) rural policy
    (b) social thinking
    (c) urban policy
    (d) economic thinking

14. Colonial policy and modernisation led to the destruction of
    (a) major industrial infrastructure
    (b) irrigation infrastructure
    (c) urban infrastructure
    (d) rural infrastructure

15. Gandhi's active non-violence is derived from
    (a) Moral restraint of not injuring another being
    (b) Having liberties, desires and acquisitiveness
    (c) Freedom of action
    (d) Nature-blind technology and enslavement of human spirit and energies

16. DTH service was started in the year
    (a) 2000 (b) 2002
    (c) 2004 (d) 2006

17. National Press day is celebrated on
    (a) 16th November (b) 19th November
    (c) 21st November (d) 30th November

18. The total number of members in the Press Council of India are
    (a) 28 (b) 14
    (c) 17 (d) 20

19. The right to impart and receive information is guaranteed in the Constitution of India by Article
    (a) 19(2)(a) (b) 19(16)
    (c) 19(2) (d) 19(1)(a)

20. Use of radio for higher education is based on the presumption of
    (a) Enriching curriculum-based instruction
    (b) Replacing teacher in the long run
    (c) Everybody having access to a radio set
    (d) Other means of instruction getting outdated

21. Find out the number which should come at the place of question mark which will complete the following series.
    5, 4, 9, 17, 35, ? = 139
    (a) 149 (b) 79
    (c) 49 (d) 69

Questions 22 to 24 are based on the following diagram in which there are three interlocking circles I, S and P, where circle I stands for Indians, circle S for Scientists and circle P for Politicians. Different regions in the figure are lettered from a to f.

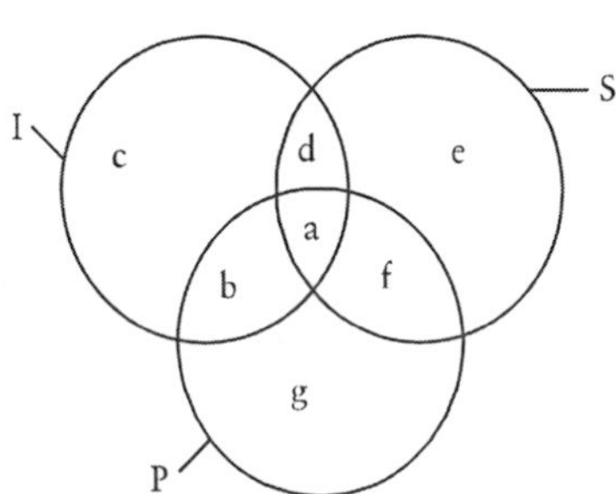

22. The region which represents Non-Indian Scientists who are Politicians.
    (a) f (b) d
    (c) a (d) c

23. The region which represents Indians who are neither Scientists nor Politicians.
    (a) g (b) c
    (c) f (d) a

24. The region which represents Politicians who are Indians as well as Scientists.
    (a) b (b) c
    (c) a (d) d

25. Which number is missing in the following series?
    2, 5, 10, 17, 26, 37, 50, ?
    (a) 63 (b) 65
    (c) 67 (d) 69

26. The function of measurement includes
    (a) Prognosis (b) Diagnosis
    (c) Prediction (d) All of the above

27. Logical arguments are based on
    (a) Scientific reasoning
    (b) Customary reasoning
    (c) Mathematical reasoning
    (d) Syllogistic reasoning

28. Insert the missing number 4 : 17 : : 7 : ?
    (a) 48 (b) 49
    (c) 50 (d) 51

29. Choose the odd word.
    (a) Nun (b) Knight
    (c) Monk (d) Priest

30. Choose the number which is different from others in the group.
    (a) 49 (b) 63
    (c) 77 (d) 81

31. Probability sampling implies.
    (a) Stratified Random Sampling
    (b) Systematic Random Sampling
    (c) Simple Random Sampling
    (d) All of the above

32. Insert the missing number.
    $\frac{36}{62}, \frac{39}{63}, \frac{43}{61}, \frac{48}{64}, ?$

(a) $\frac{51}{65}$ (b) $\frac{56}{60}$
(c) $\frac{54}{65}$ (d) $\frac{33}{60}$

33. At what time between 3 and 4 O'clock will the hands of a watch point in opposite directions?
(a) 40 minutes past three
(b) 45 minutes past three
(c) 50 minutes past three
(d) 55 minutes past three

34. Mary has three children. What is the probability that none of the three children is a boy?
(a) $\frac{1}{2}$ (b) $\frac{1}{3}$
(c) $\frac{3}{4}$ (d) 1

35. If the radius of a circle is increased by 50 percent. Its area is increased by
(a) 125 percent (b) 100 percent
(c) 75 percent (d) 50 percent

36. CD ROM stands for
(a) Computer Disk Read Only Memory
(b) Compact Disk Read Over Memory
(c) Compact Disk Read Only Memory
(d) Computer Disk Read Over Memory

37. The 'brain' of a computer which keeps peripherals under its control is called
(a) Common Power Unit
(b) Common Processing Unit
(c) Central Power Unit
(d) Central Processing Unit

38. Data can be saved on backing storage medium known as
(a) Compact Disk Recordable
(b) Computer Disk Rewritable
(c) Compact Disk Rewritable
(d) Computer Data Rewritable

39. RAM means
(a) Random Access Memory
(b) Rigid Access Memory
(c) Rapid Access Memory
(d) Revolving Access Memory

40. www represents
(a) who what and where
(b) weird wide web
(c) word wide web
(d) world wide web

41. Deforestation during the recent decades has led to
(a) Soil erosion
(b) Landslides
(c) Loss of bio-diversity
(d) All of the above

42. Which one of the following natural hazards is responsible for causing highest human disaster?
(a) Earthquakes
(b) Volcanic eruptions
(c) Snowstorms
(d) Tsunami

43. Which one of the following is appropriate for natural hazard mitigation?
(a) International AID
(b) Timely Warning System
(c) Rehabilitation
(d) Community Participation

44. Slums in metro city are the result of
(a) Rural to urban migration
(b) Poverty of the city-scape
(c) Lack of urban infrastructure
(d) Urban-governance

45. The great Indian Bustard bird is found in
(a) Thar Desert of India
(b) Coastal regions of India
(c) Temperate Forests in the Himalaya
(d) Tarai zones of the Himalayan Foot

46. The first Indian Satellite for serving the educational sector is known as
(a) SATEDU (b) INSAT-B
(c) EDUSAT (d) INSAT-C

47. Exclusive educational channel of IGNOU is known as
   (a) Gyan Darshan (b) Gyan Vani
   (c) Door Darshan (d) Prasar Bharati

48. The headquarter of Mahatma Gandhi Antarrashtriya Hindi Vishwavidyalaya is situated in
   (a) Sevagram (b) New Delhi
   (c) Wardha (d) Ahmedabad

49. Match List I with List II and select the correct answer using the codes given below.

   List I (Institutes)
   A. Central Institute of English and Foreign Languages
   B. Gramodaya Vishwavidyalaya
   C. Central Institute of Higher Tibetan Studies
   D. IGNOU

   List II (Locations)
   1. Chitrakoot 2. Hyderabad
   3. New Delhi 4. Dharmasala

Codes:	A	B	C	D
(a)	2	1	4	3
(b)	4	3	2	1
(c)	3	4	1	2
(d)	1	2	4	3

50. The aim of vocationalisation of education is
   (a) preparing students for a vocation along with knowledge
   (b) converting liberal education into vocational education
   (c) giving more importance to vocational than general education
   (d) making liberal education job-oriented

ANSWERS

1. (b)	2. (a)	3. (b)	4. (a)	5. (a)
6. (c)	7. (c)	8. (c)	9. (d)	10. (c)
11. (c)	12. (a)	13. (b)	14. (c)	15. (a)
16. (d)	17. (a)	18. (a)	19. (d)	20. (b)
21. (d)	22. (a)	23. (b)	24. (d)	25. (b)
26. (d)	27. (d)	28. (c)	29. (b)	30. (c)
31. (d)	32. (c)	33. (c)	34. (d)	35. (a)
36. (c)	37. (d)	38. (c)	39. (a)	40. (d)
41. (d)	42. (a)	43. (b)	44. (a)	45. (a)
46. (c)	47. (a)	48. (c)	49. (a)	50. (d)

PAPER–II

Note: This paper contains fifty (50) objective type questions, each question carrying two (2) marks. All questions are compulsory.

1. "Secularism as the basic structure of the constitution has been held to be so on the basis of more than 50 years' experience of the working of the constitution. The complete apathy for all kinds of religious teachings in institutions of the State have not helped in removing mutual misunderstanding and intolerance inter se between sections of the people of different religious faith and beliefs." This was stated by the Supreme Court of India in:
   (a) Aruna Roy V/s Union of India
   (b) Arunditi Roy V/s Union of India
   (c) P.A. Inamdar V/s State of Maharashtra
   (d) Unni Krishnan V/s State of A.P.

2. University of Petroleum, Energy, Gas and Oil has been created by a statute of a State on self-financing scheme. It:
   (a) Shall not be "the State" under Article 12

(b) Shall be "the State" having the trappings of the State under Article 12
(c) Shall not be "the State" with no liability and obligations to the public under Article 12
(d) Shall not be "the State" because of its governing relationship with other people under Article 12

3. Sexual harassment of women at working place was recognised as violation of human right to human dignity in:
(a) Sarla Mudgal V/s State of T.N.
(b) Vishakha V/s State of Rajasthan
(c) Nargesh Mirza V/s Air India
(d) Menaka Gandhi V/s Union of India

4. The Fundamental Right to move the Supreme Court has been described as the cornerstone of the democratic edifice raised by the Constitution and as such the Supreme Court must always regard it as its solemn duty to protect the said Fundamental rights zealously and vigilantly. This has been stated by the Supreme Court in:
(a) Daryao V/s State of U.P. 1962
(b) Bandhua Mukti Morcha V/s Union of India 1984
(c) Sheela Barse V/s Union of India 1988
(d) M.C. Mehta V/s Union of India 1989

5. Which of the following Articles do not contain the power of the highest Court of the Country to punish for the contempts of the Court:
(a) Article 141 (b) Article 142
(c) Article 129 (d) Both (a) and (b)

6. Match the following:
(A) National Emergency
(B) President's Rule
(C) Financial Emergency
(D) Public Service Commission for Union

(i) Article 316 (ii) Article 360
(iii) Article 356 (iv) Article 352

Codes:	**A**	**B**	**C**	**D**
(a)	(iv)	(iii)	(ii)	(i)
(b)	(ii)	(iii)	(i)	(iv)
(c)	(iii)	(ii)	(i)	(iv)
(d)	(i)	(ii)	(iv)	(iii)

7. Schedule IX was inserted in the Constitution of India by:
(a) 1st amendment 1951
(b) 42nd amendment 1976
(c) 44th amendment 1978
(d) 52nd amendment 1985

8. Hugo Gratius is regarded as the father of:
(a) Realist School
(b) Analytical School
(c) Historical School
(d) Philosophical School

9. "The task of Social engineering is to build as efficient structure of the society as possible with minimum friction and waste," it is said by:
(a) Kelsen (b) Karl Marx
(c) Roscoe Pound (d) Savigny

10. The difference between possession and ownership is as follows:
(a) Full enjoyment of the property is restricted in possession and there is no restriction in ownership
(b) The right of ownership consists of excluding others from using it and there is no such right in possession
(c) Both (a) and (b)
(d) None of the above

11. Precedent is a source of Law in:
(a) Common law system
(b) Civil law system
(c) International law
(d) All the above systems

12. The meaning of per in urium is as follows:
    (a) A decision which ignores a statute on the subject
    (b) A decision which ignores the case law on the subject
    (c) A decision which ignores the constitution on the subject
    (d) All of the above

13. An incorporated service of successive person is called:
    (a) Corporate person
    (b) Corporate aggregate
    (c) Corporate animation
    (d) Incorporial possession

14. Savigny's Volkgeist theory reveals:
    (a) Decision of the Court
    (b) Juristic opinion
    (c) Spirit of the people
    (d) None of the above

15. The World Court refused to give its advisory opinion in:
    (a) The Genocide convention case
    (b) The legality of the use by a state of Nuclear Weapons in Armed conflict
    (c) Interpretation of Peace Treaties case
    (d) Legality of the threat or use of Nuclear Weapons case

16. UN Human Rights Council has taken the place of:
    (a) Human Rights Committee
    (b) Human Rights Commission
    (c) U.N. Centre for Human Rights
    (d) Economic, Social and Cultural Rights Committee

17. Which of the following pairs are not correctly matched?

(a)	Doctrine of legitimacy	Tobar
(b)	Doctrine of non-recognition	Stimson
(c)	Doctrine of automatic recognition	Estrada
(d)	Doctrine of Effective control	Nixon

18. Arrange the following treaties in order in which they appeared. Use the code given below:
    (i) Convention Relating to the status of refugees
    (ii) European Convention on Human Rights
    (iii) Convention on the Prevention of Genocide
    (iv) The pact of Paris

Codes:

(a)	(i)	(iv)	(iii)	(ii)
(b)	(iii)	(ii)	(iv)	(i)
(c)	(ii)	(iv)	(i)	(iii)
(d)	(iv)	(iii)	(ii)	(i)

19. The purpose of the United Nations are:
    (i) To maintain International Peace and Security
    (ii) To establish World Government
    (iii) To develop friendly relations among Member States
    (iv) To secure international cooperation in solving problems of social, economic and humanitarian character

    Of these following are correct:
    (a) (i), (ii) and (iii) (b) (ii), (iii) and (iv)
    (c) (ii) and (iii) (d) (i), (iii) and (iv)

20. **Assertion (A):** International law is not potent enough to restrain a powerful state which has no respect for public opinion.

    Reason (R): Sanctions behind international law are weak.

    Codes:
    (a) Both (A) and (R) are correct and (R) is the correct explanation
    (b) Both (A) and (R) are correct, but (R) is not the correct explanation
    (c) (A) is true, but (R) is false
    (d) (A) is false, but (R) is true

21. When two persons are descendants of a common ancestor but by different wives, they are said to be related to each other by:
(a) Full blood (b) Uterine blood
(c) Half blood (d) None of these

22. Rules relating to Sapinda relationship are based on the principle of:
(a) Polygamy (b) Monogamy
(c) Endogamy (d) Exogamy

23. The term Hindu denotes the persons:
(i) Professing Hindu religion
(ii) Professing Buddh, Jain or Sikh religion
(iii) Who are not professing Muslim, Christian, Parsi or Jew religion
In respect of the aforesaid propositions which is correct?
(a) (i) and (ii) are correct and (iii) is incorrect
(b) (ii) and (iii) are correct and (i) is incorrect
(c) (i) and (iii) are incorrect but (ii) is correct
(d) (i), (ii) and (iii) are all correct

24. Marriages of all persons who are citizens of India belonging to various religions should be made compulsorily registrable in their respective states where the marriage is solemnized. This was held by the Supreme Court in case of:
(a) Githa Hariharn v/s R.B.I.
(b) Seema v/s Ashwani Kumar
(c) John Vallamattom v/s U.O.I.
(d) None of the above

25. Arrange the grounds of divorce in the order in which they appear in the Hindu Marriage Act 1955. Use the code given below:
(i) Mutual Consent (ii) Breakdown
(iii) Fault (iv) Customary

Codes:

(a)	(iii)	(ii)	(i)	(iv)
(b)	(ii)	(iii)	(iv)	(i)
(c)	(i)	(ii)	(iii)	(iv)
(d)	(iv)	(i)	(iii)	(ii)

26. 'Tuhr' means:
(a) Period of iddat
(b) Period of menstruation
(c) Period between menstruations
(d) None of the above

27. To convert a proposal into a promise the acceptance must be:
(a) Qualified
(b) Unqualified
(c) General
(d) Absolute and Unqualified

28. In which of the following statements "Undue Influence" does not exist:
(a) When dominating party holds real or apparent authority
(b) When a person's mental capacity is affected because of bodily distress
(c) When a person threatens another to commit suicide
(d) When the party holds fiduciary relationship

29. **Assertion (A):** Agreement between 'A' and 'B' is void:
Reason (R):
(a) Consent of a party was caused by coercion
(b) Both the parties were under mistake as to a fact essential to the agreement
(c) Consideration in the contract is inadequate
(d) Consent was given under mistaken conception as to the value of the subject matter of contract.

30. In a Wrestling 'A' tells 'B' that Wrestler no. 1 will win. 'B' challenges the statement

of 'A'. They bet with each other over the result of the match. This is:
(a) Unlawful agreement
(b) Wagering agreement
(c) Contingent contract
(d) Voidable contract

31. A valuable consideration in the sense of the law may consist either in some right or interest or benefit accruing to one party on some forebearance, detriment, loss, responsibility given, suffered or undertaken by the other is well explained in:
(a) Currie Vs. Misa
(b) Abdul Aziz Vs. Manzum Ali
(c) Gopal Co. Ltd. Vs. Hazarilal Co. Ltd.
(d) Kedarnath Vs. Gauri Mohammed

32. Contract becomes impossible of performance if:
(a) The goods are not available in the market
(b) Workers are on strike
(c) Subject matter of the contract was destroyed at the time of contract
(d) Money is not available

33. In Denough V/s Stevenson, the duty of a manufacturer was fixed towards:
(a) Retailer only
(b) Buyer from retailer
(c) Ultimate consumer
(d) None of the above

34. The rule laid down in Ryland V/s Fletcher is not applicable to:
(a) When the escape is due to 'Vismajor' or act of God
(b) When the damage is due to the wrongful or malicious act of a stranger
(c) When the escape is due to the plaintiff's own fault
(d) All of the above

35. Whether the doctrine of 'Common Employment' is applied in India:
(a) Yes (b) No
(c) Partly applied (d) All are incorrect

36. The legal maxim 'Qui facit peralium facit perse' means:
(a) The act of an agent is the act of principal
(b) The act of husband is the act of wife
(c) The act of a master is the act of a servant
(d) All of the above

37. Ryland V/s Fletcher was decided by:
(a) the Privy Council
(b) the Kings Division Bench
(c) the House of Lords
(d) None of the above

38. The characteristic feature of a Tort is:
(a) Tort is a civil wrong
(b) Tort is both civil and criminal wrong
(c) Tort is only criminal wrong
(d) None of the above

39. 'A' a child is in a house with 'Z' which has caught fire. Neighbouring people spreads a blanket to save the child. 'Z' in the interest of the child throws him on the blanket, but the child dies. 'Z' has committed an offence of:
(a) Murder
(b) Culpable homicide amounting to murder
(c) Culpable homicide covered under exception to section 300 of Indian Penal Code
(d) Not committed any offence

40. Which of the following statements is true in relation to abetment of an offence?
(a) It is not necessary that the offence abetted has been committed
(b) There is no question of abetment unless the offence abetted has been committed

(c) That to prove offence of abetment it is necessary to prove that the abettor has extended helping hand in the commission of the offence
(d) None of the above

41. Because of grave and sudden provocation of 'Z' 'A' fires at 'Z', but 'Z' does not die. 'A' has committed the offence of:
(a) Attempt to murder
(b) Culpable homicide not amounting to murder
(c) Attempt to commit culpable homicide
(d) Grievious hurt

42. 'X' dishonestly taken possession from 'Y' a box containing jewellary. While going home 'X' save 'Y' is chasing him. 'X' left the box and started pelting stones on 'Y' to stop him from chasing. 'X' has committed:
(a) No offence at all
(b) Offence of theft
(c) Offence of robbery
(d) Offence of extortion

43. Match List I and List II and give the correct answer using the code given below:

List I (Subject)
(A) Defence of insanity
(B) Common intention
(C) Necessity
(D) Causing death due to grave and sudden provocation

List II (Decided Cases)
(i) King V/s Virendra Kumar Ghosh
(ii) King V/s Mechnaughtan
(iii) State V/s K.M. Nanawati
(iv) King V/s Dadle Stephens

Codes:	A	B	C	D
(a)	(i)	(ii)	(iii)	(iv)
(b)	(ii)	(i)	(iv)	(iii)
(c)	(iii)	(ii)	(iv)	(i)
(d)	(iv)	(ii)	(iii)	(i)

44. Consider the following statements:
(i) Joinder is an ingredient of conspiracy and unlawfullness is implied in it for causing injury Joinder is a cause of action
(ii) Where the fact of joinder is absent the cause of action becomes irrelevant
(iii) For serving his own legal interest Joinder will not create a cause of action

Which of the statement is true in the above statements?
(a) (i) and (ii) (b) (ii) and (iii)
(c) (i) and (iii) (d) (i), (ii) and (iii)

45. In which of the following cases the Supreme Court of India has laid down 'Triple Test' for the identification of an industry within the ambit of section 2(j) of the IDA.
(a) D.N. Banerjee V/s P.R. Mukherjee
(b) H.K. Makwana V/s State of Gujarat and others
(c) Hotel Imperial, New Delhi V/s Hotel worker's union
(d) Bangalore water supply V/s A. Rajappa

46. The term 'Workman' under IDA includes:
(a) a person employed for doing any manual unskilled, skilled, technical, clerical or supervisory work for hire or reward
(b) a person employed mainly for managerial or administrative capacity
(c) (a) and (b) are correct
(d) (a) is correct

47. Under which of the following sections, a Registered Trade union is immuned from its criminal liability where an act done by the members infurtherance of their Trade Disputes:
(a) Section 15 of the Trade Union Act, 1926

(b) Section 16 of the Trade Union Act, 1926
(c) Section 17 of the Trade Union Act, 1926
(d) Section 20 of the Trade Union Act, 1926

48. In which of the following cases it is well established that, any settlement between the employer and with one or more concerned union in a conciliation proceeding would bind all other workmen unions who were not made parties to the settlement:
(a) Ramnagar Cane and Sugar Co. Ltd. V/s Jatin Chakravarthy
(b) Shanbhu Nath Goel V/s Bank of Baroda
(c) Workers of Dimakuchi Tea Estate V/s Management of Dimakuchi
(d) None of the above

49. The word 'Lock-out' is defined under Section 2(1) of the IDA, 1947 as:
(a) The temporary closure of a place of employment or suspension of work
(b) Refusal to continue the employment of the existing workers
(c) (a) is correct
(d) Both (a) and (b) are correct

50. Under Section 2(OO) of the Industrial Disputes Act 1947, the word 'Retrenchment' doesn't include:
(a) Termination of the Service of a workman
(b) Termination of the Service of a workman as punishment inflicted by way of disciplinary action
(c) Voluntary Retirement of the woman
(d) Both (a) and (b) are correct

ANSWERS

1. (a)	2. (d)	3. (b)	4. (a)	5. (a)
6. (a)	7. (a)	8. (d)	9. (c)	10. (c)
11. (d)	12. (b)	13. (b)	14. (c)	15. (b)
16. (d)	17. (d)	18. (d)	19. (d)	20. (a)
21. (c)	22. (b)	23. (d)	24. (b)	25. (a)
26. (b)	27. (d)	28. (b)	29. (a)	30. (b)
31. (a)	32. (c)	33. (c)	34. (d)	35. (c)
36. (a)	37. (a)	38. (a)	39. (d)	40. (a)
41. (b)	42. (b)	43. (b)	44. (b)	45. (d)
46. (d)	47. (c)	48. (d)	49. (d)	50. (d)

JUNE–2007

Note: This paper contains fifty (50) objective type questions, each question carrying two (2) marks. All questions are compulsory.

PAPER–I

1. Teacher uses visual-aids to make learning
   (a) simple
   (b) more knowledgeable
   (c) quicker
   (d) interesting

2. The teacher's role at the higher educational level is to
   (a) provide information to students
   (b) promote self-learning in students
   (c) encourage healthy competition among students
   (d) help students to solve their personal problems

3. Which one of the following teachers would you like the most?
   (a) Punctual
   (b) Having research aptitude
   (c) Loving and having high idealistic philosophy
   (d) Who often amuses his students

4. Micro teaching is most effective for the student-teacher
   (a) during the practice-teaching
   (b) after the practice-teaching
   (c) before the practice-teaching
   (d) None of the above

5. Which is the least important factor in teaching?
   (a) Punishing the students
   (b) Maintaining discipline in the class
   (c) Lecturing in impressive way
   (d) Drawing sketches and diagrams on the blackboard

6. To test null hypothesis, a researcher uses
   (a) t test
   (b) ANOVA
   (c) χ^2
   (d) factorial analysis

7. A research problem is feasible only when
   (a) it has utility and relevance
   (b) it is researchable
   (c) it is new and adds something to knowledge
   (d) All of the above

8. Bibliography given in a research report
   (a) shows vast knowledge of the researcher
   (b) helps those interested in further research
   (c) has no relevance to research
   (d) All of the above

9. Fundamental research reflects the ability to
   (a) Synthesise new ideals
   (b) Expound new principles
   (c) Evaluate the existing material concerning research
   (d) Study the existing literature regarding various topics

10. The study in which the investigators attempt to trace an effect is known as
    (a) Survey Research
    (b) *Ex-post Facto* Research

(c) Historical Research
(d) Summative Research

Read the following passage and answer the questions 11 to 15:

All political systems need to mediate the relationship between private wealth and public power. Those that fail risk a dysfunctional government captured by wealthy interests. Corruption is one symptom of such failure with private willingness-to-pay trumping public goals. Private individuals and business firms pay to get routine services and to get to the head of the bureaucratic queue. They pay to limit their taxes, avoid costly regulations, obtain contracts at inflated prices and get concessions and privatised firms at low prices. If corruption is endemic, public officials—both bureaucrats and elected officials—may redesign programs and propose public projects with few public benefits and many opportunities for private profit. Of course, corruption, in the sense of bribes, pay-offs and kickbacks, is only one type of government failure. Efforts to promote "good governance" must be broader than anti-corruption campaigns. Governments may be honest but inefficient because no one has an incentive to work productively, and narrow elites may capture the state and exert excess influence on policy. Bribery may induce the lazy to work hard and permit those not in the inner circle of cronies to obtain benefits. However, even in such cases, corruption cannot be confined to 'functional' areas. It will be a temptation whenever private benefits are positive. It may be a reasonable response to a harsh reality but, over time, it can facilitate a spiral into an even worse situation.

11. The governments which fail to focus on the relationship between private wealth and public power are likely to become
    (a) Functional
    (b) Dysfunctional
    (c) Normal functioning
    (d) Good governance

12. One important symptom of bad governance is
    (a) Corruption
    (b) High taxes
    (c) Complicated rules and regulations
    (d) High prices

13. When corruption is rampant, public officials always aim at many opportunities for:
    (a) Public benefits (b) Public profit
    (c) Private profit (d) Corporate gains

14. Productivity linked incentives to public/private officials is one of the indicatives for
    (a) Efficient government
    (b) Bad governance
    (c) Inefficient government
    (d) Corruption

15. The spiralling corruption can only be contained by promoting
    (a) Private profit
    (b) Anti-corruption campaign
    (c) Good governance
    (d) Pay-offs and kickbacks

16. Press Council of India is located at
    (a) Chennai (b) Mumbai
    (c) Kolkata (d) Delhi

17. Adjusting the photo for publication by cutting is technically known as
    (a) Photo cutting
    (b) Photo bleeding
    (c) Photo cropping
    (d) Photo adjustment

18. Feedback of a message comes from
    (a) Satellite (b) Media
    (c) Audience (d) Communicator

19. Collection of information in advance before designing communication strategy is known as

(a) Feedback (b) Feed-forward
(c) Research study (d) Opinion poll

20. The aspect ratio of TV screen is
(a) 4:3 (b) 4:2
(c) 3:5 (d) 2:3

21. Which is the number that comes next in the sequence?
9, 8, 8, 8, 7, 8, 6, __
(a) 5 (b) 6
(c) 8 (d) 4

22. If in a certain language PUNCTUAL is coded as 16598623, how would ACTUPULN be coded?
(a) 834536 (b) 29861635
(c) 834530 (d) 834539

23. The question to be answered by factorial analysis of the quantitative data does not explain one of the following
(a) Is 'X' related to 'Y'?
(b) How is 'X' related to 'Y'?
(c) How does 'X' affect the dependent variable 'Y' at different levels of another independent variable 'K' or 'M'?
(d) How is 'X' by 'K' related to 'M'?

24. January 12, 1980 was Saturday, what day was January 12, 1979?
(a) Saturday (b) Friday
(c) Sunday (d) Thursday

25. How many Mondays are there in a particular month of a particular year, if the month ends on Wednesday?
(a) 5 (b) 4
(c) 3 (d) None of these

26. From the given four statements, select the two which cannot be true but yet both can be false. Choose the right pair.
1. All men are mortal
2. Some men are mortal
3. No man is mortal
4. Some men are not mortal
(a) 1 and 2 (b) 3 and 4
(c) 1 and 3 (d) 2 and 4

27. A Syllogism must have
(a) Three terms (b) Four terms
(c) Six terms (d) Five terms

28. Copula is that part of proposition which denotes the relationship between
(a) Subject and predicate
(b) Known and unknown
(c) Major premise and minor premise
(d) Subject and object

29. "E" denotes
(a) Universal Negative Proposition
(b) Particular Affirmative Proposition
(c) Universal Affirmative Proposition
(d) Particular Negative Proposition

30. 'A' is the father of 'C' and 'D' is the son of 'B'. 'E' is the brother of 'A'. If 'C' is the sister of 'D' how is 'B' related to 'E'?
(a) Daughter (b) Husband
(c) Sister-in-law (d) Brother-in-law

31. Which of the following methods will you choose to prepare choropleth map of India showing urban density of population?
(a) Quartiles (b) Quintiles
(c) Mean and SD (d) Break-point

32. Which of the following methods is best suited to show on a map the types of crops being grown in a region?
(a) Choropleth (b) Chorochromatic
(c) Choroschematic (d) Isopleth

33. A ratio represents the relation between
(a) Part and Part
(b) Part and Whole
(c) Whole and Whole
(d) All of the above

34. Out of four numbers, the average of the first three numbers is thrice the fourth number. If the average of the four numbers is 5, the fourth number is

(a) 4.5 (b) 5
(c) 2 (d) 4

35. Circle graphs are used to show
(a) How various sections share in the whole
(b) How various parts are related to the whole
(c) How one whole is related to other wholes
(d) How one part is related to other parts

36. On the keyboard of computer each character has an "ASCII" value which stands for
(a) American Stock Code for Information Interchange
(b) American Standard Code for Information Interchange
(c) African Standard Code for Information Interchange
(d) Adaptable Standard Code for Information Change

37. Which part of the Central Processing Unit (CPU) performs calculation and makes decisions
(a) Arithmetic Logic Unit
(b) Alternating Logic Unit
(c) Alternate Local Unit
(d) American Logic Unit

38. "Dpi" stands for
(a) Dots per inch
(b) Digits per unit
(c) Dots pixel inch
(d) Diagrams per inch

39. The process of laying out a document with text, graphics, headlines and photographs is involved in
(a) Deck Top Publishing
(b) Desk Top Printing
(c) Desk Top Publishing
(d) Deck Top Printing

40. Transfer of data from one application to another line is known as
(a) Dynamic Disk Exchange
(b) Dodgy Data Exchange
(c) Dogmatic Data Exchange
(d) Dynamic Data Exchange

41. Tsunami occurs due to
(a) Mild earthquakes and landslides in the oceans
(b) Strong earthquakes and landslides in the oceans
(c) Strong earthquakes and landslides in mountains
(d) Strong earthquakes and landslides in deserts

42. Which of the natural hazards have big effect on Indian people each year?
(a) Cyclones (b) Floods
(c) Earthquakes (d) Landslides

43. Comparative Environment Impact Assessment study is to be conducted for
(a) the whole year
(b) three seasons excluding monsoon
(c) any three seasons
(d) the worst season

44. Sea level rise results primarily due to
(a) Heavy rainfall
(b) Melting of glaciers
(c) Submarine volcanism
(d) Seafloor spreading

45. The plume rise in a coal based power plant depends on
1. Buoyancy
2. Atmospheric stability
3. Momentum of exhaust gases
Identify the correct code
Codes:
(a) Both (1) and (2) (b) Both (2) and (3)
(c) Both (1) and (3) (d) (1), (2) and (3)

46. Value education makes a student
(a) Good citizen
(b) Successful businessman

(c) Popular teacher
(d) Efficient manager

47. Networking of libraries through electronic media is known as
(a) Inflibnet (b) Libinfnet
(c) Internet (d) HTML

48. The University which telecasts interactive educational programs through its own channel is
(a) B.R. Ambedkar Open University, Hyderabad
(b) I.G.N.O.U.
(c) University of Pune
(d) Annamalai University

49. The Government established the University Grants Commission by an Act of Parliament in the year
(a) 1980 (b) 1948
(c) 1950 (d) 1956

50. Universities having central campus for imparting education are called
(a) Central Universities
(b) Deemed Universities
(c) Residential Universities
(d) Open Universities

ANSWERS

1. (d)	2. (a)	3. (a)	4. (b)	5. (a)
6. (c)	7. (d)	8. (b)	9. (b)	10. (b)
11. (b)	12. (a)	13. (c)	14. (a)	15. (c)
16. (d)	17. (c)	18. (c)	19. (d)	20. (a)
21. (c)	22. (b)	23. (c)	24. (b)	25. (d)
26. (b)	27. (a)	28. (b)	29. (a)	30. (d)
31. (b)	32. (c)	33. (b)	34. (c)	35. (a)
36. (a)	37. (a)	38. (a)	39. (c)	40. (d)
41. (b)	42. (b)	43. (a)	44. (b)	45. (d)
46. (a)	47. (a)	48. (b)	49. (d)	50. (b)

PAPER–II

Note: This paper contains fifty (50) objective type questions, each question carrying two (2) marks. All questions are compulsory.

1. Constitution of India assures the "Dignity of the Individual" in the language of:
(a) Article 14 (b) Article 19
(c) Article 21 (d) Preamble

2. Secularism is one of the five constituents of the Constitution of India and has been held to be the only permissible religion in a pluralistic Indian Society in the case of:
(a) I.C. Golaknath v. State of Punjab
(b) Kesavananda Bharathi v. State of Kerala
(c) S.R. Bommai v. Union of India
(d) S.L. Kapoor v. Union of India

3. Article 21A and Article 51A(k) are:
(a) interrelated and integrated as right and obligation
(b) not interrelated and integrated as right and obligation
(c) mutually exclusive
(d) independent and not inter-dependent

4. With the deletion of Article 31 from the Fundamental Rights of the Constitution of India, Schedule IX seems to have outlived its utility:
(a) False (b) True
(c) Not True (d) Both (a) and (c)

5. The doctrine of prospective overruling established in the case of I.C. Golaknath v. State of Punjab 1967 can be applied:
(a) by any Court of the Country
(b) by any Administrative Tribunal of the Country
(c) only by the highest Court of the Country
(d) only by the revenue authorities under the Land Ceiling Acts

6. Which one is not correctly matched:
   (a) Freedom of Speech and Expression — include freedom of Press and Right of Information
   (b) Freedom of Conscience — includes right to wear and carry Kirpans by Sikhs
   (c) Right to personal liberty — includes right to carry on the trade or business
   (d) Right to equality — includes principles of natural justice
7. Non-amendability of the Basic Structure of the Constitution was declared firstly in:
   (a) Sajjan Singh v. State of Rajasthan, 1965
   (b) Minerva Mills v. Union of India, 1983
   (c) Sankari Prasad v. Union of India, 1951
   (d) Kesavananda Bharathi v. State of Kerala, 1973
8. Who among the following is related to historical school of jurisprudence?
   (a) Salmond (b) Bentham
   (c) Rawls (d) Henry Maine
9. Who propounded the "Pure theory of law"?
   (a) Austin (b) Kelsen
   (c) Salmond (d) H.L.A. Hart
10. Which one of the following is correct?
   (a) Liberty and duty are jural opposites
   (b) Duty cancels out liberty
   (c) Both (a) and (b)
   (d) None of the above
11. Realist school is a branch of:
   (a) Sociological approach
   (b) Positive approach
   (c) Historical approach
   (d) Analytical approach
12. The interest theory of legal rights is propounded by:
   (a) Durkeim (b) Dicey
   (c) Paton (d) Ihering
13. The rights which are available against persons generally is termed as:
   (a) Rights in realiena
   (b) Rights in personam
   (c) Rights in rem
   (d) Rights in re-propria
14. Ratio decidendi may be defined as:
   (a) Statement of law applied to the legal problems disclosed by facts
   (b) Finding of material facts, direct and inferential, based on earlier case law
   (c) Both (a) and (b)
   (d) None of the above
15. The legal terminology of 'opinio juris' was first formulated by:
   (a) George Scelle
   (b) Schwarzenberger
   (c) Francois Geny
   (d) Quincy Wright
16. **Assertion (A):** International customs continue to be a significant source of International Law.
   Reason (R): It develops slowly but spontaneously and mirrors the mean of contemporary international society.
   (a) Both (A) and (R) are true and (R) is the correct explanation
   (b) Both (A) and (R) are true but (R) is not the correct explanation
   (c) (A) is true, but (R) is false
   (d) (A) is false, but (R) is true
17. Which of the following are not correctly matched?
   (a) The Reparation case — Legal personality of International Institution
   (b) The Genocide case — Reservation to treaties
   (c) The Nottebohm case — Measurement of territorial sea
   (d) Anglo-Norwegian Fisheries case — Principle of non-use of force

18. Using the code given below Match List I and List II:

List I (Judicial decision)

(A) The Temple case
(B) The Corfue Channel case
(C) The Nuclear Tests case
(D) The German interests in Polish Upper Silesia

List II (Principle)

(i) Admissibility of indirect evidence
(ii) Estopped
(iii) Respect for acquired rights
(iv) Good faith

Codes:	A	B	C	D
(a)	(iii)	(ii)	(i)	(iv)
(b)	(ii)	(i)	(iv)	(iii)
(c)	(ii)	(iii)	(iv)	(i)
(d)	(iv)	(iii)	(i)	(ii)

19. Consider the following statements:
(i) Universal Declaration of Human Rights is an international Magnacarta of Human Rights
(ii) India is a party to Protocol of the International Covenant on Civil and Political Rights
(iii) India has signed and ratified the 1984 Anti-Torture Convention

Of these, following are correct:
(a) (i) and (ii) are correct
(b) (ii) and (iii) are correct
(c) (i) alone is correct
(d) (ii) alone is correct

20. Arrange the following decisions in order in which they appeared. Use the code given below:
(i) East Timor case
(ii) Western Sahara
(iii) Namibia case
(iv) South West Africa case

Codes:	A	B	C	D
(a)	(ii)	(iii)	(i)	(iv)
(b)	(i)	(iv)	(ii)	(iii)
(c)	(iii)	(i)	(ii)	(iv)
(d)	(iv)	(iii)	(ii)	(i)

21. Ceremonies of Hindu marriage have been laid down in minute detail in:
(a) Dharma sutra (b) Dharma shastra
(c) Grhiya sutra (d) None of these

22. Prohibited degree and sapinda relationship are:
(a) mutually exculsive
(b) dependent on each other
(c) may overlap each other
(d) None of the above

23. Propositions are:
(i) Consent theory makes the divorce very easy.
(ii) Consent theory makes the divorce very difficult.

Which of the following is correct in respect of the aforesaid propositions:
(a) (i) is correct but (ii) is incorrect
(b) (i) and (ii) both are correct
(c) (ii) is correct but (i) is incorrect
(d) (i) and (ii) both are incorrect

24. The Hindu Marriage Act, 1955, provides for _______ theory/theories of divorce:
(a) breakdown (b) fault
(c) consent (d) All the above

25. Propositions are:
(i) A void marriage remains valid until a decree annulling it has been passed by a competent court.
(ii) A void marriage is never a valid marriage and there is no necessity of any decree annulling it.
(iii) A voidable marriage is regarded as a valid subsisting marriage until a decree annulling it has been passed by a competent court.

In respect of the aforesaid propositions which is correct:
(a) (i) and (ii) are correct and (iii) is incorrect

(b) (ii) and (iii) are correct and (i) is incorrect
(c) (i), (ii) and (iii) all are correct
(d) (i) and (iii) are incorrect but (ii) is correct

26. 'Iddat' is a period during which a Muslim woman is prohibited from marrying on dissolution of marriage:
(a) by death
(b) by divorce
(c) only (a) and not (b)
(d) both (a) and (b)

27. Communication of acceptance is complete:
(a) before the offer is revoked
(b) when acceptance is put in the course of transmission
(c) even the acceptance is lost in transit
(d) after the revocation of acceptance reaches the offeror

28. Generally offer to the world at large does not make it necessary on the part of the acceptor to communicate his acceptance. This is well explained in:
(a) Entores Ltd. vs. Miles Far East Corporation
(b) Carlil vs. Carbolic Smoke Ball Company
(c) Lalman Shukla vs. Gauridatta
(d) Hadley vs. Baxendale

29. Arrange the sequence of following concepts in a contract. Use the code given below:
(i) Fraud (ii) Mistake
(iii) Coercion (iv) Quasi Contract

Codes:	A	B	C	D
(a)	(iv)	(ii)	(i)	(iii)
(b)	(i)	(ii)	(iii)	(iv)
(c)	(iii)	(iv)	(ii)	(i)
(d)	(iii)	(i)	(ii)	(iv)

30. The following rule as to consideration is true:
(a) It must be adequate
(b) It must move at the desire of the promisor
(c) It must be present or future only
(d) It must move at the desire of the promisee

31. When a minor is supplied with necessaries of life, the supplier:
(a) Cannot recover the price
(b) Can recover the price
(c) Can recover the price from the property of the minor
(d) Can file a criminal case

32. Under which of the following sections of the Indian Contract Act, 1872, remedies for breach of contract are available?
(a) Section 72 (b) Section 73
(c) Section 74 (d) Section 32

33. "Tortious liability arises from the breach of a duty primarily fixed by law; this duty is towards persons generally and its breach is redressible by an action for unliquidated damages"—This statement is made by:
(a) Salmond (b) Winfield
(c) Dias (d) Julius Stone

34. In which of the following cases the House of Lords held that 'volenti non fit injuria' had no application to harm sustained by a workman from the negligence of his employers in not warning him of the moment of a recurring danger, although the man knew and understood that he personally ran risk of injury if and when the danger did occur.
(a) Smith v. Baker
(b) Hynes v. Harwood
(c) Lane v. Holloway
(d) None of the above

35. The maxim 'injuria sine damno' has been explained in the following case:

(a) Donough v. Stevenson
(b) Ryland v. Fletcher
(c) Ashby v. White
(d) Braford v. Pickles

36. Under the doctrine of 'vicarious liability', a master is liable for the acts of his servant:
(a) only if the servant is under the control of the master as regards the manner in which work is to be done
(b) only if the servant is not under the control of the master as regards the manner of doing work
(c) irrespective of whether the servant is under the control of the master or not as regards the manner of doing the work
(d) None of the above

37. The verdict of the 'Donough v. Stevenson' was delivered by the following Judge:
(a) Justice Black Stone
(b) J. Douglas
(c) Lord Denning
(d) Lord Atkin

38. The decision given in M.C. Mehta v. Union of India is on:
(a) Vicarious liability
(b) Absolute liability
(c) Strict liability
(d) Simple liability

39. Wrist watch of 'X' was stolen. Some days after 'X' saw 'Y' is in possession of his wrist watch. In this context which of the following statements is true?
(a) 'X' has a right to private defence
(b) 'X' has right to private defence and can take back his wrist watch by force
(c) Right of private defence to 'X' is no more available
(d) As soon as 'X' saw his wrist watch in possession of 'Y', his right of private defence of property has been revived

40. 'X' gives poisonous apple to 'Y' with intention to cause his death. 'Y' comes to know of the fact that apple is poisonous. 'Y' gives that apple to a minor child for eating. Child eats that and dies. In this case:
(a) 'X' is accused of murder and 'Y' is accused of abetment of murder
(b) 'X' and 'Y' both are accused of murder
(c) 'Y' has committed the offence of murder and 'X' has not committed any offence
(d) 'X' is accused of attempt to murder and 'Y' is accused of murder

41. 'A' with intention to commit theft instigates 'B' to take possession of property of 'Z' from 'Z's possession. For this 'A' gives impression to 'B' that the property belongs to him. 'B' with the impression that the property belongs to 'A' takes possession of property bonafidely.

In relation to above statement
Statement (A): 'A' is accused of abetment to commit theft and 'B' has not committed any offence.
Reason (R): Abetter's liability is not dependent on the liability of the principal offender.
(a) Both statement (A) and reason (R) are correct and (R) explains (A) properly
(b) Both statement (A) and reason (R) are correct but (R) does not explain (A)
(c) (A) is true but (R) is false
(d) (A) is false but (R) is true

42. Carefully read the following statements:
(i) According to Section 34 of Indian Penal Code, requirement is of two persons, where as under Section 149 of I.P.C., requirement is of five persons

(ii) According to Section 34 of I.P.C., common intention is required whereas under Section 149 I.P.C., common object is required
(iii) Previous consent is required under Sections 34 and 149 of I.P.C.
(iv) Section 34 of I.P.C. and Section 149 of I.P.C. constitutes a specific offence

Which of the above statements is true?
(a) (i) and (iii) (b) (ii) and (iii)
(c) (i) and (ii) (d) (ii) and (iv)

43. 'A', a police constable tortured a person under the order of his senior police officer. The person lost one eye because of the torture. Which of the following will be the basis of defence which can be invoked by the accused police constable?
(a) torture was under the order of senior police officer
(b) torture was given because he was under the threat of losing service
(c) torture was given because he was under the threat of suspension from service
(d) torture was given because there was imminent threat to death

44. Preparation and attempt are two stages for commission of an offence. Preparation is generally not punishable. The reason for not making preparation punishable is:
(a) Lack of relationship between preparation and attempt
(b) Possibility of change in mind before commission of the offence
(c) Absence of intention
(d) Absence of attempt

45. Who among the following is a workman under Section 2(3) of the Industrial Disputes Act, 1947:
(a) Medical representative
(b) Teacher
(c) Probationer
(d) Legal representative of deceased workman

46. The institution of Works Committee was introduced in India through:
(a) The Trade Disputes Act
(b) The Industrial Disputes Act
(c) The Trade Unions Act
(d) The Employment Standing Order Act

47. Match the List I with List II. Use the code given below:

List I (Subject)
(A) Right to Strike (B) Industry
(C) Lay-off (D) Retrenchment

List II (Judicial Decisions)
(i) University of Delhi v. Ramnath
(ii) Gujarat Steel Tubes v. G.S.T. Mazdoor Sabha
(iii) Piplaich Sugar Mills Mazdoor Union
(iv) Workmen v. Firestone Tyre and Rubber Co.

Codes:	A	B	C	D
(a)	(iii)	(iv)	(i)	(ii)
(b)	(iv)	(ii)	(iii)	(i)
(c)	(ii)	(i)	(iv)	(iii)
(d)	(iv)	(iii)	(ii)	(i)

48. Giving financial aid to illegal strikes is punishable under:
(a) Section 25, Industrial Disputes Act
(b) Section 28, Industrial Disputes Act
(c) Section 26, Industrial Disputes Act
(d) Section 27, Industrial Disputes Act

49. Consider the following statements:
(i) The Trade Unions Act prescribe time limit for the grant of registration of Trade Unions
(ii) The certificate of registration issued by Registrar is a conclusive evidence.
(iii) The Registrar of Trade Unions is duty bound to hear existing unions before granting registration to a new Trade Union

Of these, following are correct:
(a) (i) alone (b) (i) and (ii)
(c) (i), (ii) and (iii) (d) (ii) alone

50. Arrange the following decisions in the order in which they appeared. Use the code given below:
(i) Baroda Borough Municipality
(ii) D.N. Banerji v. P.R. Mukherjee
(iii) Samish Dubey v. City Board, Etawah
(iv) Lalit Hari Ayurvedic College Pharmacy case

Codes:
(a) (i), (ii), (iii), and (iv)
(b) (ii), (i), (iv) and (iii)
(c) (iii), (iv), (ii) and (i)
(d) (iv), (ii), (iii) and (i)

ANSWERS

1. (c)	2. (c)	3. (c)	4. (c)	5. (c)
6. (b)	7. (d)	8. (d)	9. (b)	10. (c)
11. (a)	12. (d)	13. (b)	14. (c)	15. (c)
16. (a)	17. (b)	18. (c)	19. (a)	20. (d)
21. (b)	22. (c)	23. (b)	24. (d)	25. (c)
26. (d)	27. (a)	28. (b)	29. (d)	30. (b)
31. (c)	32. (b)	33. (c)	34. (a)	35. (c)
36. (a)	37. (d)	38. (b)	39. (d)	40. (b)
41. (a)	42. (c)	43. (c)	44. (b)	45. (a)
46. (b)	47. (c)	48. (b)	49. (c)	50. (b)

DECEMBER–2008

Note: This paper contains fifty (50) objective type questions, each question carrying two (2) marks. All questions are compulsory.

PAPER–I

1. According to Swami Vivekananda, teacher's success depends on
   (a) His renunciation of personal gain and service to others
   (b) His professional training and creativity
   (c) His concentration on his work and duties with a spirit of obedience to God
   (d) His mastery on the subject and capacity in controlling the students
2. Which of the following teacher will be liked most?
   (a) A teacher of high idealistic attitude
   (b) A loving teacher
   (c) A teacher who is disciplined
   (d) A teacher who often amuses his students
3. A teacher's most important challenge is
   (a) To make students do their home work
   (b) To make teaching-learning process enjoyable
   (c) To maintain discipline in the class-room
   (d) To prepare the question paper
4. Value-education stands for
   (a) making a student healthy
   (b) making a student to get a job
   (c) inculcation of virtues
   (d) all-round development of personality
5. When a normal student behaves in an erratic manner in the class, you would
   (a) pull up the student then and there
   (b) talk to the student after the class
   (c) ask the student to leave the class
   (d) ignore the student
6. The research is always
   (a) verifying the old knowledge
   (b) exploring new knowledge
   (c) filling the gap between knowledge
   (d) All of these
7. The research that applies the laws at the time of field study to draw more and more clear ideas about the problem is
   (a) Applied research
   (b) Action research
   (c) Experimental research
   (d) None of these
8. When a research problem is related to heterogeneous population, the most suitable sampling method is
   (a) Cluster Sampling
   (b) Stratified Sampling
   (c) Convenient Sampling
   (d) Lottery Method
9. The process not needed in experimental research is
   (a) Observation
   (b) Manipulation and replication
   (c) Controlling
   (d) Reference collection
10. A research problem is not feasible only when

(a) it is researchable
(b) it is new and adds something to knowledge
(c) it consists of independent and dependent variables
(d) it has utility and relevance

Read the following passage carefully and answer the questions 11 to 15:

Radically changing monsoon patterns, reduction in the winter rice harvest and a quantum increase in respiratory diseases all part of the environmental doomsday scenario which is reportedly playing out in South Asia. According to a United Nations Environment Program report, a deadly three-kilometer deep blanket of pollution comprising a fearsome, cocktail of ash, acids, aerosols and other particles has enveloped in this region. For India, already struggling to cope with a drought, the implication of this are devastating and further crop failure will amount to a life and death question for many Indians. The increase in premature deaths will have adverse social and economic consequences and a rise in morbidities will place an unbearable burden on our crumbling health system. And there is no one to blame but ourselves. Both official and corporate India has always been allergic to any mention of clean technology. Most mechanical two wheelers roll of the assembly line without proper pollution control system. Little effort is made for R&D on simple technologies, which could make a vital difference to people's lives and the environment.

However, while there is no denying that South Asia must clean up its act, skeptics might question the timing of the haze report. The Kyoto meet on climate change is just two weeks away and the stage is set for the usual battle between the developing world and the West, particularly the Unites States of America. President Mr. Bush has adamantly refused to sign any protocol, which would mean a change in American consumption level. U.N. environment report will likely find a place in the U.S. arsenal as it plants an accusing finger towards controls like India and China. Yet the U.S.A. can hardly deny its own dubious role in the matter of erasing trading quotas.

Richer countries can simply buy up excess credits from poorer countries and continue to pollute. Rather than try to get the better of developing countries, who undoubtedly have taken up environmental shortcuts in their bid to catch up with the West, the USA should take a look at the environmental profigacy, which is going on within. From opening up virgin territories for oil exploration to relaxing the standards for drinking water, Mr. Bush's policies are not exactly beneficial, not even to America's interests. We realise that we are all in this together and that pollution anywhere should be a global concern otherwise there will only be more tunnels at the end of the tunnel.

11. Both official and corporate India is allergic to
    (a) Failure of Monsoon
    (b) Poverty and Inequality
    (c) Slowdown in Industrial Production
    (d) Mention of Clean Technology
12. If the rate of premature death increases it will
    (a) Exert added burden on the crumbling economy
    (b) Have adverse social and economic consequences
    (c) Make positive effect on our effort to control population
    (d) Have less job aspirants in the society
13. According to the passage, the two-wheeler industry is not adequately concerned about
    (a) Passenger safety on the roads
    (b) Life cover insurance of the vehicle owner

(c) Pollution control system in the vehicle
(d) Rising cost of the two wheelers

14. What could be the reason behind timing of the haze report just before the Kyoto meet?
(a) United Nations is working hand-in-glove with U.S.A.
(b) Organisers of the forthcoming meet to teach a lesson to the U.S.A.
(c) Drawing attention of the world towards devastating effects of environment degradation.
(d) U.S.A. wants to use it as a handle against the developing countries in the forthcoming meet.

15. Which of the following is the indication of environmental degradation in South Asia?
(a) Social and economic inequality
(b) Crumbling health care system
(c) Inadequate pollution control system
(d) Radically changing monsoon pattern

16. Community Radio is a type of radio service that caters to the interest of
(a) Local audience (b) Education
(c) Entertainment (d) News

17. Orkut is a part of
(a) Intrapersonal Communication
(b) Mass Communication
(c) Group Communication
(d) Interpersonal Communication

18. Match List I with List II and select the correct answer using the codes given below.

List I (Artists)
A. Amrita Shergill
B. T. Swaminathan Pillai
C. Bhimsen Joshi
D. Padma Subramaniyam

List II (Art)
1. Flute 2. Classical Song
3. Painting 4. Bharat Natyam

Codes:	A	B	C	D
(a)	3	1	2	4
(b)	2	3	1	4
(c)	4	2	3	1
(d)	1	4	2	3

19. Which is not correct in latest communication award?
(a) Salman Rushdie - Booker's Prize—July 20, 2008
(b) Dilip Sanghavi - Business Standard CEO Award, July 22, 2008
(c) Tapan Sinha - Dada Saheb Falke Award, July 21, 2008
(d) Gautam Ghosh - Osians Lifetime Achievement Award, July 11, 2008

20. Firewalls are used to protect a communication network system against
(a) Unauthorised attacks
(b) Virus attacks
(c) Data-driven attacks
(d) Fire-attacks

21. Insert the missing number in the following

$\frac{2}{7}, \frac{4}{7}, ?, \frac{11}{21}, \frac{16}{31},$

(a) $\frac{10}{8}$ (b) $\frac{6}{10}$
(c) $\frac{5}{10}$ (d) $\frac{7}{13}$

22. In a certain code, GAMESMAN is written as AGMEMSAN. How would DISCLOSE be written in that code?
(a) IDSCOLSE (b) IDCSOLES
(c) IDSCOLES (d) IDSCLOSE

23. The letters in the first set have a certain relationship. On the basis of this

relationship mark the right choice for the second set : AST : BRU :: NQV: ?

(a) ORW (b) MPU
(c) MRW (d) OPW

24. On what dates of April, 1994 did Sunday fall?
(a) 2, 9, 16, 23, 30
(b) 3, 10, 17, 24
(c) 4, 11, 18, 25
(d) 1, 8, 15, 22, 29

25. Find out the wrong number in the sequence.
125, 127, 130, 135, 142, 153, 165
(a) 130 (b) 142
(c) 153 (d) 165

26. There are five books A, B, C, D and E. The book C lies above D, the book E is below A and B is below E. Which is at the bottom?
(a) E (b) B
(c) A (d) C

27. Logical reasoning is based on
(a) Truth of involved propositions
(b) Valid relation among the involved propositions
(c) Employment of symbolic language
(d) Employment of ordinary language

28. Two propositions with the same subject and predicate terms but different in quality are
(a) Contradictory (b) Contrary
(c) Subaltern (d) Identical

29. The premises of a valid deductive argument
(a) Provide some evidence for its conclusion
(b) Provide no evidence for its conclusion
(c) Are irrelevant for its conclusion
(d) Provide conclusive evidence for its conclusion

30. Syllogistic reasoning is
(a) Deductive (b) Inductive
(c) Experimental (d) Hypothetical

Study the following Venn diagram and answer questions nos. 31 to 33.

Three circles representing GRADUATES, CLERKS and GOVERNMENT EMPLOYEES are intersecting. The intersections are marked A, B, C, e, f, g and h. Which part best represents the statements in questions 31 to 33?

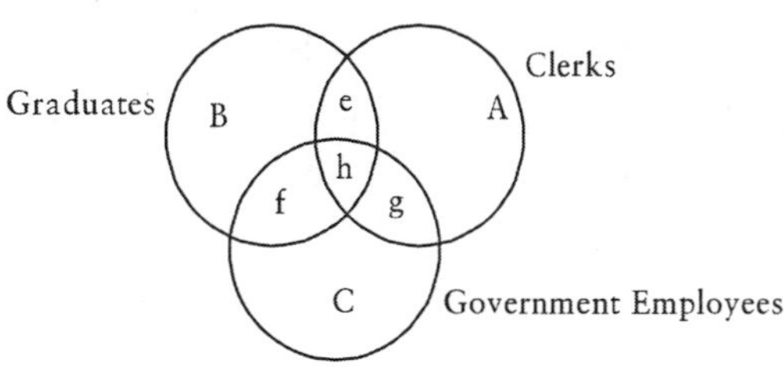

31. Some Graduates are Government employees but not as Clerks.
(a) h (b) g
(c) f (d) e

32. Clerks who are Graduates as well as Government employees.
(a) e (b) f
(c) g (d) h

33. Some Graduates are Clerks but not Government employees.
(a) f (b) g
(c) h (d) e

Study the following graph and answer questions numbers from 34 to 35

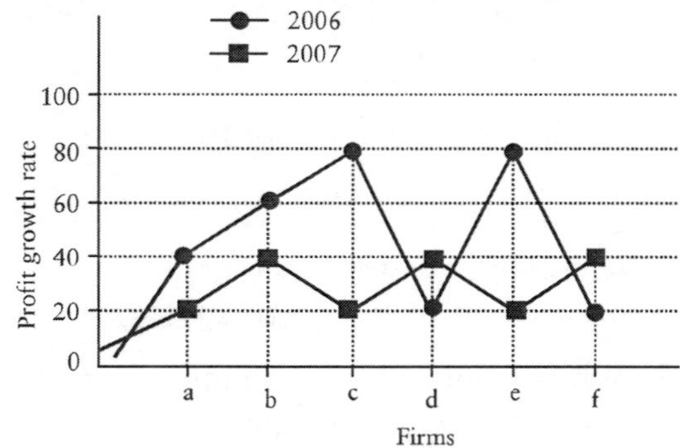

34. Which of the firms got maximum profit growth rate in the year 2006?
(a) ab (b) ce
(c) cd (d) ef

35. Which of the firms got maximum profit growth rate in the year 2007?
(a) bdf (b) acf
(c) bed (d) ace

36. The accounting software 'Tally' was developed by
(a) HCL (b) TCS
(c) Infosys (d) Wipro

37. Errors in computer programs are called
(a) Follies (b) Mistakes
(c) Bugs (d) Spam

38. HTML is basically used to design
(a) Webpage
(b) Website
(c) Graphics
(d) Tables and Frames

39. 'Micro Processing' is made for
(a) Computer
(b) Digital System
(c) Calculator
(d) Electronic Goods

40. Information, a combination of graphics, text, sound, video and animation is called
(a) Multiprogram (b) Multifacet
(c) Multimedia (d) Multiprocess

41. Which of the following pairs regarding typical composition of hospital wastes is incorrect?
(a) Plastic - 9-12%
(b) Metals - 1-2%
(c) Ceramic - 8-10%
(d) Biodegradable - 35-40%

42. Freshwater achieves its greatest density at
(a) –4°C (b) 0°C
(c) 4°C (d) –2.5°C

43. Which one of the following is not associated with earthquakes?
(a) Focus (b) Epicenter
(c) Seismograph (d) Swells

44. The tallest trees in the world are found in the region
(a) Equatorial region
(b) Temperate region
(c) Monsoon region
(d) Mediterranean region

45. Match List I with List II and select the correct answer from the codes given below.

List I (National Parks)
A. Periyar
B. Nandan Kanan
C. Corbett National Park
D. Sariska Tiger Reserve

List II (States)
1. Orissa 2. Kerala
3. Rajasthan 4. Uttarakhand

Codes:	A	B	C	D
(a)	2	1	4	3
(b)	1	2	4	3
(c)	3	2	1	4
(d)	1	2	3	4

46. According to Radhakrishnan Commission, the aim of Higher Education is
(a) To develop the democratic values, peace and harmony
(b) To develop great personalities who can give their contributions in politics, administration, industry and commerce
(c) Both (a) and (b)
(d) None of these

47. The National Museum at New Delhi is attached to
(a) Delhi University
(b) a Deemed University
(c) a Subordinate Office of the JNU
(d) Part of Ministry of Tourism and Culture

48. Match List I with List II and select the correct answer from the code given below.

List I (Institutions)

A. National Law Institute
B. Indian Institute of Advanced Studies
C. National Judicial Academy
D. National Savings Institute

List II (Locations)

1. Shimla 2. Bhopal
3. Hyderabad 4. Nagpur

Codes:	A	B	C	D
(a)	3	2	4	1
(b)	1	2	3	4
(c)	4	3	1	2
(d)	3	1	2	4

49. Election of Rural and Urban local bodies are conducted and ultimately supervised by
(a) Election Commission of India
(b) State Election Commission
(c) District Collector and District Magistrate
(d) Concerned Returning Officer

50. Which opinion is not correct?
(a) Education is a subject of concurrent list of VII schedule of Constitution of India
(b) University Grants Commission is a statutory body
(c) Patent, inventions, design, copyright and trade marks are the subject of concurrent list
(d) Indian Council of Social Science Research is a statutory body related to research in social sciences

ANSWERS

1. (d)	2. (c)	3. (b)	4. (c)	5. (b)
6. (d)	7. (a)	8. (b)	9. (d)	10. (b)
11. (d)	12. (b)	13. (c)	14. (c)	15. (d)
16. (a)	17. (d)	18. (a)	19. (b)	20. (a)
21. (d)	22. (a)	23. (d)	24. (b)	25. (d)
26. (b)	27. (b)	28. (a)	29. (d)	30. (a)
31. (c)	32. (d)	33. (d)	34. (b)	35. (a)
36. (b)	37. (c)	38. (a)	39. (a)	40. (c)
41. (d)	42. (c)	43. (d)	44. (b)	45. (a)
46. (c)	47. (d)	48. (d)	49. (b)	50. (c)

PAPER–II

Note: This paper contains fifty (50) objective type questions, each question carrying two (2) marks. All questions are compulsory.

1. Consider the following Judgements of the Supreme Court, which dealt with the appointment and transfer of Judges of the Supreme Court and High Courts:
(i) S.P. Gupta Vs Union of India
(ii) Sankal Chand Vs Union of India
(iii) In re special Reference No. 1 of 1998
(iv) Supreme Court Advocate on Record Association Vs Union of India

Which one of the following is correct chronological order in which the above judgements were delivered?

(a)	(i)	(ii)	(iii)	(iv)
(b)	(ii)	(i)	(iii)	(iv)
(c)	(ii)	(i)	(iv)	(iii)
(d)	(i)	(ii)	(iv)	(iii)

2. Which one of the following is the correct statement? 'Full Faith and Credit' clause of the constitution does not apply to
(a) Public records
(b) Judicial proceedings
(c) Acts of Corporation
(d) Public acts

3. In which case has the Supreme Court of India held that there is no reason to

compel non-smokers to be helpless victims of air pollution?

(a) Salem Advocate Bar Association Tamil Nadu Vs Union of India
(b) Onkar Lal Bizoe Vs Union of India
(c) Ramkrishnan Vs State of Kerala
(d) Murli S. Deora Vs Union of India

4. Joint Session of the Parliament was summoned by the President of India to pass:
(a) Dowry Prohibition on Act
(b) Banking Service Commission Act
(c) Prevention of Terrorism Act
(d) All the above Acts

5. Match List I and List II and select the correct answer using the code given below the lists:

List I
(a) Liberty of thought and expression
(b) Freedom of speech and expression
(c) Making special provision for women and children
(d) Protection of interest of minorities

List II
(i) Right to freedom
(ii) Cultural and education rights
(iii) Preamble
(iv) Life and liberty
(v) Right to equality

Codes:	**A**	**B**	**C**	**D**
(a)	(iii)	(iv)	(v)	(ii)
(b)	(ii)	(v)	(iv)	(i)
(c)	(iii)	(v)	(iv)	(ii)
(d)	(ii)	(iv)	(v)	(i)

6. Which one of the following is the correct statement? *Double Jeopardy* means:
(a) trying a person for two offences committed by him in one incident
(b) putting the same person on trial twice for the same offence
(c) trying the same person for two offences at two different times
(d) trying two persons jointly for the same offence

7. Which one of the following is the correct statement? The theory of repugnancy has application in a case where:
(a) both Union and State occupy two different fields in different lists
(b) both Union and State laws are enacted under the concurrent list
(c) the Union law is enacted under List III and State law in enacted under List II
(d) the Union and State laws enacted under the State list

8. Which one of the following is not expressly covered as a Fundamental Right under the Constitution of India?
(a) Right to form association
(b) Right to equality before law
(c) Right to freedom of press
(d) Right to assemble peaceably and without arms

9. Which set of the following is the concepts of law?
(a) Precedent and Legislation
(b) Judicial Process and Judicial Activism
(c) Rights and Duties
(d) Ratio and Obiter

10. "Jurisprudence was designed to defend the stability of a particular economic system and protect the interests of the middle class. A legal theory built on these premises can hardly be called value-free or impartial". It is said by
(a) Austin (b) Salmond
(c) Holland (d) Hart

11. Which one of the following is not a source of law?
(a) Legal theory (b) Custom
(c) Precedent (d) Legislation

12. Match List I with List II using the code given below:

List I (Theory)

(A) Retributive theory
(B) Sociological theory
(C) Theory of Precedent
(D) Theory of Property

List II (Subject)

(i) Legal Right (ii) Source of law
(iii) Punishment (iv) Roscoe pound

Codes:	A	B	C	D
(a)	(i)	(iv)	(iii)	(ii)
(b)	(iii)	(iv)	(ii)	(i)
(c)	(iii)	(ii)	(i)	(iv)
(d)	(iv)	(iii)	(i)	(ii)

13. Law is a means of:
(a) Social Theory
(b) Individual Development in Society
(c) State Action
(d) Social Control

14. Kelsen propounded one of the following theories:
(a) Realist theory
(b) Natural law theory
(c) Pure theory
(d) Sociological theory

15. The weaknesses of International Law are:
(i) Lack of institutions
(ii) Lack of certainty
(iii) Vital interests
(iv) Lack of sanctions

Codes:
(a) (iii) and (iv) are correct
(b) (ii) and (iv) are correct
(c) (i), (ii), (iii) and (iv) are correct
(d) (i), (ii) and (iii) are correct

16. Match List I with List II using the code given below:

List I (Principles)

(A) Concept of limited liability
(B) Principle of subrogation
(C) Concept of trust
(D) Duty to pay compensation for

List II (Decisions)

(i) The South West Africa case
(ii) The Barcelona traction case
(iii) The Danube case
(iv) The Mavrommatis Palestine proven injury concessions case
(v) Frontier Dispute case

Codes:	A	B	C	D
(a)	(ii)	(i)	(v)	(iii)
(b)	(ii)	(iv)	(i)	(iii)
(c)	(i)	(ii)	(iii)	(v)
(d)	(iii)	(iv)	(ii)	(i)

17. An interim government of 'Romalia' seeks control over certain funds belonging to the Republic of Romalia. Romalia is in a state of civil war. An application is filed before a UK. Court by the Interim Government. The evidence before the court is that the UK Government has no dealings with the Interim Government. The court comes to the conclusion that there is no effective government of Romalia. The court:
(a) will accept the application because the applicant is an interim government
(b) will not accept the application because the government has not been recognized by U.K.
(c) will not accept the application because if has no jurisdiction
(d) will not accept the application because the interim government is not in its determination a sovereign government

18. **Assertion (A):** Only states may be parties in cases before the International Court of Justice.

Reason (R): Non-parties may have access to the Court with the prior approval of the secretary-general.

Codes:

(a) Both (A) and (R) are true and (R) is a correct explanation of (A)
(b) Both (A) and (R) are true but (R) is not a correct explanation of (A)
(c) (A) is true but (R) is false
(d) (A) is false but (R) is true

19. Indicate the correct order in which the following decisions appeared:
(i) Namibia case
(ii) Naulilaa case
(iii) Nauru Vs Australia
(iv) Nicaragua Vs Honduras

Codes:

(a) (i), (iii), (iv) and (ii)
(b) (ii), (i), (iii) and (iv)
(c) (iii), (iv), (ii) and (i)
(d) (iv), (iii), (ii) and (iii)

20. Human Rights Council has taken the place of:
(a) International Human Rights Institute
(b) Human Rights Committee
(c) Centre for Human Rights
(d) Human Rights Commission

21. Dower in Muslim law is:
(i) Dowry
(ii) An obligation imposed upon husband as a mark of respect for wife
(iii) Sale price of woman
(iv) Consideration for Marriage

Select the correct answer by using the code given below:

Codes:

(a) (i), (iii) and (iv) (b) (ii) and (iii)
(c) (ii) and (iv) (d) (i) and (iii)

22. In which of the following cases S.C. held 'Talakul Biddat' is not a valid divorce?
(a) Bai Tahira Vs Ali Hussain Fissalli
(b) Shamim Ara Vs Union of India
(c) Mohd Ahmad Khan Vs Shah Bano
(d) Yusuf Vs Sawarama

23. Marriage in Fosterage relationship is:
(a) Valid (b) Irregular
(c) Void (d) None of these

24. In which of the following the Supreme Court held that the Registration of Marriage should be made compulsory:
(a) Ashok kumar Vs Rupa Hura
(b) Seema Vs Ashawani Kumar
(c) Hafizunnissan Vs Mohd. Yasin khan
(d) T. Sareetha Vs T. Venkatta Subhaiah

25. Match the List I and List II using following code:

List I

(A) Registration of Marriage
(B) Presumption of Marriage
(C) Presumption of legitimacy of child
(D) Marriage religious ceremonies

List II

(i) S. 112 Evidence Act
(ii) S. 7 HM Act
(iii) S. 114 Evidence Act
(iv) S. 8 HM Act

Codes:	**A**	**B**	**C**	**D**
(a)	(i)	(ii)	(iii)	(iv)
(b)	(iv)	(iii)	(i)	(ii)
(c)	(iii)	(iv)	(ii)	(i)
(d)	(ii)	(iii)	(iv)	(i)

26. **Assertion (A):** A Bigamous marriage is void under Hindu law.

Reason (R): A child born out of void marriage is legitimate child of his parent.

Codes:

(a) Both (A) and (R) are true and (R) is the correct explanation of (A)
(b) Both (A) and (R) are true but (R) is not the correct explanation of (A)
(c) (A) is true but (R) is false
(d) (A) is false but (R) is true

27. When consent is not free, agreement will be:
(a) Voidable (b) Void
(c) Illegal (d) Void or Voidable

28. **Assertion (A):** Law of contract recently facing a problem due to frequent use of contract of Adhesion.
    Reason (R): One party to contract has no choice to negotiate but to accept it.
    Codes:
    (a) (A) is right but (R) is wrong
    (b) (A) is wrong but (R) is right
    (c) (A) and (R) both right and (R) is right explanation of (A)
    (d) (A) and (R) both right but (R) is not right explanation of (A)

29. Voidable agreements are declared in:
    (a) Section 2 of the contract Act
    (b) Section 30
    (c) Section 19
    (d) Section 60

30. Which one of the following pairs is correctly matched?
    (a) Mohiribibi Vs Dharmodas Ghose — Proposal
    (b) Hadley Vs Baxandale — Free Consent
    (c) Satyabrat Ghose Vs Magniram — Frustration of contract
    (d) Lalman Shukla Vs Gauri Dutt — Capacity to contract

31. A promise to pay subscription for charitable purpose will be enforced if:
    (a) promise is made in writing
    (b) steps have been taken in furtherance of promise
    (c) amount is not excessive
    (d) part payment has been made

32. An agreement will be void, if mistake is:
    (a) of facts as well as of law
    (b) of law
    (c) of facts
    (d) neither of facts or nor of law

33. Match the following:
    (A) Gillick Vs West Norfolk and Wiseback Area Health Authority
    (B) Wagon Mound II
    (C) Ashby Vs White
    (D) M.C. Mehta Vs Union of India
    (E) Priestley Vs Fowler
    (i) Strict Liability
    (ii) Violation of absolute rights
    (iii) Remoteness of damages
    (iv) Doctrine of common employment
    (v) Volenti non fit injuria

Codes:	A	B	C	D	E
(a)	(v)	(iii)	(ii)	(i)	(iv)
(b)	(iii)	(ii)	(iv)	(i)	(v)
(c)	(ii)	(iii)	(v)	(i)	(iv)
(d)	(iv)	(iii)	(ii)	(i)	(v)

34. **Assertion (A):** Attempt to commit suicide is punishable under the Indian law.
    Reason (R): In English law also attempt to commit suicide is punishable.
    Codes:
    (a) Both (A) and (R) are true and (R) is a good explanation of (A)
    (b) Both (A) and (R) are true but (R) is not a correct explanation of (A)
    (c) (A) is true but (R) is false
    (d) (A) is false but (R) is true

35. The term MALFEA ANCE applies to:
    (a) the commission of an unlawful act
    (b) the improper performance of some lawful act
    (c) the failure to perform some act for which there is an obligation to perform
    (d) (a), (b) and (c) all are correct

36. *Salus Populi Suprema Lex* means:
    (a) The welfare of the people is the supreme law
    (b) Law is more important than the people
    (c) The supremacy of law can never be questioned
    (d) Public opinion is superior to law

37. In India, the Railways:

(a) Have direct statutory duty to erect gates and employ gatemen at the level crossings
(b) Have no duty until the central government so requires by a requisition under Section 13 of the Railways Act.
(c) Being engaged in an inherently dangerous activity are bound by the common law duty on the principle of neighborhood
(d) Both (b) and (c) are correct

38. Exemplary damages are awarded:
(a) When it is considered that an action should never have been bought
(b) When the purpose of the action is merely to establish a right
(c) When it is necessary to compensate the plaintiff
(d) To punish the defendant and to deter him from similar conduct in future

39. Nothing is an offence which is committed by a child below the age of:
(a) 5 years (b) 7 years
(c) 9 years (d) 12 years

40. **Assertion (A):** Nothing is an offence which causes slight harm.
Reason (R): Law does not take care of trivials.
Codes:
(a) Both (A) and (R) are true and (R) is a correct explanation of (A)
(b) Both (A) and (R) are true but (R) is not a correct explanation of (A)
(c) (A) is true but (R) is false
(d) (A) is false but (R) is true

41. Match List I and List II with the help of codes given below:
List I
(A) Kehar Singh Vs State of Delhi
(B) Visakha Vs State of Rajasthan
(C) Roopa Deol Bajaj Vs K.P.S. Gill
(D) Gurdatta Mal Vs State of U.P.

List II
(i) common object
(ii) outraging the modesty of woman
(iii) murder
(iv) sexual harassment

Codes:	A	B	C	D
(a)	(i)	(ii)	(iv)	(iii)
(b)	(iii)	(iv)	(ii)	(i)
(c)	(iv)	(ii)	(i)	(iii)
(d)	(ii)	(iii)	(iv)	(i)

42. Ignorantia facit doth excusat means:
(a) Ignorance of law is no excuse
(b) Ignorance of law is an excuse in certain cases
(c) Ignorance of fact is an excuse
(d) Ignorance of law and fact both are excusable

43. 'A' an insane person kills 'B' by firing from a loaded gun. A has committed:
(a) An offence of culpable homicide not amounting to murder
(b) An offence of murder
(c) An offence of grievious hurt
(d) No offence at all

44. Under which of the sections of the Indian Penal Code, 1860 a person can be convicted for the offence of Bigamy?
(a) Section 375 (b) Section 377
(c) Section 494 (d) Section 498

45. **Assertion (A):** Only a section of labour force is protected under section 17 of the trade unions Act.
Reason (R): Protection is available only to office-bearers and member of registered trade unions.
Codes:
(a) Both (A) and (R) are true and (R) is a correct explanation of (A)
(b) Both (A) and (R) are true but (R) is not a correct explanation of (A)
(c) (A) is true but (R) is false
(d) (A) is false but (R) is true

46. Which of the following is an 'industry'?
 (i) Radio and Doordarshan
 (ii) Central Institute of Fisheries
 (iii) Postal and Telegraph Department
 (iv) Public Service Commission

Codes:
(a) (i), (ii) and (iii) are correct
(b) (ii) and (iv) are correct
(c) (i), (iii) and (iv) are correct
(d) only (i) is correct

47. Who among the following is a workman?
(a) Legal Representative of deceased workman
(b) Research fellow
(c) Probationer
(d) A member of armed force

48. A workman had worked intermittently in the past. His appointment was made on contractual basis with a stipulation that his services could be terminated as and when the council deemed necessary. His services were terminated subsequently. But retrenchment compensation provisions were not followed. He is:
(a) entitled to be reinstated with full back wages
(b) not entitled to any compensation
(c) entitled to retrenchment compensation
(d) entitled to wages as determined by the court

49. Match List I and List II using the codes given below:

List I (Industry)
(A) Cooperatives
(B) Charitable Institution
(C) Educational Institution run by a
(D) Chartered accountants

List II (Judicial Decision)
(i) Corporation of city of Nagpur case
(ii) Prabhudayal Vs Alwar Shakari Bhumi Vikas
(iii) Ramkrishna Iyyar Vaidyanathan corporation Vs Fifth Industrial Tribunal
(iv) Bombay pinjarapole case

Codes:	**A**	**B**	**C**	**D**
(a)	(iv)	(i)	(ii)	(iii)
(b)	(iii)	(ii)	(iv)	(i)
(c)	(ii)	(iv)	(i)	(iii)
(d)	(ii)	(iii)	(i)	(iv)

50. Consider the following decisions on the meaning of the employer under section 2(g) of the Industrial Disputes Act. Identify the correct order in which they appeared:
(i) Bombay Dock Labour Board Vs Stevedone workers
(ii) Western India Automobile Association Vs Industrial Tribunal
(iii) Kays Construction Co (P) Ltd Vs Its workmen
(iv) Anakapalle cooperative Agricultural and Industrial Society Vs Its workmen

Codes:

(a)	(ii)	(iv)	(iii)	(i)
(b)	(iii)	(ii)	(i)	(iv)
(c)	(ii)	(i)	(iii)	(iv)
(d)	(i)	(iii)	(iv)	(ii)

ANSWERS

1. (a)	2. (c)	3. (d)	4. (c)	5. (a)
6. (b)	7. (d)	8. (c)	9. (c)	10. (a)
11. (a)	12. (b)	13. (d)	14. (c)	15. (b)
16. (a)	17. (d)	18. (a)	19. (b)	20. (a)
21. (c)	22. (b)	23. (c)	24. (b)	25. (b)
26. (b)	27. (b)	28. (c)	29. (c)	30. (c)
31. (b)	32. (a)	33. (c)	34. (b)	35. (a)
36. (a)	37. (a)	38. (d)	39. (b)	40. (a)
41. (b)	42. (a)	43. (d)	44. (c)	45. (a)
46. (a)	47. (a)	48. (c)	49. (c)	50. (c)

JUNE–2008

Note: This paper contains fifty (50) objective type questions, each question carrying two (2) marks. All questions are compulsory.

PAPER–I

1. The teacher has been glorified by the phrase "Friend, philosopher and guide" because
   (a) He has to play all vital roles in the context of society
   (b) He transmits the high value of humanity to students
   (c) He is the great reformer of the society
   (d) He is a great patriot

2. The most important cause of failure for teacher lies in the area of
   (a) interpersonal relationship
   (b) lack of command over the knowledge of the subject
   (c) verbal ability
   (d) strict handling of the students

3. A teacher can establish rapport with his students by
   (a) becoming a figure of authority
   (b) impressing students with knowledge and skill
   (c) playing the role of a guide
   (d) becoming a friend to the students

4. Education is a powerful instrument of
   (a) Social transformation
   (b) Personal transformation
   (c) Cultural transformation
   (d) All of the above

5. A teacher's major contribution towards the maximum self-realisation of the student is affected through
   (a) Constant fulfilment of the students' needs
   (b) Strict control of classroom activities
   (c) Sensitivity to students' needs, goals and purposes
   (d) Strict reinforcement of academic standards

6. Research problem is selected from the standpoint of
   (a) Researcher's interest
   (b) Financial support
   (c) Social relevance
   (d) Availability of relevant literature

7. Which one is called non-probability sampling?
   (a) Cluster sampling
   (b) Quota sampling
   (c) Systematic sampling
   (d) Stratified random sampling

8. Formulation of hypothesis may not be required in
   (a) Survey method
   (b) Historical studies
   (c) Experimental studies
   (d) Normative studies

9. Field-work based research is classified as
   (a) Empirical (b) Historical
   (c) Experimental (d) Biographical

10. Which of the following sampling methods is appropriate to study the prevalence of AIDS amongst male and female in India in 1976, 1986, 1996 and 2006?

(a) Cluster sampling
(b) Systematic sampling
(c) Quota sampling
(d) Stratified random sampling

Read the following passage and answer the questions 11 to 15:

The fundamental principle is that Article 14 forbids class legislation but permits reasonable classification for the purpose of legislation which classification must satisfy the twin tests of classification being founded on an intelligible differentia which distinguishes persons or things that are grouped together from those that are left out of the group and that differentia must have a rational nexus to the object sought to be achieved by the Statute in question. The thrust of Article 14 is that the citizen is entitled to equality before law and equal protection of laws. In the very nature of things the society being composed of unequals a welfare State will have to strive by both executive and legislative action to help the less fortunate in society to ameliorate their condition so that the social and economic inequality in the society may be bridged. This would necessitate a legislative application to a group of citizens otherwise unequal and amelioration of whose lot is the object of state affirmative action. In the absence of the doctrine of classification such legislation is likely to flounder on the bedrock of equality enshrined in Article 14. The Court realistically appraising the social and economic inequality and keeping in view the guidelines on which the State action must move as constitutionally laid down in Part IV of the Constitution evolved the doctrine of classification. The doctrine was evolved to sustain a legislation or State action designed to help weaker sections of the society or some such segments of the society in need of succour. Legislative and executive action may accordingly be sustained if it satisfies the twin tests of reasonable classification and the rational principle correlated to the object sought to be achieved.

The concept of equality before the law does not involve the idea of absolute equality among human beings which is a physical impossibility. All that Article 14 guarantees is a similarity of treatment contra-distinguished from identical treatment. Equality before law means that among equals the law should be equal and should be equally administered and that the likes should be treated alike. Equality before the law does not mean that things which are different shall be as though they are the same. It of course means denial of any special privilege by reason of birth, creed or the like. The legislation as well as the executive government, while dealing with diverse problems arising out of an infinite variety of human relations must of necessity have the power of making special laws, to attain any particular object and to achieve that object it must have the power of selection or classification of persons and things upon which such laws are to operate.

11. Right to equality, one of the fundamental rights, is enunciated in the Constitution under Part III, Article
    (a) 12 (b) 13
    (c) 14 (d) 15
12. The main thrust of Right to equality is that it permits
    (a) class legislation
    (b) equality before law and equal protection under the law
    (c) absolute equality
    (d) special privilege by reason of birth
13. The social and economic inequality in the society can be bridged by
    (a) executive and legislative action
    (b) universal suffrage
    (c) identical treatment
    (d) None of the above

14. The doctrine of classification is evolved to
    (a) Help weaker sections of the society
    (b) Provide absolute equality
    (c) Provide identical treatment
    (d) None of the above

15. While dealing with diverse problems arising out of an infinite variety of human relations, the government
    (a) must have the power of making special laws
    (b) must not have any power to make special laws
    (c) must have power to withdraw equal rights
    (d) None of the above

16. Communication with oneself is known as
    (a) Group communication
    (b) Grapevine communication
    (c) Interpersonal communication
    (d) Intrapersonal communication

17. Which broadcasting system for TV is followed in India?
    (a) NTSE (b) PAL
    (c) SECAM (d) NTCS

18. All India Radio before 1936 was known as
    (a) Indian Radio Broadcasting
    (b) Broadcasting Service of India
    (c) Indian State Broadcasting Service
    (d) All India Broadcasting Service

19. The biggest news agency of India is
    (a) PTI
    (b) UNI
    (c) NANAP
    (d) Samachar Bharati

20. Prasar Bharati was launched in the year
    (a) 1995 (b) 1997
    (c) 1999 (d) 2001

21. A statistical measure based upon the entire population is called parameter while measure based upon a sample is known as
    (a) Sample parameter
    (b) Inference
    (c) Statistics
    (d) None of these

22. The importance of the correlation co-efficient lies in the fact that
    (a) There is a linear relationship between the correlated variables
    (b) It is one of the most valid measure of statistics
    (c) It allows one to determine the degree or strength of the association between two variables
    (d) It is a non-parametric method of statistical analysis

23. The F-test
    (a) is essentially a two-tailed test
    (b) is essentially a one-tailed test
    (c) can be one tailed as well as two tailed depending on the hypothesis
    (d) can never be a one-tailed test

24. What will be the next letter in the following series
    DCXW, FEVU, HGTS, ______
    (a) AKPO (b) JBYZ
    (c) JIRQ (d) LMRS

25. The following question is based on the diagram given below. If the two small circles represent formal classroom education and distance education and the big circle stands for university system of education, which figure represents the university systems.

    (a)  (b) 

    (c) (d) 

26. The statement, 'To be non-violent is good' is a

(a) Moral judgement
(b) Factual judgement
(c) Religious judgement
(d) Value judgement

27. **Assertion (A):** Man is a rational being.
Reason (R): Man is a social being.
(a) Both (A) and (R) are true and (R) is the correct explanation of (A)
(b) Both (A) and (R) are true but (R) is not the correct explanation of (A)
(c) (A) is true but (R) is false
(d) (A) is false but (R) is true

28. Value Judgements are
(a) Factual Judgements
(b) Ordinary Judgements
(c) Normative Judgements
(d) Expression of public opinion

29. Deductive reasoning proceeds from
(a) general to particular
(b) particular to general
(c) one general conclusion to another general conclusion
(d) one particular conclusion to another particular conclusion

30. AGARTALA is written in code as 14168171, the code for AGRA is
(a) 1641 (b) 1416
(c) 1441 (d) 1461

31. Which one of the following is the most comprehensive source of population data?
(a) National Family Health Surveys
(b) National Sample Surveys
(c) Census
(d) Demographic Health Surveys

32. Which one of the following principles is not applicable to sampling?
(a) Sample units must be clearly defined
(b) Sample units must be dependent on each other
(c) Same units of sample should be used throughout the study
(d) Sample units must be chosen in a systematic and objective manner

33. If January 1st, 2007 is Monday, what was the day on 1st January 1995?
(a) Sunday (b) Monday
(c) Friday (d) Saturday

34. Insert the missing number in the following series
4 16 8 64 ? 256
(a) 16 (b) 24
(c) 32 (d) 20

35. If an article is sold for ₹ 178 at a loss of 11%; what would be its selling price in order to earn a profit of 11%?
(a) ₹ 222.50 (b) ₹ 267
(c) ₹ 222 (d) ₹ 220

36. WYSIWYG—describes the display of a document on screen as it will actually print
(a) What you state is what you get
(b) What you see is what you get
(c) What you save is what you get
(d) What you suggest is what you get

37. Which of the following is not a Computer language?
(a) PASCAL (b) UNIX
(c) FORTRAN (d) COBOL

38. A keyboard has at least
(a) 91 keys (b) 101 keys
(c) 111 keys (d) 121 keys

39. An E-mail address is composed of
(a) two parts (b) three parts
(c) four parts (d) five parts

40. Corel Draw is a popular
(a) Illustration program
(b) Programming language
(c) Text program
(d) None of the above

41. Human ear is most sensitive to noise in which of the following ranges
(a) 1-2 kHz (b) 100-500 Hz
(c) 10-12 kHz (d) 13-16 kHz

42. Which one of the following units is used to measure intensity of noise?
(a) Decible (b) Hz
(c) Phon (d) Watts/m^2

43. If the population growth follows a logistic curve, the maximum sustainable yield
(a) is equal to half the carrying capacity
(b) is equal to the carrying capacity
(c) depends on growth rates
(d) depends on the initial population

44. Chemical weathering of rocks is largely dependent upon
(a) high temperature
(b) strong wind action
(c) heavy rainfall
(d) glaciation

45. Structure of earth's system consists of the following: Match List I with List II and give the correct answer.
List I (Zone)
A. Atmosphere B. Biosphere
C. Hydrosphere D. Lithosphere
List II (Chemical Character)
1. Inert gases
2. Salt, freshwater, snow and ice
3. Organic substances, skeleton matter
4. Light silicates

Codes:	A	B	C	D
(a)	2	3	1	4
(b)	1	3	2	4
(c)	2	1	3	4
(d)	3	1	2	4

46. NAAC is an autonomous institution under the aegis of
(a) ICSSR (b) CSIR
(c) AICTE (d) UGC

47. National Council for Women's Education was established in
(a) 1958 (b) 1976
(c) 1989 (d) 2000

48. Which one of the following is not situated in New Delhi?
(a) Indian Council of Cultural Relations
(b) Indian Council of Scientific Research
(c) National Council of Educational Research and Training
(d) Indian Institute of Advanced Studies

49. Autonomy in higher education implies freedom in
(a) Administration
(b) Policy-making
(c) Finance
(d) Curriculum development

50. Match List I with List II and select the correct answer from the code given below
List I (Institutions)
A. Dr. Hari Singh Gour University
B. S.N.D.T. University
C. M.S. University
D. J.N. Vyas University
List II (Locations)
1. Mumbai 2. Baroda
3. Jodhpur 4. Sagar

Codes:	A	B	C	D
(a)	4	1	2	3
(b)	1	2	3	4
(c)	3	1	2	4
(d)	2	4	1	3

ANSWERS

1. (b)	2. (b)	3. (b)	4. (d)	5. (c)
6. (c)	7. (b)	8. (b)	9. (a)	10. (d)
11. (c)	12. (b)	13. (a)	14. (a)	15. (a)
16. (d)	17. (b)	18. (c)	19. (a)	20. (b)
21. (a)	22. (c)	23. (c)	24. (c)	25. (b)
26. (a)	27. (b)	28. (c)	29. (a)	30. (d)
31. (c)	32. (b)	33. (d)	34. (a)	35. (c)
36. (b)	37. (b)	38. (b)	39. (a)	40. (a)
41. (b)	42. (a)	43. (a)	44. (c)	45. (b)
46. (d)	47. (a)	48. (d)	49. (c)	50. (a)

PAPER–II

Note: This paper contains fifty (50) objective type questions, each question carrying two (2) marks. All questions are compulsory.

1. Consider the following statements:

   An accused person can be compelled to:
   (i) give his finger prints
   (ii) give evidence against himself
   (iii) participate in the identification parade

   Which of the above statements are correct?
   (a) (i), (ii) and (iii) (b) (ii) and (iii)
   (c) (i) and (ii) (d) (i) and (iii)

2. In which of the constitutional Amendment it has been laid down that the total number of Ministers including Prime Minister in the Union council of Ministers, shall not exceed 15 per cent of the total members of the House of people?
   (a) The Constitution [Eighty-Eighth Amendment] Act
   (b) The Constitution [Eighty-Nineth Amendment] Act
   (c) The Constitution [Ninety-First Amendment] Act
   (d) The Constitution [Ninety-Third Amendment] Act

3. "What cannot be done directly, cannot be done indirectly". This statement relates to the:
   (a) Doctrine of pith and substance
   (b) Doctrine of colourable legislation
   (c) Doctrine of ancillary powers
   (d) Doctrine of implied powers

4. In which case the Supreme Court of India held that the voters have a right to know the antecedents of contesting candidates?
   (a) Shakila Abdul Gaffor Vs. Vasant R. Dhoble
   (b) Shyam Narain Chowksey Vs. Union of India
   (c) Union of India Vs. Association for Democratic Reform
   (d) Saurabh Chowdhery Vs. Union of India

5. Recently the Supreme Court of India, while holding right to marriage, a right protected under Article 21 of the Constitution, directed the police and administrations not to harass or subject to act of threat or violence, those who marry outside their caste or religion. It was so held in:
   (a) Lata Singh Vs. State of Uttar Pradesh
   (b) Ashok Kumar Vs. West Bengal State
   (c) P.U.C.L Vs. Union of India
   (d) Priyanka Vs. State of M.P.

6. A 2003 enactment provided for doing away with the requirement of a candidate to be resident of a particular state, to contest the election to the Rajya Sabha. In 2006 the Supreme Court of India has held such enactment:
   (a) Unconstitutional
   (b) Constitutional
   (c) Partly valid end partly invalid
   (d) Subject to judicial review

7. A five judge Constitution bench of the Supreme Court in October 2006 has held that the exclusion of 'Creamy Layer' among the Scheduled Castes and Scheduled Tribes is:
   (a) Subject to Judicial review
   (b) Unconstitutional
   (c) Constitutional directive
   (d) A matter of policy decision of the government

8. Which one of the following is a Fundamental Duty of every citizen of India?

(a) To be truthful to one's duties
(b) To renounce the practices derogatory to the dignity of children
(c) To renounce the practices derogatory of human beings
(d) To renounce the practices derogatory to the dignity of a woman

9. Possession is called:
(a) 8 points in Law
(b) 10 points in Law
(c) 9 points in Law
(d) 7 points in Law

10. "True Law is right reason in agreement with nature; it is of Universal application, un-changing and everlasting...it is a sin to try to alter this law, nor is it allowable to attempt to repeal any part of it and it is impossible to abolish it entirely.... God is the author of this law, its promulgator and its enforcing Judge". This passage highlights the importance of...
(a) Customary law
(b) Natural law
(c) Positive law
(d) Anthropological law

11. "The limits are set by rational Principles of Justice", it is said by
(a) Holland (b) Henry Maine
(c) Kelson (d) Rawls

12. Match List I with List II giving the code given below:

List I
(A) Human Vulnerability
(B) Approximate Equality
(C) Limited Altruism
(D) Limited Sources

List II
(i) We are in general selfish
(ii) Even the strongest must sleep at times
(iii) We need food, clothes and shelter,
(iv) We are susceptible to physical attacks

Codes:	A	B	C	D
(a)	(i)	(iii)	(ii)	(iv)
(b)	(iii)	(i)	(iv)	(ii)
(c)	(ii)	(iv)	(i)	(iii)
(d)	(iv)	(ii)	(i)	(iii)

13. The Jural Correlative of 'Right' is:
(a) Privilege (b) Possession
(c) Duty (d) Obligation

14. Which of the following is the recommended theory of punishment in view of Human Rights:
(a) Reformative theory
(b) Retributive theory
(c) Preventive theory
(d) Deterrent theory

15. The basis of International Law is:
(a) Ubi societas, ubijus
(b) Jus gentium
(c) Jus Cogens
(d) Droit des gens

16. The reasons why international law does work are:
(i) The common good
(ii) The flexible nature of international law
(iii) Practitioners of international law are lawyers
(iv) The effective institutions

Codes:
(a) only (i) and (ii) are correct
(b) only (iii) and (iv) are correct
(c) (i), (ii), (iii) and (iv) are correct
(d) (i), (ii) and (iii) are correct

17. Match List I with List II using the code given below:
List I (Subject Matter)
(A) Territorial boundary treaty
(B) Regional custom
(C) Principle of estoppel
(D) Principle of equity

List II (Decisions)
(i) Rann of Kutch Arbitration
(ii) Temple of Preah Vihear case
(iii) The Asylum case
(iv) Case concerning Kasikili/Sedudu Island
(v) The Danube Dam case

Codes:	A	B	C	D
(a)	(iii)	(v)	(i)	(iv)
(b)	(iv)	(v)	(iii)	(ii)
(c)	(iv)	(iii)	(ii)	(i)
(d)	(v)	(iv)	(ii)	(iii)

18. Identify the correct order in which the following bases of Jurisdiction appear in the statute of the International Criminal Justice:
(i) Consent ad hoc
(ii) As provided in the U.N. Charter
(iii) Consent under the optional system
(iv) Transferred Jurisdiction

Codes:
(a) (iv), (iii), (i) and (ii)
(b) (iii), (i), (ii) and (iv)
(c) (ii), (i), (iii) and (iv)
(d) (i), (ii), (iv) and (iii)

19. **Assertion (A):** Doctrine of stare decisis is not applicable to International Court of Justice.
Reason (R): Decision of the International Court of Justice is binding on parties and only in respect of that case.

Codes:
(a) Both (A) and (R) are true and (R) is a correct explanation of (A)
(b) Both (A) and (R) are true but (R) is not a correct explanation of (A)
(c) (A) is true but (R) is false
(d) (A) is false but (R) is true

20. In Gur corporation's case the issue before an English court was whether the Government of Ciskei could sue as claimant in its own name. The court of Appeal answered this question in the affirmative by applying:
(a) The foreign corporation Act.
(b) Foreign Relations Act.
(c) Doctrine of acts of a delegated sovereign.
(d) Estrada doctrine.

21. 'Coparcenary property' of a Hindu:
(a) devolves by succession
(b) devolves by survivorship
(c) can be partitioned
(d) can not be partitioned

22. Match List I and List II and select the correct answer using the code given below the lists:

List I
(A) Marriage between parties within degree of prohibited relationship
(B) Impotency
(C) Marriage between two sapindas of each other
(D) Pregnancy of wife at the time of marriage by some person other then petitioner

List II
(i) Voidable (ii) Void
(iii) Voidable (iv) Void

Codes:	A	B	C	D
(a)	(ii)	(i)	(iv)	(iii)
(b)	(ii)	(iii)	(i)	(iv)
(c)	(ii)	(i)	(iii)	(iv)
(d)	(ii)	(iv)	(i)	(iii)

23. In which of the following cases the Court held that Doctrine of acknowledgment is a part of the substantive Muslim Law of Inheritance and not a rule of Evidence:
(a) S.A. Hussain Vs. Rajamma
(b) Mohd Amin Vs. Vakil Ahmad
(c) Mohammed Allahadad Khan Vs. Mohammed Ismail Khan
(d) Habibur Rehman Vs. Altaf Ali

24. A gift by the husband to the wife in lieu of her dower is recognised as:
(a) Hiba-bil-iwaz
(b) Hiba-ba-shartul-iwaz
(c) Hiba
(d) Will

25. Match List I and List II with the help of code given below:
List I
(A) Mohd Ahmad Vs. Shah Bano
(B) Mukku Rathod Vs. State of Kerala
(C) Maina Bibi Vs. Chaudhry Vakil Ahmad
(D) Nawazish Ali Khan Vs. Ali Raza Khan
List II
(i) Oral gift (ii) Maintenance
(iii) Life Interest (iv) Dower

Codes:	A	B	C	D
(a)	(ii)	(i)	(iv)	(iii)
(b)	(i)	(ii)	(iii)	(iv)
(c)	(ii)	(iii)	(iv)	(i)
(d)	(i)	(iv)	(iii)	(ii)

26. The statement while there is no rose which has no thorn but if what you hold is all thorn and no rose, better throw it away, relates to:
(a) Restituation of Conjugal Rights
(b) Judicial Separation
(c) Divorce by Mutual consent
(d) Irretrievable break down of marriage theory of divorce

27. **Assertion (A):** There is no actual loss to the party on breach of contract, even nominal compensation will be paid.
Reason (R): There is a right, there should be remedy.
Codes:
(a) (A) is right but (R) is wrong
(b) (A) is wrong but (R) is right
(c) (A) and (R) both right and (R) is right explanation of (A)
(d) (A) and (R) both right but (R) is not explanation of (A)

28. Which one is not matching:
(a) Proposal (b) Consideration
(c) Acceptance (d) Quasi contract

29. In case amount of compensation is stipulated in contract and breach of contract occurs; compensation will be allowed:
(a) Stipulated amount
(b) More than stipulated amount
(c) Less than stipulated amount
(d) At the discretion of court but not more than stipulated amount

30. An agreement in restraint of marriage is void, if restraint is:
(a) Absolute
(b) Partial
(c) Absolute or partial
(d) None of above

31. A bid at an auction is provisionally accepted but that is subject to final approval of an authority:
(a) Contract is final
(b) It will not become contract
(c) Contract will be final on approval of authority
(d) None of above

32. Wagering agreements are void but collateral transactions will be:
(a) void
(b) voidable
(c) valid
(d) valid, at the discretion of court

33. A tort is a violation of:
(a) Right in Personal
(b) Right in Rem
(c) Either right in personal or right in rem
(d) Imperfect right

34. In torts, exemplary damages are awarded:
(a) in all cases
(b) in most of the cases
(c) in restrictive category of cases
(d) never awarded at all

35. The justification from Civil liability for acts prima facie wrongful are based principally upon:
(a) Private grounds
(b) Public grounds
(c) Both private and public grounds
(d) Equitable grounds

36. The exception to the rule that the employer is not liable for the acts of the independent contractor:
(a) Technical exceptions
(b) Because of the absence of vicarious liability of the employer for the fault of the contractor
(c) Because of breach of duty
(d) Cases where the employer is made liable for his own fault or breach of duty

37. Res Ipsa Loquitur means:
(a) The thing speaks for itself
(b) The thing speaks for others
(c) The thing does not speak for itself
(d) The thing is a manifestation of others

38. Act of God is applicable to:
(a) All cases of inevitable accident
(b) Those who have their origin in part to the agency of man
(c) Those which are occasioned by the elementary forces of nature unconnected with the agency of man
(d) Those which are occasioned partly by the elementary forces of nature and partly by the agency of man

39. Cohabitation caused by a man deceitfully inducing a belief of lawful marriage is punishable with:

Codes:
(a) Imprisonment upto ten years and fine also
(b) Imprisonment upto seven years
(c) Imprisonment for a term of five years and fine
(d) Punishment with fine only

40. Which of the following does not fall in the category of General Exceptions in the Indian Penal Code, 1860:

Codes:
(a) Accident in doing a lawful act
(b) Insanity
(c) Involuntary intoxication of any degree
(d) Well calculated Murder

41. Match List I and List II with the help of codes given below:

List I
(A) Bhaurao Shankar Lokhande Vs. State of Maharashtra
(B) Gul Mohammad Vs. Emperor
(C) Pawan Kumar Vs. State of Haryana
(D) Barendra Kumar Ghosh Vs. King Emperor

List II
(i) Adultery
(ii) Cruelty
(iii) Joint Liability
(iv) Bigamy

Codes:	**A**	**B**	**C**	**D**
(a)	(iv)	(i)	(ii)	(iii)
(b)	(i)	(ii)	(iv)	(iii)
(c)	(ii)	(i)	(iv)	(iii)
(d)	(iv)	(ii)	(iii)	(i)

42. **Assertion (A):** Right of Private Defence extends to causing death if property sought to be protected is public property.
Reason (R): Public property must be protected even at any cost.

Codes:
(a) Both (A) and (R) are true but (R) is not a correct explanation of (A)

(b) Both (A) and (R) are true and (R) is a correct explanation of (A)
(c) (A) is true but (R) is false
(d) (A) is false but (R) is true

43. Which of the following section-wise sequence is correct:
(i) Rape (ii) Attempt
(iii) Conspiracy (iv) Joint Liability

Codes:

(a)	(i)	(iv)	(ii)	and	(iii)
(b)	(iii)	(ii)	(iv)	and	(i)
(c)	(iv)	(iii)	(i)	and	(ii)
(d)	(i)	(iii)	(iv)	and	(ii)

44. **Assertion (A):** Necessity knows no law.
Reason (R): Necessity does not justify indiscriminate throwing of passengers over board to save sinking boat.
Codes:
(a) Both (A) and (R) are true and (R) is a correct explanation of (A)
(b) Both (A) and (R) are true but (R) is not a correct explanation of (A)
(c) (A) is true but (R) is false
(d) (A) is false but (R) is true

45. **Assertion (A):** No protection is available to the members of a trade union under sections 17 and 18 of the trade unions Act in respect of Gherao.
Reason (R): In *Rookes* Vs. *Barnard* the court held that trade unions were liable for the tort of intimidation.
Codes:
(a) Both (A) and (R) are true and (R) is the correct explanation of (A)
(b) Both (A) and (R) are true but (R) is not the correct explanation of (A)
(c) (A) is true but (R) is false
(d) (A) is false but (R) is true

46. In view of the change in economic policy of the country it might not now be proper to allow the employees to break the discipline. The Supreme Court held so in:
(a) Management of Pandian Roadways Corporation Vs. Labour Court
(b) B. Srinivasa Reddy Vs. Karnataka Urban Water supply and Drainage Board Employees Association
(c) Electronics Corporation of India Vs. Service Engineering Ltd.
(c) Hombegowda Educational Trust Vs. State of Karnataka

47. Match List I with List II using the code given below:
List I (Judicial decision)
(A) Coir Board Ernakulam
(B) Pipraich Sugar Mills Ltd. Vs. Pipraich Sugar Mills Mazdoor Union
(C) Sundarmbal Vs. Govt. of Goa
(D) Western India Automobile Association Vs. I.T.
List II (Items)
(i) Employer (ii) Industry
(iii) Workman (iv) Retrenchment

Codes:	**A**	**B**	**C**	**D**
(a)	(iii)	(ii)	(iv)	(i)
(b)	(ii)	(iv)	(iii)	(i)
(c)	(i)	(ii)	(iii)	(iv)
(d)	(iv)	(iii)	(i)	(ii)

48. An individual dispute becomes an industrial dispute when it is espoused by:
(i) a trade union
(ii) the appreciable number of workmen
(iii) falls under section 2A of the industrial Disputes Act
(iv) One-fifth of the total work force in the concerned establishment

Codes:
(a) (i) (iii) and (iv) are correct
(b) (ii) and (iii) are correct
(c) (i), (ii) and (iii) are correct
(d) only (iv) is correct

49. 'A's' services were terminated without complying with retrenchment compensation provision:

(a) A is entitled to reinstatement without back wages
(b) A is entitled to back wages
(c) A is entitled to retrenchment compensation
(d) A is entitled to reinstatement and back wages as determined by the Court

50. Indicate the order in which the following words appear in the definition of 'workmen' as given in section 2(s) of the Industrial Disputes Act:
(i) Operational (ii) Manual
(iii) Technical (iv) Supervisory Work

Codes:
(a) (iii), (ii) (i) and (iv)
(b) (ii), (iii), (iv) and (i)
(c) (i), (ii), (iii) and (iv)
(d) (ii), (iv), (iii) and (i)

ANSWERS

1. (d)	2. (c)	3. (b)	4. (c)	5. (a)
6. (b)	7. (c)	8. (c)	9. (c)	10. (b)
11. (d)	12. (d)	13. (c)	14. (a)	15. (c)
16. (a)	17. (c)	18. (c)	19. (a)	20. (a)
21. (a)	22. (a)	23. (c)	24. (c)	25. (a)
26. (b)	27. (c)	28. (d)	29. (d)	30. (c)
31. (c)	32. (d)	33. (c)	34. (b)	35. (d)
36. (a)	37. (a)	38. (c)	39. (a)	40. (d)
41. (a)	42. (a)	43. (c)	44. (b)	45. (a)
46. (c)	47. (b)	48. (c)	49. (d)	50. (a)

DECEMBER–2009

Note: This paper contains Sixty (60) multiple-choice questions, each question carrying two (2) marks. Candidate is expected to answer any Fifty (50) questions. In case more than Fifty (50) questions are attempted, only the first Fifty (50) questions will be evaluated.

PAPER–I

1. The University which telecasts interaction educational programs through its own channel is
   (a) Osmania University
   (b) University of Pune
   (c) Annamalai University
   (d) Indira Gandhi National University (IGNOU)

2. Which of the following skills are needed for present-day teacher to adjust effectively with the classroom teaching?
   1. Knowledge of technology
   2. Use of technology in teaching learning
   3. Knowledge of students' needs
   4. Content mastery

   (a) 1 and 3 (b) 2 and 3
   (c) 2, 3 and 4 (d) 2 and 4

3. Who has signed an MoU for Accreditation of Teacher Education Institutions in India?
   (a) NAAC and UGC
   (b) NCTE and NAAC
   (c) UGC and NCTE
   (d) NCTE and IGNOU

4. The primary duty of the teacher is to
   (a) raise the intellectual standard of the students
   (b) improve the physical standard of the students
   (c) help all-round development of the students
   (d) imbibe value system in the students

5. Micro teaching is more effective
   (a) during the preparation for teaching-practice
   (b) during the teaching-practice
   (c) after the teaching-practice
   (d) always

6. What quality the students like the most in a teacher?
   (a) Idealist philosophy
   (b) Compassion
   (c) Discipline
   (d) Entertaining

7. A null hypothesis is
   (a) when there is no difference between the variables
   (b) the same as research hypothesis
   (c) subjective in nature
   (d) when there is difference between the variables

8. The research which is exploring new facts through the study of the past is called
   (a) Philosophical research
   (b) Historical research
   (c) Mythological research
   (d) Content analysis

9. Action research is
   (a) An applied research
   (b) A research carried out to solve immediate problems
   (c) A longitudinal research
   (d) Simulative research

10. The process not needed in Experimental Researches is
    (a) Observation (b) Manipulation
    (c) Controlling (d) Content Analysis
11. Manipulation is always a part of
    (a) Historical research
    (b) Fundamental research
    (c) Descriptive research
    (d) Experimental research
12. Which correlation co-efficient best explains the relationship between creativity and intelligence?
    (a) 1.00 (b) 0.6
    (c) 0.5 (d) 0.3

Read the following passage and answer the Question Nos. 13 to 18:

The decisive shift in British Policy really came about under mass pressure in the autumn and winter of 1945 to 46—the months which Penderel Moon while editing Wavell's Journal has perceptively described as 'The Edge of a Volcano'. Very foolishly, the British initially decided to hold public trials of several hundreds of the 20,000 I.N.A. prisoners (as well as dismissing from service and detaining without trial no less than 7,000). They compounded the folly by holding the first trial in the Red Fort, Delhi in November 1945, and putting on the dock together a Hindu, a Muslim and a Sikh (P.K. Sehgal, Shah Nawaz, Gurbaksh Singh Dhillon). Bhulabhai Desai, Tejbahadur Sapru and Nehru appeared for the defence (the latter putting on his barrister's gown after 25 years), and the Muslim League also joined the countrywide protest. On 20 November, an Intelligence Bureau note admitted that "there has seldom been a matter which has attracted so much Indian public interest and, it is safe to say, sympathy...this particular brand of sympathy cuts across communal barriers". A journalist (B. Shiva Rao) visiting the Red Fort prisoners on the same day reported that 'There is not the slightest feeling among them of Hindu and Muslim.... A majority of the men now awaiting trial in the Red Fort is Muslim. Some of these men are bitter that Mr. Jinnah is keeping alive a controversy about Pakistan.' The British became extremely nervous about the I.N.A. spirit spreading to the Indian Army, and in January the Punjab Governor reported that a Lahore reception for released I.N.A. prisoners had been attended by Indian soldiers in uniform.

13. Which heading is more appropriate to assign to the above passage?
    (a) Wavell's Journal
    (b) Role of Muslim League
    (c) I.N.A. Trials
    (d) Red Fort Prisoners
14. The trial of P.K. Sehgal, Shah Nawaz and Gurbaksh Singh Dhillon symbolises
    (a) communal harmony
    (b) threat to all religious persons
    (c) threat to persons fighting for the freedom
    (d) British reaction against the natives
15. I.N.A. stands for
    (a) Indian National Assembly
    (b) Indian National Association
    (c) Inter-national Association
    (d) Indian National Army
16. "There has seldom been a matter which has attracted so much Indian Public Interest and, it is safe to say, sympathy... this particular brand of sympathy cuts across communal barriers." Who sympathises to whom and against whom?
    (a) Muslims sympathised with Shah Nawaz against the British
    (b) Hindus sympathised with P.K. Sehgal against the British
    (c) Sikhs sympathised with Gurbaksh Singh Dhillon against the British
    (d) Indians sympathised with the persons who were to be trialled

17. The majority of people waiting for trial outside the Red Fort and criticising Jinnah were the
    (a) Hindus
    (b) Muslims
    (c) Sikhs
    (d) Hindus and Muslims both
18. The sympathy of Indian soldiers in uniform with the released I.N.A. prisoners at Lahore indicates
    (a) Feeling of Nationalism and Fraternity
    (b) Rebellion nature of Indian soldiers
    (c) Simply to participate in the reception party
    (d) None of the above
19. The country which has the distinction of having the two largest circulated newspapers in the world is
    (a) Great Britain
    (b) The United States
    (c) Japan
    (d) China
20. The chronological order of non-verbal communication is
    (a) Signs, symbols, codes, colours
    (b) Symbols, codes, signs, colours
    (c) Colours, signs, codes, symbols
    (d) Codes, colours, symbols, signs
21. Which of the following statements is not connected with communication?
    (a) Medium is the message.
    (b) The world is an electronic cocoon.
    (c) Information is power.
    (d) Telepathy is technological.
22. Communication becomes circular when
    (a) the decoder becomes an encoder
    (b) the feedback is absent
    (c) the source is credible
    (d) the channel is clear
23. The site that played a major role during the terrorist attack on Mumbai (26/11) in 2008 was
    (a) Orkut (b) Facebook
    (c) Amazon.com (d) Twitter
24. **Assertion (A):** For an effective classroom communication at times it is desirable to use the projection technology.
    Reason (R): Using the projection technology facilitates extensive coverage of course contents.
    (a) Both (A) and (R) are true, and (R) is the correct explanation.
    (b) Both (A) and (R) are true, but (R) is not the correct explanation.
    (c) (A) is true, but (R) is false.
    (d) (A) is false, but (R) is true.
25. January 1, 1995 was a Sunday. What day of the week lies on January 1, 1996?
    (a) Sunday (b) Monday
    (c) Wednesday (d) Saturday
26. When an error of 1% is made in the length and breadth of a rectangle, the percentage error (%) in the area of a rectangle will be
    (a) 0 (b) 1
    (c) 2 (d) 4
27. The next number in the series 2, 5, 9, 19, 37, ? will be
    (a) 74 (b) 75
    (c) 76 (d) None of these
28. There are 10 true-false questions in an examination. Then these questions can be answered in
    (a) 20 ways (b) 100 ways
    (c) 240 ways (d) 1024 ways
29. What will be the next term in the following?
    DCXW, FEVU, HGTS, ?
    (a) AKPO (b) ABYZ
    (c) JIRQ (d) LMRS
30. Three individuals X, Y, Z hired a car on a sharing basis and paid ₹ 1,040. They used it for 7, 8, 11 hours, respectively. What are the charges paid by Y?

(a) ₹ 290 (b) ₹ 320
(c) ₹ 360 (d) ₹ 440

31. Deductive argument involves
(a) sufficient evidence
(b) critical thinking
(c) seeing logical relations
(d) repeated observation

32. Inductive reasoning is based on or presupposes
(a) uniformity of nature
(b) God created the world
(c) unity of nature
(d) laws of nature

33. To be critical, thinking must be
(a) practical
(b) socially relevant
(c) individually satisfying
(d) analytical

34. Which of the following is an analogous statement?
(a) Man is like God
(b) God is great
(c) Gandhiji is the Father of the Nation
(d) Man is a rational being

Questions from 35-36 are based on the following diagram in which there are three intersecting circles. H representing The Hindu, I representing Indian Express and T representing The Times of India. A total of 50 persons were surveyed and the number in the Venn diagram indicates the number of persons reading the newspapers.

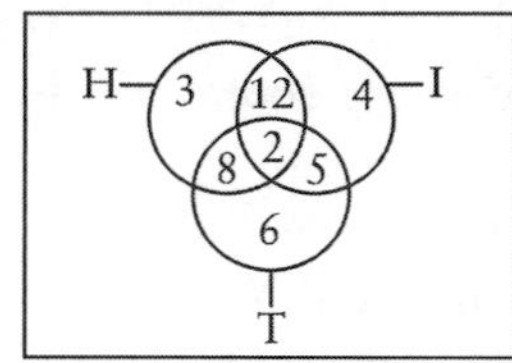

35. How many persons would be reading at least two newspapers?
(a) 23 (b) 25
(c) 27 (d) 29

36. How many persons would be reading almost two newspapers?
(a) 23 (b) 25
(c) 27 (d) 48

37. Which of the following graphs does not represent regular (periodic) behaviour of the variable f(t)?

1. 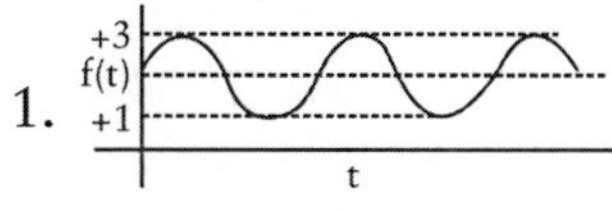

2. 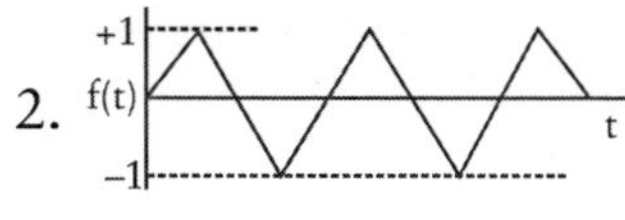

3. 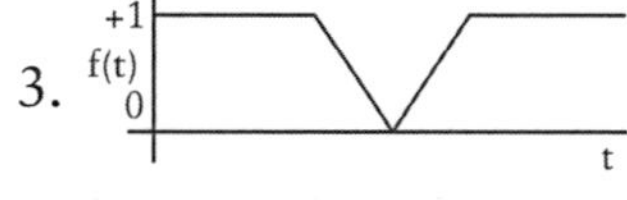

4. 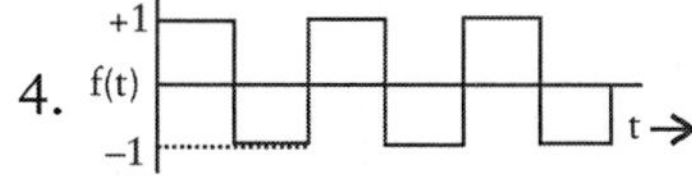

(a) 1 (b) 2
(c) 3 (d) 4

Study the following graph and answer the questions 38 to 40.

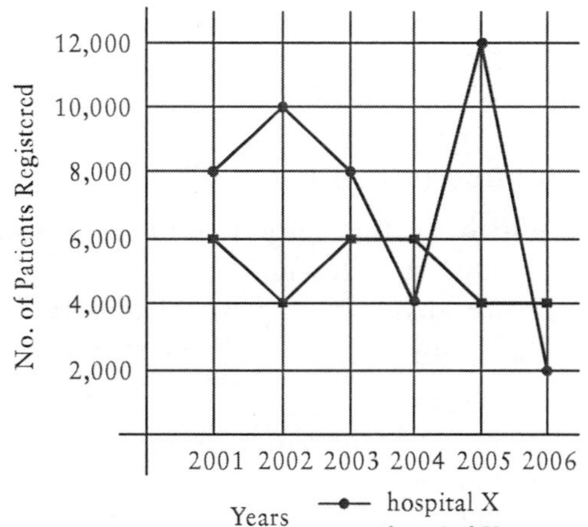

38. In which year total number of patients registered in hospital X and hospital Y was the maximum?
(a) 2003 (b) 2004
(c) 2005 (d) 2006

39. What is the maximum dispersion in the registration of patients in the two hospitals in a year?
(a) 8000 (b) 6000
(c) 4000 (d) 2000

40. In which year there was maximum decrease in registration of patients in hospital X?
(a) 2003 (b) 2004
(c) 2005 (d) 2006

41. Which of the following sources of data is not based on primary data collection?
(a) Census of India
(b) National Sample Survey
(c) Statistical Abstracts of India
(d) National Family Health Survey

42. Which of the four data sets have more dispersion?

(a)	88	91	90	92	89	91
(b)	0	1	1	0	–1	–2
(c)	3	5	2	4	1	5
(d)	0	5	8	10	–2	–8

43. Which of the following is not related to information security on the Internet?
(a) Data Encryption
(b) Water Marking
(c) Data Hiding
(d) Information Retrieval

44. Which is the largest unit of storage among the following?
(a) Terabyte (b) Megabyte
(c) Kilobyte (d) Gigabyte

45. Bit stands for
(a) binary information term
(b) binary digit
(c) binary tree
(d) Bivariate Theory

46. Which one of the following is not a linear data structure?
(a) Array (b) Binary Tree
(c) Queue (d) Stack

47. Which one of the following is not a network device?
(a) Router (b) Switch
(c) Hub (d) CPU

48. A compiler is used to convert the following to object code which can be executed
(a) High-level language
(b) Low-level language
(c) Assembly language
(d) Natural language

49. The great Indian Bustard bird is found in
(a) Thar Desert of Rajasthan
(b) Malabar Coast
(c) Coastal regions of India
(d) Delta regions

50. The Sagarmanthan National Park has been established to preserve the eco-system of which mountain peak?
(a) Kanchenjunga (b) Mount Everest
(c) Annapurna (d) Dhaulavira

51. Maximum soot is released from
(a) Petrol vehicles
(b) CNG vehicles
(c) Diesel vehicles
(d) Thermal Power Plants

52. Surface Ozone is produced from
(a) Transport sector
(b) Cement plants
(c) Textile industry
(d) Chemical industry

53. Which one of the following non-conventional energy sources can be exploited most economically?
(a) Solar
(b) Wind
(c) Geo-thermal
(d) Ocean Thermal Energy Conversion (OTEC)

54. The most recurring natural hazard in India is

(a) Earthquakes (b) Floods
(c) Landslides (d) Volcanoes

55. The recommendation of National Knowledge Commission for the establishment of 1500 universities is to
(a) create more teaching jobs
(b) ensure increase in student enrolment in higher education
(c) replace or substitute the privately managed higher education institutions by public institutions
(d) enable increased movement of students from rural areas to urban areas

56. According to Article 120 of the Constitution of India, the business in Parliament shall be transacted in
(a) Only English
(b) Only Hindi
(c) Both English and Hindi
(d) All the languages included in Eighth Schedule of the Constitution

57. Which of the following is more interactive and student centric?
(a) Seminar
(b) Workshop
(c) Lecture
(d) Group Discussion

58. The Parliament in India is composed of
(a) Lok Sabha and Rajya Sabha
(b) Lok Sabha, Rajya Sabha and Vice President
(c) Lok Sabha, Rajya Sabha and President
(d) Lok Sabha, Rajya Sabha with their Secretariats

59. The enrolment in higher education in India is contributed both by Formal System of Education and by System of Distance Education. Distance education contributes
(a) 50% of formal system
(b) 25% of formal system
(c) 10% of the formal system
(d) Distance education system's contribution is not taken into account whileconsidering the figures of enrolment in higher education

60. **Assertion (A):** The UGC Academic Staff Colleges came into existence to improve the quality of teachers.
Reason (R): University and college teachers have to undergo both orientation and refresher courses.
(a) Both (A) and (R) are true and (R) is the correct explanation.
(b) Both (A) and (R) are correct but (R) is not the correct explanation of (A).
(c) (A) is correct and (R) is false.
(d) (A) is false and (R) is correct.

ANSWERS

1. (d)	2. (c)	3. (b)	4. (c)	5. (b)
6. (c)	7. (a)	8. (b)	9. (b)	10. (b)
11. (c)	12. (b)	13. (c)	14. (a)	15. (d)
16. (d)	17. (b)	18. (a)	19. (c)	20. (a)
21. (d)	22. (a)	23. (a)	24. (a)	25. (b)
26. (c)	27. (b)	28. (d)	29. (c)	30. (b)
31. (c)	32. (a)	33. (b)	34. (a)	35. (c)
36. (d)	37. (c)	38. (c)	39. (a)	40. (d)
41. (c)	42. (d)	43. (d)	44. (a)	45. (b)
46. (b)	47. (d)	48. (a)	49. (a)	50. (b)
51. (d)	52. (a)	53. (a)	54. (b)	55. (b)
56. (c)	57. (d)	58. (c)	59. (b)	60. (a)

PAPER–II

Note: This paper contains fifty (50) objective type questions, each question carrying two (2) marks. Attempt all the questions.

1. Consider the following Judgements of the Supreme Court which dealt with the appointment and transfer of Judges of the Supreme Court and High Courts:
   1. S.P. Gupta Vs. Union of India
   2. Sankal Chand Vs. Union of India
   3. President's Special Reference No. 1
   4. Supreme Court Advocate on Record Association Vs. Union of India

   Which one of the following is correct chronological order in which the above judgements were delivered ?

(a)	1	2	3	4
(b)	2	1	3	4
(c)	2	1	4	3
(d)	1	2	4	3

2. Which one of the following is the correct statement?
   "Full faith and credit" clause of the Constitution does not apply to
   (a) Public records
   (b) Judicial proceedings
   (c) Acts of Corporations
   (d) Public acts

3. In which of the following cases the Supreme Court held that allowing medical examination of a woman to prove her virginity, amounts to violation of her right to privacy, guaranteed under Article 21 of the Constitution ?
   (a) Surjeet Singh Thind Vs. Kanwaljit Kaur
   (b) Phillipa Anne Vs. State of Tamilnadu State
   (c) Hameeda Sarfaraj Vs. M. S. Kashekar
   (d) Kavita Vs. State of Maharashtra

4. By which Constitutional Amendment, Article 21A providing for right to education was inserted in the Constitution of India?
   (a) The Constitution [Eighty Third Amendment] Act
   (b) The Constitution [Eighty Sixth Amendment] Act
   (c) The Constitution [Ninetieth Amendment] Act
   (d) The Constitution [Ninety Second Amendment] Act

5. Joint-session of the Parliament was summoned by the President of India to pass
   (a) Dowry Prohibition Act
   (b) Banking Service Commission Act
   (c) POTA
   (d) All the above Act

6. Justice Verma's Committee Report relates to
   (a) Effectuation of Fundamental Duties
   (b) Duty to vote in Election
   (c) Freedom of Religion
   (d) National Judicial Commission

7. By which Constitutional Amendment, Article 51A(K) which provides for the eleventh duty of a citizen was added?
   (a) The Constitution [Ninety-Third Amendment] Act
   (b) The Constitution [Ninety-First Amendment] Act
   (c) The Constitution [Eighty Sixth Amendment] Act
   (d) The Constitution [Eighty Fourth Amendment] Act

8. Who submitted the Report of the "National Commission to Review the working of the Constitution"?

(a) Justice B.P. Jeevan Reddy
(b) Justice A.S. Anand
(c) Justice R.S. Sarkaria
(d) Justice M.N. Venkatachalliah

9. Who has first coined the term 'Legal theory'?
(a) Kelsen (b) W. Friedman
(c) Bentham (d) Roscoe Pound

10. Who propounded the 'Utilitarian theory'?
(a) Kelsen (b) Henry Maine
(c) Bentham (d) Julius Stone

11. In which of the following cases the jurisprudential basis of the principle to award compensation for violating Human Rights has been laid down by the Supreme Court?
(a) Konda Reddy Vs. State
(b) Ratlam Municipality Vs. Verdhichand
(c) Visakha Vs. State of Rajasthan
(d) Nilabhati Behra Vs. State of Orissa

12. Rights and duties are
(a) Postulates (b) Correlatives
(c) Opposites (d) Parallels

13. Match the following:

List I
(I) Retributive theory
(II) Immemorial Antiquity
(III) Ground norm
(IV) Locus Standi

List II
1. Public Interest Litigation
2. Punishment
3. Custom
4. Hans Kelson

Codes:	(I)	(II)	(III)	(IV)
(a)	2	4	3	1
(b)	1	3	4	2
(c)	2	3	4	1
(d)	3	4	1	2

14. 'Law must be changed in a manner to get pleasure and to avoid painful change with social circumstances' is the contribution of
(a) Historical theory
(b) Sociological theory
(c) Anthropological theory
(d) Analytical theory

15. The theme of the 60th Anniversary celebrations of the Universal Declaration of Human Rights, 1948 is
(a) Human Rights for all.
(b) All Human Rights for all.
(c) Justice and dignity for all.
(d) Human Rights for Human Dignity.

16. Principal modes of peaceful settlement of disputes are
(a) 5 (b) 6
(c) 4 (d) 3

17. Who said "International Law is the vanishing point of jurisprudence"?
(a) Austin (b) Holland
(c) Kelson (d) Bentham

18. The era of law making treaties began with
(a) Treaty of Vienna
(b) Treaty of Versailles
(c) Kellogg Briard Act
(d) Treaty of Westphalia

19. The Arrantzazu Mendi case deals with
(a) Human Rights
(b) Recognition
(c) Nature of International Law
(d) Peaceful settlement of disputes

20. Match the following:

List I
(I) Paquete Habana Case
(II) Dumparton Oaks Conference
(III) Vienna Declaration, 1993
(IV) Custom

List II
1. South West Africa Case
2. Text Book Writers

3. United Nations
4. Human Rights

Codes:	(I)	(II)	(III)	(IV)
(a)	2	3	4	1
(b)	3	4	2	1
(c)	4	3	1	2
(d)	4	3	2	1

21. Where a Hindu Male and a Hindu Female contract their Marriage under the Special Marriages Act 1954, Hindu Personal Law
(a) Applies to such marriage
(b) Does not apply
(c) Applies with some modifications
(d) Applies with the Indian Contract Act

22. Abortion of child by wife without the consent of the husband is a ground for
(a) Nullity of marriage
(b) Judicial separation
(c) Divorce
(d) None of the above

23. 'A' marries 'B', the widow of his elder brother. The marriage is
(a) Valid (b) Void
(c) Voidable (d) None of these

24. A Muslim woman observising iddat period marries with another man. The marriage is
(a) Sahih (b) Batil
(c) Fasid (d) None of these

25. In which of the following cases, the court held that 'Triple divorce' is not a Valid Talaq?
(a) Ziauddin Vs. Anwari Begum
(b) Mohammad Ahmad Khan Vs. Shah Bano
(c) Bai Tahira V. Ali Hussain
(d) None of the above

26. A marriage under Muslim Law between persons with Fosterage relationship is
(a) Sahih (b) Batil
(c) Fasid (d) None of these

27. Arrange the sequence of the following events in which they occur in a contract, using the code
(i) Communication of offer
(ii) Invitation to offer
(iii) Fraud
(iv) Damages

Codes:

(a)	(ii)	(i)	(iii)	(iv)
(b)	(i)	(ii)	(iii)	(iv)
(c)	(iv)	(ii)	(i)	(iii)
(d)	(iv)	(iii)	(ii)	(i)

28. Find correct explanation from following assertion and reason from code.
Assertion (A): Damages must be reasonable for breach of a contract.
Reason (R): Because reasonable damages are agreed upon in a contract.
Code:
(a) Assertion (A) and Reason (R) are right.
(c) Assertion (A) and Reason are (R) wrong.
(c) Assertion (A) is right, Reason (R) is wrong.
(d) Assertion (A) is wrong, Reason (R) is right.

29. Frustration of contract is provided by which Section of the Indian Contact Act?
(a) 73 (b) 70
(c) 2(d) (d) 56

30. Some, all or none of the following statements are right. Answer using the code.
(i) A minor is liable for breach of a contract to which he is a party.
(ii) A minor is liable to pay for necessaries for his spouse.
(iii) Supply of necessaries to a minor is a contract.
(iv) Necessaries supplied to a minor need not be according to his station in life, for the supplier to claim damages.

Codes:
(a) All statements are right.
(b) All statements are wrong.
(c) Only statement (ii) is right.
(d) Only statement (ii) is wrong.

31. Promissory estoppel against government agencies is decided in
(a) Tweedle Vs. Atkinson, 4LT468
(b) Dutton Vs. Poole, 83LR523
(c) Delhi Cloth and General Mills Ltd. Vs. Union of India, AIR 1987 SC 2414
(d) Kedar Nath Vs. Gorie Mohd., ILR (1886) 14 Col. 64

32. Which one of the following statements is right?
(a) Two or more persons are said to consent when they agree upon some thing in some sense.
(b) Two or more persons are said to consent when they agree upon the same thing in the same sense.
(c) Two or more persons are said to enter into a contract when they agree upon the same thing in the same sense.
(d) Two or more persons are said to enter a quasi contract when they agree upon the same thing in the same sense.

33. If a person enters voluntarily into a sports event and receives grave injury, he has
(a) a claim in torts for medical expenses though not for a loss of income.
(b) a claim in torts for loss of earning capacity.
(c) no claim in torts because the injury was not intentionally caused.
(d) no claim in torts because of the principle volenti non fit injuria.

34. 'Qui facit per alium facit perse' establishes the
(a) Liability under the Indian Penal Code
(b) Liability under the law of torts
(c) Vicarious liability
(d) Liability under the Indian Contract Act

35. The rule of Absolute Liability was first laid down by
(a) Lord Atkin in 1635
(b) Justice Blackburn in 1868
(c) Winfield in 1765
(d) Chief Justice Holt in 1868

36. Res ipsa Loquitur is
(a) weapon of defence
(b) weapon of offence
(c) a defence of some factor which was beyond the control of the person who caused injury
(d) a dangerous weapon

37. If A gives lift in his car to B upto a certain place and on the way due to negligence of A an accident is caused. A has
(a) no responsibility towards B.
(b) no legal duty to take care of B's safety.
(c) a legal duty to take care of B also and is liable for compensation.
(d) All of the above.

38. For an action of nuisance defendant can put up the following defence.
I. The place is suitable for the purpose.
II. It is for the benefit of the residents of the locality.
III. It is done under statutory authority.
IV. Plaintiff has consented to the act.

Of the above statement
(a) I, II and III are correct.
(b) II, III and IV are correct.
(c) I, III and IV are correct.
(d) III and IV are correct.

39. Which of the following is the offence which is punishable in four stages?

(a) Robbery (b) Dacoity
(c) Murder (d) Rape

40. 'a', 'b' and 'c' are joint owners of some property. 'a' removes the property.
(a) 'a' is not guilty of theft as property belongs to him.
(b) 'a' is guilty of theft as he is only a joint owner.
(c) 'a' is guilty of criminal misappropriation.
(d) 'a' is guilty of breach of trust.

41. Which of the following statements is correct?
(a) Sec. 34 of I.P.C. is only a rule of evidence.
(b) Sec. 34 of I.P.C. does not create a substantive offence.
(c) Both (a) and (b) are correct.
(d) None of these.

42. A instigates B to kidnap son of Z. B instigates C to do so and C kidnaps son of Z.
(a) Only B is guilty of abetting C.
(b) Only A is guilty of abetment.
(c) Both A and B are guilty of abetment.
(d) None of these

43. **Assertion (A):** X and Y had independently entertained the idea to kill Z. Accordingly, each separately inflicts wounds on Z. Z dies. X and Y can be tried jointly.
Reason (R): Two or more persons can be tried jointly if the act, resulting in an offence, is done in furtherance of a common intention.

Select your answer using the codes given below:
Codes:
(a) Both (A) and (R) are true, and (R) is the correct explanation of (A).
(b) Both (A) and (R) are true, but (R) is not a correct explanation of (A).
(c) (A) is true, but (R) is false.
(d) (A) is false, but (R) is true.

44. 'Y' picks 'X's pocket. Next day, 'X' while buying paan near his office finds 'Y' paying money from his (X's) purse. 'X' catches hold of 'Y' and tries to take back his purse. 'Y' resists. 'X' twists 'Y's' arm with such force that it is broken. 'X' is charged with causing hurt to 'Y'. In his defence 'X' can
(a) say that he was acting under right of private defence of property.
(b) not raise the plea of right of private defence since he had time to seek the help of public authorities.
(c) say that his right of private defence revived as soon as he saw Y with his purse.
(d) say that he did not use more force than was required.

45. Given below are two statements. One is labelled as Assertion (A) and other is labelled as Reason (R). Select correct code combination.
Assertion (A): Physical Research Laboratory, Ahmedabad was held not to be an 'industry' by the Supreme Court.
Reason (R): Since it is carrying on research not for the benefit of self. Moreover, it is not engaged in commercial activities.
Codes:
(a) (A) is correct, but (R) is wrong.
(b) Both (A) and (R) are wrong.
(c) (A) is wrong, but (R) is correct.
(d) Both (A) and (R) are correct.

46. Select correct code combination relating to "Closure".
(A) Employment relationship severed.
(B) Suspension of Employment relationship.

(C) End of bargaining.
(D) To compel workmen to accept terms and conditions in the course of bargaining.
(E) Permanent closing down of employer's business.
(F) Deliberate temporary closing of a place of employment.
(G) Not in consequence of an industrial dispute.

Codes:
(a) (A), (C), (E) and (G)
(b) (B), (D), (F) and (G)
(c) (C), (E), (F) and (G)
(d) (B), (C), (E) and (F)

47. Which one of the following is not an 'Industry'?
(a) Forest Department of State
(b) Indian Red Cross Society
(c) Federation of Indian Chamber of Commerce & Industries
(d) Khadi and Village Industries Board

48. Which of the following does not relate to "industrial dispute"?
(a) Dispute or difference connected with employment of.
(b) Dispute or difference connected with non-employment of.
(c) Dispute or difference connected with the terms of employment or with the conditions of labour.
(d) Dispute or difference connected with the election of a trade union.

49. A certificate of registration of a trade union is
(a) Rebuttable evidence
(b) Irrebuttable evidence
(c) Conclusive evidence
(d) None of the above

50. Which of the following is related to "settlement"?
(a) Strike (b) Lock-out
(c) Retrenchment (d) Conciliation

ANSWERS

1. (b)	2. (c)	3. (a)	4. (a)	5. (d)
6. (a)	7. (c)	8. (d)	9. (a)	10. (c)
11. (d)	12. (c)	13. (c)	14. (b)	15. (c)
16. (d)	17. (b)	18. (d)	19. (b)	20. (a)
21. (a)	22. (d)	23. (a)	24. (b)	25. (b)
26. (b)	27. (a)	28. (c)	29. (a)	30. (c)
31. (c)	32. (c)	33. (d)	34. (c)	35. (b)
36. (a)	37. (c)	38. (c)	39. (b)	40. (a)
41. (c)	42. (a)	43. (a)	44. (b)	45. (a)
46. (d)	47. (b)	48. (d)	49. (c)	50. (d)

JUNE–2009

Note: This paper contains Sixty (60) multiple-choice questions, each question carrying two (2) marks. Candidate is expected to answer any Fifty (50) questions. In case more than Fifty (50) questions are attempted, only the first Fifty (50) questions will be evaluated.

PAPER–I

1. Good evaluation of written material should not be based on
   (a) Linguistic expression
   (b) Logical presentation
   (c) Ability to reproduce whatever is read
   (d) Comprehension of subject

2. Why do teachers use teaching aid?
   (a) To make teaching fun-filled
   (b) To teach within understanding level of students
   (c) For students' attention
   (d) To make students attentive

3. Attitudes, concepts, skills and knowledge are products of
   (a) Learning (b) Research
   (c) Heredity (d) Explanation

4. Which among the following gives more freedom to the learner to interact?
   (a) Use of film
   (b) Small group discussion
   (c) Lectures by experts
   (d) Viewing country-wide classroom program on TV

5. Which of the following is not a product of learning?
   (a) Attitudes (b) Concepts
   (c) Knowledge (d) Maturation

6. How can the objectivity of the research be enhanced?
   (a) Through its impartiality
   (b) Through its reliability
   (c) Through its validity
   (d) All of these

7. Action-research is
   (a) An applied research
   (b) A research carried out to solve immediate problems
   (c) A longitudinal research
   (d) All of the above

8. The basis on which assumptions are formulated
   (a) Cultural background of the country
   (b) Universities
   (c) Specific characteristics of the castes
   (d) All of the these

9. Which of the following is classified in the category of the developmental research?
   (a) Philosophical research
   (b) Action research
   (c) Descriptive research
   (d) All of the above

10. We use Factorial Analysis
    (a) To know the relationship between two variables
    (b) To test the Hypothesis
    (c) To know the difference between two variables
    (d) To know the difference among the many variables

Read the following passage and answer the questions 11 to 15:

While the British rule in India was detrimental to the economic development of the country, it did help in starting of the process of modernising Indian society and formed several progressive institutions during that process. One of the most beneficial institutions, which were initiated by the British, was democracy. Nobody can dispute that despite its many shortcomings, democracy was and is far better alternative to the arbitrary rule of the rajas and nawabs, which prevailed in India in the pre-British days.

However, one of the harmful traditions of British democracy inherited by India was that of conflict instead of cooperation between elected members. This was its essential feature. The party, which got the support of the majority of elected members, formed the government while the others constituted a standing opposition. The existence of the opposition to those in power was and is regarded as a hallmark of democracy.

In principle, democracy consists of rule by the people; but where direct rule is not possible, it's rule by persons elected by the people. It is natural that there would be some differences of opinion among the elected members as in the rest of the society.

Normally, members of any organisations have differences of opinion between themselves on different issues but they manage to work on the basis of a consensus and they do not normally form a division between some who are in majority and are placed in power, while treating the others as in opposition.

The members of an organisation usually work on consensus. Consensus simply means that after an adequate discussion, members agree that the majority opinion may prevail for the time being. Thus persons who form a majority on one issue and whose opinion is allowed to prevail may not be on the same side if there is a difference on some other issue.

It was largely by accident that instead of this normal procedure, a two-party system came to prevail in Britain and that is now being generally taken as the best method of democratic rule.

Many democratically inclined persons in India regret that such a two-party system was not brought about in the country. It appears that to have two parties in India—of more or less equal strength—is a virtual impossibility. Those who regret the absence of a two-party system should take the reasons into consideration.

When the two-party system got established in Britain, there were two groups among the rules (consisting of a limited electorate) who had the same economic interests among themselves and who therefore formed two groups within the selected members of Parliament.

There were members of the British aristocracy (which landed interests and consisting of lord, barons, etc.) and members of the new commercial class consisting of merchants and artisans. These groups were more or less of equal strength and they were able to establish their separate rule at different times.

Answer the following questions:

11. In pre-British period, when India was ruled by the independent rulers
    (a) Peace and prosperity prevailed in the society
    (b) People were isolated from political affairs
    (c) Public opinion was inevitable for policy making
    (d) Law was equal for one and all

12. What is the distinguishing feature of the democracy practised in Britain?
    (a) End to the rule of might is right.
    (b) Rule of the people, by the people and for the people.
    (c) It has stood the test of time.
    (d) Cooperation between elected members.

13. Democracy is practised where
    (a) Elected members form a uniform opinion regarding policy matter.
    (b) Opposition is more powerful than the ruling combine.
    (c) Representatives of masses.
    (d) None of these.

14. Which of the following is true about the British rule in India?
    (a) It was behind the modernisation of the Indian society.
    (b) India gained economically during that period.
    (c) Various establishments were formed for the purpose of progress.
    (d) None of these.

15. Who became the members of the new commercial class during that time?
    (a) British Aristocrats
    (b) Lord and Barons
    (c) Political Persons
    (d) Merchants and Artisans

16. Which one of the following Telephonic Conferencing with a radio link is very popular throughout the world?
    (a) TPS (b) Telepresence
    (c) Video conference (d) Video teletext

17. Which is not 24 hours news channel?
    (a) NDTV 24×7
    (b) ZEE News
    (c) Aajtak
    (d) Lok Sabha Channel

18. The main objective of FM station in radio is
    (a) Information, Entertainment and Tourism
    (b) Entertainment, Information and Interaction
    (c) Tourism, Interaction and Entertainment
    (d) Entertainment only

19. In communication chatting on Internet is
    (a) Verbal communication
    (b) Non-verbal communication
    (c) Parallel communication
    (d) Grapevine communication

20. Match List I with List II and select the correct answer using the codes given below:

    List I (Artists)
    A. Pandit Jasraj B. Kishan Maharaj
    C. Ravi Shankar D. Udai Shankar

    List II (Art)
    1. Hindustani vocalist
    2. Sitar
    3. Tabla
    4. Dance

Codes:	A	B	C	D
(a)	1	2	3	4
(b)	1	3	4	2
(c)	1	3	2	4
(d)	3	2	1	4

21. Insert the missing number in the following.
    3, 8, 18, 23, 33, ?, 48
    (a) 37 (b) 40
    (c) 38 (d) 45

22. In a certain code, CLOCK is written as KCOLC. How would STEPS be written in that code?
    (a) SPEST (b) SPSET
    (c) SPETS (d) SEPTS

23. The letters in the first set have a certain relationship. On the basis of this relationship mark the right choice for the second set
    BDFH : OMKI :: GHIK : ?
    (a) FHJL (b) RPNL
    (c) LNPR (d) LJHF

24. What was the day of the week on 1st January 2001?
    (a) Friday (b) Monday
    (c) Sunday (d) Wednesday

25. Find out the wrong number in the sequence.
52, 51, 48, 43, 34, 27, 16
(a) 27 (b) 34
(c) 43 (d) 48

26. In a deductive argument conclusion is
(a) Summing up of the premises
(b) Not necessarily based on premises
(c) Entailed by the premises
(d) Additional to the premises

27. 'No man are mortal' is contradictory of
(a) Some man are mortal
(b) Some man are not mortal
(c) All men are mortal
(d) No mortal is man

28. A deductive argument is valid if
(a) premises are false and conclusion is true
(b) premises are false and conclusion is also false
(c) premises are true and conclusion is false
(d) premises are true and conclusion is true

29. Structure of logical argument is based on
(a) Formal validity
(b) Material truth
(c) Linguistic expression
(d) Aptness of examples

30. Two ladies and two men are playing bridge and seated at North, East, South and West of a table. No lady is facing East. Persons sitting opposite to each other are not of the same sex. One man is facing South. Which direction are the ladies facing to?
(a) East and West
(b) North and West
(c) South and East
(d) None of these

Questions 31 and 32 are based on the following Venn diagram in which there are three intersecting circles representing Hindi knowing persons, English knowing persons and persons who are working as teachers. Different regions so obtained in the figure are marked as a, b, c, d, e, f and g.

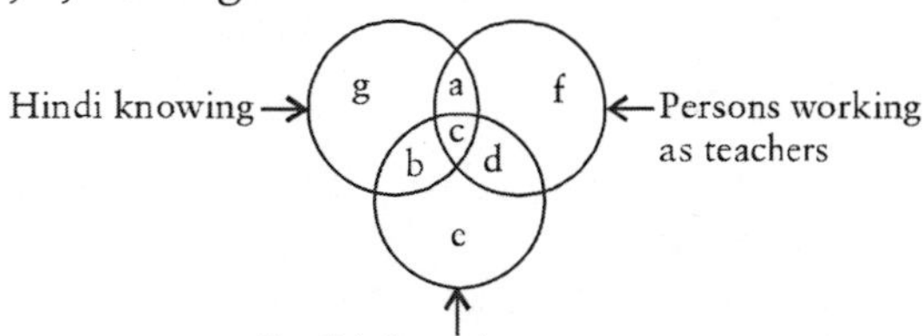

31. If you want to select Hindi and English knowing teachers, which of the following is to be selected?
(a) g (b) b
(c) c (d) e

32. If you want to select persons, who do not know English and are not teachers, which of the region is to be selected?
(a) e (b) g
(c) b (d) a

Study the following graph carefully and answer questions 33 to 35.

Export of Engineering Goods

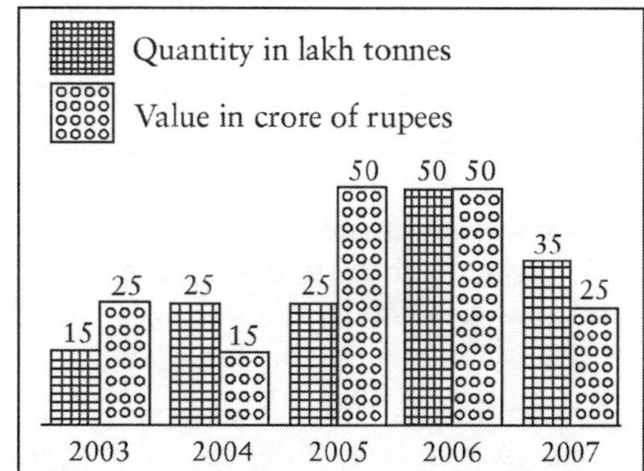

33. In which year the quantity of engineering goods' exports was maximum?
(a) 2005 (b) 2006
(c) 2004 (d) 2007

34. In which year the value of engineering goods decreased by 50 percent compared to the previous year?

(a) 2004 (b) 2007
(c) 2005 (d) 2006

35. In which year the quantity of exports was 100 percent higher than the quantity of previous year?
(a) 2004 (b) 2005
(c) 2006 (d) 2007

36. What do you need to put your web pages on the www?
(a) a connection to internet
(b) a web browser
(c) a web server
(d) All of the above

37. Which was the first company to launch mobile phone services in India?
(a) Essar (b) BPL
(c) Hutchinson (d) Airtel

38. Chandrayan I was launched on 22nd October, 2008 in India from
(a) Bengaluru (b) Sri Harikota
(c) Chennai (d) Ahmedabad

39. What is blog?
(a) Online music
(b) Intranet
(c) A personal or corporate website in the form of an online journal
(d) A personal or corporate Google search

40. Which is not online Indian Matrimonial website?
(a) www.jeevansathi.com
(b) www.bharatmatrimony.com
(c) www.shaadi.com
(d) www.u.k.singlemuslim.com

41. Environmental impact assessment is an objective analysis of the probable changes in
(a) physical characteristics of the environment
(b) biophysical characteristics of the environment
(c) socio-economic characteristics of the environment
(d) All of the above

42. Bog is a wetland that receives water from
(a) nearby water bodies
(b) melting
(c) Only rainfall
(d) Only sea

43. Which of the following regions is in the very high risk zone of earthquakes?
(a) Central Indian Highland
(b) Coastal region
(c) Himalayan region
(d) Indian desert

44. Match List I with List II and select the correct answer using the codes given below.

List I (Institutes)
A. Central Arid Zone Institute
B. Space Application Centre
C. Indian Institute of Public Administration
D. Headquarters of Indian Science Congress

List II (Cities)
1. Kolkata 2. New Delhi
3. Ahmedabad 4. Jodhpur

Codes:	**A**	**B**	**C**	**D**
(a)	4	3	2	1
(b)	4	2	1	3
(c)	3	1	2	4
(d)	1	2	4	3

45. Indian coastal areas experienced Tsunami disaster in the year
(a) 2005 (b) 2004
(c) 2006 (d) 2007

46. The Kothari Commission's report was entitled on
(a) Education and National Development
(b) Learning to be adventure
(c) Diversification of Education
(d) Education and socialisation in democracy

47. Which of the following is not a Dual mode University?
(a) Delhi University
(b) Bangalore University

(c) Madras University
(d) Indira Gandhi National Open University

48. Which part of the Constitution of India is known as "Code of Administrators"?
(a) Part I (b) Part II
(c) Part III (d) Part IV

49. Which article of the constitution provides safeguards to Naga Customary and their social practices against any act of Parliament?
(a) Article 371A (b) Article 371B
(c) Article 371C (d) Article 263

50. Which one of the following is not the tool of good governance?
(a) Right to Information
(b) Citizens' Charter
(c) Social Auditing
(d) Judicial Activism

ANSWERS

1. (a)	2. (a)	3. (a)	4. (b)	5. (d)
6. (d)	7. (b)	8. (a)	9. (d)	10. (d)
11. (b)	12. (d)	13. (a)	14. (c)	15. (a)
16. (b)	17. (d)	18. (b)	19. (b)	20. (c)
21. (c)	22. (c)	23. (b)	24. (b)	25. (b)
26. (c)	27. (c)	28. (d)	29. (b)	30. (b)
31. (c)	32. (b)	33. (b)	34. (b)	35. (c)
36. (d)	37. (d)	38. (b)	39. (c)	40. (d)
41. (d)	42. (a)	43. (b)	44. (a)	45. (b)
46. (a)	47. (d)	48. (d)	49. (a)	50. (d)

PAPER–II

Note: This paper contains fifty (50) objective type questions, each question carrying two (2) marks. Attempt all the questions.

1. If 'X' hires a taxi for going to railway station and the taxi driver 'V' negligently hits 'Z' who will be liable?
(a) X (b) V
(c) Z (d) None of these

2. Who defines liability as the bond of necessity that exists between the wrongdoer and the remedy of the wrong?
(a) Blackstone (b) Winfield
(c) Salmond (d) Austin

3. In a civil wrong, the liability is measured by which factor?
(a) Wrongful act
(b) The punishment
(c) The intention
(d) Condition

4. Two kinds of liability are civil and criminal. Which one of the following is connected with criminal liability?
(a) Remedial liability
(b) Strict liability
(c) Penal liability
(d) Absolute liability

5. Abetment by aid requires
(a) Intentional aiding
(b) Passive aiding
(c) Active aiding
(d) All of the above

6. A with a guilty intention, abets a child B to set fire to a dwelling house
(a) A is not guilty as there is no question of setting fire for him
(b) A is guilty of abetting B
(c) Both are guilty
(d) None of the above

7. A instigates B to kidnap son of Z, B instigates C to do so and C kidnaps son of Z.
(a) Only A is guilty of abetment
(b) Both A and B are guilty of abetment
(c) Only Bis guilty of abetting
(d) None of the above

8. A offers a bribe to B, a public servant as a reward for showing A some favour in the exercise of B's official functions. B accepts the bribe
   (a) A is guilty of abetting
   (b) B is guilty
   (c) Both A and B are guilty
   (d) None of the above

9. A knowing that dacoity is about to be committed at B falsely informs the Magistrate that a dacoity is about to be committed at C, a place in an opposite direction, and thereby misleads the Magistrate with intent to facilitate the commission of the offence. The dacoity is committed at B in pursuance of the design. A is
   (a) Not guilty
   (b) Guilty
   (c) The magistrate is guilty
   (d) None of the above

10. Section 34 applies when
   (a) A criminal act is done in furtherance of the common intention of all the offender
   (b) Public servant concealing design to commit offence
   (c) Abettor is present
   (d) None of the above

11. The President gets a salary of
   (a) ₹ 50,000 per month
   (b) ₹ 45,000 per month
   (c) ₹ 40,000 per month
   (d) ₹ 1,00,000 per month

12. Which one of the following is not a qualification for election as President of India
   (a) Citizen of India
   (b) Thirty-five years of age
   (c) Qualified for election as a member of the House of the People
   (d) Should be a Graduate

13. How much pension does the President get after his retirement
   (a) ₹ 1,00,000 per annum
   (b) ₹ 2,00,000 per annum
   (c) ₹ 3,00,000 per annum
   (d) ₹ 4,00,000 per annum

14. "The executive power of the Union shall be vested in the President and shall be exercised by him either directly or through officers subordinate to him in accordance with this Constitution". This has been mentioned under Article
   (a) 51 (b) 52
   (c) 53 (d) 54

15. The manner of the election of the President has been mentioned under Article
   (a) 51 (b) 53
   (c) 54 (d) 55

16. Fundamental Rights are
   (a) Those basic conditions of social life without which a citizen cannot be at his best self
   (b) The rights of the rulers
   (c) The rights of the police
   (d) Those rights which men enjoyed in the State of Nature

17. From which Constitution of the world have we borrowed the concept of Fundamental Rights?
   (a) U.K. (b) Canada
   (c) U.S.S.R. (d) U.S.A.

18. In the Indian Constitution the Fundamental Rights have been included in
   (a) Part IV of the Constitution
   (b) Part III of the Constitution
   (c) Part II of the Constitution
   (d) Part V of the Constitution

19. How many freedoms were originally provided under Article 19?

(a) 5 (b) 6
(c) 7 (d) 8

20. The Fundamental Rights granted to the Indian citizens are
(a) Justiciable
(b) Non-justiciable
(c) Sometimes justiciable and sometimes non-justiciable
(d) None of the above

Direction: The following items consist of two statements, one labelled the Assertion (A) and the other labelled the Reason (R). You are to examine these two statements carefully and decide if the Assertion (A) and the Reason (R) are individually true and if so whether the reason is a correct explanation of the Assertion. Select your answer to these items using the codes given below and mark your answer sheet accordingly.

(a) Both (A) and (R) are true and (R) is the correct explanation of (A).
(b) Both (A) and (R) are true but R is not the correct explanation of (A).
(c) (A) is true but (R) is false.
(d) (A) is false but (R) is true.

21. **Assertion (A):** Supreme Court is a court of record.
Reason (R): Its judicial proceeding are enrolled for perpetual memory it has power to punish contempt of itself.

22. **Assertion (A):** Writ of Habeas Corpus, is a process to release a person from illegal confinement.
Reason (R): The detention should be in accordance with procedure established by law.

23. **Assertion (A):** Animus should based on a legal claim to the object.
Reason (R): Animus must be of exclusive claim to the object.

24. **Assertion (A):** Parliament has power to make any law for implementation of any treaty, agreement or convention with any other country.
Reason (R): Power to enter in to international treaties is conferred on Parliament.

25. The League of Nations was established on
(a) April 21, 1919
(b) January 8, 1918
(c) January 10, 1920
(d) June 28, 1919

26. Who defined Natural Law is a divine law (written in the hearts of all men, obliging them to do those things which are necessarily consonant to the rational nature of mankind, and to refrain from those things which are repugnant to it?
(a) Austin
(b) Hobbes
(c) Bentham
(d) Christian Thomasius

27. The idea of codification of the law of nations was first mooted by
(a) Austin (b) Starke
(c) Fenwick (d) Bentham

28. Which article of the charter of the United Nations gives ample scope for the codification of International Law?
(a) Article 12 (b) Article 14
(c) Article 13 (d) Article 20

29. Which of the following is true about the various theories regarding subjects of International Law?
(a) States alone are subjects of International Law
(b) Individuals alone are the subjects of International Law
(c) States are the main subjects of International Law, but to lesser extent individuals and certain non-state entities
(d) All of the above

30. When was the Twenty-eighth Amendment passed?
(a) 1972 (b) 1973
(c) 1974 (d) 1975

31. Which Amendment laid down that the decision of the President regarding the declaration of the emergency in the country could not be challenged in a court of law?
(a) Thirty-seventh (b) Thirty-eighth
(c) Thirty-ninth (d) Fortieth

32. When was the Thirty-ninth Amendment passed?
(a) 1972 (b) 1973
(c) 1974 (d) 1975

33. Which Amendment laid down the rule that the election disputes relating to President, Vice-President, the Prime Minister and the Speaker would be decided only by a Special Tribunal Inter-established by the Parliament?
(a) Thirty-ninth (b) Fortieth
(c) Forty-First (d) None of these

34. When was the Fourtieth Amendment passed?
(a) 1975 (b) 1976
(c) 1977 (d) 1978

35. The Maritime Jurisdiction of our country was laid down in the
(a) Fortieth Amendment
(b) Forty-first Amendment
(c) Forty-second Amendment
(d) Forty-third Amendment

36. Arrange the following advisory opinion given by the Supreme Court under Art. 143.
1. Kerala Education Bill
2. The Special Court Bill
3. Presidential Poll Re.
4. Customs Berubari Union and Exchange of Enclave Re.
(a) 1, 2, 3 & 4 (b) 4, 2, 3 & 1
(c) 1, 4, 3 & 2 (d) 1, 2, 3 & 4

37. Enlargement of the jurisdiction of the Supreme Court may be done by,
(a) Parliament
(b) Chief Justice of India
(c) President
(d) Council of Minister

38. Which of the following is not a condition for evoking appellate jurisdiction of Supreme Court in civil matters?
1. the decision appealed against must be a judgement, decree or final order of a High Court.
2. a certificate of the High Court to the effect, that the case involves a substantial question of law.
3. in the opinion of the Supreme Court that question needs to be decided by Supreme Court.
4. no appeal shall be to the Supreme Court from the judgement, decree or final order of a single judge of a High Court.
(a) 2 & 3 (b) 1, 3 & 4
(c) 1, 2, 3 & 4 (d) 2, 3 & 4

39. During financial emergency, President can issue direction for the reduction of salaries of
(a) Judges of High Court
(b) Judges of Supreme Court
(c) None of the above
(d) Both of the above

40. Which of the following case is known as bibe of delegated legislation?
(a) Delhi Law Act 1912 Re
(b) Field Vs. Clark
(c) Ram Jaway Vs. State of Punjab
(d) Edward Mills Co., Vs. State of Ajmer

41. In which of the following case, free and fair election has been held as basic structure of Indian Constitution?

(a) Indira Nehru Gandhi Vs. Raj Narain
(b) Keshavanand Bharti's Case
(c) Golak Nath's Case
(d) Waman Rao Vs. Union of India

42. Section 323, deals with reports of public service commission, which of the following are directed to submit their report to concerned Governor?
(a) Joint commission
(b) State commission
(c) Union commission
(d) Both (a) and (b)

43. Indian Government enters into an agreement with U.S.A. and make law on the subject matter of the agreement to give it effect. However the subject matter is covered under the state list,
(a) the impugned legislation is void because it amounts to encroachment and the state list
(b) this law may be framed only after having the consent of the states
(c) it is a valid law, it has been framed for giving effect to international agreement
(d) distribution of power is a fundamental feature of Indian Constitution it cannot be abrogated

44. *Actus non facit ream nisi mensitrea* implies,
(a) The act does not constitute guilt unless done with a guilty intent
(b) The act constitute guilt even it done with a bona fide intent
(c) Intent of the accused should not be considered in a criminal case
(d) None of the above

45. Match List I with List II and select the correct answer by using codes given below.

List I
W. Common intention
X. Good faith
Y. Dishonest intention
Z. Common Object

List II
1. S. 34 2. S. 149
3. Theft 4. Mistake of feet

Codes:	W	X	Y	Z
(a)	1	4	3	2
(b)	1	2	3	4
(c)	4	3	2	1
(d)	4	1	2	3

46. Which of the following statements is true?
(a) Employer is liable for the tortious act committed by an independent contractor
(b) Employer is not liable for tortious act committed by an independent contractor
(c) Employer is liable for tortious act committed by an independent contractor in case of strict liability
(d) None of the above

47. X wife of Y gets injured because of the combined negligence of Y and Z, X recoveres full amount of compensation from Z, Z dues Y for his contribution
(a) Y is liable to contribute
(b) Y's liable to contribute, if there is a direction from the court
(c) Y is not liable, being husband of X
(d) Z and Y both are jointly liable

48. Which of the following statements is true?
(a) There should be direct evidence of negligence to prove negligence
(b) Evidence of negligence may be direct or indirect
(c) There is no need of evidence to prove
(d) None of the above

49. "Res ipsa loquitar" implies,
(a) the things speak for itself
(b) the law speaks for the victim

(c) you must speak for the justified cause
(d) None of the above

50. A, an editor of a newspaper, published a report of parliament proceedings in his newspaper without the authority of parliament, in this case,
(a) A is liable for unauthorised publication of matter.
(b) A can claim qualified privilege, if the publication is made without malice and for public good.
(c) qualified privilege is available to A, even if he publishes the matter maliciously.
(d) None of the above.

ANSWERS

1. (a)	2. (c)	3. (d)	4. (d)	5. (b)
6. (c)	7. (d)	8. (c)	9. (a)	10. (b)
11. (d)	12. (d)	13. (c)	14. (c)	15. (d)
16. (a)	17. (d)	18. (b)	19. (c)	20. (a)
21. (a)	22. (a)	23. (c)	24. (a)	25. (c)
26. (b)	27. (d)	28. (c)	29. (d)	30. (a)
31. (b)	32. (d)	33. (a)	34. (b)	35. (a)
36. (c)	37. (a)	38. (c)	39. (d)	40. (a)
41. (a)	42. (d)	43. (c)	44. (a)	45. (a)
46. (c)	47. (c)	48. (b)	49. (a)	50. (b)

DECEMBER–2010

Note: This paper contains Sixty (60) multiple-choice questions, each question carrying two (2) marks. Candidate is expected to answer any Fifty (50) questions. In case more than Fifty (50) questions are attempted, only the first Fifty (50) questions will be evaluated.

PAPER–I

1. Which of the following variables cannot be expressed in quantitative terms?
   (a) Socio-economic Status
   (b) Marital Status
   (c) Numerical Aptitude
   (d) Professional Attitude

2. A doctor studies the relative effectiveness of two drugs of dengue fever. His research would be classified as
   (a) Descriptive Survey
   (b) Experimental Research
   (c) Case Study
   (d) Ethnography

3. The term 'phenomenology' is associated with the process of
   (a) Qualitative Research
   (b) Analysis of Variance
   (c) Correlational Study
   (d) Probability Sampling

4. The 'Sociogram' technique is used to study
   (a) Vocational Interest
   (b) Professional Competence
   (c) Human Relations
   (d) Achievement Motivation

Read the following passage carefully and answer questions from 5 to 10.

It should be remembered that the nationalist movement in India, like all nationalist movements, was essentially a bourgeois movement. It represented the natural historical stage of development, and to consider it or to criticise it as a working-class movement is wrong. Gandhi represented that movement and the Indian masses in relation to that movement to a supreme degree, and he became the voice of Indian people to that extent. The main contribution of Gandhi to India and the Indian masses has been through the powerful movements which he launched through the National Congress. Through nation-wide action he sought to mould the millions, and largely succeeded in doing so, and changing them from a demoralised, timid and hopeless mass, bullied and crushed by every dominant interest, and incapable of resistance, into a people with self-respect and self-reliance, resisting tyranny, and capable of united action and sacrifice for a larger cause.

Gandhi made people think of political and economic issues and every village and every bazaar hummed with argument and debate on the new ideas and hopes that filled the people. That was an amazing psychological change. The time was ripe for it, of course, and circumstances and world conditions worked for this change. But a great leader is necessary to take advantage of circumstances and conditions. Gandhi was that leader, and he released many of the bonds that imprisoned and disabled our minds, and none of us who experienced it can ever forget that great feeling of release and exhilaration that came over the Indian people.

Gandhi has played a revolutionary role in India of the greatest importance because he knew how to make the most of the objective conditions and could reach the heart of the masses, while groups with a more advanced ideology functioned largely in the air because they did not fit in with those conditions and could therefore not evoke any substantial response from the masses.

It is perfectly true that Gandhi, functioning in the nationalist plane, does not think in terms of the conflict of classes, and tries to compose their differences. But the action he has indulged and taught the people has inevitably raised mass consciousness tremendously and made social issues vital. Gandhi and the Congress must be judged by the policies they pursue and the action they indulge in. But behind this, personality counts and colours those policies and activities. In the case of very exceptional person like Gandhi the question of personality becomes especially important in order to understand and appraise him. To us he has represented the spirit and honour of India, the yearning of her sorrowing millions to be rid of their innumerable burdens, and an insult to him by the British Government or others has been an insult to India and her people.

5. Which one of the following is true of the given passage?
   (a) The passage is a critique of Gandhi's role in Indian movement for independence
   (b) The passage hails the role of Gandhi in India's freedom movement
   (c) The author is neutral on Gandhi's role in India's freedom movement
   (d) It is an account of Indian National Congress's support to the working-class movement
6. The change that the Gandhian movement brought among the Indian masses was
   (a) Physical (b) Cultural
   (c) Technological (d) Psychological
7. To consider the nationalist movement or to criticise it as a working-class movement was wrong because it was a
   (a) historical movement
   (b) voice of the Indian people
   (c) bourgeois movement
   (d) movement represented by Gandhi
8. Gandhi played a revolutionary role in India because he could
   (a) preach morality
   (b) reach the heart of Indians
   (c) see the conflict of classes
   (d) lead the Indian National Congress
9. Groups with advanced ideology functioned in the air as they did not fit in with
   (a) objective conditions of masses
   (b) the Gandhian ideology
   (c) the class consciousness of the people
   (d) the differences among masses
10. The author concludes the passage by
    (a) criticising the Indian masses
    (b) the Gandhian movement
    (c) pointing out the importance of the personality of Gandhi
    (d) identifying the sorrows of millions of Indians
11. Media that exist in an interconnected series of communication—points are referred to as
    (a) Networked media
    (b) Connective media
    (c) Nodal media
    (d) Multimedia
12. The information function of mass communication is described as
    (a) Diffusion (b) Publicity
    (c) Surveillance (d) Diversion
13. An example of asynchronous medium is

(a) Radio (b) Television
(c) Film (d) Newspaper

14. In communication, connotative words are
(a) Explicit (b) Abstract
(c) Simple (d) Cultural

15. A message beneath a message is labelled as
(a) embedded text (b) internal text
(c) inter-text (d) sub-text

16. In analogue mass communication, stories are
(a) Static (b) Dynamic
(c) Interactive (d) Exploratory

17. Determine the relationship between the pair of words ALWAYS : NEVER and then select from the following pair of words which have a similar relationship
(a) often : rarely
(b) frequently : occasionally
(c) constantly : frequently
(d) intermittently : casually

18. Find the wrong number in the sequence 52, 51, 48, 43, 34, 27, 16
(a) 27 (b) 34
(c) 43 (d) 48

19. In a certain code, PAN is written as 31 and PAR as 35, then PAT is written in the same code as
(a) 30 (b) 37
(c) 39 (d) 41

20. The letters in the first set have certain relationship. On the basis of this relationship, make the right choice for the second set:
AF : IK : : LQ : ?
(a) MO (b) NP
(c) OR (d) TV

21. If 5472 = 9, 6342 = 6, 7584 = 6, what is 9236?
(a) 2 (b) 3
(c) 4 (d) 5

22. In an examination, 35% of the total students failed in Hindi, 45% failed in English and 20% in both. The percentage of those who passed in both subjects is
(a) 10 (b) 20
(c) 30 (d) 40

23. Two statements I and II given below are followed by two conclusions (a) and (b). Supposing the statements are true, which of the following conclusions can logically follow?

Statements:
I. Some flowers are red.
II. Some flowers are blue.

Conclusions:
(A) Some flowers are neither red nor blue.
(B) Some flowers are both red and blue.
(a) Only (A) follows
(b) Only (B) follows
(c) Both (A) and (B) follow
(d) Neither (A) nor (B) follows

24. If the statement 'all students are intelligent' is true, which of the following statements are false?
(i) No students are intelligent.
(ii) Some students are intelligent.
(iii) Some students are not intelligent.
(a) (i) and (ii) (b) (i) and (iii)
(c) (ii) and (iii) (d) Only (i)

25. A reasoning where we start with certain particular statements and conclude with a universal statement is called
(a) Deductive Reasoning
(b) Inductive Reasoning
(c) Abnormal Reasoning
(d) Transcendental Reasoning

26. What is the smallest number of ducks that could swim in this formation—two ducks in front of a duck, two ducks behind a duck and a duck between two ducks?

(a) 5 (b) 7
(c) 4 (d) 3

27. Mr. A, Miss B, Mr. C and Miss D are sitting around a table and discussing their trades.
(i) Mr. A sits opposite to the cook.
(ii) Miss B sits right to the barber.
(iii) The washerman sits right to the barber.
(iv) Miss D sits opposite to Mr. C.
What are the trades of A and B?
(a) Tailor and barber
(b) Barber and cook
(c) Tailor and cook
(d) Tailor and washerman

28. Which one of the following methods serve to measure correlation between two variables?
(a) Scatter Diagram
(b) Frequency Distribution
(c) Two-way table
(d) Coefficient of Rank Correlation

29. Which one of the following is not an Internet Service Provider (ISP)?
(a) MTNL
(b) BSNL
(c) ERNET India
(d) Infotech India Ltd.

30. The hexadecimal number system consists of the symbols
(a) 0 — 7 (b) 0 — 9, A — F
(c) 0 — 7, A — F (d) None of these

31. The binary equivalent of $(-15)_{10}$ is (2's complement system is used)
(a) 11110001 (b) 11110000
(c) 10001111 (d) None of these

32. 1 GB is equal to
(a) 2^{30} bits (b) 2^{30} bytes
(c) 2^{20} bits (d) 2^{20} bytes

33. The set of computer programs that manage the hardware/software of a computer is called
(a) Compiler system
(b) Operation system
(c) Operating system
(d) None of these

34. SMIME in Internet technology stands for
(a) Secure Multipurpose Internet Mail Extension
(b) Secure Multimedia Internet Mail Extension
(c) Simple Multipurpose Internet Mail Extension
(d) Simple Multimedia Internet Mail Extension

35. Which of the following is not covered in 8 missions under the Climate Action Plan of Government of India?
(a) Solar power
(b) Waste to energy conversion
(c) Afforestation
(d) Nuclear energy

36. The concentration of Total Dissolved Solids (TDS) in drinking water should not exceed
(a) 500 mg/L (b) 400 mg/L
(c) 300 mg/L (d) 200 mg/L

37. 'Chipko' movement was first started by
(a) Arundhati Roy
(b) Medha Patkar
(c) Ila Bhatt
(d) Sunderlal Bahuguna

38. The constituents of photochemical smog responsible for eye irritation are
(a) SO_2 and O_3
(b) SO_2 and NO_2
(c) HCHO and PAN
(d) SO_2 and SPM

39. **Assertion (A):** Some carbonaceous aerosols may be carcinogenic.
Reason (R): They may contain polycyclic aromatic hydrocarbons (PAHs).
(a) Both (A) and (R) are correct and (R) is the correct explanation of (A).

(b) Both (A) and (R) are correct but (R) is not the correct explanation of (A).
(c) (A) is correct, but (R) is false.
(d) (A) is false, but (R) is correct.

40. Volcanic eruptions affect
(a) atmosphere and hydrosphere
(b) hydrosphere and biosphere
(c) lithosphere, biosphere and atmosphere
(d) lithosphere, hydrosphere and atmosphere

41. India's first Defence University is in the State of
(a) Haryana
(b) Andhra Pradesh
(c) Uttar Pradesh
(d) Punjab

42. Most of the universities in India
(a) conduct teaching and research only
(b) affiliate colleges and conduct examinations
(c) conduct teaching/research and examinations
(d) promote research only

43. Which one of the following is not a Constitutional Body?
(a) Election Commission
(b) Finance Commission
(c) Union Public Service Commission
(d) Planning Commission

44. Which one of the following statements is not correct?
(a) Indian Parliament is supreme.
(b) The Supreme Court of India has the power of judicial review.
(c) There is a division of powers between the Centre and the States.
(d) There is a Council of Ministers to aid and advise the President.

45. Which one of the following statements reflects the republic character of Indian democracy?
(a) Written constitution
(b) No State religion
(c) Devolution of power to local government institutions
(d) Elected President and directly or indirectly elected Parliament

46. Who among the following appointed by the Governor can be removed by only the President of India?
(a) Chief Minister of a State
(b) A member of the State Public Service Commission
(c) Advocate-General
(d) Vice-Chancellor of a State University

47. If two small circles represent the class of the 'men' and the class of the 'plants' and the big circle represents 'mortality', which one of the following figures represent the proposition 'All men are mortal?.'

(a) 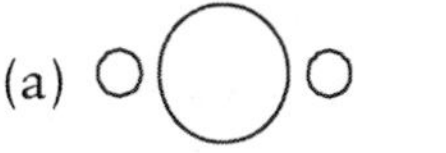
(b) 
(c) 
(d) 

The following table presents the production of electronic items (TVs and LCDs) in a factory during the period from 2006 to 2010. Study the table carefully and answer the questions from 48 to 52:

Year	2006	2007	2008	2009	2010
TVs	6000	9000	13000	11000	8000
LCDs	7000	9400	9000	10000	12000

48. In which year, the total production of electronic items is maximum?
(a) 2006 (b) 2007
(c) 2008 (d) 2010

49. What is the difference between averages of production of LCDs and TVs from 2006 to 2008?

(a) 3000 (b) 2867
(c) 3015 (d) None of these

50. What is the year in which production of TVs is half the production of LCDs in the year 2010?
(a) 2007 (b) 2006
(c) 2009 (d) 2008

51. What is the ratio of production of LCDs in the years 2008 and 2010?
(a) 4:3 (b) 3:4
(c) 1:3 (d) 2:3

52. What is the ratio of production of TVs in the years 2006 and 2007?
(a) 6:7 (b) 7:6
(c) 2:3 (d) 3:2

53. Some students in a class exhibit great curiosity for learning. It may be because such children
(a) Are gifted
(b) Come from rich families
(c) Show artificial behaviour
(d) Create indiscipline in the class

54. The most important quality of a good teacher is
(a) Sound knowledge of subject matter
(b) Good communication skills
(c) Concern for students' welfare
(d) Effective leadership qualities

55. Which one of the following is appropriate in respect of teacher-student relationship?
(a) Very informal and intimate
(b) Limited to classroom only
(c) Cordial and respectful
(d) Indifferent

56. The academic performance of students can be improved if parents are encouraged to
(a) supervise the work of their wards
(b) arrange for extra tuition
(c) remain unconcerned about it
(d) interact with teachers frequently

57. In a lively classroom situation, there is likely to be
(a) occasional roars of laughter
(b) complete silence
(c) frequent teacher-student dialogue
(d) loud discussion among students

58. If a parent approaches the teacher to do some favour to his/her ward in the examination, the teacher should
(a) try to help him
(b) ask him not to talk in those terms
(c) refuse politely and firmly
(d) ask him rudely to go away

59. Which of the following phrases is not relevant to describe the meaning of research as a process?
(a) Systematic Activity
(b) Objective Observation
(c) Trial and Error
(d) Problem Solving

60. Which of the following is not an example of a continuous variable?
(a) Family size (b) Intelligence
(c) Height (d) Altitude

ANSWERS

1. (d)	2. (b)	3. (a)	4. (c)	5. (b)
6. (d)	7. (c)	8. (b)	9. (a)	10. (c)
11. (a)	12. (c)	13. (d)	14. (d)	15. (d)
16. (a)	17. (a)	18. (b)	19. (b)	20. (d)
21. (a)	22. (b)	23. (c)	24. (d)	25. (b)
26. (a)	27. (c)	28. (d)	29. (d)	30. (b)
31. (d)	32. (b)	33. (c)	34. (a)	35. (d)
36. (a)	37. (d)	38. (b)	39. (a)	40. (d)
41. (a)	42. (c)	43. (d)	44. (b)	45. (d)
46. (b)	47. (c)	48. (c)	49. (d)	50. (b)
51. (b)	52. (c)	53. (a)	54. (b)	55. (c)
56. (d)	57. (c)	58. (c)	59. (c)	60. (c)

PAPER–II

1. The term 'secularism' implies that
   (a) Parliament should support religions
   (b) State and religion are inseparable
   (c) State does not recognise any religion as a State religion
   (d) People are free to worship State recognised religion

2. In which of the following cases the Supreme Court held that, "if a body is an agency or instrumentality of Government it may be an authority under Article 12"?
   (a) Ujjambai V. State of Uttar Pradesh
   (b) Ramana Dayaram Shetty V. The International Airport Authority of India
   (c) Electricity Board, Rajasthan V. Mohanlal
   (d) P.D. Shamdasaru V. Central Bank of India

3. The Supreme Court of India for the first time struck down the 'Carry forward Rule' as unconstitutional in the following case:
   (a) Balaji V. State of Mysore
   (b) Rangachari V. General Manager, Southern Railway
   (c) Ashok Kumar Thakur V. State of Bihar
   (d) Devadasan V. Union of India

4. A Judge of a Supreme Court or High Court may be removed from his service by
   (a) The President of India
   (b) The Chief Justice of the Supreme Court
   (c) Parliament through impeachment motion
   (d) National Judicial Academy

5. Which of the following case is popularly known as 'the Fundamental Rights' case?
   (a) M.C. Mehta V. Union of India
   (b) Keshavanand Bharati V. State of Kerala
   (c) S.P. Gupta V. Union of India
   (d) Champakam Dorairajan V. State of Madras

6. Match List I with List II and select the correct answer using the codes given below the lists:

   List I
   I. Right to go abroad
   II. Right to livelihood
   III. Right against sexual harassment
   IV. Right to education

   List II
   A. Olga Tellis's case
   B. Mohini Jain's case
   C. Menaka Gandhi's case
   D. Vishakas' case

Codes:	**I**	**II**	**III**	**IV**
(a)	D	B	A	C
(b)	B	C	D	A
(c)	C	A	D	B
(d)	B	A	C	D

7. Consider the following statements relating to Kelsen's pure theory of law:
   I. Law is a coercive order.
   II. Law are ought propositions.
   III. Law is a system of social rules.
   IV. There is a hierarchy of norms, each norm being valid on the presupposed validity of some other.

   Codes:
   (a) I, II and IV are correct.
   (b) II, III and IV are correct.
   (c) I and III are correct.
   (d) II and IV are correct.

8. **Assertion (A):** Ownership subject to condition subsequent is vested ownership.

Reason (R): Possession and ownership do not differ in their mode of acquisition.

Codes:

(a) Both (A) and (R) are true and (R) is the correct explanation of (A).
(b) Both (A) and (R) are true, but (R) is not the correct explanation of (A).
(c) (A) is true, but (R) is false.
(d) (A) is false, but (R) is true.

9. Law according to Joseph Raz is a
(a) Social engineering
(b) Social fact
(c) Political principle
(d) Normative science

10. Match List I with List II and select the correct answer using the codes given below:

List I (Concepts)

I. Minimum content of law
II. Inner morality of law
III. Law with a variable content
IV. Law as a phenomenon of civilization

List II (Jurists)

1. Fuller 2. Hart
3. Kohler 4. Stammler

Codes:	I	II	III	IV
(a)	3	1	2	4
(b)	2	3	4	1
(c)	2	1	4	3
(d)	1	2	3	4

11. X, an accused drove off amongst his own lambs, without knowing it, a lamb belonging to Y. After X discovered the error, he sold the lamb belonging to Y with his own lambs. X is guilty of
(a) theft
(b) theft and continuing trespass
(c) continuing trespass
(d) none of the above

12. Consider the names of the following jurists associated with sociology of law and sociological jurisprudence:

I. Max Weber II. Leon Duguit
III. Ehrlich IV. Ihering

The correct chronological order in which these jurists appeared on the science is
(a) II, IV, I and III (b) IV, I, III and II
(c) I, III, IV and II (d) III, IV, II and I

13. The Charter of the United Nations requires that the organization and its members shall act in accordance with the principles enumerated in the Charter. Which of the following is not one of such principles?
(a) Sovereign equality
(b) Settlement of international disputes by peaceful means
(c) Promotion of human rights
(d) Prohibition of threat or use of force

14. Human Rights Commission has been discarded in 2006 and its successor is
(a) Human Rights Committee
(b) Human Rights Council
(c) International Committee of Red Cross
(d) Amnesty International

15. Read Assertion (A) and Reason (R) and with the help of codes given below, point out the correct answer:

Assertion (A): The jurisdiction of International Court of Justice is based on the consent of the parties to the dispute.

Reason (R): Principle of reciprocity underlies the jurisdiction of International Court of Justice.

Codes:

(a) Both (A) and (R) are true and (R) is good explanation of (A).
(b) Both (A) and (R) are true, but (R) is not correct explanation of (A).
(c) (A) is true, but (R) is false.
(d) (A) is false, but (R) is true.

16. Arrange the following international instruments in order in which they were adopted. Use the codes given below:

I. The Charter of United Nations.
II. Universal Declaration of Human Rights.
III. International Covenant for the Protection of Civil and Political Rights.
IV. International Convention on Elimination of All Forms of Racial Discrimination.

Codes:

(a)	I	IV	II	III
(b)	II	IV	I	III
(c)	I	II	IV	III
(d)	I	III	IV	II

17. Match the case decided by International Court of Justice mentioned in List I with the year of decision mentioned in List II and with the help of codes given below, point out the correct answer:

List I
I. North Sea Continental Shelf Cases
II. Corfu Channel Case
III. South West Africa Case
IV. Right of Passage Over Indian Territories

List II
1. 1969 2. 1949
3. 1955 4. 1960

Codes:	I	II	III	IV
(a)	1	2	3	4
(b)	2	3	1	4
(c)	3	4	1	2
(d)	4	3	1	2

18. In India, treaty-making is
(a) Legislative Act
(b) Executive Act
(c) Judicial Act
(d) Legislative and Judicial Act

19. Which section of the Hindu Marriage Act, 1955 provides the remedy of "Restitution of Conjugal Rights"?
(a) Section 5 (b) Section 9
(c) Section 11 (d) Section 13

20. Which of the following refers to the irrevocable form of Talaq?
(a) Talaq-ul-ahsan
(b) Talaq-ul-Hasan
(c) Talaq-ul-Biddat
(d) Talaq-i-Tafweez

21. The Special Marriage Act was enacted in the year
(a) 1932 (b) 1947
(c) 1954 (d) 1956

22. **Assertion (A):** Break down of marriage as such is not a ground for divorce.
Reason (R): It may result into an easy way of dissolution of marriage and shall result into instability in the society.
Codes:
(a) Both (A) and (R) are correct.
(b) (A) is correct, but (R) is incorrect.
(c) Both (A) and (R) are wrong.
(d) (R) is correct, but (A) is wrong.

23. The main sources of Muslim law are, Holy Quran, Sunna and Ahadhis and Ijmaa.
(a) True
(b) False
(c) Partly true and partly false
(d) None of the above

24. The Supreme Court of India gave direction to the fact that the marriages of all persons, citizen of India, belonging to various religions should be made compulsorily registerable in those respective States where marriage is solemnized. These directions were issued in which of the following cases?
(a) R.D. Upadhyay V. State of A.P.
(b) Shastri V. Muldas
(c) Seema V. Ashwanikumar
(d) Kailash Sarkar V. Maya Devi

25. Consensus ad idem means
(a) Common Intention
(b) Meeting of Minds

(c) Common Object
(d) None of the above

26. When consent is given by mistake, agreement will be
(a) Voidable (b) Void
(c) Illegal (d) Valid

27. Two statements are given in this question. One is labelled as Assertion (A) and the other is labelled as Reason (R). Examine these statements and select the correct combination of the codes.
Assertion (A): Collateral transaction to wagering agreement is enforceable by law.
Reason (R): Wagering agreement is not illegal.
Codes:
(a) Both Assertion (A) and Reason (R) are correct.
(b) Assertion (A) is correct, but Reason (R) is wrong.
(c) Both Assertion (A) and Reason (R) are wrong.
(d) Reason (R) is correct, but Assertion (A) is wrong.

28. Match List I with List II and select the correct answer using the codes given below:
List I
(A) General offer
(B) Contract by telephonic communication
(C) Acceptance given in ignorance of proposal
(D) Remoteness of damages
List II
(i) Bhagwandas V. Girdharilal
(ii) Lalman V. Gauridatt
(iii) Carlil V. Carbolic Smoke Ball Co.
(iv) Hadley V. Baxendale

Codes:	**(A)**	**(B)**	**(C)**	**(D)**
(a)	(i)	(ii)	(iii)	(iv)
(b)	(iii)	(i)	(ii)	(iv)
(c)	(ii)	(iv)	(i)	(iii)
(d)	(i)	(iv)	(iii)	(ii)

29. When the parties to the contract agree to substitute the existing contract with new contract, it is called
(a) Alteration in Contract
(b) Rescission of Contract
(c) Novation of Contract
(d) All of the above

30. Where a contract contains a stipulation by way of penalty on breach of contract, the aggrieved party is entitled for compensation:
(a) Stipulated amount, if actual loss is proved
(b) Stipulated amount, even actual loss is not proved
(c) Reasonable amount but not more than stipulated amount
(d) Reasonable amount, even more than stipulated amount if loss is proved

31. Torts is defined as a civil wrong for which remedy is an action for
(a) Unliquidated damages
(b) Liquidated damages
(c) Damages of all kinds
(d) No damages

32. The exercise of ordinary rights for a lawful purpose and in a lawful manner is no wrong even if it causes damage. This is known as
(a) Volenti non fit injuria
(b) Injuria sine damnum
(c) Damnum sine injuria
(d) None of the above

33. 'Respondent superior' means
(a) respondent is superior than plaintiff
(b) master is superior
(c) servant is not liable
(d) master is vicariously liable

34. In remoteness of damages the main tests to determine whether damage is remote or not are

I. Test of reasonable Foresight
II. Test of Remoteness
III. Test of Directness
IV. Test of Foresightedness

(a) II, III (b) II, IV
(c) III, IV (d) I only

35. **Assertion (A):** For an 'Act of God' to be an exception, there is to be working of the natural forces so unexpected that no human force or skill could reasonably be expected to anticipate it.
Reason (R): It is not an absolute exception and can be overlooked.
Codes:
(a) (A) is correct, but (R) is wrong.
(b) (R) is correct, but (A) is wrong.
(c) Both (A) and (R) are correct.
(d) Both (A) and (R) are wrong.

36. **Assertion (A):** If a dangerous thing is brought on one's land, its use is non-natural and if it escapes, the person can plead lack of 'mens rea' as a plea.
Reason (R): The rule of strict liability cannot be applied to every such situation.
Codes:
(a) (A) is correct, but (R) is wrong.
(b) (R) is correct, but (A) is wrong.
(c) Both (A) and (R) are correct.
(d) Both (A) and (R) are wrong.

37. The demarcating line between intention and knowledge is
(a) Non-existing (b) Existing
(c) Thin (d) Wide

38. The feeling of hatredness exciting an individual is an offence of
(a) Conspiracy (b) Abetment
(c) Defamation (d) None of above

39. Sex with a girl with fraudulent consent amounts to
(a) Simple physical assault
(b) Molestation
(c) Outraging of modesty
(d) Rape

40. The requirement for fixing joint liability lies particularly on the confederation of parties because of
(a) Common object
(b) Common intention
(c) Vicarious liability
(d) Deemed to be guilty

41. An aggravated form of wrongful confinement of a girl amounts to
(a) Kidnapping (b) Abduction
(c) Enticing (d) Taking away

42. In order to prove the offence of dowry related act the law prescribes that
(a) The demand for dowry should have been made within seven years of marriage.
(b) There must be cruelty against the woman to infer dowry demand.
(c) There must be a conduct of harassment only for such demand.
(d) All of them.

43. Permanent closing down of a part of place of work is called
(a) Lay-off (b) Retrenchment
(c) Closure (d) Lockout

44. Match List I with List II and select the correct answer using the codes given below:

List I (Subjects)
I. Lockout II. Lay-off
III. Industrial Dispute IV. Industry

List II (Judicial Decisions)
1. Lalit Hari Ayurvedic College Pharmacy V. Workers and Hospital Union
2. A.P. Dairy Development Co-Op. Federation Ltd. V. Presiding Officer, Labour Court Guntur
3. Workman V. Firestone Tyre & Rubber Co.
4. Kairbeta Estate V. Rajmanickam

Codes:	I	II	III	IV
(a)	1	2	4	3
(b)	3	4	1	2
(c)	2	1	3	4
(d)	4	3	2	1

45. Consider the following judicial decisions:
    I. Hindustan Steel Ltd. V. Presiding Officer
    II. Management of KSRT Corp., Bangalore V. M. Boraih
    III. Pipraich Sugar Mills V. Mazdoor Union
    IV. Management of W.B. India Ltd. V. Jaganath

    The correct sequence in which these judicial decisions were rendered is

    Codes:
    (a) I, IV, II and III (b) IV, II, III and I
    (c) II, III, I and IV (d) III, II, IV and I

46. **Assertion (A):** Definition of lay-off as given under the Industrial Disputes Act does not confer any power on the management to lay-off.

    Reason (R): Financial stringency cannot constitute a ground for lay-off.

    Codes:
    (a) Both (A) and (R) are true and (R) is the correct explanation of (A).
    (b) Both (A) and (R) are true, but (R) is not the correct explanation of (A).
    (c) (A) is true, but (R) is false.
    (d) (A) is false, but (R) is true.

47. Consider the following statements:
    I. Lock-out indicates the closure of the place of business.
    II. Lock-out indicates the closure of the business itself.
    III. Suspension of work due to trade reasons constitute lockout.
    IV. Lock-out does not include discharge.

    Codes:
    (a) I, II and III are correct.
    (b) II and III are correct.
    (c) I and IV are correct.
    (d) II and III are correct.

48. A union leader or an office-bearer of the trade union has immunity from
    (a) transfer
    (b) misconduct
    (c) civil proceedings
    (d) deliberate trespass

49. The maxim Res ipsa loquitur is a rule of
    (a) evidence
    (b) criminal law
    (c) refutal of evidence
    (d) vicarious liability

50. Which of the following pairs is not correctly matched?
    (a) Distinction between defacto and dejure recognition is political – The Arantzaju Mendi's Case
    (b) Status of customary international law in England – Maclaine Watson's Case
    (c) Treaty making power of the central executive – Shrikrishna Sharma V. State of West Bengal
    (d) Binding character of an arbitral award – Maganbhai Ishwarbhai V. Union of India

ANSWERS

1. (b)	2. (a)	3. (a)	4. (a)	5. (c)
6. (c)	7. (b)	8. (b)	9. (d)	10. (a)
11. (d)	12. (c)	13. (c)	14. (a)	15. (c)
16. (c)	17. (b)	18. (b)	19. (a)	20. (a)
21. (d)	22. (d)	23. (c)	24. (b)	25. (c)
26. (a)	27. (a)	28. (b)	29. (c)	30. (c)
31. (b)	32. (b)	33. (a)	34. (c)	35. (d)
36. (d)	37. (d)	38. (a)	39. (c)	40. (b)
41. (a)	42. (a)	43. (c)	44. (b)	45. (c)
46. (d)	47. (d)	48. (b)	49. (b)	50. (a)

JUNE–2010

Note: This paper contains Sixty (60) multiple-choice questions, each question carrying two (2) marks. Candidate is expected to answer any Fifty (50) questions. In case more than Fifty (50) questions are attempted, only the first Fifty (50) questions will be evaluated.

PAPER–I

1. Which one of the following is the most important quality of a good teacher?
   (a) Punctuality and sincerity
   (b) Content mastery
   (c) Content mastery and reactive
   (d) Content mastery and sociable

2. The primary responsibility for the teacher's adjustment lies with
   (a) The children
   (b) The principal
   (c) The teacher himself
   (d) The community

3. As per the NCTE norms, what should be the staff strength for a unit of 100 students at B.Ed. level?
   (a) 1 + 7 (b) 1 + 9
   (c) 1 + 10 (d) 1 + 5

4. Research has shown that the most frequent symptom of nervous instability among teachers is
   (a) Digestive upsets
   (b) Explosive behaviour
   (c) Fatigue
   (d) Worry

5. Which one of the following statements is correct?
   (a) Syllabus is an annexure to the curriculum.
   (b) Curriculum is the same in all educational institutions.
   (c) Curriculum includes both formal and informal education.
   (d) Curriculum does not include methods of evaluation.

6. A successful teacher is one who is
   (a) Compassionate and disciplinarian
   (b) Quite and reactive
   (c) Tolerant and dominating
   (d) Passive and active

Read the following passage carefully and answer the questions 7 to 12.

The phrase "What is it like?" stands for a fundamental thought-process. How does one go about observing and reporting on things and events that occupy segments of earth space? Of all the infinite variety of phenomena on the face of the earth, how does one decide what phenomena to observe? There is no such thing as a complete description of the earth or any part of it, for every microscopic point on the earth's surface differs from every other such point. Experience shows that the things observed are already familiar, because they are like phenomena that occur at home or because they resemble the abstract images and models developed in the human mind.

How are abstract images formed? Humans alone among the animals possess language; their words symbolise not only specific things but also mental images of classes of things. People can remember what they have seen or experienced because they attach a word symbol to them.

During the long record of our efforts to gain more and more knowledge about the face of the earth as the human habitat, there has been a continuing interplay between things and events. The direct observation through the senses is described as a percept; the mental image is described as a concept. Percepts are what some people describe as reality, in contrast to mental images, which are theoretical, implying that they are not real.

The relation of Percept to Concept is not as simple as the definition implies. It is now quite clear that people of different cultures or even individuals in the same culture develop different mental images of reality and what they perceive is a reflection of these preconceptions. The direct observation of things and events on the face of the earth is so clearly a function of the mental images of the mind of the observer that the whole idea of reality must be reconsidered.

Concepts determine what the observer perceives, yet concepts are derived from the generalisations of previous percepts. What happens is that the educated observer is taught to accept a set of concepts and then sharpens or changes these concepts during a professional career. In any one field of scholarship, professional opinion at one time determines what concepts and procedures are acceptable, and these form a kind of model of scholarly behaviour.

7. The problem raised in the passage reflects on
   (a) thought-process
   (b) human behaviour
   (c) cultural perceptions
   (d) professional opinion
8. According to the passage, human beings have mostly in mind
   (a) Observation of things
   (b) Preparation of mental images
   (c) Expression through language
   (d) To gain knowledge
9. Concept means
   (a) A mental image
   (b) A reality
   (c) An idea expressed in language form
   (d) All of the above
10. The relation of Percept to Concept is
    (a) Positive (b) Negative
    (c) Reflective (d) Absolute
11. In the passage, the earth is taken as
    (a) The Globe
    (b) The Human Habitat
    (c) A Celestial Body
    (d) A Planet
12. Percept means
    (a) Direct observation through the senses
    (b) A conceived idea
    (c) Ends of a spectrum
    (d) An abstract image
13. Action research means
    (a) A longitudinal research
    (b) An applied research
    (c) A research initiated to solve an immediate problem
    (d) A research with socio-economic objective
14. Research is
    (a) Searching again and again
    (b) Finding solution to any problem
    (c) Working in a scientific way to search for truth of any problem
    (d) None of the above
15. A common test in research demands much priority on
    (a) Reliability (b) Usability
    (c) Objectivity (d) All of the above
16. Which of the following is the first step in starting the research process?
    (a) Searching sources of information to locate problem
    (b) Survey of related literature
    (c) Identification of problem
    (d) Searching for solutions to the problem
17. If a researcher conducts a research on finding out which administrative style

contributes more to institutional effectiveness? This will be an example of
(a) Basic Research
(b) Action Research
(c) Applied Research
(d) None of the above

18. Normal Probability Curve should be
(a) Positively skewed
(b) Negatively skewed
(c) Leptokurtic skewed
(d) Zero skewed

19. In communication, a major barrier to reception of messages is
(a) audience attitude
(b) audience knowledge
(c) audience education
(d) audience income

20. Post-modernism is associated with
(a) Newspapers (b) Magazines
(c) Radio (d) Television

21. Didactic communication is
(a) Intra-porsonal (b) Inter-personal
(c) Organisational (d) Relational

22. In communication, the language is
(a) the non-verbal code
(b) the verbal code
(c) the symbolic code
(d) the iconic code

23. Identify the correct sequence of the following:
(a) Source, channel, message, receiver
(b) Source, receiver, channel, message
(c) Source, message, receiver, channel
(d) Source, message, channel, receiver

24. **Assertion (A):** Mass media promote a culture of violence in the society.
Reason (R): Because violence sells in the market as people themselves are violent in character.
(a) Both (A) and (R) are true and (R) is the correct explanation of (A).
(b) Both (A) and (R) are true, but (R) is not the correct explanation of (A).
(c) (A) is true, but (R) is false.
(d) Both (A) and (R) are false.

25. When an error of 1% is made in the length of a square, the percentage error in the area of a square will be
(a) 0 (b) 1/2
(c) 1 (d) 2

26. On January 12, 1980, it was a Saturday. The day of the week on January 12, 1979 was
(a) Thursday (b) Friday
(c) Saturday (d) Sunday

27. If water is called food, food is called tree, tree is called earth, earth is called world, which of the following grows a fruit?
(a) Water (b) Tree
(c) World (d) Earth

28. E is the son of A, D is the son of B, E is married to C, C is the daughter of E. How is D related to E?
(a) Brother (b) Uncle
(c) Father-in-law (d) Brother-in-law

29. If INSURANCE is coded as ECNARUSNI, how HINDRANCE will be coded?
(a) CADNHIWCE (b) HANODEINR
(c) AENIRHDCN (d) ECNARDNIH

30. Find the next number in the following series: 2, 5, 10, 17, 26, 37, 50, ?
(a) 63 (b) 65
(c) 67 (d) 69

31. Which of the following is an example of circular argument?
(a) God created man in his image and man created God in his own image.
(b) God is the source of a scripture and the scripture is the source of our knowledge of God.
(c) Some of the Indians are great because India is great.
(d) Rama is great because he is Rama.

32. Lakshmana is a morally good person because
    (a) he is religious (b) he is educated
    (c) he is rich (d) he is rational

33. Two statements I and II given below are followed by two conclusions (a) and (b). Supposing the statements are true, which of the following conclusions can logically follow?

    Statements:

    I. Some religious people are morally good.
    II. Some religious people are rational.

    Conclusion:

    (A) Rationally religious people are good morally.
    (B) Non-rational religious persons are not morally good.
    (a) Only (A) follows
    (b) Only (B) follows
    (c) Both (A) and (B) follow
    (d) Neither (A) nor (B) follows

34. Certainty is
    (a) an objective fact
    (b) emotionally satisfying
    (c) logical
    (d) ontological

Questions from 35 to 36 are based on the following diagram in which there are three intersecting circles I, S and P where circle I stands for Indians, circle S stands for Scientists and circle P for Politicians. Different regions of the figure are lettered from a to g.

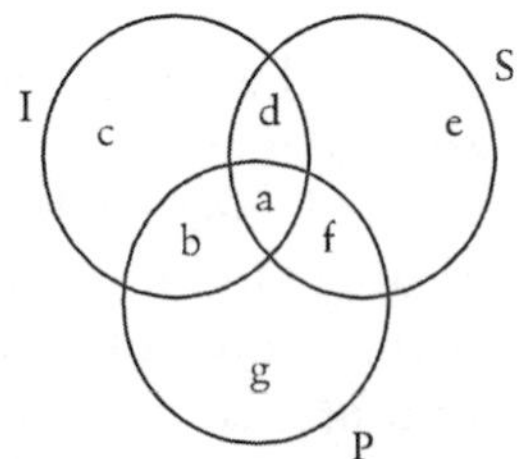

35. The region which represents non-scientists who are politicians.
    (a) f (b) d
    (c) a (d) c

36. The region which represents politicians who are Indians as well as scientists.
    (a) b (b) c
    (c) a (d) d

37. The population of a city is plotted as a function of time (years) in graphic form below:

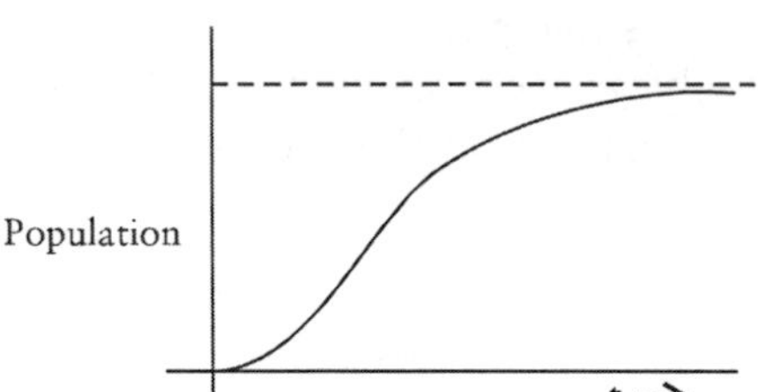

Which of the following inferences can be drawn from above plot?
    (a) The population increases exponentially.
    (b) The population increases in parabolic fashion.
    (c) The population initially increases in a linear fashion and then stabilises.
    (d) The population initially increases exponentially and then stabilises.

In the following chart, the price of logs is shown in per cubic metre and that of Plywood and Saw Timber in per tonnes. Study the chart and answer the following questions 38, 39 and 40.

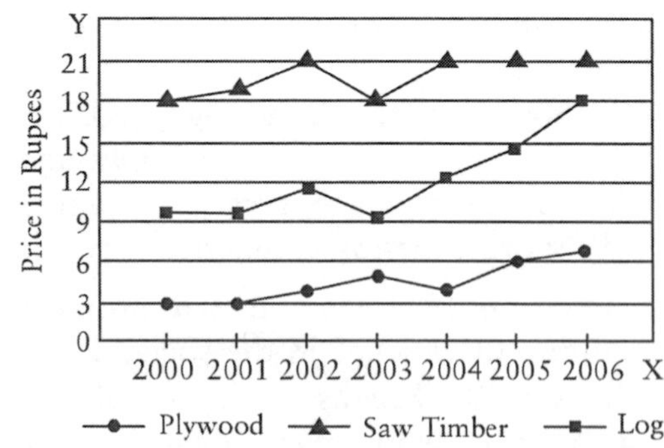

38. Which product shows the maximum percentage increase in price over the period?

(a) Saw timber (b) Plywood
(c) Log (d) None of these

39. What is the maximum percentage increase in price per cubic metre of log?
(a) 6 (b) 12
(c) 18 (d) None of these

40. In which year the prices of two products decreased and that of the third increased?
(a) 2000 (b) 2002
(c) 2003 (d) 2006

41. Which one of the following is the oldest Archival source of data in India?
(a) National Sample Surveys
(b) Agricultural Statistics
(c) Census
(d) Vital Statistics

42. In a large random data set following normal distribution, the ratio (%) of number of data points which are in the range of (mean ± standard deviation) to the total number of data points, is
(a) ~ 50% (b) ~ 67%
(c) ~ 97% (d) ~ 47%

43. Which number system is usually followed in a typical 32-bit computer?
(a) 2 (b) 8
(c) 10 (d) 16

44. Which one of the following is an example of Operating System?
(a) Microsoft Word
(b) Microsoft Excel
(c) Microsoft Access
(d) Microsoft Windows

45. Which one of the following represents the binary equivalent of the decimal number 23?
(a) 01011 (b) 10111
(c) 10011 (d) None of these

46. Which one of the following is different from other members?
(a) Google (b) Windows
(c) Linux (d) Mac

47. Where does a computer add and compare its data?
(a) CPU (b) Memory
(c) Hard disk (d) Floppy disk

48. Computers on an Internet are identified by
(a) e-mail address
(b) street address
(c) IP address
(d) None of the above

49. The Right to Information Act, 2005 makes the provision of
(a) Dissemination of all types of information by all Public authorities to any person
(b) Establishment of Central, State and District Level Information Commissions as an appellate body
(c) Transparency and accountability in Public authorities
(d) All of the above

50. Which type of natural hazards cause maximum damage to property and lives?
(a) Hydrological
(b) Hydro-meteorological
(c) Geological
(d) Geo-chemical

51. Dioxins are produced from
(a) Wastelands
(b) Power plants
(c) Sugar factories
(d) Combustion of plastics

52. The slogan "A tree for each child" was coined for
(a) Social forestry program
(b) Clean Air program
(c) Soil conservation program
(d) Environmental protection program

53. The main constituents of biogas are
(a) Methane and Carbon dioxide
(b) Methane and Nitric oxide
(c) Methane, Hydrogen and Nitric oxide
(d) Methane and Sulphur dioxide

54. **Assertion (A):** In the world as a whole, the environment has degraded during past several decades.
Reason (R): The population of the world has been growing significantly.
(a) (A) is correct, (R) is correct and (R) is the correct explanation of (A).
(b) (A) is correct, (R) is correct and (R) is not the correct explanation of (A).
(c) (A) is correct, but (R) is false.
(d) (A) is false, but (R) is correct.

55. Climate change has implications for
1. soil moisture 2. forest fires
3. biodiversity 4. groundwater
Identify the correct combination according to the code:
Codes:
(a) 1 and 3 (b) 1, 2 and 3
(c) 1, 3 and 4 (d) 1, 2, 3 and 4

56. The accreditation process by National Assessment and Accreditation Council (NAAC) differs from that of National Board of Accreditation (NBA) in terms of
(a) Disciplines covered by both being the same, there is duplication of efforts.
(b) One has institutional grading approach and the other has program grading approach.
(c) Once get accredited by NBA or NAAC, the institution is free from renewal of grading, which is not a progressive decision.
(d) This accreditation amounts to approval of minimum standards in the quality of education in the institution concerned.

57. Which option is not correct?
(a) Most of the educational institutions of national repute in scientific and technical sphere fall under 64th entry of Union list.
(b) Education, in general, is the subject of concurrent list since 42nd Constitutional Amendment Act 1976.
(c) Central Advisory Board on Education (CABE) was first established in 1920.
(d) India had implemented the right to Free and Compulsory Primary Education in 2002 through 86th Constitutional Amendment.

58. Which statement is not correct about the "National Education Day" of India?
(a) It is celebrated on 5th September every year.
(b) It is celebrated on 11th November every year.
(c) It is celebrated in the memory of India's first Union Minister of Education, Dr. Abul Kalam Azad.
(d) It is being celebrated since 2008.

59. Match List I with List II and select the correct answer from the codes given below:
List I (Articles of the Constitution)
A. Article 280 B. Article 324
C. Article 323 D. Article 315
List II (Institutions)
1. Administrative Tribunals
2. Election Commission of India
3. Finance Commission at Union level
4. Union Public Service Commission

Codes:	A	B	C	D
(a)	1	2	3	4
(b)	3	2	1	4
(c)	2	3	4	1
(d)	2	4	3	1

60. Deemed Universities declared by UGC under Section 3 of the UGC Act 1956, are not permitted to
(a) offer programs in higher education and issue degrees
(b) give affiliation to any institute of higher education

(c) open off-campus and off-shore campus anywhere in the country and overseas respectively without the permission of the UGC
(d) offer distance education programs without the approval of the Distance Education Council

ANSWERS

1. (b)	2. (c)	3. (c)	4. (b)	5. (c)
6. (a)	7. (c)	8. (a)	9. (a)	10. (c)
11. (b)	12. (a)	13. (c)	14. (c)	15. (d)
16. (c)	17. (c)	18. (d)	19. (c)	20. (d)
21. (b)	22. (b)	23. (d)	24. (d)	25. (d)
26. (b)	27. (c)	28. (d)	29. (d)	30. (b)
31. (b)	32. (a)	33. (d)	34. (c)	35. (a)
36. (c)	37. (d)	38. (c)	39. (d)	40. (b)
41. (c)	42. (b)	43. (a)	44. (d)	45. (b)
46. (b)	47. (a)	48. (c)	49. (d)	50. (c)
51. (d)	52. (d)	53. (a)	54. (b)	55. (d)
56. (c)	57. (a)	58. (a)	59. (b)	60. (b)

PAPER–II

1. Requirement of 'reasonableness' runs like a golden thread through the entire fabric of fundamental rights is held in
   (a) Keshavananda Bharthi V. State of Kerala
   (b) Indra Sawhney V. Union of India
   (c) Vishaka V. State of Rajasthan
   (d) Maneka Gandhi V. Union of India
2. 'Right to life' does not include 'right to die'. It has been held in case of
   (a) P. Rathinam V. Union of India
   (b) Bandhua Mukti Morcha V. Union of India
   (c) A.K. Gopalan V. State of Madras
   (d) Gian Kaur V. State of Punjab
3. Fundamental Rights are
   (a) Unrestricted Rights
   (b) Absolute Rights
   (c) Restricted Rights
   (d) None of the above
4. Right against 'Double Jeopardy' is guaranteed under
   (a) Article 21 (b) Article 20(1)
   (c) Article 20(2) (d) Article 22(1)
5. **Assertion (A):** An accused person cannot be compelled to give his thumb impression, except for comparison.
   Reason (R): It amounts to self-incrimination.
   Codes:
   (a) Both (A) and (R) are true and (R) is the correct explanation of (A).
   (b) Both (A) and (R) are true and (R) is not correct explanation of (A).
   (c) (A) is true, but (R) is false.
   (d) (A) is false, but (R) is true.
6. Which of the following writ can be issued against the usurpation of Public Office?
   (a) Writ of Mandamus
   (b) Writ of Certiorari
   (c) Writ of Quo warranto
   (d) Writ of Prohibition
7. Consider the following statements:
   I. Equitable ownership always pre-supposes the existence of a legal ownership.
   II. When property is given by A to B for the benefit of C, B becomes the legal owner and C the equitable owner.
   III. In many cases, equity recognizes ownership whereas law does not recognize ownership owing to some flaw or defect.

IV. Contingent ownership is spes successionis

Codes:
(a) I, II and III are correct
(b) II and III are correct
(c) I and II are correct
(d) III and IV are correct

8. **Assertion (A):** Ownership is not only a juridical concept but also a social concept and an instrument of social policy.
Reason (R): The right of alienation is not a necessary incident of ownership.
Codes:
(a) Both (A) and (R) are true and (R) is the correct explanation of (A).
(b) Both (A) and (R) are true, but (R) is not the correct explanation of (A).
(c) (A) is true, but (R) is false.
(d) (A) is false, but (R) is true.

9. H.L.A. Hart is a
(a) Linguistic philosopher
(b) Realist philosopher
(c) Socialist philosopher
(d) Post-modernist philosopher

10. Match List I with List II and select the correct answer using the codes given below:

List I (Theories)	**List II (Jurists)**
I. The general will theory	1. Kelsen
II. Justice as common good	2. Ihering
III. Law as a means to achieve social ends	3. Rousseau
IV. Grundnorm theory	4. Finnis

Codes:	I	II	III	IV
(a)	2	4	1	3
(b)	2	3	4	1
(c)	3	2	1	4
(d)	3	4	2	1

11. X, plaintiff found a parcel of notes on the floor of Y, the defendant's shop. Who is in possession of notes?
(a) X (b) Y
(c) Government (d) Both X and Y

12. Consider the names of the following natural law jurists:
I. Morris II. Stammler
III. Rawls IV. Jerome Hall
The chronological order in which these jurists appeared on the scene:
(a) IV, II, I and III
(b) I, III, II and IV
(c) III, II, IV and I
(d) II, III, I and IV

13. Which of the following is principal organ of the United Nations ?
(a) Human Rights Committee
(b) Economic and Social Council
(c) International Labour Organization
(d) International Law Association

14. India is not a party to
(a) International Covenant on Economic, Social and Cultural Rights, 1966.
(b) International Covenant on Civil and Political Rights, 1966.
(c) Optional Protocol to International Covenant on Civil and Political Rights, 1966.
(d) Convention on Elimination of Discrimination against Women (CEDAW), 1979.

15. Treaty, in principle, binds the States parties to the treaty. A State becomes party to the treaty by
(a) signing the treaty
(b) ratifying or acceding to the treaty
(c) enacting domestic legislation to implement the treaty
(d) enforcing the treaty by way of conduct

16. Which of the following can request the International Court of Justice to give an advisory opinion?
(a) State
(b) General Assembly

(c) International Law Commission
(d) Individual

17. Read Assertion (A) and Reason (R) and with the help of codes given below, point out the correct answer.

Assertion (A): To promote and encourage respect for human rights is one of the purposes of the United Nations.

Reason (R): The Charter of United Nations conceptualizes, substantiates and spells out human rights which are to be promoted by the member States.

Codes:
(a) Both (A) and (R) are true, but (R) is good explanation of (A).
(b) Both (A) and (R) are true, but (R) is not a correct explanation of (A).
(c) (A) is true, but (R) is false.
(d) (A) is false, but (R) is true.

18. Match the statement in List I with its author in List II and with the help of codes given below, point out the correct answer.

List I (Statement)

I. International law is not true law but positive international morality.
II. International customary law is deemed automatically to be part of common law.
III. *Opino juris sive* necessitatis is not a condition precedent for the existence of international custom.
IV. General Assembly Resolutions, in general, do not create legal obligation to comply with them but a resolution recommending to an administering State a specific course of action creates some legal obligation.

List II (Author)

1. John Austin
2. William Blackstone
3. Michael Akehurst
4. Hersch Lauterpacht

Codes:	I	II	III	IV
(a)	1	2	3	4
(b)	2	3	1	4
(c)	3	4	1	2
(d)	4	2	3	1

19. According to Muslim law, marriage is not solemnized only for the sexual enjoyment between two spouses, it is an act of ibadat.
(a) True
(b) False
(c) Partly true and partly false
(d) None of the above

20. Which of the following is not a ground for Divorce under Hindu Marriage Act?
(a) Cruelty
(b) Desertion
(c) Adultery
(d) Incompatible Temperamental Adjustment

21. Children born out of a union which is either void or voidable under Sections 11 and 12 of Hindu Marriage Act, 1955 shall be
(a) Bastard
(b) Deemed to be legitimate
(c) Illegitimate
(d) Legitimate

22. **A.** Nikah is a regular and permanent form of marriage among Muslims.
R. Muta is contractual form of marriage and is most uncommon in India.
(a) A and R above are correct.
(b) A is correct, R is false.
(c) R is correct, but A is wrong.
(d) Neither A is correct nor R is correct.

23. Which of the following is not a ground for divorce under the Dissolution of Muslim Marriage Act, 1939?
(a) Treating the wife with cruelty.
(b) That the whereabouts of the Husband have not been known for a period for more than four years.

(c) The husband has been sentenced to imprisonment for a period of two years or upwards.
(d) That the husband has been insane for a period of two years or more.

24. Any Hindu Marriage which is not properly solemnized, it shall be
(a) Valid (b) Voidable
(c) Void ab-initio (d) None of these

25. An acceptance given by post
(a) can be revoked at any time
(b) cannot be revoked at all
(c) can be revoked, if it does not reach to the proposer
(d) can be revoked, even if it comes to the knowledge of proposer

26. A promise to pay time barred debt is
(a) not enforceable
(b) enforceable at the discretion of debtor
(c) enforceable under exception
(d) none of the above

27. Which of the following statements is correct?
(a) Third party can always sue for breach of contract.
(b) Wagering agreements are illegal.
(c) When consent is not free, agreement will always be voidable.
(d) Catalogue is an invitation to offer.

28. Two statements are given in this question. One is labelled as Assertion (A) and the other is labelled as Reason (R). Examine these statements and select the correct combination of the codes.
Assertion (A): Partial acceptance is not acceptance.
Reason (R): Acceptance must be absolute and unconditional.
Codes:
(a) Both (A) and (R) are correct.
(b) Both (A) and (R) are wrong.
(c) (A) is correct, but (R) is wrong.
(d) (A) is false, but (R) is correct.

29. A counter offer is
(a) an invitation to offer
(b) an acceptance to offer
(c) a rejection of the offer
(d) a conditional acceptance

30. An agreement with minor is void, hence
(a) Minor is never allowed to enforce such agreement.
(b) Minor is allowed to enforce such agreement, if it was made for his benefit.
(c) Minor is always allowed to enforce such agreement.
(d) Minor is allowed to enforce such contract when other party makes no objection.

31. Tort is a violation of
(a) Right in personam
(b) Right in rem
(c) Both (a) and (b)
(d) None of the above

32. Which of the following is not correctly matched?
(a) ubi Jus ibi remedium — where there is a right there is a remedy
(b) res ipsa loquitur — things speak for themselves
(c) damnum sine injuria — damage without injury
(d) injuria sine damnum — injury with damage

33. Limitations on the scope of the doctrine *volenti non-fit injuria* are
(a) Rescue cases
(b) Statutory authority
(c) Both (a) and (b)
(d) None of the above

34. Injustice would manifest itself if a person is held responsible for all consequences

of his act. Therefore, he is responsible only for consequences not too

(a) Remote (b) Near
(c) In and around (d) Far sighted

35. **A.** Law of Torts is concerned with allocation and distribution of losses and awarding compensation to the victim.
R. This is a branch of law governing actions for damages for injuries to private legal rights.
(a) A is correct, but R is wrong.
(b) R is correct, but A is wrong.
(c) Both A and R are correct.
(d) Both A and R are wrong.

36. **A.** The consequences of a wrongful act may be endless or there may be consequences of consequences.
R. The 'Test of reasonable foresight' is followed usually in such cases which is based on the Wagen Mound case.
(a) A is correct, but R is wrong.
(b) R is correct, but A is wrong.
(c) Both A and R are correct.
(d) Both A and R are wrong.

37. Conspiracy is an offence having mens rea without any actus rea?
(a) Yes
(b) No
(c) Depends upon circumstances
(d) Depends upon judicial discretion

38. The right of private defence is available to
(a) The aggressor
(b) The person who has attacked
(c) The aggressor and the victim
(d) The act done in defence of a person who was attacked

39. In abetment of an offence can be constituted by
(a) Instigation
(b) Conspiracy
(c) Intentional aid
(d) All of the above

40. Buggery is an offence against
(a) Having carnal knowledge with a woman.
(b) Offence committed without use of force.
(c) Depravity against natural order of sex.
(d) Manipulation and movement of male organ.

41. Illicit intercourse implies
(a) Rape
(b) Prostitution
(c) Sex between two persons not united by lawful marriage
(d) Sex with a sleeping woman

42. A police officer arrested and detained a girl in the lock-up despite bail order. The police officer shall be guilty of
(a) Kidnapping
(b) Abduction
(c) Intimidation
(d) Wrongful confinement

43. **Assertion (A):** Priest in a temple is a workman for the purposes of the Industrial Disputes Act.
Reason (R): He cannot be considered as a workman as he is not doing any manual or clerical services to the devotees of the temple.
Codes:
(a) Both (A) and (R) are true and (R) is the correct explanation of (A).
(b) Both (A) and (R) are true, but (R) is not the correct explanation of (A).
(c) (A) is true, but (R) is false.
(d) (A) is false, but (R) is true.

44. Consider the following judicial decision on the meaning of industry:

I. Indian Red Cross Society V. Additional Labour Court, Chandigarh.
II. Dhanrajgiri Hospital V. Workmen.
III. State of Punjab V. Kuldeep Singh.
IV. Prema Govinda V. Karnataka Small Scale Industries Association, Bangalore.

The correct order in which these judicial decisions were rendered is
(a) II, III, I and IV
(b) III, II, IV and I
(c) IV, III, I and II
(d) II, I, III and IV

45. Consider the following statements on industrial dispute.
I. Industrial dispute will subsist in spite of closure of industry.
II. An industrial dispute can arise when a demand is made by the workman and denied by the employer.
III. Once a dispute is referred for adjudication, the presumption is that it is an industrial dispute.
IV. Employer's failure to keep his verbal assurances is an industrial dispute.

Codes:
(a) I and II are correct.
(b) II and III are correct.
(c) III and IV are correct.
(d) I, II and III are correct.

46. Unfair labour practices mean any of the practices specified in the
(a) Fourth Schedule of the Industrial Disputes Act
(b) Fifth Schedule of the Industrial Disputes Act
(c) Sixth Schedule of the Industrial Disputes Act
(d) Third Schedule of the Industrial Disputes Act

47. Which of the following is not a leading case on immunity of trade unions from criminal proceedings?
(a) Jay Engineering Works Ltd. V. State of West Bengal.
(b) Standard Chartered Grindlays Bank Ltd. V. Grindlays Bank Employees.
(c) Onkarnath Tiwari V. Chief Engineer, Minor Irrigation Department.
(d) Piperaich Sugar Mills Ltd.

48. Which of the following pairs are not matched?
(a) Individual dispute whether industrial dispute — Newspapers Ltd. Allahabad V. Industrial Tribunal.
(b) Meaning of Employer — Western Automobile Association V. Industrial Tribunal.
(c) Solicitor's professionnot an industry — National Union of Commercial Employees V. Industrial Tribunal.
(d) Go-Slow as a serious case of misconduct — Bijay Cotton Mills V. Workmen.

Read the following paragraph and answer the Question Nos. 49 and 50.

Protection of society and stamping out criminal proclivity must be the object of Law, which must be achieved by imposing appropriate sentence. Therefore, law as a cornerstone of the edifice of "order" should meet the challenges confronting the society. In operating the sentencing system law should adopt the corrective machinery or the deterrence based on factual matrix. By deft modulation sentencing process be stern where it should be and tempered with mercy where it warrants to be. The facts and given circumstances in each case, the nature of crime, the manner in which it was planned and committed, the motive for the commission of crime, the conduct of the accused, the nature of weapons used and all other attending circumstances are relevant facts which would enter into the area of consideration.

49. What is the object of law?
   (a) Safeguarding individual interests.
   (b) Permitting the individual to earn and become rich.
   (c) Protection of society and stamping out criminal proclivity.
   (d) None of the above.

50. While imposing sentence what are the relevant considerations?
   (a) The nature of crime only
   (b) The manner in which it was planned and committed only
   (c) The motive for the commission of crime only
   (d) All the above are relevant considerations

ANSWERS

1. (c)	2. (b)	3. (d)	4. (c)	5. (b)
6. (c)	7. (a)	8. (c)	9. (b)	10. (c)
11. (a)	12. (b)	13. (c)	14. (b)	15. (c)
16. (c)	17. (a)	18. (b)	19. (b)	20. (c)
21. (c)	22. (a)	23. (a)	24. (c)	25. (b)
26. (b)	27. (d)	28. (b)	29. (d)	30. (c)
31. (a)	32. (c)	33. (d)	34. (d)	35. (b)
36. (a)	37. (c)	38. (c)	39. (d)	40. (b)
41. (c)	42. (d)	43. (c)	44. (d)	45. (d)
46. (b)	47. (b)	48. (c)	49. (a)	50. (b)

DECEMBER–2011

Note: This paper contains Sixty (60) multiple-choice questions, each question carrying two (2) marks. Candidate is expected to answer any Fifty (50) questions. In case more than Fifty (50) questions are attempted, only the first Fifty (50) questions will be evaluated.

PAPER–I

1. Photo bleeding means
   (a) Photo cropping
   (b) Photo placement
   (c) Photo cutting
   (d) Photo colour adjustment

2. While designing communication strategy feed-forward studies are conducted by
   (a) Audience (b) Communicator
   (c) Satellite (d) Media

3. In which language the newspapers have highest circulation?
   (a) English (b) Hindi
   (c) Bengali (d) Tamil

4. Aspect ratio of TV screen is
   (a) 4 : 3 (b) 3 : 4
   (c) 2 : 3 (d) 2 : 4

5. Communication with oneself is known as
   (a) Organisational Communication
   (b) Grapevine Communication
   (c) Interpersonal Communication
   (d) Intrapersonal Communication

6. The term 'SITE' stands for
   (a) Satellite Indian Television Experiment
   (b) Satellite International Television Experiment
   (c) Satellite Instructional Television Experiment
   (d) Satellite Instructional Teachers Education

7. What is the number that comes next in the sequence?
   2, 5, 9, 19, 37, ___
   (a) 76 (b) 74
   (c) 75 (d) 50

8. Find the next letter for the series MPSV.....
   (a) X (b) Y
   (c) Z (d) A

9. If '367' means 'I am happy'; '748' means 'you are sad' and '469' means 'happy and sad' in a given code, then which of the following represents 'and' in that code?
   (a) 3 (b) 6
   (c) 9 (d) 4

10. The basis of the following classification is 'animal', 'man', 'house', 'book', and 'student':
    (a) Definite descriptions
    (b) Proper names
    (c) Descriptive phrases
    (d) Common names

11. **Assertion (A):** The coin when flipped next time will come up tails.
    Reason (R): Because the coin was flipped five times in a row, and each time it came up heads.
    Choose the correct answer from below:
    (a) Both (A) and (R) are true, and (R) is the correct explanation of (A).
    (b) Both (A) and (R) are false, and (R) is the correct explanation of (A).

(c) (A) is doubtful, (R) is true, and (R) is not the correct explanation of (A).
(d) (A) is doubtful, (R) is false, and (R) is the correct explanation of (A).

12. The relation 'is a sister of' is
(a) Non-symmetrical (b) Symmetrical
(c) Asymmetrical (d) Transitive

13. If the proposition "Vegetarians are not meat eaters" is false, then which of the following inferences is correct? Choose from the codes given below:
1. "Some vegetarians are meat eaters" is true.
2. "All vegetarians are meat eaters" is doubtful.
3. "Some vegetarians are not meat eaters" is true.
4. "Some vegetarians are not meat eaters" is doubtful.

Codes:
(a) 1, 2 and 3 (b) 2, 3 and 4
(c) 1, 3 and 4 (d) 1, 2 and 4

14. Determine the nature of the following definition:
'Poor' means having an annual income of ₹ 10,000.
(a) Persuasive (b) Precising
(c) Lexical (d) Stipulative

15. Which one of the following is not an argument?
(a) If today is Tuesday, tomorrow will be Wednesday.
(b) Since today is Tuesday, tomorrow will be Wednesday.
(c) Ram insulted me so I punched him in the nose.
(d) Ram is not at home, so he must have gone to town.

16. Venn diagram is a kind of diagram to
(a) represent and assess the truth of elementary inferences with the help of Boolean Algebra of classes.
(b) represent and assess the validity of elementary inferences with the help of Boolean Algebra of classes.
(c) represent but not assess the validity of elementary inferences with the help of Boolean Algebra of classes.
(d) assess but not represent the validity of elementary inferences with the help of Boolean Algebra of classes.

17. Inductive logic studies the way in which a premise may
(a) support and entail a conclusion
(b) not support but entail a conclusion
(c) neither support nor entail a conclusion
(d) support a conclusion without entailing it

18. Which of the following statements are true? Choose from the codes given below.
1. Some arguments, while not completely valid, are almost valid.
2. A sound argument may be invalid.
3. A cogent argument may have a probably false conclusion.
4. A statement may be true or false.

Codes:
(a) 1 and 2 (b) 1, 3 and 4
(c) Only 4 (d) 3 and 4

19. If the side of the square increases by 40%, then the area of the square increases by
(a) 60% (b) 40%
(c) 196% (d) 96%

20. There are 10 lamps in a hall. Each one of them can be switched on independently. The number of ways in which hall can be illuminated is
(a) 10^2 (b) 1023
(c) 2^{10} (d) 10!

21. How many numbers between 100 and 300 begin or end with 2?
(a) 100 (b) 110
(c) 120 (d) 180

22. In a college having 300 students, every student reads 5 newspapers and every newspaper is read by 60 students. The number of newspapers required is
(a) at least 30 (b) at most 20
(c) exactly 25 (d) exactly 5

The total CO_2 emissions from various sectors are 5 mmt. In the Pie Chart given below, the percentage contribution to CO_2 emissions from various sectors is indicated.

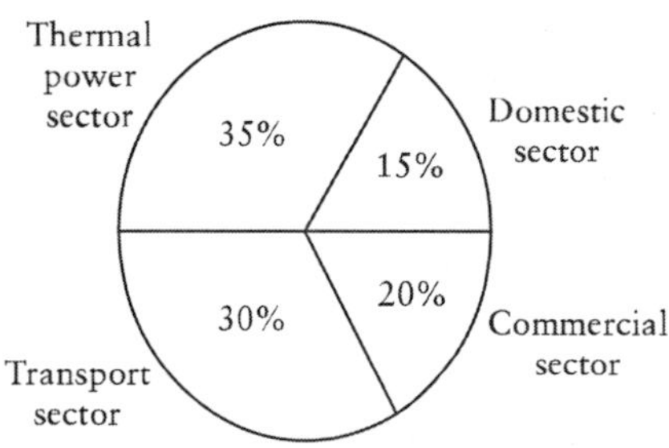

23. What is the absolute CO_2 emission from domestic sector?
(a) 1.5 mmt (b) 2.5 mmt
(c) 1.75 mmt (d) 0.75 mmt

24. What is the absolute CO_2 emission for combined thermal power and transport sectors?
(a) 3.25 mmt (b) 1.5 mmt
(c) 2.5 mmt (d) 4 mmt

25. Which of the following operating system is used on mobile phones?
(a) Windows Vista
(b) Android
(c) Windows XP
(d) All of the above

26. If $(y)_x$ represents a number y in base x, then which of the following numbers is smallest of all?
(a) $(1111)_2$ (b) $(1111)_8$
(c) $(1111)_{10}$ (d) $(1111)_{16}$

27. High-level programming language can be converted to machine language using which of the following?
(a) Oracle (b) Compiler
(c) Mat lab (d) Assembler

28. HTML is used to create
(a) machine language program
(b) high-level program
(c) web page
(d) web server

29. The term DNS stands for
(a) Domain Name System
(b) Defense Nuclear System
(c) Downloadable New Software
(d) Dependent Name Server

30. IPv4 and IPv6 are addresses used to identify computers on the Internet. Find the correct statement out of the following:
(a) Number of bits required for IPv4 address is more than number of bits required for IPv6 address.
(b) Number of bits required for IPv4 address is same as number of bits required for IPv6 address.
(c) Number of bits required for IPv4 address is less than number of bits required for IPv6 address.
(d) Number of bits required for IPv4 address is 64.

31. Which of the following pollutants affects the respiratory tract in humans?
(a) Carbon monoxide
(b) Nitric oxide
(c) Sulphur dioxide
(d) Aerosols

32. Which of the following pollutants is not emitted from the transport sector?
(a) Oxides of nitrogen
(b) Chlorofluorocarbons
(c) Carbon monoxide
(d) Poly aromatic hydrocarbons

33. Which of the following sources of energy has the maximum potential in India?
(a) Solar energy
(b) Wind energy
(c) Ocean thermal energy
(d) Tidal energy

34. Which of the following is not a source of pollution in soil?
(a) Transport sector
(b) Agriculture sector
(c) Thermal power plants
(d) Hydropower plants

35. Which of the following is not a natural hazard?
(a) Earthquake (b) Tsunami
(c) Flash floods (d) Nuclear accident

36. Ecological footprint represents
(a) area of productive land and water to meet the resources requirement
(b) energy consumption
(c) CO_2 emissions per person
(d) forest cover

37. The aim of value education to inculcate in students is
(a) the moral values
(b) the social values
(c) the political values
(d) the economic values

38. Indicate the number of Regional Offices of University Grants Commission of India.
(a) 10 (b) 07
(c) 08 (d) 09

39. One-rupee currency note in India bears the signature of
(a) The President of India
(b) Finance Minister of India
(c) Governor, Reserve Bank of India
(d) Finance Secretary of Government of India

40. Match the List I with the List II and select the correct answer from the codes given below:

List I (Commissions and Committees)
A. First Administrative Reforms Commission
B. Paul H. Appleby Committee I
C. K. Santhanam Committee
D. Second Administrative Reforms Commission

List II (Year)
1. 2005 2. 1962
3. 1966 4. 1953

Codes:	A	B	C	D
(a)	1	3	2	4
(b)	3	4	2	1
(c)	4	2	3	1
(d)	2	1	4	3

41. Constitutionally the registration and recognition of political parties is the function performed by
(a) The State Election Commission of respective States
(b) The Law Ministry of Government of India
(c) The Election Commission of India
(d) Election Department of the State Governments

42. The members of Gram Sabha are
(a) Sarpanch, Upsarpanch and all elected Panchas
(b) Sarpanch, Upsarpanch and Village level worker
(c) Sarpanch, Gram Sevak and elected Panchas
(d) Registered voters of Village Panchayat

43. By which of the following methods the true evaluation of the students is possible?
(a) Evaluation at the end of the course
(b) Evaluation twice in a year
(c) Continuous evaluation
(d) Formative evaluation

44. Suppose a student wants to share his problems with his teacher and he visits the teacher's house for the purpose, the teacher should

(a) contact the student's parents and solve his problem
(b) suggest him that he should never visit his house
(c) suggest him to meet the principal and solve the problem
(d) extend reasonable help and boost his morale

45. When some students are deliberately attempting to disturb the discipline of the class by making mischief, what will be your role as a teacher?
(a) Expelling those students
(b) Isolate those students
(c) Reform the group with your authority
(d) Giving them an opportunity for introspection and improve their behaviour

46. Which of the following belongs to a projected aid?
(a) Blackboard (b) Diorama
(c) Epidiascope (d) Globe

47. A teacher is said to be fluent in asking questions, if he can ask
(a) meaningful questions
(b) as many questions as possible
(c) maximum number of questions in a fixed time
(d) many meaningful questions in a fixed time

48. Which of the following qualities is most essential for a teacher?
(a) He should be a learned person
(b) He should be a well-dressed person
(c) He should have patience
(d) He should be an expert in his subject

49. A hypothesis is a
(a) Law (b) Canon
(c) Postulate (d) Supposition

50. Suppose you want to investigate the working efficiency of nationalised bank in India, which one of the following would you follow?
(a) Area Sampling
(b) Multi-stage Sampling
(c) Sequential Sampling
(d) Quota Sampling

51. Controlled group condition is applied in
(a) Survey Research
(b) Historical Research
(c) Experimental Research
(d) Descriptive Research

52. Workshops are meant for
(a) giving lectures
(b) multiple target groups
(c) showcase new theories
(d) hands on training/experience

53. Which one of the following is a research tool?
(a) Graph (b) Illustration
(c) Questionnaire (d) Diagram

54. Research is not considered ethical if it
(a) tries to prove a particular point.
(b) does not ensure privacy and anonymity of the respondent.
(c) does not investigate the data scientifically.
(d) is not of a very high standard.

Read the following passage carefully and answer the questions (55 to 60):

The catalytic fact of the twentieth century is uncontrollable development, consumerist society, political materialism, and spiritual devaluation. This inordinate development has led to the transcendental 'second reality' of sacred perception that biologically transcendence is a part of human life. As the century closes, it dawns with imperative vigour that the 'first reality' of enlightened rationalism and the 'second reality' of the Beyond have to be harmonised in a worthy state of man. The *de facto* values describe what we are, they portray the 'is' of our ethic, they are *est* values (Latin *est* means is). The ideal values tell us what we ought to be, they are *esto* values (Latin *esto* 'ought to be'). Both have to be in the ebb and flow of consciousness. The ever new science and technology and the ever-perennial faith are two modes of one certainty, that is the wholeness of man, his courage to be, his share in Being.

The materialistic foundations of science have crumbled down. Science itself has proved that matter is energy, processes are as valid as facts, and affirmed the non-materiality of the universe. The encounter of the 'two cultures', the scientific and the humane, will restore the normal vision, and will be the bedrock of a 'science of understanding' in the new century. It will give new meaning to the ancient perception that quantity (measure) and quality (value) coexist at the root of nature. Human endeavours cannot afford to be humanistically irresponsible.

55. The problem raised in the passage reflects overall on
   (a) Consumerism
   (b) Materialism
   (c) Spiritual devaluation
   (d) Inordinate development

56. The *de facto* values in the passage means
   (a) What is
   (b) What ought to be
   (c) What can be
   (d) Where it is

57. According to the passage, the 'first reality' constitutes
   (a) Economic prosperity
   (b) Political development
   (c) Sacred perception of life
   (d) Enlightened rationalism

58. Encounter of the 'two cultures', the scientific and the human implies
   (a) Restoration of normal vision
   (b) Universe is both material and non-material
   (c) Man is superior to nature
   (d) Co-existence of quantity and quality in nature

59. The contents of the passage are
   (a) Descriptive (b) Prescriptive
   (c) Axiomatic (d) Optional

60. The passage indicates that science has proved that
   (a) universe is material
   (b) matter is energy
   (c) nature has abundance
   (d) humans are irresponsible

ANSWERS

1. (a)	2. (b)	3. (b)	4. (a)	5. (d)
6. (c)	7. (c)	8. (b)	9. (c)	10. (d)
11. (c)	12. (b)	13. (a)	14. (b)	15. (a)
16. (b)	17. (d)	18. (d)	19. (d)	20. (b)
21. (b)	22. (c)	23. (d)	24. (a)	25. (b)
26. (a)	27. (b)	28. (c)	29. (a)	30. (c)
31. (a)	32. (b)	33. (b)	34. (d)	35. (d)
36. (a)	37. (a)	38. (b)	39. (d)	40. (b)
41. (c)	42. (d)	43. (d)	44. (d)	45. (d)
46. (c)	47. (d)	48. (c)	49. (d)	50. (b)
51. (c)	52. (d)	53. (c)	54. (b)	55. (c)
56. (a)	57. (d)	58. (a)	59. (a)	60. (b)

JUNE–2011

Note: This paper contains Sixty (60) multiple-choice questions, each question carrying two (2) marks. Candidate is expected to answer any Fifty (50) questions. In case more than Fifty (50) questions are attempted, only the first Fifty (50) questions will be evaluated.

PAPER–I

1. A research paper is a brief report of research work based on
   (a) Primary Data only
   (b) Secondary Data only
   (c) Both Primary and Secondary Data
   (d) None of the above

2. Newton gave three basic laws of motion. This research is categorised as
   (a) Descriptive Research
   (b) Sample Survey
   (c) Fundamental Research
   (d) Applied Research

3. A group of experts in a specific area of knowledge assembled at a place and prepared a syllabus for a new course. The process may be termed as
   (a) Seminar (b) Workshop
   (c) Conference (d) Symposium

4. In the process of conducting research "Formulation of Hypothesis" is followed by
   (a) Statement of Objectives
   (b) Analysis of Data
   (c) Selection of Research Tools
   (d) Collection of Data

Read the following passage carefully and answer questions 5 to 10:

All historians are interpreters of text if they be private letters, Government records or parish birthlists or whatever. For most kinds of historians, these are only the necessary means to understanding something other than the texts themselves, such as a political action or a historical trend, whereas for the intellectual historian, a full understanding of his chosen texts is itself the aim of his enquiries. Of course, the intellectual history is particularly prone to draw on the focus of other disciplines that are habitually interpreting texts for purposes of their own, probing the reasoning that ostensibly connects premises and conclusions. Furthermore, the boundaries with adjacent subdisciplines are shifting and indistinct: the history of art and the history of science both claim a certain autonomy, partly just because they require specialised technical skills, but both can also be seen as part of a wider intellectual history, as is evident when one considers, for example, the common stock of knowledge about cosmological beliefs or moral ideals of a period.

Like all historians, the intellectual historian is a consumer rather than a producer of 'methods'. His distinctiveness lies in which aspect of the past he is trying to illuminate, not in having exclusive possession of either a corpus of evidence or a body of techniques. That being said, it does seem that the label 'intellectual history' attracts a disproportionate share of misunderstanding.

It is alleged that intellectual history is the history of something that never really mattered. The long dominance of the historical profession by political historians bred a kind of philistinism, an unspoken belief that power and its exercise was 'what mattered'. The prejudice was reinforced by the assertion that political action was never really the outcome of principles or ideas that were 'more flapdoodle'. The legacy of this precept is still discernible in the tendency to require ideas to have 'licensed' the political class before they can be deemed worthy of intellectual attention, as if there were some reasons why the history of art or science, of philosophy or literature, were somehow of interest and significance than the history of Parties or Parliaments. Perhaps in recent years the mirror-image of this philistinism has been more common in the claim that ideas of any one is of systematic expression or sophistication do not matter, as if they were only held by a minority.

Answer the following questions:

5. An intellectual historian aims to fully understand
   (a) the chosen texts of his own
   (b) political actions
   (c) historical trends
   (d) his enquiries
6. Intellectual historians do not claim exclusive possession of
   (a) conclusions
   (b) any corpus of evidence
   (c) distinctiveness
   (d) habitual interpretation
7. The misconceptions about intellectual history stem from
   (a) a body of techniques
   (b) the common stock of knowledge
   (c) the dominance of political historians
   (d) cosmological beliefs
8. What is philistinism?
   (a) Reinforcement of prejudice
   (b) Fabrication of reasons
   (c) The hold of land-owning classes
   (d) Belief that power and its exercise matter
9. Knowledge of cosmological beliefs or moral ideas of a period can be drawn as part of
   (a) literary criticism
   (b) history of science
   (c) history of philosophy
   (d) intellectual history
10. The claim that ideas of any one is of systematic expression do not matter, as if they were held by a minority, is
    (a) to have a licensed political class
    (b) a political action
    (c) a philosophy of literature
    (d) the mirror-image of philistinism
11. Public communication tends to occur within a more
    (a) complex structure
    (b) political structure
    (c) convenient structure
    (d) formal structure
12. Transforming thoughts, ideas and messages into verbal and non-verbal signs is referred to as
    (a) Channelisation (b) Mediation
    (c) Encoding (d) Decoding
13. Effective communication needs a supportive
    (a) economic environment
    (b) political environment
    (c) social environment
    (d) multi-cultural environment
14. A major barrier in the transmission of cognitive data in the process of communication is an individual's
    (a) personality (b) expectation
    (c) social status (d) coding ability
15. When communicated, institutionalised stereotypes become
    (a) Myths (b) Reasons
    (c) Experiences (d) Convictions

16. In mass communication, selective perception is dependent on the receiver's
(a) Competence (b) Pre-disposition
(c) Receptivity (d) Ethnicity

17. Determine the relationship between the pair of words NUMERATOR : DENOMINATOR and then select the pair of words from the following which have a similar relationship:
(a) fraction : decimal
(b) divisor : quotient
(c) top : bottom
(d) dividend : divisor

18. Find the wrong number in the sequence
125, 127, 130, 135, 142, 153, 165
(a) 130 (b) 142
(c) 153 (d) 165

19. If HOBBY is coded as IOBY and LOBBY is coded as MOBY; then BOBBY is coded as
(a) BOBY (b) COBY
(c) DOBY (d) OOBY

20. The letters in the first set have certain relationship. On the basis of this relationship, make the right choice for the second set
K/T : 11/20 :: J/R : ?
(a) 10/8 (b) 10/18
(c) 11/19 (d) 10/19

21. If A = 5, B = 6, C = 7, D = 8 and so on, what do the following numbers stand for?
17, 19, 20, 9, 8
(a) Plane (b) Moped
(c) Motor (d) Tonga

22. The price of oil is increased by 25%. If the expenditure is not allowed to increase, the ratio between the reduction in consumption and the original consumption is
(a) 1:3 (b) 1:4
(c) 1:5 (d) 1:6

23. How many 8s are there in the following sequence which are preceded by 5 but not immediately followed by 3?
5 8 3 7 5 8 6 3 8 5 4 5 8 4 7 6
5 5 8 3 5 8 7 5 8 2 8 5
(a) 4 (b) 5
(c) 7 (d) 3

24. If a rectangle were called a circle, a circle a point, a point a triangle and a triangle a square, the shape of a wheel is
(a) Rectangle (b) Circle
(c) Point (d) Triangle

25. Which one of the following methods is best suited for mapping the distribution of different crops as provided in the standard classification of crops in India?
(a) Pie diagram
(b) Chorochromatic technique
(c) Isopleth technique
(d) Dot method

26. Which one of the following does not come under the methods of data classification?
(a) Qualitative (b) Normative
(c) Spatial (d) Quantitative

27. Which one of the following is not a source of data?
(a) Administrative records
(b) Population census
(c) GIS
(d) Sample survey

28. If the statement 'some men are cruel' is false, which of the following statements/statement are/is true?
(i) All men are cruel.
(ii) No men are cruel.
(iii) Some men are not cruel.
(a) (i) and (iii) (b) (i) and (ii)
(c) (ii) and (iii) (d) Only (iii)

29. The octal number system consists of the following symbols
   (a) 0 – 7 (b) 0 – 9
   (c) 0 – 9, A – F (d) None of these

30. The binary equivalent of $(-19)_{10}$ in signed magnitude system is
   (a) 11101100 (b) 11101101
   (c) 10010011 (d) None of these

31. DNS in internet technology stands for
   (a) Dynamic Name System
   (b) Domain Name System
   (c) Distributed Name System
   (d) None of these

32. HTML stands for
   (a) Hyper Text Markup Language
   (b) Hyper Text Manipulation Language
   (c) Hyper Text Managing Links
   (d) Hyper Text Manipulating Links

33. Which of the following is type of LAN?
   (a) Ethernet (b) Token Ring
   (c) FDDI (d) All of the above

34. Which of the following statements is true?
   (a) Smart cards do not require an operating system.
   (b) Smart cards and PCs use some operating system.
   (c) COS is smart card operating system.
   (d) The communication between reader and card is in full duplex mode.

35. The Ganga Action Plan was initiated during the year
   (a) 1986 (b) 1988
   (c) 1990 (d) 1992

36. Identify the correct sequence of energy sources in order of their share in the power sector in India.
   (a) Thermal > nuclear > hydro > wind
   (b) Thermal > hydro > nuclear > wind
   (c) Hydro > nuclear > thermal > wind
   (d) Nuclear > hydro > wind > thermal

37. Chromium as a contaminant in drinking water in excess of permissible levels, causes
   (a) Skeletal damage
   (b) Gastrointestinal problem
   (c) Dermal and nervous problems
   (d) Liver/Kidney problems

38. The main precursors of winter smog are
   (a) N_2O and hydrocarbons
   (b) NO_x and hydrocarbons
   (c) SO_2 and hydrocarbons
   (d) SO_2 and ozone

39. Flash floods are caused when
   (a) the atmosphere is convectively unstable and there is considerable vertical wind shear
   (b) the atmosphere is stable
   (c) the atmosphere is convectively unstable with no vertical windshear
   (d) winds are catabatic

40. In mega cities of India, the dominant source of air pollution is
   (a) transport sector
   (b) thermal power
   (c) municipal waste
   (d) commercial sector

41. The first Open University in India was set up in the State of
   (a) Andhra Pradesh
   (b) Delhi
   (c) Himachal Pradesh
   (d) Tamil Nadu

42. Most of the Universities in India are funded by
   (a) the Central Government
   (b) the State Governments
   (c) the University Grants Commission
   (d) Private bodies and Individuals

43. Which of the following organisations looks after the quality of Technical and Management education in India?
   (a) NCTE (b) MCI
   (c) AICTE (d) CSIR

44. Consider the following statements: Identify the statement which implies natural justice.
    (a) The principle of natural justice is followed by the Courts.
    (b) Justice delayed is justice denied.
    (c) Natural justice is an inalienable right of a citizen.
    (d) A reasonable opportunity of being heard must be given.
45. The President of India is
    (a) the Head of State
    (b) the Head of Government
    (c) both Head of the State and the Head of the Government
    (d) None of the above
46. Who among the following holds office during the pleasure of the President of India?
    (a) Chief Election Commissioner
    (b) Comptroller and Auditor General of India
    (c) Chairman of the Union Public Service Commission
    (d) Governor of a State

Questions 47 to 49 are based upon the following diagram in which there are three interlocking circles A, P and S where A stands for Artists, circle P for Professors and circle S for Sportspersons. Different regions in the figure are lettered from a to f:

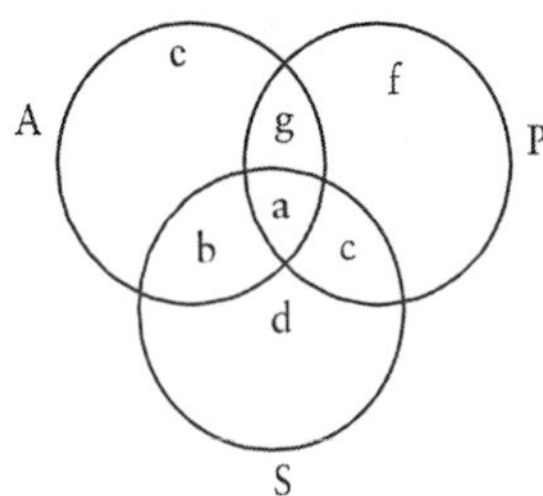

47. The region which represents artists who are neither sportsmen nor professors.
    (a) d (b) e
    (c) b (d) g
48. The region which represents professors, who are both artists and sportspersons.
    (a) a (b) c
    (c) d (d) g
49. The region which represents professors, who are also sportspersons, but not artists.
    (a) e (b) f
    (c) c (d) g

Questions 50 to 52 are based on the following data:

Measurements of some variable X were made at an interval of 1 minute from 10 A.M. to 10:20 A.M. The data, thus, obtained is as follows:

X: 60, 62, 65, 64, 63, 61, 66, 65, 70, 68 63, 62, 64, 69, 65, 64, 66, 67, 66, 64

50. The value of X, which is exceeded 10% of the time in the duration of measurement, is
    (a) 69 (b) 68
    (c) 67 (d) 66
51. The value of X, which is exceeded 90% of the time in the duration of measurement, is
    (a) 63 (b) 62
    (c) 61 (d) 60
52. The value of X, which is exceeded 50% of the time in the duration of measurement, is
    (a) 66 (b) 65
    (c) 64 (d) 63
53. For maintaining an effective discipline in the class, the teacher should
    (a) Allow students to do what they like.
    (b) Deal with the students strictly.
    (c) Give the students some problem to solve.
    (d) Deal with them politely and firmly.
54. An effective teaching aid is one which
    (a) is colourful and good looking
    (b) activates all faculties

(c) is visible to all students
(d) easy to prepare and use

55. Those teachers are popular among students who
(a) develop intimacy with them
(b) help them solve their problems
(c) award good grades
(d) take classes on extra tuition fee

56. The essence of an effective classroom environment is
(a) a variety of teaching aids
(b) lively student-teacher interaction
(c) pin-drop silence
(d) strict discipline

57. On the first day of his class, if a teacher is asked by the students to introduce himself, he should
(a) ask them to meet after the class
(b) tell them about himself in brief
(c) ignore the demand and start teaching
(d) scold the student for this unwanted demand

58. Moral values can be effectively inculcated among the students when the teacher
(a) frequently talks about values
(b) himself practices them
(c) tells stories of great persons
(d) talks of Gods and Goddesses

59. The essential qualities of a researcher are
(a) spirit of free enquiry
(b) reliance on observation and evidence
(c) systematisation or theorising of knowledge
(d) All of the above

60. Research is conducted to
1. Generate new knowledge
2. Not to develop a theory
3. Obtain research degree
4. Reinterpret existing knowledge

Which of the above are correct?
(a) 1, 3 & 2 (b) 3, 2 & 4
(c) 2, 1 & 3 (d) 1, 3 & 4

ANSWERS

1. (c)	2. (c)	3. (b)	4. (c)	5. (a)
6. (b)	7. (c)	8. (d)	9. (d)	10. (d)
11. (d)	12. (c)	13. (d)	14. (c)	15. (d)
16. (b)	17. (d)	18. (d)	19. (b)	20. (b)
21. (b)	22. (c)	23. (a)	24. (c)	25. (a)
26. (b)	27. (a)	28. (b)	29. (a)	30. (d)
31. (b)	32. (a)	33. (d)	34. (c)	35. (a)
36. (b)	37. (d)	38. (c)	39. (a)	40. (a)
41. (a)	42. (c)	43. (c)	44. (d)	45. (b)
46. (d)	47. (b)	48. (a)	49. (c)	50. (c)
51. (b)	52. (d)	53. (d)	54. (b)	55. (b)
56. (b)	57. (b)	58. (b)	59. (d)	60. (d)

PAPER–II

Note: This paper contains fifty (50) objective type questions, each question carrying two (2) marks. Attempt all the questions.

1. The Supreme Court of India has adopted new approach for the interpretation of the concept 'Equality' in
(a) State of West Bengal V. Anwarli Sarkar
(b) EP Royappa V. State of Tamil Nadu
(c) Keshavanand Bharati V. State of Kerala
(d) State of Karnataka V. Appa Balu Ingale

2. In which of the following case the Supreme Court said 'Right to Life does not include Right to Die'?
(a) P. Rathinam V. Union of India
(b) M.C. Mehta V. Union of India

(c) Gan Kaur V. State of Punjab
(d) Sunil Batra V. Superintendent, Delhi Administration

3. Which one of the following privileges is guaranteed to the President of India under Article 361 of the Constitution?
   (a) Not to participate in the Parliamentary proceedings.
   (b) He is answerable to the Chief Justice of India.
   (c) He is not to be answerable to any court during the term of his office.
   (d) Can address both the Houses of Parliament at the time of joint session.

4. Money Bills can be introduced only
   (a) in Rajya Sabha
   (b) in both Houses of Parliament
   (c) in Lok Sabha only
   (d) None of the above

5. Who has the power to dissolve the House of the People?
   (a) The Council of Ministers
   (b) The Prime Minister
   (c) The Speaker of the Lok Sabha
   (d) The President

6. Judicial review in the Indian Constitution is based on
   (a) Procedure established by law
   (b) Due process of law
   (c) Rule of law
   (d) Precedents and Conventions

7. 'Limits of Jurisprudence Defined' written by
   (a) Jeremy Bentham (b) John Austin
   (c) T.E. Holland (d) H.L.A. Hart

8. H.L.A. Hart remarks that Law is a
   (a) Union of primary and secondary rules.
   (b) Union of Public and Private law.
   (c) Union of Central and State law.
   (d) Union of effective rules.

9. The term 'Legal theory' has been first time coined by
   (a) Hans Kelsen
   (b) W. Friedman
   (c) Salmond
   (d) Ronald Dworkin

10. There are ______ theories of punishment.
   (a) two (b) three
   (c) four (d) five

11. Which one of the following statements is true?
   (a) Animus is necessary for the acquisition or commencement of possession.
   (b) Corpus is necessary for the acquisition or commencement of possession.
   (c) Animus and corpus are not necessary for the acquisition or commencement of possession.
   (d) Animus and corpus are necessary for the acquisition or commencement of possession.

12. The 'Will Theory' was criticised by
   (a) Locke (b) Holmes
   (c) Puchta (d) Duguit

13. Boundary delimitation treaties are binding even on non-party states because they are valid ergo omnes. The International Court of Justice held so in
   (a) The Asylum Case
   (b) The case concerning Kasikili/Sedudu Island (Botswana V. Namibia)
   (c) The case concerning the Gabcikobo-Nagymaros Project (Hungary V. Slovakia)
   (d) The Anglo-Norwegian Fisheries case

14. "A treaty is a contract between the Governments of two or more sovereign States." Lord Templeman said so in
   (a) The S.S. Lotus case
   (b) The Gulf of Maine case
   (c) James Buchanan & Co. V. Babco Forwarding and Shipping
   (d) Maclaine Watson V. Dept. of Trade and Industry

15. **Assertion (A):** International Law is generally not enforceable.
Reason (R): International Law is generally observed by States in practice.
Codes:
(a) Both (A) and (R) are true and (R) is the correct explanation of (A).
(b) Both (A) and (R) are true, but (R) is not the correct explanation of (A).
(c) (A) is true, but (R) is false.
(d) (A) is false, but (R) is true.

16. Match List I with List II and select the correct answer using the codes given below:
List I (Themes)
I. Unilateral statements can become legally binding
II. Arbitration
III. International Organizations as a subject of International Law
IV. Concept of subrogation
List II (Decisions)
1. Island of Palmas case
2. Nuclear Test cases
3. Mavrommatis Palestine Concessions case
4. Advisory opinion on the legality of the threat or use of Nuclear Weapons.

Codes:	I	II	III	IV
(a)	1	2	3	4
(b)	2	3	4	1
(c)	2	1	4	3
(d)	3	2	1	4

17. According to proponents of dualism both international law and municipal law differ
1. terms of their subjects
2. terms of their basis
3. terms of binding nature
4. terms of their existence
Codes:
(a) 1, 2 and 3 are correct.
(b) 2, 3 and 4 are correct.
(c) 1 and 2 are correct.
(d) 2 and 4 are correct.

18. An interim Government of Lomalia seeks control over certain funds belonging to the Republic of Lomalia. Lomalia is at present in a state of civil war, with no faction in effective control of the State. The court asks the foreign office to give its opinion on status of the interim Government and the foreign office informs the Court that the U.K. no longer recognized the Government and that the attitude of the government is to be inferred from the nature of its dealings with the regime concerned on a Government to Government basis. In this circumstance the Court can decide the case by relying on
(a) the doctrine of de facto recognition
(b) the doctrine of de jure recognition
(c) the doctrine of rebus sic stantibus
(d) the doctrine of legality, effectiveness and in marginal cases, recognition

19. Consider the following Propositions.
I. A void marriage remains valid until a decree annulling it has been passed by a competent court.
II. A void marriage is never a valid marriage and there is no necessity of any decree annulling it.
III. A voidable marriage is regarded as a valid marriage until a decree annulling it has been passed by a competent court.
Codes:
(a) I, II and III are correct.
(b) I and II are correct.
(c) II and III are correct.
(d) I and III are correct.

20. Where the marriage has not been consummated, Iddat has to be observed in case of

(a) Death
(b) Divorce
(c) Both death and divorce
(d) Neither death nor divorce

21. Now a marriage solemnised between any two persons in violation of the requirement of age may be
(a) Valid (b) Void
(c) Voidable (d) All of above

22. A child may be given in adoption by the
(a) Father (b) Mother
(c) Guardian (d) All the above

23. "Marriages of all persons who are citizens of India belonging to various religions should be made compulsorily registerable in their respective States where the marriage is solemnized." This was held by the Supreme Court in case of
(a) John Vallamattom V. U.O.I.
(b) Seema V. Ashwani Kumar
(c) Githa Hariharan V. R.B.I.
(d) A. Jayachandra V. Aneel Kaur

24. To mature as a ground of divorce, the desertion under the Hindu Marriage Act, 1955 must continue for a minimum period of
(a) One year (b) Two years
(c) Three years (d) Four years

25. An agreement enforceable at law is a
(a) Legal agreement
(b) Moral agreement
(c) Acceptance
(d) Contract

26. Every promise and every set of promises, forming the consideration for each other is
(a) Contract (b) Offer
(c) Acceptance (d) Agreement

27. Void agreement signifies
(a) Illegal agreement
(b) Legally unenforceable agreement
(c) Agreement without contract
(d) Agreement without substance

28. An agreement obtained by coercion is
(a) Void (b) Voidable
(c) Valid (d) Illegal

29. An agreement shall be void on account of
(a) Mistake of law
(b) Mistake of fact by one party
(c) Mistake of fact by both the parties
(d) Mistake apparent on face of record

30. A contingent contract
(a) becomes void when the event becomes impossible
(b) is voidable
(c) is void
(d) never becomes void

31. A, a competent contractor, constructed a reservoir of water for the mill of B. During the construction of the reservoir, A came across some old shafts and tunnels, but he did not get them blocked. When the reservoir was filled, the water burst through the old shafts and tunnels flooding the nearby mines of C. C sued B. What defences, if any, are available to B?
(a) Inevitable accident
(b) If any negligence has been committed, it is by A and not by B.
(c) B has no defence. He is responsible for the escape of water.
(d) Third Party's negligence.

32. Give the correct response.
(a) The liability of master and servant is joint.
(b) The liability of master and servant is several.
(c) The liability of master and servant is joint and several.
(d) The liability of master and servant is joint and several in exceptional cases.

33. Match the following:
(A) Common employment
(B) Respondent superior
(C) Agreement to injure the other in the trade
(D) Egg-shell skull rule
1. Conspiracy
2. Master and servant
3. Servant and servant
4. Tort feasor takes his victim as he finds

Codes:	(A)	(B)	(C)	(D)
(a)	3	2	1	4
(b)	3	2	4	1
(c)	2	3	4	1
(d)	2	3	1	4

34. Generally mens-rea is an essential element in a criminal offence. Mens-rea in tort.
(a) is relevant and crucial
(b) has no relevance whatsoever
(c) is generally not important
(d) is relevant in certain tortious actions

35. Last Opportunity Rule is associated with
(a) Remoteness of damage
(b) Volunti nor fit injuria
(c) Contributory negligence
(d) Negligence

36. Give the correct match:

I
(A) Act of God
(B) Remoteness of damage
(C) Act of State
(D) Negligence

II
1. Secretary of State for India vs Hari Bhaji
2. Nichols Vs. Marsland
3. Donoghue Vs. Stevenson
4. Smith Vs. Lindon & South Western Rly. Co.

Codes:	(A)	(B)	(C)	(D)
(a)	3	1	2	4
(b)	2	4	1	3
(c)	1	2	3	4
(d)	4	3	2	1

37. The chief elements of crime are
(a) To act in a particular way otherwise to undergo punishment
(b) An act committed or omitted in furtherance of criminal intent
(c) An act causing injury to another individual or society
(d) All the above

38. Wantonly means
(a) Things done recklessly
(b) Things done malignantly
(c) Acts done through mischief
(d) All the above

39. The law on bigamy does not apply where
(a) There was no mens rea
(b) Bona fide reasons to believe that the spouse was dead
(c) The other spouse was living in a shared house
(d) None of the above

40. Loosing wrongfully means
(a) When the property is put to auction.
(b) When such person is wrongfully deprived of property.
(c) When such person is wrongfully kept out of the property.
(d) All the above.

41. Denotion of mens rea is inferred through
(a) Reason to believe
(b) Voluntarily
(c) Dishonestly
(d) All the above

42. Right to private defence is not available on
(a) All acts of self-defence
(b) All acts of aggression

(c) All acts where danger is sensed
(d) All the above

43. In which of the following cases the GHERAO was declared illegal?
(a) Bangalore Water Supply & Sewerage Board V. Rajappa
(b) Jay Engneering Works Ltd. V. State of West Bengal
(c) Hindustan Motors Ltd. V. Tapan Kumar
(d) O.P. Gupta V. Union of India

44. Retrenchment means
(a) Voluntary retirement of workman
(b) Termination of the service of a workman on the ground of continued ill-health
(c) Termination by the employer of the service of workman for any reason whatsoever
(d) Termination of the service of the workman as a result of the non-renewal of the contract of employment

45. How many members may apply for registration of trade union under the Trade Union Act, 1926?
(a) Two or more
(b) Five or more
(c) Ten or more
(d) Seven or more

46. Contribution to political fund of trade union is
(a) compulsory for all members
(b) not compulsory for all members
(c) compulsory for office bearer
(d) compulsory, if employer wants

Read the following paragraph and answer the Question Nos. 47 to 50:

Broadly speaking, legal theory involves a study of the characteristic features essential to law and common to legal systems and analysis of the basic elements of law which made it law and distinguish it from other forms of rules and standards, from systems which cannot be described as legal systems and from other social phenomena. In fact, it is not possible to reach our dogmatic answer to the question 'what is law' or provide exclusive answers to many questions which are asked about its essential nature. The nature of legal theory lies in a study of the light which other theories may shed on the distinctive attributes of law, by an examination of the relative merits and demerits of the principal expositions of the subject. In the same strain Friedman says, 'legal theory' is linked at one end with philosophy and, at other end, with political theory. Sometimes, the starting point is philosophy and political ideology plays a secondary part.... Sometimes the theory of knowledge and political ideology are welded into one coherent system, of course, it is true that some legal philosophies have been philosophers first and foremost and jurists incidentally and other politicians first and foremost and jurists because they felt the need to express their political thought in legal form.... In short, before the nineteenth century legal theory was essentially a by-product of philosophy, religion, ethics or politics. The new era of legal philosophy arises mainly from the confrontation of professional lawyers, in his legal work, with problems of social justice. The modern jurists legal theory, no less than scholastic philosopher's, is based on ultimate beliefs whose inspiration comes from outside the law itself. In the light of above, answer the following:

47. As the science of law or philosophy of law emerged, which of the following approach came into existence?
(a) Analytical positivist approach
(b) Realist approach
(c) Socio-logical approach
(d) Historical approach

48. Law must remain free from social sciences, metaphysical, ethical and moral elements. This was propounded by
(a) Hart (b) Bentham
(c) Salmond (d) Kelson

49. Law is always in a state of continual change. This is the basic tenet of
(a) Sociological jurisprudence
(b) Historical jurisprudence
(c) Realist jurisprudence
(d) Philosophical school

50. Who defined jurisprudence as a formal science of positive law?
(a) Austin (b) Salmond
(c) Holland (d) Hobbes

ANSWERS

1. (c)	2. (a)	3. (c)	4. (c)	5. (d)
6. (a)	7. (a)	8. (a)	9. (d)	10. (c)
11. (d)	12. (d)	13. (a)	14. (d)	15. (b)
16. (c)	17. (b)	18. (d)	19. (c)	20. (b)
21. (b)	22. (d)	23. (b)	24. (d)	25. (a)
26. (c)	27. (b)	28. (d)	29. (d)	30. (a)
31. (c)	32. (b)	33. (b)	34. (d)	35. (c)
36. (b)	37. (d)	38. (d)	39. (b)	40. (b)
41. (d)	42. (d)	43. (b)	44. (c)	45. (a)
46. (a)	47. (c)	48. (d)	49. (c)	50. (b)

DECEMBER–2012

Note: This paper contains Sixty (60) multiple-choice questions, each question carrying two (2) marks. Candidate is expected to answer any Fifty (50) questions. In case more than Fifty (50) questions are attempted, only the first Fifty (50) questions will be evaluated.

PAPER–I

1. The English word 'Communication' is derived from the words
   (a) Communis and Communicare
   (b) Communist and Commune
   (c) Communism and Communalism
   (d) Communion and Common sense

2. Chinese Cultural Revolution leader Mao Zedong used a type of communication to talk to the masses is known as
   (a) Mass line communication
   (b) Group communication
   (c) Participatory communication
   (d) Dialogue communication

3. Conversing with the spirits and ancestors is termed as
   (a) Transpersonal communication
   (b) Intrapersonal communication
   (c) Interpersonal communication
   (d) Face-to-face communication

4. The largest circulated daily newspaper among the following is
   (a) *The Times of India*
   (b) *The Indian Express*
   (c) *The Hindu*
   (d) *The Deccan Herald*

5. The pioneer of the silent feature film in India was
   (a) K.A. Abbas
   (b) Satyajit Ray
   (c) B.R. Chopra
   (d) Dada Sahib Phalke

6. Classroom communication of a teacher rests on the principle of
   (a) Infotainment (b) Edutainment
   (c) Entertainment (d) Power equation

7. The missing number in the series:
   0, 6, 24, 60, 120, ?, 336, is
   (a) 240 (b) 220
   (c) 280 (d) 210

8. A group of 7 members having a majority of boys is to be formed out of 6 boys and 4 girls. The number of ways the group can be formed is
   (a) 80 (b) 100
   (c) 90 (d) 110

9. The number of observations in a group is 40. The average of the first 10 members is 4.5 and the average of the remaining 30 members is 3.5. The average of the whole group is
   (a) 4 (b) 15/2
   (c) 15/4 (d) 6

10. If MOHAN is represented by the code KMFYL, then COUNT will be represented by
    (a) AMSLR (b) MSLAR
    (c) MASRL (d) SAMLR

11. The sum of the ages of two persons A and B is 50. 5 years ago, the ratio of their

ages was 5/3. The present age of A and B are

(a) 30, 20 (b) 35, 15
(c) 38, 12 (d) 40, 10

12. Let a means minus (–), b means multiplied by (×), C means divided by (÷) and D means plus (+). The value of 90 D 9 a 29 C 10 b 2 is

(a) 8 (b) 10
(c) 12 (d) 14

13. Consider the Assertion I and Assertion II and select the right code given below:

Assertion I: Even Bank-lockers are not safe. Thieves can break them and take away your wealth. But thieves cannot go to heaven. So you should keep your wealth in heaven.

Assertion II: The difference of skin-colour of beings is because of the distance from the sun and not because of some permanent traits. Skin-colour is the result of body's reaction to the sun and its rays.

Codes:

(a) Both the assertions I and II are forms of argument.
(b) The assertion I is an argument but the assertion II is not.
(c) The assertion II is an argument but the assertion I is not.
(d) Both the assertions are explanations of facts.

14. By which of the following proposition, the proposition 'some men are not honest' is contradicted?

(a) All men are honest.
(b) Some men are honest.
(c) No men are honest.
(d) All of the above.

15. A stipulative definition is

(a) always true
(b) always false
(c) sometimes true sometimes false
(d) neither true nor false

16. Choose the appropriate alternative given in the codes to replace the question mark.
Examiner – Examinee, Pleader – Client, Preceptor – ?

(a) Customer (b) Path-finder
(c) Perceiver (d) Disciple

17. If the statement 'most of the students are obedient' is taken to be true, which one of the following pair of statements can be claimed to be true?

I. All obedient persons are students.
II. All students are obedient.
III. Some students are obedient.
IV. Some students are not disobedient.

Codes:

(a) I & II (b) II & III
(c) III & IV (d) II & IV

18. Choose the right code:
A deductive argument claims that:

I. The conclusion does not claim something more than that which is contained in the premises.
II. The conclusion is supported by the premise/premises conclusively.
III. If the conclusion is false, then premise/premises may be either true or false.
IV. If premise/combination of premises is true, then conclusion must be true.

Codes:

(a) I and II (b) I and III
(c) II and III (d) All the above

On the basis of the data given in the following table, give answers to questions from 19 to 24:

Government Expenditures on Social Services
(As percent of total expenditure)

Sl.No.	Items	2007-08	2008-09	2009-10	2010-11
	Social Services	11.06	12.94	13.06	14.02
(a)	Education, sports & youth affairs	4.02	4.04	3.96	4.46
(b)	Health & family welfare	2.05	1.91	1.90	2.03
(c)	Water supply, housing, etc.	2.02	2.31	2.20	2.27
(d)	Information & broadcasting	0.22	0.22	0.20	0.22
(e)	Welfare to SC/ST & OBC	0.36	0.35	0.41	0.63
(f)	Labour and employment	0.27	0.27	0.22	0.25
(g)	Social welfare & nutrition	0.82	0.72	0.79	1.06
(h)	North-eastern areas	0.00	1.56	1.50	1.75
(i)	Other social services	1.29	1.55	1.87	1.34
	Total Government expenditure	100.00	100.00	100.00	100.00

19. How many activities in the social services are there where the expenditure has been less than 5 percent of the total expenditures incurred on the social services in 2008-09?
(a) One (b) Three
(c) Five (d) All the above

20. In which year, the expenditures on the social services have increased at the highest rate?
(a) 2007-08 (b) 2008-09
(c) 2009-10 (d) 2010-11

21. Which of the following activities remains almost stagnant in terms of share of expenditures?
(a) North-eastern areas
(b) Welfare to SC/ST & OBC
(c) Information & broadcasting
(d) Social welfare and nutrition

22. Which of the following item's expenditure share is almost equal to the remaining three items in the given years?
(a) Information & broadcasting
(b) Welfare to SC/ST and OBC
(c) Labour and employment
(d) Social welfare & nutrition

23. Which of the following items of social services has registered the highest rate of increase in expenditures during 2007-08 to 2010-11?
(a) Education, sports & youth affairs
(b) Welfare to SC/ST & OBC
(c) Social welfare & nutrition
(d) Overall social services

24. Which of the following items has registered the highest rate of decline in terms of expenditure during 2007-08 to 2009-10?
(a) Labour and employment
(b) Health & family welfare
(c) Social welfare & nutrition
(d) Education, sports & youth affairs

25. ALU stands for
(a) American Logic Unit
(b) Alternate Local Unit
(c) Alternating Logic Unit
(d) Arithmetic Logic Unit

26. A Personal Computer uses a number of chips mounted on a circuit board called
(a) Microprocessor (b) System Board
(c) Daughter Board (d) Mother Board

27. Computer Virus is a
    (a) Hardware (b) Bacteria
    (c) Software (d) None of these

28. Which one of the following is correct?
    (a) $(17)_{10} = (17)_{16}$
    (b) $(17)_{10} = (17)_{8}$
    (c) $(17)_{10} = (10111)_{2}$
    (d) $(17)_{10} = (10001)_{2}$

29. The file extension of MS-Word document in Office 2007 is ______.
    (a) .pdf (b) .doc
    (c) .docx (d) .txt

30. ______ is a protocol used by e-mail clients to download e-mails to your computer.
    (a) TCP (b) FTP
    (c) SMTP (d) POP

31. Which of the following is a source of methane?
    (a) Wetlands
    (b) Foam Industry
    (c) Thermal Power Plants
    (d) Cement Industry

32. 'Minamata disaster' in Japan was caused by pollution due to
    (a) Lead (b) Mercury
    (c) Cadmium (d) Zinc

33. Biomagnification means increase in the
    (a) concentration of pollutants in living organisms
    (b) number of species
    (c) size of living organisms
    (d) biomass

34. Nagoya Protocol is related to
    (a) Climate change
    (b) Ozone depletion
    (c) Hazardous waste
    (d) Biodiversity

35. The second most important source after fossil fuels contributing to India's energy needs is
    (a) Solar energy (b) Nuclear energy
    (c) Hydropower (d) Wind energy

36. In case of earthquakes, an increase of magnitude 1 on Richter Scale implies
    (a) a ten-fold increase in the amplitude of seismic waves.
    (b) a ten-fold increase in the energy of the seismic waves.
    (c) two-fold increase in the amplitude of seismic waves.
    (d) two-fold increase in the energy of seismic waves.

37. Which of the following is not a measure of Human Development Index?
    (a) Literacy Rate
    (b) Gross Enrolment
    (c) Sex Ratio
    (d) Life Expectancy

38. India has the highest number of students in colleges after
    (a) the U.K. (b) the U.S.A.
    (c) Australia (d) Canada

39. Which of the following statement(s) is/are not correct about the Attorney General of India?
    1. The President appoints a person, who is qualified to be a Judge of a High Court, to be the Attorney General of India.
    2. He has the right of audience in all the Courts of the country.
    3. He has the right to take part in the proceedings of the Lok Sabha and the Rajya Sabha.
    4. He has a fixed tenure.

    Select the correct answer from the codes given below:

    Codes:
    (a) 1 and 4 (b) 2, 3 and 4
    (c) 3 and 4 (d) 3 only

40. Which of the following prefix President Pranab Mukherjee desires to be discontinued while interacting with Indian dignitaries as well as in official notings?

1. His Excellency 2. Mahamahim
3. Hon'ble 4. Shri/Smt.

Select the correct answer from the codes given below:

Codes:

(a) 1 and 3 (b) 2 and 3
(c) 1 and 2 (d) 1, 2 and 3

41. Which of the following can be done under conditions of financial emergency?
   1. State Legislative Assemblies can be abolished.
   2. Central Government can acquire control over the budget and expenditure of States.
   3. Salaries of the Judges of the High Courts and the Supreme Court can be reduced.
   4. Right to Constitutional Remedies can be suspended.

   Select the correct answer from the codes given below:

   Codes:

   (a) 1, 2 and 3 (b) 2, 3 and 4
   (c) 1 and 2 (d) 2 and 3

42. Match List I with List II and select the correct answer from the codes given below:

   List I
   (A) Poverty Reduction Programme
   (B) Human Development Scheme
   (C) Social Assistance Scheme
   (D) Minimum Need Scheme

   List II
   (i) Mid-day Meals
   (ii) Indira Awas Yojana (IAY)
   (iii) National Old Age Pension (NOAP)
   (iv) MNREGA

Codes:	(A)	(B)	(C)	(D)
(a)	(iv)	(i)	(iii)	(ii)
(b)	(ii)	(iii)	(iv)	(i)
(c)	(iii)	(iv)	(i)	(ii)
(d)	(iv)	(iii)	(ii)	(i)

43. For an efficient and durable learning, learner should have
   (a) ability to learn only
   (b) requisite level of motivation only
   (c) opportunities to learn only
   (d) desired level of ability and motivation

44. Classroom communication must be
   (a) Teacher centric
   (b) Student centric
   (c) General centric
   (d) Textbook centric

45. The best method of teaching is to
   (a) impart information
   (b) ask students to read books
   (c) suggest good reference material
   (d) initiate a discussion and participate in it

46. Interaction inside the classroom should generate
   (a) Argument (b) Information
   (c) Ideas (d) Controversy

47. "Spare the rod and spoil the child", gives the message that
   (a) punishment in the class should be banned.
   (b) corporal punishment is not acceptable.
   (c) undesirable behaviour must be punished.
   (d) children should be beaten with rods.

48. The type of communication that the teacher has in the classroom, is termed as
   (a) Interpersonal
   (b) Mass communication
   (c) Group communication
   (d) Face-to-face communication

49. Which one of the following is an indication of the quality of a research journal?
   (a) Impact factor (b) h-index
   (c) g-index (d) i10-index

50. Good 'research ethics' means
   (a) Not disclosing the holdings of shares/ stocks in a company that sponsors your research.
   (b) Assigning a particular research problem to one Ph.D./research student only.
   (c) Discussing with your colleagues confidential data from a research paper that you are reviewing for an academic journal.
   (d) Submitting the same research manuscript for publishing in more than one journal.

51. Which of the following sampling methods is based on probability?
   (a) Convenience sampling
   (b) Quota sampling
   (c) Judgement sampling
   (d) Stratified sampling

52. Which one of the following references is written according to American Psychological Association (APA) format?
   (a) Sharma, V. (2010). Fundamentals of Computer Science.
   New Delhi: Tata McGraw Hill
   (b) Sharma, V. 2010. Fundamentals of Computer Science.
   New Delhi: Tata McGraw Hill
   (c) Sharma.V. 2010. Fundamentals of Computer Science,
   New Delhi: Tata McGraw Hill
   (d) Sharma, V. (2010), Fundamentals of Computer Science,
   New Delhi: Tata McGraw Hill

53. Arrange the following steps of research in correct sequence:
   1. Identification of research problem
   2. Listing of research objectives
   3. Collection of data
   4. Methodology
   5. Data analysis
   6. Results and discussion

   (a) 1, 2, 3, 4, 5, 6 (b) 1, 2, 4, 3, 5, 6
   (c) 2, 1, 3, 4, 5, 6 (d) 2, 1, 4, 3, 5, 6

54. Identify the incorrect statement:
   (a) A hypothesis is made on the basis of limited evidence as a starting point for further investigations.
   (b) A hypothesis is a basis for reasoning without any assumption of its truth.
   (c) Hypothesis is a proposed explanation for a phenomenon.
   (d) Scientific hypothesis is a scientific theory.

Read the following passage carefully and answer the questions (55 to 60):

The popular view of towns and cities in developing countries and of urbanization process is that despite the benefits and comforts it brings, the emergence of such cities connotes environmental degradation, generation of slums and squatters, urban poverty, unemployment, crimes, lawlessness, traffic chaos, etc. But what is the reality? Given the unprecedental increase in urban population over the last 50 years from 300 million in 1950 to 2 billion in 2000 in developing countries, the wonder really is how well the world has coped, and not how badly.

In general, the urban quality of life has improved in terms of availability of water and sanitation, power, health and education, communication and transport. By way of illustration, a large number of urban residents have been provided with improved water in urban areas in Asia's largest countries such as China, India, Indonesia and Philippines. Despite that, the access to improved water in terms of percentage of total urban population seems to have declined during the last decade of 20th century, though in absolute numbers, millions of additional urbanites, have been provided improved services. These countries have made significant progress in the provision of sanitation services too, together, providing for an additional population of more than 293 million citizens within a decade (1990-2000). These improvements must be viewed against the backdrop of rapidly increasing urban population, fiscal crunch and strained human resources and efficient and quality-oriented public management.

55. The popular view about the process of urbanization in developing countries is
    (a) Positive (b) Negative
    (c) Neutral (d) Unspecified
56. The average annual increase in the number of urbanites in developing countries, from 1950 to 2000 A.D. was close to
    (a) 30 million (b) 40 million
    (c) 50 million (d) 60 million
57. The reality of urbanization is reflected in
    (a) How well the situation has been managed.
    (b) How badly the situation has gone out of control.
    (c) How fast has been the tempo of urbanization.
    (d) How fast the environment has degraded.
58. Which one of the following is not considered as an indicator of urban quality of life?
    (a) Tempo of urbanization
    (b) Provision of basic services
    (c) Access to social amenities
    (d) All of the above
59. The author in this passage has tried to focus on
    (a) Extension of Knowledge
    (b) Generation of Environmental Consciousness
    (c) Analytical Reasoning
    (d) Descriptive Statement
60. In the above passage, the author intends to state
    (a) The hazards of the urban life
    (b) The sufferings of the urban life
    (c) The awareness of human progress
    (d) The limits to growth

ANSWERS

1. (a)	2. (d)	3. (a)	4. (a)	5. (d)
6. (b)	7. (d)	8. (b)	9. (c)	10. (a)
11. (a)	12. (d)	13. (a)	14. (a)	15. (d)
16. (dc)	17. (c)	18. (d)	19. (d)	20. (d)
21. (c)	22. (d)	23. (d)	24. (b)	25. (d)
26. (d)	27. (c)	28. (d)	29. (b)	30. (d)
31. (a)	32. (b)	33. (a)	34. (d)	35. (c)
36. (a)	37. (c)	38. (b)	39. (d)	40. (c)
41. (c)	42. (a)	43. (d)	44. (b)	45. (d)
46. (c)	47. (c)	48. (c)	49. (a)	50. (a)
51. (d)	52. (a)	53. (b)	54. (d)	55. (b)
56. (a)	57. (a)	58. (a)	59. (d)	60. (d)

PAPER–II

Note: This paper contains fifty (50) objective type questions of two (2) marks each. All questions are compulsory.

1. Clause (4) of Article 15 has been added to the Constitution by
    (a) The Constitution First Amendment Act.
    (b) The Constitution Second Amendment Act.
    (c) The Constitution Fourth Amendment Act.
    (d) The Constitution Sixth Amendment Act.

2. The State shall endeavour to secure for the citizens a Uniform Civil Code throughout the territory of India as per
   (a) Article 40 (b) Article 43
   (c) Article 44 (d) Article 48

3. In India sovereignty lies with
   (a) The Constitution
   (b) The Supreme Court
   (c) The Parliament
   (d) The People

4. The Supreme Court of India formulated the doctrine of eclipse in
   (a) Bhikaji Narain Dhakras Vs State of M.P.
   (b) Bashesharnath Vs Income Tax Commissioner.
   (c) State of W.B. Vs Anwar Ali Sarka.
   (d) Maneka Gandhi Vs Union of India

5. The satisfaction of the President means the satisfaction of the Council of Ministers and not his personal satisfaction, held in
   (a) Samsher Singh Vs State of Punjab
   (b) U.N. Rao Vs Indira Gandhi
   (c) Ram Jawaya Kapoor Vs State of Punjab
   (d) Sardar Lal Vs Union Government

6. "The Concurrent List was described as a 'Twilight Zone', as it were for both the Union and the States are competent to legislate in this field without coming in to conflict" is stated by
   (a) Basu, D.D. (b) Dicey, A.V.
   (c) Pyle, M.V. (d) Ambedkar, B.

7. Article 360 has been invoked
   (a) only one time.
   (b) two times.
   (c) three times.
   (d) never invoked.

8. "Jurisprudence is concerned primarily with the effects of law upon society and only to a lesser extent with questions about the social determination of law." Who said it?
   (a) Roscoe Pound (b) Eugen Ehrlich
   (c) Emile Durkheim (d) Max Weber

9. "True law is that which has right reason in agreement with nature" was propagated by
   (a) Cicero (b) Hart
   (c) Grotius (d) Salmond

10. Match List I with List II and select the correct answer using the codes given below the lists:

    List I
    I. Privilege II. Duty
    III. Power IV. Absolute Duty

    List II
    A. Gives content to the claim of a person
    B. Freedom from claim of another
    C. Have no correlative claim according to Austin
    D. Ability of a person to change legal relations

Codes:	**I**	**II**	**III**	**IV**
(a)	A	B	D	C
(b)	B	A	D	C
(c)	A	B	C	D
(d)	B	A	C	D

11. 'X' a servant finds a bag at the basement of the shop. He hands it over to 'Y' the owner of the shop, who asks him to place it in the almirah. Now, the bag is in possession of
    (a) 'X' because he was the finder.
    (b) 'Y' because he was the owner of the shop.
    (c) 'X' because he has kept it in the almirah.
    (d) 'Y' because in him there was union of corpus and animus.

12. Which one of the following jurists emphasised that "We cannot understand

what a thing is unless we study what it does"?
(a) Salmond (b) Roscoe Pound
(c) Kelsen (d) Austin

13. Who defines "ownership as planary control over an object"?
(a) Austin (b) Salmond
(c) Holland (d) Savigny

14. **Assertion (A):** A legal right is a legally protected interest.
Reason (R): An element of advantage is essential to constitute right.
Codes:
(a) Both (A) and (R) are true, and (R) is the correct explanation of (A).
(b) Both (A) and (R) are true, but (R) is not correct explanation of (A).
(c) (A) is true, but (R) is false.
(d) (A) is false, but (R) is true.

15. **Assertion (A):** International Law Commission has initiated studies and prepared draft codes on diverse fields in international law.
Reason (R): International Law Commission was established under General Assembly Resolution No. 174 (11) adopted on 21 November 1947 with an object to promote, progressively develop and codify international law.
Codes:
(a) Both (A) and (R) are true.
(b) (A) is true but (R) is false.
(c) (R) is true but (A) is false.
(d) Both (A) and (R) are false.

16. Match List I with List II.
List I Declaration/Treaty/Convention
(A) Universal Declaration of Human Rights
(B) International Convention on Civil and Political Rights
(C) Convention on the Rights of the Child
(D) Convention on the Rights of Persons with Disabilities

List II Year of Adoption
i. 1948 ii. 1966
iii. 2006 iv. 1999

Codes:	A	B	C	D
(a)	i	ii	iv	iii
(b)	ii	i	iv	iii
(c)	iv	iii	ii	i
(d)	iii	ii	iv	i

17. Jus Cogens means
(a) Peremptory norm of international law.
(b) Norm of international law.
(c) Peremptory norm which does not permit derogation.
(d) None of the above.

18. Which one of the following is primary source of international law?
(a) Decisions of International Court of Justice.
(b) Resolutions of U.N. General Assembly.
(c) General Principles of law recognized by Civilized Nations.
(d) None of the above.

19. Which one of the following is not a permanent member of the U.N. Security Council?
(a) U.K. (b) U.S.A.
(c) Japan (d) China

20. "Recognition operates retroactively not to invalidate the acts of a former government, but to validate the acts of a *de facto* government which has become the new *de jure* government." has been held by the court in the case of:
(a) Civil Air Transport Inc. Vs Central Air Transport Corporation.
(b) A.M. Luther Vs Sagar & Co.
(c) The Arantzazu Mendi.
(d) Gdynia Ameryka Linie Vs Boguslawski.

21. Rules relating to sapinda relationship are based on

(a) Principle of Endogamy
(b) Principle of Exogamy
(c) Principle of Polygamy
(d) Principle of Monogamy

22. On the ground of barrenness or sterility, marriage can be
(a) voidable
(b) void
(c) Both (a) and (b)
(d) Neither (a) nor (b)

23. Breakdown theory of divorce is reflected in
(a) Section 13 (1) of Hindu Marriage Act, 1955.
(b) Section 13 (2) of Hindu Marriage Act, 1955.
(c) Section 13 (IA) of Hindu Marriage Act, 1955.
(d) Section 13 (B) of Hindu Marriage Act, 1955.

24. Match List I with List II and indicate the correct answer using the codes given below:

List I
(A) Ashok Hura Vs Rupa Hura case
(B) Bipin Chandra Vs Prabhavati
(C) Sarla Mudugal Vs Union of India
(D) T. Sareetha Vs State of A.P.

List II
i. Restitution of Conjugal Rights
ii. Uniform Civil Code
iii. Dessertion
iv. Divorce by Mutual Consent

Codes:	(A)	(B)	(C)	(D)
(a)	i	ii	iii	iv
(b)	iv	iii	ii	i
(c)	ii	iii	i	iv
(d)	iv	iii	i	ii

25. Arrange the grounds of divorce in the order in which they appear in the Hindu Marriage Act, 1955. Use the codes given below:
(I) Mutual consent (II) Break down
(III) Fault (IV) Customary

Codes:

(a)	III	II	I	IV
(b)	II	III	IV	I
(c)	I	II	III	IV
(d)	IV	III	I	II

26. The petition for divorce by mutual consent may be presented if the spouses have been living separately for a period of
(a) One year (b) Two years
(c) Three years (d) None of these

27. An offer and an acceptance to it must be in the
(a) same time (b) same place
(c) same sense (d) none of above

28. Which of the following statements are true?
(i) Past consideration is no consideration under Indian and English Law.
(ii) Past consideration is no consideration under Indian Law.
(iii) Past consideration is no consideration under English Law.
(iv) Past consideration is made in past.

Codes:
(a) (i) and (ii) (b) (ii) and (iii)
(c) (iii) and (iv) (d) (iv) and (i)

29. **Assertion (A):** When subject matter of a contract is destroyed, the contract is frustrated.
Reason (R): Frustration of a contract frustrates a party to the contract.

Codes:
(a) Both (A) and (R) are true and (R) is the correct explanation of (A).
(b) Both (A) and (R) are true, but (R) is not correct explanation of (A).
(c) (A) is true, but (R) is false.
(d) (A) is false, but (R) is true.

30. Arrange the following concepts in which they appeared. Use the code given below:
    (i) Invitation to offer (ii) Damage
    (iii) Offer (iv) Damages

    Codes:
    (a) (i), (iii), (ii), (iv)
    (b) (i), (iii), (iv), (ii)
    (c) (iii), (i), (ii), (iv)
    (d) (i), (iv), (iii), (ii)

31. Match an item in List I with an item in List II, using code given below:

List I	List II
I. Capacity	1. Breach
II. Damages	2. Unruly horse
III. Remedy	3. Compensation
IV. Public policy	4. Sound mind

Codes:	I	II	III	IV
(a)	4	3	2	1
(b)	1	2	4	3
(c)	3	4	1	2
(d)	4	3	1	2

32. Which one of the following pairs does not match?
    (a) Novation of contract - Section 62
    (b) Agreement in restraint of legal proceedings - Section 29
    (c) Tender of performance - Section 38
    (d) Unlawful object and consideration - Section 23

33. Which one of the following is not an example of vicarious liability?
    (a) Liability of the principal for the tort of his agent.
    (b) Liability of partners for each others' tort.
    (c) Liability of the master for the tort of his servant.
    (d) Liability of the parents for the tort of the children.

34. Match List I and List II, select the correct answer by using codes given below:

    List I
    (A) Injuria sine damnum
    (B) Damnum sine injuria
    (C) Strict liability
    (D) Defence of consent

    List II
    1. Reylands Vs Fletcher
    2. Gloucester's Case
    3. Volenti non fit injuria
    4. Ashby Vs White

Codes:	A	B	C	D
(a)	4	2	1	3
(b)	2	4	1	3
(c)	1	2	3	4
(d)	4	3	2	1

35. Rule of absolute liability was propounded by
    (a) Justice Bhagwati
    (b) Justice Sodhi
    (c) Justice Ahmadi
    (d) Justice Kuldeep Singh

36. Which one of the defence to strict liability is based on the maxim, volenti non fit injuria?
    (a) Consent of the plaintiff
    (b) Act of God
    (c) Act of Third Party
    (d) Statutory Authority

37. Mental condition of the wrong-doer at the time of wrong doing is
    (a) relevant in all torts.
    (b) relevant to torts based on fault.
    (c) relevant in torts based on strict liability.
    (d) not relevant in tortious liability.

38. Consider the following set of legal propositions:
    (1) A person can claim damages for all wrongs he has suffered.
    (2) A person can claim damages for wrongs only if they are caused intentionally.

(3) A person can claim damages for a wrong if it is caused by infringement of the legal right.
(4) A person can claim damages even if he has suffered no loss.

Of these above propositions which are correct?

(a) (1) and (2) (b) (3) and (4)
(c) (1) and (3) (d) (2) and (4)

39. Which of the meaning given for the maxim "Actus me invite factus non est mens actus" is correct?
(a) Merely a voluntary act by me will not be a crime with a criminal intention.
(b) An act done by me against my will is not my act.
(c) Neither I nor my person can be held liable for an act done under compulsion.
(d) All of them.

40. The general principles as to protection of an accused is based on:
(i) Autrefois acquit and Autrefois convict.
(ii) Reasonable doubt as to presumption of innocence.
(iii) Natural Justice.
(iv) Conviction cannot be based without proving the guilt even if it was admitted.

Which statement is correct?
(a) (i) is correct.
(b) (i) and (ii) are correct.
(c) (i), (ii) and (iii) are correct.
(d) (i), (ii), (iii) and (iv) are correct.

41. Fill in the blanks with appropriate words: The distinctive features of riot and unlawful assembly are an activity which is accompanied by ____
(a) use of force and violence.
(b) causing alarm.
(c) violence on a common purpose.
(d) All of them.

42. The offence of __________ homicide supposes knowledge of likelihood of causing death.
(a) unlawful (b) abnormal
(c) culpable (d) all types of

43. The expression 'Seduced' used in Section 366A of Indian Penal Code means to ________ a woman to submit to illicit intercourse at any time.
(a) use of force by stress
(b) deceitfully induce
(c) willfully influence
(d) None of them

44. Preparation consists in devising or arranging means necessary for the commission of the offence. Such attempt is not punishable because
(i) the motive was harmless.
(ii) impossibility to reach wrongful end.
(iii) does not affect the security of any person.
(iv) it remained without culmination.

The reasoned answer is
(a) Only (i) is correct.
(b) The most probability is (i) and (ii).
(c) There is quite likelihood of (i) and (iii).
(d) All the reasons (i), (ii), (iii) and (iv) have to be examined.

45. No person employed in a public utility service shall go on strike
(I) without giving notice of strike to employer.
(II) within 14 days of giving such notice.
(III) after expiry of date specified in notice for strike.
(IV) within 7 days of conclusion of conciliation proceeding.

Codes:
(a) I and IV (b) I and III
(c) I and II (d) II and III

46. There can be lay-off for
 (a) One day
 (b) More than one day
 (c) Maximum seven days
 (d) Any period, even less than one day

47. In which of the following cases the court reiterated the well-known legal position that even a temporary worker can claim retrenchment compensation, if he is covered by the provisions of Section 25F of the Industrial Disputes Act, 1947?
 (a) Tatanagar Foundary Co. Vs Their Workmen.
 (b) Management of Willcox Buckwell (India) Ltd. Vs Jagannath.
 (c) Barsi Light Railway Co. Ltd. Vs Joglekar.
 (d) Modern Stores Vs Krishandas.

48. Which one of the following statements is true?
 (a) All government departments are industries.
 (b) No government department can be industry.
 (c) Government department carrying on business or trade may be industry.
 (d) Government department carrying on only sovereign function may be industry.

49. According to Section 9 A of the Trade Union Act, 1926 minimum requirement about membership of a trade union is
 (a) Seven
 (b) Ten percent or one hundred of the workmen.
 (c) Ten percent or one hundred of the workmen, whichever is less.
 (d) Ten percent or one hundred of the workmen, whichever is less, subject to minimum seven.

50. To be a member of trade union, a person must attain the age of
 (a) 18 years (b) 16 years
 (c) 15 years (d) 21 years

ANSWERS

1. (a)	2. (c)	3. (d)	4. (a)	5. (a)
6. (c)	7. (d)	8. (a)	9. (c)	10. (b)
11. (d)	12. (a)	13. (c)	14. (c)	15. (a)
16. (a)	17. (c)	18. (c)	19. (c)	20. (a)
21. (b)	22. (a)	23. (c)	24. (b)	25. (d)
26. (a)	27. (c)	28. (c)	29. (b)	30. (a)
31. (d)	32. (b)	33. (d)	34. (a)	35. (a)
36. (a)	37. (b)	38. (b)	39. (b)	40. (d)
41. (a)	42. (c)	43. (b)	44. (d)	45. (c)
46. (d)	47. (b)	48. (c)	49. (d)	50. (c)

PAPER–III

Note: This paper contains seventy-five (75) objective type questions of two (2) marks each. All questions are compulsory.

1. Democracy and Federalism are essential features of our Constitution and basic feature of its structure. This observation was made in S.R. Bommai Vs. Union of India by the Judge.
 (a) Justice P.B. Sawant
 (b) Justice S.R. Pandyan
 (c) Justice J.S. Verma
 (d) Justice A.M. Ahmadi

2. According to A.V. Dicey in India the 'Rule of Law' is embodied in
 (a) Article 12 of the Constitution of India
 (b) Article 13 of the Constitution of India
 (c) Article 14 of the Constitution of India
 (d) Article 21 of the Constitution of India

3. When the court declare that certain provisions of the Act as invalid, it does not affect the validity of the Act and it remains as it is. The principle is known as:
   (a) Doctrine of prospective over ruling.
   (b) Doctrine of severability.
   (c) Doctrine of pleasure.
   (d) Doctrine of eclipse.

4. **Assertion (A):** A Bill which contains a taxation clause besides clauses dealing with other matters may also be a Money Bill.
   Reason (R): All Bills dealing with taxes are Money Bills.
   Codes:
   (a) Both (A) and (R) are true, but (R) is not the correct explanation of (A).
   (b) Both (A) and (R) are true and (R) is the correct explanation of (A).
   (c) (A) is false, but (R) is true.
   (d) (A) is true, but (R) is false.

5. Article 40 of the Constitution of India deals with
   (a) Provision for Just and humane conditions of work and maternity relief.
   (b) Living wages, etc. for workers.
   (c) Duty of the State to raise the level of nutrition.
   (d) Organisation of Village Panchayats.

6. Article 20 and Article 21 has been taken from the purview of Article 359 of the Constitution of India by
   (a) 42nd Amendment
   (b) 43rd Amendment
   (c) 44th Amendment
   (d) 59th Amendment

7. The Chairperson of Delimitation Commission
   (a) Justice Kuldeep Singh
   (b) Justice R.S. Sarkaria
   (c) Justice R.S. Pathak
   (d) Justice S.N. Phukan

8. Representation of House of People is based on
   (a) Literacy of State
   (b) Area of the State
   (c) Population
   (d) Community

9. Find correct answer:
   Administrative law is the law relating to the powers and procedures of
   (a) The Parliament
   (b) The Legislature
   (c) The Administrative Authorities
   (d) Judiciary

10. Find the correct answer:
    The principles of natural justice are:
    (i) No person can be judge in his own case.
    (ii) No person shall be condemned unheard.
    Codes:
    (a) Only (i) is correct.
    (b) Only (ii) is correct.
    (c) (i) and (ii) are correct.
    (d) None of the above are correct.

11. Find correct answer:
    Administrative Tribunals exercises:
    (a) Purely Administrative functions
    (b) Purely Judicial functions
    (c) Purely Legislative functions
    (d) Quasi Judicial functions

12. What is the effect of violation of the rule: "Audi Alteram Partem" on an administrative action?
    (a) Mere irregularity
    (b) Null and void
    (c) An illegality
    (d) Voidable

13. In which of the following cases, the Supreme Court held that the principles

of natural justice are applicable to administrative proceedings?
(a) M.C. Mehta Vs. Union of India.
(b) Maneka Gandhi Vs. Union of India.
(c) A.K. Kraipak Vs. Union of India.
(d) Smt. Indira Nehru Gandhi Vs. Raj Narain.

14. Find correct answer:
The writ of prohibition may be issued, when there is
(a) an absence of jurisdiction or abuse of jurisdiction.
(b) violation of principles of natural justice and fraud.
(c) any kind of contravention of the law of the land.
(d) all of the above.

15. Find correct answer:
The writ of certiorari necessarily implies that
(a) An error of fact, cannot corrected.
(b) An error of law apparent on the face of the record, can be corrected.
(c) Violation of natural justice.
(d) None of the above.

16. "Common law is essentially a Judge made law".
This opinion was expressed by
(a) Pollock (b) Austin
(c) Paton (d) Salmond

17. Match the following:

List I	List II
A. Enacted law	1. Legislation
B. Case law	2. Agreement
C. Customary law	3. Precedent
D. Conventional law	4. Custom

Codes:	A	B	C	D
(a)	1	2	4	3
(b)	1	2	3	4
(c)	1	3	4	2
(d)	3	1	4	2

18. State the legal status of Hindu Joint family.
(a) Hindu Joint family is a legal person.
(b) Hindu Joint family is a natural person.
(c) Hindu Joint family is both a legal and natural person.
(d) None of the above.

19. "Case-law is gold in the mine—a few grains of precious metal to the tons of useless matter, while the statute law is coin of the state which ready for immediate use".
Who gave this statement?
(a) Bentham (b) Salmond
(c) Kelsen (d) Holland

20. "Law is the guarantee of the conditions of life of society, assured by the States" power of constraint" who said it?
(a) Dvguit (b) Ihering
(c) Savigny (d) Ehrlich

21. Match List I (Legal Right) with List II (Nature of Legal Right) and select the correct answer by using the codes given below the lists:

List I
A. Time barred debt
B. Right to reputation
C. Right to physical integrity
D. Right arising out of a contract

List II
1. Personal Right
2. Right in Personam
3. Imperfect Right
4. Right in Rem

Codes:	A	B	C	D
(a)	3	4	2	1
(b)	3	2	1	4
(c)	2	3	1	4
(d)	3	4	1	2

22. Right in re aliena means a right over
  (a) his own property.
  (b) a property of someone else.
  (c) a property situated in a foreign country.
  (d) a property situated in one's own country.
23. The birth and death of legal person is determined by
  (a) Nature (b) Custom
  (c) Law (d) Precedent
24. Read the following passage and match the column:
  The social tolerance towards crime establishes the concept of crime. No longer people accept that crime is related to sin by which people feel remorse and undergo penance to seek exoneration from punishment. But there is a general opinion that crime is relatively connected to individual behaviour, which very often changes. To resolve the conflict, the general view is that, anything which is injurious to public welfare is a crime.

Column 'P'	Column 'Q'
i. Russell	– Crime is not absolute as it depends upon social tolerance.
ii. Black Stone	– Changing concept of crime as it is related to sin.
iii. H.J. Klare	– Crime is known through attributes as it is related to behavior.
iv. G.W. Patton	– Act which does not attract law is not a crime.

  Correct answer is
  (a) i (b) ii
  (c) iii (d) iv
25. Fill in the gap.
  Contributory negligence is ______ defense to a criminal charge.
  (a) genuine (b) accurate
  (c) sharp (d) no
26. The accused fired two shots with a revolver at point blank range at the Acting Governor but the bullets failed to produce the desired result because of some defect in the ammunition or intervention of leather wallet. What offence is caused?
  (a) Culpable Homicide
  (b) Attempt to Murder
  (c) Attempt to harm
  (d) None of them
27. In a case where a minor girl was in the custody of her mother. Later the mother obtained divorce from her husband and thereafter the father forcefully removed the daughter from the school. What offence is created by the father?
  (a) Abduction (b) Kidnapping
  (c) Confinement (d) Custody
28. Can a woman be prosecuted for gang rape?
  (a) Occasionally
  (b) As the case demands
  (c) Not at all
  (d) When she is a party to it
29. Criminal breach of trust is an offence which signifies:
  (a) Entrustment
  (b) Demand
  (c) Refusal
  (d) Wrongful intention
30. 'X' a Police Officer while executing a warrant of arrest against 'Y' asks 'Z' to identify 'Y'. 'Z' knowingly tells that 'M' is 'Y' and consequently 'M' is arrested. What offence is committed by 'Z'?

(a) Abetment by Instigation
(b) Abetment by Aiding
(c) Abetment by False representation
(d) Abetment by Mischie

31. A married man commits adultery if he commits sexual intercourse with
(a) A teen aged girl.
(b) An unmarried woman.
(c) Any woman who is not his wife.
(d) Married woman.

32. In which of the following cases, the Supreme Court applied the doctrine of public trust that the State as a trustee of all natural resources is under a legal duty to protect the natural resources.
These natural resources are meant for public use and cannot be converted into private ownership?
(a) M.C. Mehta Vs. Kamalnath and Others.
(b) M.C. Mehta Vs. Union of India (Ganga Water Pollution case).
(c) M.C. Mehta Vs. Union of India (Replacing diesel vehicles by CNG vehicles).
(d) Church of God (Full Gospel) in India Vs. KKR Majestic Colony Welfare Association.

33. In which of the following cases, the Supreme Court discussed the development of the precautionary principle?
(a) A.P. Pollution Control Board Vs. M.V. Nayudu.
(b) Rural Litigation and Entitlement Kendra Vs. State of U.P.
(c) M.C. Mehta Vs. Union of India (Ganga Water Pollution case).
(d) Olga Tellis (1986) case.

34. The term "environment" under Section 2(a) of the Environment (Protection) Act, 1986 means
(a) Air, Water and Land only.
(b) Water, Air, Land and interrelationship between air, water, and land only.
(c) Water, Air, Land, and the interrelationship between water, air and land and human beings, other living creatures, plants, micro organism and property.
(d) None of the above.

35. **Assertion (A):** The right to clean drinking water and right to free air to breath are attributes of the right to life.
Reason (R): Because they are the basic elements which sustain life.

Codes:
(a) (A) and (R) are true. (R) is good explanation of (A).
(b) Both (A) and (R) are true. But (R) is not a good explanation of (A).
(c) (A) is true, (R) is false.
(d) (A) is false, (R) is true.

36. In which of the following cases, the Supreme Court observed that, "When there is a state of uncertainty due to the lack of data or material about the extent of damage or pollution likely to be caused, then in order to maintain the ecological balance, the burden of proof that the said balance will be maintained must necessarily be on the industry or the unit which is likely to cause pollution"?
(a) M.C. Mehta Vs. Union of India.
(b) Olga Tellis Vs. Bombay Municipal Corporation.
(c) Taj Trapezium case.
(d) None of the above.

37. In which of the following cases, the Supreme Court directed closing down and demolition of shrimp industries in coastal regulation zone and implement the "precautionary principle" and "the polluter pays principle and held them liable for payment of compensation for

reversing the ecology and compensate the individual for loss suffered?

(a) S. Jagannath Vs. Union of India.
(b) Vellore Citizens Welfare Forum Vs. Union of India.
(c) M.C. Mehta Vs. Union of India.
(d) Church of God (Full Gospels) in India Vs. KKR Majestic Colony Welfare Association.

38. In which of the following cases, the Supreme Court upheld the governmental direction to close down the lime-stone mining operations and quarrying permanently, holding it the duty of the lessee to protest and safeguard the right of the people to live in a healthy environment with minimal disturbance of ecological balance?

(a) All India Council for Enviro Legal Action Vs. Union of India.
(b) Rural Litigation and Entitlement Kendra Vs. State of Uttar Pradesh.
(c) Vellore Citizens Welfare Forum Vs. Union of India.
(d) M.C. Mehta Vs. Union of India.

39. Match the correct answer from List B to the item in List A.

List A

(A) The polluter pays principle

List B

(a) Each generation should be obligated to conserve the diversity of natural and cultural resources base so that it does not restrict options of the future generations.
(b) Affirmative State Action for efficient management of resources and empowers the citizens to question ineffective management of natural resources.
(c) The pollutant not only has an obligation to make good the loss to the victims but has to bear the costs of restoring the environment to its original state.
(d) State's obligation to devise and implement a cohesive and coordinated programme to meet its obligation to sustainable development.

40. "If International Law were only a kind of morality, the framers of state papers concerning foreign policy would throw all strength on moral argument. But as a matter of fact, this is not what they do. They appeal not to the general feeling of moral rightness, but to precedents, to treaties, and to opinions of specialists. They assume the existence among statesmen and publicists of a series of legal as distinguished from moral obligations in the affairs of nations." This observation is made by

(a) Frederick Pollock
(b) L. Oppenheim
(c) Hans Kelsen
(d) P.C. Corbett

41. What are essential tests for the existence of International Custom?

(a) Uniform practice of States and longevity of time period.
(b) Uniform practice of States and opino juris sine necessitatis.
(c) Uniform practice of States, longevity of time period and opino juris sine necessitatis.
(d) None of the above.

42. In which of the following cases, Judge Alvarez evolved a doctrine that General Assembly resolutions are virtually binding upon States in a legislative sense?

(a) South West Africa Voting Procedure case, ICJ Reports, 1975, p. 12
(b) Western Sahara case, ICJ Reports, 1975, p. 12
(c) Anglo-Norwegian Fisheries case, ICJ Reports, 1951, p. 152

(d) South West Africa Voting Procedure case, ICJ Reports, 1955, p. 67

43. Which of the following cases relates to nationality of an individual which is an evidence of the link of an individual with the State?
(a) Nottebohm case (Leichtenstein V. Guatemala), ICJ Reports, 1955, p. 4
(b) South West Africa, Advisory Opinion, ICJ Reports, 1971, p. 16
(c) Reservations to the Genocide Convention case, ICJ Reports, 1951, p. 15
(d) United States Diplomatic and Consular Staff in Tehran, ICJ Reports, 1980, p. 3

44. The non-permanent members of the Security Council of United Nations are elected for a term of
(a) Three years (b) Five years
(c) One year (d) Two years

45. Which of the following has the power to give effect to the judgment of the International Court of Justice if a party to the case fails to perform the obligations incumbent upon it under a judgment?
(a) General Assembly
(b) Security Council
(c) Highest National Court in the concerned State
(d) International Court of Justice

46. In which of the following cases, International Court of Justice refused to give advisory opinion at the request of World Health Organization?
(a) Legality of the Threat of Use of Nuclear Weapons.
(b) Nicaragua Vs. U.S.A.
(c) Competence of Assembly regarding admission to United Nations.
(d) North Sea Continental Shelf cases.

47. In which of the following case the Supreme Court held that "The Three Talaks" would be treated as a "Single Talak" and not a valid Talak?
(a) Shamim Ara Vs. State of U.P. AIR 2002 SCR 4162.
(b) Mohd. Ahmed Khan Vs. Shah Bano AIR 1985 SC 365.
(c) Bai Tahira Vs. Ali Hussain AIR 1979 SC 362.
(d) None of the above.

48. Ceremonies of Hindu Marriage have been laid down in Minute details in
(a) Dharma Sutra
(b) Dharma Shastra
(c) Grhiya Sutra
(d) None of the above

49. To mature as a ground of Divorce the 'Desertion', under the Hindu Marriage Act, 1955, must continue for a minimum period of
(a) One year (b) Two years
(c) Three years (d) None of these

50. In which of its following Reports the Law Commission recommended, the "Breakdown Principle" to be accepted as the additional ground of Divorce?
(a) 70th Report
(b) 71st Report
(c) 72nd Report
(d) None of the above

51. Which of the following Ceremony/ Ceremonies is/are obligatory under the Hindu Marriage Act ?
(a) Kanyadan (b) Panigrahan
(c) Saptapadi (d) All of the above

52. Children born to annuled voidable marriages or void marriages under Section 11 and 12 of the Hindu Marriage Act are:
(a) Illegitimate.
(b) Illegitimate but can inherit the property of their parents.
(c) Legitimate and can inherit all family property.

(d) Legitimate but can inherit only the property of their parents.

53. In which of the following cases, the court held that "Dower (Mehar) is a sale price of women"?
(a) Humara Begum case
(b) Aziz Bano Vs. Mohammed
(c) Shah Bano case
(d) Abdul Kadir case

54. "Iddat" is a period during which a Muslim woman is prohibited from marrying on dissolution of marriage.
(a) By Death of husband
(b) By Divorce
(c) Only (a) and not (b)
(d) Both (a) and (b)

55. Indicate the order in which the following words appear in the definition of 'Human Rights' as given in Section 2(d) of the Protection of Human Rights Act, 1993.
(i) Life (ii) Liberty
(iii) Equality (iv) Dignity
Codes:
(a) (i), (iii), (ii) and (iv)
(b) (ii), (iii), (iv) and (i)
(c) (i), (ii), (iv) and (iii)
(d) (i), (ii), (iii) and (iv)

56. Who is the Chairperson of NHRC?
(a) Justice J.S. Verma
(b) Justice K.G. Bala Krishnan
(c) Justice A.S. Anand
(d) Justice M.N. Venkatachalaiah

57. Match List I with List II and select the correct answer with the help of codes attached.
List I
A. Magna Carta
B. International Convention on Civil and Political Rights
C. Universal Declaration of Human Rights
D. Convention on the Rights of Child
List II
1. 1948 2. 1989
3. 1215 4. 1966

Codes:	A	B	C	D
(a)	3	4	1	2
(b)	2	3	1	4
(c)	1	2	3	4
(d)	4	2	1	3

58. India is not a party to
(a) International Convention on Civil and Political Rights.
(b) International Convention on Economic, Social and Cultural Rights.
(c) Convention on the Rights of Child.
(d) Optional Protocol to International Civil and Political Rights.

59. The 'Convention on Elimination of All Forms of Discrimination Against Women' was entered into force in the year
(a) 1979 (b) 1981
(c) 1989 (d) 1992

60. The Committee on Economic, Social and Cultural Rights was established under ECOSOC Resolution No. 17 adopted on
(a) 28th May, 1985
(b) 30th May, 1985
(c) 26th April, 1986
(d) 24th May, 1986

61. Which one of the following is the fourth generation of Human Right?
(a) Right to Life
(b) Right to Health
(c) Right to Environment
(d) Right to Communication

62. Which of the following statements is true?
1. Under English Law Libel is actionable per se.
2. Under Indian Law 'Libel' as well as Slander are actionable per se.
3. Under English Law, only 'Libel' is a crime.

4. Under Indian Law both 'Libel' and 'Slander' are crime.

(a) 1, 2 and 3 are correct.
(b) 1, 2, 3 and 4 are correct.
(c) 2, 3 and 4 are correct.
(d) 1, 3 and 4 are correct.

63. Match List I with List II and select the correct answer by using the codes given below:

List I

A. Deficiency of services
B. Grounds of making a complaint
C. Findings of the District Forum and relief
D. An ex-parte unreasoned order can be recalled

List II

1. Section 12
2. Section 2(1)(g)
3. Indian Oil Corporation Vs. Lakshmi Shankar Narain (1999) 9 S.C.C. 2
4. Section 14

Note: Sections above are from the Consumer Protection Act.

Codes:	A	B	C	D
(a)	1	2	4	3
(b)	2	1	4	3
(c)	2	1	3	4
(d)	3	4	2	1

64. Nuisance is a form of Tort

(a) Which is actionable per se.
(b) Which is not actionable per se.
(c) Actionable per se if plaintiff suffers pecuniary loss.
(d) None of the above.

65. **Assertion (A):** Services rendered to a patient by a Medical Practitioner, by way of consultation, diagnosis and treatment would fall within the ambit of 'services' as defined, in Section 2(1)(O) of the Consumer Protection Act.

Reason (R): Like other professions, Medical Practitioner should also conduct himself by using of reasonable skill and care.

Find correct answer using codes given below:

Codes:

(a) (A) is true and (R) is false.
(b) (R) is true, but (A) is false.
(c) (A) and (R), both are true, but (R) is not correct explanation of (A).
(d) (A) and (R) both are true and (R) is correct explanation of (A).

66. Which of the following is an essential constituent of negligence?

1. Defendant was under a legal duty to exercise due care.
2. This duty was owed to plaintiff.
3. Defendant committed breach of such duty.
4. That the breach of such duty was the direct and proximate cause of the damage alleged.

(a) 1, 2 and 3 are correct.
(b) 1, 2, 3 and 4 are correct.
(c) 2, 3 and 4 are correct.
(d) 1, 2 and 4 are correct.

67. The Rule of 'Absolute Liability' was laid down in the case

(a) M.C. Mehta Vs. Union of India
(b) Madras Railways Co. Vs. Zamidar
(c) K. Nagireddi Vs. State of A.P.
(d) Minu B. Mehta Vs. Balakrishna

68. Consider the following elements:

1. Infringement of a legal right
2. Legal damage
3. Any damage
4. Existence of legal right

Right to claim damages in Tort would arise only if:

(a) 1 and 2 are present.
(b) 1, 2 and 4 are present.
(c) 1, 3 and 4 are present.
(d) 3 and 4 are present.

69. Which statements are correct?
Directors are
(i) Trustees of Company
(ii) Managers of Company
(iii) Agents of Company
(iv) Owners of Company
Codes:
(a) (i) and (ii) are correct.
(b) (ii) and (iii) are correct.
(c) (iii) and (iv) are correct.
(d) (i) and (iii) are correct.

70. Which one of the following is correct statement?
(a) Every agency is partnership.
(b) Every partnership is agency.
(c) Every partnership is limited company.
(d) Every private limited company is partnership.

71. Read the following passage and match the column.
No suit to enforce a right arising from a contract shall be initiated in any court by any person suing as a partner in a non-registered firm. Registration of firms is not compulsory. There is no penalty for non-registration. An unregistered firm cannot sue any third person for the enforcement of any right arising from contract.
Column P
A. Registration
B. Non-registration
C. Partner of a registered firm
D. Partner of a nonregistered firm
Column Q
1. No penalty
2. Optional
3. Unenforceability of his rights
4. Can sue

Codes:	A	B	C	D
(a)	1	2	3	4
(b)	2	1	4	3
(c)	2	1	3	4
(d)	1	3	2	4

72. **Assertion (A):** Doctrine of Indoor Management protects an outsider dealing with a company from irregularities inside a company.
Reason (R): Doctrine of ultra vires protects an outsider dealing with a company for corporate capacity not mentioned in the objects clause.
Choose correct answer from below:
Codes:
(a) (A) is true, but (R) is false.
(b) (A) is false, but (R) is true.
(c) (A) and (R) are true, but (R) is not an explanation of (A).
(d) (A) and (R) are true, and (R) is an explanation of (A).

73. Match items in Column P with items in Column Q, according to provisions of the Negotiable Instrument Act.
Column P
A. Definition of promissory note
B. Drawer of cheque
C. Holder's right to duplicate
D. Dishonour
Column Q
1. Section 30
2. Section 45A
3. Section 135
4. Section 4

Codes:	A	B	C	D
(a)	2	4	1	3
(b)	4	2	3	1
(c)	4	1	3	2
(d)	4	1	2	3

74. Which statements are correct?
(i) Partners have right to profit.
(ii) Partners have right to attend general meeting.
(iii) Partners have right to interest.
(iv) Partners have right to appoint proxy.

Codes:
(a) (i) and (ii) are correct.
(b) (ii) and (iii) are correct.
(c) (iii) and (iv) are correct.
(d) (i) and (iii) are correct.

75. Match an item in List P with an item in List Q.

List P
A. Prohibition of assignment of office by Director.
B. Appointment of alternate Director.
C. Disqualifications to be a Director.
D. Officer who is in default.

List Q
1. Section 267
2. Section 312
3. Section 5
4. Section 313

Codes:	**A**	**B**	**C**	**D**
(a)	4	2	1	3
(b)	2	4	1	3
(c)	2	4	3	1
(d)	2	3	1	4

ANSWERS

1. (a)	2. (c)	3. (b)	4. (a)	5. (d)
6. (c)	7. (a)	8. (c)	9. (c)	10. (c)
11. (d)	12. (b)	13. (c)	14. (d)	15. (b)
16. (d)	17. (c)	18. (a)	19. (b)	20. (b)
21. (d)	22. (b)	23. (c)	24. (a)	25. (d)
26. (b)	27. (b)	28. (c)	29. (a)	30. (c)
31. (d)	32. (a)	33. (a)	34. (c)	35. (a)
36. (d)	37. (a)	38. (b)	39. (c)	40. (a)
41. (b)	42. (c)	43. (a)	44. (d)	45. (b)
46. (a)	47. (a)	48. (c)	49. (b)	50. (b)
51. (c)	52. (d)	53. (d)	54. (d)	55. (d)
56. (b)	57. (a)	58. (d)	59. (b)	60. (a)
61. (d)	62. (c)	63. (b)	64. (b)	65. (c)
66. (b)	67. (a)	68. (b)	69. (d)	70. (b)
71. (b)	72. (c)	73. (d)	74. (d)	75. (b)

JUNE–2012

Note: This paper contains Sixty (60) multiple-choice questions, each question carrying two (2) marks. Candidate is expected to answer any Fifty (50) questions. In case more than Fifty (50) questions are attempted, only the first Fifty (50) questions will be evaluated.

PAPER–I

1. Video-Conferencing can be classified as one of the following types of communication:
   (a) Visual one way
   (b) Audio-Visual one way
   (c) Audio-Visual two way
   (d) Visual two way

2. MC National University of Journalism and Communication is located at
   (a) Lucknow (b) Bhopal
   (c) Chennai (d) Mumbai

3. All India Radio (A.I.R.) for broadcasting was named in the year
   (a) 1926 (b) 1936
   (c) 1946 (d) 1956

4. In India for broadcasting TV programmes which system is followed?
   (a) NTCS (b) PAL
   (c) NTSE (d) SECAM

5. The term 'DAVP' stands for
   (a) Directorate of Advertising & Vocal Publicity
   (b) Division of Audio-Visual Publicity
   (c) Department of Audio-Visual Publicity
   (d) Directorate of Advertising & Visual Publicity

6. The term "TRP" is associated with TV shows stands for
   (a) Total Rating Points
   (b) Time Rating Points
   (c) Thematic Rating Points
   (d) Television Rating Points

7. Which is the number that comes next in the following sequence?
   2, 6, 12, 20, 30, 42, 56, ______
   (a) 60 (b) 64
   (c) 72 (d) 70

8. Find the next letter for the series YVSP ....
   (a) N (b) M
   (c) O (d) L

9. Given that in a code language, '645' means 'day is warm'; '42' means 'warm spring' and '634' means 'spring is sunny'; which digit represents 'sunny'?
   (a) 3 (b) 2
   (c) 4 (d) 5

10. The basis of the following classification is:
    'first President of India', 'author of Godan', 'books in my library', 'blue things' and 'students who work hard'
    (a) Common names
    (b) Proper names
    (c) Descriptive phrases
    (d) Indefinite description

11. In the expression 'Nothing is larger than itself' the relation 'is larger than' is
    (a) Antisymmetric (b) Asymmetrical
    (c) Intransitive (d) Irreflexive

12. **Assertion (A):** There are more laws on the books today than ever before, and more crimes being committed than ever before.

Reason (R): Because to reduce crime we must eliminate the laws.

Choose the correct answer from below:

(a) (A) is true, (R) is doubtful and (R) is not the correct explanation of (A).
(b) (A) is false, (R) is true and (R) is the correct explanation of (A).
(c) (A) is doubtful, (R) is doubtful and (R) is not the correct explanation of (A).
(d) (A) is doubtful, (R) is true and (R) is not the correct explanation of (A).

13. If the proposition "All men are not mortal" is true then which of the following inferences is correct? Choose from the code given below:
   1. "All men are mortal" is true.
   2. "Some men are mortal" is false.
   3. "No men are mortal" is doubtful.
   4. "All men are mortal" is false.

   Codes:

   (a) 1, 2 and 3 (b) 2, 3 and 4
   (c) 1, 3 and 4 (d) 1 and 3

14. Determine the nature of the following definition: "Abortion" means the ruthless murdering of innocent beings.

   (a) Lexical (b) Persuasive
   (c) Stipulative (d) Theoretical

15. Which one of the following is not an argument?

   (a) Devadutt does not eat in the day so he must be eating at night.
   (b) If Devadutt is growing fat and if he does not eat during the day, he will be eating at night.
   (c) Devadutt eats in the night so he does not eat during the day.
   (d) Since Devadutt does not eat in the day, he must be eating in the night.

16. Venn diagram is a kind of diagram to

   (a) represent and assess the validity of elementary inferences of syllogistic form.
   (b) represent but not assess the validity of elementary inferences of syllogistic form.
   (c) represent and assess the truth of elementary inferences of syllogistic form.
   (d) assess but not represent the truth of elementary inferences of syllogistic form.

17. Reasoning by analogy leads to

   (a) certainty
   (b) definite conclusion
   (c) predictive conjecture
   (d) surety

18. Which of the following statements are false? Choose from the code given below:
   1. Inductive arguments always proceed from the particular to the general.
   2. A cogent argument must be inductively strong.
   3. A valid argument may have a false premise and a false conclusion.
   4. An argument may legitimately be spoken of as 'true' or 'false'.

   Codes:

   (a) 2, 3 and 4 (b) 1 and 3
   (c) 2 and 4 (d) 1 and 2

19. Six persons A, B, C, D, E and F are standing in a circle. B is between F and C, A is between E and D, F is to the left of D. Who is between A and F?

   (a) B (b) C
   (c) D (d) E

20. The price of petrol increases by 25%. By what percentage must a customer reduce the consumption so that the earlier bill on the petrol does not alter?

   (a) 20% (b) 25%
   (c) 30% (d) 33.33%

21. If Ram knows that y is an integer greater than 2 and less than 7 and Hari knows that y is an integer greater than 5 and

less than 10, then they may correctly conclude that

(a) y can be exactly determined
(b) y may be either of two values
(c) y may be any of three values
(d) there is no value of y satisfying these conditions

22. Four pipes can fill a reservoir in 15, 20, 30 and 60 hours respectively. The first one was opened at 6 AM, second at 7 AM, third at 8 AM and the fourth at 9 AM. When will the reservoir be filled?
(a) 11 AM (b) 12 Noon
(c) 1 PM (d) 1:30 PM

The total electricity generation in a country is 97 GW. The contribution of various energy sources is indicated in percentage terms in the Pie Chart given below:

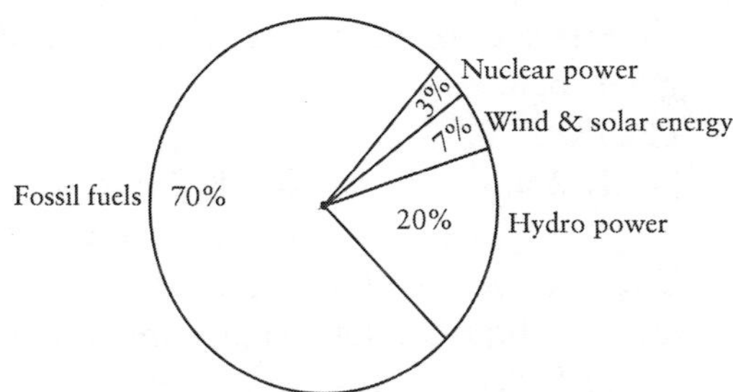

23. What is the contribution of wind and solar power in absolute terms in the electricity generation?
(a) 6.79 GW (b) 19.4 GW
(c) 9.7 GW (d) 29.1 GW

24. 10 is the mean of a set of 7 observations and 5 is the mean of a set of 3 observations. The mean of the combined set is given by
(a) 7.5 (b) 8.5
(c) 10 (d) 15

25. TCP/IP is necessary if one is to connect to the
(a) Phone lines (b) LAN
(c) Internet (d) a Server

26. Each character on the keyboard of computer has an ASCII value which stands for
(a) American Stock Code for Information Interchange
(b) American Standard Code for Information Interchange
(c) African Standard Code for Information Interchange
(d) Adaptable Standard Code for Information Change

27. Which of the following is not a programming language?
(a) Pascal (b) Microsoft Office
(c) Java (d) C++

28. Minimum number of bits required to store any 3 digit decimal number is equal to
(a) 3 (b) 5
(c) 8 (d) 10

29. Internet explorer is a type of
(a) Operating System (b) Compiler
(c) Browser (d) IP address

30. POP3 and IMAP are e-mail accounts in which
(a) One automatically gets one's mail everyday
(b) One has to be connected to the server to read or write one's mail
(c) One only has to be connected to the server to send and receive e-mail
(d) One does not need any telephone lines

31. Irritation in eyes is caused by the pollutant
(a) Sulphur dioxide (b) Ozone
(c) PAN (d) Nitrous oxide

32. Which is the source of chloro-fluoro-carbons?
(a) Thermal power plants
(b) Automobiles
(c) Refrigeration and Airconditioning
(d) Fertilizers

33. Which of the following is not a renewable natural resource?
(a) Clean air (b) Fertile soil
(c) Fresh water (d) Salt

34. Which of the following parameters is not used as a pollution indicator in water?
(a) Total dissolved solids
(b) Coliform count
(c) Dissolved oxygen
(d) Density

35. S and P waves are associated with
(a) floods (b) wind energy
(c) earthquakes (d) tidal energy

36. Match List I and List II and select the correct answer from the codes given below:

List I	List II
(A) Ozone hole	(i) Tsunami
(B) Greenhouse effect	(ii) UV radiations
(C) Natural hazards	(iii) Methane
(D) Sustainable development	(iv) Eco-centrism

Codes:	A	B	C	D
(a)	(ii)	(iii)	(i)	(iv)
(b)	(iii)	(ii)	(i)	(iv)
(c)	(iv)	(iii)	(i)	(ii)
(d)	(iv)	(ii)	(iii)	(i)

37. Indian Institute of Advanced Study is located at
(a) Dharmshala (b) Shimla
(c) Solan (d) Chandigarh

38. Indicate the number of Regional Offices of National Council of Teacher Education.
(a) 04 (b) 05
(c) 06 (d) 08

39. Which of the following rights was considered the "Heart and Soul" of the Indian Constitution by Dr. B.R. Ambedkar?
(a) Freedom of Speech
(b) Right to Equality
(c) Right to Freedom of Religion
(d) Right to Constitutional Remedies

40. Who among the following created the office of the District Collector in India?
(a) Lord Cornwallis
(b) Warren Hastings
(c) The Royal Commission on Decentralisation
(d) Sir Charles Metcalfe

41. The Fundamental Duties of a citizen include
1. Respect for the Constitution, the National Flag and the National Anthem.
2. To develop the scientific temper.
3. Respect for the Government.
4. To protect Wildlife.

Choose the correct answer from the codes given below:

Codes:
(a) 1, 2 and 3 (b) 1, 2 and 4
(c) 2, 3 and 4 (d) 1, 3, 4 and 2

42. The President of India takes oath
(a) to uphold the sovereignty and integrity of India.
(b) to bear true faith and allegiance to the Constitution of India.
(c) to uphold the Constitution and Laws of the country.
(d) to preserve, protect and defend the Constitution and the law of the country.

43. If you get an opportunity to teach a visually challenged student along with normal students, what type of treatment would you like to give him in the class?
(a) Not giving extra attention because majority may suffer.
(b) Take care of him sympathetically in the classroom.

(c) You will think that blindness is his destiny and hence you cannot do anything.
(d) Arrange a seat in the front row and try to teach at a pace convenient to him.

44. Which of the following is not a characteristic of a good achievement test?
(a) Reliability (b) Objectivity
(c) Ambiguity (d) Validity

45. Which of the following does not belong to a projected aid?
(a) Overhead projector
(b) Blackboard
(c) Epidiascope
(d) Slide projector

46. For a teacher, which of the following methods would be correct for writing on the blackboard?
(a) Writing fast and as clearly as possible.
(b) Writing the matter first and then asking students to read it.
(c) Asking a question to students and then writing the answer as stated by them.
(d) Writing the important points as clearly as possible.

47. A teacher can be successful if he/she
(a) helps students in becoming better citizens
(b) imparts subject knowledge to students
(c) prepares students to pass the examination
(d) presents the subject matter in a well organized manner

48. Dynamic approach to teaching means
(a) Teaching should be forceful and effective
(b) Teachers should be energetic and dynamic
(c) The topics of teaching should not be static, but dynamic
(d) The students should be required to learn through activities

49. The research that aims at immediate application is
(a) Action Research
(b) Empirical Research
(c) Conceptual Research
(d) Fundamental Research

50. When two or more successive footnotes refer to the same work which one of the following expressions is used?
(a) ibid. (b) et al.
(c) op. cit. (d) loc. cit.

51. Nine year olds are taller than seven year olds. This is an example of a reference drawn from
(a) Vertical study
(b) Cross-sectional study
(c) Time series study
(d) Experimental study

52. Conferences are meant for
(a) Multiple target groups
(b) Group discussions
(c) Show-casing new research
(d) All of the above

53. Ex Post Facto research means
(a) The research is carried out after the incident.
(b) The research is carried out prior to the incident.
(c) The research is carried out along with the happening of an incident.
(d) The research is carried out keeping in mind the possibilities of an incident.

54. Research ethics do not include
(a) Honesty (b) Subjectivity
(c) Integrity (d) Objectivity

Read the following passage carefully and answer the questions 55 to 60:

James Madison said, "A people who mean to be their own governors must arm themselves with power that knowledge gives." In India, the Official Secrets Act, 1923 was a convenient smokescreen to deny members of the public access to information. Public functioning has traditionally been shrouded in secrecy. But in a democracy in which people govern themselves, it is necessary to have more openness. In the maturing of our democracy, right to information is a major step forward; it enables citizens to participate fully in the decision-making process that affects their lives so profoundly. It is in this context that the address of the Prime Minister in the Lok Sabha is significant. He said, "I would only like to see that everyone, particularly our civil servants, should see the Bill in a positive spirit; not as a draconian law for paralyzing Government, but as an instrument for improving Government-Citizen interface resulting in a friendly, caring and effective Government functioning for the good of our People." He further said, "This is an innovative Bill, where there will be scope to review its functioning as we gain experience. Therefore, this is a piece of legislation, whose working will be kept under constant reviews."

The Commission, in its Report, has dealt with the application of the Right to Information in Executive, Legislature and Judiciary. The judiciary could be a pioneer in implementing the Act in letter and spirit because much of the work that the Judiciary does is open to public scrutiny, Government of India has sanctioned an e-governance project in the Judiciary for about ₹700 crores which would bring about systematic classification, standardization and categorization of records. This would help the judiciary to fulfil its mandate under the Act. Similar capacity building would be required in all other public authorities. The transformation from non-transparency to transparency and public accountability is the responsibility of all three organs of State.

55. A person gets power
 (a) by acquiring knowledge
 (b) from the Official Secrets Act, 1923
 (c) through openings
 (d) by denying public information

56. Right to Information is a major step forward to
 (a) enable citizens to participate fully in the decision-making process
 (b) to make the people aware of the Act
 (c) to gain knowledge of administration
 (d) to make the people Government friendly

57. The Prime Minister considered the Bill
 (a) to provide power to the civil servants
 (b) as an instrument for improving Government-Citizen interface resulting in a friendly, caring and effective Government
 (c) a draconian law against the officials
 (d) to check the harassment of the people

58. The Commission made the Bill effective by
 (a) extending power to the executive authorities
 (b) combining the executive and legislative power
 (c) recognizing Judiciary a pioneer in implementing the act in letter and spirit
 (d) educating the people before its implementation

59. The Prime Minister considered the Bill innovative and hoped that
 (a) It could be reviewed based on the experience gained on its functioning.
 (b) The civil servants would see the Bill in a positive spirit.
 (c) It would not be considered as a draconian law for paralyzing Government.
 (d) All of the above.

60. The transparency and public accountability is the responsibility of

three organs of the State. These three organs are
(a) Lok Sabha, Rajya Sabha and Judiciary
(b) Lok Sabha, Rajya Sabha and Executive
(c) Judiciary, Legislature and the Commission
(d) Legislature, Executive and Judiciary

ANSWERS

1. (c)	2. (b)	3. (b)	4. (b)	5. (d)
6. (a)	7. (c)	8. (b)	9. (a)	10. (c)
11. (d)	12. (a)	13. (b)	14. (b)	15. (b)
16. (a)	17. (c)	18. (c)	19. (c)	20. (a)
21. (a)	22. (c)	23. (a)	24. (b)	25. (c)
26. (b)	27. (b)	28. (d)	29. (c)	30. (c)
31. (c)	32. (c)	33. (d)	34. (d)	35. (c)
36. (a)	37. (b)	38. (a)	39. (d)	40. (b)
41. (b)	42. (d)	43. (d)	44. (c)	45. (b)
46. (d)	47. (a)	48. (d)	49. (a)	50. (a)
51. (b)	52. (d)	53. (a)	54. (b)	55. (a)
56. (a)	57. (b)	58. (c)	59. (d)	60. (d)

PAPER–II

Note: This paper contains fifty (50) objective type questions of two (2) marks each. All questions are compulsory.

1. The Supreme Court held in which of the following cases that preamble is not the part of the Constitution of India
(a) Berubari case
(b) A.K. Gopalan case
(c) Balaji Case
(d) Minerva Mill's case

2. Article 16(4A) which gives power to the State to make laws regarding reservation in favour of Scheduled Castes and Scheduled Tribes was added by the
(a) 75th Amendment to the Constitution of India.
(b) 76th Amendment to the Constitution of India.
(c) 77th Amendment to the Constitution of India.
(d) 78th Amendment to the Constitution of India.

3. The protection and improvement of environment including forests and wild life of the country is
(a) Directive Principle of State Policy
(b) Fundamental National Policy
(c) Fundamental Duty of a Citizen
(d) Both Directive Principle of State Policy and Fundamental Duty of a Citizen

4. Originally the Supreme Court consisted of a Chief Justice and
(a) Seven other judges
(b) Twelve other judges
(c) Thirteen other judges
(d) Fifteen other judges

5. A resolution passed under Clause (1) of Article 249 shall remain in force for such period not exceeding
(a) Three months
(b) Six months
(c) Nine months
(d) Twelve months

6. The President's rule under Article 356 of the Constitution of India remains valid in the State for maximum period of
(a) One month (b) Three months
(c) Six months (d) One year

7. The power of the Parliament to a mend the Constitution of India is a constituent power laid down in Article 368 by
(a) Twenty-Fourth Amendment Act
(b) Twenty-Sixth Amendment Act
(c) Forty-Second Amendment Act
(d) Forty-Fourth Amendment Act

8. "Jurisprudence is as big as law and bigger". Who said this?
   (a) Austin (b) Lloyds
   (c) Lewellyn (d) Holland

9. "Rousseau is a Janus like figure in the history of national law"—who said this?
   (a) Hobbes (b) J.S. Mill
   (c) Locke (d) Barker

10. Match List I (Jurist) with List II (Assumption) and select the correct answer using the codes given below the lists:

List I	List II
I. Acquinars	(A) Jural postulates
II. Pound	(B) Spirit of people
III. Kelsen	(C) Ground norm
IV. Savigny	(D) Reason and will in law

Codes:	I	II	III	IV
(a)	(B)	(D)	(C)	(A)
(b)	(D)	(B)	(C)	(A)
(c)	(B)	(D)	(A)	(C)
(d)	(D)	(B)	(A)	(C)

11. Match List I with List II and select the correct answer using the codes given below the lists

List I

I. Law in a changing society
II. Human Law and Human Justice
III. The morality of law
IV. Ancient law

List II

(A) Fuller (B) Friedmann
(C) Stone (D) Main

Codes:	I	II	III	IV
(a)	(A)	(C)	(B)	(D)
(b)	(C)	(A)	(B)	(D)
(c)	(B)	(A)	(D)	(C)
(d)	(A)	(B)	(D)	(C)

12. Which one of the following schools of Jurisprudence considers that "a reasoned scale of values can be discovered as a basis for legal development"?
   (a) Sociological (b) Historical
   (c) Analytical (d) Philosophical

13. According to Salmond, the correlative of liberty is
   (a) Duty (b) No rights
   (c) Subjection (d) Disabilities

14. **Assertion (A):** Customs to have the force of law must be immemorial.
   Reason (R): Custom represents common consciousness of people.
   Codes:
   (a) Both (A) and (R) are true and (R) is the correct explanation of (A).
   (b) Both (A) and (R) are true and (R) is not a correct explanation of (A).
   (c) (A) is true, but (R) is false.
   (d) (A) is false, but (R) is true.

15. **Assertion (A):** International Court of Justice has power to decide cases on the basis of equity.
   Reason (R): Equity is one of the General Principles of Law recognized by Civilized Nations.
   Codes:
   (a) Both (A) and (R) are true and (R) is correct explanation of (A).
   (b) Both (A) and (R) are true, but (R) is not a correct explanation of (A).
   (c) (A) is true, but (R) is false.
   (d) (A) is false, but (R) is true.

16. Match List I with List II:
   List I (Subject Matter)
   A. International Custom
   B. Res Judicata
   C. Legal status of General Assembly Resolutions on decolonization and self determination
   D. Human Rights

List II (Cases)

(i) S.S. Lotus (France v. Turkey) PCIJ, Series A, No. 10
(ii) U.N. Administrative Tribunal case, International Law Reports, 1954, P. 310
(iii) Western Sahara Case, Advisory Opinion, ICJ Rep., 1975, P. 12
(iv) Lawless Case, American Journal of International Law, Vol. 56, 1962, P. 187

Codes:	(A)	(B)	(C)	(D)
(a)	(i)	(ii)	(iii)	(iv)
(b)	(ii)	(i)	(iii)	(iv)
(c)	(iii)	(ii)	(i)	(iv)
(d)	(iv)	(ii)	(iii)	(i)

17. U.N. Commission on Human Rights has been discarded and replaced by
(a) Economic, Social and Cultural Rights Committee
(b) Amnesty International
(c) Human Rights Committee
(d) Human Rights Council

18. Which of the following is not a primary source of International Law?
(a) International Treaty
(b) Decision of International Court of Justice
(c) International Custom
(d) General Principle of Law recognized by Civilized Nations

19. Which of the following cases relates to retroactive nature of the act of recognition of government?
(a) Aksionairnoye Obschestro A.M. Luthar V. James Sagor & Co. (1921) 3 K.B. P. 532
(b) Trendtex Trading Corporation V. Central Bank of Nigeria (1977) B.P. 529
(c) Central Air Transport Inc. V. Central Air Transport Corporation (1953) A.C.P. 70
(d) Nicaragua V. U.S.A., ICJ Rep., 1984, P. 169.

20. In a case concerning the legality of the Threat or use of Nuclear Weapons, the International Court of Justice gave advisory opinion at the request of:
(a) U.N. Security Council
(b) U.N. General Assembly
(c) World Health Organization
(d) United Nations Educational and Cultural Organization

21. Which is not the modern source of Hindu Law?
(a) Equity, Justice and Good Conscience
(b) Precedent
(c) Sruti
(d) Legislation

22. Consider the following propositions and give the correct answer
I. A void marriage remains valid until a decree annulling it has been passed by a competent court.
II. A void marriage is never a valid marriage and there is no necessity of any decree annulling it.
III. A voidable marriage is regarded as a valid marriage until a decree annulling it has been passed by a competent court.

Codes:
(a) I, II and III are correct
(b) I and II are correct
(c) II and III are correct
(d) I and III are correct

23. **Assertion (A):** Break down of marriage as such is not a ground for divorce.
Reason (R): It may result into an easy way of dissolution of marriage and shall result into instability in the society.

Codes:
(a) Both (A) and (R) are correct.
(b) (A) is correct, but (R) is incorrect.

(c) Both (A) and (R) are wrong.
(d) (R) is correct, but (A) is wrong.

24. Dastane Vs. Dastane is a case decided by the Supreme Court relating to:
(a) Adultery (b) Dessertion
(c) Cruelty (d) None of these

25. Marriages of all persons who are citizens of India belonging to various religions should by made compulsory registrable in their respective States where the marriage is solemnised. This was held by the Supreme Court in the case of:
(a) Githa Hariharn Vs. RBI
(b) Seema Vs. Ashwani Kumar
(c) John Vallamathom Vs. Union of India
(d) None of the above

26. **Assertion (A):** The Hindu Marriage Act, 1955 brought changes like prohibition of polygamy and prigamy and permission for inter-caste marriages.
Reason (R): The changes were brought under social pressure.
Codes:
(a) Both (A) and (R) are true and (R) is correct explanation of (A).
(b) Both (A) and (R) are true but (R) is not the correct explanation of (A).
(c) (A) is correct but (R) is false.
(d) (A) is false but (R) is true.

27. An agreement made by mistake is
(a) Void (b) Voidable
(c) Illegal (d) Immoral

28. Which of the following statements are true?
(i) Minor's contract can be ratified on attaining majority.
(ii) Minor's contract cannot be ratified on attaining majority.
(iii) Minor's contract can be ratified jointly by both the parties to the contract.
(iv) Minor is not liable under minor's contract.
Codes:
(a) (i) and (iii) (b) (ii) and (iv)
(c) (i) and (ii) (d) (ii) and (iii)

29. **Assertion (A):** Damages must be related to damage.
Reason (R): Damage is damaging and damages are compensating.
Codes:
(a) Both (A) and (R) are true, but (R) is not correct explanation of (A).
(b) Both (A) and (R) are true, and (R) is correct explanation of (A).
(c) (A) is true, but (R) is false.
(d) (A) is false, but (R) is true.

30. Arrange the following concepts in sequence in which they appeared.
Use the codes given below:
(i) Offer by x to y
(ii) Undue influence of x over y
(iii) Demand of damages by y from x
(iv) Acceptance of the offer by y.
Codes:
(a) (i) (ii) (iii) (iv)
(b) (i) (iv) (iii) (ii)
(c) (ii) (i) (iv) (iii)
(d) (ii) (iv) (i) (iii)

31. Which one of the following pairs is correctly matched?
(a) In India, consideration must follow... from promisee only.
(b) In India, consideration must follow... from only promisor or only promisee.
(c) In India, consideration must follow... from promisor or any other person.
(d) In India, consideration must follow... promisee or any other person.

32. **Assertion (A):** Collateral transactions to wagering agreements are valid.
Reason (R): Only wagering agreements are declared void under Section 30 of the Indian Contract Act.

Codes:

(a) (A) is true, but (R) is false.
(b) (A) is false, but (R) is true.
(c) Both (A) and (R) are true, but (R) is not correct explanation of (A).
(d) Both (A) and (R) are true and (R) is correct explanation of (A).

33. Liability in torts depends on
(a) quantum of damages suffered
(b) involvement of intention
(c) infringement of legal right
(d) effect of public interest

34. Which of the following ingredients are essential to make master liable for the acts of the servant?
(1) Tort was committed by the servant.
(2) Tort was committed in the course of employment.
(3) Express authority was given by master.
(4) Master has knowledge of all constituent offers of tort.

Codes:

(a) 1, 2, 3 (b) 1, 2, 4
(c) 3, 4 (d) 1, 2

35. Which of the following is an essential constituent of negligence?
(1) Defendant was under or legal duty to exercise due care
(2) This duty was owed to plantiff
(3) Defendant committed breach of such duty
(4) That the breach of such duty was the direct and proximate cause of the damage alleged.

Codes:

(a) 1, 2 and 3 (b) 1, 2, 3 and 4
(c) 2, 3 and 4 (d) 1, 2 and 4

36. Which one of the following is not a good defence in suits for damages or negligence?
(a) Contributory negligence
(b) Express contract with plantiff
(c) Express contract where statute prohibits
(d) Voluntary assumptions of risk

37. Match List I with List II and select the correct answer using the codes given below the lists

List I

A. Rayland Vs Fletcher
B. Donoghue Vs Stevenson
C. Gludster Grammer School Case
D. Rose Vs Ford

List II

1. Compensation for pain and suffering
2. Loss caused by competition in business
3. Strict liability
4. Liability of minor for tests
5. Liability for negligence

Codes:	A	B	C	D
(a)	1	2	3	4
(b)	2	3	4	5
(c)	3	5	2	1
(d)	3	4	2	1

38. **Assertion (A):** Tort is a civil wrong redressible by an action for unliquidated damages only.
Reason (R): Law does not provide compensation in the nature of liquidated damages.

Codes:

(a) Both (A) and (R) are true and (R) is correct explanation of (A).
(b) Both (A) and (R) are true but (R) is not the correct explanation of (A).
(c) (A) is true but (R) is false.
(d) (A) is false but (R) is true.

39. 'Z' while walking along a deserted road at night during winter saw a just born baby abandoned on a side. For a moment be realized that he could save the baby without appreciable trouble, expense or loss of his time and also felt that if the

baby is left over unprotected, it might die. But he did nothing and went away. 'P' another person also passed through that road and saw the baby and acted just like 'Z' and went away. Next morning the infant baby died of exposure.

Decide who is responsible?

(a) Only 'Z' who saw first
(b) 'P' for omitting to be compassionate
(c) Both 'Z' and 'P' for negligence
(d) Neither 'Z' nor 'P' is responsible

40. Decide on whom criminal liability can be fixed on the following:

The accused 'P' caught hold of the victim and exhorted on the main accused 'L' to strike the victim; upon which he inflicted a kirpan wound and consequently the victim died.

Assertions:

(i) 'P' is liable for punishment.
(ii) 'P' and 'L' are both liable for common intention.
(iii) 'P' and 'L' are both responsible for victims death for having common object.
(iv) 'P' is not liable for any offence.

Reasons:

(a) (i) is quite possible
(b) (ii) is reasonable
(c) (iii) is as occasion demands
(d) (iv) is most accurate

41. 'M' a quack, an uneducated in matters of surgery, had performed an operation on a man for internal piles with the help of ordinary Knife, unlike previous occasions, for which the man died due to haemorrhage. Decide on 'M's liability.

(i) 'M' is a recognised quack and hence not liable.
(ii) 'M's' profession is not legally acceptable hence liable.
(iii) 'M' is not liable because the man consented for such operation.
(iv) 'M' is not liable because it was a post-operational syndrome

The probable answer is:

(a) Statement (i) is correct
(b) Statement (ii) is correct
(c) Statement (iii) is correct
(d) Statements (iii) and (iv) are correct

42. Fill in the gap. 'P' in support of a just claim of 'Q' has stated against 'Z', for a sum of Rupees one thousand and falsely sweared on a trial that he heard 'Z' admitted as to the just claim of 'Q'. The court decides that it was an affirmation of ________.

(a) Statement of truth
(b) False evidence
(c) Making a declaration
(d) None of them

43. One of the essentials of holding a person responsible for dowry death is

(a) subjected to harassment by peer groups
(b) subjected to harassment for dowry
(c) subjected to harassment under suspicious circumstances
(d) All of them

44. Fill in the gap:

An act of grievous hurt is always inferred through enormity to ________ and not merely a slight more than a frolic.

(a) Murder
(b) Bodily injury
(c) Amputation
(d) All of them

45. **Assertion (A):** Before Bangalore Water Supply case educational institutions were excluded from the definition of an industry.

Reason (R): Main purpose of such institutions is to impart education, and not to run business or trade.

Codes:

(a) Both (A) and (R) are true and (R) is the correct explanation.

(b) Both (A) and (R) are true but (R) is not the correct explanation.
(c) (A) is true but (R) is false.
(d) (A) is false but (R) is true.

46. An individual dispute becomes industrial dispute when it is taken up by
(a) Union only.
(b) Union or substantial number of workmen.
(c) Continuous support of union.
(d) Subsequent support of union.

47. Which of the following statements are true?
I. All employees are workmen.
II. All employees are not workmen.
III. All workmen are employees.
IV. All managerial staff are workmen.
Codes:
(a) I and II (b) II and III
(c) III and IV (d) I and III

48. In which of the following cases the Supreme Court held that medical representative is not workman?
(a) Standard Vacuum Oil Company V. Commissioner of Labour
(b) Anand Bazar Patrika V. Its Workmen
(c) Workmen V. Greaves Cotton & Co.
(d) J&J Dechane V. State of Kerala

49. Which one of the following statements is true?
(a) The general funds of a registered trade union shall not be spent on the payment of salaries.
(b) A registered Trade Union may constitute a separate fund for the promotion of the civic and political interests.
(c) No appeal lies against the order of refusal of the Registrar to register a Trade union.
(d) Every registered Trade Union shall not be a body corporate.

50. Match List I with List II and select the correct answer using the codes given below:
List I (Subject)
(i) Appointment of Registrar
(ii) Appeal
(iii) Amalgamation of Trade Unions
(iv) Cancellation of registration
List II (Provisions of Trade Union Act, 1926)
1. Section 24 2. Section 10
3. Section 3 4. Section 11

Codes:	I	II	III	IV
(a)	2	4	1	3
(b)	4	1	3	2
(c)	3	4	1	2
(d)	1	3	2	1

ANSWERS

1. (a)	2. (c)	3. (d)	4. (a)	5. (d)
6. (b)	7. (a)	8. (c)	9. (d)	10. (a)
11. (b)	12. (d)	13. (b)	14. (d)	15. (a)
16. (a)	17. (d)	18. (b)	19. (c)	20. (b)
21. (c)	22. (c)	23. (a)	24. (c)	25. (b)
26. (c)	27. (a)	28. (b)	29. (d)	30. (c)
31. (d)	32. (d)	33. (c)	34. (d)	35. (b)
36. (c)	37. (c)	38. (c)	39. (d)	40. (d)
41. (b)	42. (b)	43. (b)	44. (a)	45. (a)
46. (b)	47. (b)	48. (d)	49. (b)	50. (c)

PAPER-III

Note: This paper contains seventy-five (75) objective type questions of two (2) marks each. All questions are compulsory.

1. "The new Constitution establishes, indeed a system of Government which is at the

most quasi-federal, almost devolutionary in character, a unitary state with subsidiary federal features rather than the federal state with unitary features" said by

(a) Dr. K.C. Wheare
(b) Dr. Rajendra Prasad
(c) Dr. B.R. Ambedkar
(d) Pandit Jawaharlal Nehru

2. In which of the following cases it was held that 'Right to Life does not include Right to Die'?
(a) Gian Kaur Vs. State of Punjab
(b) Chenna Jagdeshwar Vs. State of A.P.
(c) State of U.P. Vs. Sanjay Kumar Bhatia
(d) Deena Vs. Union Bank of India

3. **Assertion (A):** An accused person cannot be compelled to give his signature or thumb impression.
Reason (R): An accused person cannot be compelled to be a witness against himself.
Codes:
(a) (A) is true but (R) is false.
(b) (A) is false but (R) is true.
(c) Both (A) and (R) are true.
(d) Both (A) and (R) are false.

4. After a Money Bill has been passed by the House of the People, within how many days it is transmitted to the Council of States for its recommendations?
(a) Thirty days (b) Twenty-four days
(c) Sixty days (d) Fourteen days

5. **Assertion (A):** Directive Principles are not enforceable by any Court.
Reason (R): Directive Principles are more or less fundamental in the governance of the country.
Codes:
(a) Both (A) and (R) are true but (R) is not the correct explanation of (A).
(b) Both (A) and (R) are true and (R) is the correct explanation of (A).
(c) (A) is false but (R) is true.
(d) (A) is true but (R) is false.

6. The Supreme Court does not have original jurisdiction regarding a dispute between
(a) a citizen and a State
(b) the Government of India and one State
(c) two States
(d) the Government of India and one State on one side and one State on the other side

7. In the Constitution of India, provision relating to the formation of new States can be amended by
(a) A Parliamentary resolution which should be ratified by majority of State Legislatures.
(b) A simple majority in each House of Parliament.
(c) 3/4th majority in the Parliament.
(d) 2/3rd majority in the each House of Parliament provided they also constitute the majority of total members of each House.

8. Holding of periodic, free and fair elections by the Election Commission is part of the basic structure of the Constitution as per the following:
(a) Election Commission of India Vs. AIADMK
(b) S.S. Dhanoa Vs. Union of India
(c) In Gujarat Assembly Election matter
(d) Sadiq Ali Vs. Election Commission of India

9. Writ of *Mandamus* cannot be issued, where a fundamental right is infringed by
(a) A Statute
(b) A Statutory Order
(c) An Executive Order
(d) Private Body

10. **Assertion (A):** The principles of natural justice ensures fair hearing.

Reason (R): It requires unbiased judge to decide after hearing all parties.

Codes:

(a) Both (A) and (R) are true and (R) is good explanation of (A).
(b) Both (A) and (R) are true and (R) is not a good explanation of (A).
(c) (A) is true, but (R) is false.
(d) (A) is false, but (R) is true.

11. Prerogative writs to review an administrative action are:
(a) **Two** : Writ of Habeas Corpus and Writ of Mandamus.
(b) **Three** : Writ of Habeas Corpus and Writ of Mandamus and Writ of Prohibition.
(c) **Four** : Writ of Habeas Corpus and Writ of Mandamus and Writ of Prohibition and Writ of Certiorari and Writ of Quo Warranto.
(d) **Five** : Writ of Habeas Corpus, Writ of Mandamus, Writ of Quo warranto, Writ of Certiorari and Writ of Prohibition.

12. A mandatory procedural requirement for an administrative tribunal must be
(a) Legal representation
(b) Cross examination
(c) Reasoned decision
(d) All of the above

13. Judicial review of an administrative action means
(a) Review by the Parliament
(b) Review by the Government
(c) Review by the Legislative Assembly
(d) Review by the Judiciary

14. Match an item in List I with correct answer in List II.

List I

Institution of Lokpal and Lokayukta

List II

(a) Law should be able to control the numerous wide discretionary powers
(b) Ensure fair hearing
(c) Evaporate maladministration and corruption to bring good governance
(d) Check and control abuse of power and executive excesses

15. Find correct answer:
(a) Administrative law is a branch of public law and is only a part of Constitutional law. It cannot control the Constitutional law.
(b) Administrative law is a branch of private law.
(c) Administrative law is independent to Constitutional law.
(d) Administrative law is neither the branch of public law nor of private law, but a part of Constitutional law.

16. Bentham's definition of law is imperative in nature because
(a) law is an assembling of signs.
(b) law is declaration of volition conceived or adopted by sovereign in a State.
(c) because it is adopted by nonsovereign State.
(d) (a) and (b) both

17. The term 'Legal theory' has been first time used by
(a) Llewlyne (b) Ihring
(c) Salmond (d) W. Friedman

18. Bracket theory of corporate personality is also known as
(a) Concession theory
(b) Symbolist theory
(c) Fiction theory
(d) Will theory

19. 'A' says to 'B' that he will give a sum of rupees five thousand if 'B' marries his daughter, this is
(a) Vested Right
(b) Contingent Right
(c) Primary Right
(d) Secondary Right

20. **Assertion (A):** Kelsen follows Kant in distinguishing between 'is' and 'ought'.
Reason (R): Kelsen is a forerunner of philosophical school.
Codes:
(a) Both (A) and (R) are true, and (R) is the correct explanation of (A).
(b) Both (A) and (R) are true but (R) is not a correct explanation of (A).
(c) (A) is true, but (R) is false.
(d) (A) is false, but (R) is true.

21. The possession is the
(a) five point in ownership
(b) seven point in ownership
(c) nine point in ownership
(d) ten point in ownership

22. Which of the following duties have been included by Austin in the category of 'absolute duties'?
I. Duties owed to persons indefinitely
II. Self-regarding duties
III. Duties owed to the sovereign
IV. Duties owed to the parents
Select the correct answer using the codes
Codes:
(a) I, III and IV (b) II, III and IV
(c) I, II and IV (d) I, II and III

23. Which one of the following get along correctly?
(a) Trust and co-ownership
(b) Legal and contingent ownership
(c) Sole and limited ownership
(d) Legal and equitable ownership

24. A person who causes bodily injury to another who is labouring under a disorder, disease or bodily infirmity and thereby accelerates the death of the person. Under which it shall be deemed to have caused his death?
(a) Explanation I to Section 299
(b) Explanation I to Section 300
(c) Explanation II to Section 299
(d) Explanation II to Section 300

25. In which provision of Indian Penal Code the definition of 'valuable security' is explained?
(a) Section 29 (b) Section 30
(c) Section 31 (d) Section 13

26. State the age limit prescribed under Section 82 of Indian Penal Code in which if a child commits an overt act is not considered as an offence?
(a) Under the age of 12 years.
(b) Under the age of 7 years.
(c) Under the age of 16 years.
(d) Under the age of 18 years.

27. When the injury is intentional and sufficient to cause death in the ordinary course of nature and death follows. The offence is of the category:
(a) Attempt to murder
(b) Culpable homicide not amounting to murder
(c) Murder
(d) Attempt to suicide

28. **Principle:** Theft + Violence or Threat to violence = Robbery.
Facts: M meets B and her child on a river bridge. M takes the child and threatens to fling it down to the river unless B delivers her purse. B in consequence delivers her purse.
What offence 'M' has committed?
(a) M is liable for theft.
(b) M is liable for coercion.
(c) M is liable for robbery.
(d) M is liable for extortion.

29. Fill in the gap:
A disability for _______ days constitutes grievous hurt.
(a) A week
(b) A fortnight

(c) A month
(d) A minimum of twenty days

30. Fill in the gap with appropriate word: Wrongful restraint means keeping a person from out of his ________ of his residence.
(a) house (b) place
(c) hotel (d) guest house

31. Fill in the gap which is more appropriate. Inducing a girl under 18 years of age to go away with him from ________ is an offence.
(a) Normal home (b) Place of work
(c) Domestic area (d) Any place

32. Find the correct answer:
The principle of intergenerational equity envisages:
(a) Conservation of options
(b) Conservation of quality
(c) Conservation of access
(d) All of the above

33. Find the correct answer:
The Supreme Court allowed compensation of ₹ 23.84 lakhs and later allowed additional compensation of ₹ 47 lakhs to the farmers whose crops got damaged, being irrigated by subsoil water drawn from a stream which was polluted from untreated effluents of 22 industries. It was decided in the case of
(a) Vellore Citizens Welfare Forum vs. Union of India
(b) Indian Council For Environment Action vs. Union of India
(c) S. Jagannath vs. Union of India
(d) Narmada Bachao Andolan vs. Union of India

34. The concept of sustainable development contains which of the following essentials?
(a) The precautionary principle
(b) The polluter pays principle
(c) The doctrine of public trust
(d) All of the above

35. **Assertion (A):** The Supreme Court in Banwasi Seva Ashram vs. State of Uttar Pradesh, permitted the government agency to acquire the forest land, ousting certain tribal dwellers to implement a power project only after they agreed to provide certain facilities approved by the Court.
Reason (R): Because the governmental action had an environmental impact that threatened to dislocate poor forest dwellers and disrupt their lifestyle infringing their fundamental right to life, which include the right to livelihood.
Codes:
(a) (A) is true and (R) is false.
(b) (A) and (R) both are true, but (R) is not a correct explanation of (A).
(c) (A) is false and (R) is true.
(d) Both (A) and (R) are true and (R) is good explanation of (A).

36. The Supreme Court observed that noise pollution cannot be tolerated, even if such noise was a direct result of and was connected with religious activities in the case of
(a) A.P. Pollution Control Board vs. Prof M.V. Naidu
(b) Church of God (Full Gospel) in India vs. KKR Majestic Colony Welfare Association.
(c) K.M. Chinappa vs. Union of India
(d) Narmada Bachao Andolan vs. Union of India

37. **Assertion (A):** Nobody can claim a fundamental right to create noise pollution by amplifying the sound of his speech with the help of loudspeaker.
Reason (R): While one has a right to speech, others have a right to listen or

decline to listen. Anyone who wishes to live in peace, comfort and quiet within his house has a fundamental right to prevent the noise as pollutantion reaching him.

Codes:

(a) (A) is true, but (R) is false.
(b) (A) is false, but (R) is true.
(c) Both (A) and (R) are true, but (R) is not a correct explanation.
(d) Both (A) and (R) are true and (R) is good explanation of (A).

38. In which of the following cases it was held that there is no reason to compel non-smokers to be helpless victims of air pollution?
(a) Samantha vs. State of A.P.
(b) M.C. Mehta vs. Union of India
(c) Murli Deora vs. Union of India
(d) Sheela Barse vs. Union of India

39. Protection and improvement of environment and safeguarding forests and wildlife is
(a) A fundamental right.
(b) One of the Directive Principles of State Policy.
(c) One of the Fundamental Duties.
(d) Both one of the Directive Principles of State Policy and one of the Fundamental Duties.

40. Who stated that international law is not true law but 'positive international morality' only, analogous to the rules binding a club or society?
(a) Oscar Schachter (b) John Austin
(c) Louis Flenkin (d) Hans Kelson

41. *Opino juris sive necessitatis* means
(a) Opinions of jurists is necessary evidence for determining rules of international custom
(b) Opinions of jurists is not necessary for ascertaining the rules of international law
(c) The feeling on the part of States that in acting as they do they are fulfilling a legal obligation
(d) None of the above

42. Which of the following cases supports constitutive theory of recognition, namely the act of recognition alone confers international personality on an entity purporting to be a state or clothes new government with an authority to enter into international relations?
(a) The Arantzazu Mendi, (1939) A.C. P 256
(b) A.M. Luther Vs. James Sagor & Co, (1921) 3 K.B. P. 532
(c) Tinoco Concessions, (1923) 1 United Nations Reports of International Arbitral Awards P. 369
(d) None of the above

43. Which of the following statements is true?
(a) Nationality is the evidence of the link or relations of an individual with the State whereas domicile denotes *de facto* residence of an individual in a State with an intention to permanently settle there.
(b) Nationality is an evidence of residence of an individual with an intention to permanently settle there.
(c) Domicile denotes the link or relations of an individual with the State.
(d) None of the above.

44. The Charter of the Untied Nations came into force on
(a) 26 June 1945
(b) 10 December 1945
(c) 24 October 1945
(d) 1 November 1945

45. A member of the United Nations which has persistently violated the principles contained in the Charter may be expelled from the United Nations by the

(a) Security Council
(b) General Assembly
(c) General Assembly upon the recommendation of the Security Council
(d) Security Council upon the recommendation of the General Assembly

46. The Judges of the International Court of Justice are elected by the
(a) General Assembly
(b) Security Council
(c) General Assembly upon recommendation of the Security Council
(d) General Assembly and the Security Council independently of one another

47. Under Section 6 of the Hindu Minority and Guardianship Act, 1956 the natural guardian of a minor child is
(a) Mother
(b) Father
(c) Both Mother and Father
(d) Either Mother or Father

48. A Muslim wife can relinquish her Mahr
(a) When she is minor
(b) When she has attained the age of puberty
(c) When she is not less than 18 years of age
(d) When she is not less than 21 years of age.

49. In Islamic Law "Faskh" means
(a) Restitution of conjugal rights.
(b) Judicial separation.
(c) Dissolution or rescission of the contract of marriage by judicial decree at the instance of the husband.
(d) Dissolution on rescission of the contract of marriage by judicial decree at the instance of the wife.

50. Muta marriage is recognised by
(a) Hanafi School
(b) Maliki School
(c) Ithna Ashari School
(d) Hanbali School

51. The term 'Hindu' denotes the person
(i) Professing Hindu Religion
(ii) Professing Buddh, Jain or Sikh Religion
(iii) Who are not professing Muslim, Christian, Parsi or Jew Religion. In respect of the aforesaid propositions which is correct?
(a) (i) and (ii) are correct but (iii) is incorrect.
(b) (ii) and (iii) are correct and (i) is incorrect.
(c) (i) and (iii) are correct and (ii) is incorrect.
(d) (i), (ii) and (iii) are all correct.

52. Match the List I with List II using the codes given below:

List I
A. Void Marriages
B. Voidable marriages
C. Divorce
D. Restitution of Conjugal Rights

List II
(i) Section 9 (ii) Section 11
(iii) Section 13 (iv) Section 12

Codes:	**(A)**	**(B)**	**(C)**	**(D)**
(a)	(ii)	(iv)	(iii)	(i)
(b)	(iv)	(iii)	(ii)	(i)
(c)	(iii)	(i)	(ii)	(iv)
(d)	(i)	(ii)	(iii)	(iv)

53. In which of the following case the Court held that Section 9 of the Hindu Marriage Act was Constitutionally violative of right to Human dignity and privacy?
(a) Bipin Chandra vs. Prabhavati
(b) T. Sareetha vs. T. Venkatasubah

(c) Lachman vs. Meena
(d) None of the above

54. Match the List I with List II and indicate the correct answer using the codes given below:

List I
A. Pre-Marriage Pregnancy
B. Marriage within Prohibited Degree Relationship
C. Cruelty
D. When any spouse without reasonable excuse withdraws from the society of the other

List II
(i) Divorce
(ii) Voidable Marriage
(iii) Void Marriage
(iv) Restitution of Conjugal Rights

Codes:	**(A)**	**(B)**	**(C)**	**(D)**
(a)	(ii)	(iv)	(i)	(iii)
(b)	(ii)	(iii)	(i)	(iv)
(c)	(iv)	(ii)	(iii)	(i)
(d)	(i)	(ii)	(iii)	(iv)

55. International Women's Day is celebrated every year on
(a) 2nd March (b) 4th March
(c) 6th March (d) 8th March

56. Which one of the following is correct according to Art I of the Universal Declaration of Human Rights, 1948?
(a) All human beings are born free and equal in rights.
(b) All human beings are born free, equal and dignity.
(c) All human beings are equal in dignity and rights.
(d) All human beings are born free and equal in rights and dignity.

57. Regional Human Rights Court does not exist in
(a) Africa (b) Europe
(c) America (d) Asia

58. Which protocol to the European Convention on Human Rights has abolished European Commission of Human Rights?
(a) Protocol 1 (b) Protocol 2
(c) Protocol 3 (d) Protocol 11

59. Which one of the following convention has neither interstate communication procedure nor individual communication procedure?
(a) International Convention on Civil and Political Rights
(b) International Convention on Economic, Social and Cultural Rights
(c) Convention on the Rights of Child
(d) Convention on the Rights of persons with Disabilities

60. The term of the office of the Chairperson and Members of the NHRC under Protection of Human Rights Act, 1993 is
(a) 5 years from the date on which he enters the office or until he attains the age of 70 years whichever is earlier.
(b) 4 years from the date on which he enters the office or until he attains the age of 70 years whichever is earlier.
(c) 3 years from the date on which he enters the office or until he attains the age of 68 years whichever is earlier.
(d) 5 years from the date on which he enters the office or until he attains the age of 68 years whichever is earlier.

61. The Chairperson of National Commission on Minorities shall be deemed member of
(a) Human Rights Council
(b) Law Commission of India
(c) National Human Rights Commission
(d) International Law Commission

62. Which one of the following is an 'actionable' wrong?
(a) Injuria sine damnum
(b) Damnum sine injuria
(c) Both of the above
(d) None of the above

63. Which of the following is the gist of tortious liability?
(a) Legal damages
(b) Violation of legal right
(c) Availability of legal duty
(d) None of the above

64. The Rule of Absolute Liability is subject to
(a) All the exceptions mentioned in the rule of Rylands vs. Fletcher
(b) Half of the exceptions mentioned in the rule of Rylands vs. Fletcher
(c) None of the exceptions mentioned in the rule of Rylands vs. Fletcher
(d) All the exceptions mentioned in rule of M.C. Mehta vs. Union of India

65. **Assertion (A):** If a person speaks ill of the business which X is doing, it amounts to defamation.
Reason (R): Slander is actionable *per se.*
Codes:
(a) Both (A) and (R) are true and (R) is the correct explanation of (A).
(b) Both (A) and (R) are true but (R) is not the correct explanation of (A).
(c) (A) is true but (R) is false.
(d) (A) is false but (R) is true.

66. In *res Ipsa Loquitor*:
(1) Presumption of negligence is there.
(2) Plaintiff has to bring direct evidence.
(3) Plaintiff is discharged from the duty of proving negligence on the part of the defendant.
(4) Court does not give chance to defendant to avoid his liability.
Codes:
(a) (1) and (2) are correct.
(b) (1), (2) and (4) are correct.
(c) (1), (2) and (3) are correct.
(d) (1) and (3) are correct.

67. Which one of the following statements is true?
(a) Both public and private nuisance are punishable under criminal law.
(b) Only private nuisance is punishable under criminal law, while there is no punishment for general nuisance.
(c) Public nuisance is punishable under criminal law while private nuisance is a moral wrong only.
(d) Public nuisance is punishable under criminal law, while private nuisance under civil law.

68. For constituting tort of nuisance, there should be
(a) Unreasonable interference
(b) Interference should be with the use of enjoyment of land
(c) Damage
(d) All of the above

69. Partnership is based on
(a) Mutual trust (b) Mutual benefit
(c) Mutual interest (d) Mutual agency

70. Which statements are correct?
(i) An undisclosed principal can intervene against express terms.
(ii) An undisclosed principal cannot intervene against express terms.
(iii) An undisclosed principal cannot intervene when he knows that the other party would not have dealt with him.
(iv) An undisclosed principal can intervene when he knows that the other party would not have dealt with him.

Codes:
(a) (i) and (ii) are correct.
(b) (ii) and (iii) are correct.
(c) (iii) and (iv) are correct.
(d) (iv) and (i) are correct.

71. Read the following passage, and match the column:

A negotiable instrument contains a contract and therefore must be supported by consideration. In order to be a holder in due course, the holder must have obtained the instrument before its maturity. An instrument payable on demand is current at least as long as no demand for payment is made. To make a holder in due course, the instrument must be complete and regular. A postdated cheque may not be complete and regular.

Column P
A. Negotiable instrument
B. Holder in due course
C. Currency of instrument
D. Complete and regular

Column Q
(i) Before maturity
(ii) Demand for payment
(iii) Post dated cheque
(iv) Consideration

Codes:	**(A)**	**(B)**	**(C)**	**(D)**
(a)	(i)	(iv)	(ii)	(iii)
(b)	(ii)	(iii)	(i)	(iv)
(c)	(iv)	(i)	(ii)	(iii)
(d)	(iv)	(iii)	(i)	(ii)

72. **Assertion (A):** Every public company shall have at least three and every private company at least two Directors.

Reason (R): Directors are trustees for the company and not for individual shareholders.

Codes:
(a) (A) and (R) are true, but (R) is not an explanation for (A).
(b) (A) and (R) are true and (R) is an explanation for (A).
(c) (A) is true, but (R) is false.
(d) (R) is true, but (A) is false.

73. Arrange the following concepts in a sequence in which they appeared. Use the code given below:
(i) Right of an unpaid seller to stop goods in transit.
(ii) Agreement to sell goods.
(iii) Damages for breach of contract of sale of goods.
(iv) Conditions and warranties.

Codes:
(a) (ii), (iv), (iii), (i)
(b) (iv), (ii), (i), (iii)
(c) (ii), (i), (iv), (iii)
(d) (i), (ii), (iv), (iii)

74. Which statements are correct?
(i) Partner has a duty of good faith.
(ii) Partner has duty not to compete.
(iii) Partner has duty of due diligence.
(iv) Partner has duty to indemnify for fraud.

Codes:
(a) Only (i) is correct.
(b) Only (i) and (ii) are correct.
(c) Only (i), (ii) and (iii) are correct.
(d) (i), (ii), (iii) and (iv) are correct.

75. Match an item in List P with an item in List Q:

List P
(A) Removal of Directors by Company Law Board
(B) Duty of Directors to disclose interest
(C) Compensation for loss of office of Director
(D) Director with unlimited liability

List Q
(i) Section 318
(ii) Sections 299-300
(iii) Section 402
(iv) Sections 322-323

Codes:	(A)	(B)	(C)	(D)
(a)	(iii)	(ii)	(i)	(iv)
(b)	(ii)	(iii)	(i)	(iv)
(c)	(ii)	(iii)	(iv)	(i)
(d)	(ii)	(i)	(iii)	(iv)

ANSWERS

1. (a)	2. (a)	3. (c)	4. (d)	5. (a)
6. (a)	7. (b)	8. (c)	9. (d)	10. (a)
11. (d)	12. (d)	13. (d)	14. (b)	15. (a)
16. (d)	17. (d)	18. (b)	19. (b)	20. (a)
21. (c)	22. (d)	23. (d)	24. (a)	25. (b)
26. (b)	27. (c)	28. (c)	29. (d)	30. (b)
31. (d)	32. (d)	33. (b)	34. (d)	35. (d)
36. (b)	37. (d)	38. (c)	39. (d)	40. (b)
41. (c)	42. (d)	43. (a)	44. (c)	45. (c)
46. (d)	47. (b)	48. (c)	49. (c)	50. (c)
51. (d)	52. (a)	53. (b)	54. (b)	55. (d)
56. (c)	57. (d)	58. (d)	59. (c)	60. (a)
61. (c)	62. (a)	63. (b)	64. (c)	65. (c)
66. (d)	67. (c)	68. (d)	69. (d)	70. (b)
71. (c)	72. (a)	73. (b)	74. (d)	75. (a)

DECEMBER–2013

Note: This paper contains Sixty (60) multiple-choice questions, each question carrying two (2) marks. Candidate is expected to answer any Fifty (50) questions. In case more than Fifty (50) questions are attempted, only the first Fifty (50) questions will be evaluated.

PAPER–I

1. The post-industrial society is designated as
   (a) Information society
   (b) Technology society
   (c) Mediated society
   (d) Non-agricultural society

2. The initial efforts for Internet-based communication was for
   (a) Commercial communication
   (b) Military purposes
   (c) Personal interaction
   (d) Political campaigns

3. Internal communication within institutions is done through
   (a) LAN (b) WAN
   (c) EBB (d) MMS

4. Virtual reality provides
   (a) Sharp pictures
   (b) Individual audio
   (c) Participatory experience
   (d) Preview of new films

5. The first virtual university of India came up in
   (a) Andhra Pradesh
   (b) Maharashtra
   (c) Uttar Pradesh
   (d) Tamil Nadu

6. Arrange the following books in chronological order in which they appeared. Use the codes given below:
   (i) Limits to Growth
   (ii) Silent Spring
   (iii) Our Common Future
   (iv) Resourceful Earth

   Codes:
   (a) (i), (iii), (iv), (ii)
   (b) (ii), (iii), (i), (iv)
   (c) (ii), (i), (iii), (iv)
   (d) (i), (ii), (iii), (iv)

7. Which one of the following continents is at a greater risk of desertification?
   (a) Africa (b) Asia
   (c) South America (d) North America

8. "Women are closer to nature than men." What kind of perspective is this?
   (a) Realist (b) Essentialist
   (c) Feminist (d) Deep ecology

9. Which one of the following is not a matter a global concern in the removal of tropical forests?
   (a) Their ability to absorb the chemicals that contribute to depletion of ozone layer.
   (b) Their role in maintaining the oxygen and carbon balance of the earth.
   (c) Their ability to regulate surface and air temperatures, moisture content and reflectivity.
   (d) Their contribution to the biological diversity of the planet.

10. The most comprehensive approach to address the problems of man-environment interaction is one of the following:

(a) Natural Resource Conservation Approach
(b) Urban-industrial Growth Oriented Approach
(c) Rural-agricultural Growth Oriented Approach
(d) Watershed Development Approach

11. The major source of the pollutant gas, carbon monooxide (CO), in urban areas is
(a) Thermal power sector
(b) Transport sector
(c) Industrial sector
(d) Domestic sector

12. In a fuel cell driven vehicle, the energy is obtained from the combustion of
(a) Methane (b) Hydrogen
(c) LPG (d) CNG

13. Which one of the following Councils has been disbanded in 2013?
(a) Distance Education Council (DEC)
(b) National Council for Teacher Education (NCTE)
(c) National Council of Educational Research and Training (NCERT)
(d) National Assessment and Accreditation Council (NAAC)

14. Which of the following statements are correct about the National Assessment and Accreditation Council?
1. It is an autonomous institution.
2. It is tasked with the responsibility of assessing and accrediting institutions of higher education.
3. It is located in Delhi.
4. It has regional offices.

Select the correct answer from the codes given below:

Codes:
(a) 1 and 3 (b) 1 and 2
(c) 1, 2 and 4 (d) 2, 3 and 4

15. The power of the Supreme Court of India to decide disputes between two or more States falls under its
(a) Advisory Jurisdiction
(b) Appellate Jurisdiction
(c) Original Jurisdiction
(d) Writ Jurisdiction

16. Which of the following statements are correct?
1. There are seven Union Territories in India.
2. Two Union Territories have Legislative Assemblies
3. One Union Territory has a High Court.
4. One Union Territory is the capital of two States.

Select the correct answer from the codes given below:

Codes:
(a) 1 and 3
(b) 2 and 4
(c) 2, 3 and 4
(d) 1, 2, 3 and 4

17. Which of the following statements are correct about the Central Information Commission?
1. The Central Information Commission is a statutory body.
2. The Chief Information Commissioner and other Information Commissioners are appointed by the President of India.
3. The Commission can impose a penalty upto a maximum of ₹ 25,000
4. It can punish an errant officer.

Select the correct answer from the codes given below:

Codes:
(a) 1 and 2 (b) 1, 2 and 4
(c) 1, 2 and 3 (d) 2, 3 and 4

18. Who among the following conducted the CNN-IBN-The Hindu 2013 Election

Tracker Survey across 267 constituencies in 18 States?
(a) The Centre for the Study of Developing Societies (CSDS)
(b) The Association for Democratic Reforms (ADR)
(c) CNN and IBN
(d) CNN, IBN and The Hindu

19. In certain code TEACHER is written as VGCEJGT. The code of CHILDREN will be
(a) EKNJFTGP (b) EJKNFTGP
(c) KNJFGTP (d) None of these

20. A person has to buy both apples and mangoes. The cost of one apple is ₹ 7 whereas that of a mango is ₹ 5. If the person has ₹ 38, the number of apples he can buy is
(a) 1 (b) 2
(c) 3 (d) 4

21. A man pointing to a lady said, "The son of her only brother is the brother of my wife". The lady is related to the man as
(a) Mother's sister
(b) Grandmother
(c) Mother-in-law
(d) Sister of father-in-law

22. In this series
6, 4, 1, 2, 2, 8, 7, 4, 2, 1, 5, 3, 8, 6, 2, 2, 7, 1, 4, 1, 3, 5, 8, 6, how many pairs of successive numbers have a difference of 2 each?
(a) 4 (b) 5
(c) 6 (d) 8

23. The mean marks obtained by a class of 40 students is 65. The mean marks of half of the students is found to be 45. The mean marks of the remaining students is
(a) 85 (b) 60
(c) 70 (d) 65

24. Anil is twice as old as Sunita. Three years ago, he was three times as old as Sunita. The present age of Anil is
(a) 6 years (b) 8 years
(c) 12 years (d) 16 years

25. Which of the following is a social network?
(a) amazon.com (b) eBay
(c) gmail.com (d) Twitter

26. The population information is called parameter while the corresponding sample information is known as
(a) Universe
(b) Inference
(c) Sampling design
(d) Statistics

Read the following passage carefully and answer questions 27 to 32:

Heritage conservation practices improved worldwide after the International Centre for the Study of the Preservation and Restoration of Cultural Property (ICCROM) was established with UNESCO's assistance in 1959. The inter-governmental organisation with 126 member states has done a commendable job by training more than 4,000 professionals, providing practice standards, and sharing technical expertise. In this golden jubilee year, as we acknowledge its key role in global conservation, an assessment of international practices would be meaningful to the Indian conservation movement. Consistent investment, rigorous attention, and dedicated research and dissemination are some of the positive lessons to imbibe. Countries such as Italy have demonstrated that prioritising heritage with significant budget provision pays. On the other hand, India, which is no less endowed in terms of cultural capital, has a long way to go. Surveys indicate that in addition to the 6,600 protected monuments, there are over 60,000 equally valuable heritage structures that await attention. Besides the small group in the service of Archaeological Survey of India, there are only about 150 trained conservation professionals. In order to overcome this severe shortage the emphasis has been on setting up dedicated labs and training institutions. It would make much better sense for conservation to be made part of mainstream research and engineering institutes, as has been done in Europe.

Increasing funding and building institutions are the relatively easy part. The real challenge is to redefine international approaches to address local contexts. Conservation cannot limit itself to enhancing the art-historical value of the heritage structures, which international charters perhaps overemphasise. The effort has to be broad-based. It must also serve as a means to improving the quality of life in the area where the heritage structures are located. The first task therefore is to integrate conservation efforts with sound development plans that take care of people living in the heritage vicinity. Unlike in western countries, many traditional building crafts survive in India, and conservation practices offer an avenue to support them. This has been acknowledged by the Indian National Trust for Art and Cultural Heritage charter for conservation but is yet to receive substantial state support. More strength for heritage conservation can be mobilised by aligning it with the green building movement. Heritage structures are essentially eco-friendly and conservation could become a vital part of the sustainable building practices campaign in future.

27. The outlook for conservation heritage changed
    (a) after the establishment of the International Centre for the Study of the Preservation and Restoration of Cultural Property.
    (b) after training the specialists in the field.
    (c) after extending UNESCO's assistance to the educational institutions.
    (d) after ASI's measures to protect the monuments.

28. The inter-government organization was appreciated because of
    (a) increasing number of members to 126.
    (b) imparting training to professionals and sharing technical expertise.
    (c) consistent investment in conservation.
    (d) its proactive role in renovation and restoration.

29. Indian conservation movement will be successful if there would be
    (a) Financial support from the Government of India.
    (b) Non-governmental organisation's role and participation in the conservation movement.
    (c) consistent investment, rigorous attention, and dedicated research and dissemination of awareness for conservation.
    (d) Archaeological Survey of India's meaningful assistance.

30. As per the surveys of historical monuments in India, there is very small number of protected monuments. As per given the total number of monuments and enlisted number of protected monuments, percentage comes to
    (a) 10 percent (b) 11 percent
    (c) 12 percent (d) 13 percent

31. What should India learn from Europe to conserve our cultural heritage?
    (i) There should be significant budget provision to conserve our cultural heritage.
    (ii) Establish dedicated labs and training institutions.
    (iii) Force the government to provide sufficient funds.
    (iv) Conservation should be made part of mainstream research and engineering institutes.

Choose correct answer from the codes given below:
(a) (i), (ii), (iii), (iv)
(b) (i), (ii), (iv)
(c) (i), (ii)
(d) (i), (iii), (iv)

32. INTACH is known for its contribution for conservation of our cultural heritage. The full form of INTACH is
(a) International Trust for Art and Cultural Heritage.
(b) Intra-national Trust for Art and Cultural Heritage
(c) Integrated Trust for Art and Cultural Heritage
(d) Indian National Trust for Art and Cultural Heritage

33. While delivering lecture if there is some disturbance in the class, a teacher should
(a) keep quiet for a while and then continue.
(b) punish those causing disturbance.
(c) motivate to teach those causing disturbance.
(d) not bother of what is happening in the class.

34. Effective teaching is a function of
(a) Teacher's satisfaction.
(b) Teacher's honesty and commitment.
(c) Teacher's making students learn and understand.
(d) Teacher's liking for professional excellence.

35. The most appropriate meaning of learning is
(a) Acquisition of skills
(b) Modification of behaviour
(c) Personal adjustment
(d) Inculcation of knowledge

36. Arrange the following teaching process in order:
(i) Relate the present knowledge with previous one
(ii) Evaluation
(iii) Reteaching
(iv) Formulating instructional objectives
(v) Presentation of instructional materials
(a) (i), (ii), (iii), (iv), (v)
(b) (ii), (i), (iii), (iv), (v)
(c) (v), (iv), (iii), (i), (ii)
(d) (iv), (i), (v), (ii), (iii)

37. CIET stands for
(a) Centre for Integrated Education and Technology
(b) Central Institute for Engineering and Technology
(c) Central Institute for Education Technology
(d) Centre for Integrated Evaluation Techniques.

38. Teacher's role at higher education level is to
(a) provide information to students.
(b) promote self-learning in students.
(c) encourage healthy competition among students.
(d) help students to solve their problems.

39. The Verstehen School of Understanding was popularised by
(a) German Social Scientists
(b) American Philosophers
(c) British Academicians
(d) Italian Political Analysts

40. The sequential operations in scientific research are
(a) Co-variation, Elimination of Spurious Relations, Generalisation, Theorisation
(b) Generalisation, Co-variation, Theorisation, Elimination of Spurious Relations
(c) Theorisation, Generalisation, Elimination of Spurious Relations, Co-variation
(d) Elimination of Spurious Relations, Theorisation, Generalisation, Co-variation.

41. In sampling, the lottery method is used for
(a) Interpretation
(b) Theorisation
(c) Conceptualisation
(d) Randomisation

42. Which is the main objective of research?
(a) To review the literature
(b) To summarize what is already known
(c) To get an academic degree
(d) To discover new facts or to make fresh interpretation of known facts

43. Sampling error decreases with the
(a) decrease in sample size
(b) increase in sample size
(c) process of randomization
(d) process of analysis

44. The principles of fundamental research are used in
(a) action research
(b) applied research
(c) philosophical research
(d) historical research

45. Users who use media for their own ends are identified as
(a) Passive audience
(b) Active audience
(c) Positive audience
(d) Negative audience

46. Classroom communication can be described as
(a) Exploration
(b) Institutionalisation
(c) Unsignified narration
(d) Discourse

47. Ideological codes shape our collective
(a) Productions (b) Perceptions
(c) Consumptions (d) Creations

48. In communication, myths have power, but are
(a) Uncultural (b) Insignificant
(c) Imprecise (d) Unpreferred

49. The first multi-lingual news agency of India was
(a) Samachar
(b) API
(c) Hindustan Samachar
(d) Samachar Bharati

50. Organisational communication can also be equated with
(a) intra-personal communication
(b) inter-personal communication
(c) group communication
(d) mass communication

51. If two propositions having the same subject and predicate terms are such that one is the denial of the other, the relationship between them is called
(a) Contradictory (b) Contrary
(c) Sub-contrary (d) Sub-alternation

52. Ananya and Krishna can speak and follow English. Bulbul can write and speak Hindi as Archana does. Archana talks with Ananya also in Bengali. Krishna cannot follow Bengali. Bulbul talks with Ananya in Hindi. Who can speak and follow English, Hindi and Bengali?
(a) Archana (b) Bulbul
(c) Ananya (d) Krishna

53. A stipulative definition may be said to be
(a) Always true
(b) Always false
(c) Sometimes true, sometimes false
(d) Neither true nor false

54. When the conclusion of an argument follows from its premise/premises conclusively, the argument is called
(a) Circular argument
(b) Inductive argument
(c) Deductive argument
(d) Analogical argument

55. Saturn and Mars are planets like the Earth. They borrow light from the Sun

and moves around the Sun as the Earth does. So those planets are inhabited by various orders of creatures as the Earth is.

What type of argument is contained in the above passage?

(a) Deductive (b) Astrological
(c) Analogical (d) Mathematical

56. Given below are two premises. Four conclusions are drawn from those two premises in four codes. Select the code that states the conclusion validly drawn.

Premises:

(i) All saints are religious. (major)
(ii) Some honest persons are saints. (minor)

Codes:

(a) All saints are honest.
(b) Some saints are honest.
(c) Some honest persons are religious.
(d) All religious persons are honest

Following table provides details about the Foreign Tourist Arrivals (FTAs) in India from different regions of the world in different years. Study the table carefully and answer questions from 57 to 60 based on this table.

Region	Number of Foreign Tourist Arrivals		
	2007	2008	2009
Western Europe	1686083	1799525	1610086
North America	1007276	1027297	1024469
South Asia	982428	1051846	982633
South East Asia	303475	332925	348495
East Asia	352037	355230	318292
West Asia	171661	215542	201110
Total FTAs in India	5081504	5282603	5108579

57. Find out the region that contributed around 20 percent of the total foreign tourist arrivals in India in 2009.

(a) Western Europe (b) North America
(c) South Asia (d) South East Asia

58. Which of the following regions has recorded the highest negative growth rate of foreign tourist arrivals in India in 2009?

(a) Western Europe (b) North America
(c) South Asia (d) West Asia

59. Find out the region that has been showing declining trend in terms of share of foreign tourist arrivals in India in 2008 and 2009.

(a) Western Europe (b) South East Asia
(c) East Asia (d) West Asia

60. Identify the region that has shown hyper growth rate of foreign tourist arrivals than the growth rate of the total FTAs in India in 2008.

(a) Western Europe (b) North America
(c) South Asia (d) East Asia

ANSWERS

1. (a)	2. (b)	3. (a)	4. (c)	5. (d)
6. (c)	7. (a)	8. (b)	9. (a)	10. (d)
11. (b)	12. (b)	13. (a)	14. (b)	15. (c)
16. (d)	17. (c)	18. (a)	19. (b)	20. (d)
21. (d)	22. (c)	23. (a)	24. (c)	25. (d)
26. (d)	27. (a)	28. (b)	29. (c)	30. (b)
31. (b)	32. (d)	33. (c)	34. (c)	35. (b)
36. (d)	37. (c)	38. (b)	39. (a)	40. (a)
41. (d)	42. (d)	43. (b)	44. (b)	45. (b)
46. (d)	47. (b)	48. (c)	49. (c)	50. (c)
51. (a)	52. (c)	53. (d)	54. (c)	55. (c)
56. (c)	57. (b)	58. (d)	59. (a)	60. (c)

PAPER–II

Note: This paper contains fifty (50) objective type questions, each question carrying two (2) marks. All questions are compulsory.

1. Social, economic and political justice is
   (a) an idea enshrined in the Preamble to the Constitution of India
   (b) guaranteed by Fundamental Rights in the Constitution of India
   (c) a Directive Principle of State Policy taken into consideration while making enactments
   (d) guaranteed to the people by the writs issued by the High Courts and Supreme Court

2. Without paying proper remuneration, labour taken from the prisoners is 'forced labour' and violation of
   (a) Art. 20 of the Constitution of India
   (b) Art. 21 of the Constitution of India
   (c) Art. 22 of the Constitution of India
   (d) Art. 23 of the Constitution of India

3. Art. 51A of the Constitution of India provides for the Fundamental Duties of
   (a) Citizens of India
   (b) Public Servants
   (c) All those who run public and private sectors
   (d) Prime Minister and his Council of Ministers

4. The appropriate writ issued by Supreme Court to quash the appointment of a person to a public office is
   (a) Certiorari (b) Mandamus
   (c) Prohibition (d) Quo-Warranto

5. The power of the President of India to issue an ordinance is a
   (a) Legislative power
   (b) Executive power
   (c) Quasi-judicial power
   (d) Judicial power

6. The jurisdiction of Supreme Court of India may be enlarged by
   (a) The President of India
   (b) The Parliament by resolution
   (c) The Parliament by Law
   (d) The President in consultation with the Chief Justice of India

7. At the first instance, the President can issue a proclamation of financial emergency for a period of
   (a) Fifteen days (b) Two months
   (c) One month (d) Six months

8. Legal Theory is based on
   (a) a systematic study of positive laws
   (b) purely logical and empirical study
   (c) concepts like morality, justice and ethics
   (d) total exclusion of customary practices, morality and social vagaries

9. Who separated jurisprudence from religion?
   (a) Kant (b) Hugo Grotius
   (c) Salmond (d) Jethro Brown

10. Under how many categories the five theories of punishment can be divided?
    (a) 2 (b) 4
    (c) 5 (d) 3

11. On which one of the following one can have corporeal ownership?
    (a) A right
    (b) Trademark
    (c) Movable property
    (d) A debt

12. "Sovereignty must be determinate, it is essential, is indivisible and is unlimited and illimitable." Who conceived this about the sovereignty?
    (a) Hobbes (b) Austin
    (c) Jean Bodin (d) Plato

13. Consider the following statements:
    1. Statements, which are not partaking of the character of ratio decidendi can be ignored while deciding the latter case.
    2. The ratio decidendi is not the reason of decision.
    3. Only that part of the judgment in an earlier decision is binding which constitutes the ratio decidendi of that case.
    4. A judicial decision has a binding force for subsequent cases but the whole judgment is not binding, only a part of it is biding.

    Which of the above statement(s) is/are correct ?

    (a) 1, 3, 4 (b) 1, 2, 3
    (c) 2, 3, 4 (d) 1, 2, 4

14. "Case law is gold in the mine, a few grains of the precious metal to the tons of useless matter, while statute law is coin of the realm ready for immediate use." Who said these words?

    (a) Ihering (b) Austin
    (c) Kelson (d) Salmond

15. Which of the following statements are true?
    1. There is no rule to determine when usage shall give rise to a custom.
    2. Customary rules of International Law are diminishing and are being replaced by Treaties and Conventions.
    3. Treaty contracts are not direct source of International Law.
    4. International Law is a positive morality.

    Codes:

    (a) 1, 2, 3 & 4 (b) 2, 3 & 4
    (c) 1, 2 & 3 (d) 1 & 2

16. "The Law of National or International Law may be defined as the body of rules and principles of actions which are binding upon civilized states in their relations with one-another."

    This definition of International law was given by

    (a) J.L. Brierly (b) Torsten Vitel
    (c) Hackworth (d) None of these

17. Match the following:

    List-I

    A. Recognition only and exclusively bestows a State with rights and duties under International Law.
    B. It is a first step towards final recognition.
    C. It is a final recognition by a State.
    D. International personality of a State does not depend upon recognition.

    List-II

    i. De-facto recognition
    ii. De-Jure recognition
    iii. Declaratory Theory
    iv. Constitutive Theory

Codes:	A	B	C	D
(a)	iv	i	ii	iii
(b)	i	ii	iii	iv
(c)	iv	iii	ii	i
(d)	iii	ii	i	iv

18. The Charter of the United Nations can be amended by
    (a) Five-thirds of the members of General Assembly.
    (b) The Security Council only
    (c) Two-thirds of the members of the U.N. including all permanent members of the Security Council after recommendations by a two-thirds vote of a conference convened for the purpose, is received.
    (d) Two-thirds of the members of the Security Council including five permanent member

19. In which of the following cases, International Court of Justice denied existence of customary rule?

(a) North Sea Continental Shelf case.
(b) The Lotus case.
(c) Both of the above.
(d) None of the above.

20. Which organ of the United Nations has been given responsibility of promoting international co-operation in the realisation of human rights?
(a) General Assembly
(b) Security Council
(c) Both of the above
(d) None of the above

21. In which of the following cases the Supreme Court held that even the wife of a void marriage is entitled to maintenance?
(a) Amarjeet Kaur Vs. Harbhajan Singh (2003) 10 SCC 228.
(b) Chand Dhawan Vs. Jawaharlal Dhawan (1993) 3 SCC 406.
(c) Nirmala Devi Vs. Ram Dass (2001) 2 SCC 4.
(d) Ramesh Chandra Vs. Veena Kausal AIR 1978 SC 1807.

22. In which of the following cases, the court held that "Dower is a sale price of woman"?
(a) Maina Bibi case
(b) Humara Bibi case
(c) Subrunnisan case
(d) Abdul Kadir case

23. Read Assertion (A) and Reason (R). Find correct answer using codes given below:
Assertion (A): "Option of Puberty" is an easy process to repudiate the marriage under Hindu Law.
Reason (R): "Option of Puberty" is not an easy process to repudiate the marriage under Muslim Law.
Codes:
(a) (A) is correct, but (R) is incorrect.
(b) (A) and (R) both are correct.
(c) (R) is correct, but (A) is incorrect.
(d) (A) and (R) both are incorrect.

24. 'Tuhr' means
(a) Period of menstruation
(b) Period of iddat
(c) Period between menstruation
(d) None of the above

25. Match an item in List–I with correct answer in List–II using the codes given below:

List–I
A. Gujarat Women's Workers Association Vs. Union of India
B. Humara Bibi Vs. Zubaida Bibi Divorce
C. Anwari Begum Vs. Ziauddin
D. Bai Tahira Vs. Ali Hussain Fissalli

List–II
i. Dower
ii. Triple
iii. Uniform Civil Code
iv. Maintenance

Codes:	A	B	C	D
(a)	i	iv	ii	iii
(b)	i	ii	iii	iv
(c)	iii	i	ii	iv
(d)	ii	iii	iv	i

26. Which form of talaq is revocable during period of 'iddat'?
(a) Talaq-i-Ahsan
(b) Talaq-i-Hasan
(c) Triple Talaq
(d) None of the above

27. Essentials of valid contract is
(a) Meeting of minds
(b) Meeting of parties
(c) Meeting to discuss consideration
(d) Meeting to discuss proposal and acceptance

28. Read Assertion (A) and Reason (R) and with help of codes given below, point out the correct explanation.

Assertion (A): A proposal, when accepted, results in an agreement.
Reason (R): It is only after the acceptance of the proposal that a contract between the two parties can arise.

Codes:
(a) Both (A) and (R) are true and (R) is good explanation of (A).
(b) Both (A) and (R) are true, but (R) is not a correct explanation of (A).
(c) (A) is true, but (R) is false.
(d) (A) is false, but (R) is true.

29. A minor is son of a beggar. He is told by a law professor that he would not be liable for any goods he purchases. The minor purchases a car and a bread loaf. Decide liability for payment of car and bread loaf, using codes given below.
(a) The minor is liable to pay price of car and bread loaf.
(b) The minor is liable to pay reasonable compensation for car.
(c) The minor is liable to pay price of bread.
(d) The minor's parent/guardian is liable to pay reasonable compensation for bread loaf.

30. Arrange following concepts in sequence in which they occur, using codes given below:
(i) Offer (ii) Acceptance
(iii) Damage (iv) Damages
Codes:
(a) (iv), (iii), (ii), (i)
(b) (i), (ii), (iv), (iii)
(c) (i), (iv), (ii), (iii)
(d) (i), (ii), (iii), (iv)

31. A contract may be vitiated by:
(i) Fraud
(ii) Mistake
(iii) Frustration
(iv) Undue influence
Find correct answer, using codes:
Codes:
(a) Only (i) is correct.
(b) Only (i) and (ii) are correct.
(c) Only (i), (ii) and (iii) are correct.
(d) All are correct.

32. Match items in Table A with items in Table B, using codes given below:
Table – A
A. Promise
B. Frustration
C. Effect of refusal to accept offer of performance
D. Agreement in restraint of marriage
Table – B
i. Section 56 ii. Section 2(d)
iii. Section 26 iv. Section 38

Codes:	i	ii	iii	iv
(a)	B	D	A	C
(b)	B	A	D	C
(c)	A	B	D	C
(d)	A	B	C	D

33. P, owner of a car, asked his friend Q to drive the car to Bombay where he would join him. As the car was about five kilometres from Bombay, it hit a pedestrian R, on account of Q's negligent driving and injured him seriously. R sued P for damages. In this case:
(a) P is not liable.
(b) The liability is solely of Q, as P was not accompanying him.
(c) Since Q was driving P's car was under his authority, P is liable.
(d) P has the defence of inevitable accident.

34. "If it was lawful act, however ill the motive might be, the defendant had a right to do it." This observation was made by the court in one of the following cases:

(a) Mayor of Bradford Corporation Vs. Pickles
(b) Ashby Vs. White
(c) Christie Vs. Davey
(d) Hollywood Silver Fox Farm Ltd. Vs. Emmet

35. P and Q, unknown to R, sought and got a lift in R's car, but on account of some mechanical defect in the car, of which R was not aware, one of the front wheels of the car got detached and flew away, and the car toppled. P and Q got serious injuries and later on, P died of his injuries. Q and P's next kin sued R for damages for negligent driving. What defence R has?
(a) Volenti non fit injuria
(b) No responsibility towards P and Q who got a free lift
(c) Inevitable accident
(d) No defence

36. In contributory negligence:
(a) Both parties have contributed to the negligence equally.
(b) Only one party is negligent and other has not taken due care.
(c) One party is negligent resulting in injury while the other has taken due care.
(d) When lack of care is equal on both sides.

37. P shoot at Q with the view to kill him. When Q was being taken to hospital, a tree fell upon Q on the way and Q died in the hospital a few days later. If it was proved that the falling of the tree caused Q's death, then
(a) P shall be responsible for the death of Q.
(b) Falling of tree has broken the chain of causation.
(c) P is not liable to pay compensation to the dependents of Q.
(d) P is responsible for the death of Q as Q's death was the direct consequence of P's act.

38. Which one of the following has been laid down as basis of responsibility by the rule in Rylands Vs. Fletcher?
(a) Fault liability
(b) Conditional liability
(c) Strict liability
(d) Insurance liability

39. Read Assertion I and Reason II and with the help of codes given below decide what offence if any was committed?
Assertion I: A and Z agree to fence with each other for a game. But because of foul, despite playing fairly, Z was injured.
Reason II:
A. No offence by virtue of consent between A and Z.
B. Consent was obtained in good faith to gain prize, so no offence by A.
C. A is criminally liable because he had knowledge about the likelihood of injury.
D. Despite implied consent the intention was bad so A is liable.
Codes:
(a) Reason 'A' is true when 'B', 'C' and 'D' are not asserted.
(b) Reason 'B' is true when 'A', 'C' and 'D' are not asserted.
(c) Reason 'C' is true when 'A', 'B' and 'D' are not asserted.
(d) Reason 'D' is true when 'A', 'B' and 'C' are not asserted.

40. Read Assertion I and Reason II and with the help of codes given below select the correct answer:
Assertion I: Common intention is asserted.
Reason II:
A. A period which is anterior in time among the offenders.
B. From the facts of pre-arranged plan.

C. From the act of conduct resulting from prior concert.
D. From the totality of circumstances in which the act was committed.

Codes:

(a) 'A' is false because 'B', 'C' and 'D' do not support it.
(b) 'D' is true as 'A', 'B' and 'C' support it.
(c) 'C' is true irrespective of support of 'A', 'B' and 'D'.
(d) 'B' is true being supported by 'A', 'C' and 'D'.

41. Select the statement that is most suitable in law:
Culpable homicide is not murder when one is deprived of the power of self-control resulting from:
(a) Grave and sudden provocation
(b) When death results by voluntary provocation.
(c) Where death results in course of obedience of law.
(d) When death results by mistake.

42. B a married man commits sex with C a girl child of 16 years with her consent. What offence B has committed?
(a) Adultery
(b) Rape
(c) No offence
(d) Sexual outraging

43. Fill in the blank:
Extortion is ______, when it is committed under fear of instant hurt.
(a) Theft
(b) Attempt to steal property
(c) Robbery
(d) Wrongful restraint

44. Find answer of the following question: What is the distinctive feature between false information and false charging?
(a) Using lawful power to cause annoyance so as to institute a criminal proceeding.
(b) To omit act which ought not to be done.
(c) A case for false information can only be started by a complaint while false charge can be initiated by police.
(d) There is no real distinction.

45. Collective bargaining serves purposes:
(a) Regulating wages and conditions of service.
(b) Regulating labour management relations.
(c) Both (a) and (b).
(d) None of the above.

46. In which country where statutes make it obligatory to negotiate non-performance of the obligation invites penalty, failure to carry obligation is treated as unfair labour practice?
(a) U.K. (b) U.S.A.
(c) France (d) India

47. In which of the following cases, the Supreme Court held that "there was no rule of thumb that in every case of termination of workman's service in violation of Section 25F of ID Act relief of re-instatement should be granted?
(a) Talwara Co-operative Credit & Service Society Ltd. Vs. Sushil Kumar (2009) I LLJ 326 S.C.
(b) Gujarat Steel Tubes Ltd. Vs. G.S.T. Mazdoor Sabha (1980) I LLJ 137 S.C.
(c) Mavji C. Lakum Vs. Central Bank of India (2008) III LLJ.1. S.C.
(d) None of the above.

48. The Registrar to Pensions Appeal Tribunal was appointed as presiding officer of a Labour Court. The appointment is

(a) Valid
(b) Void
(c) Void ab-initio
(d) None of the above

49. Match List I with List II and select the correct answer using the codes given below:

List I (Subject)
A. Tribunal
B. Wages
C. Unfair Labour Practices
D. Village Industries

List II (Provisions of ID Act)
i. Section 2(ra) ii. Section 2(r)
iii. Section 2 (rb) iv. Section 2 (rr)

Codes:	A	B	C	D
(a)	i	iv	iii	ii
(b)	ii	iii	i	iv
(c)	ii	iv	i	iii
(d)	i	iii	ii	iv

50. Read Assertion (A) and Reason (R), using codes given below, select correct answer:
Assertion (A): Strike is individual stoppage of work to press management to get more pay.
Reason (R): Individual has fundamental right of strike.

Codes:
(a) (A) and (R) are true and (R) is correct explanation of (A).
(b) (A) and (R) are true, but (R) is not correct explanation of (A).
(c) (A) and (R) are false.
(d) (A) is true, but (R) is false.

ANSWERS

1. (a)	2. (d)	3. (a)	4. (d)	5. (a)
6. (c)	7. (b)	8. (c)	9. (b)	10. (d)
11. (c)	12. (b)	13. (a)	14. (d)	15. (c)
16. (a)	17. (a)	18. (d)	19. (c)	20. (c)
21. (b)	22. (c)	23. (b)	24. (c)	25. (c)
26. (a)	27. (a)	28. (a)	29. (d)	30. (d)
31. (d)	32. (b)	33. (c)	34. (a)	35. (c)
36. (b)	37. (b)	38. (c)	39. (a)	40. (b)
41. (a)	42. (c)	43. (c)	44. (b)	45. (c)
46. (b)	47. (a)	48. (c)	49. (c)	50. (c)

PAPER–III

Note: This paper contains seventy-five (75) objective type questions of two (2) marks each. All questions are compulsory.

1. Who among the following expressed the view that the Indian Constitution is Federal as much as it establishes what may be called a dual polity?
(a) Dr. B.R. Ambedkar
(b) Sir Ivor Jennings
(c) Prof. K.C. Wheare
(d) Sir B.N. Rau

2. In which of the following amendments the words 'Nothing in Article 13 shall apply to any amendment made under Article 368' were inserted?
(a) 22nd Amendment
(b) 24th Amendment
(c) 42nd Amendment
(d) 44th Amendment

3. The Supreme Court of India held in which of the following cases that the views expressed by it in exercise of its advisory jurisdiction are binding on all courts within the territory of India?
(a) In Re-Berubari case
(b) In Re-Cauvery Water Disputes Tribunal case
(c) In Re-Kerala Education Bill
(d) In Re-Special Courts Bill

4. In which one of the following cases has the Supreme Court upheld the Constitutional validity of the Constitution (93rd Amendment) introducing Article 15(5)?
   (a) TMA Pai Foundation Vs. State of Karnataka
   (b) Indra Sawhney Vs. Union of India
   (c) M. Nagaraj Vs. Union of India
   (d) Ashok Kumar Thakur Vs. Union of India

5. Match List 'A' with List 'B' and select the correct answer using the codes given below:

   List 'A'
   A. Independence of the Judiciary
   B. Executive Legislation
   C. Quasi-Judicial function
   D. Collective responsibility

   List 'B'
   i. Administrative adjudication
   ii. Parliamentary form of Government
   iii. Appointment of Judges
   iv. Ordinance

Codes:	A	B	C	D
(a)	ii	i	iv	iii
(b)	iii	iv	i	ii
(c)	ii	iv	i	iii
(d)	iii	i	iv	ii

6. Read Assertion (A) and Reason (R) and find correct answer using codes given below:
   Assertion (A): The Council of Ministers is the hub of the Parliamentary form of Government.
   Reason (R): The Government is formed from the majority party.
   Codes:
   (a) Both (A) and (R) are true but (R) is not the correct explanation of (A).
   (b) Both (A) and (R) are true and (R) is the correct explanation of (A).
   (c) (A) is true, (R) is false.
   (d) (A) is false, but (R) is true.

7. The jurisdiction of the Supreme Court of India may be enlarged by
   (a) The President of India
   (b) The President of India in consultation with the Prime Minister and Chief Justice of India
   (c) The Parliament by resolution
   (d) The Parliament by law

8. What are exceptions to the rule of natural justice? Answer using codes given below:
   i. Exclusion by statutory provisions.
   ii. Exclusion by Constitutional provision.
   iii. Exclusion in case of legislative act.
   iv. Exclusion in public interest.

   Codes:
   (a) Only i is correct.
   (b) Only i and ii are correct.
   (c) Only i, ii and iii are correct.
   (d) All of above are correct.

9. Read Assertion (A) and Reason (R) and find correct answer using codes given below:
   Assertion (A): In India the order passed in violation of the principles of natural justice is void.
   Reason (R): In India there is void in the area of principles of justice by nature.

   Codes:
   (a) (A) and (R) are true and (R) is correct explanation of (A).
   (b) (A) and (R) are true, but (R) is not correct explanation of (A).
   (c) (A) is true and (R) is false.
   (d) (A) is false and (R) is true.

10. In which of the following conditions, the abuse of discretionary power is inferred?
    i. Use for improper purpose
    ii. Mala fide
    iii. Relevant consideration
    iv. Leaving out irrelevant consideration

Answer using codes given below:

Codes:

(a) Only i is correct.
(b) Only i and ii are correct.
(c) Only i, ii and iii are correct.
(d) All of above are correct.

11. Read Assertion (A) and Reason (R) and find correct answer using codes given below:

Assertion (A): Equality is antithetic to arbitrariness.

Reason (R): Article 14 of the Indian Constitution prevents arbitrary discretion being vested in the executive.

Codes:

(a) Both (A) and (R) are true and (R) is correct explanation of (A).
(b) Both (A) and (R) are true, but (R) is not correct explanation of (A).
(c) (A) is true, but (R) is false.
(d) (A) is false, but (R) is true.

12. The writ of habeas corpus will be issued if

(a) Detention is legal.
(b) Detention is prima facie legal.
(c) Detention is prima facie illegal.
(d) Detention is primarily illegal.

13. Reading Assertion (A) and Reason (R), select correct answer using codes given below:

Assertion (A): Lokpal is the demand of time.

Reason (R): Lokpal is a time saving institution.

Codes:

(a) Both (A) and (R) are true, and (R) is correct explanation of (A).
(b) Both (A) and (R) are true, but (R) is not correct explanation of (A).
(c) (A) is true, but (R) is false.
(d) (A) is false, but (R) is true.

14. "Administrative Law is the law concerning the powers and procedures of administrative agencies, including especially the law governing judicial review of administrative action." This definition of Administrative Law is given by:

(a) Ivor Jenning (b) Garner
(c) K.C. Davis (d) Wade

15. In which of the following grounds, a writ of certiorari may be issued?

(a) Error of jurisdiction
(b) Error apparent on face of record
(c) Violation of natural justice
(d) All of the above

16. Who propounded the Doctrine of 'Moral Reasoning'?

(a) Kohler (b) Pound
(c) H.L.A. Hart (d) Kant

17. Which of the following avoid any dogmatic formulation and concentrate on the decisions given by law courts?

(a) Realist school
(b) Analytical school
(c) Philosophical school
(d) Sociological school

18. 'Jus civile', 'Jus gentium' and 'Jus naturale' are found in

(a) American Law (b) Greek Law
(c) Roman Law (d) French Law

19. Match the following:

A. Ancient theories
B. Modern theories
C. Renaissance theories
D. Medieval theories

i. Grotius, Hobbes & Locke
ii. Thomas Acquinas
iii. Stamler & Kohler
iv. Socrates, Aristotle and Plato

Codes:	A	B	C	D
(a)	iii	iv	ii	i
(b)	i	ii	iii	iv
(c)	ii	iii	iv	i
(d)	iv	iii	i	ii

20. "Law is without doubt a remedy for greater evil, yet it brings with it evils of its own." Who said it?
   (a) Blackstone (b) Friedman
   (c) Salmond (d) Hobbes

21. According to Salmond, every right involves a three-fold relation.
   I. It is a right against some person or persons.
   II. It is a right to some act or omission of such person or persons.
   III. It is a right over or to something to which that act or omission relates.

   Codes:
   (a) I and II are false.
   (b) I, II and III are true.
   (c) II and III are false.
   (d) Only I is true.

22. **Assertion (A):** Srutis and Smritis form the greatest treasure house of Hinduism.
   Reason (R): Srutis and Smritis are considered immemorial, timeless and eternal. Examine the above statement (A) and Reason (R) and select whether the reason is a correct explanation of the assertion, using the codes given below:
   Codes:
   (a) Both (A) and (R) are true, but (R) is not the correct explanation of (A).
   (b) Both (A) and (R) are true and (R) is the correct explanation of (A).
   (c) (A) is true, but (R) is false.
   (d) (A) is false, but (R) is true.

23. Personality is a very vague and wide term and it has a variety of meanings. It is derived from the word persona which is a
   (a) Latin word
   (b) French word
   (c) German word
   (d) Greek word

24. Fill in the blank with appropriate offence: Extortion is ______, when it is committed under fear of instant hurt.
   (a) Theft
   (b) Attempt to murder
   (c) Robbery
   (d) Wrongful restraint

25. Fill in the blank with suitable statement: Z dies in possession of gold ring, gold chain and a gold wrist watch during the course of an accident. A, before anyone entitled to such possession, dishonestly misappropriates the same causing ______.
   (a) An aggravated form of misappropriation as per Section 404 of IPC.
   (b) A type of possession by some process as per Section 405 of IPC.
   (c) No offence because the property in question was entrusted to A before the death of Z.
   (d) No offence because the property in question was possessed by some casualty.

26. Fill in the blank with correct proposition of law:
   The malicious injury to property as per maxim *Sic Utre tuo ut allenum non leadas* (to use your own property so as not to injure your neighbour's property as provided in ______.
   (a) Damage of property as per Section 427 IPC.
   (b) Mischief as per Section 425 IPC.
   (c) Mischief to cause wrongful restraint as per Section 440 IPC.
   (d) Destruction of landmark as per Section 433 IPC.

27. Read Assertion I and Reason II and with the help of codes given below write the appropriate answer:

I. Assertion: The distinctive feature between preparation and attempt must be based on.

II. Reason: Preparation consists in devising means necessary for the commission of offence while attempt is the direct movement towords commission.

Codes:

(a) Both I and II are true but II is not correct explanation of I.
(b) Both I and II are true while II is the correct explanation of I.
(c) I is true, but II is false.
(d) II is true, but I is only a stage of crime.

28. The accused caused bodily pain, disease or infirmity. But it is cognizable, bailable or compoundable. What offence, if any, has been committed by the accused?
(a) Voluntary causing grievous hurt as per Section 322 IPC.
(b) Voluntary causing serious hurt as per Section 325 IPC.
(c) Voluntary causing grievous hurt by dangerous weapon as per Section 324 IPC.
(d) Voluntary causing grievous hurt by dangerous weapon as per Section 326 IPC.

29. An individual's act of abridgement of another's right to movement could be an offence of:
(a) wrongful confinement as per Section 340 IPC.
(b) an act of abridgement of right to movement was done in good faith and hence no offence.
(c) the movement route being diverted so assault results.
(d) wrongful restraint as per Section 329 IPC.

30. Match the statement that *mens rea* is a loose term of elastic significance with that of the meaning in sequential order.
(A) Foresight of the consequences of the act.
(B) Criminal intention of deepest dye.
(C) An act which is visible.
(D) It depends upon knowledge and belief.

Matching probabilities:
(a) It is the bare capacity to know in the sequence of (A), (B), (C) and (D).
(b) It is essential ingredient of criminal offence in the sequence of (D), (C), (B) and (A).
(c) It is a presumption to fix criminal liability in the sequence of (C), (B), (A) and (D).
(d) Applicability of the principle becomes essential by the sequence of (B), (A), (D) and (C).

31. Read Assertion I and Reason II and with the help of codes given below point out the correct explanation.

I. Assertion: Generally a master is not criminally liable merely because his servant has committed a negligent act.

II. Reason: In ordinary course of employment a master may be criminally liable against the negligent acts of the servant.

Codes:
(a) Both I and II are true, but II is not the correct explanation of I.
(b) I is true and II is the genuine reason of I.
(c) II is true, but I is not absolutely correct.
(d) II is false, but I is only an assertion.

32. On which date & place the Earth Summit was held at?
(a) 6th June 1997 at Geneva.
(b) 20th June 1997 at London.
(c) 21st June 1992 at Rio.
(d) 27th June 1992 at Rio.

33. "In case of violation of Article 21 by disturbing the environment, the court

could award damages not only for the restoration of the ecological balance but also for the victim who have suffered due to that disturbance."

In which case the Supreme Court of India has made above observations?

(a) M.C. Mehta Vs. Union of India, AIR 1997 SC 734
(b) M.C. Mehta Vs. Kamal Nath 1997 1 SCC 388
(c) M.C. Mehta Vs. Kamal Nath AIR 2000 SC 1997
(d) M.C. Mehta Vs. Kamal Nath 2000 (2) SCALE 654

34. In which of the following cases the constitutionality, legal validity, propriety and fairness of the settlement of the claims of the victims in a mass tort action relating to Bhopal Gas Leak Disaster has been challenged in Supreme Court of India?

(a) Union Carbide Corp. Vs. Union of India, AIR 1990 SC 273
(b) M.C. Mehta Vs. Union of India, AIR 1987 SC 1086
(c) Union Carbide Corp. Vs. Union of India, AIR 1992 SC 248
(d) Charanlal Sahu Vs. Union of India, AIR 1990 SC 1480

35. Under which Article of the Constitution Environment (Protection) Act, 1986 was enacted?

(a) Article 253 (b) Article 258
(c) Article 255 (d) Article 254

36. The problem of the pollution of river Ganga by the inaction of the municipalities was brought to light in which of the following case?

(a) Indian Council for Enviro-Legal Action Vs. Union of India, AIR 1996 SC 1446
(b) A.P. Pollution Control Board Vs. M.V. Nayudu, AIR 1999 SC 812
(c) S. Jagannath Vs. Union of India, AIR 1997 SC 811
(d) M.C. Mehta Vs. Union of India, AIR 1988 SC 111

37. Which one of the following cases relates to Sariska Tiger Park?

(a) Tarun Bharat Sangh Vs. Union of India, AIR 1992 SC 514
(b) Consumer Education and Research Society Vs. Union of India, AIR 2000 SC 975
(c) Pradeep Krishen Vs. Union of India, AIR 1997 SC 2040
(d) Animal and Environmental Legal Defence Fund case, AIR 1997 SC 1070

38. Which of the following cases relates to transfer of Tribal lands by government to non-tribal people?

(a) Shri Manchegowda Vs. State of Karnataka, AIR 1984 SC 1151
(b) Samatha Vs. State of Andhra Pradesh, AIR 1997 SC 3297
(c) Suresh Lohiya Vs. State of Maharashtra (1996) 10 SCC
(d) Fatesang Gimba Vasava Vs. State of Gujarat, AIR 1987 Guj. 09

39. Match List I with List II and select the correct answer:

List I

A. Suspension of Members
B. Veto power
C. Appointment of Secretary-General
D. Objective of the Trusteeship System

List II

i. Article 5 ii. Article 6
iii. Article 27 iv. Article 76
v. Article 97

Codes:	**A**	**B**	**C**	**D**
(a)	i	ii	iii	iv
(b)	i	iii	iv	v
(c)	i	iii	v	iv
(d)	iii	ii	v	i

40. Which of the following Jurist regard the controversy "whether international law is a law, a dispute about words and not things"?
(a) Lawrence (b) Austin
(c) Hobbes (d) Hart

41. What should be the order of the use of material source of International Law?
1. Treaties and Conventions.
2. Customs.
3. General principles of law recognised by civilised States.
4. Judicial decisions and juristic opinion as subsidiary means for the determination of law.
(a) 4, 3, 2, 1 (b) 2, 3, 1, 4
(c) 4, 2, 1, 3 (d) 1, 2, 3, 4

42. Which of the Article of the Statute of International Court of Justice makes it clear that the decision of the court will have no binding force except between the parties and in respect of that particular case only?
(a) Article 60 (b) Article 59
(c) Article 68 (d) Article 38(1)

43. Which of the following functions are performed by Economic and Social Council?
1. It may make or initiate studies with respect to international economic, social, cultural, educational, health and related matters.
2. It may make recommendations for the purpose of promoting respect for and observance of human rights.
3. It may make recommendations to promote friendly relations and understanding amongst member States.
4. It may prepare draft conventions for submission to the General Assembly on any of the subjects falling within its competence.

Select the correct answer using the codes given below:
Codes:
(a) 1, 2, 3, 4 (b) 1, 3, 4
(c) 1, 2, 4 (d) 2, 3, 4

44. Match List I with List II and select the correct answer:
List I
A. The Covenant on Civil and Political Rights 1966
B. The Declaration on Human Rights
C. Convention on the Rights of Child
D. American Convention on Human Rights
List II
i. 16th Dec. ii. 1948
iii. 1990 iv. 1969

Codes:	**A**	**B**	**C**	**D**
(a)	iv	iii	ii	i
(b)	ii	iii	iv	i
(c)	i	ii	iii	iv
(d)	iv	ii	iii	i

45. **Assertion (A):** International Law is not a law.
Reason (R): It lacks determinate superior political authority to enforce its rules.
Using the codes given below give the correct answer.
Codes:
(a) Both (A) and (R) are true and (R) is the correct explanation of (A).
(b) Both (A) and (R) are true, but (R) is not the correct explanation of (A).
(c) (A) is true, but (R) is false.
(d) (A) is false, but (R) is true.

46. The junior widow has adopted a child without the consent of senior widow. Decide the adoption.
(a) Valid
(b) Void
(c) Voidable
(d) None of the above

47. In which State, where a widow may adopt a child without an express authority from her husband, before the HA&M Act, 1956?
   (a) Bihar and M.P.
   (b) U.P. and Haryana
   (c) Madras and Bombay
   (d) Orissa and Andhra Pradesh

48. In ancient Hindu Marriage, which one is not approved form of Marriage?
   (a) Brahma (b) Davia
   (c) Prajapatya (d) Asura

49. Read Assertion (A) and Reason (R) and with the help of codes given below select the correct explanation.
   Assertion (A): The Muslim Women (Protection of Divorce Rights) Act, 1986 brought changes like limit the period of maintenance to Muslim divorcee till 'iddat' period and in case of no relatives the liability on Wakf Boards.
   Reason (R): The changes were brought under Muslim's pressure.
   Codes:
   (a) Both (A) and (R) are true and (R) is correct explanation of (A).
   (b) Both (A) and (R) are true, but (R) is not correct explanation of (A).
   (c) (A) is correct, but (R) is false.
   (d) (A) is false, but (R) is true.

50. Read Assertion (A) and Reason (R) and with the help of codes given below select the correct explanation.
   Assertion (A): The Dissolution of Muslim Marriages Act, 1939 brought different grounds for dissolution of marriage and based on Maliki schools.
   Reason (R): The DMM Act, 1939 is brought on the opinion of Ulema (Ijma).
   Codes:
   (a) (A) and (R) are true, (R) is correct explanation of (A).
   (b) (A) and (R) are true, but (R) is not correct explanation of (A).
   (c) (A) is correct, but (R) is false.
   (d) (A) is false, but (R) is true.

51. A Muslim husband has failed to have 'sexual intercourse' continuously for four months with wife. It could be a form of divorce and is called
   (a) Illa (b) Mubarrah
   (c) Zihar (d) Khula

52. Match List I with List II and select correct answer from the codes:
   List I
   A. Judicial separation
   B. Divorce
   C. Voidable Marriages
   D. Restitution of Conjugal Rights
   List II
   i. Section 9 ii. Section 10
   iii. Section 13 iv. Section 12

Codes:	A	B	C	D
(a)	i	iii	ii	iv
(b)	ii	iv	iii	i
(c)	i	ii	iv	iii
(d)	ii	iii	iv	i

53. Match List I with List II and select correct answer from the codes:
   List I
   A. Impotency of Husband
   B. Marriage within Sapinda Relationship
   C. Pre-marriage Pregnancy
   D. Option of Puberty
   List II
   i. Divorce
   ii. Voidable Marriage
   iii. Nullity of Marriage
   iv. Void Marriage

Codes:	A	B	C	D
(a)	iv	iii	i	ii
(b)	iii	iv	ii	i
(c)	i	iii	iv	ii
(d)	ii	iv	i	iii

54. The Human Rights has been classified into three categories, viz.
(A) The Human Rights of first generation
(B) The Human Rights of second generation and
(C) The Human Rights of third generation, by
(a) Louis B. Sohan
(b) Theodoor C. Bowen
(c) R. Dworkin
(d) Bernard Mayo

55. "Everyone has the right to recognition everywhere as a person before the law". This has been stated in which of the following Article of Universal Declaration of Human Rights?
(a) Article 6 (b) Article 7
(c) Article 8 (d) Article 9

56. The United Nations High Commission for Refugees was established in which of the following year by the General Assembly?
(a) 1951 (b) 1953
(c) 1955 (d) 1957

57. "The most glaring instance of violation of Human Rights is the continuing poverty among masses in the country." Said by
(a) Justice A.S. Anand
(b) Justice N. Venkatachalaiah
(c) Justice P.N. Bhagwati
(d) Justice Koka Subba Rao

58. Match List I with List II and select the correct answer:
List I
A. The Magna Carta
B. The Petition of Rights
C. The English Bill of Rights
D. The U.N. Bill of Rights
List II
i. 1628 ii. 1789
iii. 1215 iv. 1689

Codes:	**A**	**B**	**C**	**D**
(a)	iii	i	iv	ii
(b)	i	iii	iv	ii
(c)	iii	ii	iv	i
(d)	iii	i	ii	iv

59. Gurupadaswamy Committee 1979 was constituted to look into the working conditions of:
(a) Minorities (b) Women
(c) Children (d) N.G.Os.

60. Using codes, arrange following instruments according to sequence of their enactment starting from past towards present:
(i) The Convention on the Political Rights of Women.
(ii) The Declaration on the elimination of discrimination against women.
(iii) The Convention on consent to marriage, minimum age for marriage and registration of marriage.
(iv) The Convention on the nationality of married women.
Codes:

(a)	i	iv	iii	ii
(b)	iv	iii	ii	i
(c)	iii	ii	i	iv
(d)	ii	i	iv	iii

61. Which one of the following statements is not correct?
(a) In tort, there is a breach of duty which is primarily fixed by law.
(b) In tort, there is a violation of a right in rem.
(c) In tort, the motive for breach of duty is immaterial.
(d) In tort, the damages are fixed according to the terms and conditions.

62. **Assertion (A):** A wooden chair while being used by a guest caused injury to

him due to defective manufacture. The guest is entitled to claim damages from the maker.

Reason (R): Manufacturer owes a duty of care to the ultimate user.

Select the correct answer using the codes below:

Codes:

(a) Both (A) and (R) are true and (R) is the correct explanation of (A).

(b) Both (A) and (R) are true, but (R) is not the correct explanation of (A).

(c) (A) is true, but (R) is false.

(d) (A) is false, but (R) is true.

63. In which of the following situations is slander actionable per se in India?

(a) An imputation that a certain female player is of unchaste character.

(b) An imputation that a certain person is a habitual smuggler.

(c) An imputation that a certain person is liar.

(d) An imputation that the wrestler is womanizer.

64. Match List I with List II and indicate the correct answer using the codes given below:

List I

A. A patient is a consumer

B. Doctor's duty to maintain secrecy

C. Free service

D. Contract of personal service

List II

i. Vasantha P. Nair Vs. Smt. V.P. Nair

ii. K. Rangaswami Vs. Jaya Vital & others

iii. Indian Medical Association Vs. V.P. Shantha

iv. Dr. Tokugha Vs. Apollo Hospital Enterprises Ltd.

Codes:	**A**	**B**	**C**	**D**
(a)	i	ii	iii	iv
(b)	iv	ii	i	iii
(c)	i	iv	iii	ii
(d)	iii	ii	i	iv

65. State in which of the following cases, it amounts to nuisance?

(a) Planting of trees on another's land.

(b) When branches of trees project on the land of their neighbour.

(c) Construction of a pond on the land of another.

(d) All of the above.

66. In which of the following cases, the rule of absolute liability laid down by the Supreme Court of India was followed?

(a) Indian Council for Enviro-Legal Action Vs. Union of India, A.I.R. 1996 SC 1446

(b) Klaus Mittelbachert Vs. East India Hotels Ltd., A.I.R. 1997 Del. 201

(c) Both (a) and (b) above.

(d) None of the above.

67. Match List I with List II and indicate the correct answer using the codes given below:

List I

A. The Wagon Mound case

B. Re Polemis and Furness Withy & Co. Ltd.

C. Scott Vs. Shepherd

D. Fardon Vs. Harcourt Rivington

List II

i. Remote but proximate

ii. The test of reasonable foresight

iii. The test of directness

iv. Reasonable foreseeability

Codes:	**A**	**B**	**C**	**D**
(a)	i	ii	iii	iv
(b)	ii	iii	i	iv
(c)	i	iv	iii	ii
(d)	ii	i	iv	iii

68. Find right answer from following statements:

(a) Every partnership is based on mutual agency.

(b) Every agency is based on mutual partnership.
(c) Every agent is a partner.
(d) Every partner is a sleeping partner.

69. Which statements are correct, answer using codes given below:
i. Directors are trustees of company.
ii. Directors are mentors of company.
iii. Directors are agents of company.
iv. Director are agents of shareholders.
Codes:
(a) i and ii are correct.
(b) i and iii are correct.
(c) i and iv are correct.
(d) ii and iv are correct.

70. Read Assertion (A) and Reason (R) and with help of codes given below, point out the correct explanation:
Assertion (A): The doctrine of indoor management seeks to protect the company against the outsider.
Reason (R): The company has right to privacy.
Codes:
(a) Both (A) and (R) are true and (R) is correct explanation of (A).
(b) Both (A) and (R) are true, but (R) is not correct explanation of (A).
(c) (A) is true, but (R) is false.
(d) (A) is false, but (R) is true.

71. Match items in Table A with items in Table B, using codes given below:
Table A
A. Essentials of partnership
B. Partnership at will
C. Effect of non-registration of firm
D. Compulsory dissolution of firm

Table B
i. Section 41 ii. Section 4
iii. Section 7 iv. Section 69

Codes:	A	B	C	D
(a)	i	ii	iv	iii
(b)	ii	iii	iv	i
(c)	iii	iv	i	ii
(d)	i	ii	iii	iv

72. Find correct answer, using codes given below:
(i) Bulk shall correspond with sample, is an implied condition.
(ii) Buyer shall have a reasonable opportunity of comparing bulk with sample, is an implied condition.
(iii) Goods should be free from any defect rendering them unmerchantable, is an implied condition.
(iv) There is an implied condition that the buyer shall have and enjoy possession of the goods.
Codes:
(a) (i) only is correct.
(b) (i) and (ii) only are correct.
(c) (i), (ii) and (iii) only are correct.
(d) All of above are correct.

73. Choose correct statement from following:
(a) Right against the goods can be exercised only by a paid seller.
(b) Right against the goods can be exercised only by an unpaid seller.
(c) Right against the goods can be exercised only by a paid buyer.
(d) Right against the goods can be exercised only by an unpaid buyer.

74. Match items in Table A with items in Table B, using codes given below:
Table A
A. Prabhu Dayal Vs. Jwala Bank, ILR 1938 All. 634
B. Discharge from liability by cancellation
C. Payment in due course
D. Protest
Table B
i. Section 100
ii. Section 10
iii. Forgery of signature
iv. Section 82

Codes:	A	B	C	D
(a)	i	iii	ii	iv
(b)	iii	iv	ii	i
(c)	iv	iii	ii	i
(d)	ii	i	iii	iv

75. Find correct legal principle from following statements:
   (a) While collecting a cheque for a banker, the customer is under an obligation to present it promptly so as to avoid any loss due to change of circumstances.
   (b) While collecting a cheque for a customer, the banker is under an obligation to present it properly so as to avoid any loss due to change of circumstances.
   (c) While collecting a cheque for a customer, the banker is under no obligation to present it properly so as to avoid any loss due to change of circumstances.
   (d) While collecting a cheque for a banker, the customer is under no obligation to present it promptly so as to avoid any loss due to change of circumstances.

ANSWERS

1. (a)	2. (b)	3. (d)	4. (c)	5. (b)
6. (a)	7. (d)	8. (d)	9. (c)	10. (b)
11. (a)	12. (c)	13. (b)	14. (c)	15. (d)
16. (a)	17. (a)	18. (c)	19. (d)	20. (c)
21. (b)	22. (b)	23. (d)	24. (c)	25. (a)
26. (b)	27. (b)	28. (c)	29. (d)	30. (d)
31. (b)	32. (c)	33. (d)	34. (c)	35. (a)
36. (d)	37. (a)	38. (b)	39. (c)	40. (a)
41. (d)	42. (a)	43. (a)	44. (c)	45. (b)
46. (c)	47. (c)	48. (d)	49. (a)	50. (a)
51. (a)	52. (d)	53. (b)	54. (a)	55. (a)
56. (a)	57. (a)	58. (a)	59. (c)	60. (a)
61. (d)	62. (a)	63. (a)	64. (c)	65. (d)
66. (c)	67. (b)	68. (a)	69. (b)	70. (c)
71. (b)	72. (c)	73. (b)	74. (b)	75. (b)

JUNE–2013

Note: This paper contains Sixty (60) multiple-choice questions, each question carrying two (2) marks. Candidate is expected to answer any Fifty (50) questions. In case more than Fifty (50) questions are attempted, only the first Fifty (50) questions will be evaluated.

PAPER–I

1. Which one of the following references is written as per Modern Language Association (MLA) format?
   (a) Hall, Donald. Fundamentals of Electronics,
   New Delhi: Prentice Hall of India, 2005
   (b) Hall, Donald, Fundamentals of Electronics,
   New Delhi: Prentice Hall of India, 2005
   (c) Hall, Donald, Fundamentals of Electronics,
   New Delhi: Prentice Hall of India, 2005
   (d) Hall, Donald. Fundamentals of Electronics.
   New Delhi: Prentice Hall of India, 2005
2. A workshop is
   (a) a conference for discussion on a topic.
   (b) a meeting for discussion on a topic.
   (c) a class at a college or a university in which a teacher and the students discuss a topic.
   (d) a brief intensive course for a small group emphasizing the development of a skill or technique for solving a specific problem.
3. A working hypothesis is
   (a) a proven hypothesis for an argument.
   (b) not required to be tested.
   (c) a provisionally accepted hypothesis for further research.
   (d) a scientific theory.

Read the following passage carefully and answer the questions (4 to 9):

The Taj Mahal has become one of the world's best known monuments. This domed white marble structure is situated on a high plinth at the southern end of a four-quartered garden, evoking the gardens of paradise, enclosed within walls measuring 305 by 549 metres. Outside the walls, in an area known as Mumtazabad, were living quarters for attendants, markets, serais and other structures built by local merchants and nobles. The tomb complex and the other imperial structures of Mumtazabad were maintained by the income of thirty villages given specifically for the tomb's support. The name Taj Mahal is unknown in Mughal chronicles, but it is used by contemporary Europeans in India, suggesting that this was the tomb's popular name. In contemporary texts, it is generally called simply the Illuminated Tomb (Rauza-i-Munavvara).

Mumtaz Mahal died shortly after delivering her fourteenth child in 1631. The Mughal court was then residing in Burhanpur. Her remains were temporarily buried by the grief-stricken emperor in a spacious garden known as Zainabad on the bank of the river Tapti. Six months later her body was transported to Agra, where it was interred in land chosen for the mausoleum. This land, situated south of the Mughal city on the bank of the Jamuna, had belonged to the Kachhwaha rajas since the time of Raja Man Singh and was purchased from the then current raja, Jai Singh. Although contemporary chronicles indicate Jai Singh's willing cooperation in this exchange, extant *farmans* (imperial commands) indicate that the final price was not settled until almost two years after the mausoleum's commencement. Jai Singh's further cooperation was insured by imperial orders issued between 1632 and 1637 demanding that he provide stone masons and carts to transport marble from the mines at Makrana, within his "ancestral domain", to Agra where both the Taj Mahal and Shah Jahan's additions to the Agra fort were constructed concurrently.

Work on the mausoleum was commenced early in 1632. Inscriptional evidence indicates much of the tomb was completed by 1636. By 1643, when Shah Jahan most lavishly celebrated the 'Urs ceremony for Mumtaz Mahal', the entire complex was virtually complete.

4. Marble stone used for the construction of the Taj Mahal was brought from the ancestral domain of Raja Jai Singh. The name of the place where mines of marble is
   (a) Burhanpur (b) Makrana
   (c) Amber (d) Jaipur
5. The popular name Taj Mahal was given by
   (a) Shah Jahan
   (b) Tourists
   (c) Public
   (d) European travellers
6. Point out the true statement from the following:
   (a) Marble was not used for the construction of the Taj Mahal.
   (b) Red sand stone is non-visible in the Taj Mahal complex.
   (c) The Taj Mahal is surrounded by a four-quartered garden known as Char Bagh.
   (d) The Taj Mahal was constructed to celebrate the 'Urs ceremony for Mumtaz Mahal'.
7. In the contemporary texts the Taj Mahal is known
   (a) Mumtazabad
   (b) Mumtaz Mahal
   (c) Zainabad
   (d) Rauza-i-Munavvara
8. The construction of the Taj Mahal was completed between the period
   (a) 1632 – 1636 A.D.
   (b) 1630 – 1643 A.D.
   (c) 1632 – 1643 A.D.
   (d) 1636 – 1643 A.D.
9. The documents indicating the ownership of land, where the Taj Mahal was built, known as
   (a) Farman
   (b) Sale Deed
   (c) Sale-Purchase Deed
   (d) None of the above
10. In the process of communication, which one of the following is in the chronological order?
    (a) Communicator, Medium, Receiver, Effect, Message
    (b) Medium, Communicator, Message, Receiver, Effect
    (c) Communicator, Message, Medium, Receiver, Effect
    (d) Message, Communicator, Medium, Receiver, Effect
11. *Bengal Gazette*, the first Newspaper in India was started in 1780 by
    (a) Dr. Annie Besant
    (b) James Augustus Hicky
    (c) Lord Cripson
    (d) A.O. Hume

12. Press censorship in India was imposed during the tenure of the Prime Minister
(a) Rajeev Gandhi
(b) Narasimha Rao
(c) Indira Gandhi
(d) Deve Gowda

13. Communication via New media such as computers, teleshopping, Internet and mobile telephony is termed as
(a) Entertainment
(b) Interactive communication
(c) Developmental communication
(d) Communitarian

14. Classroom communication of a teacher rests on the principle of
(a) Infotainment
(b) Edutainment
(c) Entertainment
(d) Enlightenment

15. ________ is important when a teacher communicates with his/her student.
(a) Sympathy (b) Empathy
(c) Apathy (d) Antipathy

16. In a certain code GALIB is represented by HBMJC. TIGER will be represented by
(a) UJHFS (b) UHJSF
(c) JHUSF (d) HUJSF

17. In a certain cricket tournament 45 matches were played. Each team played once against each of the other teams. The number of teams participated in the tournament is
(a) 8 (b) 10
(c) 12 (d) 14

18. The missing number in the series 40, 120, 60, 180, 90, ?, 135 is
(a) 110 (b) 270
(c) 105 (d) 210

19. The odd numbers from 1 to 45 which are exactly divisible by 3 are arranged in an ascending order. The number at 6th position is
(a) 18 (b) 24
(c) 33 (d) 36

20. The mean of four numbers a, b, c, d is 100. If c = 70, then the mean of the remaining numbers is
(a) 30 (b) $\frac{85}{2}$
(c) $\frac{170}{3}$ (d) 110

21. If the radius of a circle is increased by 50%, the perimeter of the circle will increase by
(a) 20% (b) 30%
(c) 40% (d) 50%

22. If the statement 'some men are honest' is false, which among the following statements will be true. Choose the correct code given below:
(i) All men are honest.
(ii) No men are honest.
(iii) Some men are not honest.
(iv) All men are dishonest.

Codes:
(a) (i), (ii) and (iii)
(b) (ii), (iii) and (iv)
(c) (i), (iii) and (iv)
(d) (ii), (i) and (iv)

23. Choose the proper alternative given in the codes to replace the question mark.
Bee – Honey, Cow – Milk, Teacher – ?
(a) Intelligence (b) Marks
(c) Lessons (d) Wisdom

24. P is the father of R and S is the son of Q and T is the brother of P. If R is the sister of S, how is Q related to T?
(a) Wife
(b) Sister-in-law
(c) Brother-in-law
(d) Daughter-in-law

25. A definition put forward to resolve a dispute by influencing attitudes or stirring emotions is called
    (a) Lexical (b) Persuasive
    (c) Stipulative (d) Precisions

26. Which of the codes given below contains only the correct statements?

    Statements:
    (i) Venn diagram is a clear method of notation.
    (ii) Venn diagram is the most direct method of testing the validity of categorical syllogisms.
    (iii) In Venn diagram method the premises and the conclusion of a categorical syllogism is diagrammed.
    (iv) In Venn diagram method the three overlapping circles are drawn for testing a categorical syllogism.

    Codes:
    (a) (i), (ii) & (iii)
    (b) (i), (ii) & (iv)
    (c) (ii), (iii) & (iv)
    (d) (i), (iii) & (iv)

27. Inductive reasoning presupposes
    (a) unity in human nature
    (b) integrity in human nature
    (c) uniformity in human nature
    (d) harmony in human nature

Read the table below and based on this table answer questions from 28 to 33:

Area under Major Horticulture Crops

(in lakh hectares)

Year	Fruits	Vegetables	Flowers	Total Horti-culture Area
2005-06	53	72	1	187
2006-07	56	75	1	194
2007-08	58	78	2	202
2008-09	61	79	2	207
2009-10	63	79	2	209

28. Which of the following two years have recorded the highest rate of increase in area under the total horticulture?
    (a) 2005-06 & 2006-07
    (b) 2006-07 & 2008-09
    (c) 2007-08 & 2008-09
    (d) 2006-07 & 2007-08

29. Shares of the area under flowers, vegetables and fruits in the area under total horticulture are respectively:
    (a) 1, 38 and 30 percent
    (b) 30, 38 and 1 percent
    (c) 38, 30 and 1 percent
    (d) 35, 36 and 2 percent

30. Which of the following has recorded the highest rate of increase in area during 2005-06 to 2009-10?
    (a) Fruits
    (b) Vegetables
    (c) Flowers
    (d) Total horticulture

31. Find out the horticultural crop that has recorded an increase of area by around 10 percent from 2005-06 to 2009-10.
    (a) Fruits
    (b) Vegetables
    (c) Flowers
    (d) Total horticulture

32. What has been the share of area under fruits, vegetables and flowers in the area under total horticulture in 2007-08?
    (a) 53 percent (b) 68 percent
    (c) 79 percent (d) 100 percent

33. In which year, area under fruits has recorded the highest rate of increase?
    (a) 2006-07 (b) 2007-08
    (c) 2008-09 (d) 2009-10

34. 'www' stands for
    (a) work with web
    (b) word wide web
    (c) world wide web
    (d) worth while web

35. A hard disk is divided into tracks which is further subdivided into
(a) Clusters (b) Sectors
(c) Vectors (d) Heads

36. A computer program that translates a program statement by statement into machine language is called a/an
(a) Compiler (b) Simulator
(c) Translator (d) Interpreter

37. A Gigabyte is equal to
(a) 1024 Megabytes (b) 1024 Kilobytes
(c) 1024 Terabytes (d) 1024 Bytes

38. A Compiler is a software which converts
(a) characters to bits
(b) high level language to machine language
(c) machine language to high level language
(d) words to bits

39. Virtual memory is
(a) an extremely large main memory.
(b) an extremely large secondary memory.
(c) an illusion of extremely large main memory.
(d) a type of memory used in super computers.

40. The phrase 'tragedy of commons' is in the context of
(a) tragic event related to damage caused by release of poisonous gases.
(b) tragic conditions of poor people.
(c) degradation of renewable free access resources.
(d) climate change.

41. Kyoto Protocol is related to
(a) Ozone depletion
(b) Hazardous waste
(c) Climate change
(d) Nuclear energy

42. Which of the following is a source of emissions leading to the eventual formation of surface ozone as a pollutant?
(a) Transport sector
(b) Refrigeration and Airconditioning
(c) Wetlands
(d) Fertilizers

43. The smog in cities in India mainly consists of
(a) Oxides of sulphur
(b) Oxides of nitrogen and unburnt hydrocarbons
(c) Carbon monoxide and SPM
(d) Oxides of sulphur and ozone

44. Which of the following types of natural hazards have the highest potential to cause damage to humans?
(a) Earthquakes
(b) Forest fires
(c) Volcanic eruptions
(d) Droughts and floods

45. The percentage share of renewable energy sources in the power production in India is around
(a) 2-3% (b) 22-25%
(c) 10-12% (d) < 1%

46. In which of the following categories the enrolment of students in higher education in 2010-11 was beyond the percentage of seats reserved?
(a) OBC students
(b) SC students
(c) ST students
(d) Woman students

47. Which one of the following statements is not correct about the University Grants Commission (UGC)?
(a) It was established in 1956 by an Act of Parliament.
(b) It is tasked with promoting and coordinating higher education.
(c) It receives Plan and non-Plan funds from the Central Government.
(d) It receives funds from State Governments in respect of State Universities.

48. Consider the statement which is followed by two arguments (I) and (II):
Statement: Should India switch over to a two party system?
Arguments: (I) Yes, it will lead to stability of government.
(II) No, it will limit the choice of voters.
(a) Only argument (I) is strong.
(b) Only argument (II) is strong.
(c) Both the arguments are strong.
(d) Neither of the arguments is strong.

49. Consider the statement which is followed by two arguments (I) and (II):
Statement: Should persons with criminal background be banned from contesting elections?
Arguments: (I) Yes, it will decriminalise politics.
(II) No, it will encourage the ruling party to file frivolous cases against their political opponents.
(a) Only argument (I) is strong.
(b) Only argument (II) is strong.
(c) Both the arguments are strong.
(d) Neither of the arguments is strong.

50. Which of the following statement(s) is/are correct about a Judge of the Supreme Court of India?
1. A Judge of the Supreme Court is appointed by the President of India.
2. He holds office during the pleasure of the President.
3. He can be suspended, pending an inquiry.
4. He can be removed for proven misbehaviour or incapacity.

Select the correct answer from the codes given below:
Codes:
(a) 1, 2 and 3 (b) 1, 3 and 4
(c) 1 and 3 (d) 1 and 4

51. In the warrant of precedence, the Speaker of the Lok Sabha comes next only to
(a) The President
(b) The Vice-President
(c) The Prime Minister
(d) The Cabinet Ministers

52. The blackboard can be utilised best by a teacher for
(a) putting the matter of teaching in black and white
(b) making the students attentive
(c) writing the important and notable points
(d) highlighting the teacher himself

53. Nowadays the most effective mode of learning is
(a) self-study
(b) face-to-face learning
(c) e-learning
(d) blended learning

54. At the primary school stage, most of the teachers should be women because they
(a) can teach children better than men.
(b) know basic content better than men.
(c) are available on lower salaries.
(d) can deal with children with love and affection.

55. Which one is the highest order of learning?
(a) Chain learning
(b) Problem-solving learning
(c) Stimulus-response learning
(d) Conditioned-reflex learning

56. A person can enjoy teaching as a profession when he
(a) has control over students.
(b) commands respect from students.
(c) is more qualified than his colleagues.
(d) is very close to higher authorities.

57. "A diagram speaks more than 1000 words." The statement means that the teacher should

(a) use diagrams in teaching.
(b) speak more and more in the class.
(c) use teaching aids in the class.
(d) not speak too much in the class.

58. A research paper
(a) is a compilation of information on a topic.
(b) contains original research as deemed by the author.
(c) contains peer-reviewed original research or evaluation of research conducted by others.
(d) can be published in more than one journal.

59. Which one of the following belongs to the category of good 'research ethics'?
(a) Publishing the same paper in two research journals without telling the editors.
(b) Conducting a review of the literature that acknowledges the contributions of other people in the relevant field or relevant prior work.
(c) Trimming outliers from a data set without discussing your reasons in a research paper.
(d) Including a colleague as an author on a research paper in return for a favour even though the colleague did not make a serious contribution to the paper.

60. Which of the following sampling methods is not based on probability?
(a) Simple Random Sampling
(b) Stratified Sampling
(c) Quota Sampling
(d) Cluster Sampling

ANSWERS

1. (d)	2. (d)	3. (c)	4. (b)	5. (d)
6. (c)	7. (d)	8. (c)	9. (a)	10. (c)
11. (b)	12. (c)	13. (b)	14. (b)	15. (b)
16. (a)	17. (b)	18. (b)	19. (c)	20. (d)
21. (d)	22. (b)	23. (d)	24. (b)	25. (b)
26. (b)	27. (c)	28. (d)	29. (a)	30. (c)
31. (b)	32. (b)	33. (a)	34. (c)	35. (b)
36. (d)	37. (a)	38. (b)	39. (c)	40. (c)
41. (c)	42. (a)	43. (b)	44. (d)	45. (c)
46. (a)	47. (d)	48. (c)	49. (a)	50. (d)
51. (c)	52. (c)	53. (d)	54. (d)	55. (d)
56. (b)	57. (c)	58. (c)	59. (b)	60. (c)

PAPER–II

Note: This paper contains fifty (50) objective type questions, each question carrying two (2) marks. All questions are compulsory.

1. "It is likely that free India may be federal India, though in any event there would be a great deal of Unitary Control." This statement was made by
(a) Sir Alladi Krishna Swami Iyyer
(b) Dr. B.R. Ambedkar
(c) Pt. Jawaharlal Nehru
(d) Sardar Vallabhbhai Patel

2. Judicial Review in the Constitution of India is based on
(a) Precedents and conventions
(b) Rule of law
(c) Due process of law
(d) Procedure established by law

3. The Constitution of India embodies the parliamentary form of government because
(a) The Council of Ministers is collectively responsible to the Lok Sabha.

(b) The Council of Ministers is responsible to Lok Sabha and Rajya Sabha.
(c) The President, the head of the executive, is answerable to Parliament.
(d) The Prime Minister, the Head of the Cabinet, is accountable to Parliament.

4. The Supreme Court held that Election Commissioners cannot be placed on par with the Chief Election Commissioner in terms of power and authority in the following case:
(a) S.S. Dhannoa Vs Union of India
(b) T.N. Seshan Vs Union of India
(c) A.C. Jose Vs Sivan Pillai
(d) Venkatachalam Vs A. Swamickan

5. The maximum interval between the two sessions of each House of Parliament is
(a) Three months (b) Four months
(c) Five months (d) Six months

6. The Supreme Court observed that "Parliamentary proceedings are not subject to Fundamental Rights" in the following case:
(a) Keshav Singh Vs Speaker, U.P. Assembly
(b) Gunapati Vs Habibul Hasan
(c) M.S.M. Sharma Vs Srikrishna Sinha
(d) State of Punjab Vs Satpal Dang

7. For the purpose of creating a new State in India an amendment to the Constitution of India must be passed by
(a) 2/3rd majority of the members of both Houses of Parliament present and voting.
(b) 2/3rd majority of the members of both Houses of Parliament and ratification by not less than 2/3rd majority of the States.
(c) A simple majority in Parliament and ratification by not less than half of the States.
(d) A simple majority by the Parliament.

8. Match the following:

A. Perfect right	(i)	Which has correlative positive duty.
B. Negative right	(ii)	Which has a correlative duty that can be legally enforced.
C. Imperfect right	(iii)	A has a right to receive damage.
D. Positive right	(iv)	That right which although recognised by State but not enforceable.

Codes:	A	B	C	D
(a)	(iii)	(iv)	(i)	(ii)
(b)	(ii)	(iii)	(iv)	(i)
(c)	(iv)	(iii)	(ii)	(i)
(d)	(i)	(ii)	(iii)	(iv)

9. According to which school, "the purpose of jurisprudence is to analyse and dissect the law of the land as it exists today"?
(a) Analytical Jurisprudence
(b) Historical Jurisprudence
(c) Sociological Jurisprudence
(d) Philosophical Jurisprudence

10. "The one who holds the property is the owner."
Give your correct response from following on the basis of above statement:
(a) The holder of property may be mere possessor or bailee.
(b) The holder of property need not be the owner.
(c) This statement is not correct.
(d) This statement is correct.

11. The sources of law have been divided into two classes. These are
(a) Divine sources and human sources
(b) Formal sources and material sources
(c) Natural sources and universal sources
(d) (a) and (b) both of the above

12. According to whose theory, "Law is not universal in its nature; like language it varies with people and age"?
    (a) Bentham's theory
    (b) Austin's theory
    (c) Savigny's theory
    (d) Montesquieu's theory

13. Which one of the following pairs is not correctly matched?

(a) Law properly so-called (in regard to notion of law)	:	Which is distinct from morals.
(b) Law improperly so-called (in regard to notion of law)	:	Other laws.
(c) Audi alteram partem	:	Rule of natural justice.
(d) Conspectus of justice	:	Justice denied.

14. **Assertion (A):** The Maneka Gandhi's case is a landmark decision from the point of human rights and remedial jurisprudence.
    Reason (R): From the positivist point of view, equality is antithetic to arbitrariness.
    Examine the above statements (A) and (R) and select whether the Reason is a correct explanation of the Assertion using the codes given below:
    Codes:
    (a) Both (A) and (R) are true and (R) is the correct explanation of (A).
    (b) Both (A) and (R) are true, but (R) is not the correct explanation of (A).
    (c) (A) is true, but (R) is false.
    (d) (A) is false, but (R) is true.

15. Who among the following said that the law of nation is "the body of legal rules which apply between states and such entities as have been granted international personality"?
    (a) Fenwick (b) Oppeheim
    (c) Schwarzenberger (d) Verdoss

16. The main difference between de-facto and de-jure recognition is
    1. De-facto recognition may be withdrawn while de-jure recognition is full and final.
    2. Only de-jure recognised states can represent the old states, for the purpose of state succession.
    3. In de-jure recognition, formal diplomatic relations are established while in case of de-facto they may not be entered into.
    4. Former is legal and the latter is a factual recognition.
    (a) 1, 2 & 3 (b) 2, 3 & 4
    (c) 2 & 3 (d) 1 & 2

17. A member of the United Nations can be suspended from the exercise of rights and privileges of membership by the
    (a) General Assembly
    (b) Security Council
    (c) General Assembly on the recommendations of the Security Council
    (d) Secretary General on the recommendations of the Security Council

18. Read Assertion (A) and Reason (R) and with the help of codes given below select the correct answer.
    Assertion (A): International Law consists for the most part of customary rules.
    Reason (R): Customary rules are the original and oldest source of International Law.
    Codes:
    (a) Both (A) and (R) are true, and (R) is the correct explanation of (A).
    (b) Both (A) and (R) are true, but (R) is not the correct explanation of (A).

(c) (A) is true, but (R) is false.
(d) (A) is false and (R) is true.

19. Universal Declaration of Human Rights was adopted on
(a) December 10, 1948
(b) November 10, 1948
(c) October 20, 1948
(d) January 21, 1948

20. Read Assertion (A) and Reason (R) and with the help of codes given below select the correct answer.
Assertion (A): Human Rights occupy a significant place in the UN Charter.
Reason (R): Members of the UN have committed themselves to promote respect for and observance of human rights and fundamental rights.
Codes:
(a) Both (A) and (R) are individually true and (R) is the correct explanation of (A).
(b) Both (A) and (R) are individually true, but (R) is not the correct explanation of (A).
(c) (A) is true, but (R) is false.
(d) (A) is false, but (R) is true.

21. Adultery by a Hindu husband is
(a) Ground of divorce only
(b) Not a ground of divorce
(c) Ground of judicial separation
(d) None of the above

22. 'A' marries 'B', the widow of the elder brother. The marriage is
(a) Valid (b) Void
(c) Voidable (d) None of these

23. Marriage with an impotent and has not been consummated. The marriage is
(a) Valid (b) Void
(c) Nullity (d) Irregular

24. 'Khula' is a form of divorce by
(a) Sale (b) Purchase
(c) Agreement (d) Coercion

25. Muta marriage could not be dissolved
(a) Ipso facto by the efflux of the period
(b) By death
(c) By divorce
(d) By Hiba-i-Mudat

26. By which of the following way a Muslim marriage can be dissolved by a Muslim husband?
(a) Talaq (b) Illa
(c) Zihar (d) All of the above

27. When a person making a false statement believes the statement to be true and does not intend to mislead to the other party to the contract, it is known as
(a) Mistake
(b) Fraud
(c) Misrepresentation
(d) Undue influence

28. Read Assertion (A) and Reason (R) and with help of codes given below, point out the correct explanation.
Assertion (A): An agreement not enforceable by law is said to be void.
Reason (R): Law has no force.
Codes:
(a) Both (A) and (R) are true and (R) is good explanation of (A).
(b) Both (A) and (R) are true, but (R) is not correct explanation of (A).
(c) (A) is true, but (R) is false.
(d) (A) is false, but (R) is true.

29. A and B are friends. A told to B to show him a new movie in a posh theatre, upon which A promised to offer him lunch in a 5-star hotel. B showed him a movie in a posh theatre, but A gave lunch to B in a road side dhaba. Decide A's liability using codes given below:
Codes:
(a) A is liable because there was intention to create legal relation between A and B.

(b) A is not liable because there was no intention to crate legal relation between A and B.
(c) B was mistaken.
(d) A was mistaken.

30. Arrange the following concepts in sequence in which they occur, using codes given below:
(i) Offer is communicated.
(ii) Counter offer is made.
(iii) Offer is rejected.
(iv) Counter offer is accepted.

Codes:
(a) (i), (ii), (iii), (iv) (b) (i), (iii), (ii), (iv)
(c) (i), (iv), (ii), (iii) (d) (ii), (i), (iii), (iv)

31. Following are essentials of valid contract:
(i) Parties to contract should have capacity to contract.
(ii) Parties to contract should have legal mind.
(iii) Parties to contract should be intelligent.
(iv) Invitation to offer should be accepted.

Find correct answer, using codes:
(a) Only (i) is correct.
(b) Only (i) and (iv) are correct.
(c) All of above are correct.
(d) Only (ii) is correct.

32. Match items in Table A with items in Table B, using codes given below:

Table A
A. Ambiguous and uncertain agreements
B. Coercion
C. Past consideration
D. Remoteness of damage

Table B
(i) Section 15 (ii) Section 25(2)
(iii) Section 73 (iv) Section 29

Codes:	**(i)**	**(ii)**	**(iii)**	**(iv)**
(a)	(B)	(C)	(D)	(A)
(b)	(C)	(B)	(D)	(A)
(c)	(C)	(B)	(A)	(D)
(d)	(A)	(D)	(C)	(B)

33. Which one of the following statements is incorrect?
(a) Tort is a civil wrong in which claim for unliquidated damages is made.
(b) In tort, action lies against the wrong-doer in a civil court.
(c) For a tortious liability, a jail term can also be awarded.
(d) In some torts an injunction can also be issued against the wrong-doer.

34. Which one of the following defences is not available in Law of Tort?
(a) Volenti non-fit injuria
(b) Act of God
(c) Contributory negligence
(d) Inevitable accident

35. "Sometimes it happens that the legal right of a person is violated but he does not suffer any harm." From which one of the following maxim we can attribute it?
(a) Damnum sine injuria
(b) Injuria sine damno
(c) Volenti non-fit injuria
(d) Res ipsa loquitur

36. The rule of 'absolute liability' was laid down by the Supreme Court of India in the following case:
(a) Rylands Vs Fletcher
(b) M.C. Mehta (Sriram Food and Fertilizer Co.) Vs Union of India
(c) M.C. Mehta (C.N.G. Fuel case) Vs Union of India
(d) None of the above

37. In which of the following cases did the Supreme Court of India gave the ruling that sovereign immunity of the State is subject to the Fundamental
(a) Kasturilal Ralia Ram Jain Vs State of U.P.

(b) State of Rajasthan Vs Vidhyawati
(c) People's Union for Democratic Rights Vs State of Bihar
(d) Shyam Sundar Vs State of Rajasthan

38. The rule laid down in Re Polemis case is that the defendant shall be liable for all
(a) direct consequences of his act.
(b) direct consequences of his act, if he could foresee some damage to the plaintiff from his act.
(c) direct consequences of his act, only if he could foresee the kind of damage which has actually occurred.
(d) foreseeable damage.

39. Match List I (Jurists) with List II (Assumptions) and select the correct answer using the codes given below:
List I
(A) Lord T.B. Macauley
(B) Jermy Bentham
(C) Kelson
(D) Sir Barnes Peacock
List II
(i) Preparation of Penal Code of India
(ii) Unwritten jurisprudence on Penal principles
(iii) Substantive law on crimes
(iv) Revision of Penal law

Codes:	**(A)**	**(B)**	**(C)**	**(D)**
(a)	(i)	(ii)	(iii)	(iv)
(b)	(ii)	(i)	(iv)	(iii)
(c)	(iii)	(iv)	(i)	(ii)
(d)	(iv)	(i)	(ii)	(iii)

40. Match List I (Objectives) with List II (Propositions) and select the correct answer using the codes given below:
List I
(A) Inchoate crime (B) Attempt
(C) Preparation (D) Intention
List II
(i) 'Whaton' says it is the begining but not complete.
(ii) It does not act towards the commission of offence.
(iii) Culprit commences to do something.
(iv) When preparation merges itself with attempt.

Codes:	**(A)**	**(B)**	**(C)**	**(D)**
(a)	(ii)	(iii)	(iv)	(i)
(b)	(i)	(ii)	(iii)	(iv)
(c)	(iii)	(iv)	(i)	(ii)
(d)	(iv)	(i)	(ii)	(iii)

41. Fill in the blank using appropriate statement.
Non Compos Mentis means ______
(a) Not of sound mind.
(b) Who lacks the requisite mensrea.
(c) Unable to know that the act is either wrong or contrary to law.
(d) A concussion of brain.

42. Fill in the blank using appropriate reason. Right to private defence by a friend is generally not available because ______
(a) There was no specified circumstances.
(b) Explanation II of Section 300.
(c) The act was not with an intention to protect the friend.
(d) The offending party was an aggressor.

43. Read Assertion (I) and Reason (II) and with the help of codes given below select the correct explanation.
Assertion (I): Section 95 of IPC is intended to prevent penalisation of negligible wrongs of trivial character because:
Reasons (II):
(A) The injury is negligible.
(B) The victim and the wrongdoer were related to each other.
(C) The injured and the offender were not related by circumstances.
(D) The nature of injury was very minor.

Codes:
(a) (A) is true and (D) is the reason while (B) and (C) are not true.
(b) (B) is true and (C) is the reason while (A) and (D) are false.
(c) (C) is true and (D) is the reason while (A) and (B) are not true.
(d) (D) is the only reason while all others (A), (B) and (C) are false.

44. Fill in the blank:
Deceiving dishonestly by inducing a person to retain the property is known as offence.
(a) Concealment
(b) Deception by false pretention
(c) Cheating
(d) Fraud

45. Which of the following amount to Industrial Dispute?
(a) Any dispute between Employers and Employees.
(b) Between Employers and Workmen.
(c) Between Workmen and Workmen.
(d) All of these.

46. In which of the following cases, the Supreme Court held that "the benefit of running allowance had to be taken into consideration for computing pension only once, at the time of retirement of the employee, not for any future calculation"?
(a) U.O.I. Vs Dhingara and others (2008) I LLJ 867(SC)
(b) Bennet Coleman & Co. Vs Punya Priyadas AIR 1970 SC 426
(c) State Bank of Patiala Vs phoolpati (2005) II LLJ 473 (SC)
(d) Pearlite Lines Pvt. Ltd. Vs Manorama Sirse (2004) I LLJ 1041 (SC)

47. Which rights remain unaffected, during the pendency of a proceeding before a court of inquiry under Sections 22, 23 and 33 of the I.D. Act, 1947?
(a) Workmen to go on strike.
(b) The rights of Employer to dismiss or to punish the workmen.
(c) Employer to lock-out his business.
(d) All the above.

48. Read Assertion (A) and Reason (R), using codes given below, select the correct answer.
Assertion (A): Termination of service does not amount to retrenchment.
Reason (R): Amount of loss of retrenchment is more than amount of termination.
Codes:
(a) (A) and (R) are true, and (R) is correct explanation of (A).
(b) (A) and (R) are true, but (R) is not correct explanation of (A).
(c) (A) is true, but (R) is false.
(d) (A) is false, but (R) is true.

49. Read Assertion (A) and Reason (R) and using codes given below choose correct answer.
Assertion (A): Strike is stoppage of work by a body of persons employed in any service acting in combination.
Reason (R): Combined work is service oriented.
Codes:
(a) (A) and (R) are true, and (R) is correct explanation of (A).
(b) (A) and (R) are true, but (R) is not correct explanation of (A).
(c) (A) and (R) are false.
(d) (A) is true, (R) is false.

50. Trade unionism to be fully effective demands
(a) Union of trade
(b) Trade of union
(c) Democratic spirit and education
(d) Soul-elevating and democratic spirits

ANSWERS

1. (c)	2. (d)	3. (a)	4. (a)	5. (d)
6. (c)	7. (d)	8. (b)	9. (a)	10. (b)
11. (a)	12. (c)	13. (d)	14. (b)	15. (c)
16. (a)	17. (c)	18. (b)	19. (a)	20. (b)
21. (d)	22. (b)	23. (c)	24. (b)	25. (c)
26. (d)	27. (c)	28. (c)	29. (b)	30. (b)
31. (a)	32. (a)	33. (c)	34. (c)	35. (b)
36. (b)	37. (c)	38. (b)	39. (a)	40. (b)
41. (a)	42. (b)	43. (a)	44. (c)	45. (d)
46. (a)	47. (d)	48. (c)	49. (c)	50. (c)

PAPER–III

Note: This paper contains seventy-five (75) objective type questions of two (2) marks each. All questions are compulsory.

1. In E.P. Royappa case which of the Supreme Court Judge propounded the new concept of Equality as "Equality is a dynamic concept with many aspects and dimensions and it cannot be 'crippled, combined and confined' within traditional and doctrinaire limits"?
   (a) Justice Y.V. Chandrachud
   (b) Justice P.N. Bhagawati
   (c) Justice V.R. Krishna Iyer
   (d) Justice O.P. Chinnapa Reddy
2. The State shall make provisions for securing just and humane conditions of work and for maternity relief is found
   (a) As a part of the Preamble to the Constitution of India.
   (b) As a Fundamental Right under Art. 21 of the Constitution of India.
   (c) As a Directive Principle of the State Policy.
   (d) As a Fundamental Duty of the State.
3. Fundamental duties under Part IVA was inserted in the Constitution by
   (a) 17th Amendment
   (b) 25th Amendment
   (c) 42nd Amendment
   (d) 44th Amendment
4. The powers of the President of India are
   (a) Supra-Constitutional
   (b) Beyond the Constitution
   (c) In accordance with the Parliament of India
   (d) In accordance with the Constitution of India
5. Which one of the following has been considered as authority of power?
   (a) The Constitution of India
   (b) The President of India
   (c) The Parliament of India
   (d) The Supreme Court of India
6. In which of the following judgements it was held that according to Art. 226, Courts are flooded with large number of PIL, so it is desirable for Courts to filter out frivolous petitions and dismiss them with costs?
   (a) Deepak Sharma Vs Vineeta Sharma
   (b) Dharampal Vs State of Uttar Pradesh
   (c) Holicow Pictures Pvt. Ltd. Vs Premchandra Mishra
   (d) M.C. Mehta Vs Union of India
7. A resolution for the revocation of the proclamation of National Emergency may be moved by
   (a) Ten members of Lok Sabha
   (b) One-fifth of the total membership of the Lok Sabha.
   (c) One-tenth of the total membership of the Lok Sabha.
   (d) One-fifteenth of the total membership of the Lok Sabha.

8. Answer the following using the codes given below:
Administrative Law deals with:
(i) Composition, powers and functions of the administrative authorities.
(ii) Procedures to be followed by the administrative authorities in the exercise of their powers and functions.
(iii) Methods of control of powers of the administrative authorities.
(iv) Remedies available to a person in case of violation of his rights by the administrative authorities.
Codes:
(a) Only (i) is correct.
(b) Only (i) and (ii) are correct.
(c) Only (i), (ii) and (iii) are correct.
(d) All of the above are correct.

9. Read Assertion (A) and Reason (R) and with the help of codes given below, point out the correct explanation:
Assertion (A): One of the principles of natural justice is, 'No man shall be judge in his own cause'.
Reason (R): Principles of natural justice require fair play in action.
Codes:
(a) (A) and (R) are true and (R) is the correct explanation of (A).
(b) (A) and (R) are true, but (R) is not the correct explanation of (A).
(c) (A) is true and (R) is false.
(d) (A) is false and (R) is true.

10. Match List I with List II and indicate the correct answer using the codes given below:
List I
(A) A.K. Kraipak Vs. Union of India
(B) Manak Lal Vs. Dr. Prem Chand
(C) Maneka Gandhi Vs. Union of India
(D) Olga Tellis Vs. Bombay Municipal Corporation
List II
(i) Post-decisional hearing
(ii) Personal bias
(iii) Pecuniary bias
(iv) Reasonable opportunity of hearing

Codes:	**(A)**	**(B)**	**(C)**	**(D)**
(a)	(i)	(ii)	(iii)	(iv)
(b)	(i)	(iii)	(iv)	(ii)
(c)	(ii)	(iii)	(i)	(iv)
(d)	(iii)	(ii)	(iv)	(i)

11. Answer the following using the codes given below:
Which of the following doctrines were developed by the Court to control the administrative actions?
(i) Doctrine of Promissory Estoppel.
(ii) Doctrine of Legitimate Expectations.
(iii) Doctrine of Separation of Power and Rule of Law.
(iv) Judicial Activism.
Codes:
(a) Only (i), (ii) and (iii) are correct.
(b) Only (ii) and (iv) are correct.
(c) Only (i) and (iii) are correct.
(d) All of the above are correct.

12. Answer the following using the codes given below:
In which of the following grounds the judicial review of an administrative action be made?
(i) Abuse of discretion
(ii) Mala fide or Bad faith
(iii) Irrelevant consideration
(iv) Unreasonableness
Codes:
(a) Only (i), (ii) and (iii) are correct.
(b) Only (i) and (ii) are correct.
(c) Only (ii) and (iii) are correct.
(d) All (i), (ii), (iii) and (iv) are correct.

13. A writ of mandamus will not lie against
(a) President of India
(b) Parliament

(c) Local authorities
(d) Courts and Tribunals

14. Match List I with List II and indicate the correct answer using the codes given below:

List I
(A) Bring the body before the Court
(B) Petitioner's legal right to compel the performance of public duty
(C) By what authority a person is holding the public post
(D) Action of subordinate Court in violation of the principles of natural justice

List II
(i) Writ of Mandamus
(ii) Writ of Certiorari
(iii) Writ of Habeas Corpus
(iv) Writ of Quowarranto

Codes:	(A)	(B)	(C)	(D)
(a)	(i)	(ii)	(iii)	(iv)
(b)	(iii)	(i)	(iv)	(ii)
(c)	(iii)	(ii)	(i)	(iv)
(d)	(iii)	(iv)	(ii)	(i)

15. Which one of the following States has not yet established the institution of Lokayukta?
(a) Uttar Pradesh
(b) Karnataka
(c) Uttarakhand
(d) None of the above

16. "A legal person is any subject matter other than a human being to which law attributes personality." Who said these words?
(a) Savigny (b) Bentham
(c) Austin (d) Salmond

17. "Pure theory of Law is an exercise in logic and not life." This observation was made by
(a) Pound (b) Savigny
(c) Maine (d) Harold Laski

18. "Law is derived from social facts and not dependent on State authority but on social compulsion." Who said this?
(a) Putchta (b) Ehrlich
(c) Friedman (d) Pound

19. Which one of the following pairs is not correctly matched?
(a) Sie utere tero out alierum non laedas : To use your own property as not to injure your neighbour's right
(b) Re Legitima Portis : A person cannot dispose of his entire property
(c) Jus turtii : To set up title of a third person other than himself or the plaintiff
(d) Nec vi nec calur precario : Possession must show to the competitor

20. **Assertion (A):** In India the distinction between legal and equitable ownership is not recognised.
Reason (R): The trustees are, subject to the law relating to trust and trustees, bound to carry out the trust according to the dictates of the maker of the trust.
Examine the above statements (A) and Reason (R) and select whether the reason is a correct explanation of the assertion using the codes given below:
Codes:
(a) Both (A) and (R) are true and (R) is the correct explanation of (A).
(b) Both (A) and (R) are true, but (R) is not the correct explanation of (A).
(c) (A) is true, but (R) is false.
(d) (A) is false, but (R) is true.

21. The purpose theory is based on the assumption that "person is applicable only to human beings; they alone can be the subjects of rural relations".

Who developed this theory of Brinz in England?

(a) Barker (b) Duguit

(c) Salmond (d) Hoffman

22. "Ownership in its comprehensive signification, denotes the relation between a person and any right that is vested in him. That which a man owns in this sense is in all cases a right."

Who is the exponent of this theory?

(a) Miss Tay (b) Maitland

(c) Salmond (d) Fuller

23. "Legal rights are institutional rights to decisions in Courts. Institutions about justice presuppose a fundamental right, namely, the right to equality, which I call the right to equal concern and respect."

Who propounded this theory in relation to natural rights?

(a) Dworkin (b) Fuller

(c) Jerome Hall (d) Professor Hart

24. Fill in the gap that is most appropriate.

Who ever entices a girl child of less than 16 years has said to have caused kidnapping out of the keeping of the lawful ______.

(a) Parents (b) Foster parents

(c) Adopted parents (d) Guardians

25. Fill in the gap with the offence that the accused has committed.

Who ever dishonestly uses any moveable property to his own advantage has committed the offence of ______.

(a) Breach of trust

(b) Wrongful gain

(c) Misappropriation

(d) None of the above

26. Read Assertion I and Reason II and with the help of codes given below point out the correct explanation.

Assertion I: Moral derangement is a state of will and turns to be the vehicle of vicious actions.

Reason II: Crime is committed under the influence of instructive and irresistible impulse.

Codes:

(a) Moral insanity or imbecility are not exempted from criminal liability as per Section 53 of IPC.

(b) Both I and II are correct statements to attract criminal liability as per Section 53 IPC as both are diabolical criminal conduct.

(c) Only by II criminal responsibility can be fixed but not with the help of I.

(d) McNaghten's Rule can be applied in I but not in II.

27. Read Assertion I and Reason II and with the help of given codes point out the correct explanation.

Assertion I: Consent of husband or wife of the victim does not grant immunity from the offence of bigamy.

Reason II: Sexual offence with the consent of one spouse does not fix liability for adultery.

Codes:

(a) I is correct, but not with the reason of II.

(b) I is correct, but with the support of II.

(c) II is only the correct proposition while I is void.

(d) II is valid when I is not admissible.

28. Read Assertion I and Reason II and with the help of codes given below point out the correct explanation.

Assertion I: To establish a charge of conspiracy, knowledge about indulgence in an illegal act by certain legal means, is necessary.

Reason II: The normal rule is that when a particular unlawful use being intended has to be inferred from the chain of actions.

Codes:
(a) I is the judicious cause of conspiracy, because II is the correct explanation.
(b) II is more appropriate explanation than merely fixing charge as per I.
(c) I is the correct proposition as II is optional.
(d) I is not correct because as per II there must be pre-meditation.

29. Read Assertion I and Reason II and with the help of codes given below point out the correct explanation.

Assertion I: Publishing a report of proceedings of a court will not amount to defamation.

Reason II: It is an exception to the principle of defamation.

Codes:
(a) I is true, because II is the specific objective.
(b) I is true, but II is not the correct proposition.
(c) II is always true, because I is not dependent.
(d) II is false, because I is always independent of criminal liability.

30. Read Assertion I and Reason II and with the help of codes given below point out the correct explanation.

Assertion I: Independently putting a person in fear of injury to another is extortion.

Reason II: It is an exception to the rule of delivering the valuable security.

Codes:
(a) I is true, but II is not the correct statement.
(b) I is true, because II is the correct proposition.
(c) Both I and II are independent of proof.
(d) Both I and II are false.

31. Read Assertion I and Reason II and with the help of codes given below find out the correct explanation.

Assertion I: Disorder of mind which impairs the mental faculties is known as unsoundness of mind as such it acts as defence to a criminal charge.

Reason II: Insanity is the mental abnormality and when it impairs the cognitive faculty and if an act results during that period criminal liability could be exempted.

Codes:
(a) By I there is transgression of harmful acts while II refers to established rules of society for which no prosecution stands.
(b) Both I and II are correct explanations as per Section 84 of IPC.
(c) II is more precise while I is only a supportive factor.
(d) The true test of I and II is to apply Mc Naghten's Rule.

32. The Air (Prevention and Control of Pollution) Act, 1981, and the Environment (Protection) Act, 1986, were passed by the Parliament under:
(a) Article 252 of the Constitution of India.
(b) Article 253 of the Constitution of India.
(c) Article 250 of the Constitution of India.
(d) None of the above.

33. Which of the following Judges of the Supreme Court is famously known as the "Green Judge"?
(a) Justice V.R. Krishna Iyyar
(b) Justice P.N. Bhagwati
(c) Justice Kuldip Singh
(d) Justice B.N. Kirpal

34. Which of the following Articles of the Constitution of India have been mostly used by the Supreme Court to protect environment?
(a) Article 32
(b) Article 21
(c) Both Articles 21 and 32
(d) None of the above

35. What is the period of notice required to be served upon the Central Government for filing a criminal complaint by any person, under the provisions of Environment (Protection) Act, 1986?
(a) Not less than 30 days
(b) Not less than 60 days
(c) Not less than 90 days
(d) None of the above

36. Which one of the following cases is considered as "High Water-mark case in Forest Protection" decided by the Supreme Court?
(a) Salebhai Mulla Mohmadali Vs. State of Gujarat.
(b) T.N. Godavarman Tirumulkpad Vs. Union of India.
(c) Narmada Bachao Andolan Vs. Union of India.
(d) Samatha Vs. State of Andhra Pradesh.

37. The Parliament enacted the Water (Prevention and Control of Pollution) Act, 1974 for the control of water pollution:
(a) On the request from States.
(b) Of his own.
(c) On the direction of United Nations.
(d) On the direction of Supreme Court.

38. Under which of the following Article of the Constitution of India, the provisions regarding duty of the State "to protect and improvement of environment and safeguard the forest and wildlife", exist?
(a) Article 51(g) (b) Article 47
(c) Article 48A (d) None of these

39. Read Assertion (A) and Reason (R) and with the help of codes given below write the correct answer.
Assertion (A): Under International Law extradition is mostly a matter of bilateral treaties.
Reason (R): There is no general duty of States in respect of extradition of criminals.
Codes:
(a) Both (A) and (R) are individually true and (R) is the correct explanation of (A).
(b) Both (A) and (R) are individually true, but (R) is not the correct explanation of (A).
(c) (A) is true, but (R) is false.
(d) (A) is false, but (R) is true.

40. Which of the following cases does not concern with the judgement that a non-recognised State cannot sue in the courts of the State which was not recognised?
(a) Russian Socialist Federated Soviet Republic Vs. Cibraria.
(b) Guarantee Trust Company of New York Vs. United States.
(c) U.S. Vs. Pink.
(d) Bank of Ethopia Vs. National Bank of Egypt and Liquori.

41. Match List I with List II and select the correct answer:
List I (Name of the Case)
(A) The Caroline case
(B) The Nottebohm case
(C) Re Castioni case
(D) U.S. Vs. Rouscher
List II (Principle Propounded)
(i) Self-Defence
(ii) Effective Nationality
(iii) Non-Extradition of Political Criminals
(iv) Rule of Speciality

Codes:	(A)	(B)	(C)	(D)
(a)	(i)	(ii)	(iii)	(iv)
(b)	(iv)	(iii)	(ii)	(i)
(c)	(iii)	(iv)	(i)	(ii)
(d)	(ii)	(i)	(iv)	(iii)

42. Match List I with List II and select the correct answer:

List I

(A) Australia and Prussia exercised joint sovereignty over

(B) Great Britain and France exercised joint sovereignty over

(C) Great Britain exercised sovereignty over

(D) In 1898 China leased the district of Kiaochow to

List II

(i) New Helarides

(ii) Schleswig Holstein Anenburg

(iii) Germany

(iv) Turkish Island

Codes:	(A)	(B)	(C)	(D)
(a)	(ii)	(i)	(iv)	(iii)
(b)	(i)	(ii)	(iii)	(iv)
(c)	(iv)	(iii)	(ii)	(i)
(d)	(iii)	(iv)	(i)	(ii)

43. Which of the following statements is correct?

A de-facto government is government:

(a) Whose origin and existence is contrary to the Constitutional law of the State concerned and legality is challenged in International Law.

(b) Whose origin and existence is in conformity with the Constitutional law of the State represented and whose legality is uncontested in International Law.

(c) Which exercise control over a Foreign State.

(d) Which has been forced to leave the territory of its State due to enemy occupation or civil war.

44. Under which of the following Article of the U.N. Charter there is an obligation to inform the Security Council if the regional arrangements take any enforcement action for maintenance of peace and security?

(a) Article 51 (b) Article 54

(c) Article 107 (d) Article 108

45. In which one of the following cases the permanent Court of International Justice held, "it is a generally acceptable principle of international law that in relations, between powers, who are contracting parties to a treaty, the provisions of the municipal law cannot prevail over the treaty"?

(a) Navlilaa Incident Case

(b) Greco, Bulgarian Communities Case

(c) Panevezys Saldutiskis Railway Case

(d) Polish Postal Service Case

46. The wife's sister's daughter's son can be adopted. The adoption is

(a) void

(b) valid

(c) voidable

(d) None of the above

47. Kritrima Adoption is prevalent in which areas of India?

(a) Madras (b) Banaras

(c) Avadh (d) Mithila

48. In which case the Supreme Court held that "Cohabitation leads to presumption that person are living as husband and wife"?

(a) Balasubramaniyam Vs Suruttayan AIR 1992 SC 756

(b) Seema Vs Ashwin Kumar AIR 2006 SC 1158

(c) Vishnu Prakash Vs Sheela Devi (2001) 4 SCC 729

(d) None of the above

49. In which of the case, the Supreme Court held that it is desirable that "all marriages should be Compulsorily Registered in the State, where they are solemnized"?
(a) S. Nagalingam Vs. Sivagani AIR (2001) SC 3576
(b) Shanti Dev Berma Vs K.P. Devi AIR (1991) SC 816
(c) Seema Vs Ashwin Kumar AIR 2006 SC 1158
(d) None of the above

50. Rules relating to prohibited degrees are based on the principle of
(a) Monogamy (b) Polygamy
(c) Exogamy (d) Endogamy

51. In Islamic Law, marriage is both 'Ibadt' and 'Mammulat'. Who said this?
(a) Amir Ali Justice
(b) Dr. Fayzee
(c) Abdur-Rahim
(d) Mahmood Justice

52. A Muslim husband can delegate his right of Talaq to
(a) Any other person
(b) Wife only
(c) Both (a) and (b)
(d) None of the above

53. A Muslim minor wife can cease her right to repudiate the marriage in case:
(a) when she attained the age of puberty.
(b) when the marriage was consummated before attaining the age of puberty.
(c) when she is less than 18 years of age.
(d) none of the above.

54. Find correct answer using codes given below:
Following are main approaches to explain nature and meaning of human rights:
(i) The scientific right theory
(ii) The moral right theory
(iii) The natural right theory
(iv) The legal right theory

Codes:
(a) (i) and (ii) are correct.
(b) (ii) and (iii) are correct.
(c) (iii) and (iv) are correct.
(d) (iv) and (i) are correct.

55. Read Assertion (A) and Reason (R). Find correct answer using codes given below:
Assertion (A): The purpose of Human Rights is to provide protection against the abuse of power committed by the organs of State.
Reason (R): Due to absence of Lok Pal the misuse of power by the State cannot be effectively checked.
Codes:
(a) (A) and (R) are correct and (R) is correct explanation of (A).
(b) (A) and (R) are correct, but (R) is not correct explanation of (A).
(c) (A) is true and (R) is false.
(d) (A) is false and (R) is true.

56. Match item in Table A with items in Table B using codes given below:
Table A
(A) The first generation of Human Rights
(B) The second generation of Human Rights
(C) The third generation of Human Rights
(D) Theoretical approach to Human Rights
Table B
(i) Idealistic Theory of Law
(ii) Collective Rights
(iii) Civil and Political Rights
(iv) Economic, Social and Cultural Rights

Codes:	**(A)**	**(B)**	**(C)**	**(D)**
(a)	(i)	(iii)	(ii)	(iv)
(b)	(iii)	(iv)	(ii)	(i)
(c)	(iv)	(iii)	(ii)	(i)
(d)	(iii)	(iv)	(i)	(ii)

57. In Indian Constitution, Civil and Political Rights given in its

(a) Part II (b) Part III
(c) Part IV (d) Part IX

58. "No one shall be subjected to arbitrary arrest, detention or exile." Above law is in
(a) Article 21 of the Indian Constitution
(b) Criminal Procedure Code
(c) Civil Procedure Code
(d) Article 9 of the Universal Declaration of Human Rights

59. Read Assertion (A) and Reason (R) and find correct answer using codes given below:
Assertion (A): Advancement of rights of women has been the concern of world community since the end of Second World War.
Reason (R): In Second World War, population of men was significantly decreased.
Codes:
(a) (A) and (R) are true and (R) is correct explanation of (A).
(b) (A) and (R) are true, but (R) is not correct explanation of (A).
(c) (A) is true and (R) is false.
(d) (A) is false, but (R) is true.

60. Read Assertion (A) and Reason (R) and find correct answer using codes given below:
Assertion (A): The child must be given the means requisite for his normal development, both materially and spiritually.
Reason (R): Spirituality is material and material is spiritual.
Codes:
(a) (A) and (R) are true and (R) is correct explanation of (A).
(b) (A) and (R) are true, but (R) is not correct explanation of (A).
(c) (A) is true, but (R) is false.
(d) (A) is false, but (R) is true.

61. State which of the following statements is incorrect?
(a) Liability in tort arises from breach of duty primarily fixed by law.
(b) The duty, breach of which results in tortious liability, is towards the public generally.
(c) The duty, breach of which results in liability in tort, is towards some person in particular.
(d) The breach of duty, which results in liability in tort, is redressable by an action for unliquidated damages.

62. The plaintiff was watching a cricket match at a stadium organized by the Cricket Club of India. He was seriously injured by a mighty hit from the batsman. In this case, who is liable to pay the damages to the plaintiff ?
(a) The Batsman
(b) The Cricket Club of India
(c) Both (a) and (b) above
(d) None of the above

63. Which one of the following sets correctly identifies the specific defence available in an action for defamation?
(a) Privilege, Truth, Fair comment.
(b) Privilege, Mistake, Fair comment.
(c) Truth, Mistake, Fair comment.
(d) Truth, Privilege, Mistake.

64. Read Assertion (A) and Reason (R) and with the help of codes given below, point out the correct explanation.
Assertion (A): Pleading lack of intention to defame someone does not absolve one from liability for defamation.
Reason (R): The essence of defamation lies in the lowering a person in the estimation of the right thinking members of the society, even without intention.

Codes:
(a) Both (A) and (R) are true and (R) is the correct explanation of (A).
(b) Both (A) and (R) are true and (R) is not the correct explanation of (A).
(c) (A) is true, but (R) is false.
(d) (A) is false, but (R) is true.

65. **Assertion (A):** In India, defendants collecting water in reservoirs have not been held liable for damage caused due to the escape of water from these reservoirs in absence of negligence.
Reason (R): The rule of strict liability laid down in Rylands Vs Fletcher case has been held to be not applicable in India.
Select the correct answer using the codes given below:
Codes:
(a) Both (A) and (R) are true and (R) is the correct explanation of (A).
(b) Both (A) and (R) are true, but (R) is not the correct explanation of (A).
(c) (A) is true, but (R) is false.
(d) (A) is false, but (R) is true.

66. **Assertion (A):** In tort of nuisance, interference by the defendant may cause damage to the plaintiff's property or personal discomfort in the enjoyment of property.
Reason (R): Every interference in the use of property is a nuisance.
Select the correct answer using the codes given below:
Codes:
(a) Both (A) and (R) are individually true and (R) is the correct explanation of (A).
(b) Both (A) and (R) are individually true, but (R) is not the correct explanation of (A).
(c) (A) is true, but (R) is false.
(d) (A) is false, but (R) is true.

67. Match List I with List II and indicate the correct answer using the codes given below:
List I
(A) Composition of the District Forum
(B) Complaint to be accompanied by court fee
(C) Jurisdiction of the State Commission
(D) Appeals from National Commission to the Supreme Court
List II
(i) Section 10, C.P. Act
(ii) Section 17, C.P. Act
(iii) Section 23, C.P. Act
(iv) Section 12(2), C.P. Act

Codes:	(A)	(B)	(C)	(D)
(a)	(i)	(ii)	(iii)	(iv)
(b)	(i)	(iv)	(ii)	(iii)
(c)	(ii)	(iv)	(i)	(iii)
(d)	(iv)	(iii)	(ii)	(i)

68. Find correct legal principle from following statements:
(a) A company may do an act which is necessary for or incidental to the attainment of its objects or which is otherwise not authorized by the Act.
(b) A company may not do an act which is necessary for or incidental to the attainment of its objects which is otherwise not authorized by the Act.
(c) A company may do an act which is necessary for or incidental to the attainment of its objects or which is therwise authorized by the Act.
(d) A company may do an act which is unnecessary for or not incidental to attainment of its goals or which is otherwise barred by the Act.

69. Match items from Table A with items in Table B, using codes given below:
Table A
(A) Lakshmi Ratan Cotton Mills Vs. J.K. Jute Mills Co., AIR 1957 All 311

(B) Automatic Self-cleansing Filter Syndicate Co. Ltd. Vs. Cuninghame, (1906) 2 Ch. 34
(C) G. Ramesh Vs. ROC (2007) 135 Comp Cas 655
(D) City Equitable Fire Insurance Company, Re (1924) All E Rep 485

Table B

(i) Director's duty of care, diligence and skill
(ii) Statutory protection to Directors against liability
(iii) Powers of Directors
(iv) Scope of authority of Directors

Codes:	(A)	(B)	(C)	(D)
(a)	(iv)	(iii)	(ii)	(i)
(b)	(iii)	(ii)	(i)	(iv)
(c)	(ii)	(i)	(iv)	(iii)
(d)	(i)	(iv)	(iii)	(ii)

70. Read Assertion (A) and Reason (R) and with help of codes given below, point out the correct explanation.

Assertion (A): A contract of sale may be absolute or conditional.

Reason (R): There is no absolute condition for a contract of sale.

Codes:

(a) Both (A) and (R) are true and (R) is correct explanation of (A).
(b) Both (A) and (R) are true, but (R) is not correct explanation of (A).
(c) (A) is true, but (R) is false.
(d) (A) is false, but (R) is true.

71. "Where under a contract of sale the property in the goods is transferred from the seller to the buyer, the contract is called a sale, but where the transfer of the property in the goods is to take place at a future time or subject to some condition thereafter to be fulfilled, the contract is called an agreement to sell."

Read above statement and find correct answer, using codes given below:

Codes:

(a) Contract of sale is conditional.
(b) Contract of agreement to sell is conditional.
(c) There is no difference between sale and agreement to sell, as both are contracts.
(d) Sale is a contract, agreement to sell is not a contract.

72. Essential feature of a partnership is

(i) Agreement
(ii) Object to carry on a business
(iii) To share profits
(iv) Business is to be carried by all or any of them acting for all

Codes:

(a) Only (i) is correct.
(b) Only (i) and (ii) are correct.
(c) Only (i), (ii) and (iii) are correct.
(d) All of above are correct.

73. Find the correct legal statement from following statements:

(a) Every partner is liable, severally with all the other partners and jointly for all acts of the firm done while he is a partner.
(b) Every partner is liable, jointly with all the other partners and severally for all acts of the firm done while he is a partner.
(c) Every partner is liable only for acts done by him as acts of the firm done while he is a partner.
(d) Sleeping partner is not liable for acts done by him as acts of the firm done while he is a partner.

74. Read Assertion (A) and Reason (R) and with help of codes given below, point out the correct explanation.

Assertion (A): It is the duty of the banker to be acquainted with the customer's handwriting.
Reason (R): A banker must be hand writing expert.
Codes:
(a) Both (A) and (R) are true and (R) is correct explanation of (A).
(b) Both (A) and (R) are true, but (R) is not correct explanation of (A).
(c) (A) is true, but (R) is false.
(d) (A) is false, but (R) is true.

75. When a negotiable instrument is dishonoured, the party liable to pay, becomes bound to pay compensation to
(a) The bank
(b) The endorser
(c) Holder or endorsee
(d) The Court

ANSWERS

1. (d)	2. (a)	3. (a)	4. (c)	5. (d)
6. (c)	7. (a)	8. (c)	9. (b)	10. (d)
11. (a)	12. (b)	13. (c)	14. (b)	15. (d)
16. (c)	17. (a)	18. (a)	19. (d)	20. (d)
21. (d)	22. (c)	23. (c)	24. (d)	25. (a)
26. (c)	27. (d)	28. (d)	29. (d)	30. (b)
31. (b)	32. (b)	33. (b)	34. (b)	35. (d)
36. (d)	37. (a)	38. (c)	39. (a)	40. (d)
41. (b)	42. (a)	43. (a)	44. (d)	45. (a)
46. (d)	47. (c)	48. (b)	49. (d)	50. (a)
51. (c)	52. (c)	53. (c)	54. (c)	55. (b)
56. (a)	57. (b)	58. (b)	59. (d)	60. (a)
61. (d)	62. (a)	63. (b)	64. (c)	65. (d)
66. (d)	67. (d)	68. (b)	69. (d)	70. (b)
71. (d)	72. (c)	73. (c)	74. (d)	75. (c)

DECEMBER–2014

Note: This paper contains Sixty (60) multiple-choice questions, each question carrying two (2) marks. Candidate is expected to answer any Fifty (50) questions. In case more than Fifty (50) questions are attempted, only the first Fifty (50) questions will be evaluated.

PAPER I

1. The term 'Yellow Journalism' refers to
   (a) sensational news about terrorism and violence
   (b) sensationalism and exaggeration to attract readers/viewers.
   (c) sensational news about arts and culture
   (d) sensational news prints in yellow paper.

2. In the classroom, the teacher sends the message either as words or images. The students are really
   (a) Encoders (b) Decoders
   (c) Agitators (d) Propagators

3. Media is known as
   (a) First Estate (b) Second Estate
   (c) Third Estate (d) Fourth Estate

4. The mode of communication that involves a single source transmitting information to a large number of receivers simultaneously, is called
   (a) Group Communication
   (b) Mass Communication
   (c) Intrapersonal Communication
   (d) Interpersonal Communication

5. A smart classroom is a teaching space which has
   (i) Smart portion with a touch panel control system.
   (ii) PC/Laptop connection and DVD/VCR player.
   (iii) Document camera and specialized software.
   (iv) Projector and screen.

   Select the correct answer from the codes given below:
   (a) (i) and (ii) only
   (b) (ii) and (iv) only
   (c) (i), (ii) and (iii) only
   (d) (i), (ii), (iii) and (iv)

6. Digital Empowerment means
   (i) Universal digit literacy.
   (ii) Universal access to all digital resources.
   (iii) Collaborative digital platform for participative governance.
   (iv) Probability of all entitlements for individuals through cloud.

   Choose the correct answer from the codes given below:
   (a) (i) and (ii) only
   (b) (ii) and (iii) only
   (c) (i), (ii) and (iii) only
   (d) (i), (ii), (iii) and (iv)

7. The next term in the series:
   2, 7, 28, 63, 126, ____ is
   (a) 215 (b) 245
   (c) 276 (d) 296

8. The next term in the series:
   AB, ED, IH, NM, ______ is

(a) TS (b) ST
(c) TU (d) SU

9. If STREAMERS is coded as UVTGALDQR, then KNOWLEDGE will be coded as
(a) MQPYLCDFD (b) MPQYLDCFD
(c) PMYQLDFCD (d) YMQPLDDFC

10. A is brother of B. B is the brother of C. C is the husband of D. E is the father of A. D is related to E as
(a) Daughter
(b) Daughter-in-law
(c) Sister-in-law
(d) Sister

11. Two numbers are in the ratio 3 : 5. If 9 is subtracted from the numbers, the ratio becomes 12 : 23. The numbers are
(a) 30, 50 (b) 36, 60
(c) 33, 55 (d) 42, 70

12. The mean of the ages of father and his son is 27 years. After 18 years, father will be twice as old as his son. Their present ages are
(a) 42, 12 (b) 40, 14
(c) 30, 24 (d) 36, 18

Read the following passage carefully and answer questions 13 to 17:

The literary distaste for politics, however, seems to be focused not so much on the largely murky practice of politics in itself as a subject of literary representation but rather more on how it is often depicted in literature, i.e., on the very politics of such representation. A political novel often turns out to be not merely a novel about politics but a novel with a politics of its own, for it seeks not merely to show us how things are but has fairly definite ideas about how things should be, and precisely what one should think and do in order to make things move in that desired direction. In short, it seeks to convert and enlist the reader to a particular cause or ideology; it often is (in an only too familiar phrase) not literature but propaganda. This is said to violate the very spirit of literature which is to broaden our understanding of the world and the range of our sympathies rather than to narrow them down through partisan commitment. As John Keats said, "We hate poetry that has a palpable design upon us".

Another reason why politics does not seem amenable to the highest kind of literary representation seems to arise from the fact that politics by its very nature is constituted of ideas and ideologies. If political situations do not lend themselves to happy literary treatment, political ideas present perhaps an even greater problem in this regard. Literature, it is argued, is about human experiences rather than about intellectual abstractions; it deals in what is called the 'felt reality' of human flesh and blood, and in sap and savour (*rasa*) rather than in arid and lifeless ideas. In an extensive discussion of the matter in her book *Ideas and the Novel*, the American novelist Mary McCarthy observed that 'ideas are still today felt to be unsightly in the novel' though that was not so in 'former days', i.e., in the 18th and 19th centuries. Her formulation of the precise nature of the incompatibility between ideas on the one hand and the novel on the other betrays perhaps a divided conscience in the matter and a sense of dilemma shared by many writers and readers: "An idea cannot have loose ends, but a novel, I almost think, needs them. Nevertheless, there is enough in common for the novelists to feel...the attraction of ideas while taking up arms against them—most often with weapons of mockery."

13. According to the passage, a political novel often turns out to be a
(a) Literary distaste for politics
(b) Literary representation of politics
(c) Novel with its own politics
(d) Depiction of murky practice of politics

14. A political novel reveals
    (a) Reality of the things
    (b) Writer's perception
    (c) Particular ideology of the readers
    (d) The spirit of literature

15. The constructs of politics by its nature is
    (a) Prevalent political situation
    (b) Ideas and ideologies
    (c) Political propaganda
    (d) Understanding of human nature

16. Literature deals with
    (a) Human experiences in politics
    (b) Intellectual abstractions
    (c) Dry and empty ideas
    (d) Felt reality of human life

17. The observation of the novelist, Mary McCarthy reveals
    (a) unseen felt ideas of today in the novel
    (b) dichotomy of conscience on political ideas and novels
    (c) compatibility between idea and novel
    (d) endless ideas and novels

18. When in a group of propositions, one proposition is claimed to follow from the others, that group of propositions is called
    (a) An argument
    (b) A valid argument
    (c) An explanation
    (d) An invalid argument

19. Namita and Samita are brilliant and studious. Anita and Karabi are obedient and irregular. Babita and Namita are irregular but brilliant. Samita and Kabita are regular and obedient. Who among them is/are brilliant, obedient, regular and studious?
    (a) Samita alone
    (b) Namita and Samita
    (c) Kabita alone
    (d) Anita alone

20. Warrior is related to sword, carpenter is related to saw, farmer is related to plough. In the same way, the author is related to
    (a) Book (b) Fame
    (c) Reader (d) Pen

21. Given below is a diagram of three circles A, B and C over-lapping each other. The circle A represents the class of honest people, the circle B represents the class of sincere people and circle C represents the class of politicians. p, q, r, s, U, X, Y represent different regions. Select the code that represents the region indicating the class of honest politicians who are not sincere.

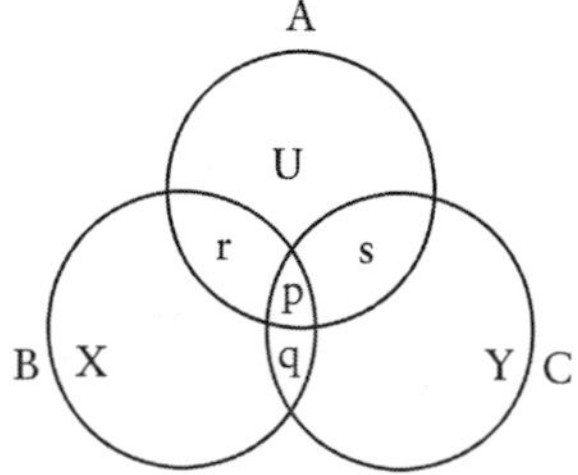

Codes:
(a) X (b) q
(c) p (d) s

22. "A man ought no more to value himself for being wiser than a woman if he owes his advantage to a better education, than he ought to boast of his courage for beating a man when his hands were tied."
    The above passage is an instance of
    (a) Deductive argument
    (b) Hypothetical argument
    (c) Analogical argument
    (d) Factual argument

23. By which of the following proposition, the proposition 'wise men are hardly afraid of death' is contradicted?
    (a) Some wise men are afraid of death.
    (b) All wise men are afraid of death.
    (c) No wise men is afraid of death.
    (d) Some wise men are not afraid of death.

For a country CO_2 emissions (million metric tons) from various sectors are given in the following table. Answer the questions (24 to 29) based on the data given:

	CO_2 emissions (million metric tons)				
Year/Sector	Power	Industry	Commercial	Agriculture	Domestic
2005	500	200	150	80	100
2006	600	300	200	90	110
2007	650	320	250	100	120
2008	700	400	300	150	150
2009	800	450	320	200	180

24. What is the percentage (%) growth of CO_2 emissions from power sector during 2005 to 2009?
(a) 60 (b) 50
(c) 40 (d) 80

25. Which sector has recorded maximum growth in CO_2 emissions during 2005 to 2009?
(a) Power (b) Industry
(c) Commercial (d) Agriculture

26. By what percentage (%), the total emissions of CO_2 have increased from 2005 to 2009?
(a) ~89.32% (b) ~57.62%
(c) ~40.32% (d) ~113.12%

27. What is the average annual growth rate of CO_2 emissions in power sector?
(a) ~12.57% (b) ~16.87%
(c) ~30.81% (d) ~50.25%

28. What is the percentage contribution of power sector to total CO_2 emissions in the year 2008?
(a) ~30.82% (b) ~41.18%
(c) ~51.38% (d) ~60.25%

29. In which year, the contribution (%) of industry to total sectoral CO_2 emissions was minimum?
(a) 2005 (b) 2006
(c) 2007 (d) 2009

30. Symbols A-F are used in which one of the following?
(a) Binary number system
(b) Decimal number system
(c) Hexadecimal number system
(d) Octal number system

31. Which one of the following is not a search engine?
(a) Google (b) Chrome
(c) Yahoo (d) Bing

32. CSS stands for
(a) Cascading Style Sheets
(b) Collecting Style Sheets
(c) Comparative Style Sheets
(d) Comprehensive Style Sheets

33. MOOC stands for
(a) Media Online Open Course
(b) Massachusetts Open Online Course
(c) Massive Open Online Course
(d) Myrind Open Online Course

34. Binary equivalent of decimal number 35 is
(a) 100011 (b) 110001
(c) 110101 (d) 101011

35. gif, jpg, bmp, png are used as extensions for files which store
(a) audio data (b) image data
(c) video data (d) text data

36. Which of the anthropogenic activity accounts for more than two-third of global water consumption?
(a) Agriculture
(b) Hydropower generation
(c) Industry
(d) Domestic and Municipal usage

37. One of the anthropogenic sources of gaseous pollutants chlorofluorocarbons (CFCs) in air is
(a) Cement industry
(b) Fertiliser industry
(c) Foam industry
(d) Pesticide industry

38. In terms of total CO_2 emissions from a country, identify the correct sequence:

(a) U.S.A. > China > India > Russia
(b) China > U.S.A. > India > Russia
(c) China > U.S.A. > Russia > India
(d) U.S.A. > China > Russia > India

39. Match List-I and List-II and identify the correct code:

List-I
A. World Health Day
B. World Population Day
C. World Ozone Day
D. World AIDS Day

List-II
(i) 16th September (ii) 1st December
(iii) 11th July (iv) 7th April

Codes:	A	B	C	D
(a)	(i)	(ii)	(iii)	(iv)
(b)	(iv)	(iii)	(i)	(ii)
(c)	(ii)	(iii)	(iv)	(i)
(d)	(iii)	(iv)	(ii)	(i)

40. The cyclone 'Hudhud' hit the coast of which State?
(a) Andhra Pradesh (b) Karnataka
(c) Kerala (d) Gujarat

41. Which of the following is not a renewable natural resource?
(a) Clean air (b) Fresh water
(c) Fertile soil (d) Salt

42. The maximum number of fake institutions/universities as identified by the UGC in the year 2014 are in the State/Union territory of
(a) Bihar (b) Uttar Pradesh
(c) Tamil Nadu (d) Delhi

43. Which of the following institutions are empowered to confer or grant degrees under the UGC Act, 1956?
1. A university established by an Act of Parliament.
2. A university established by an Act of Legislature.
3. A university/institution established by a linguistic minority.
4. An institution which is a deemed to be university.

Select the correct answer from the codes given below:
(a) 1 and 2 (b) 1, 2 and 3
(c) 1, 2 and 4 (d) 1, 2, 3 and 4

44. Which of the following are the tools of good governance?
1. Social Audit
2. Separation of Powers
3. Citizen's Charter
4. Right to Information

Select the correct answer from the codes given below:
(a) 1, 3 and 4 (b) 2, 3 and 4
(c) 1 and 4 (d) 1, 2, 3 and 4

45. Which of the following powers, the President has in relation to Lok Sabha?
1. Summoning
2. Adjournment—sine die
3. Prorogation
4. Dissolution

Select the correct answer from the codes given below:
(a) 1 and 4 (b) 1, 2 and 3
(c) 1, 3 and 4 (d) 1, 2, 3 and 4

46. The interval between two sessions of Parliament must not exceed
(a) 3 months (b) 6 months
(c) 4 months (d) 100 days

47. Right to Privacy as a Fundamental Right is implied in
(a) Right to Freedom
(b) Right to Life and Personal Liberty
(c) Right to Equality
(d) Right against Exploitation

48. Which of the following organizations deals with 'capacity building program' on Educational Planning?
(a) NCERT (b) UGC
(c) NAAC (d) NUEPA

49. "Education is the manifestation of perfection already in man" was stated by

(a) M.K. Gandhi
(b) R.N. Tagore
(c) Swami Vivekanand
(d) Sri Aurobindo

50. Which of the following is not a prescribed level of teaching?
(a) Memory (b) Understanding
(c) Reflective (d) Differentiation

51. Maximum participation of students during teaching is possible through
(a) Lecture method
(b) Demonstration method
(c) Inductive method
(d) Textbook method

52. Diagnostic evaluation ascertains
(a) Students performance at the beginning of instructions.
(b) Learning progress and failures during instructions.
(c) Degree of achievement of instructions at the end.
(d) Causes and remedies of persistent learning problems during instructions.

53. Instructional aids are used by the teacher to
(a) glorify the class
(b) attract the students
(c) clarify the concepts
(d) ensure discipline

54. Attitude of the teacher that affects teaching pertains to
(a) Affective domain
(b) Cognitive domain
(c) Connative domain
(d) Psychomotor domain

55. When planning to do as social research, it is better to
(a) approach the topic with an open mind
(b) do a pilot study before getting stuck into it
(c) be familiar with literature on the topic
(d) forget about theory because this is a very practical

56. When academicians are called to deliver lecture or presentation to an audience on certain topics or a set of topics of educational nature, it is called
(a) Training Program
(b) Seminar
(c) Workshop
(d) Symposium

57. The core elements of a dissertation are
(a) Introduction; Data Collection; Data Analysis; Conclusions and Recommendations
(b) Executive Summary; Literature Review; Data gathered; Conclusions; Bibliography
(c) Research Plan; Research Data; Analysis; References
(d) Introduction; Literature Review; Research Methodology; Results; Discussion and Conclusion

58. What is a Research Design?
(a) A way of conducting research that is not grounded in theory.
(b) The choice between using qualitative or quantitative methods.
(c) The style in which you present your research findings e.g. a graph.
(d) A framework for every stage of the collection and analysis of data.

59. 'Sampling Cases' means
(a) Sampling using a sampling frame
(b) Identifying people who are suitable for research
(c) Literally the researcher's brief case
(d) Sampling of people, newspapers, television programmes etc.

60. The frequency distribution of a research data which is symmetrical in shape similar to a normal distribution but center peak is much higher, is

(a) Skewed (b) Mesokurtic
(c) Leptokurtic (d) Platykurtic

ANSWERS

1. (b)	2. (b)	3. (d)	4. (b)	5. (d)
6. (d)	7. (a)	8. (a)	9. (b)	10. (b)
11. (c)	12. (a)	13. (c)	14. (b)	15. (c)
16. (d)	17. (b)	18. (a)	19. (a)	20. (d)
21. (d)	22. (c)	23. (b)	24. (a)	25. (d)
26. (a)	27. (a)	28. (b)	29. (a)	30. (c)
31. (b)	32. (a)	33. (c)	34. (a)	35. (b)
36. (a)	37. (d)	38. (b)	39. (b)	40. (a)
41. (c)	42. (b)	43. (c)	44. (d)	45. (b)
46. (b)	47. (b)	48. (d)	49. (c)	50. (d)
51. (c)	52. (d)	53. (c)	54. (a)	55. (a)
56. (b)	57. (d)	58. (d)	59. (d)	60. (c)

PAPER II

Note: This paper contains fifty (50) objective type questions of two (2) marks each. All questions are compulsory.

1. Which of the following statements is right?
   (a) Law consist of rules in accordance with reason and nature has formed the basis of imperative law.
   (b) Natural law is a type of command.
   (c) Law, according to positivist, is made through medium of courts.
   (d) Hart talks in terms of conduct supplemented by an attitude of mind to the effect that the conduct in question is obligatory because it is required by rule.
2. Right *in re aliena* means a right over
   (a) his own property
   (b) a property of someone else
   (c) property situated in a foreign country
   (d) property situated in one's own country
3. **Assertion (A):** A perfect duty is one which a man not merely ought to perform, but may be justly compelled to perform.
   Reason (R): A perfect duty is one which is not merely recognised by law but enforced.
   1. (A) is true, but (R) is false.
   2. (A) is false, but (R) is true.
   3. Both (A) and (R) are true.
   4. Both (A) and (R) are false.

   (a) 1 and 2 (b) 2 and 3
   (c) 3 alone (d) 4 alone
4. Possession is prima facie evidence of tittle of ownership. Hence—
   (a) long adverse possession confers tittle even to a property which originally belonged to another.
   (b) in all cases possession leads to ownership.
   (c) transfer of possession is not a mode of transferring ownership.
   (d) long possession do not confer tittle to the property which originally belonged to government.
5. Who among the following said that there is in essence no difference between the legal personality of a company and that of an individual?
   (a) Maitland (b) Dicey
   (c) Gierke (d) Kelson
6. Ownership of Goodwill of a business is
   (a) Limited ownership
   (b) Corporeal ownership
   (c) Incorporeal ownership
   (d) Beneficial ownership
7. It was remarked in 'Golaknath Vs. State of Punjab' that our 'Preamble to the Constitution contains in a nutshell its

ideals and aspirations' by one of the judges?
(a) Justice V.R. Krishna Iyer
(b) Justice K. Subba Rao
(c) Justice A.N. Ray
(d) Justice H.R. Khanna

8. Right of eligible employees to be considered for promotion is virtually a part of Fundamental Right of employees, was decided by the Supreme Court in:
(a) Union of India Vs. Hemraj Singh Chauhan
(b) Supreme Court Employees Association Vs. Union of India
(c) John Vallamattam Vs. Union of India
(d) St. Stephens College Vs. University of Delhi

9. In Vishram Singh Raghubanshi Vs. State of Uttar Pradesh (AIR2011 SC2275) the court held that:
(a) It is the duty of Superior Courts to protect the reputation of judicial officers of subordinate courts.
(b) Procedure laid down in the appointment of officers of subordinate courts.
(c) Procedure laid down in the salaries and service conditions of the judicial officers of the lower judiciary.
(d) Transfer of the Judges of the High Court.

10. In which of these cases, Fundamental Duties are judicially invoked? Answer using codes given below:
i. Prem Prakash Vs. Punjab University
ii. Suresh Koshy George Vs. University of Kerala
iii. Rural Litigation and Entitlement Kendra Vs. State of Uttar Pradesh
iv. Shri Sachidanand Pandey Vs. State of West Bengal

Codes:
(a) i and ii are correct.
(b) ii and iii are correct.
(c) iii and iv are correct.
(d) i, ii, iii and iv are correct.

11. Match List-I with List-II using codes given below:

List-I
A. Executive power must be exercised in accordance with the Constitution.
B. Executive power is the residue of functions of government, which are not legislative or judicial
C. Executive power may be exercised without prior legislative support.
D. The President is not bound to hear a petitioner for mercy before he rejects the petition.

List-II
1. H.H. Maharajadhiraja Madhav Rao Jivaji Rao Scindia Bahadur Vs. Union of India
2. Maganbhai Ishwarbhai Patel Vs. Union of India
3. Kehar Singh Vs. Union of India
4. A. Sanjeevi Naidu Vs. State of Madras

Codes:	A	B	C	D
(a)	4	1	2	3
(b)	1	4	2	3
(c)	4	1	3	2
(d)	2	3	1	4

12. The Supreme Court has laid down guidelines for imposing emergency under Art. 356 in one of the following cases:
(a) A.K. Roy Vs. Union of India
(b) S.R. Bommai Vs. Union of India
(c) State of Rajasthan Vs. Union of India
(d) Rameswar Prasad Vs. Union of India

13. By which constitutional amendment "The total number of ministers, including the

Prime Minister, in the Council of Ministers shall not exceed fifteen percent of the total number of members of the House of the people"?

(a) Ninety First (b) Ninety Second
(c) Ninety Third (d) Ninety Fifth

14. Match List-I with List-II and give correct answers by using the codes given below:

List-I (Principles applied by the Courts)
1. Law must be based on justice, equity and good conscience
2. Subrogation
3. Res-Judicata
4. Estoppel

List-II (Cases)
A. R.V. Keyn
B. Chorzaw Factory (Indemnity) Case
C. Mavrommatis Palestine Concessions Case
D. Barcelona Traction Case

Codes:	A	B	C	D
(a)	3	2	4	1
(b)	1	3	2	4
(c)	2	4	3	2
(d)	1	2	3	4

15. Who is not the Exponent of the Constitutive Theory of 'Recognition'?

(a) Hegel (b) Oppenheim
(c) Hall (d) Anzilloti

16. Match List-I with List-II and give the correct answer by using the codes given below:

List-I (Sources of Public International Law)
1. General principles of law recognised by the civilized countries
2. Juristic Work
3. International Customs
4. Justice and Equity

List-II (Case-related)
A. North Continental Self case
B. Burkina Faso Vs. Mali
C. Portugal Vs. India
D. Paquete Habaana case

Codes:	A	B	C	D
(a)	1	2	3	4
(b)	2	3	4	1
(c)	3	4	1	2
(d)	4	1	3	2

17. **Statement-I:** Subject to Rules of Jus Cogens, local customary law can supplement or derogate from general custom.

Statement-II: International law does not recognise the concept of local custom.

Using the codes given below give the correct answer:

(a) Both the statements are individually true and Statement-II is the correct explanation of statement-I.
(b) Both the Statements are individually true but Statement-II is not the correct explanation of Statement-I.
(c) Statement-I is true, but Statement-II is false.
(d) Statement-I is false, but Statement-II is true.

18. Using the codes given below indicate the chronological sequence in which the following judgements were delivered by the International Court of Justice:

1. Right of passage over Indian Territory case.
2. South-West Africa case.
3. Frontier Dispute.
4. Temple of Preah Vihear

Codes:

(a) 1, 2, 3, 4 (b) 2, 4, 1, 3
(c) 1, 4, 2, 3 (d) 3, 2, 4, 1

19. Match List-I with List-II and give the correct answer by using the codes given below:

List-I (Provisions under Statute of International Court of Justice)

1. Binding force of decrees of International Court of Justice.
2. Methods of conferring Jurisdiction upon the court.
3. Advisory Jurisdiction of the Court.
4. Courts power to allow a state to intervene in case to which it is not a party.

List-II (Related Articles)

(A) Article 65 (B) Article 62
(C) Article 59 (D) Article 36

Codes:	A	B	C	D
(a)	3	4	1	2
(b)	2	3	4	1
(c)	4	2	3	1
(d)	1	2	3	4

20. In which of the following cases, a child could not be a 'Hindu' under the Hindu Marriage Act, 1955?
   I. Only one parent is a Hindu and the child was brought up as a Hindu.
   II. If after the birth of a child both the parents convert to Buddhism.
   III. Only one parent is Jain and the child was not brought up as a Jain.
   IV. If after the birth of a child both the parents convert to Muslim religion and in the exercise of parental right the child is also converted to Muslim religion.

   Codes:
   (a) I, II and IV (b) III and IV
   (c) II and I (d) I, II and III

21. When two Hindus are descendants of a common ancestress but by different husbands, they are said to be related to each other by
   (a) Uterine Blood (b) Half Blood
   (c) Full Blood (d) Fosterage

22. A 'Muta' marriage is:
   I. A temporary marriage.
   II. Recognized under Sunni law.
   III. Recognized under Shia law.
   IV. For a fixed period.

   Codes:
   (a) II and IV only (b) I, II, III and IV
   (c) I, III and IV (d) II and III

23. A decree of judicial separation:
   I. dissolve the matrimonial bond.
   II. does not dissolve the matrimonial bond but merely suspends marital rights and obligations during the subsistence of the decree.
   III. mandates that the parties still continue to be husband and wife but not obliged to live together.
   IV. provides that if the parties have not resumed cohabitation for a period of one year either party may seek divorce.

   Codes:
   (a) I, II and IV (b) I, II, III and IV
   (c) I and IV (d) II, III and IV

24. Match List-I with List-II and select the correct answer with the help of codes given below:

   List-I
   (A) Ijma (B) Faskh
   (C) Mahr-ul-misl (D) Qiyas

   List-II
   1. Cancellation of marriage
   2. Opinion of one individual only
   3. Collective opinion of commentators
   4. Customary dower

Codes:	A	B	C	D
(a)	3	1	4	2
(b)	1	2	3	4
(c)	3	4	2	1
(d)	4	2	1	3

25. Rules relating to spinda relationship are based on the principle of
(a) Polygyny (b) Endogamy
(c) Exogamy (d) Polyandry

26. Divorce by Zihar is a species of
(a) actual divorce
(b) inchoate divorce
(c) khula divorce
(d) constructive divorce

27. For a valid contract acceptance should be
(a) absolute and qualified
(b) partial but unqualified
(c) absolute and unqualified
(d) absolutely qualified

28. According to Explanation 2 to Section 25 of the Indian Contract Act, which of the following statements are correct?
i. An agreement to which the consent of the promisor is not freely given is valid because consideration is adequate.
ii. An agreement to which the consent of promisor is freely given is valid even if consideration is inadequate.
iii. Consideration must be legal.
iv. Consideration can be illegal.

Codes:
(a) i and ii are correct.
(b) ii and iii are correct.
(c) iii and iv are correct.
(d) i and iv are correct.

29. In Jyotindra Bhattacharjee Vs. Mrs. Sona Balon Bora, it was held that
(a) the onus of proving soundness of mind of a person always rests upon a person who alleges such state of mind of another person.
(b) the onus of proving unsoundness of mind of a person always rests upon a person who alleges such state of mind of another person.
(c) the onus of proving unsoundness of mind rests upon person of unsound mind.
(d) the onus of proving unsoundness of mind is on the judge deciding the case involving person of unsound mind.

30. Read Assertion (A) and Reason (R) and give the correct explanation with the help of codes given below:
Assertion (A): Agreement is void when both parties are under mistake as to the matter of law.
Reason (R): Parties entering into a contract are legally obliged to know the law relating to the contract.

Codes:
(a) (A) and (R) are correct and (R) is correct reason for (A).
(b) (A) is correct, but (R) is wrong.
(c) (R) is correct, but (A) is wrong.
(d) Both (A) and (R) are wrong.

31. Where, a law promulgated after the contract is made, makes the performance of the agreement impossible, the agreement becomes
(a) Voidable (b) Valid
(c) Void (d) Absolutely binding

32. Match List-I with List-II and select the correct answer using the codes given below:

List-I
A. Damages arising in the usual course of things
B. Compensation for mental anguish
C. Measure of damages
D. Compensation for breach of contract where penalty is stipulated for

List-II
1. Ghaziabad Dev. Authority Vs. Union of India
2. Hadley Vs. Baxendale

3. M/s. Ganga Maruthi Vs. Nagaraj
4. Jamal Vs. Moolla Dawood

Codes:	A	B	C	D
(a)	2	1	4	3
(b)	1	2	4	3
(c)	2	1	3	4
(d)	4	3	1	2

33. Who is the propounder of 'Pigeon hole' theory?
(a) Winfield (b) Salmond
(c) Flemming (d) Paton

34. The owner of the bus instructed the driver not to race and compete with other omnibuses on a particular route. Driver still tried to obstruct a rival omnibus and caused an accident. What shall be the nature of liability?
(a) The driver shall be liable for the accident because he did not follow the instructions of his owner.
(b) It shall be the liability of the owner of bus because he has no authority to give instruction to his driver and his act was totally wrong.
(c) The owner of the bus shall be vicariously liable for the accident committed by his driver during the course of employment.
(d) Neither owner nor driver shall be liable.

35. Which of the following is NOT a sovereign function of the State?
(a) Construction of military road.
(b) Injury to the plaintiff during the lathi-charge by the police to disperse the unlawful crowd.
(c) A Government jeep being taken from the workshop to the collector's bungalow for his use.
(d) Distribution of meals to army personnel.

36. **Assertion (A):** A wooden chair while being used by a guest, caused an injury to him due to defective manufacture. The guest is entitled to claim damages from the manufacturer.
Reason (R): The manufacturer owes a duty to take care only towards the lawful buyer under the Consumer Protection Act.

Codes:
(a) Both (A) and (R) are true and (R) is the correct explanation of (A).
(b) Both (A) and (R) are true, but (R) is not the correct explanation of (A).
(c) (A) is true, but (R) is false.
(d) (A) is false, but (R) is true.

37. If a journalist publishes an article in a leading newspaper that all lawyers were thieves, no particular lawyer could sue him unless there is something to point to the particular individual. It refers to
(a) Defamation of a company
(b) Innuendo
(c) Defamation of public figures
(d) Defamation of class of persons

38. Match the List-I (Name of Case) with List-II (Name of Court):

List-I
A. Municipal Corporation Vs. Subhagwanti
B. Roop Lal Vs. Union of India
C. State Vs. Chironji Lal
D. Rural Transport Service Vs. Bezlum Bibi

List-II
1. High Court of Madhya Pradesh
2. High Court of Jammu & Kashmir
3. High Court of Calcutta
4. Supreme Court

Codes:	A	B	C	D
(a)	4	2	1	3
(b)	2	1	4	3
(c)	3	4	2	1
(d)	4	1	3	2

39. The Revenue Inspector knowingly disobeys the direction to conduct enquiry at a place for demarcation, what offence, if any, has been caused by him under IPC?
    (a) An offence as per Sec. 166-A.
    (b) For continuing to remain in an unlawful assembly as per Sec. 145.
    (c) For touching any point material as per Sec. 199.
    (d) For giving false information as per Sec. 201.

40. A man has committed physical contact involving unwelcome sexual overture against a female. What offence has been caused by him under IPC?
    (a) Requesting for sexual favour as per Sec. 354-A(1)(ii).
    (b) Sexual harassment as per Sec. 354(1)(i).
    (c) Out-raging of modesty as per Sec. 354.
    (d) Attempt to rape as per Sec. 370(A).

41. Read the Assertion (A) and the Reason (R) given below to answer the correct explanation using the codes:
    Assertion (A): The legal right involves freedom from penalty.
    Reason (R): A legal right is one which is either enforceable or recognised.
    Codes:
    (a) Both (A) and (R) are correct, but (R) is not the correct explanation of (A).
    (b) Both (A) and (R) are true and (R) is the correct explanation of (A).
    (c) Assertion (A) is correct, but Reason (R) is wrong.
    (d) Assertion (A) is incorrect because Reason (R) fixes liability when not enforceable or derecognised.

42. The maxim 'ream linguam non facit nisi mens rea' is propounded by
    (a) Coke (b) Lord Kenyon
    (c) Augustine (d) Lord Arbinger

43. Fill in the gap:
    Disobedience of law is not ordinarily a crime unless that act is declared as crime by some________.
    (a) law (b) method
    (c) society (d) All the above

44. The Indian Penal Code prohibits fixing of liability on a person so long he is authorised or gives assent to it. But there is an exceptional situation arising out of:
    (a) Libel
    (b) Public nuisance
    (c) Contempt of Court
    (d) All of them

45. Who among the following moved a resolution in the Central Legislative Assembly recommending that the Government should introduce a legislation for registration and protection of Trade Union in the year 1921?
    (a) B.P. Wadia (b) M.N. Joshi
    (c) N.M. Lokhanddey (d) V.V. Giri

46. "Works Committee under the Industrial Disputes Act should be substituted by an 'Industrial Relations Committee' to promote in-house dispute settlement." This recommendation was made by
    (a) Royal Commission on Labour
    (b) National Commission on Labour 1969
    (c) National Commission on Labour 2002
    (d) National Commission for enterprises in the Unorganised Sector

47. Who is a protected workman under the Industrial Disputes Act? Answer from the codes given below:
    1. A workman who is a member of a registered Trade Union.
    2. Recognised by the Registrar of the Trade Union as protected workman.

3. A workman who is a member of the Executive or other office bearer of a registered Trade Union connected with the establishment.
4. Recognised as protected workman under the rules applicable to the establishment.

Codes:

(a) 1 and 2 (b) 2 and 4
(c) 3 and 4 (d) 1 and 3

48. Failure of the conciliation proceedings under the Industrial Disputes Act leads to refer the matter to adjudication by
(a) the conciliation officer
(b) both employer and employee
(c) the employer
(d) the appropriate government

49. The power of the Government to refer a Dispute under the Industrial Disputes Act is
(a) Mandatory
(b) Discretionary
(c) Recommendatory
(d) Either mandatory or discretionary

50. Read the Assertion (A) and Reason (R). Write the correct answer using the codes given below:

Assertion (A): The conciliation officer has no power under the Industrial Disputes Act when neither industrial disputes exists or apprehended.

Reason (R): Conciliation officer only investigates the Industrial disputes which exists or apprehended.

Codes:

(a) Both (A) and (R) are wrong.
(b) Both (A) and (R) are correct.
(c) (A) is correct and (R) is wrong.
(d) (A) is wrong and (R) is correct.

ANSWERS

1. (d)	2. (b)	3. (c)	4. (a)	5. (d)
6. (c)	7. (b)	8. (a)	9. (a)	10. (c)
11. (a)	12. (b)	13. (a)	14. (b)	15. (c)
16. (d)	17. (c)	18. (c)	19. (a)	20. (b)
21. (a)	22. (c)	23. (d)	24. (a)	25. (c)
26. (b)	27. (c)	28. (b)	29. (b)	30. (d)
31. (c)	32. (a)	33. (b)	34. (c)	35. (c)
36. (c)	37. (d)	38. (a)	39. (a)	40. (b)
41. (b)	42. (c)	43. (a)	44. (d)	45. (b)
46. (c)	47. (c)	48. (d)	49. (b)	50. (b)

PAPER III

Note: This paper contains seventy-fifty (75) objective type questions of two (2) marks each. All questions are compulsory.

1. Read Assertion (A) and Reason (R) and answer using the codes given below:

Assertion (A): The writ of Habeas Corpus can be granted to enable the detainee to argue his case in person.

Reason (R): Because R Vs. Secretary of State for Home Department ex parte Wynne (1992) decided so.

Codes:

(a) (A) and (R) are right and (R) is right reason for (A).
(b) (A) is right, but (R) is wrong.
(c) (A) is wrong, but (R) is right.
(d) Both (A) and (R) are wrong.

2. Which of the following are matched incorrectly?
i. Habeas Corpus - 'To produce the body'

ii. Quo warranto - 'Issued to a lower court to stop proceedings in a case'

iii. Prohibition - 'Issued to a lower court quashing a decision or order'

iv. Mandamus - 'Commands a person to perform a public duty'

(a) i, ii and iii (b) ii and iii
(c) ii, iii and iv (d) ii and iv

3. Art. 51 A of the Constitution of India is confined to
(a) All citizens of India
(b) All persons of India
(c) All Non-Residents of India
(d) All students of India

4. Read Assertion (A) and Reason (R) and answer using codes given below:
Assertion (A): Code of conduct has statutory force.
Reason (R): Because Article 102 of the Constitution says so.

Codes:
(a) (A) and (R) are right and (R) is right reason for (A).
(b) Both (A) and (R) are wrong.
(c) (A) is right, but (R) is wrong.
(d) (R) is right, but (A) is wrong.

5. Read Assertion (A) and Reason (R) to answer using codes given below:
Assertion (A): One of the two Acts enacted under List I Entry 66 and the other under List III Entry 25 can be repugnant to each other.
Reason (R): Because in Annamalai University Vs. Secretary of Inf. and Tourism Department decided so.

Codes:
(a) (A) and (R) are right and (R) is right reason for (A).
(b) (A) is right, but (R) is wrong.
(c) (A) is wrong, but (R) is right.
(d) Both (A) and (R) are wrong.

6. If the Government is defeated on the floor of Rajya Sabha, what is the consequence?
(a) Parliament is dissolved.
(b) Prime Minister has to submit his resignation.
(c) President's rule is imposed immediately.
(d) Nothing happens.

7. Read Assertion (A) and Reason (R) and answer using the codes given below:

Assertion (A): The power under 368 of the Constitution is a constituent power subject to the constitutional scheme as to distribution of legislative power according to entries in the Seventh Schedule.

Reason (R): Because Sasanka Sekhar Maity Vs. Union of India decided so.
(a) Both (A) and (R) are wrong.
(b) Both (A) and (R) are right, but (R) is not right reason for (A).
(c) (A) is right and (R) is wrong.
(d) (A) is wrong and (R) is right.

8. Using codes given below, find out correct answers:
Administrative law deals with
i. the powers of constitutional authorities
ii. the powers of judicial authorities
iii. the powers of the administrative authorities
iv. the powers of the legislative authorities.

Codes:
(a) Only i and ii are correct.
(b) Only ii is correct.
(c) Only iii is correct.
(d) i, ii, iii and iv are correct.

9. Match List-I with List-II using codes given below:

List-I

A. There is no rigid formula for principles of natural justice.
B. Choice of application of rules of natural justice.
C. Justice should not only be done, but manifestly and undoubtedly be seen to be done.
D. Meaning of bias.

List-II

i. R.S. Dass Vs. Union of India
ii. R. Vs. Sussex Justices
iii. Union of India Vs. P.K. Roy
iv. Secy. to Govt. Transport Dept. Vs. Munuswamy

Codes:	A	B	C	D
(a)	ii	iv	i	iii
(b)	iii	i	iv	ii
(c)	i	iii	ii	iv
(d)	iii	i	ii	iv

10. Read Assertion (A) and Reason (R) and find out correct answer using codes given below:

Assertion (A): Legitimate expectation does not grant an absolute right to a claimant.

Reason (R): Legitimate expectation protects the right of fair hearing before a decision which results in negating a promise or withdrawing an undertaking is taken.

Codes:

(a) (A) and (R) are true and (R) is correct explanation of (A).
(b) (A) and (R) are true, but (R) is not correct explanation of (A).
(c) (A) is true and (R) is false.
(d) (A) is false and (R) is true.

11. Which of the following statement is correct?

(a) Gullappalli Nageswara Rao Vs. State of AP, is about bias.
(b) K.L. Tripathi Vs. State Bank of India, is about right of cross examination.
(c) General Medical Council Vs. Spaekmen, is about irrelevance of principles of natural justice; if in reaching a decision, the principles make no difference.
(d) N. Kalindi Vs. Tata Locomotives, is about the right of representation by a lawyer being considered to be a part of natural justice and it can be claimed as of right.

12. Which one of the following is the correct statement?

(a) While certiorari can be issued against judicial or quasi-judicial authorities, mandamus can be issued against administrative authorities also.
(b) Mandamus can be issued for a declaration that an Act is ultra vires the Constitution and certiorari can also be issued for correcting that defect.
(c) Certiorari can be issued against a quasi-judicial authority to prevent it from exercising jurisdiction not vested in it. Mandamus cannot be issued for that purpose.
(d) Certiorari cannot be issued against usurping a public officer, but Mandamus can be issued for that purpose.

13. Abuse of discretion can be inferred from the following circumstances. Find out the answer from the codes given below:

i. Non-application of mind.
ii. Colourable exercise of power.
iii. Non-observance of audi alteram partem.
iv. Irreevant considerations.

Codes:

(a) Only (i) is correct.
(b) Only (i) and (ii) are correct.
(c) Only (ii) and (iii) are correct.
(d) Only (ii), (iii) and (iv) are correct.

14. What was the principle laid down by the Supreme Court in A.K. Kraipak Vs. Union of India? Find correct answer from the following statements:
   (a) Rule of law is embedded in Article 14 of the Constitution of India.
   (b) Judicial review is a part of basic structure of the Constitution.
   (c) Principles of natural justice are applicable to administrative proceedings.
   (d) Post-decisional hearing would be sufficient for the observance of principles of natural justice.

15. Find correct answer from the following statement:
   (a) A quasi-judicial body may never review its own decision unless authorised by the statute.
   (b) A quasi-judicial body may review its own decision if there is grave error of law in it.
   (c) A quasi-judicial body may review its own decision if there is violation of natural justice.
   (d) All tribunals may review their decisions.

16. Select the correct answer using the code given below on the following decided cases about possession:
   1. Cartwright Vs. Green
   2. R.Vs. Hudson
   3. Daimler Co. Vs. Continental Tyre and Rubber Co.

   Codes:

   (a) 3 only (b) 2 and 3
   (c) 1 and 3 (d) 1 and 2

17. Austin described ownership as a right over determinate thing with reference to one of the following. Specify the correct answer.
   (a) Restricted in point of disposition
   (b) Indefinite in point of user
   (c) Unlimited in point of duration
   (d) Unlimited in point of space

18. Consider the following statements regarding vested and contingent rights:
   1. A vested right creates an immediate interest and is transferable and heritable.
   2. A contingent right creates an immediate interest and is defeated when the required facts have not occurred.

   Which of the Statement given above is/are correct?

   (a) 1 only (b) 2 only
   (c) Both 1 and 2 (d) Neither 1 nor 2

19. There is a clear cut division between the spheres of legislature and judiciary. The former makes the laws and the latter applies them. Which of the school propounds this doctrine?
   (a) Analytical jurisprudence
   (b) Historical jurisprudence
   (c) Sociological jurisprudence
   (d) Philosophical jurisprudence

20. In which one of the following cases was it observed by the Supreme Court that precedent should not be petrified nor judicial dicta divorced from the socio-economic mores of the age?
   (a) Mamleshwar Vs. Kanahaiya Lal
   (b) Bengal Immunity Company Ltd. Vs. State of Bihar
   (c) State of West Bengal Vs. Corporation of Calcutta
   (d) K.C. Dora Vs. G. Annamanaidu

21. Who among the following divided the sources of Law into formal sources and material sources?
    (a) Gray (b) Keaton
    (c) Allen (d) Solmond

22. According to Professor Goodhart a *ratio decidendi* of a case is
    (a) the principle of law laid down in a decision which is the decisive element
    (b) the conclusion reached by the judge on the basis of the material facts of the case
    (c) the reason given by the court for its decision
    (d) any opinion of the court on a question of law

23. Read Assertion (A) and Reason (R) and with the help of codes given below find the correct explanation:
    Assertion (A): Nullum Crimen is an injunction to the legislature not to implicate all the suspected persons to be prosecuted.
    Reason (R): To avoid impossibility and to settle the question, the legislature must have to use administrative ruling.

    Codes:
    (a) Both (A) and (R) are true, but (R) is not the correct explanation of (A).
    (b) Both (A) and (R) are true and (R) is the correct explanation of (A).
    (c) (A) is correct, but (R) is false.
    (d) (A) is false, but (R) is true.

24. Read Assertion (A) and Reason (R) and with the help of codes given below find the correct explanation:
    Assertion (A): Participation in some manner in the act constituting the offence of common intention by all the persons to be prosecuted is necessary.
    Reason (R): Physical presence at the time of commission of crimes is not mandatory in all cases.

    Codes:
    (a) Both (A) and (R) are true, but (R) is not the correct explanation of (A).
    (b) Both (A) and (R) are true and (R) is the correct explanation of (A).
    (c) (A) is correct, but (R) is false.
    (d) (A) is false, but (R) is true.

25. Which of the mitigating factors do not justify the award of death penalty?
    (a) Where the murder has been previously planned.
    (b) Such murder involves exceptional depravity.
    (c) When such murder was against a public servant while on duty.
    (d) When the offence was committed by the accused under the influence of extreme mental disturbance.

26. Read Assertion (A) and Reason (R) and with the help of codes given below find the correct explanation:
    Assertion (A): The gist of conspiracy lies in forming the scheme between two or more persons to perform the overt act.
    Reason (R): The alleged agreement must provide circumstantial evidence about the participation by all to establish conspiracy.

    Codes:
    (a) Both (A) and (R) are true and (R) is the correct explanation of (A).
    (b) Both (A) and (R) are true, but (R) is not the correct explanation of (A).
    (c) (A) is correct, but (R) is false.
    (d) (A) is false, but (R) is true.

27. Which of these facts do not constitute the degree of knowledge for holding a person to be criminally liable for adducing false evidence?

(a) A statement known to be false.
(b) A statement believed to be false.
(c) A statement not believed to be true.
(d) An offence committed but not affirmed.

28. What offence, if any, has been caused by the accused 'X' in the following facts:
'X' had some verbal wrangle with his wife 'Y' and incourse of that he gave her a blow with great force and after an interval for two hours 'Y' died. Medical evidence provided the causative factor as rapture in the spleen.
(a) Culpable homicide not amounting to murder
(b) Grievous hurt
(c) Homicide
(d) Simple hurt

29. Which of the following properties could not be held to be an offence of theft, when committed/taken by a person?
(a) Durga Idol
(b) Cooking Gas
(c) Running Electricity
(d) Forgotten Umbrella

30. Read Assertion (A) and Reason (R) and using codes given below, answer:
Assertion (A): In criminal breach of trust, there is conversion of property held by a person in a fiduciary capacity.
Reason (R): A person has a right to convert property held by him in a fiduciary capacity.

Codes:
(a) Both (A) and (R) are right and (R) is correct reason for (A).
(b) (A) is right, but (R) is wrong.
(c) (A) is wrong, but (R) is right.
(d) Both (A) and (R) are wrong.

31. The main objective of the Air (Prevention and Control of Pollution) Act is:
(a) To provide for the prevention, control and abatement of air pollution.
(b) To provide for ensuring standards for emission from automobiles.
(c) To put restrictions on the establishment of certain industrial plants.
(d) To establish air laboratory for air quality standards.

32. The definition of 'environmental pollution' under the Environment (Protection Act) is:
(a) Any pollution of air, water and soil
(b) The presence of any solid, liquid or gaseous substance in the environment that causes injuries to man
(c) The presence in the environment of any environmental pollutant
(d) Any pollution in land, sea and air

33. **Assertion (A):** A company was unlawfully polluting streams and rivers by discharging trade effluents which raised pollution level beyond permissible limits.
Reason (R): The court decided that the company could not be held liable under Water Act, 1974.

Codes:
(a) Both (A) and (R) are true and (R) is the correct explanation of (A).
(b) Both (A) and (R) are true, but (R) is not the correct explanation of (A).
(c) (A) is true, but (R) is false.
(d) (A) is false, but (R) is true.

34. The National Environment Tribunal Act provides for compensation on the basis of no fault liability in the cases of
I. Death of any person
II. Injury to any person
III. Death and injury to workman
IV. Damage to any property

Codes:
(a) I and II are correct.
(b) II and III are correct.
(c) IV only is correct.
(d) I, II and IV are correct.

35. Arrange the following cases in the chronological order on the basis of the year in which they have been decided by the Supreme Court on Public Trust doctrine under Environment law. Use the code given below:
I. M.C. Mehta Vs. Kamal Nath
II. M.I. Builders Pvt. Ltd. Vs. Radhey Shyam Sahu
III. Hinch Lal Tiwari Vs. Kamala Devi
IV. Intellectual Forum, Thirupathi Vs. State of Andhra Pradesh

Codes:
(a) IV, III, I, II (b) III, II, IV, I
(c) III, I, IV, II (d) I, II, III, IV

36. Match items in List-I with items in List-II using codes given below:

List-I
A. Intergenerational Equity
B. Sustainable Development
C. Precautionary Principle
D. Polluter Pays Principle

List-II
1. Earth Summit, 1992, Principle 15
2. Rio Declaration, 1992, Principle 16
3. Stockholm Declaration 1972, Principles 1 & 2
4. Rio Declaration, 1992, Principle 3

Codes:	A	B	C	D
(a)	4	3	1	2
(b)	1	3	2	4
(c)	2	4	1	3
(d)	3	4	1	2

37. For which special purpose a conditional permit for hunting any wild animal, cannot be granted under the Wild Life (Protection) Act?
(a) Preparation of snake venom for manufacturing of life saving drugs.
(b) Collection of specimen for zoos and museums.
(c) Scientific research.
(d) Research in traditional and established Universities.

38. Under whose specification the recycling of plastic is undertaken as per the Plastic Manufacture, Sales and Usage Rules, 1999?
(a) Indian Standard Institution
(b) Bureau of Indian Standards
(c) Indian Standard Organisation
(d) Indian Plastic Bureau

39. "International law may be defined in broad terms as the body of general principles and specific rules which are binding upon the members of the International Community in their mutual relations". Who has given this definition of Public International Law?
(a) J.G. Starke (b) Charles G. Fenwick
(c) Whiteman (d) Torsten Gihl

40. Match List-I with List-II and give the correct answer by using the codes given below:

List-I (Name of Cases)
A. Portugal Vs. India
B. Burkina Faso Vs. Mali
C. Spain Vs. Canada
D. Columbia Vs. Peru

List-II (Popular Names)
1. The Asylum Case
2. Fisheries Jurisdiction Case
3. Frontier Dispute Case
4. Right of Passage over Indian Territory Case

Codes:	A	B	C	D
(a)	1	2	3	4
(b)	4	3	2	1

(c)	2	4	1	3
(d)	3	1	4	2

41. Match List-I with List-II and give the correct answer by using the codes given below:

List-I

A. Recognition clothes the recognized State with rights and duties under International law.
B. Recognition is merely a formal acknowledgement through which established facts are accepted
C. State recognized possesses the essential elements of statehood and fit to be subject of international law.
D. Recognition is final and once granted cannot be withdrawn

List-II

1. De Facto Recognition
2. Constitutive Theory of Recognition
3. De-Jure Recognition
4. Declaratory Theory of Recognition

Codes:	A	B	C	D
(a)	2	4	1	3
(b)	1	2	3	4
(c)	3	4	2	1
(d)	4	3	1	2

42. The Estrada Doctrine was propounded by
(a) The Home Minister of Mexico
(b) The Foreign Minister of Mexico
(c) The External Secretary of U.S.A.
(d) The Prime Minister of U.K.

43. Provision, "that the U.N.O. has no competence to intervene in matters which are essentially within the domestic jurisdiction of any State", has been provided under which Article of U.N. Charter?
(a) Article 1(7) (b) Article 2(7)
(c) Article 7(2) (d) Article 98(7)

44. Match List-I with List-II and give the correct answer by using the codes given below:

List-I (Name of Cases)

A. Lether Vs. Sagor
B. Bank of Ethiopia Vs. National Bank of Egypt
C. Arantzazu Mendi Case
D. U.S. Vs. Pink

List-II (Years of Decision)

1. 1939 2. 1942
3. 1937 4. 1921

Codes:	A	B	C	D
(a)	1	2	3	4
(b)	3	4	2	1
(c)	2	1	4	3
(d)	4	3	1	2

45. Give the chronological order of the following in which they came into existence:
i. Charter of United Nations.
ii. Universal Declaration of Human Rights.
iii. International Covenant on Civil and Political Rights.
iv. International Covenant on Economic, Social and Cultural Rights.

Codes:

(a)	i	iii	ii	iv
(b)	iv	ii	i	iii
(c)	i	ii	iv	iii
(d)	iii	iv	ii	i

46. Propositions are:
I. A void marriage remains valid until a decree annulling it has been passed by a competent court.
II. A void marriage is never a valid marriage and there is no necessity of any decree annulling it.
III. A voidable marriage is a valid subsisting marriage until a decree

annulling it has been passed by a court of competent jurisdiction.

In respect of the aforesaid propositions which is correct?

(a) I and III are correct, but II is incorrect.
(b) II and III are correct, but I is incorrect.
(c) I and III are incorrect, but II is correct.
(d) I and II are incorrect, but III is correct.

47. As per Section 5 of the Hindu Marriage Act, 1955 the essential conditions of a Hindu marriage are:

I. Monogamy
II. Mental capacity
III. The bridegroom has completed the age of 21 years and the bride of 18 years
IV. No prohibited degree and sapinda relationship unless saved by custom.

Codes:

(a) I, II and IV (b) II, III, and IV
(c) I, II and III (d) I, II, III and IV

48. Section 9 of the Hindu Marriage Act, 1955 was held to be 'intra-vires' the Constitution by the Supreme Court in the case of

(a) T. Sareetha Vs. T.V. Subbhiah
(b) Saroj Rani Vs. Sudarshan
(c) Harvinder Kaur Vs. Harmandar Singh
(d) Sarla Mudgil Vs. Union of India

49. A Muslim has given Triple Talaaq to his wife and now wants to marry her again. He can do so

(a) without any restriction
(b) only on request of such wife
(c) cannot marry her
(d) only if such woman marry another man, the marriage is consummated and he has [second Husband] divorced her

50. In giving a child in adoption by the Hindu father, the requirement of the consent of the mother, can be dispensed with if

I. She has been declared to be of unsound mind by the Court of Competent jurisdiction.
II. She has finally and completely renounced the world.
III. She has ceased to be a Hindu.
IV. Her age is less than 18 years.

Codes:

(a) II, III and IV (b) I, II, III and IV
(c) I, II and III (d) I, III and IV

51. "A Hindu mother can be natural guardian of her minor child during the life of father of the child if he is not taking due care of the child." This was held by the Supreme Court of India in case of

(a) M.M. Ganguli Vs. Jayanti Ganguli
(b) Jijabai Vs. Pathan Khan
(c) Sarla Mudgil Vs. Union of India
(d) Githa Hariharan Vs. Reserve Bank of India

52. Match List-I with List-II in the light of Section 2 of the Dissolution of Muslim Marriage Act, 1939 and select the correct answer using the codes given below:

List-I

A. Imprisonment of Husband
B. Option of puberty
C. Husband missing
D. Impotency of husband

List-II

i. Sec. 2(vii) ii. Sec. 2(iii)
iii. Sec. 2(v) iv. Sec. 2(i)

Codes:	**A**	**B**	**C**	**D**
(a)	ii	i	iv	iii
(b)	i	ii	iii	iv
(c)	iv	ii	i	iii
(d)	iii	i	ii	iv

53. Which of the following has not yet been statutorily recognized as a theory of divorce under the Hindu Marriage Act, 1955?

(a) Fault Theory
(b) Will Theory
(c) Breakdown Theory
(d) Mutual Consent Theory

54. Read Assertion (A) and Reason (R) and answer using codes given below:

Assertion (A): Human Rights are regarded as those fundamental but alienable rights which are preferred for life as human being.

Reason (R): Change is general rule of life. Therefore legislatures are free to change human rights according to changing needs and circumstances.

Codes:

(a) Both (A) and (R) are right and (R) is correct reason for (A).
(b) Both (A) and (R) are right, but (R) is not correct reason for (A).
(c) Both (A) and (R) are wrong.
(d) (A) is wrong and (R) is right.

55. Which of the following statements are wrong? Answer using codes:

i. Human rights are created by legislation.
ii. Legal duty to protect human rights is not duty to respect them.
iii. International concern with human rights as enshrined in the United Nations Charter is a modern innovation.
iv. A human right violation is now conceived as violation of those personally and directly aggrieved, but not of everyone.

Codes:

(a) i, ii (b) ii, iii
(c) iii, iv (d) i, ii, iii and iv

56. Read Assertion (A) and Reason (R) and answer using codes given below:

Assertion (A): The purpose of the United Nation is to maintain national security and peace.

Reason (R): Because Article-I of the Charter of the United Nations says so.

Codes:

(a) Both (A) and (R) are right and (R) is right reason for (A).
(b) Both (A) and (R) are wrong.
(c) (A) is right and (R) is wrong.
(d) (A) is wrong and (R) is right.

57. Right to nationality, right to marry and to found a family are the rights under

i. Only women rights
ii. Social and cultural rights
iii. Civil and political rights
iv. Inherent rights

Codes:

(a) i, ii and iv (b) ii, iii and iv
(c) ii and iii (d) iii

58. Which of the following court normally is/are notified by the State Governments to act as Human Rights Court for speedy trial of offences violating Human Rights?

i. Munsiff Courts
ii. Lok Adalats
iii. Senior Civil Judge Court
iv. Sessions Court

Codes:

(a) i and iv (b) i, iii and iv
(c) ii and iv (d) iv

59. The power of 'enquiry and investigation' was given to Human Rights Commission under the following sections of the protection of Human Rights Act 1993

i. Sec. 13 ii. Sec. 14
iii. Sec. 9 iv. Sec. 10

Codes:

(a) i and ii (b) i and iii
(c) ii and iii (d) iii and iv

60. Read Assertion (A) and Reason (R) and answer using codes given below:

Assertion (A): A refugee means any person who, owing to well-founded fear of being prosecuted for reason of race, religion, nationality, membership of a particular social group or political opinion, is outside the country of his nationality.

Reason (R): Because the United Nations Convention on the Refugees 1951 in its Article 1A says so.

Codes:

(a) Both (A) and (R) are right and (R) is right reason of (A).

(b) (A) is wrong and (R) is right.

(c) (A) is right and (R) is wrong.

(d) Both (R) and (A) are wrong.

61. Match the List-I (Name of Maxim) with List-II (Meaning of Maxim) by using the codes given below:

List-I

A. Scienti non fit injuria

B. Qui facit per alium facit per se

C. Ubi jus ibi remedium

D. Ubi remedium ibi jus

List-II

i. Where there is remedy there is a right

ii. He who does an act through another is deemed in law to do it himself.

iii. No injury is done to one who knowingly does an act

iv. Where there is wrong there is remedy

Codes:	**A**	**B**	**C**	**D**
(a)	iii	iv	i	ii
(b)	iv	iii	ii	i
(c)	iii	ii	iv	i
(d)	i	ii	iii	iv

62. Which of the following is an effective defence in the tort of nuisance?

I. Public good

II. Prescription

III. Statutory authority

IV. Reasonable care

Codes:

(a) I and III are correct.

(b) II and IV are correct.

(c) II and III are correct.

(d) I and IV are correct.

63. **Assertion (A):** Negligence as a tort is the breach of legal duty to take care which results in damage.

Reason (R): In the tort of negligence law takes cognizance of carelessness only if it is supported by the legal duty to care.

Codes:

(a) Both (A) and (R) are true and (R) is the correct explanation of (A).

(b) Both (A) and (R) are true but (R) is not the correct explanation of (A).

(c) (A) is true, but (R) is false.

(d) (A) is false, but (R) is true.

64. In the tort of slander it is essential that some special damage has been resulted from the use of word by the defendant. In which of the following case an action of slander may be maintained, without proof of special damage? Answer using the codes:

I. Words imputing criminal offence to the plaintiff.

II. Words imputing to the plaintiff that he has an infectious disease.

III. Words prejudice the plaintiff in his office, profession etc.

IV. Words imputing unchastity to a woman.

Codes:

(a) I and II are correct.

(b) I, II and III are correct.

(c) I, II and IV are correct.
(d) I, II, III and IV are correct.

65. Which of the following is not an exception to the strict liability principle laid down in Rylands Vs. Flecher?
(a) Independent contractor
(b) Statutory authority
(c) Act of God
(d) Consent of the plaintiff

66. Which of the following is the right of the consumer under Consumer Protection Act, 1986?
I. Right to consumer education
II. Right to seek redressal
III. Access to a variety of goods and services at competitive prices
IV. Take goods and services free of cost

Codes:
(a) I and III are correct.
(b) I, II and III are correct.
(c) I and II are correct.
(d) I, II, III and IV are correct.

67. What is the pecuniary jurisdiction of the State Commission under the Consumer Protection Act?
(a) Exceeds rupees fifty lakhs but does not exceed rupees one crore.
(b) Exceeds rupees twenty lakhs but does not exceed rupees one crore.
(c) Exceeds rupees ten lakhs but does not exceed rupees one crore.
(d) Exceeds rupees one crore.

68. According to Section 12 of the Partnership Act, any difference arising as to ordinary matters connected with the business of partnership may be decided by
(a) the seniormost partner
(b) an arbitrator
(c) a majority of partners
(d) a judge

69. Which are essentials of a contract of sale of goods? Answer using codes given below:
i. Offer
ii. Acceptance of offer
iii. Exchange of goods for money
iv. Transfer of property in goods from seller to buyer

Codes:
(a) Only i and ii (b) Only iii and iv
(c) Only ii and iii (d) i, ii, iii and iv

70. Read Assertion (A) and Reason (R) and answer using the codes below:
Assertion (A): Where under a contract of sale the property in the goods has passed to the buyer and the buyer wrongfully neglects to pay for the goods according to the terms of the contract, the buyer may sue the seller for the price of the goods.
Reason (R): The seller is entitled to get the contractual price.

Codes:
(a) Both (A) and (R) are correct, and (R) is correct reason for (A).
(b) Both (A) and (R) are wrong.
(c) (A) is wrong, but (R) is right.
(d) (R) is wrong, but (A) is right.

71. Match List-I with List-II and select the correct answer using the codes given below:

List-I
A. Intention of parties to pass property in goods
B. Ascertainment of intention to pass property in goods
C. Passing of property in goods
D. Specific goods in deliverable State

List-II
i. Ghasiram Vs. State
ii. Badriprasad Vs. State of Madhya Pradesh

iii. United Breweries Ltd. Vs. State of Andhra Pradesh
iv. Usha Beltron Ltd. Vs. State of Punjab

Codes:	A	B	C	D
(a)	ii	iv	i	iii
(b)	iii	i	ii	iv
(c)	i	iii	iv	ii
(d)	iii	i	iv	ii

72. Which one statement is correct from the following statements:
(a) If the contract is inconsistent with the public documents, the person contracting will not be prejudiced by irregularities that may be set the outdoor working of the company.
(b) If the contract is consistent with the public documents, the person contracting will not be prejudiced by irregularities that may be set the indoor working of the company.
(c) The doctrine of indoor management seeks to protect the company against the outsider.
(d) The doctrine of ultra vires seeks to protect the outsider against internal irregularities of the company.

73. Match List-I with List-II and select the correct answer using the codes given below:

List-I
A. Directors with unlimited liability
B. Prevention of management of a company by undesirable persons.
C. A director cannot assign his office in favour of any one else.
D. Appointment to a place of profit under the company.

List-II
i. Section 202 and 203 of the Companies Act
ii. Section 312 of the Companies Act.
iii. Section 322 and 323 of the Companies Act.
iv. Section 314 of the Companies Act

Codes:	A	B	C	D
(a)	i	iii	ii	iv
(b)	iii	i	ii	iv
(c)	iii	i	iv	ii
(d)	ii	iv	i	iii

74. Match List-I with List-II and select the correct answer using the codes given below:

List-I
A. Inchoate stamped instrument
B. Liability of acceptor of a negotiable instrument
C. Liability of an endorser
D. Liability of the drawee of a cheque.

List-II
i. Union Bank of India Vs. Ankur Corp.
ii. Section 31 of the Negotiable Instrument Act
iii. Section 35 of the Negotiable Instrument Act.
iv. Section 20 of the Negotiable Instrument Act.

Codes:	A	B	C	D
(a)	i	iv	iii	ii
(b)	iv	i	iii	ii
(c)	iv	i	ii	iii
(d)	iii	ii	i	iv

75. Which of the following statements are correct ? Answer using codes given below:

In order that a person can be called a holder in due course, he must show:
i. that he is the drawer of the negotiable instrument.
ii. that he has obtained it without consideration.
iii. that he has obtained it before the maturity of the negotiable instrument.
iv. that he has obtained the negotiable instrument in good faith.

Codes:

(a) i and ii are correct.
(b) ii and iii are correct.
(c) iii and iv are correct.
(d) i and iv are correct.

ANSWERS

1. (d)	2. (b)	3. (a)	4. (b)	5. (d)
6. (d)	7. (a)	8. (c)	9. (d)	10. (a)
11. (b)	12. (a)	13. (d)	14. (c)	15. (a)
16. (d)	17. (b)	18. (a)	19. (a)	20. (b)
21. (d)	22. (b)	23. (a)	24. (b)	25. (d)
26. (a)	27. (d)	28. (b)	29. (c)	30. (b)
31. (a)	32. (c)	33. (c)	34. (d)	35. (d)
36. (d)	37. (d)	38. (d)	39. (b)	40. (b)
41. (a)	42. (b)	43. (b)	44. (d)	45. (c)
46. (b)	47. (d)	48. (b)	49. (d)	50. (c)
51. (d)	52. (a)	53. (b)	54. (c)	55. (d)
56. (b)	57. (d)	58. (d)	59. (a)	60. (d)
61. (c)	62. (c)	63. (a)	64. (d)	65. (a)
66. (b)	67. (b)	68. (c)	69. (d)	70. (c)
71. (d)	72. (b)	73. (b)	74. (b)	75. (c)

JUNE–2014

Note: This paper contains Sixty (60) multiple-choice questions, each question carrying two (2) marks. Candidate is expected to answer any Fifty (50) questions. In case more than Fifty (50) questions are attempted, only the first Fifty (50) questions will be evaluated.

PAPER I

1. Break-down in verbal communication is described as
   (a) Short circuit
   (b) Contradiction
   (c) Unevenness
   (d) Entropy
2. The Telephone Model of Communication was first developed in the area of
   (a) Technological theory
   (b) Dispersion theory
   (c) Minimal effects theory
   (d) Information theory
3. The Dada Saheb Phalke Award for 2013 has been conferred on
   (a) Karan Johar (b) Amir Khan
   (c) Asha Bhonsle (d) Gulzar
4. Photographs are not easy to
   (a) publish (b) secure
   (c) decode (d) change
5. The grains that appear on a television set when operated are also referred to as
   (a) sparks (b) green dots
   (c) snow (d) rain drops
6. In circular communication, the encoder becomes a decoder when there is
   (a) noise (b) audience
   (c) criticality (d) feedback
7. In a post-office, stamps of three different denominations of ₹ 7, ₹ 8, ₹ 10 are available. The exact amount for which one cannot buy stamps is
   (a) 19 (b) 20
   (c) 23 (d) 29
8. In certain coding method, the word QUESTION is encoded as DOMESTIC. In this coding, what is the code word for the word RESPONSE?
   (a) OMESUCEM
   (b) OMESICSM
   (c) OMESICEM
   (d) OMESISCM
9. If the series 4, 5, 8, 13, 14, 17, 22, ... is continued in the same pattern, which one of the following is not a term of this series?
   (a) 31 (b) 32
   (c) 33 (d) 35
10. Complete the series BB, FE, II, ML, PP, ... by choosing one of the following option given:
    (a) TS (b) ST
    (c) RS (d) SR
11. A man started walking from his house towards south. After walking 6 km, he turned to his left and walked 5 km. Then he walked further 3 km after turning left. He then turned to his left and continued his walk for 9 km. How far is he away from his house?
    (a) 3 km (B) 4 km
    (c) 5 km (d) 6 km

12. One writes all numbers from 50 to 99 without the digits 2 and 7. How many numbers have been written?
    (a) 32 (b) 36
    (c) 40 (d) 38

13. "If a large diamond is cut up into little bits, it will lose its value just as an army is divided up into small units of soldiers, it loses its strength."
    The argument put above may be called as
    (a) Analogical (b) Deductive
    (c) Statistical (d) Causal

14. Given below are some characteristics of logical argument. Select the code which expresses a characteristic which is not of inductive in character.
    (a) The conclusion is claimed to follow from its premises.
    (b) The conclusion is based on causal relation.
    (c) The conclusion conclusively follows from its premises.
    (d) The conclusion is based on observation and experiment.

15. If two propositions having the same subject and predicate terms can both be true but cannot both be false, the relation between those two propositions is called
    (a) contradictory (b) contrary
    (c) subcontrary (d) subaltern

16. Given below are two premises and four conclusions drawn from those premises. Select the code that expresses conclusion drawn validly from the premises (separately or jointly).
    Premises:
    (a) All dogs are mammals.
    (b) No cats are dogs.
    Conclusions:
    (i) No cats are mammals.
    (ii) Some cats are mammals.
    (iii) No dogs are cats.
    (iv) No dogs are non-mammals.
    Codes:
    (a) (i) only (b) (i) and (ii)
    (c) (iii) and (iv) (d) (ii) and (iii)

17. Given below is a diagram of three circles A, B and C inter-related with each other. The circle A represents the class of Indians, the circle B represents the class of scientists and circle C represents the class of politicians. p, q, r, s...represent different regions. Select the code containing the region that indicates the class of Indian scientists who are not politicians.

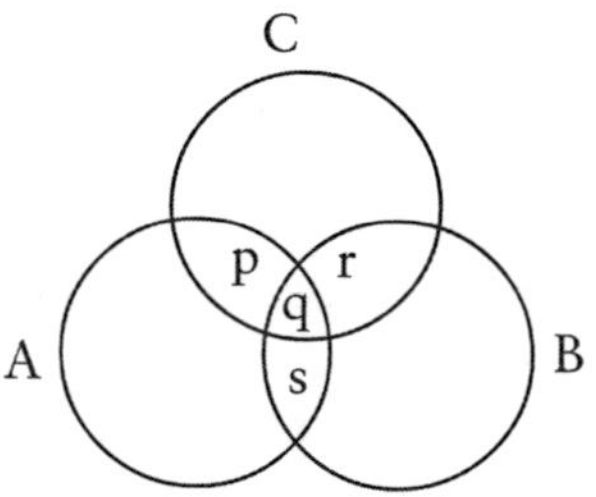

Codes:
(a) q and s only
(b) s only
(c) s and r only
(d) p, q and s only

18. Read the following table carefully. Based upon this table answer questions from 18 to 22:
    Net Area under Irrigation by sources in a country (Thousand Hectares)

Year	Government canals	Private canals	Tanks	Tube wells & other wells	Other sources	Total
1997-98	17117	211	2593	32090	3102	55173
1998-99	17093	212	2792	33988	3326	57411
1999-00	16842	194	2535	34623	2915	57109
2000-01	15748	203	2449	33796	2880	55076
2001-02	15031	209	2179	34906	4347	56672
2002-03	13863	206	1802	34250	3657	53778
2003-04	14444	206	1908	35779	4281	56618
2004-05	14696	206	1727	34785	7453	58867
2005-06	15268	207	2034	35372	7314	60196

18. Which of the following sources of irrigation has registered the largest percentage of decline in Net area under irrigation during 1997-98 and 2005-06?
(a) Government canals
(b) Private canals
(c) Tanks
(d) Other sources

19. Find out the source of irrigation that has registered the maximum improvement in terms of percentage of Net irrigated area during 2002-03 and 2003-04.
(a) Government canals
(b) Tanks
(c) Tube wells and other wells
(d) Other sources

20. In which of the following years, Net irrigation by tanks increased at the highest rate?
(a) 1998-99 (b) 2000-01
(c) 2003-04 (d) 2005-06

21. Identify the source of irrigation that has recorded the maximum incidence of negative growth in terms of Net irrigated area during the years given in the table.
(a) Government canals
(b) Private canals
(c) Tube wells and other wells
(d) Other sources

22. In which of the following years, share of the tube wells and other wells in the total net irrigated area was the highest?
(a) 1998-99 (b) 2000-01
(c) 2002-03 (d) 2004-05

23. The acronym FTP stands for
(a) File Transfer Protocol
(b) Fast Transfer Protocol
(c) File Tracking Protocol
(d) File Transfer Procedure

24. Which one of the following is not a/an image/graphic file format?
(a) PNG (b) GIF
(c) BMP (d) GUI

25. The first web browser is
(a) Internet Explorer
(b) Netscape
(c) World Wide Web
(d) Firefox

26. When a computer is booting, BIOS is loaded to the memory by
(a) RAM (b) ROM
(c) CD-ROM (d) TCP

27. Which one of the following is not the same as the other three?
(a) MAC address
(b) Hardware address
(c) Physical address
(d) IP address

28. Identify the IP address from the following:
(a) 300 · 215 · 317 · 3
(b) 302 · 215@ · 417 · 5
(c) 202 · 50 · 20 · 148
(d) 202 - 50 - 20 - 148

29. The population of India is about 1.2 billion. Take the average consumption of energy per person per year in India as 30 Mega Joules. If this consumption is met by carbon based fuels and the rate of carbon emissions per kilojoule is 15×10^6 kgs, the total carbon emissions per year from India will be
(a) 54 million metric tons
(b) 540 million metric tons
(c) 5400 million metric tons
(d) 2400 million metric tons

30. Which of the following cities has been worst affected by urban smog in recent times?
(a) Paris (b) London
(c) Los Angeles (d) Beijing

31. The primary source of organic pollution in fresh water bodies is

(a) run-off urban areas
(b) run-off from agricultural forms
(c) sewage effluents
(d) industrial effluents

32. 'Lahar' is a natural disaster involving
(a) eruption of large amount of material
(b) strong winds
(c) strong water waves
(d) strong winds and water waves

33. In order to avoid catastrophic consequences of climate change, there is general agreement among the countries of the world to limit the rise in average surface temperature of earth compared to that of pre-industrial times by
(a) 1.5°C to 2°C
(b) 2.0°C to 3.5°C
(c) 0.5°C to 1.0°C
(d) 0.25°C to 0.5°C

34. The National Disaster Management Authority functions under the Union Ministry of
(a) Environment
(b) Water Resources
(c) Home Affairs
(d) Defence

35. Match List-I and List-II and select the correct answer from the codes given below:

List-I

A. Flood B. Drought
C. Earthquake D. Volcano

List-II

1. Lack of rainfall of sufficient duration
2. Tremors produced by the passage of vibratory waves through the rocks of the earth
3. A vent through which molted substances come out
4. Excess rain and uneven distribution of water

Codes:	A	B	C	D
(a)	4	1	2	3
(b)	2	3	4	1
(c)	3	4	2	1
(d)	4	3	1	2

36. Which one of the following greenhouse gases has the shortest residence time in the atmosphere?
(a) Chlorofluorocarbon
(b) Carbon dioxide
(c) Methane
(d) Nitrous oxide

37. Consider the following statements and select the correct answer from the code given below:
i. Rajasthan receives the highest solar radiation in the country.
ii. India has the fifth largest installed wind power in the world.
iii. The maximum amount of wind power is contributed by Tamil Nadu.
iv. The primary source of uranium in India is Jaduguda.

Codes:
(a) i and ii (b) i, ii and iii
(c) ii and iii (d) i and iv

38. Who among the following is the de facto executive head of the Planning Commission?
(a) Chairman
(b) Deputy Chairman
(c) Minister of State for Planning
(d) Member Secretary

39. Education as a subject of legislation figures in the
(a) Union List
(b) State List
(c) Concurrent List
(d) Residuary Powers

40. Which of the following are Central Universities?

1. Pondicherry University
2. Vishwa Bharati
3. H.N.B. Garhwal University
4. Kurukshetra University

Select the correct answer from the code given below:

Codes:

(a) 1, 2 and 3 (b) 1, 3 and 4
(c) 2, 3 and 4 (d) 1, 2 and 4

41. Consider the statement which is followed by two arguments (i) and (ii).

Statement: India should have a very strong and powerful Lokpal.

Arguments: (i) Yes, it will go a long in eliminating corruption in bureaucracy.

(ii) No, it will discourage honest officers from making quick decisions.

Codes:

(a) Only argument (i) is strong.
(b) Only argument (ii) is strong.
(c) Both the arguments are strong.
(d) Neither of the arguments is strong.

42. Which of the following universities has adopted the meta university concept?
(a) Assam University
(b) Delhi University
(c) Hyderabad University
(d) Pondicherry University

43. Which of the following statements are correct about a Central University?
1. Central University is established under an Act of Parliament.
2. The President of India acts as the visitor of the University.
3. The President has the power to nominate some members to the Executive Committee or the Board of Management of the University.
4. The President occasionally presides over the meetings of the Executive Committee or Court.

Select the correct answer from the code given below:

Codes:

(a) 1, 2 and 4 (b) 1, 3 and 4
(c) 1, 2 and 3 (d) 1, 2, 3 and 4

44. Which one of the following is considered a sign of motivated teaching?
(a) Students asking questions
(b) Maximum attendance of the students
(c) Pin drop silence in the classroom
(d) Students taking notes

45. Which one of the following is the best method of teaching?
(a) Lecture (b) Discussion
(c) Demonstration (d) Narration

46. Dyslexia is associated with
(a) mental disorder
(b) behavioural disorder
(c) reading disorder
(d) writing disorder

47. The e-content generation for undergraduate courses has been assigned by the Ministry of Human Resource Development to
(a) INFLIBNET
(b) Consortium for Educational Communication
(c) National Knowledge Commission
(d) Indira Gandhi National Open University

48. Classroom communication is normally considered as
(a) effective (b) cognitive
(c) affective (d) selective

49. Who among the following, propounded the concept of paradigm?
(a) Peter Haggett (b) Von Thunen
(c) Thomas Kuhn (d) John K. Wright

50. In a thesis, figures and tables are included in
(a) the appendix
(b) a separate chapter
(c) the concluding chapter
(d) the text itself

51. A thesis statement is
 (a) an observation (b) a fact
 (c) an assertion (d) a discussion

52. The research approach of Max Weber to understand how people create meanings in natural settings is identified as
 (a) positive paradigm
 (b) critical paradigm
 (c) natural paradigm
 (d) interpretative paradigm

53. Which one of the following is a non-probability sampling?
 (a) Simple random
 (b) Purposive
 (c) Systematic
 (d) Stratified

54. Identify the category of evaluation that assesses the learning progress to provide continuous feedback to the students during instruction.
 (a) Placement (b) Diagnostic
 (c) Formative (d) Summative

55. The research stream of immediate application is
 (a) Conceptual research
 (b) Action research
 (c) Fundamental research
 (d) Empirical research

Read the following passage carefully and answer questions 56 to 60:

Traditional Indian values must be viewed both from the angle of the individual and from that of the geographically delimited agglomeration of peoples or groups enjoying a common system of leadership which we call the 'State'. The Indian 'State's' special feature is the peaceful, or perhaps mostly peaceful, co-existence of social groups of various historical provenances which mutually adhere in a geographical, economic, and political sense, without ever assimilating to each other in social terms, in ways of thinking, or even in language. Modern Indian law will determine certain rules, especially in relation to the regime of the family, upon the basis of how the loin-cloth is tied, or how the turban is worn, for this may identify the litigants as members of a regional group, and therefore as participants in its traditional law, though their ancestors left the region three or four centuries earlier. The use of the word 'State' above must not mislead us. There was no such thing as a conflict between the individual and the State, atleast before foreign governments became established, just as there was no concept of state 'sovereignty' or of any church-and-state dichotomy.

Modern Indian 'secularism' has an admittedly peculiar feature: It requires the state to make a fair distribution of attention and support amongst all religions. These blessed aspects of India's famed tolerance (Indian kings so rarely persecuted religious groups that the exceptions prove the rule) at once struck Portuguese and other European visitors to the West Coast of India in the sixteenth century, and the impression made upon them in this and other ways gave rise, at one remove, to the basic constitution of Thomas More's Utopia. There is little about modern India that strikes one at once as Utopian: but the insistence upon the inculcation of norms, and the absence of bigotry and institutionalized exploitation of human or natural resources, are two very different features which link the realities of India and her tradition with the essence of all Utopians.

56. Which of the following is a special feature of the Indian State?
 (a) Peaceful co-existence of people under a common system of leadership
 (b) Peaceful co-existence of social groups of different historical provenances attached to each other in a geographical, economic and political sense

(c) Social integration of all groups
(d) Cultural assimilation of all social groups.

57. The author uses the word 'State' to highlight
(a) Antagonistic relationship between the state and the individual throughout the period of history.
(b) Absence of conflict between the state and the individuals upto a point in time.
(c) The concept of state sovereignty.
(d) Dependence on religion.

58. Which one is the peculiar feature of modern Indian 'Secularism'?
(a) No discrimination on religious considerations
(b) Total indifference to religion
(c) No space for social identity
(d) Disregard for social law

59. The basic construction of Thomas More's Utopia was inspired by
(a) Indian tradition of religious tolerance.
(b) Persecution of religious groups by Indian rulers.
(c) Social inequality in India.
(d) European perception of Indian State.

60. What is the striking feature of modern India?
(a) A replica of Utopian State
(b) Uniform laws
(c) Adherence to traditional values
(d) Absence of Bigotry

ANSWERS

1. (d)	2. (d)	3. (d)	4. (c)	5. (c)
6. (d)	7. (a)	8. (c)	9. (c)	10. (a)
11. (c)	12. (a)	13. (a)	14. (c)	15. (c)
16. (c)	17. (b)	18. (c)	19. (d)	20. (d)
21. (a)	22. (c)	23. (a)	24. (d)	25. (c)
26. (b)	27. (d)	28. (c)	29. (b)	30. (d)
31. (c)	32. (a)	33. (a)	34. (c)	35. (a)
36. (c)	37. (d)	38. (b)	39. (c)	40. (a)
41. (a)	42. (b)	43. (c)	44. (a)	45. (c)
46. (c)	47. (b)	48. (c)	49. (c)	50. (d)
51. (c)	52. (d)	53. (b)	54. (c)	55. (b)
56. (b)	57. (d)	58. (a)	59. (a)	60. (d)

PAPER II

Note: This paper contains fifty (50) objective type questions of two (2) marks each. All questions are compulsory.

1. In which of the following cases, the Supreme Court held that 'the preamble is the part of the constitution'?
(a) Berubari union and Exchange of enclave
(b) Golaknath v/s State of Punjab
(c) Kesavananda Bharati v/s State of Kerala
(d) None of the above

2. Clause (5) of Article 15 has been added to the constitution by:
(a) Constitution (First Amendment) Act
(b) Constitution (Seventh Amendment) Act
(c) Constitution (Forty-second Amendment) Act
(d) Constitution (Ninety-third Amendment) Act

3. Match List-I with List-II and select the correct answer using the codes given below the lists:

List-I
i. Equal justice and free legal aid
ii. Uniform civil code for citizens
iii. Protection and improvement of environment and safeguarding of forests and wild life.

iv. Promotion of international peace and security

List-II

A. Article 44 B. Article 48A
C. Article 39A D. Article 51

Codes:	i	ii	iii	iv
(a)	C	B	D	A
(b)	C	A	B	D
(c)	A	B	C	D
(d)	D	A	B	C

4. Rights of a citizen under Article 19 are automatically suspended during the period of emergency, if emergency under Article 352 is declared on the grounds of:
   (a) war, external aggression or armed rebellion
   (b) war or armed rebellion
   (c) external aggression or armed rebellion
   (d) war or external aggression

5. In which of the following cases the Supreme Court has held that the word 'law' in Article 21 does not mean merely an enacted piece of law but must be just, fair and reasonable law?
   (a) A.K. Gopalan v/s State of Madras
   (b) Maneka Gandhi v/s Union of India
   (c) Both (a) and (b) above
   (d) None of the above

6. A distinguished jurist can be appointed as a judge of the:
   (a) High court only
   (b) Supreme court only
   (c) High court or supreme court both
   (d) None of the above

7. 'Which cannot be done directly, cannot be done indirectly.'—This statement epitomises the doctrine of:
   (a) colourable legislation
   (b) pith and substance
   (c) harmonious construction
   (d) eclipse

8. Match List-I with List-II by using the codes given below:
   Possession must be protected because:

List-I

1. Kent 2. Hegal
3. Hollard 4. Savigny

List-II

A. Man by taking possession has brought the object within his sphere of will.
B. In possession there is manifestation of individual's will.
C. Every act of violence is unlawful.
D. It is essential for preservation of peace.

Codes:	1	2	3	4
(a)	C	B	D	A
(b)	A	D	B	C
(c)	B	D	C	A
(d)	A	B	C	D

9. Which one of the following statements is not correct?
   (a) Austin and Kelson did much to rescue jurisprudence from the so-called confusion of social sciences.
   (b) Historical school of jurisprudence was a reaction against a prior methods of reasoning of eighteen century natural law.
   (c) Cujas and Hugo also applied the historical approach in the study of law.
   (d) Savigny did not discard the principle of natural law.

10. Match List-I (Name of Books) with List-II (Name of Writers) and select the correct answer:

List-I

A. *Pure Theory of Law*
B. *Three Lectures on Vedanta Philosophy*
C. *Judiciary Attacks and Survivals*
D. *The Growth of Law*

List-II

1. Hans Kelson
2. Max Muller
3. Justice V.D. Tulzapurkar
4. Justice Cardozo

Codes:	A	B	C	D
(a)	1	2	3	4
(b)	4	3	2	1
(c)	3	1	4	2
(d)	2	4	1	3

11. The term 'Legal Theory' has been first time coined by:
    (a) Hans Kelson
    (b) W. Friedman
    (c) Salmond
    (d) Ronald Dworkin

12. Which of the following statements is not true about the conformity of custom?
    (a) It should be in conformity with public policy.
    (b) It should be in conformity with statutory law.
    (c) In England, custom will be recognised even if it is m conflict with some fundamental principles of law.
    (d) The custom must not be in conflict with tradition.

13. "No one has any other right than always to do his duty." It was stated by:
    (a) Kelsen (b) Prof. Duguit
    (c) Holland (d) Salmond

14. **Assertion (A):** Custom is per se law, independent of its prior recognition by the sovereign or the judge.
    Reason (R): Custom is a source of law.
    Codes:
    (a) Both (A) and (R) are true but (R) is the correct explanation of (A).
    (b) Both (A) and (R) are true but (R) is not a correct explanation of (A).
    (c) (A) is true but (R) is false.
    (d) (A) is false but (R) is true.

15. **Assertion (A):** According to John Austin, international law is true law and not negative international morality.
    Reason (R): Three elements in Austin's definition of law, namely command of the sovereign, duty of inferiors and sanction in case of inferior who commit breach of the command are absent in international law.
    Codes:
    (a) Both (A) and (R) are true and (R) is the correct explanation of (A).
    (b) Both (A) and (R) are true but (R) is not a correct explanation of (A).
    (c) (A) is true but (R) is false.
    (d) (A) is false but (R) is true.

16. "International law is international morality or ethics, international courtesy or convention in the social sense of the word, comity as distinguished from rule of law." Above statement is attributed to:
    (a) Hobbes (b) Pufendorf
    (c) Bentham (d) Kelsen

17. Match List-I with List-II and select the correct answer using the codes given below:

List-I

i. International custom
ii. United Nations
iii Enforcing judgement of international court of justice
iv. Nirmal bose v/s Union of India, AIR Calcutta, p. 506

List-II

A. Peace keeping
B. Source of international law
C. Entry 14, list I read with Article 73
D. Political mechanism

Codes:	i	ii	iii	iv
(a)	B	A	D	C
(b)	A	B	D	C

(c)	A	B	C	D
(d)	D	B	A	C

18. Estrada doctrine relates to
    (a) Necessity of recognition
    (b) Form of recognition
    (c) No necessity of recognition
    (d) Recognition is superficial

19. Principle of United Nation is
    (a) Some sovereigns are more equal than others.
    (b) Member nations have rights but no obligations.
    (c) All members shall settle their international disputes by peaceful means.
    (d) All members shall settle their national disputes by peaceful means.

20. Doctrine of forum prorogatum means
    (a) Jurisdiction cannot be conferred upon an existing tribunal not otherwise competent by the litigants during the proceedings.
    (b) Jurisdiction can be conferred upon an existing tribunal not otherwise competent by the litigants during the proceedings.
    (c) Jurisdiction can be conferred upon an existing tribunal not otherwise competent by the litigants after the proceedings.
    (d) None of the above.

21. **Assertion (A):** Nikah is a regular and permanent form of marriage among Muslims.
    Reason (R): Muta is contractual form of marriage and is most uncommon in India.
    Codes:
    (a) Both (A) and (R) are correct.
    (b) (A) is correct but (R) is false.
    (c) (R) is correct but (A) is wrong.
    (d) Neither (A) is correct nor (R) is correct.

22. Where a Hindu male and Hindu female contract their marriage under the special Marriage Act, 1954, Hindu personal law:
    (a) Applies to such marriage
    (b) Does not apply
    (c) Applies with some modifications
    (d) Applies with Indian Contract Act

23. When two persons are descendants of a common ancestor but by different wives, they are said to be related to each other by:
    (a) Full Blood (b) Uterine Blood
    (c) Half-Blood (d) None of these

24. The term "Hindu" denotes the persons:
    (i) professing Hindu religion
    (ii) professing Buddh, Jain or Sikh religion
    (iii) who are not professing Muslims Christian, Parsi or Jain religion.
    In respect of the aforesaid propositions which is correct?
    (a) (i) and (ii) are correct and (iii) is incorrect.
    (b) (ii) and (iii) are correct and (i) is incorrect.
    (c) (i) and (iii) are incorrect but (ii) is correct.
    (d) (i), (ii) and (iii) all are correct.

25. **Assertion (A):** A having a wife alive, marries another wife. The marriage is void.
    Reason (R): Monogamy is the Law.
    Codes:
    (a) Both (A) and (R) are true.
    (b) Both (A) and (R) are false.
    (c) (A) is true but (R) is false.
    (d) (A) is false but (R) is true.

26. A marriage under Muslim law between persons with fosterage relationship is:
    (a) Sahih (b) Batil
    (c) Fasid (d) None of these

27. Under the Indian Contract Act, acceptance of proposal should be

(a) Conditional or Unconditional
(b) Conditional but not absolute
(c) Unconditional and absolute
(d) Unconditional but not absolute

28. In Indian Contract Act, the term voidable contract has been defined under:
(a) Section 2(e) (b) Section 2(h)
(c) Section 2(i) (d) Section 2(g)

29. Contractual liability arises, where
(a) there is offer and acceptance only
(b) there is intention to create legal relation
(c) there is loss to one party
(d) the loss of one party is the gain of other party

30. There may be a contract without consideration, if
(a) agreement is in writing and registered.
(b) parties to the agreement are in near relationship.
(c) agreement is made due to natural love and affection.
(d) All the above elements are present.

31. An agreement of trade combination to regulate legal trade in organised way is
(a) Void (c) Legal
(b) Voidable (d) Illegal

32. Which one of the following statements is true?
(a) Intimation of minimum price is proposal.
(b) An agreement against public policy is voidable.
(c) An agreement, the meaning of which is not certain is void.
(d) Contingent contracts are illegal.

33. Which one of the following is correct?
(a) Damages can be dispensed with in tort
(b) Damages cannot be awarded in tort when other remedies are provided by a statute
(c) A remedy by way of damages is essential ingredient of tort
(d) Damages can be awarded only if there is a physical injury

34. After considering the following, choose the right choice:
1. infringement of a legal right
2. legal damage
3. any damage
4. existence of a legal right

Right to claim damages in tort would arise only if:
(a) 1, 2 and 3 are present.
(b) 1, 2 and 4 are present.
(c) 1, 3 and 4 are present.
(d) All 1, 2, 3, 4 are present.

35. Mental condition of the wrong doer is
(a) relevant in all torts
(b) not relevant in tortious liability
(c) relevant in case of strict liability
(d) relevant in torts based on fault

36. P voluntarily accepted lift from D who was drunk and driving the car. D was affected by the drink and this was known to P. D caused the accident in which P suffered injury. Here,
(a) D can escape the liability because P was aware of risk.
(b) D is liable because P did not agree to suffer the harm.
(c) D is not liable because he gave free lift to P.
(d) D is liable because the degree of intoxication was not to such an extent that it can be assumed that there was voluntary assumption of risk by P.

37. A rickshaw was being pulled by the rickshaw puller with three passengers on board, which was against law. A bus was being driven rashly and negligently by its driver. The bus collides with rickshaw

resulting into damage to rickshaw and injury to rickshaw passengers. Here

(a) passengers cannot claim compensation from bus operator for the injury as they themselves were not acting according to law.
(b) passengers cannot claim compensation from bus operator as there was contributory negligence on their part.
(c) passengers can claim full compensation from bus operator as their negligence has not contributed to their injury.
(d) passengers are entitled for compensation which shall be proportionally reduced taking into account their illegal act.

38. Consider the following and then select the right code:
   1. Absolute liability implies liability without fault.
   2. In case of absolute liability defendant is liable for the injury if his act is the direct and proximate cause of plaintiff's injury.
   3. Absolute liability is the liability of the defendant without any defence.
   4. In absolute liability, defendant can escape the liability if he can prove that the damage was the result of an act of stranger.

   Codes:
   (a) 1, 2 and 4 are correct.
   (b) 2 and 3 are correct.
   (c) 1, 2 and 3 are correct.
   (d) 1 and 4 are correct.

39. Causing one thing to resemble another thing is known as:
   (a) Counterfeit (b) Deception
   (c) Cheating (d) All of them

40. A private libel is not considered as strict liability because:
   (a) There is no common injury or danger inferred from the facts
   (b) It was the result of bonafide belief
   (c) It is not a statutory offence
   (d) The principles of Rayland v/s Fletcher is not applicable

41. **Assertion (A):** The principle of common intention applies when a criminal act is done by several persons in furtherance of that intention.
   Reason (R): A intentional cooperation for committing an offence culminated from several acts.
   Codes:
   (a) (A) is true but (R) is not the reason.
   (b) Both (A) and (R) are true and (R) is the reasonable explanation of (A) .
   (c) Both are distinctive offences and (A) is not dependent on (R).
   (d) (A) is false but (R) is true.

42. **Assertion (A):** The right of private defence does not depend upon the actual criminality of the aggressor but on the wrongful character of the act attempted.
   Reason (R): Even if an act is treated as offence the right of private defence arises against the author despite his personal incapacity.
   Codes:
   (a) (A) is correct principle because (R) is the right reason.
   (b) (A) is untenable under law while (R) is the justifiable cause.
   (c) (A) is the law on an unlawful act while (R) results without mens rea.
   (d) (A) is not true while (R) is false.

43. The maxim "De Minimis non curat" relates to ____.
   (a) Slight harm
   (b) Trifles
   (c) Exhibition of disrespect
   (d) Annoyance

44. Instigating or engaging in a conspiracy or intentionally aiding a person to commit an offence is better known as _____.
   (a) Principal Crime
   (b) Second Degree Crime
   (c) Wilful mis-representation
   (d) Abetment

45. The First Come Last Go, and the Last Come First Go rule is associated with
   (a) Strike (b) Lockout
   (c) Retrenchment (d) Closure

46. One of the following is not the duty of works committee under the Industrial Disputes Act.
   (a) To promote measures for securing and preserving amity and good relations between the employees and workmen.
   (b) To form groups among workmen and strengthen mediation between employer and employee.
   (c) To achieve the object, it is their duty to comment upon matter of common interest or concern of employers and workmen.
   (d) to endeavour to compose any material difference of opinion in respect of matters of common interest or concern between employers and workmen.

47. An unregistered trade union has one of the following disadvantage:
   (a) It can acquire and hold both movable and immovable property.
   (b) It has no corporate existence.
   (c) It can contract through agents.
   (d) It is a legal entity.

48. In order to entitle the workmen to wages for the period of strike, the strike should be legal as well as justified. The above principle was laid down in one of the following cases by the apex court:
   (a) Crompton Greaves v/s The Workmen AIR 1978 SC.
   (b) Ballarpur Collieries v/s C.G.I.T Dhanbad AIR 1972 SC.
   (c) Management of India Radiatiors Ltd and Another v/s Presiding Officer and Another AIR 2003 II LU (Mad)
   (d) Workmen of Motor Industries Co. Ltd v/s Management of Motor Industires Co Ltd AIR 1969 SC.

49. In one of the following cases the Supreme Court held that when retrenchment of a workmen is invalid reinstatement can be ordered:
   (a) Harindara Singh v/s Punjab State Warehousing Corporation 2010IILU SC
   (b) Surendara Kumar Verma v/s Central Govt. Indl. Tribunal 1981 ILU SC
   (c) Management W.B. India Ltd v/s Jagannath AIR 1974 SC
   (d) Pioneer Ltd v/s Tajdar Hussain AIR 1974 SC

50. In which of the following, the members of the registered trade union can claim immunity in criminal cases?
   (a) The combination of two or more members of a registered trade union act in furtherance of a trade dispute.
   (b) The combination of two or more members of a registered trade union act with an intention to create loss or damage to the properties of the employer.
   (c) The trade union leaders in exercise of the managerial powers direct the workers from abstaining to do the work.
   (d) The members of a trade union act in combination with an intention to coerce the employer to acced to their demands.

ANSWERS

1. (c)	2. (d)	3. (b)	4. (d)	5. (b)
6. (b)	7. (a)	8. (b)	9. (d)	10. (a)
11. (d)	12. (c)	13. (b)	14. (a)	15. (c)
16. (c)	17. (a)	18. (c)	19. (c)	20. (b)
21. (a)	22. (a)	23. (c)	24. (d)	25. (a)
26. (b)	27. (c)	28. (c)	29. (b)	30. (d)
31. (c)	32. (c)	33. (c)	34. (b)	35. (a)
36. (d)	37. (c)	38. (c)	39. (c)	40. (a)
41. (c)	42. (a)	43. (a)	44. (d)	45. (c)
46. (b)	47. (b)	48. (a)	49. (b)	50. (a)

PAPER III

Note: This paper contains seventy-five (75) objective type questions of two (2) marks each. All questions are compulsory.

1. "The constitution establishes a system of government which is almost quasi-federal ...a unitary state with subsidiary federal features rather than a federal state with subsidiary unitary features." This is the opinion of:
   (a) K.C. Wheare (b) Jennings
   (c) A.V. Dicey (d) None of these

2. Match List-I with List-II and select the correct answer using the codes given below:

   List-I
   i. Appointment of Judges
   ii. A Court of Record
   iii. Appeal in civil cases
   iv. Certificate for appeal to Supreme Court

   List-II
   A. Article 124 B. Article 129
   C. Article 133 D. Article 134A

Codes:	i	ii	iii	iv
(a)	A	B	C	D
(b)	A	C	B	D
(c)	A	B	D	C
(d)	B	A	D	C

3. The constitution of Election Commission is provided in the constitution under:
   (a) Article 323 (b) Article 324
   (c) Article 327 (d) Article 329

4. Match List-I with List-II and select the correct answer using the codes given below:

   List-I
   i. Doctrine of Eclipse
   ii. Doctrine of severability
   iii. Doctrine of Waiver
   iv. Doctrine of pith and substance

   List-II
   A. RMDCv/s Union of India
   B. State of Bombay v/s F.N. Balsara
   C. Bhikaji v/s State of M.P.
   D. Bashesher Nath v/s Income Tax Commissioner

Codes:	i	ii	iii	iv
(a)	C	B	D	A
(b)	B	C	A	D
(c)	C	A	D	B
(d)	D	B	C	A

5. In case there is any inconsistency between the laws made by parliament and the laws made by the state legislature, which one of the following shall prevail?
   (a) The law made by parliament only if it is passed before the law made by state legislature.
   (b) The law made by parliament only if it is passed after the law made by state legislature.
   (c) The law made by parliament whether it is passed before or after the law made by state legislature.
   (d) The law made by state if it is passed after the law made by parliament.

6. Which of the following statements is true?
   (a) All self-incriminatory statements are valid.
   (b) All self-incriminatory statements are violative of Article 20(3).
   (c) Self-incriminatory statements furnished under compulsion are violative of Article 20(3).
   (d) None of the above.

7. **Assertion (A):** Under Article 368, the parliament can amend any part of the constitution of India.
   Reason (R): The parliament is supreme legislative body elected by people of India.
   Codes:
   (a) Both (A) and (R) are true and (R) is the correct explanation of (A).
   (b) Both (A) and (R) are true but (R) is not the correct explanation of (A).
   (c) (A) is true, but (R) is false.
   (d) (A) is false, but (R) is true.

8. Match List-I with List-II and select the correct answer using the codes given below:
   List-I
   i. Seperation of judiciary from executive
   ii. Promotion of international peace and security
   iii. Organisation of village panchayats
   iv. Protection and improvement of forests and wild life

   List-II
   A. Article 51 B. Article 48A
   C. Article 50 D. Article 40

Codes:	i	ii	iii	iv
(a)	A	B	C	D
(b)	C	A	D	B
(c)	C	B	D	A
(d)	B	A	C	D

9. Lokpal or Lokayukta is competent to
   (a) Discharge the functions of administrative officer.
   (b) Investigate complaints involving grievances in respect of administrative actions.
   (c) Conduct inquiry against administrative officer for disciplinary action.
   (d) Give observations and recommendations in respect of administrative actions to the government.

10. **Assertion (A):** Indian Constitution has not recognized the doctrine of separation of power in its absolute rigidity.
    Reason (R): Doctrine of separation of power accommodates a system of checks and balances.
    Codes:
    (a) Both (A) and (R) are true and (R) is the correct explanation of (A).
    (b) Both (A) and (R) are true but (R) is not the correct explanation of (A).
    (c) (A) is true, but (R) is false.
    (d) (R) is true, but (A) is false.

11. Administrative law is concerned with the operation and control of the powers of administrative authorities with emphasis on functions rather than on structure. This definition was given by
    (a) K.C. Davis (b) Jennings
    (c) A.V. Dicey (d) Wade

12. Which one of the following is not basic source of administrative law?
    (a) Custom
    (b) Delegated legislation
    (c) Ordinance promulgated by Governor
    (d) Reports of the committees and Commission

13. Doctrine of pleasure is related to
    (a) Fundamental duties
    (b) Fundamental rights
    (c) Directive principles of state policy
    (d) None of the above

14. Which of the following statements is true?
   (a) Mandamus lies against quasi-judicial order.
   (b) Mandamus is issued where inferior court declined jurisdiction.
   (c) Mandamus may be issued, even if alternate remedy is available.
   (d) Mandamus may be issued even no legal right of petitioner subsists.

15. The rule of 'Audi alteram partem' requires reasonable opportunity of hearing. Hearing may be
   (a) only in writing
   (b) only orally
   (c) written or oral
   (d) written and oral both

16. The high court can exercise the supervisory jurisdiction over the courts and tribunals subordinate to it under
   (a) Article 32 (b) Article 226
   (c) Article 227 (d) Article 141

17. Fiction theory is related to which one of the following concepts?
   (a) Ownership
   (b) Justice
   (c) Legal personality
   (d) None of the above

18. "We must admit openly that precedent makes law as well as declare it.... Original precedents are the outcome of the international exercise by the courts of their privileges of developing the law at the same time that they administer it." Who said it?
   (a) Salmond (b) Redcliffe
   (c) Lord Denning (d) Starke

19. Prof. Holland distinguishes a legal right from:
   (a) Moral and Natural rights
   (b) External and Internal rights
   (c) Might and Moral rights
   (d) Sight and Moral rights

20. Match List-I with List-II and select the correct answer using the codes given below:

   List-I (Concepts)
   i. Minimum content of law
   ii. Inner morality of law
   iii. Law with a variable content
   iv. Law as a phenomenon of civilization

   List-II (Jurists)
   A. Fuller B. Hart
   C. Kohler D. Starnmler

Codes:	i	ii	iii	iv
(a)	C	A	B	D
(b)	B	C	D	A
(c)	B	A	D	C
(d)	A	B	C	D

21. The 'Bracket Theory' contemplates:
   (a) The members of the corporation are the only persons who have rights and duties.
   (b) Law puts a bracket around the persons, by organising juristic personality.
   (c) Only human beings can have personality.
   (d) Group has a real will, read mind and real power of action.

22. Consider the following statements and give the correct answer by using the codes given below:
   I. Equitable ownership always presupposes the existence of a legal ownership.
   II. Where property is given by A to B for the benefit of C. B becomes the legal owner and C the equitable owner.
   III. In many cases, equity recognizes ownership whereas law does not recognise ownership owing to some flaw or defect.
   IV. Contingent ownership is spes successions.

Codes:
(a) I, II and III are correct.
(b) II and III are correct.
(c) I and II are correct.
(d) II and IV are correct.

23. Who defined possession as "to gain possession a man must stand in a certain physical relation to the object and to the rest of world and must have a certain intent"?
(a) Holmes (b) Salmond
(c) Pollock (d) Savigny

24. **Statement I:** Person of inheritance is the owner of the right.
Statement II: Inheritance is a means to ownership.
Codes:
(a) Both Statements I and II are individually true statements and Statement II is the correct explanation of Statement I.
(b) Both Statements I and II are individually true but Statement II is not the correct explanation of Statement I.
(c) Statement I is true but Statement IT is false.
(d) Statement I is false but statement II is true.

25. Malum Prohibitum means:
(a) Intrinsically wrong
(b) Course of law has made it otherwise
(c) Innocent but made punishable by statute.
(d) All of them.

26. Demolishing a private structure standing encroached on a public street amounts to:
(a) Gain by unlawful means.
(b) Wrongful gain for public purpose.
(c) Wrongful loss by mischief.
(d) None of above.

27. **Assertion (A):** When an act is done dishonestly it does not require deception or concealment as its ingredient.
Reason (R): Dishonesty requires an intention to cause wrongful loss or gain of property.
Codes:
(a) (A) is true, but (R) is not the reason.
(b) Both (A) and (R) are true because (R) is the right reason of (A).
(c) Both (A) and (R) are distinctive offences.
(d) (A) is false, while (R) is true.

28. **Assertion (A):** Harbouring includes supplying a person with shelter, food, money or conveyance.
Reason (R): The supply must relate to evading apprehension.
Codes:
(a) (A) is correct clarification but (R) is not the correct reason.
(b) (A) is not true while (R) is the correct explanation.
(c) Both (A) and (R) are correct proposition.
(d) Only in exceptional situation (R) is the reason of (A).

29. The real and abiding concern for the dignity of human life was decided in the case of:
(a) Rajendra Prasad v/s State of U.P.
(b) Mohindra Singh v/s Delhi Administration
(c) Javed Ahmed v/s State of Maharashtra.
(d) Bachan Singh v/s State of Punjab.

30. An unlawful assembly is a particular state of activity accompanied by the use of force or violence is riot, but it does not include:
(a) There must be five or more persons.
(b) There must be animation by a common object.

(c) Persons assembled for lawful purpose but started quarrelling without any previous intention.
(d) All of them.

31. Which of the following statements are not false evidence in discharge of public justice?
(a) A false statement given under instigation.
(b) A statement known to be false.
(c) A statement not believed to be true.
(d) None of above.

32. A ceremonial pollution is an act relating to unclean worship and is known as the offence of ___.
(a) Insult to religion
(b) Defilement
(c) Anti secularism
(d) Religious hatredness

33. One of the following cases is popularly known as "Doon Valley case":
(a) Pathumna v/s State of Kerala AIR 1978, 2 SCC.
(b) M.C. Metha v/s Union of India AIR 1987 SC.
(c) Unni Krishnan v/s State of A.P. AIR 1993, 1 SCC.
(d) R.L. & E. Kendra v/s State of UP AIR 1985 SC.

34. The polluter pays principle has been incorporated in
(a) Principle 15 of the Rio Declaration on Environment and Development
(b) Principle 27 of the Rio Declaration on Environment and Development
(c) Principle 8 of the Rio Declaration on Environment and Development
(d) Principle 16 of the Rio Declaration on Environment and Development

35. Protection and Improvement of environment and safeguarding forests and wild life is
(a) One of the Directive Principles of state policy
(b) A fundamental right
(c) Fundamental duty
(d) Both directive principles of state policy and fundamental duties

36. Two important Amendments were brought in the year 1976. One with reference to directive principles of state policy making the state responsible to protect and improve the environment and safeguard the forests and wild life of the country. The other under fundamental duties making every citizen to protect and improve the natural environment including forests, lakes, rivers and wild life and to have compassion for living creatures.
The relevant amendment is
(a) 49th Amendment
(b) 45th Amendment
(c) 43rd Amendment
(d) 42rd Amendment

37. Section 19 of the Environment (Protection) Act 1986 enables a person to file a complaint in a criminal court after giving a notice to the Pollution Control Board. Once a complaint has been made, the board is bound to make available to the complaint all relevant reports to him on demand. The board may also refuse to disclose on public interest.
Similar provisions are also available under
(a) Section 49 of the Water Act 1974 and Section 43 of the Air Act 1981
(b) Section 43 of the Water Act 1974 and Section 49 of the Air Act 1981
(c) Section 42 of the Water Act 1974 and Section 46 of the Air Act 1981
(d) Section 41 of the Water Act 1974 and Section 42 of the Air Act 1981

38. The Supreme Court of India ordered conversion from fuel to CNG on July 28, 1998. It also set up a committee to evaluate the cleanliness of various fuels on April 27, 2001. The name of the committee is
    (a) Bhurelal Committee
    (b) Santhanam Committee
    (c) Mallimath Committee
    (d) Madanlal Committee

39. "The public trust doctrine primarily rests on the principle that certain resources like air, sea, water and the forests have such a great importance to the people as a whole that it would be wholly injustified to make them a subject of private ownership."
    The above Doctrine was discussed in detail in one of the following cases:
    (a) M.C. Metha v/s Kamalnath 1997, 1 SCC.
    (b) Rural litigation and Environment Kendra v/s Union of India AIR, 1985 SC.
    (c) Vellore Citizen's welfare Forum v/s Union of India 1996, 5 SCC.
    (d) M.C. Metha v/s Union of India AIR. 1987 SC.

40. "Form of rules accepted by civilized states as determining their conduct towards each other and each other's subject, is defined as international law."
    Above statement is attributed to:
    (a) S.S. Lotus case
    (b) West Rand Central Gold Mining ltd. Co. v/s King
    (c) Queen V. Keyn
    (d) L. Oppenheim

41. **Assertion (A):** International convention is the most important source of law.
    Reason (R): International convention has generic wisdom.
    Codes:
    (a) Both (A) and (R) are true and (R) is the correct explanation of (A).
    (b) Both (A) and (R) are true but (R) is not the correct explanation of (A).
    (c) (A) is true, but (R) is false.
    (d) (A) is false, but (R) is true.

42. Which of the following statements is true?
    (a) The community to be recognized as an international person should be organised one.
    (b) Control of the community over definite territory is desirable.
    (c) The control over the territory may be permanent.
    (d) The community must be independent.

43. Which of the following statements is correct?
    (a) Primary responsibility of international peacekeeping and security is on the General Assembly.
    (b) The Security Council is a deliberative organ.
    (c) Members may not accept and carry out the advice of the security council.
    (d) Social and economic council is to discharge the responsibility of the states enshrined in Chapter IX from Articles 55-60. This council operates under the authority and supervision of general assembly.

44. Match List-I with List-II and select the correct answer using the codes given below:
    List-I
    i. Doctrine of forum prorogatum
    ii. Condition of reciprocity
    iii. Advisory jurisdiction
    iv. Reservations
    List-II
    A. Certain expenses case, ICJ Rep. 1962, p. 151

B. Nicaragua v. US, ICJ Rep. 1984, pp. 392, 421-26
C. Interhandel case, ICJ Rep. 1959, p. 6
D. Corfu channel case, (Preliminary objection), ICJ Rep. 1948, p. 28

Codes:	i	ii	iii	iv
(a)	C	D	A	B
(b)	D	C	A	B
(c)	D	C	B	A
(d)	A	B	D	C

45. Which of the following statements is true?
(a) Mere counting of heads is enough to assess the degree of authority and credibility of a resolution of General Assembly.
(b) Mere counting of heads is not enough to assess the degree of authority and credibility of a resolution of General Assembly.
(c) Mere counting of heads is enough to assess integrity of General Assembly.
(d) None of the above.

46. **Assertion (A):** Recognition of a state is not the same as recognition of its government.
Reason (R): Within existing states, governments come and go and normally the changes raise no question of recognition.
Codes:
(a) Both (A) and (R) are correct and (R) is the correct explanation of (A).
(b) Both (A) and (R) are correct but (R) is not the correct explanation of (A).
(c) (A) is true, but (R) is false.
(d) (A) is false, but (R) is true.

48. A Muslim wife may sue for divorce under the Dissolution of Muslim Marriage Act, 1939 if the husband has been insane for a period of:
(a) 1 year (b) 2 years
(c) 3 years (d) 5 years

48. Which of the following is not essential for divorce by mutual consent?
(a) They have been living separately for one year.
(b) They have not been able to live together.
(c) The wife has not received any maintenance.
(d) They have mutually agreed that the marriage should be dissolved.

49. That the respondent was, at the time of the marriage, pregnant by some person other than the petitioner, is a ground for voidable marriages under
(a) Section 12(1)(a)
(b) Section 12(1)(b)
(c) Section 12(1)(c)
(d) Section 12(1)(d)

50. A petition for the dissolution of the marriage by a decree of divorce may be presented, if cohabitation as between the parties to the marriage, after the passing of a decree of judicial separation, is not resumed for a period of:
(a) One year or upwards
(b) Two years or upwards
(c) Six months or upwards
(d) None of the above

51. Match List-I with List-II and select the correct answer using the codes given below:
List-I
A. Marriage during Iddat period is.
B. Marriage with an impotent person is.
C. Marriage below the age of 18 years is.
D. Inter-caste marriage
List-II
i. Void ii. Irregular
iii. Voidable iv. Valid

Codes:	A	B	C	D
(a)	i	ii	iii	iv
(b)	ii	i	iv	iii

(c)	iii	ii	i	iv
(d)	ii	iii	i	iv

52. Where the marriage has not been consummated, Iddat has to be observed in case of:
(a) Death of husband
(b) Divorce
(c) Both death and divorce
(d) Neither death nor divorce

53. Match List-I with List-II and select the correct answer using the codes given below:
List-I (Cases)
A. Ram Narayan v/s Rameshwari
B. Lachman v/s Meena
C. Dastane v/s Dastane
D. Mr. X v/s Hospital Z
List-II (Grounds)
i. Insanity
ii. Cruelty
iii. Desertion
iv. Venereal Diseases

Codes:	A	B	C	D
(a)	iii	i	iv	ii
(b)	ii	iv	iii	i
(c)	i	iii	ii	iv
(d)	iv	ii	i	iii

54. Under the Shia school, what is the cronical order of persons entitled to the 'Hizanat' of a minor child?
A. Father B. Mother
C. Grandfather D. Grandmother
(a) B, A, C, D (b) B, A, D, C
(c) C, B, A, D (d) D, C, B, A

55. The solidarity rights, more commonly known as 'Third Generation Human Rights' is based on:
(a) Independent needs of people
(b) Concept of universalism
(c) Right to self-determination
(d) Common heritage of mankind

56. "Human rights have two main dimensions. One of them can be called negative freedom in the sense that it is less important, it is negative because such freedom is based on a bedrock of what cannot be done, rather than what can be done."
The above is from the thoughts of
(a) Kofi Annan
(b) P.N. Bhagwati
(c) Amartya Sen
(d) M.N. Venkatachaliah

57. Match List-I containing Human rights and List-II containing related Articles of Universal Declaration of Human Rights, using the codes given below:
List-I
i. Rights to own property
ii. Freedom of religion
iii. Right to liberty and security of person
iv. Right to privacy
List-II
A. Article 18 B. Article 9
C. Article 12 D. Article 17

Codes:	i	ii	iii	iv
(a)	A	C	D	B
(b)	A	D	C	B
(c)	A	D	B	C
(d)	D	A	B	C

58. Human rights are inscribed in the hearts of the people; they were there long before law makers drafted their first proclamation. This statement was made by:
(a) Kofi Annan (b) Krishna Iyer, J.
(c) Mary Robinson (d) None of these

59. Human Rights Council has taken the place of:
(a) Human Right Committee
(b) International Human Rights Institute
(c) Centre for Human Rights
(d) Human Right Commission

60. Select the best answer using the codes given below:

The national Human Rights commission can:

1. itself take action and punish those who violate human rights.
2. recommend the government to take action.
3. initiate proceedings in the court.
4. join as a party to a case in the court involving violation of human rights.

Codes:

(a) 1 and 2 are correct.
(b) 2, 3 and 4 are correct.
(c) 1, 2 and 3 are correct.
(d) 3 and 4 are correct.

61. Some of the human rights are contained in the Indian Constitution under:

(a) Part III and Part IV-A
(b) Part III and Part IV
(c) Part IV and Part IV-A
(d) Part II and Part IV-A

62. Tort is defined as "an infringement of a right in rem of a private individual giving a right of compensation of the suit of the injured party" by

(a) Salmond (b) Pranger
(c) Winfield (d) Hemmings

63. Which of the following correctly represent the position under the law of torts?

Select from the code given below: A person is responsible for

1. all the consequences of his wrongful act.
2. consequences which directly flow from his wrongful act.
3. consequences which are not too remote.
4. all the consequences which are reasonably foreseable.

Codes:

(a) 1 and 2 are correct.
(b) 1, 2 and 3 are correct.
(c) 2 and 3 are correct.
(d) 2, 3 and 4 are correct.

64. Which of the following is not necessary in tort of defamation?

(a) The statement is defamatory.
(b) There is intention to refer to the plaintiff.
(c) The right thinking members in the society infer that the statement refers to plaintiff.
(d) The statement is made known to other members of society.

65. A film critic in his review of a film comments adversely on the cinematic values and quality of the film. The director of the film sues the film critic for defamation. Which of the following is correct, use the code given below:

1. The film critic is not liable as he can raise the defence of justification.
2. The critic is not liable because it was a fair and bonafide comment in public interest.
3. It was an expression of opinion and not assertion of facts.
4. It was a fair criticism of a film meant for public entertainment.

Codes:

(a) 1 and 4 are correct.
(b) 1 and 2 are correct.
(c) 2, 3 and 4 are correct.
(d) 1 and 3 are correct.

66. The 'standard of care' generally used in care of negligence is

(a) the care taken by an intelligent and prudent man.
(b) the skill and care taken by a qualified and competent person.

(c) the foresight of an adult person.
(d) the care and skill of a prudent and careful man belonging to defendant's calling or business or skill.

67. Which one of the following is a good defence for the tort of private nuisance?
(a) Plaintiff has come to the place of nuisance.
(b) Reasonable care was taken to prevent nuisance.
(c) The activity is for the public benefit.
(d) The activity is continuing for the past 20 years.

68. Who is a consumer under the Consumer Protect Act, 1986?
(a) A person who gives his pants for stitching to a tailor.
(b) A person who purchases goods for sale in his shop.
(c) A person who purchases a car for being used as a taxi in his taxi service.
(d) A person who avails of medical services free of cost.

69. Partnership is
(a) Trust (b) Company
(c) Mutual agency (d) Mutual fund

70. **Assertion (A):** When something of valuable nature is acquired by a partner in breach of his duty in good faith, it is taken to be acquired for the benefit of all the partners and has to be accounted for to the firm.
Reason (R): Partnership is a trust.

Codes:
(a) Both (A) and (R) are true and (R) is the correct explanation of (A).
(b) Both (A) and (R) are true but (R) is not the correct explanation of (A).
(c) (A) is true, but (R) is false.
(d) (A) is false, but (R) is true.

71. Arrange the following concepts in which sequence they appeared, using the codes given below:
(i) Damage
(ii) Breach of terms of agreement of partnership
(iii) Damaged
(iv) Agreement to share profits from business of firm

Codes:
(a) (i), (ii), (iv), (iii)
(b) (iv), (ii), (i), (iii)
(c) (ii), (iv), (i), (iii)
(d) (iii), (i), (ii), (iv)

72. Match items in List-I with items in List-II using the codes given below:

List-I
i. Liability for misappropriation by a partner
ii. Liability of a partner for torts
iii. Liability of a partner for holding out
iv. Doctrine of implied authority of a partner

List-II
A. Section 26
B. Section 27
C. Section 28
D. Sections 18 and 19

Codes:	i	ii	iii	iv
(a)	C	D	A	B
(b)	B	A	D	C
(c)	A	B	C	D
(d)	B	A	C	D

73. Which one of the following pairs does match?
(a) Definition and essentials of sale — E. & S 5 : 02 PM Ruben Ltd. V/s Faire Bros. (1949)1 KB 254
(b) Formalities of sale — Drummond & Sons V/s Van Ingen, (1887) 12 App. Cases 284

(c) Conditions implied by trade and usage — Peter Darlington Partners Ltd. V/s Gosho Co. Ltd., (1964) 1 Uoyds Rep 149
(d) Sale by sample — Rowland V/s Divali (1923) 2 KB 500, CA.

74. Which one of the following statements is true?
(a) The order contained in the bill of exchange may be conditional.
(b) A bill of exchange must contain a request to pay.
(c) Every bill of exchange is a promissory note.
(d) The payee must be certain.

75. Haward V/s Patent Ivory Manufacturing Co., (1888) 38 Ch.D. 156 is a case about
(a) Doctrine of ultra vires
(b) Doctrine of indoor management
(c) Doctrine of public notice
(d) Doctrine of social responsibility

ANSWERS

1. (a)	2. (a)	3. (b)	4. (c)	5. (c)
6. (c)	7. (d)	8. (b)	9. (b)	10. (a)
11. (d)	12. (a)	13. (d)	14. (b)	15. (c)
16. (c)	17. (c)	18. (a)	19. (c)	20. (c)
21. (b)	22. (a)	23. (a)	24. (a)	25. (c)
26. (c)	27. (b)	28. (c)	29. (d)	30. (c)
31. (a)	32. (b)	33. (d)	34. (d)	35. (d)
36. (d)	37. (a)	38. (a)	39. (a)	40. (b)
41. (b)	42. (d)	43. (d)	44. (b)	45. (b)
46. (a)	47. (b)	48. (c)	49. (d)	50. (a)
51. (d)	52. (b)	53. (c)	54. (a)	55. (b)
56. (c)	57. (d)	58. (c)	59. (b)	60. (b)
61. (b)	62. (b)	63. (d)	64. (b)	65. (c)
66. (d)	67. (d)	68. (a)	69. (c)	70. (c)
71. (b)	72. (d)	73. (c)	74. (d)	75. (b)

DECEMBER–2015

Note: This paper contains Sixty (60) multiple-choice questions, each question carrying two (2) marks. Candidate is expected to answer any Fifty (50) questions. In case more than Fifty (50) questions are attempted, only the first Fifty (50) questions will be evaluated.

PAPER–I

1. Greater the handicap of the students coming to the educational institutions, greater the demand on the
   (a) Family (b) Society
   (c) Teacher (d) State

2. What are the characteristics of Continuous and Comprehensive Evaluation?
   1. It increases the workload on students by taking multiple tests.
   2. It replaces marks with grades.
   3. It evaluates every aspect of the student.
   4. It helps in reducing examination phobia.

   Select the correct answer from the codes given below:
   Codes:
   (a) 1, 2, 3 and 4 (b) 2 and 4
   (c) 1, 2 and 3 (d) 2, 3 and 4

3. Which of the following attributes denote great strengths of a teacher?
   1. Full-time active involvement in the institutional management
   2. Setting examples
   3. Willingness to put assumptions to the test
   4. Acknowledging mistakes

   Select the correct answer from the codes given below:
   Codes:
   (a) 1, 2 and 4 (b) 2, 3 and 4
   (c) 1, 3 and 4 (d) 1, 2, 3 and 4

4. Which one of the following statements is correct in the context of multiple-choice type questions?
   (a) They are more objective than true-false type questions.
   (b) They are less objective than essay type questions.
   (c) They are more subjective than short-answer type questions.
   (d) They are more subjective than true-false type questions.

5. As Chairman of an independent commission on education, Jacques Delors report to UNESCO was titled:
   (a) International Commission on Education Report
   (b) Millennium Development Report
   (c) Learning: The Treasure Within
   (d) World Declaration on Education for All

6. What are required for good teaching?
   1. Diagnosis 2. Remedy
   3. Direction 4. Feedback

   Select the correct answer from the codes given below:
   Codes:
   (a) 1, 2, 3 and 4 (b) 1 and 2
   (c) 2, 3 and 4 (d) 3 and 4

7. Which of the following statements is not true in the context of participatory research?
   (a) It recognizes knowledge as power.
   (b) It emphasises on people as experts.
   (c) It is a collective process of enquiry.
   (d) Its sole purpose is production of knowledge.
8. Which of the following statements is true in the context of the testing of a hypothesis?
   (a) It is only the alternative hypothesis, that can be tested.
   (b) It is only the null hypothesis, that can be tested.
   (c) Both, the alternative and the null hypotheses can be tested.
   (d) Both, the alternative and the null hypotheses cannot be tested.
9. Which of the following are the basic rules of APA style of referencing format?
   1. Italicize titles of shorter works such as journal articles or essays
   2. Invert authors' names (last name first)
   3. Italicize titles of longer works such as books and journals
   4. Alphabetically index reference list

   Select the correct answer from the codes given below:

   Codes:

   (a) 1 and 2 (b) 2, 3 and 4
   (c) 3 and 4 (d) 1, 2, 3 and 4
10. Which of the following are the characteristics of a seminar?
   1. It is a form of academic instruction.
   2. It involves questioning, discussion and debates.
   3. It involves large groups of individuals.
   4. It needs involvement of skilled persons.

   Select the correct answer from the codes given below:

   Codes:

   (a) 2 and 3 (b) 2 and 4
   (c) 2, 3 and 4 (d) 1, 2 and 4
11. A researcher is interested in studying the prospects of a particular political party in an urban area. What tool should he prefer for the study?
   (a) Rating scale (b) Interview
   (c) Questionnaire (d) Schedule
12. Ethical norms in research do not involve guidelines for:
   (a) Thesis format
   (b) Copyright
   (c) Patenting policy
   (d) Data sharing policies

Read the following passage carefully and answer question numbers 13 to 17.

I did that thing recently where you have to sign a big card—which is a horror unto itself, especially as the keeper of the Big Card was leaning over me at the time. Suddenly I was on the spot, a rabbit in the headlights, torn between doing a fun message or some sort of in-joke or a drawing. Instead overwhelmed by the myriad options available to me, I decided to just write "Good luck, best, Joel".

It was then that I realised, to my horror, that I had forgotten how to write. My entire existence is "tap letters into computer". My shopping lists are hidden in the notes function of my phone. If I need to remember something I send an e-mail to myself. A pen is something I chew when I'm struggling to think. Paper is something I pile beneath my laptop to make it a more comfortable height for me to type on.

A poll of 1,000 teens by the stationers, Bic found that one in 10 don't own a pen, a third have never written a letter, and half of 13 to 19 years-old have never been forced to sit down and write a thank you letter. More than 80% have never written a love letter, 56% don't have letter paper at home. And a quarter have never known the unique torture of writing a birthday card. The most a teen ever has to use a pen is on an exam paper.

Bic, have you heard of mobile phones? Have you heard of e-mail, facebook and snap chatting? This is the future. Pens are dead. Paper is dead. Handwriting is a relic.

"Handwriting is one of the most creative outlets we have and should be given the same importance as other art forms such as sketching, painting or photography."

Answer the following questions:

13. When confronted with signing a big card, the author felt like "a rabbit in the headlight".
What does this phrase mean?
(a) A state of confusion
(b) A state of pleasure
(c) A state of anxiety
(d) A state of pain

14. According to the author, which one is not the most creative outlet of pursuit?
(a) Handwriting (b) Photography
(c) Sketching (d) Reading

15. The entire existence of the author revolves round:
1. Computer 2. Mobile phone
3. Typewriter
Identify the correct answer from the codes given below:
(a) 2 only (b) 1 and 2 only
(c) 1, 2 and 3 (d) 2 and 3 only

16. How many teens, as per the Bic survey, do not own a pen?
(a) 800 (b) 560 (c) 500 (d) 100

17. What is the main concern of the author?
(a) That the teens use social networks for communication.
(b) That the teens use mobile phones.
(c) That the teens use computer.
(d) That the teens have forgotten the art of handwriting.

18. The main objectives of student evaluation of teachers are:
1. To gather information about student weaknesses.
2. To make teachers take teaching seriously.
3. To help teachers adopt innovative methods of teaching.
4. To identify the areas of further improvement in teacher traits.
Identify the correct answer from the codes given below:
(a) 1 and 2 only
(b) 2, 3 and 4 only
(c) 1, 2 and 3 only
(d) 1 only

19. Using the central point of the classroom communication as the beginning of a dynamic pattern of ideas is referred to as:
(a) Systemisation
(b) Problem-orientation
(c) Idea protocol
(d) Mind mapping

20. Aspects of the voice, other than the speech are known as:
(a) Physical language
(b) Personal language
(c) Para language
(d) Delivery language

21. Every type of communication is affected by its:
(a) Reception (b) Transmission
(c) Non-regulation (d) Context

22. Attitudes, actions and appearances in the context of classroom communication are considered as:

(a) Verbal (b) Non-verbal
(c) Impersonal (d) Irrational

23. Most often, the teacher-student communication is:
(a) Spurious (b) Critical
(c) Utilitarian (d) Confrontational

24. In a classroom, a communicator's trust level is determined by:
(a) the use of hyperbole
(b) the change of voice level
(c) the use of abstract concepts
(d) eye contact

25. The next term in the series
2, 5, 10, 17, 26, 37, __?__ is:
(a) 50 (b) 57
(c) 62 (d) 72

26. A group of 210 students appeared in some test. The mean $\frac{1}{3}$rd of students is found to be 60. The mean of the remaining students is found to be 78. The mean of the whole group will be:
(a) 80 (b) 76
(c) 74 (d) 72

27. Anil after travelling 6 km towards East from his house realized that he has travelled in a wrong direction. He turned and travelled 12 km towards West, turned right and travelled 8 km to reach his office. The straight distance of the office from his house is:
(a) 20 km (b) 14 km
(c) 12 km (d) 10 km

28. The next term in the series:
B2E, D5H, F12K, H27N, __?__ is:
(a) J56I (b) I62Q
(c) Q62J (d) J58Q

29. A party was held in which a grandmother, father, mother, four sons, their wives and one son and two daughters to each of the sons were present. The number of females present in the party is:
(a) 12 (b) 14
(c) 18 (d) 24

30. P and Q are brothers. R and S are sisters. The son of P is brother of S. Q is related to R as:
(a) Son (b) Brother
(c) Uncle (d) Father

31. Consider the argument given below:
'Pre-employment testing of teachers is quite fair because doctors, architects and engineers who are now employed had to face such a testing.'
What type of argument it is?
(a) Deductive (b) Analogical
(c) Psychological (d) Biological

32. Among the following propositions two are related in such a way that they can both be true although they cannot both be false. Which are those propositions? Select the correct code.
Propositions:
1. Some priests are cunning.
2. No priest is cunning.
3. All priests are cunning.
4. Some priests are not cunning.

Codes:
(a) 1 and 2 (b) 3 and 4
(c) 1 and 3 (d) 1 and 4

33. A Cluster of propositions with a structure that exhibits some inference is called:
(a) An inference
(b) An argument
(c) An explanation
(d) A valid argument

34. Consider the following Assertion (A) and Reason (R) and select the correct code given below:

(A): No man is perfect.
(R): Some men are not perfect.

(a) Both (A) and (R) are true but (R) does not provide sufficient reason for (A).
(b) Both (A) and (R) are true and (R) provides sufficient reason for (A).
(c) (A) is true but (R) is false.
(d) (A) is false but (R) is true.

35. A definition that has a meaning that is deliberately assigned to some symbol is called:
(a) Lexical (b) Precising
(c) Stipulative (d) Persuasive

36. If the proposition 'No men are honest' is taken to be false which of the following proposition/propositions can be claimed certainly to be true?
Propositions:
(a) All men are honest
(b) Some men are honest
(c) Some men are not honest
(d) No honest person is man

Given below in the table is the decadal data of Population and Electrical Power Production of a country.

Year	Population (million)	Electrical Power Production (GW)*
1951	20	10
1961	21	20
1971	24	25
1981	27	40
1991	30	50
2001	32	80
2011	35	100

* 1 GW = 1000 million watt

Based on the above table, answer the questions from Sl. No. 37 to 42.

37. Which decade registered the maximum growth rate (%) of population?
(a) 1961-71 (b) 1971-81
(c) 1991-2001 (d) 2001-11

38. Average decadal growth rate (%) of population is:
(a) ~ 12.21% (b) ~ 9.82%
(c) ~ 6.73% (d) ~ 5%

39. Based on the average decadal growth rate, what will be the population in the year 2021?
(a) 40.34 million (b) 38.49 million
(c) 37.28 million (d) 36.62 million

40. In the year 1951, what was the power availability per person?
(a) 100 W (b) 200 W
(c) 400 W (d) 500 W

41. In which decade, the average power availability per person was maximum?
(a) 1981-1991 (b) 1991-2001
(c) 2001-2011 (d) 1971-1981

42. By what percentage (%) the power production increased from 1951 to 2011?
(a) 100% (b) 300%
(c) 600% (d) 900%

43. NMEICT stands for:
(a) National Mission on Education through ICT
(b) National Mission on E-governance through ICT
(c) National Mission on E-commerce through ICT
(d) National Mission on E-learning through ICT

44. Which of the following is an instant messaging application?
1. WhatsApp
2. Google Talk
3. Viber

Select the correct answer from the codes given below:

Codes:

(a) 1 and 2 only (b) 2 and 3 only
(c) 1 only (d) 1, 2 and 3

45. In a Computer a byte generally consists of:
(a) 4 bits (b) 8 bits
(c) 16 bits (d) 10 bits

46. Which of the following is not an input device?
(a) Microphone (b) Keyboard
(c) Joystick (d) Monitor

47. Which of the following is an open source software?
(a) MS Word (b) Windows
(c) Mozilla Firefox (d) Acrobat Reader

48. Which of the following enables us to send the same letter to different persons in MS Word?
(a) Mail join (b) Mail copy
(c) Mail insert (d) Mail merge

49. Inside rural homes, the source/sources of Nitrogen Oxide Pollution may be
1. Unvented gas stoves
2. Wood stoves
3. Kerosene heaters

Choose the correct code

Codes:

(a) 1 and 2 only (b) 2 and 3 only
(c) 2 only (d) 1, 2 and 3

50. Which of the following pollutants can cause cancer in humans?
(a) Pesticides (b) Mercury
(c) Lead (d) Ozone

51. **Assertion (A):** People population control measures do not necessarily help in checking environmental degradation.

Reason (R): The relationship between population growth and environmental degradation is rather complex.

Choose the correct answer from the following:

(a) Both (A) and (R) are true and (R) is the correct explanation of (A).
(b) Both (A) and (R) are true but (R) is not the correct explanation of (A).
(c) (A) is true but (R) is false.
(d) (A) is false but (R) is true.

52. Which of the following phenomena is not a natural hazard?
(a) Wildfire
(b) Lightning
(c) Landslide
(d) Chemical contamination

53. As part of National Climate Change Policy, Indian Government is planning to raise the installed capacity of renewable energy by the year 2030 to
(a) 175 GW (b) 200 GW
(c) 250 GW (d) 350 GW

54. At present, in terms of per capita energy consumption (kWh/year), identify the correct sequence.
(a) Brazil > Russia > China > India
(b) Russia > China > India > Brazil
(c) Russia > China > Brazil > India
(d) China > Russia > Brazil > India

55. Which of the following are the objectives of Rashtriya Uchchatar Shiksha Abhiyan (RUSA)?
1. To improve the overall quality of state institutions.
2. To ensure adequate availability of quality faculty.
3. To create new institutions through upgradation of existing autonomous colleges.

4. To downgrade universities with poor infrastructure into autonomous colleges.

Select the correct answer from the codes given below:

Codes:

(a) 1, 2, 3 and 4 (b) 1, 2 and 3
(c) 1, 3 and 4 (d) 1, 2 and 4

56. The grounds on which discrimination in admission to educational institutions is constitutionally prohibited are

1. Religion 2. Sex
3. Place of birth 4. Nationality

Select the correct answer from the codes given below:

Codes:

(a) 2, 3 and 4 (b) 1, 2 and 3
(c) 1, 2 and 4 (d) 1, 2, 3 and 4

57. Which of the following statements are correct about Lok Sabha?

1. The Constitution puts a limit on the size of the Lok Sabha.
2. The size and shape of the Parliamentary Constituencies is determined by the Election Commission.
3. First-past-the Post electoral system is followed.
4. The Speaker of Lok Sabha does not have a casting vote in case of an equality of votes.

Select the correct answer from the codes given below:

Codes:

(a) 1 and 3 (b) 1, 2 and 3
(c) 1, 3 and 4 (d) 1, 2, 3 and 4

58. Public Order as an item in the Constitution figures in

(a) the Union List
(b) the State List
(c) the Concurrent List
(d) the Residuary Powers

59. The term of office of the Advocate General of a State is

(a) 4 years
(b) 5 years
(c) 6 years or 65 years of age whichever is earlier
(d) not fixed

60. Which among the following States has the highest number of seats in the Lok Sabha?

(a) Maharashtra (b) Rajasthan
(c) Tamil Nadu (d) West Bengal

ANSWERS

1. (c)	2. (d)	3. (b)	4. (a)	5. (c)
6. (a)	7. (d)	8. (b)	9. (b)	10. (d)
11. (c)	12. (a)	13. (a)	14. (d)	15. (b)
16. (d)	17. (d)	18. (c)	19. (d)	20. (c)
21. (d)	22. (b)	23. (c)	24. (d)	25. (a)
26. (d)	27. (d)	28. (d)	29. (b)	30. (c)
31. (b)	32. (d)	33. (b)	34. (a)	35. (c)
36. (b)	37. (a)	38. (b)	39. (b)	40. (d)
41. (c)	42. (d)	43. (a)	44. (d)	45. (b)
46. (d)	47. (c)	48. (d)	49. (d)	50. (a)
51. (a)	52. (d)	53. (d)	54. (c)	55. (b)
56. (b)	57. (a)	58. (b)	59. (d)	60. (a)

PAPER–II

Note: This paper contains fifty (50) objective type questions of two (2) marks each. All questions are compulsory.

1. Read Assertion (A) and Reason (R) and answer using the codes given below:

Assertion (A): The preamble of the constitution of India defines the ideal philosophy of Indian democracy and its key-concepts are laid down as Justice, Liberty, Equality and Fraternity.

Reason (R): A democracy to be real must be characterised by two features.

Codes:

(a) Both (A) and (R) are true and (R) is the correct explanation of (A).

(b) Both (A) and (R) are true but (R) is not the correct explanation of (A).

(c) (A) is true but (R) is false.

(d) (A) is false but (R) is true.

2. Which of the following statements is wrong to issue Writ of Quo warranto?

(a) The office in question should be a public office

(b) The office should be held by an usurper without legal authority

(c) The petition is barred by res-judicata

(d) It is necessary for the petitioner to show that he himself suffered a personal injury nor it is necessary to show that he is seeking redress of a personal grievance

3. Match List-I with List-II and select the correct answer using the codes given below the lists:

List-I

A. S.R. Chaudhuri vs. State of Punjab

B. Murali S. Deora vs. Union of India

C. Food Corporation of India vs. Bharatiya Khadya Nigam Karmachari Sangh

D. Javed vs. State of Haryana

List-II

(i) Ban on smoking at public places

(ii) Two extra increments to the existing employees on earning Higher Qualification

(iii) Classifications based on the number of children for elected post in Panchayat

(iv) Non-member cannot be re-appointed as minister if he fails to get elected within six months.

Codes:	**(A)**	**(B)**	**(C)**	**(D)**
(a)	(iv)	(i)	(ii)	(iii)
(b)	(iv)	(ii)	(i)	(iii)
(c)	(ii)	(iii)	(i)	(iv)
(d)	(iii)	(ii)	(iv)	(i)

4. Which of the following statements are correct; use the codes and answer? Freedom of press includes:

1. Right to print and publish news
2. Distribution of printed matter
3. Criticism of public affairs
4. Pre-censorship

Codes:

(a) 1, 2, 3 and 4

(b) 1, 2 and 3

(c) 1, 3 and 4

(d) 2, 3 and 4

5. During a Financial Emergency, the executive authority of the union exercises control over state finances through the following measures:

1. It can issue directions to states to observe certain cannons of financial propriety
2. It can ask the states to reserve their money bills for the consideration of the President
3. It can direct the states to reduce the salaries and allowances of all the persons serving in connection with the affairs of the states, including the judges of the Supreme Court and High Courts.

Codes:
(a) 1 and 2 (b) 1 and 3
(c) 2 and 3 (d) 1, 2 and 3

6. Justice Pasayat held that 'pardon obtained on the basis of manifest mistake or fraud can be rescinded or cancelled' in the following case:
(a) G. Krishta Goud vs. State of A.P.
(b) Maru Ram vs. Union of India
(c) Epuru Sudhakar vs. Govt. of A.P.
(d) Kehar Singh vs. Union of India

7. Read Assertion (A) and Reason (R) and answer using the codes given below:
Assertion (A): The administrative control over the Subordinate Judiciary in the State lies with the Governor.
Reason (R): The High Court has a power of Superintendence over all courts and tribunals throughout the territory in relation to which it exercises jurisdiction, except military tribunals.

Codes:
(a) Both (A) and (R) are true and (R) is the correct explanation of (A)
(b) Both (A) and (R) are true but (R) is not the correct explanation of (A)
(c) (A) is true but (R) is false
(d) (A) is false but (R) is true

8. Who has described Jurisprudence as "The lawyer's extraversion. It is lawyer's examination of the precepts, ideals, and techniques of the law in the light derived from present knowledge in disciplines other than the law"?
(a) Paton (b) Holland
(c) Austin (d) Julius Stone

9. Who may be regarded as the leading contemporary representative of British Positivism?
(a) Holland (b) Salmond
(c) Hart (d) Hohfeld

10. Match List-I with List-II and give the correct answer by using the codes given below:

List-I
A. Justice is realised only through good law
B. Moral value needs to be included in a definition of positive law
C. Natural law with a variable content
D. A sophisticated version of Natural Law has been put forward in the tradition of Aristotle and Aquinas

List-II
(i) Jerome Hall (ii) John Finnis
(iii) Morris (iv) Stammler

Codes:	**(A)**	**(B)**	**(C)**	**(D)**
(a)	(ii)	(iv)	(i)	(iii)
(b)	(i)	(ii)	(iii)	(iv)
(c)	(iii)	(i)	(iv)	(ii)
(d)	(iv)	(iii)	(ii)	(i)

11. According to whom, whenever a person looked like an owner in relation to a thing, he had possession of it, unless possession was denied him by special rules based on practical convenience. The 'Animus' element was simply an intelligent awareness of the situation?
(a) Salmond (b) Pollock
(c) Ihering (d) Savigny

12. Match List-I with List-II and give the correct answer by using the codes given below:

List-I
A. Social Solidarity
B. Social Utilitarian
C. Social Engineering
D. Social Contract

List-II
(i) Roscoe Pound (ii) Grotius
(iii) Duguit (iv) Ihering

Codes:	(A)	(B)	(C)	(D)
(a)	(i)	(ii)	(iii)	(iv)
(b)	(ii)	(iii)	(iv)	(i)
(c)	(iv)	(i)	(ii)	(iii)
(d)	(iii)	(iv)	(i)	(ii)

13. Match List-I with List-II and give the correct answer by using the codes below:

List-I

A. No one has any other 'right' than always to do his duty.

B. 'Right' is power over an object which by means of this right he subjected to will of the person enjoying the right.

C. Legal right means, "A capacity residing in one man of controlling with the assent and assistance of the state, the acts of the other".

D. 'Right' is not the interest by itself but it is a mean by which enjoyment of interest is secured.

List-II

(i) Gray (ii) Holland

(iii) Duguit (iv) Pachta

Codes:	(A)	(B)	(C)	(D)
(a)	(iv)	(iii)	(i)	(ii)
(b)	(i)	(ii)	(iii)	(iv)
(c)	(iii)	(i)	(ii)	(iv)
(d)	(ii)	(iv)	(i)	(iii)

14. Who has stated that "As a matter of fact International law is neither a myth on the one hand nor a penacea on the other, but just one institution among others which we can use for the building of a better international order"?

(a) Prof. Louis Henkin (b) J.L. Brierly

(c) J.G. Starke (d) Oppenheim

15. Which one of the following sources of International Law does not find or mention in Article 38 of the statute of the International Court of Justice but it has now become a well recognised source?

(a) International conventions

(b) General Principles of Law Recognised by Civilized Nations

(c) Decisions of Judicial or Arbitral Tribunals and Juristic Works

(d) Decisions or Determinations of the Organs of International Institutions

16. Which of the following statement/ statements is/are correct?

1. Custom is the oldest and the original source of International as well as of law in general.
2. In Barcelona Traction case, the International Court applied the general rule of subrogation.
3. In Chorzow factory (Indemnity) case the Permanent Court of Justice ruled that the International law is based on justice, equity and good conscience.
4. In Nicaragua vs. U.S.A. The World Court has taken the view that the sources of International law are not hierarchial but are necessarily complimentary and inter related.

Codes:

(a) Only 1 is correct

(b) 1, 2, 3 are correct

(c) 1 and 4 are both correct

(d) 1, 2, 3 and 4 all are correct

17. Which of the following statement/ statements is/are incorrect?

1. There are five prominent theories of relationship between International law and Municipal law
2. According to Dualism Theory law is a unified branch of knowledge
3. 'Monism' and 'Dualism' are diametrically opposed to each other
4. Wright, Kelson and Duguit are prominent exponents of Dualism Theory

Codes:

(a) 2 and 4 are incorrect

(b) 1, 2 and 4 are incorrect

(c) Only 4 is incorrect

(d) 1, 2, 3 and 4 all are incorrect

18. Match List-I with List-II and give the correct answer by using the codes given below the lists:

List-I (Provisions)

A. Law applied by the International Court of Justice

B. Transferred Jurisdiction

C. Court power to allow a state to intervene in case to which it is not a party

D. Binding Force of the decisions of the International Court of Justice.

List-II (Articles of Statute of International Court)

(i) Article 62 (ii) Article 59

(iii) Article 38 (iv) Article 36 (5)

Codes:	**(A)**	**(B)**	**(C)**	**(D)**
(a)	(i)	(ii)	(iii)	(iv)
(b)	(iv)	(iii)	(ii)	(i)
(c)	(iii)	(iv)	(i)	(ii)
(d)	(ii)	(i)	(iv)	(iii)

19. **Assertion (A):** When a state wants to delay the de jure recognition of any state, it may, in the first stage grant de-facto recognition.

Reason (R): There is no distinction between 'de facto' and 'de jure' recognition for the purpose of giving effect to the Internal Acts of the Recognised Authority.

Use the codes below and give the correct answer.

Codes:

(a) Both (A) and (R) are correct and (R) is the correct explanation of (A)

(b) Both (A) and (R) are correct but (R) is not the correct explanation of (A)

(c) (A) is correct (R) is wrong

(d) (A) is wrong (R) is correct

20. Two persons are said to be related to each other by uterine blood when they are descended from:

(a) a common ancestor by the same wife

(b) a common ancestor but by different wives

(c) a common ancestress by the same husband

(d) a common ancestress but by different husbands

21. Match the List-I with List-II under the Hindu Marriage Act, 1955 and give the correct answer with the help of codes given below:

List-I

A. Restitution of Conjugal Rights

B. Marriagable Age

C. Customary Divorce

D. Ceremonies of Marriage

List-II

(i) Section - 5 (ii) Section-29 (2)

(iii) Section - 9 (iv) Section - 7

Codes:	**(A)**	**(B)**	**(C)**	**(D)**
(a)	(iv)	(i)	(ii)	(iii)
(b)	(iii)	(ii)	(i)	(iv)
(c)	(iii)	(i)	(ii)	(iv)
(d)	(i)	(ii)	(iii)	(iv)

22. In which of the following cases, a child could be a Hindu? Answer with the help of codes:

1. Only one parent is a Hindu and the child was brought up as a Hindu
2. Only one parent is a Hindu and the child was not brought up as a Hindu
3. If after the birth of child, father converts to non-Hindu religion

4. Both the parents are Hindu

Codes:

(a) 1, 3 and 4 only
(b) 2, 3 and 4 only
(c) 1 and 4 only
(d) 3 and 4 only

23. Under the provisions of the Hindu Marriage Act, 1955 the decree of Judicial Separation:

1. dissolve the marriage.
2. does not dissolve the marriage bond but only suspends marital rights and obligations during the subsistence of the decree.
3. the parties continue to be husband and wife but not obligated to live together and neither party is free to marry.
4. if after a decree of judicial separation the parties have not resumed cohabitation for a period of one year, either party may seek divorce.

Codes:

(a) 1, 2 and 3 (b) 2, 1 and 4
(c) 2, 3 and 4 (d) 1, 2, 3 and 4

24. Read Assertion (A) and Reason (R) and give the correct answer with the help of codes given below:

Assertion (A): The Muslim Personal Law (Shariat) Application Act, 1937 makes Muslim Law applicable expressly to all Muslims.

Reason (R): The Muslim Personal Law (Shariat) Application Act, 1937 has abrogated the customs and restored to Muslims their own personal law in almost all cases.

Codes:

(a) (A) and (R) are true and (R) is the correct explanation of (A)
(b) (A) is true but (R) is false
(c) (A) is false but (R) is true
(d) Both (A) and (R) are false

25. Observance of 'Iddat' is necessary:

(a) Where Cohabitation is lawful i.e. consummation of marriage.
(b) Where Cohabitation is unlawful i.e. illicit intercourse and the pregnancy follows the illicit intercourse.
(c) In both (a) and (b)
(d) Only in (a) and not in (b)

26. Modern sources of Hindu law are:

(a) Legislation, Precedents and Digests
(b) Legislation, Precedents, Equity etc.
(c) Precedents, Smritis, Legislation
(d) Legislation, Customs, Precedents and Commentaries

27. Match List-I with List-II and select the correct answer using the codes given below:

List-I (Heads of Public Policy)

A. Trading with enemy
B. Trafficking in public offices
C. Interference with administration of justice
D. Marriage brokage contracts

List-II (Case - Law)

(i) Girdhari Singh vs. Neeladhar Singh
(ii) Espostiv vs. Bowden
(iii) Shivsaran Lal vs. Keshav Prasad
(iv) Nand Kishor vs. Kunj Behari Lal

Codes:	(A)	(B)	(C)	(D)
(a)	(i)	(iv)	(ii)	(iii)
(b)	(iv)	(i)	(ii)	(iii)
(c)	(iv)	(i)	(iii)	(ii)
(d)	(ii)	(iii)	(i)	(iv)

28. Read Assertion (A) and Reason (R) and answer using codes given below:

Assertion (A): Compensation is recoverable for any loss or damage arising unnaturally in the unusual course of things from breach of contract, or which the parties did not know at the time of the contract as likely to result from the breach.

Reason (R): Because Section - 73 of the Indian Contract Act stipulates so.

Codes:

(a) Both (A) and (R) are right and (R) is correct reason for (A)
(b) Both (A) and (R) are wrong
(c) (A) is right, but (R) is wrong
(d) (R) is right, but (A) is wrong

29. Doctrine of frustration was laid down for the first time in:
(a) Krell vs. Henry
(b) Taylor vs. Caldwell
(c) Paradine vs. Jane
(d) Cricklewood Property and Investment Trust Ltd. vs. Leighton's Investment Trust Ltd.

30. Which of the following statements is correct?
(a) A contract is voidable because it was caused by a mistake as to any law in force in India.
(b) A mistake as to law not in force in India has the same effect as a mistake of fact.
(c) A contract is voidable merely because it was caused by one of the parties to it being under a mistake as to a matter of fact.
(d) Where both the parties to an agreement are under a mistake as to a matter of fact essential to the agreement, the agreement is not void.

31. An agreement without consideration is valid, unless:
(a) It is in writing and registered
(b) Is a promise to compensate for something done
(c) It is made by two minors
(d) Is a promise to pay a debt barred by limitation law

32. A proposal is revoked:
(a) By the notice of revocation of the proposal
(b) By the lapse of a reasonable time if the time is prescribed in the proposal
(c) By acceptance of a condition precedent to acceptance
(d) By the death or insanity of the proposer, if the fact of his death or insanity comes to the knowledge of the acceptor before acceptance

33. In order to bring an action for tort, the plaintiff has to prove that:
(a) There has been a legal damage caused to him
(b) Violation of a legal right not vested in him
(c) There has been no legal damage caused to him
(d) Violation of no legal right and has not resulted in harm to him

34. In which case it was held by the Supreme Court that state was not liable on the ground that police were acting in discharge of statutory powers and power of the police in keeping the property in the police *Malkhana* was a sovereign power?
(a) Ramawati Kaur vs. State of Bihar
(b) Radha Aggarwal vs. State of U.P.
(c) Kasturi Lal vs. State of U.P.
(d) State of Bihar vs. Rameshwar Prasad

35. Match the List-I with List-II and give the correct answer by using the codes given below:

List-I (Name of Defence)

A. Act of State B. Consent
C. Act of God D. Statutory authority

List-II (Name of Case - Law)
(i) Buron vs. Denman
(ii) Hail vs. Brookland and Auto Racing Club
(iii) Metropolitan Asylum Board vs. Hills
(iv) Nicholas vs. Marsland

Codes:	(A)	(B)	(C)	(D)
(a)	(iii)	(ii)	(i)	(iv)
(b)	(i)	(ii)	(iv)	(iii)
(c)	(iii)	(i)	(ii)	(iv)
(d)	(iv)	(i)	(iii)	(ii)

36. In which of the following cases, is the occupier of a house liable for 'negligence'?
(a) Keeping a dog, which may bite trespassers
(b) Fixing broken glass pieces on the top of a wall to prevent trespassers
(c) Setting spring guns in the premises to prevent trespassers
(d) Constructing a compound wall to prevent trespassers

37. Read Assertion (A) Reason (R) and give the correct answer with the help of codes given below:
Assertion (A): Mental element is an essential element in most of the torts.
Reason (R): State of mind of the defendant is not relevant to ascertain his liability in all branches of law of torts.
Codes:
(a) Both (A) and (R) are true and (R) is the correct explanation of (A)
(b) Both (A) and (R) are true but (R) is not the correct explanation of (A)
(c) Both (A) and (R) are true
(d) Both (A) and (R) are wrong

38. Which one of the following is not an exception to the rule of *volenti non fit injuria*?
(a) Surgeon amputates a limb of a patient to save his life
(b) Injury is caused while play-fighting with naked swords at a religion function
(c) Injury is caused while doing lawful acts under contract
(d) Injury is caused to a player in football match

39. Which of the facts do not include within the principle of joint liability?
(a) The actuated act need not be a crime or when it was foisted.
(b) An act done in a pre-arranged plan between more than one person.
(c) Mere participation in some manner in the act constituting the offence.
(d) An act done in furtherance of an intention to cause harm.

40. 'Imposing punishment implies that some one should be legally authorised to impose it upon the offender'. In which of the following cases a private person can impose such punishment?
(a) Where the law recognises moral blame worthiness.
(b) Where there is justification for punishing any person provided the offender had broken a law.
(c) Where one can establish the connection between punishment and crime.
(d) Where the act falls within a retroactive penal legislation.

41. The Apex court has shown as to how compromise is not a free choice of the rape survivor but a hidden secret of law where justice is reduced to a bargain between the victim's kin, state authorities and the accused. Identify the case law:
(a) Ravindra vs. State of M.P.
(b) Shreya Singhal vs. Union of India
(c) Sanskar Marathe vs. State of Maharashtra

(d) Khursheed Ahmed Khan vs. State of U.P.

42. There is a specific provision that the intention to screen the offender must be primary and the role object of the accused. This provision is provided in
(a) Section 202 (b) Section 201
(c) Section 199 (d) Section 203

43. Which of the following offences fall under causing hurt as well as assault?
(a) Digging a pit in the public path
(b) Flinging boiling water over a person
(c) Mixing deleterious poison in a liquid and placing the same on another table
(d) Pulling hair of a woman

44. There must be dishonest intention which should co-exist while taking a thing for an offence of theft. In which of the following situations it will not amount to theft?
(a) Taking a stick from the person to beat him
(b) Taking a sugar packet from another person in good faith while his own packet was at the shop
(c) A senior student snatching some books from a junior student with promise to return on the next day
(d) Not finding the helmet hanged on a bike, a person takes away a similar helmet from the adjacent bike, but afterwords repenting on his fault returns the same to the owner

45. The Constitution of Works Committee under the Industrial Disputes Act is to:
(a) Remove causes of friction between the employer and workmen in the day to day working of the establishment
(b) Remove causes of friction between the employer and workmen relating to wage settlement
(c) Remove causes of friction between the employer and workmen relating to standing orders
(d) Remove causes of friction between the employer and workmen relating to implementation of award

46. Under the Industrial Disputes Act, a reference to an Industrial tribunal will be:
(a) Only where both the parties to an Industrial Dispute apply for such reference
(b) Only where the appropriate government considers it expedient to do so
(c) Only where both the parties to an Industrial Dispute apply for such reference and also where the appropriate government considers it expedient to do so
(d) Only where the affected party to the dispute apply for such reference

47. To which settlement machinery can the central government refer the dispute under Rule 81-A?
(a) Conciliation (b) Arbitration
(c) Adjudication (d) Supreme Court

48. A settlement under the Industrial Disputes Act arrived at in the course of conciliation proceding, between the employer and a recognised majority union will be binding on:
(a) parties to the settlement
(b) all workmen of the establishment
(c) all workmen of a recognised majority union
(d) all workmen of a registered Trade Union

49. The permission applied for by the government shall be deemed to have been granted if the appropriate government does not communicate the order under I.D. Act, granting or refusing to grant permission within a period of:
   (a) 15 days (b) 30 days
   (c) 60 days (d) 90 days

50. "The right to strike may be controlled or restricted by appropriate industrial legislation and the validity of such legislation would have to be tested not with reference to the criteria laid down in clause (4) of Article 19 but by totally different considerations", was observed by the Supreme Court in:
   (a) Syndicate Bank vs. Umesh Nayak
   (b) All India Bank Employees Association vs. I.T.
   (c) Management of Churakulam Tea Estate (P) Ltd vs. The workmen and another
   (d) Ramnagar cane and sugar Co. vs. Jatin Chalin

ANSWERS

1. (c)	2. (c)	3. (a)	4. (b)	5. (d)
6. (c)	7. (d)	8. (d)	9. (c)	10. (a)
11. (c)	12. (d)	13. (a)	14. (b)	15. (d)
16. (c)	17. (a)	18. (c)	19. (b)	20. (d)
21. (c)	22. (a)	23. (c)	24. (a)	25. (c)
26. (b)	27. (b)	28. (b)	29. (b)	30. (b)
31. (c)	32. (d)	33. (a)	34. (c)	35. (b)
36. (c)	37. (d)	38. (d)	39. (a)	40. (b)
41. (a)	42. (b)	43. (b)	44. (a)	45. (a)
46. (c)	47. (c)	48. (b)	49. (b)	50. (b)

PAPER–III

Note: This paper contains seventy-five (75) objective type questions of two (2) marks each. All questions are compulsory.

1. Match List-I and List-II and find correct answer by using codes given below:

   List-I
   A. To renounce practices derogatory to the dignity of women
   B. Mandamus cannot be sought against an individual who does not observe a fundamental duty
   C. Respect to National Anthem
   D. Respect and dignity to National Flag

   List-II
   (i) Surya Narain Choudhary Vs. Union of India
   (ii) Union of India Vs. Naveen Jindal
   (iii) Bijoe Emmanuel Vs. State of Kerala
   (iv) Union of India Vs. Naveen Jindal

Codes:	**(A)**	**(B)**	**(C)**	**(D)**
(a)	(i)	(ii)	(iii)	(iv)
(b)	(ii)	(i)	(iii)	(iv)
(c)	(ii)	(i)	(iv)	(iii)
(d)	(iii)	(iv)	(i)	(ii)

2. Match List-I with List-II according to the provisions of the Constitution of India. Give correct answer by using the codes given below:

   List-I (Provisions)
   A. Power of Parliament to legislate with respect to a matter in the state list in the national interest
   B. Legislation for giving effect to international agreements
   C. Power of Parliament to provide for the establishment of certain additional courts

D. Power of Parliament to legislate for two or more states by consent

List-II (Articles)

(i) Article 253 (ii) Article 247

(iii) Article 252 (iv) Article 249

Codes:	**(A)**	**(B)**	**(C)**	**(D)**
(a)	(iv)	(i)	(ii)	(iii)
(b)	(i)	(ii)	(iii)	(iv)
(c)	(iv)	(iii)	(i)	(ii)
(d)	(i)	(ii)	(iv)	(iii)

3. Read Assertion (A) and Reason (R) and answer using the codes given below:
Assertion (A): The rule making power of the Supreme Court of India is not subject to any law made by the Parliament.
Reason (R): Only an impartial and independent judiciary can protect the rights of Individual without fear or favour.

Codes:
(a) Both (A) and (R) are correct and (R) is correct explanation of (A)
(b) Both (A) and (R) are correct but (R) is not the correct explanation of (A)
(c) (A) is false but (R) is true
(d) (A) is true but (R) is false

4. Who among the following shall be disqualified as a member of either House of Parliament? Give answer by selecting codes given below:
(a) Who is not a citizen of India.
(b) Who has acquired the citizenship of a foreign state.
(c) Who is under any acknowledgement to a foreign state.
(d) Who is under acknowledgement of adherence to a foreign state.

Codes:
(a) Only 1
(b) Only 1 and 2
(c) 1, 2 and 3
(d) 1, 2, 3 and 4

5. Under Article 324 of the Constitution the Election Commission of India shall be responsible to conduct elections to :
Give answers by using the codes given below:
1. Parliament and State Legislature
2. President and Vice-President
3. Zilla Parishad and Panchayats
4. Municipal Corporations and Municipal Committees

Codes:
(a) 1, 2, 3 and 4
(b) 1 and 2 only
(c) 1, 2 and 3
(d) 1, 3 and 4

6. Who among the following can establish additional court for better administration of any existing law with respect to a matter concerned in union list:
(a) Chief Justice of India
(b) Parliament
(c) The Concerned State Legislature
(d) High Court of the State Concerned

7. Which one of the following statements is correct?
Article 368 of the Constitution of India lays down:
(a) Procedure for amendment of the constitution only.
(b) Power of parliament to amend the constitution only.
(c) Power of parliament to amend the constitution and procedure therefore.
(d) Limitation on the power of the parliament to amend the constitution.

8. In which one of the following cases the Supreme Court held that, 'No election

can be challenged on the ground of defect in electoral rolls'?

(a) Inderjit Barua Vs. Election Commission of India
(b) N.P. Ponnuswami Vs. Returning Officer
(c) Kalyan Lal Omar Vs. R.K. Trivedi
(d) Mohinder Singh Gill Vs. Chief Election Commissioner

9. Who defined administrative law as; "Law relating to the Administration. It determines the organisation, powers and duties of administrative authorities"?
(a) Sir Ivor Jennings
(b) A.V. Dicey
(c) Kenneth Culp Davis
(d) Griffith and Strut

10. What was specifically declared by the Supreme Court in the Delhi Laws Act case? Answer using codes given below:
1. Legislature should not delegate its essential function.
2. Excessive delegation of powers can be struck down by courts.
3. Extension of laws with certain modification and by changing the underlying policy of legislation is allowed.
4. Legislature should itself lay down standard in the delegating Act learning the delegate with the power to make rules to execute the policy laid down in the Legislation:

Codes:

(a) 3, 1, 4 (b) 2, 4, 1
(c) 4, 3, 2 (d) 1, 2, 4

11. Which of the following is not true regarding the application of 'doctrine of promissory estoppel'?
(a) The court may refuse to apply promissory estoppel against the government if the 'public interest' suffers in fulfilling the promise.
(b) The government cannot be compelled to carry out a promise which falls outside its power and contrary to law.
(c) The promise in question may be tentative or uncertain and it need not to be unambiguous and unequivocal.
(d) There can be no promissory estoppel against the Legislature in the exercise of its legislative functions.

12. Match List-I with List-II in the light of cases decided by the Supreme Court:

List-I (Case Law)

A. Canara Bank Vs. V.K. Awasthy (2005)
B. Gullapalli Nageswara Rao Vs. A.P. State Road Transport Corporation, 1959
C. Swadeshi Cotton Mills Vs. Union of India (1981)
D. A.K. Kraipak Vs. Union of India (1970)

List-II (Principles)

(i) Duty to act fairly - in administrative functions as well
(ii) Post decisional hearing
(iii) Exclusion of rule of hearing
(iv) One who decides must hear

Codes:	**(A)**	**(B)**	**(C)**	**(D)**
(a)	(i)	(ii)	(iii)	(iv)
(b)	(iv)	(iii)	(i)	(ii)
(c)	(ii)	(iv)	(iii)	(i)
(d)	(iii)	(iv)	(ii)	(i)

13. Read Assertion (A) and Reason (R) and answer using codes given below:
Assertion (A): A High Court may decline to exercise its extra-ordinary jurisdiction under Article 226 and dismiss the writ summarily or *in limine*.

Reason (R): It would be proper for the High Court to dispose of the petition summarily or *in limine*, when no important question of law are raised in a writ petition.

Codes:

(a) Both (A) and (R) are right and (R) is correct reason of (A)

(b) Both (A) and (R) are right but (R) is not correct reason of (A)

(c) (A) is right but (R) is wrong

(d) (A) is wrong but (R) is right

14. When a writ is issued to a public authority in respect of any type of administrative, legislative, Quasi-judicial or judicial functions, it is called a writ of:

(a) Mandamus (b) Quo - warranto

(c) Certiorari (d) Prohibition

15. Read Assertion (A) and Reason (R) and answer using codes given below:

Assertion (A): In judicial review of administrative actions, generally the court would not interfere with the merits of the case by embarking upon inquiry into the facts.

Reason (R): Courts can review the procedure through which a decision has been taken by the administrative authority but courts cannot supplement its own decision and act as appellate court over the administrative authority.

Codes:

(a) Both (A) and (R) are correct and (R) is the correct explanation of (A)

(b) Both (A) and (R) are correct but (R) is not correct explanation of (A)

(c) (A) is right but (R) is wrong

(d) (A) is wrong but (R) is right

16. "The polemical version of legal realism has wielded enormous influence on the entire judicial system". Who propounded such philosophy?

(a) Gray (b) Holmes

(c) Salmond (d) Waismann

17. The *liberam arbitrium* of the courts depends upon what is right, justice, equitable or reasonable and is dependent upon:

(a) Evidence and demonstration of public

(b) Arguments submitted with reason

(c) Discovering the right or justice of the matter

(d) Pure intellectual process

18. *Obitor dicta* has no binding authority but it helps to:

(a) Rationalise legal sanctions

(b) Encourages providing solution to future litigations

(c) It allows greater prestige to the judge

(d) It makes the acceptability of precedents more flexible

19. The statement "equitable ownership of a legal right is different from the ownership of an equitable right" shows that law and equity differ with regard to:

(a) Only the existence of right

(b) Only the ownership of rights

(c) Both existence and ownership of rights

(d) The existence of a right but not regarding the consistency of a right

20. Read Assertion (A) and Reason (R) and give correct answer using codes given below:

Assertion (A): The relation of morality to a concept of law cannot be stated simply in the form of a stark alternative that the former is either externally or internally related to the later.

Reason (R): It is depending upon time-frame of reference

Codes:

(a) Both (A) and (R) are wrong

(b) Both (A) and (R) are right and (R) is correct reason of (A)

(c) (A) is wrong and (R) is right
(d) (A) is right and (R) is wrong

21. The House of Lords upheld the Attorney General's political discretion in refusing to invoke the law in face of a threatened criminal offence in deliberate defiance of an Act of Parliament, in the case of:
(a) Gouriet Vs. Union of Post Office Workers
(b) Francome Vs. Mirror Group Newspaper Ltd.
(c) R. Vs. Bourne
(d) Johnson Vs. Phillips

22. Modern doctrine of bindingness of precedents was first laid down in:
(a) London Transways Co. Vs. LCC
(b) Young Vs. Bristol Aeroplane Co. Ltd.
(c) Mirehouse Vs. Rennel
(d) Sirros Vs. Moore

23. Read Assertion (A) and Reason (R) and answer using the codes given below:
Assertion (A): Shareholders are not, in the eye of law, part owners of a company. The company is something different from the totality of the shareholders.
Reason (R): Shareholders are collective owners of the company.

Codes:
(a) Both (R) and (A) are right and (R) is correct reason of (A)
(b) Both (A) and (R) are wrong
(c) (A) is right, but (R) is wrong
(d) (R) is right, but (A) is wrong

24. An idea of inducement by exciting hope or desire on the other is known as:
(a) Seduction (b) Enticing
(c) Inciting (d) Abduction

25. A takes his own suit from the tailor without his knowledge but had the intention of returning it to the tailor later. What offence, if any has been committed by A?
(a) Stealing (b) Dishonest taking
(c) Theft (d) Unlawful retention

26. Read Assertion (A) and Reason (R) and answer using codes given below:
Assertion (A): That the act is imminently dangerous or that in all probability it will cause death.
Reason (R): Such specific principle apply to punish a person although there is no intention to cause death.

Codes:
(a) Both (A) and (R) are concurrent as per Sec. 299(c) and 300(4) respectively.
(b) Both (A) and (R) are intravivos as per Sec. 300 and Sec. 302.
(c) Both (A) and (R) are dependant upon facts based as per Sec. 299(b) and Sec. 302.
(d) Both (A) and (R) must co-exist as per Sec. 300(2) and Sec. 301.

27. The aggravated form of perjury is known from:
(a) False statement on oath
(b) False evidence in a judicial proceeding
(c) Administering oath to speak truth
(d) False affidavit before honorary Magistrate

28. Which of the following is not a crime in order to provide protection to currency?
(a) A war medal
(b) Gold Mohur
(c) Current Coin
(d) Genuine specimen of antique coin

29. Which of the following cases does not amount to robbery?
(a) Taking away ornaments from the body of a lady while she was in coma.

(b) Removal of ornaments after death of a lady.
(c) Voluntary disposition of valuables.
(d) While theft is committed along with assault.

30. Criminal liability for abandonment of a child is based on the principle of *loco-parentis*. Who else could be responsible for that offence?
(a) Adoptive father before the completion of formalities of adoption
(b) When a mother leaves the house for her husband's ill-treatment and abandons the children to the care of husband
(c) When the school master who has been teaching infants placed under him for education
(d) A mother leaves a blind child on a foot path promising to return after fetching food but never returned

31. Which of the following do not constitute an offence of forgery?
(a) The intention to induce a belief that the document was duly signed.
(b) The intention to induce a belief that the document was duly sealed.
(c) The intention to induce a belief that the document was executed by the authority of a person.
(d) Knowingly makes false entries initially in the public record on his own authority by a public officer.

32. "Where directive principles have found statutory expression in do's and dont's the court will not sit idle and allow government to become a statutory mockery for protection of environment. The law will relentlessly be enforced and the plea of poor finance will be poor alibi when people in misery cry for justice". The above was observed in Municipal Council of Ratlam Vs. Vardhichand by:
(a) Justice Chinnappa Reddy
(b) Justice V.R. Krishna Iyyer
(c) Justice P.N. Bhagavati
(d) Justice Ranganath Misra

33. Protection and Improvement of Environment and safeguarding forest and wild life is:
(a) A Fundamental Right.
(b) One of the Directive Principles of State Policy.
(c) One of the Fundamental Duties.
(d) Both Directive Principles of State Policy and Fundamental Duty.

34. In which of the following cases, the Supreme Court directed closing down and demolition of shrimp Industries in coastal regulation zone and implement the "Precautionary principle" and "the polluter pays principle" and held them liable for payment of compensation for reversing the ecology and compensate the individual for loss suffered?
(a) M.C. Mehta Vs. Union of India
(b) S. Jaganath Vs. Union of India
(c) Church of God (Full Gospels) in India Vs. K.K.R. Majestic Colony Welfare Association
(d) Vellore Citizen's Welfare Forum Vs. Union of India

35. Read Assertion (A) and Reason (R) and give the answer by using the codes given below:
Assertion (A): The right to clean drinking water and right to pollution free air to breath are attributes of "Right to Life".
Reason (R): Because they are the basic elements which sustain life.

Codes:
(a) Both (A) and (R) are true. (R) is good explanation of (A)

(b) Both (A) and (R) are true. But (R) is not a good explanation of (A)
(c) (A) is true but (R) is false
(d) (A) is false but (R) is true

36. In which of the following cases the Supreme Court applied the doctrine of public trust that the state as a trustee of all natural resources is under a legal duty to protect the natural resources. These natural resources are meant for public use and cannot be converted into private ownership?
(a) M.C. Mehta Vs. Union of India (Ganga Water Pollution Case)
(b) M.C. Mehta Vs. Kamalnath and others
(c) M.C. Mehta Vs. Union of India (Replacing diesel vehicles by CNG vehicles)
(d) Rural Litigation and Entitlement Kendra Vs. State of U.P.

37. What is the main objective of the Prohibition of Employment as Manual Scavengers and their Rehabilitation Act, 2013? Give answer by using codes below:
1. To prohibit employment of manual scavengers
2. To rehabilitate manual scavengers
3. To rehabilitate manual scavengers and their families
4. To rehabilitate manual scavengers only and not their families

Codes:
(a) Only 1 (b) Only 1 and 2
(c) 1, 2 and 3 (d) 1, 2, 3 and 4

38. Which one of the following is the main objective of the Wild Life (Protection) Act, 1972 as amended upto 2003?
(a) To check on poaching and illegal trade in domestic and wild animals.
(b) To check on poaching and on illegal trade in ivory.
(c) To check on poaching and legal trade in dog.
(d) To check on hunting and legal trade in elephant.

39. Whose observations are these on the point that whether International law is a mere positive Morality?
"If International Law were only a kind of morality, the framers of State papers concerning foreign policy would throw all their weight on moral arguments, But, as a matter of fact, this is not what they do. They appeal not to the general feeling of moral rightness, but to precedents, to treaties and to opinion of specialists".
(a) H.L.A. Hart (b) Oppenheim
(c) Edward Collins (d) Frederick Pollock

40. Which of the following statement/ Statements is/are not correct?
1. Principle of law which is recognised by domestic law of a large number of states does not automatically become a 'Principle' of International Law.
2. Para (1)(G) of Article 38 of the Statute of International Court of justice lists "General Principles of Law Recognised by Civilized States" as the Second Source of International Law.
3. General Principles of law recognised by civilized states include only substantive principles provided they have received general recognition of Civilized States.
4. The development of general principles of law recognised by civilized states as an important source of law, has given a death-knell to the positivism.

Codes:

(a) only 2 is incorrect
(b) both 2 and 3 are incorrect
(c) 1, 2 and 3 are incorrect
(d) 1, 2, 3 and 4 are incorrect

41. Which one of the following cases is not a case on the point that there is no distinction between 'De Facto' and 'De - Jure' recognition for the purpose of giving effect to the internal acts of the recognized authority?
(a) Bank of Ethopia Vs. National Bank of Egypt and Liquori
(b) Luther Vs. Sagor
(c) Civil Air Transport Incorporated Co. Vs. Central Air Transport Corporation
(d) The Arantzazu Mendi Case

42. In which one of the following cases the International Court of Justice has held that in respect of grant of nationality there is no obligation of the states if a man has no relationship with the state of Naturalisation and the court has applied the 'Principle of effective nationality'?
(a) Re Lynch Case
(b) Stoeck Vs. The Public Trustee
(c) Nottebohm's Case
(d) Paneyezys Soldutisk

43. Which one of the following institution is not authorised for requesting for 'Advisory Opinion' of the International Court of Justice?
(a) Economic and Social Council
(b) The Trusteeship Council
(c) The International Atomic Energy Agency
(d) Secretariat

44. Read both Assertion (A) and Reason (R) and give the correct answer by using the codes given below:

Assertion (A): International Law is not potent enough to restrain a powerful state which has no respect for public opinion.
Reason (R): Sanctions behind International Law are weak.

Codes:

(a) Both (A) and (R) are correct and (R) is the correct explanation of (A)
(b) Both (A) and (R) are correct but (R) is not the correct explanation of (A)
(c) (A) is true but (R) is false
(d) (A) is false but (R) is true

45. Consider the following:
The Recommendation of the Security Council made to the Member under Article 42 of U.N. Charter becomes an obligation for them which none can shirk?
1. If the Security Council decides to take action no time is given for further declarations by the General Assembly.
2. When the Security Council decides for taking enforcement measures, it also determines the part to be played by each member state.
3. All or only some members may be requested to participate but every member is to join in mutual assistance.
4. The legal requirements for military action are still not satisfied even after the council has acted.

Which of the above statement/statements is/are correct?
(a) 1, 2, 4 are correct
(b) 2, 3 and 4 are correct
(c) only 1, 2 and 3 are correct
(d) 3, 4 and 1 are correct

46. Match List-I with List-II and give the correct answer by using the codes given below:

List-I (Provisions)

A. Voting procedure of the General Assembly
B. Composition of Security Council
C. Composition of Trusteeship Council
D. Provisions regarding Membership in the United Nations

List-II (Article of UN Charter)

(i) Article 23 (ii) Article 96
(iii) Article 4 (iv) Article 18

Codes:	**(A)**	**(B)**	**(C)**	**(D)**
(a)	(ii)	(iii)	(iv)	(i)
(b)	(i)	(ii)	(iii)	(iv)
(c)	(iii)	(i)	(ii)	(iv)
(d)	(iv)	(ii)	(i)	(iii)

47. Which of the following is not a ground of Judicial Separation under the Hindu Marriage Act, 1955?
(a) Renunciation of the world
(b) Seven years absence
(c) Conversion to Non-Hindu religion
(d) Desertion for one year

48. Grounds of divorce meant exclusively for wife under section 13(2) of the Hindu Marriage Act, 1955 are:
1. Pre - Act bigamy by Husband.
2. Husband is guilty of rape, sodomy and bestiality.
3. Non-payment of maintenance and no cohabitation for one year or upwards.
4. Repudiation of marriage by wife.

Codes:
(a) 1, 3 and 4 (b) 3, 4, 1 and 2
(c) 2, 3 and 4 (d) 1, 2 and 3

49. Under the provisions of the Hindu Adoptions and Maintenance Act, 1956 an adopted child:
1. Can be given in adoption generally
2. Cannot be given in adoption
3. Can be given in adoption with the consent of natural parents
4. Can be given in adoption only with the prior permission of the court

Codes:
(a) 2 and 4 are correct but 1 and 3 are incorrect
(b) 4 is correct and 1, 2 and 3 are incorrect
(c) 2 is correct and 1, 3 and 4 are incorrect
(d) 1 and 2 are correct and 3 and 4 are incorrect

50. Match List-I with List-II in relation to the Hindu Adoptions and Maintenance Act, 1956 and give the correct answer by using the codes given below the lists:

List-I

A. Maintenance of wife
B. Maintenance of widowed daughter-in-law
C. Maintenance of parents and children
D. Maintenance of dependants

List-II

(i) Sec. 19 (ii) Sec. 22
(iii) Sec. 18 (iv) Sec. 20

Codes:	**(A)**	**(B)**	**(C)**	**(D)**
(a)	(iii)	(i)	(iv)	(ii)
(b)	(i)	(iii)	(ii)	(iv)
(c)	(iv)	(ii)	(i)	(iii)
(d)	(ii)	(i)	(iv)	(iii)

51. After the petition is presented under section 13-B of Hindu Marriage Act, 1955, the parties have to wait for a minimum period of:
(a) One year (b) Eighteen months
(c) Two years (d) Six months

52. Talaq 'ahsan' is:
(a) Revocable during the tuhr in which it has been pronounced

(b) Revocable until the next successive tuhr
(c) Revocable during the period of iddat
(d) Irrevocable

53. Match List-I with List-II in the light of the Dissolution of Muslim Marriage Act, 1939 and give the correct answer by using the codes given below:

List-I (Provision)

A. Notice to heirs of the husband when his where abouts are not known
B. Effect of conversion to another faith
C. Rights to dower not to be affected
D. Impotence of the husband as a ground of divorce

List-II (Section)

(i) Sec. 4 (ii) Sec. 3
(iii) Sec. 2(v) (iv) Sec. 5

Codes:	**(A)**	**(B)**	**(C)**	**(D)**
(a)	(i)	(iii)	(ii)	(iv)
(b)	(ii)	(i)	(iv)	(iii)
(c)	(iv)	(ii)	(i)	(iii)
(d)	(iii)	(i)	(iv)	(ii)

54. Match List-I with List-II under the Hindu Minority and Guardianship Act, 1956 and give the correct answer with the help of the codes given below:

List-I (Provision)

A. Testamentary guardian and their powers
B. Natural guardians of a Hindu Minor
C. Welfare of minor to be paramount consideration
D. De facto guardian not to deal with minor's property

List-II (Section)

(i) Sec. 6 (ii) Sec. 9
(iii) Sec. 11 (iv) Sec. 13

Codes:	**(A)**	**(B)**	**(C)**	**(D)**
(a)	(ii)	(i)	(iv)	(iii)
(b)	(i)	(iv)	(iii)	(ii)
(c)	(iv)	(ii)	(i)	(iii)
(d)	(iii)	(i)	(iv)	(ii)

55. Read both statements (A) and (R) and give the correct answer by using the codes given below:

Assertion (A): The member state of United Nations Organisation have committed to promote and the respect for observance of Human Rights.

Reason (R): The Human Rights are Inalienable, Natural, Interdependent and Indivisible. They are means to achieve human dignity.

Codes:

(a) Both (A) and (R) are true and (R) is not the correct explanation of (A)
(b) Both (A) and (R) are true and (R) is the correct explanation of (A)
(c) (A) is false but (R) is true
(d) (A) is true but (R) is false

56. The International covenant on Economic, Social and Cultural Rights came into force on:

(a) January 3, 1976
(b) January 13, 1976
(c) June 30, 1977
(d) June 13, 1977

57. UNICEF was created by the UN General Assembly to help:

(a) Children after World War I
(b) Children after World War II in Europe
(c) Children of third world countries
(d) Children of suffering from malnutrition

58. Match List-I with List-II and select the correct answer using the codes given below:

List-I

A. Mr. Jose Ayala Lasso
B. Justice Nagendra Singh
C. Kofi Annan
D. Mrs. F.D. Roosevelt

List-II

(i) President International Court of Justice
(ii) Secretary General U.N.O.
(iii) Chairperson Commission on Human Rights
(iv) U.N. High Commissioner for Human Rights

Codes:	(A)	(B)	(C)	(D)
(a)	(iv)	(i)	(ii)	(iii)
(b)	(ii)	(iv)	(iii)	(i)
(c)	(iii)	(ii)	(i)	(iv)
(d)	(iii)	(ii)	(iv)	(i)

59. The Universal Declaration of Human Rights 1948 contains provisions relating to:
    (a) Operationalization of Human Rights.
    (b) Establishment of Human Rights Institutions.
    (c) Establishment of Human Rights Committee.
    (d) Conceptualization of Human Rights.

60. Which of the following statement is correct?
    (a) The U.N. Convention on Elimination of all Forms of Discrimination Against Women (CEDAW) was adapted by the General Assembly in 1979 but, India ratified it in June 1993.
    (b) The U.N. Convention on Elimination of all Forms of Discrimination Against Women (CEDAW) was adapted by the General Assembly in 1979 but, India ratified it in December 1997.
    (c) The U.N. Convention on Elimination of all Forms of Discrimination Against Women (CEDAW) was adapted by the General Assembly in 1981 but India ratified it in June 1993.
    (d) The U.N. Convention on Elimination of all Forms of Discrimination Against Women (CEDAW) was adapted by the General Assembly in 1981 but, India ratified it in December 1997.

61. The correct chronological order of the following Human Rights documents be choosen using the codes given below:
    1. International Covenant on Civil and Political Rights.
    2. Convention on the Elimination of all Forms of Discrimination Against Women.
    3. Universal Declaration of Human Rights.
    4. Convention on the Rights of the Child.

    Codes:

    (a) 3, 2, 1, 4 (b) 3, 1, 2, 4
    (c) 4, 3, 1, 2 (d) 3, 4, 2, 1

62. Who defined law of tort as "tortious liability arises from the breach of a duty primarily fixed by the law this duty is towards persons generally and its breach is redressible by an action for unliquidated damages"?
    (a) Salmand (b) Lord Denning
    (c) Fraser (d) Winfield

63. Which of the following is not a form of *damnum sine injuria*? Choose the correct answer from the codes below:
    1. There is no right of action for damages for contempt of court.
    2. Loss inflicted on individual traders by competition.
    3. Damage is done by a man acting under necessity to prevent a greater evil.
    4. Damage caused by defamatory statements made on any occasion.

Codes:

(a) 1, 2, 3 and 4 (b) 1 and 2
(c) 2 and 4 (d) None of the above

64. Facts "The defendant was a plaintiff's landlord and was living in the same building on the floor above him. Some rats damaged a rain water box maintained by the defendant for the benefit both of himself and plaintiff and the water running through injured plaintiff's goods below." What action can be taken on the above mentioned facts in view of the exceptions to the theory of 'strict liability'?
(a) No action lie because of plaintiff's own fault
(b) Action lie because it is not act of God
(c) No action lie because of the consent of plaintiff
(d) Action lie because it is not an act of stranger

65. Read Assertion (A) and Reason (R) and give the correct answer with the help of codes given below
Assertion (A): A master is liable for the torts committed by his servant while not acting in the course of his employment.
Reason (R): Liability of the master for the act of his servant is based on the maxim *respondent superior.*
Codes:
(a) Both (A) and (R) are true and the (R) is the correct explanation of (A)
(b) Both (A) and (R) are true but (R) is not the correct explanation of (A)
(c) (A) is right but (R) is wrong
(d) (A) is wrong but (R) is right

66. Match List-I with List-II and give the correct answer by using the codes given below:
List-I (Case Laws)
A. RePolemis and Furners, Wilhy and Co. Ltd.
B. Saheli Vs. Commissioner of Police, Delhi
C. Municipal Corporation of Delhi Vs. Subhagwanti
D. South Wales Miners Federation Vs. Glamorgan Coal Company
List-II (Principles)
(i) Vicariom liability of the state
(ii) Remoteness of damages
(iii) Duty of case to plaintiff
(iv) Malice in fact

Codes:	**(A)**	**(B)**	**(C)**	**(D)**
(a)	(ii)	(i)	(iii)	(iv)
(b)	(i)	(ii)	(iv)	(iii)
(c)	(i)	(ii)	(iii)	(iv)
(d)	(ii)	(iii)	(i)	(iv)

67. What is the period of limitation under section 24 A of the Consumer Protection Act, 1986 (as amended w.e.f. 18.6.1993) for filing a complaint from the date of the cause of action?
(a) No period of limitation
(b) Three years
(c) Two years
(d) One year

68. Match the List-I with List-II and give answer by using the codes below (Re Tort of Defamation)
List-I (Name of Case Law)
A. Tolley Vs. J.S. Fry and Sons Ltd.
B. Williamson Vs. Frier
C. Alexander Vs. North Eastern Railway
D. Merivale Vs. Carson
List-II (Principle)
(i) Publication of statement
(ii) Innuendo

(iii) Fair comment
(iv) Defence of truth

Codes:	(A)	(B)	(C)	(D)
(a)	(ii)	(i)	(iv)	(iii)
(b)	(i)	(ii)	(iii)	(iv)
(c)	(iv)	(i)	(ii)	(iii)
(d)	(iii)	(ii)	(i)	(iv)

69. Match List-I with List-II and select the correct answer using the codes given below:

List-I

A. Kundan Lal Rallaram Vs. Custodian
B. C.T. Joseph Vs. I.V. Phillip
C. A.V. Murthy Vs. B.S. Nagabasavanna
D. Beni Madhavnath Vs. Jugandra Nath Balwan

List-II

(i) Presumption under section 118 of the Negotiable Instrument Act arises only if the execution of the document is proved as true
(ii) Burden of proof of failure of consideration for a negotiable instrument
(iii) A negotiable instrument is presumed to be drawn for consideration
(iv) The statutory presumption envisaged under section 118(a) of the Negotiable Instrument Act is rebuttable.

Codes:	(A)	(B)	(C)	(D)
(a)	(ii)	(i)	(iii)	(iv)
(b)	(i)	(ii)	(iii)	(iv)
(c)	(ii)	(iv)	(i)	(iii)
(d)	(iii)	(i)	(iv)	(ii)

70. Which of the following statement is incorrect?
(a) A cheque is a bill of exchange, but every bill of exchange is not a cheque.
(b) A cheque is always payable on demand.
(c) A cheque is a conditional order from the drawer of a cheque to the drawee bank to make payment of money only.
(d) A post dated cheque cannot be considered as a valid cheque till the date of maturity.

71. Which of the following cases is about doctrine of indoor management?
(a) Ashbury Railway Carriage and Iron Co. Ltd. Vs. Riche
(b) Rama Corpn. Vs. Proved tin and General Investment Co.
(c) London Country Council Vs. Attorney - General
(d) A. Lakshmana swamy Mudaliar Vs. L.I.C.

72. Read Assertion (A) and Reason (R) and answer using codes given below:

Assertion (A): For the proper exercise of the functions of a director, it is essential that he be disinterested, that is, be free from any conflicting interest.

Reason (R): Conflict is injurious to mental and physical health.

Codes:
(a) Both (A) and (R) are correct, and (R) is correct reason of (A).
(b) (A) is correct, but (R) is wrong.
(c) Both (A) and (R) are incorrect.
(d) Both (A) and (R) are correct, but (R) is not correct legal reason of (A).

73. Which are essentials of a partnership? Answer using codes given below:
1. A contract of two or more competent persons
2. Agreement to share profits
3. Mutual agency
4. Lawful business

Codes:

(a) Only 1, 2, 3 (b) Only 1, 2, 4
(c) Only 2, 3, 4 (d) 1, 2, 3, 4

74. Match List-I with List-II and select the correct answer using the codes given below

List-I

A. Section 54 of the Sale of Goods Act
B. Section 40 of the Sale of Goods Act
C. Section 37 of the Sale of Goods Act
D. Section 15 of the Sale of Goods Act

List-II

(i) Risk where goods are delivered at distant place
(ii) Delivery of wrong quantity
(iii) Sale by description
(iv) Rights of unpaid seller against the goods

Codes:	(A)	(B)	(C)	(D)
(a)	(i)	(iv)	(ii)	(iii)
(b)	(iv)	(i)	(ii)	(iii)
(c)	(iv)	(i)	(iii)	(ii)
(d)	(ii)	(iii)	(i)	(iv)

75. Which of the following cases is about performance of contract?
(a) Maruti Udyog Ltd. Vs. Susheel Kumar Gabgetra
(b) Great Northern Railway Co. Vs. Harrison
(c) Joyce Vs. Swann
(d) Behn Vs. Burness

ANSWERS

1. (d)	2. (b)	3. (a)	4. (b)	5. (d)
6. (d)	7. (a)	8. (b),(c)	9. (a)	10. (a)
11. (b)	12. (a)	13. (d)	14. (c)	15. (a)
16. (d)	17. (b)	18. (a)	19. (a)	20. (b)
21. (d)	22. (b)	23. (a)	24. (b)	25. (d)
26. (a)	27. (d)	28. (b)	29. (c)	30. (b)
31. (a)	32. (c)	33. (c)	34. (d)	35. (d)
36. (d)	37. (d)	38. (d)	39. (b)	40. (b)
41. (a)	42. (b)	43. (b)	44. (d)	45. (c)
46. (b)	47. (d)	48. (b)	49. (d)	50. (c)
51. (d)	52. (a)	53. (b)	54. (c)	55. (d)
56. (b)	57. (d)	58. (d)	59. (a)	60. (d)
61. (c)	62. (c)	63. (a)	64. (d)	65. (a)
66. (b)	67. (b)	68. (c)	69. (d)	70. (c)
71. (d)	72. (b)	73. (b)	74. (b)	75. (c)

JUNE–2015

Note: This paper contains Sixty (60) multiple-choice questions, each question carrying two (2) marks. Candidate is expected to answer any Fifty (50) questions. In case more than Fifty (50) questions are attempted, only the first Fifty (50) questions will be evaluated.

PAPER–I

1. Which of the following is the highest level of cognitive ability?
   (a) Knowing (b) Understanding
   (c) Analysing (d) Evaluating

2. Which of the following factors does not impact teaching?
   (a) Teacher's knowledge
   (b) Classroom activities that encourage learning
   (c) Socio-economic background of teachers and students
   (d) Learning through experience

3. Which of the following statements about teaching aids are correct?
   (1) They help in retaining concepts for longer duration.
   (2) They help students learn better.
   (3) They make teaching learning process interesting.
   (4) They enhance rote learning.
   Select the correct answer from the codes given below:
   (a) (1), (2), (3) and (4)
   (b) (1), (2) and (3)
   (c) (2), (3) and (4)
   (d) (1), (2) and (4)

4. Techniques used by a teacher to teach include:
   (1) Lecture
   (2) Interactive lecture
   (3) Group work
   (4) Self study
   Select the correct answer from the codes given below:
   (a) (1), (2) and (3)
   (b) (1), (2), (3) and (4)
   (c) (2), (3) and (4)
   (d) (1), (2) and (4)

5. Achievement tests are commonly used for the purpose of:
   (a) Making selections for a specific job
   (b) Selecting candidates for a course
   (c) Identifying strengths and weaknesses of learners
   (d) Assessing the amount of learning after teaching

6. A good teacher is one who:
   (a) gives useful information
   (b) explains concepts and principles
   (c) gives printed notes to students
   (d) inspires students to learn

7. Which of the following statements regarding the meaning of research are correct?
   (1) Research refers to a series of systematic activity or activities undertaken to find out the solution of a problem.

(2) It is a systematic, logical and an unbiased process wherein verification of hypothesis, data analysis, interpretation and formation of principles can be done.

(3) It is an intellectual enquiry or quest towards truth.

(4) It leads to enhancement of knowledge.

Select the correct answer from the codes given below:

(a) (1), (2) and (3)
(b) (2), (3) and (4)
(c) (1), (3) and (4)
(d) (1), (2), (3) and (4)

8. A good thesis writing should involve:
   1. reduction of punctuation and grammatical errors to a minimum.
   2. careful checking of references.
   3. consistency in the way the thesis is written.
   4. a clear and well-written abstract.

   Select the correct answer from the codes given below:

   (a) (1), (2), (3) and (4)
   (b) (1), (2) and (3)
   (c) (1), (2) and (4)
   (d) (2), (3) and (4)

9. Jean Piaget gave a theory of cognitive development of humans on the basis of his:
   (a) Fundamental Research
   (b) Applied Research
   (c) Action Research
   (d) Evaluation Research

10. "Male and female students perform equally well in a numerical aptitude test." This statement indicates a:
    (a) research hypothesis
    (b) null hypothesis
    (c) directional hypothesis
    (d) statistical hypothesis

11. The conclusions/findings of which type of research cannot be generalized to other situations?
    (a) Historical Research
    (b) Descriptive Research
    (c) Experimental Research
    (d) Causal Comparative Research

12. Which of the following steps are required to design a questionnaire?
    (1) Writing primary and secondary aims of the study.
    (2) Review of the current literature.
    (3) Prepare a draft of questionnaire.
    (4) Revision of the draft.

    Select the correct answer from the codes given below:

    (a) (1), (2) and (3)
    (b) (1), (3) and (4)
    (c) (2), (3) and (4)
    (d) (1), (2), (3) and (4)

Read the following passage carefully and answer questions 13 to 18.

Story telling is not in our genes. Neither it is an evolutionary history. It is the essence of what makes us Human.

Human beings progress by telling stories. One event can result in a great variety of stories being told about it. Sometimes those stories differ greatly. Which stories are picked up and repeated and which ones are dropped and forgotten often determines how we progress. Our history, knowledge and understanding are all the collections of the few stories that survive. This includes the stories that we tell each other about the future. And how the future will turn out depends partly, possibly largely, on which stories we collectively choose to believe.

Some stories are designed to spread fear and concern. This is because some story-tellers feel that there is a need to raise some tensions.

Some stories are frightening, they are like totemic warnings: "Fail to act now and we are all doomed." Then there are stories that indicate that all will be fine so long as we leave everything upto a few especially able adults. Currently, this trend is being led by those who call themselves "rational optimists". They tend to claim that it is human nature to compete and to succeed and also to profit at the expense of others. The rational optimists however, do not realize how humanity has progressed overtime through amiable social networks and how large groups work in less selfishness and in the process accommodate rich and poor, high and low alike. This aspect in story-telling is considered by the 'Practical Possibles', who sit between those who say all is fine and cheerful and be individualistic in your approach to a successful future, and those who ordain pessimism and fear that we are doomed.

What the future holds for us is which stories we hold on to and how we act on them.

Answer the following questions:

13. Our knowledge is a collection of:
    (a) all stories that we have heard during our life-time
    (b) some stories that we remember
    (c) a few stories that survive
    (d) some important stories
14. Story telling is:
    (a) an art
    (b) a science
    (c) in our genes
    (d) the essence of what makes us human
15. How the future will turn out to be, depends upon the stories?
    (a) We collectively choose to believe in
    (b) Which are repeatedly narrated
    (c) Designed to spread fear and tension
    (d) Designed to make prophecy
16. Rational optimists:
    (1) Look for opportunities.
    (2) Are sensible and cheerful.
    (3) Are selfishly driven.
    Identify the correct answer from the codes given below:
    (a) (1), (2) and (3) (b) (1) only
    (c) (1) and (2) only (d) (2) and (3) only
17. Humans become less selfish when:
    (a) they work in large groups
    (b) they listen to frightening stories
    (c) they listen to cheerful stories
    (d) they work in solitude
18. 'Practical Possibles' are the ones who:
    (a) follow Midway Path
    (b) are doom-mongers
    (c) are self-centred
    (d) are cheerful and carefree
19. Effectiveness of communication can be traced from which of the following?
    (1) Attitude surveys
    (2) Performance records
    (3) Students attendance
    (4) Selection of communication channel
    Select the correct answer from the codes given below:
    (a) (1), (2), (3) and (4)
    (b) (1), (2) and (3)
    (c) (2), (3) and (4)
    (d) (1), (2) and (4)
20. **Assertion (A):** Formal communication tends to be fast and flexible.
    Reason (R): Formal communication is a systematic and orderly flow of information.
    (a) Both (A) and (R) are correct and (R) is correct explanation of (A)
    (b) Both (A) and (R) are correct, but (R) is not correct explanation of (A)

(c) (A) is correct, but (R) is false
(d) (A) is false, but (R) is correct

21. Which of the following are the characteristic features of communication?
(1) Communication involves exchange of ideas, facts and opinions.
(2) Communication involves both information and understanding.
(3) Communication is a continuous process.
(4) Communication is a circular process.

Select the correct answer from the codes given below:
(a) (1), (2) and (3)
(b) (1), (2) and (4)
(c) (2), (3) and (4)
(d) (1), (2), (3) and (4)

22. The term 'grapevine' is also known as:
(a) Downward communication
(b) Informal communication
(c) Upward communication
(d) Horizontal communication

23. Which of the following is not a principle of effective communication?
(a) Persuasive and convincing dialogue
(b) Participation of the audience
(c) One-way transfer of information
(d) Strategic use of grapevine

24. In communication, the language is:
(a) The verbal code
(b) Intrapersonal
(c) The symbolic code
(d) The non-verbal code

25. The next term in the series is:
2, 5, 9, 19, 37, ?
(a) 73 (b) 75
(c) 78 (d) 80

26. In certain code MATHURA is coded as JXQEROX. The code of HOTELS will be:
(a) LEQIBP (b) ELQBIP
(c) LEBIQP (d) ELIPQB

27. One day Prakash left home and walked 10 km towards south, turned right and walked 5 km, turned right and walked 10 km and turned left and walked 10 km. How many km will he have to walk to reach his home straight?
(a) 10 (b) 20
(c) 15 (d) 30

28. A girl introduced a boy as the son of the daughter of the father of her uncle. The boy is related to the girl as
(a) Brother (b) Uncle
(c) Nephew (d) Son

29. In an examination 10,000 students appeared. The result revealed the number of students who have:
passed in all five subjects = 5583
passed in three subjects only = 1400
passed in two subjects only = 1200
passed in one subject only = 735
failed in English only = 75
failed in Physics only = 145
failed in Chemistry only = 140
failed in Mathematics only = 200
failed in Bio-science only = 157
The number of students passed in at least four subjects is:
(a) 6300 (b) 6900
(c) 7300 (d) 7900

30. At present a person is 4 times older than his son and is 3 years older than his wife. After 3 years the age of the son will be 15 years. The age of the person's wife after 5 years will be
(a) 42 (b) 48
(c) 45 (d) 50

31. If we want to seek new knowledge of facts about the world, we must rely on reason of the type:

(a) Inductive (b) Deductive
(c) Demonstrative (d) Physiological

32. A deductive argument is invalid if:
(a) Its premises and conclusions are all false
(b) Its premises are true but its conclusion is false
(c) Its premises are false but its conclusion is true
(d) Its premises and conclusions are all true

33. Inductive reasoning is grounded on:
(a) Integrity of nature
(b) Unity of nature
(c) Uniformity of nature
(d) Harmony of nature

34. Among the following statements two are contradictory to each other. Select the correct code that represents them:

Statements:
(1) All poets are philosophers.
(2) Some poets are philosophers.
(3) Some poets are not philosophers.
(4) No philosopher is a poet.

Codes:
(a) (1) and (2) (b) (1) and (4)
(c) (1) and (3) (d) (2) and (3)

35. Which of the codes given below contains only the correct statements? Select the code:

Statements:
(1) Venn diagram represents the arguments graphically.
(2) Venn diagram can enhance our understanding.
(3) Venn diagram may be called valid or invalid.
(4) Venn diagram is clear method of notation.

Codes:
(a) (1), (2) and (3) (b) (1), (2) and (4)
(c) (2), (3) and (4) (d) (1), (3) and (4)

36. When the purpose of a definition is to explain the use or to eliminate ambiguity the definition is called:
(a) Stipulative (b) Theoretical
(c) Lexical (d) Persuasive

Question numbers 37 to 42 are based on the tabulated data given below:

A company has 20 employees with their age (in years) and salary (in thousand rupees per month) mentioned against each of them:

S.No.	Age (in years)	Salary (in thousand rupees per month)
1.	44	35
2.	32	20
3.	54	45
4.	42	35
5.	31	20
6.	53	60
7.	42	50
8.	51	55
9.	34	25
10.	41	30
11.	33	30
12.	31	35
13.	30	35
14.	37	40
15.	44	45
16.	36	35
17.	34	35
18.	49	50
19.	43	45
20.	45	50

37. Classify the data of age of each employee in class interval of 5 years. Which class

interval of 5 years has the maximum average salary?
(a) 35-40 years (b) 40-45 years
(c) 45-50 years (d) 50-55 years

38. What is the frequency (%) in the class interval of 30-35 years?
(a) 20% (b) 25%
(c) 30% (d) 35%

39. What is the average age of the employees?
(a) 40.3 years (b) 38.6 years
(c) 47.2 years (d) 45.3 years

40. What is the fraction (%) of employees getting salary ≥ 40,000 per month?
(a) 45% (b) 50%
(c) 35% (d) 32%

41. What is the average salary (in thousand per month) in the age group 40-50 years?
(a) 35 (b) 42.5
(c) 40.5 (d) 36.5

42. What is the fraction of employees getting salary less than the average salary of all the employees?
(a) 45% (b) 50%
(c) 55% (d) 47%

43. Encoding or scrambling data for transmission across a network is known as:
(a) Protection (b) Detection
(c) Encryption (d) Decryption

44. Which of the following is not an output device?
(a) Printer (b) Speaker
(c) Monitor (d) Keyboard

45. Which of the following represents one billion characters?
(a) Kilobyte (b) Megabyte
(c) Gigabyte (d) Terabyte

46. Which of the following is not open source software?
(a) Internet explorer
(b) Fedora Linux
(c) Open office
(d) Apache HTTP server

47. Which one of the following represents the binary equivalent of the decimal number 25?
(a) 10101 (b) 01101
(c) 11001 (d) 11011

48. Which is an instant messenger that is used for chatting?
(a) Altavista (b) MAC
(c) Microsoft Office (d) Google Talk

49. In which of the countries per capita use of water is maximum?
(a) USA (b) European Union
(c) China (d) India

50. India's contribution to total global carbon dioxide emissions is about:
(a) ~ 3% (b) ~ 6%
(c) ~ 10% (d) ~ 15%

51. Two earthquakes A and B happen to be of magnitude 5 and 6 respectively on Richter Scale. The ratio of the energies released E_B/E_A will be approximately:
(a) ~ 8 (b) ~ 16
(c) ~ 32 (d) ~ 64

52. Which of the following combinations represent renewable natural resources?
(a) Fertile soil, fresh water and natural gas
(b) Clean air, phosphates and biological diversity
(c) Fishes, fertile soil and fresh water
(d) Oil, forests and tides

53. In the recently launched Air Quality Index in India, which of the following pollutants is not included?
(a) Carbon monoxide
(b) Fine particulate matter

(c) Ozone
(d) Chlorofluorocarbons

54. The factors which are most important in determining the impact of anthropogenic activities on environment are:
(a) Population, affluence per person, land available per person
(b) Population, affluence per person and the technology used for exploiting resources
(c) Atmospheric conditions, population and forest cover
(d) Population, forest cover and land available per person

55. The session of the parliament is summoned by:
(a) The President
(b) The Prime Minister
(c) The Speaker of the Lok Sabha
(d) The Speaker of the Lok Sabha and the Chairman of the Rajya Sabha

56. Civil Service Day is celebrated in India on:
(a) 21st April (b) 24th April
(c) 21st June (d) 7th July

57. The South Asia University is situated in the city of:
(a) Colombo (b) Dhaka
(c) New Delhi (d) Kathmandu

58. The University Grants Commission was established with which of the following aims?
(1) Promotion of research and development in higher education
(2) Identifying and sustaining institutions of potential learning
(3) Capacity building of teachers
(4) Providing autonomy to each and every higher educational institution in India
Select the correct answer from the codes given below:
(a) (1), (2), (3) and (4)
(b) (1), (2) and (3)
(c) (2), (3) and (4)
(d) (1), (2) and (4)

59. The Gross Enrolment Ratio (GER) in institutions of higher education in India at present (2015) is about:
(a) 8 percent (b) 12 percent
(c) 19 percent (d) 23 percent

60. The total number of central universities in India in April 2015 was:
(a) 08 (b) 14
(c) 27 (d) 43

ANSWERS

1. (d)	2. (c)	3. (b)	4. (b)	5. (d)
6. (d)	7. (d)	8. (b)	9. (a)	10. (b)
11. (c)	12. (b)	13. (c)	14. (d)	15. (a)
16. (d)	17. (a)	18. (a)	19. (d)	20. (d)
21. (d)	22. (b)	23. (c)	24. (a)	25. (b)
26. (b)	27. (c)	28. (a)	29. (a)	30. (d)
31. (d)	32. (b)	33. (c)	34. (b)	35. (b)
36. (b)	37. (d)	38. (b)	39. (a)	40. (a)
41. (b)	42. (c)	43. (c)	44. (d)	45. (c)
46. (a)	47. (c)	48. (d)	49. (a)	50. (b)
51. (c)	52. (c)	53. (d)	54. (c)	55. (a)
56. (a)	57. (c)	58. (b)	59. (c)	60. (d)

PAPER–II

Note: This paper contains fifty (50) objective type questions of two (2) marks each. All questions are compulsory.

1. Which of the following statement(s) is/are incorrect?

1. In Keshavananda Bharati case, the Supreme Court has said that the Preamble to the constitution is a key to open the mind of the makers.
2. "Socialist and Secular" words were added to the Preamble by 44th Amendment of the Constitution.
3. Preamble can only be amended if it violates the Basic Structure of the Constitution.
4. Since Preamble is not Articled so it is not the part of the Constitution.

Codes:

(a) only 2

(b) 3 and 4

(c) 1, 2 and 3

(d) 1, 2, 3 and 4 all are incorrect

2. Match List-I with List-II and give the correct answer by using the codes given below the Lists:

List-I

A. Article 329

B. 10th Schedule Part - 7

C. Article 31-C

D. Article 13(2)

List-II

(i) Golak Nath Vs. State of Punjab

(ii) Keshavananda Bharati Vs. State of Kerala

(iii) Indira Nehru Gandhi Vs. Raj Narain

(iv) Kihota Vs. Zachilhu

Codes:	(A)	(B)	(C)	(D)
(a)	(ii)	(i)	(iii)	(iv)
(b)	(iii)	(iv)	(ii)	(i)
(c)	(iv)	(iii)	(i)	(ii)
(d)	(i)	(ii)	(iv)	(iii)

3. "If I was asked to name any particular Article in this Constitution as the most important an Article without which this constitution would be a nullity I could not refer to any other Article except this one (Article 32).......... It is the soul of the Constitution and the very heart of it". Whose observations are these?

(a) Justice P.N. Bhagwati

(b) Dr. B.R. Ambedkar

(c) Justice V.R. Krishna Iyer

(d) Pandit Jawahar Lal Nehru

4. Which of the following statement(s) is/are incorrect?
   1. Chapter III on Fundamental Rights of the Constitution is based upon Bill of Rights of the U.S.A.
   2. 'Right to die' is a Fundamental Right Under Article 21 of the Constitution.
   3. Indian Constitution is a Complete Federal Constitution.
   4. Fundamental Rights can be waived under the Indian Constitution.

Codes:

(a) only 2 (b) 3 and 4 only

(c) 2 and 3 only (d) 2, 3 and 4

5. Match List-I with List-II and give the correct answer by using the codes given below the Lists:

List-I (Principles)

A. Equal work for Equal pay

B. "Agencies or Instrumentalition" of the State are covered under the definition of State Under Article 12 of the Constitution

C. Fundamental Rights and Directive Principles of state policy are supplementary and complimentary to each other

D. Damages can be awarded for violation of Fundamental Rights Under Article 21 of the Constitution

List-II (Case Law)

(i) R.D. Shetty Vs. The International Airport Authority of India

(ii) Rudal Sah Vs. State of Bihar
(iii) Randhir Singh Vs. Union of India
(iv) Unikrishnan Vs. State of A.P.

Codes:	(A)	(B)	(C)	(D)
(a)	(iii)	(i)	(iv)	(ii)
(b)	(i)	(ii)	(iii)	(iv)
(c)	(iv)	(iii)	(i)	(ii)
(d)	(ii)	(iv)	(iii)	(i)

6. Match List-I with List-II and give the correct answer by using the codes given under the Lists:

List-I (Added/Amended Provisions)

A. Article 15 clause (4) providing for special provisions for socially and educationally backward classes.
B. Article 13 clause (4) providing for nothing shall apply to any constitutional amendment.
C. Article 16 clause (4 A) providing for consequential seniority with promotion to SC/ST.
D. Article 21 A providing for Right to Education as Fundamental Right.

List-II (Amendment)

(i) 25th Amendment Act, 1971
(ii) Constitution (85th Amendment) Act, 2001
(iii) Constitution (86th Amendment) Act, 2002
(iv) Constitution (1st Amendment) Act, 1951

Codes:	(A)	(B)	(C)	(D)
(a)	(i)	(ii)	(iii)	(iv)
(b)	(iv)	(i)	(ii)	(iii)
(c)	(iii)	(iv)	(i)	(ii)
(d)	(ii)	(iii)	(iv)	(i)

7. **Assertion (A):** Powers and functions are distributed between the two tiers of government under the written Constitution in India.

Reason (R): Union and the States are completely independent of each other under the Indian Constitution.

Codes:

(a) (A) is correct and (R) is the correct explanation of (A).
(b) (A) is correct but (R) is not the correct explanation of (A).
(c) (A) is correct but (R) is wrong.
(d) (A) is wrong but (R) is correct.

8. Which of the following school in jurisprudence encompasses the 'functional approach'?
(a) Philosophical school
(b) Natural school
(c) Sociological school
(d) Historical school

9. A legal system which works to ensure a fair division of social benefits and burdens among the member of a community. It serves to secure a balance and equilibrium among the members of the society. What is the name of this legal system?
(a) Distributive justice
(b) Corrective justice
(c) Remedial justice
(d) Adversarial justice

10. Which of the following is not correct regarding Legislation and Precedent?
(a) Legislation reflects the formal will of the state and precedent has its source in judgement of court
(b) Legislation is the formal expression of new laws by legislature and precedent is the creation of law by recognition
(c) Legislation is general declaration of law in abstract form and precedent is the manifestation of law in action

(d) Legislations are based on the minority opinion and precedents are created or based for future decisions

11. Read Assertion (A) and Reason (R) and give the correct answer with the help of codes given below:

Assertion (A): A person in possession of a thing is deemed to be the owner of the thing possessed.

Reason (R): Possession is as good as ownership.

Codes:

(a) (A) and (R) are true, and (R) is the correct explanation of (A)
(b) (A) and (R) are true but (R) is not the correct explanation of (A)
(c) (A) is true but (R) is false
(d) (A) is false but (R) is true

12. Which of the following is not a 'kind of possession'?
(a) *De facto* and *De jure*
(b) Concurrent and duplicate
(c) Corporeal and Immediate
(d) Infinity and Antequity

13. Which of the following are elements of legal right?
(a) Responsibility, Liability and Power
(b) Subject, object and title
(c) Liability, title and Accountibility
(d) Accountibility, Responsibility and Impartiality

14. "International Law or the Law of Nations is the name of body of rules which according to the usual definitions regulate the conduct of the states in their intercourse with one another". Who has given this definition?
(a) Hack Warth (b) Charles G. Fenwick
(c) Gray (d) Whiteman

15. In which of the following cases the Parmanent Court of International Justice applied the general principle of Subrogation?
(a) Chorzow Factory (indemnity case)
(b) Case Concerning the Temple of Preah Vihear
(c) Bracelona Traction Case
(d) Mavrommatis Palestine Concessions Case

16. In which of the following cases Justice Gray remarked: "International law is a part of our law and must be ascertained and administered by the courts of justice of appropriate jurisdiction as often as questions of rights depending on it are duly presented for administration."
(a) Nicaragua Vs. U.S.
(b) Paquete Habana case
(c) U.S. Vs. Schooner
(d) U.S. Vs. Canada

17. Match List-I with List-II and give the correct answer by using the codes given below the Lists:

List-I (Charter of the United Nations) Titles

A. Membership
B. The Security Council
C. The International Court of Justice
D. The General Assembly

List-II (Number of the Chapter)

(i) Chapter XIV (ii) Chapter II
(iii) Chapter V (iv) Chapter IV

Codes:	**(A)**	**(B)**	**(C)**	**(D)**
(a)	(i)	(ii)	(iii)	(iv)
(b)	(ii)	(iii)	(iv)	(i)
(c)	(ii)	(iii)	(i)	(iv)
(d)	(iv)	(i)	(ii)	(iii)

18. Who has observed, "*De Facto* recognition is by nature provisional and may be made dependent upon conditions which the new entity has to comply. It differs from *De Jure* recognition, in that there is not yet a formal exchange of diplomatic representatives. *De Jure* recognition ....is complete, implying, full and normal diplomatic relations".
    (a) Lauterpacht (b) Philip C. Jessup
    (c) Oppenheim (d) Schwarzenberger

19. **Assertion (A):** International customs used to be the most important source of International Law in the past.
    Reason (R): The development of custom is very slow and as compared to it rapid changes made through Treaties.
    Codes:
    (a) Both (A) and (R) are correct and (R) is the correct explanation of (A)
    (b) Both (A) and (R) are correct but (R) is not the correct explanation of (A)
    (c) (A) is correct (R) is false
    (d) (A) is false (R) is correct

20. Marriage under the Hindu Marriage Act, 1955 is:
    (a) Purely contract
    (b) Purely sacramental
    (c) Semblance of contract and sacrament
    (d) Neither contract nor sacrament

21. Match the List-I with List-II under the Hindu Marriage Act, 1955 and give the correct answer with the help of codes given below:
    List-I
    A. Monogamy
    B. Judicial separation
    C. Void Marriage
    D. Divorce by Mutual Consent
    List-II
    (i) Section 10 (ii) Section 5
    (iii) Section 11 (iv) Section 13-B

Codes:	(A)	(B)	(C)	(D)
(a)	(ii)	(i)	(iii)	(iv)
(b)	(i)	(iii)	(iv)	(ii)
(c)	(ii)	(iii)	(iv)	(i)
(d)	(iv)	(iii)	(i)	(ii)

22. Which of the following are fault grounds of divorce under the Hindu Marriage Act, 1955?
    1. Extra marital sex
    2. Consent obtained by force or fraud
    3. Desertion
    4. Conversion to non Hindu religion
    Codes:
    (a) 1, 2 and 3 (b) 2, 3 and 4
    (c) 2, 1 and 4 (d) 1, 3 and 4

23. A Muslim male is prohibited from marrying the following relations:
    1. Mother, Grand mother (how high so ever)
    2. Daughter, Grand daughter (how low so ever)
    3. Aunt, Great aunt (how high so ever, whether paternal or maternal)
    4. Niece, Grand niece (how low so ever)
    Codes:
    (a) 1, 3 and 4 (b) 4, 2 and 1
    (c) 2, 3, 4 and 1 (d) 3, 2 and 4

24. The Dissolution of Muslim Marriage Act, 1939 makes available the following grounds of divorce to a Muslim woman married under Muslim Law:
    1. Seven years imprisonment of the husband.
    2. No maintenance by husband for 2 years.

3. Whereabouts of the husband are not known for a period of 4 years.
4. Failure of husband to perform marital obligation for a period of 3 years.

Codes:

(a) 3, 2 and 4 (b) 1, 2, 3 and 4
(c) 2, 3 and 1 (d) 1, 2 and 4

25. The ancient sources of Hindu Law include:
 1. Shruti
 2. Smriti
 3. Customs
 4. Digests and Commentaries

Codes:

(a) 2, 3 and 4 (b) 4, 1 and 2
(c) 1, 2 and 3 (d) 4, 3, 2 and 1

26. Originally under the Hindu Marriage Act, 1955, divorce was based on:
 (a) Fault theory only
 (b) Breakdown theory
 (c) Consent theory
 (d) Fault and consent theories

27. "A grocer supplied goods worth ₹ 6,000 on credit to A. In addition the grocer solicited a donation of ₹ 2,000 for his sons education to which A consented. Later A refused to pay both sums as he lost money on stock transaction". Which one of the following is correct while deciding the liability of A?
 1. A has already availed of the benefits in terms of goods supplied, hence consideration between the two binds A to pay.
 2. A is not bound to pay ₹ 2,000 as it a gift which is not enforceable in Law.
 3. A is liable to pay both Sums as it is a promise between A and grocer.
 4. A is not liable to pay either of the Sums as both of them are joint and not separate.

Codes:

(a) 1 and 2 (b) 1 and 3
(c) 2 and 4 (d) 3 and 4

28. "X makes an offer to Y. X dies the next day, but Y does not know of the death. Y sends a communication to the address of X accepting the offer". Is the agreement formed between the parties? Choose the correct answer.
 1. Requirements of offer followed by acceptance are met.
 2. Absence of knowledge of death will not invalidate the agreement.
 3. No meeting of minds which does not render it to agreement.
 4. Death of the offerer reduces it to nullity.

Codes:

(a) 1 and 3 (b) 1 and 2
(c) 3 and 4 (d) 2 and 4

29. Match items of Group-A with those of Group-B and choose the correct answer using codes:

Group-A

A. Food Corporation of India Vs. Ram Keshav Yadav
B. Kedar Nath Bhattacharji Vs. Gori Mohammed
C. K. Balakrishnan Vs. K. Kamalam
D. Satyabrata Goshe Vs. Mugneeram Bangar and Co.

Group-B

(i) Impossibility of performance
(ii) Capacity of minor to enter into contract
(iii) Offer and acceptance
(iv) Consideration

Codes:	**(A)**	**(B)**	**(C)**	**(D)**
(a)	(iv)	(ii)	(iii)	(i)
(b)	(iv)	(iii)	(ii)	(i)

(c)	(iii)	(iv)	(ii)	(i)
(d)	(i)	(ii)	(iii)	(iv)

30. Agreement without consideration is valid under Indian Law. Among the following statements choose the one which is against this rule:
    (a) When agreements written exist on account of natural love and affection.
    (b) When the consideration is too inadequate.
    (c) Where the consideration is past one.
    (d) Where the consideration is from third party.
31. Choose the incorrect combination:
    (a) Proposal + Acceptance = Promise
    (b) Promise + Consideration = Agreement
    (c) Agreement + Enforceability = Contract
    (d) Proposal + Consideration = Acknowledgment
32. Match items of Group-A with Group-B and answer the correct one given in the code:

    Group-A
    A. Doctrine of unjust enrichment
    B. Doctrine of absolute contract
    C. Doctrine of Estoppel
    D. Doctrine of Pari Delicto

    Group-B
    (i) Section 11 of Contract Act
    (ii) Section 56
    (iii) Section 72
    (iv) Section 23

Codes:	(A)	(B)	(C)	(D)
(a)	(i)	(iii)	(ii)	(iv)
(b)	(ii)	(iii)	(i)	(iv)
(c)	(iii)	(ii)	(i)	(iv)
(d)	(iv)	(ii)	(iii)	(i)

33. "Just as the criminal law consists of a body of rules establishing specific offence, so the law of torts consists of a body of rules establishing specific injuries". Who stated this?
    (a) Austin (b) Salmond
    (c) Winfield (d) Pollock
34. Consider the following elements:
    1. Infringement of a legal right
    2. Any damage
    3. Existence of a legal right
    4. Legal damages

    Right to claim damages in tort would arise only if:

    Codes:
    (a) 4, 2 and 1 are present
    (b) 2 and 4 are present
    (c) 1, 3 and 4 are present
    (d) 2, 3 and 1 are present
35. **Assertion (A):** X opens a food court in front of Y's 'food joint'. All the customers of Y patronise X. Y can not claim damages from X.
    Reason (R): There is a Latin maxim '*damnum sine injuria*'.
    Give the answer using the following Codes:

    Codes:
    (a) (A) is true but (R) is false
    (b) (A) is false but (R) is true
    (c) Both (A) and (R) are true but (R) is not the correct explanation of (A)
    (d) Both (A) and (R) are true and (R) is the correct explanation of (A)
36. In contributory negligence:
    (a) Only one party is negligent and other has not taken due care.
    (b) Both parties have contributed to negligence equally.
    (c) Lack of care is equal on both sides.
    (d) One party is negligent resulting in injury while the other has taken due care.

37. Match List-I with List-II and select the correct answer using the codes given below:

List-I (Principle)

A. Absolute Liability
B. *Damnum sine injuria*
C. *Injuria sine damnum*
D. Inevitable accident

List-II (Associated Case)

(i) Gloucester Grammar School
(ii) Ashby Vs. White
(iii) Stanely Vs. Powel
(iv) Ryland Vs. Fletcher

Codes:	(A)	(B)	(C)	(D)
(a)	(i)	(ii)	(iii)	(iv)
(b)	(ii)	(iii)	(iv)	(i)
(c)	(iv)	(ii)	(i)	(iii)
(d)	(iii)	(i)	(ii)	(iv)

38. Which one of the following is not a valid defence in tort?
(a) Vis major
(b) Volenti non fit injuria
(c) Inevitable accident
(d) *Scienti not fit injuria*

39. Fill in the gap:
The *actus reus* of omission commands.
(a) There must be moral duty.
(b) There should be legal duty to act.
(c) The state has option to fix criminal liability.
(d) The act performed is due to unavoidable accident.

40. Several persons can be vicariously liable for the Criminal act of another provided there is prior meeting of mind between the persons. Which of the objectives of Criminal Law is applied in such a Case?
(a) A pre-arranged plan with intention of performing the act.
(b) A pre-arranged plan for causing injury.
(c) A pre-arranged plan to kill the deceased whether fatal blow was given by that accused or not.
(d) The pre-arranged plan must be incompatible with the innocence of the accused.

41. The applicability of the principle on common object has two essential features. One purpose is that the object must import a high degree of probability; while the other purpose is:
(a) An act committed immediately connected to the common object of the assembly.
(b) The member must have prior knowledge that there is possibility of the happening of the act.
(c) The Co-accused knows that he will be responsible for offence that is likely to be committed.
(d) The object was to cause simple injury but a fatal injury resulted.

42. In which of the cases the measures of self-defence is considered to be proportionate to the quantum of force by the person accused for an offence?
(a) Aggression
(b) Accident
(c) Apprehension
(d) Assault of harmless nature

43. Ignorance of law does not permit acquittal as it is built against justification of a Crime while in extreme cases it allows:
(a) Pardon
(b) Suspended sentence
(c) Deferred sentence
(d) Paper sentence

44. In which of the circumstances an inchoate instigation to Commit a Crime is said to be incomplete?
   (a) Withdrew from the act after instigation.
   (b) The letter posted could not reach the person so sent.
   (c) When the purported crime is different from that of instigation.
   (d) When the crime results through the conspiracy of another person.

45. Read Assertion (A) and Reason (R) and answer using codes given below :
   Assertion (A): Managers collectively bargain with labourers to get cheapest labour rates and derive maximum benefit from labourers.
   Reason (R): Management must manage to maximise profits for company and give maximum dividend to shareholders. Management must be economically sound.
   Codes:
   (a) Both (A) and (R) are correct and (R) is correct reason of (A).
   (b) (A) is right, but (R) is wrong.
   (c) (A) is wrong, but (R) is right.
   (d) Both (A) and (R) are correct, but (R) is not the correct answer for (A).

46. An Independent Industrial Relation Commission to provide labour welfare in India was recommended by:
   (a) Ramanujam Committee
   (b) Madhavan Committee
   (c) Vasudevan Committee
   (d) Santhanam Committee

47. Match List-I with List-II, using codes given below. Answer in context of rights and liabilities of trade unions:
   List-I
   A. Convey Vs. Wade
   B. Rohtas Industries Staff Union Vs. Bihar
   C. Chairman, S.B.I. Vs. Orissa Bank Association
   D. Food Corporation of India Staff Union Vs. F.C.I.
   List-II
   (i) Role and right of minority trade unions
   (ii) Inducement to break a contract without violence is permissible
   (iii) Amplification of scope of immunity provisions for striking employees
   (iv) Secret ballot is valid as a credible system for determining the representative character of a trade union in a multi union establishment

Codes:	**(A)**	**(B)**	**(C)**	**(D)**
(a)	(iii)	(ii)	(i)	(iv)
(b)	(ii)	(iii)	(i)	(iv)
(c)	(iii)	(ii)	(iv)	(i)
(d)	(i)	(iv)	(ii)	(iii)

48. Read Assertion (A) and Reason (R) and answer using codes given below:
   Assertion (A): Civil servants are engaged in the task of sovereign and regal task of the Government and as such they can be included with the definition of 'workman' in an 'industry' as contemplated in Section 2(s) and 2(j) of the Industrial Disputes Act.
   Reason (R): Because Tamil Nadu, N.G.O. Union Vs. Registrar of Trade Unions decided so.
   Codes:
   (a) (A) and (R) are correct, and (R) is the correct reason of (A)
   (b) (A) and (R) are correct, but (R) is not the correct reason of (A)
   (c) (A) is correct, but (R) is wrong
   (d) Both (A) and (R) are incorrect

49. Which of the following statements, is correct?
   (a) A Trade Union cannot constitute a separate or political fund under Section 6(1) of the Trade Union Act.
   (b) The general fund of a trade union cannot be utilised for the purpose stipulated in Section 15 of Trade Union Act.
   (c) Trade Unions are not immune from civil and criminal liability.
   (d) Certain officers of trade union, who are styled as protected workmen, are given certain safeguards in the matter of alteration of service conditions and termination of service during the pendency of any proceeding in respect of an industrial dispute.

50. Which of the following is incorrect?
   (a) An Employee having less than one year of continuous service will not be retrenched.
   (b) One months notice with reasons and one months wages in lieu of such notice is necessary.
   (c) Employee is entitled to compensation equivalent to 15 days average pay for every completed one year.
   (d) Serving of notice to appropriate Government or any such authority is not mandatory.

ANSWERS

1. (d)	2. (b)	3. (b)	4. (d)	5. (a)
6. (b)	7. (c)	8. (c)	9. (a)	10. (d)
11. (c)	12. (d)	13. (b)	14. (c)	15. (d)
16. (b)	17. (c)	18. (d)	19. (b)	20. (c)
21. (a)	22. (d)	23. (c)	24. (b)	25. (d)
26. (a)	27. (a)	28. (b)	29. (b)	30. (b)
31. (d)	32. (c)	33. (b)	34. (c)	35. (d)
36. (a)	37. (b)	38. (d)	39. (b)	40. (c)
41. (a)	42. (b)	43. (a)	44. (c)	45. (c)
46. (a)	47. (b)	48. (d)	49. (d)	50. (d)

PAPER–III

Note: This paper contains seventy-five (75) objective type questions of two (2) marks each. All questions are compulsory.

1. Through 42nd Amendment to the constitution which of the following 'Expressions' were added to the Preamble?
   1. Sovereign   2. Socialist
   3. Secular   4. Integrity

   Codes:
   (a) Only 1, 2 and 3 (b) Only 2, 3 and 4
   (c) Only 1, 3 and 4 (d) 1, 2, 3 and 4

2. Match List-I with List-II and give the correct answer by using the codes given below the lists:

   List-I
   A. Compensation to persons killed in "Fake Encounter"
   B. Compensation to Rape Victims
   C. Interim Compensation to Rape Victims
   D. Protection against illegal arrest, detentions and custodial deaths.

   List-II
   (i) Delhi Domestic working women's forum v. Union of India
   (ii) Bodhisathwa Gautam v. Shubhra Chakraborty
   (iii) People's Union for Civil liberties v. Union of India
   (iv) Joginder Kumar v. State of U.P.

Codes:	(A)	(B)	(C)	(D)
(a)	(iv)	(iii)	(ii)	(i)
(b)	(iii)	(i)	(ii)	(iv)
(c)	(ii)	(iv)	(i)	(iii)
(d)	(i)	(ii)	(iii)	(iv)

3. Match List-I with List-II and give the correct answer by using the codes given below the Lists:

List-I

A. Right to speak includes Right not to speak

B. Government has no monopoly on electronic Media

C. Commercial Advertisement is part of Freedom of Speech and Expression

D. Government cannot impose prior restraint on publication of defamatory material against its officials

List-II

(i) R. Rajagopal v. State of T.N.

(ii) Tata Press Ltd. v. Mahanagar Telephone Nigam Ltd.

(iii) Secretary, Ministry I and B v. Cricket Association of Bengal (W.B.)

(iv) Bijjoe Emmanuel v. State of Kerala

Codes:	(A)	(B)	(C)	(D)
(a)	(iv)	(iii)	(ii)	(i)
(b)	(iii)	(ii)	(i)	(iv)
(c)	(i)	(iv)	(iii)	(ii)
(d)	(ii)	(i)	(iv)	(iii)

4. Which of the following statement/ statements is/are correct?

1. Fundamental Rights are not absolute. They are subject to reasonable restrictions.
2. Freedom of Press is implict in Article 19 of the Constitution.
3. Socially and economically backward classes of persons are entitled to get benefit under clause (4) of Article 15 of the Constitution.
4. 'Equal protection of laws' under Article 14 of the constitution is based upon English law.

Codes:

(a) Only 1 and 2 are correct

(b) 1, 2 and 3 are correct

(c) 3 and 4 are correct

(d) 1, 2, 3, 4 all are correct

5. Match List-I with List-II and give the correct answer by using the codes given below the lists:

List-I

A. Parliamentary Form of Government

B. Directive Principles of State Policy

C. Fundamental Rights

D. Emergency Provisions

List-II

(i) The U.S.A. Constitution

(ii) German Constitution

(iii) United Kingdom Constitution

(iv) Constitution of Ireland

Codes:	(A)	(B)	(C)	(D)
(a)	(iv)	(iii)	(i)	(ii)
(b)	(iii)	(iv)	(i)	(ii)
(c)	(i)	(ii)	(iii)	(iv)
(d)	(ii)	(i)	(iv)	(iii)

6. In which of the following cases the Supreme Court held that Art. 31-c was beyond the amending power of the parliament and was void since it destroyed the basic features of the constitution. The court observed that the constitution is founded on the bed rock of the balance between Part III and Part IV. To give absolute primary to one over the other is to disturb the harmony of the constitution which is essential feature of the Basic Structure.

(a) Minerva Mills v. Union of India

(b) In Re Kerala Education Bill Case

(c) Keshavananda Bharati v. State of Kerala
(d) Sarla Mudgal v. Union of India

7. Match List-I with List-II and give the correct answer by using the codes given below the lists:

List-I
A. Original Jurisdiction of the supreme court
B. Advisory Jurisdiction
C. Appeal by Special leave
D. Appellate Jurisdiction

List-II
(i) Article 143 (ii) Article 136
(iii) Article 132 (iv) Article 131

Codes:	(A)	(B)	(C)	(D)
(a)	(ii)	(iii)	(iv)	(i)
(b)	(i)	(ii)	(iii)	(iv)
(c)	(iv)	(i)	(ii)	(iii)
(d)	(iii)	(iv)	(i)	(ii)

8. Which of the following statement/ statements is/are correct?
   1. Predominance is given to the Union List Under Article 246 (1) of the Constitution
   2. Residuary powers are given to states under the Indian Constitution
   3. "Pith and Substance" means the true object of the legislation or a statute
   4. "Colourable Legislation" means "what you can do directly you can also do indirectly"

Codes:
(a) Only 1 and 3 are correct
(b) 1, 2 and 3 are correct
(c) 2, 3 and 4 are correct
(d) 1, 2, 3 and 4 all are correct

9. Administrative law primarily does not concern itself with which of the official functions?
(a) Rule - making
(b) Rule - application
(c) Quasi - judicial action
(d) Private law

10. Which of the following is not an exception to the principles of natural justice?
(a) Impracticability
(b) Legislative action
(c) Rule against dictation
(d) Statutory necessity

11. Match the List-I with List-II using codes given below:

List-I
A. Ram Jawaya Kapur v. State of Punjab
B. Maneka Gandhi v. Union of India
C. Vineet Narain v. Union of India
D. Union of India v. Hindustan Development Corporation

List-II
(i) Doctrine of post decisional hearing
(ii) Doctrine of public accountability
(iii) Doctrine of separation of powers
(iv) Doctrine of legitimate expectation

Codes:	(A)	(B)	(C)	(D)
(a)	(iii)	(i)	(ii)	(iv)
(b)	(iv)	(ii)	(i)	(iii)
(c)	(i)	(iv)	(iii)	(ii)
(d)	(i)	(ii)	(iii)	(iv)

12. Read Assertion (A) and Reason (R) and answer using the codes given below:
Assertion (A): It is true that in any intensive form of government, the government can not function without the exercise of some discretion by its official.
Reason (R): Giving discretion to government officials is necessary for the welfare of people.

Codes:
(a) (A) and (R) are right and (R) is the right reason for (A)

(b) (A) and (R) are right but (R) is not the correct explanation of (A)
(c) (A) is right but (R) is wrong
(d) Both (A) and (R) are wrong

13. Which of the following is correct in relation to the functioning of the institution of *Lokayukta* in Indian States?
(a) Provided with independent investigating agency
(b) They have not been given constitutional status
(c) Prosecution and final punishment power vested with them
(d) Their decision are final and not recommendentary in nature

14. Which of the following is not considered 'irrational', basing upon the *Wednesburg* principles laid down in *Associated Provincial Picture House Ltd.* V. *Wednesburg Corporation*, 1948 (KB)?
(a) Without the authority of law
(b) Based on no evidence
(c) It has sanction of law
(d) It is unreasonable

15. On which of the following ground writ of *certiosari* cannot be issued?
(a) Abuse of jurisdiction
(b) Exercise of jurisdiction
(c) Violation of principles of natural justice
(d) Error of law apparent on the face of the record

16. Which of the following is not a jural postulate of the legal system of a society as propounded by Roscoe Pound. So in a civilized society men must be able to assume:
(a) That these will be no intentional aggression
(b) That members of society will act in good faith
(c) That people will control for their beneficial use, what they have created
(d) That people will cause injury to others during their course of work

17. Who said that customs are superior to the legislation. Therefore legislations should not abrogate the customs rather synthesize them with the common consciousness of the people and society?
(a) Henry Maine (b) H.L.A. Hart
(c) Savigny (d) Hans Kelson

18. Who among the following is not the exponent of Philosophical school?
(a) Hegel (b) Kant
(c) Puchta (d) Holland

19. According to Honfield table of jural relations the jural correlative of right is duty. What are the jural correlatives of Liberty, Power and Immunity respectively?
(a) No claim, Liability and Power
(b) No claim, Responsibility and Liability
(c) No claim, Duty and Liberty
(d) No claim, Liability and Disability

20. 'The limits of jurisprudence defined' was published in 1945. It was written in 1782 by
(a) Bentham (b) Blackstone
(c) Hobbes (d) Locke

21. Who among the following has not associated his theory of the state with 'Social Contract'?
(a) Hobbes (b) Locke
(c) Henry Maine (d) Rousseau

22. Read Assertion (A) and Reason (R) and give the correct answer with the help of codes given below:
Assertion (A): Criminal is a victim of circumstances, he is sick so he requires treatment.

Reason (R): Prison reforms and juvenile schools are established to reform the criminals.

Codes:

(a) (A) and (R) are true and (R) is the correct explanation of (A).

(b) (A) and (R) are true but (R) is not the correct explanation of (A).

(c) (A) is true but (R) is false.

(d) (A) is false but (R) is true.

23. Match List-I with List-II using the codes below:

List-I

A. Right of a person not to be assaulted

B. Right of a person in his own property

C. Right of a person to enjoy his premises

D. Right of a person in the property of some one else

List-II

(i) Right in re-propria

(ii) Right in rem

(iii) Right in personam

(iv) Right in re-aliena

Codes:	(A)	(B)	(C)	(D)
(a)	(ii)	(i)	(iii)	(iv)
(b)	(iv)	(iii)	(i)	(ii)
(c)	(i)	(ii)	(iv)	(iii)
(d)	(iii)	(iv)	(ii)	(i)

24. Read the following situations and state which combination is correct to claim benefit under the broard concept of unsoundness of mind:

1. Extreme Anger
2. Somnambulism
3. Irresistible impulse
4. Hallucination

Codes:

(a) 1 and 2 both (b) 1 and 3 both

(c) 2 and 3 both (d) 1 and 4 both

25. Read the following situations and choose the correct one, where right of private defence is available:

(a) Against an act done or attempted to be done by a public servant

(b) Where there is time available to have recourse to state authorities

(c) Where there is a reasonable apprehension of causing injury to third person

(d) Where harm caused in no case should exceed the quantum of harm

26. Match cases from Group-A with relevant legal provisions from Group-B and find the correct answer:

Group-A

A. K.N. Mehra v. State of Rajasthan

B. Aruna Ramchand Shanbaugh v. Union of India

C. State (NCT of Delhi) v. Navjot Sandhu @ Afsana Guru

D. Versa Singh v. State of Punjab

Group-B

(i) Section 300 (ii) Section 120-A

(iii) Section 309 (iv) Section 378

Codes:	(A)	(B)	(C)	(D)
(a)	(i)	(iii)	(iv)	(ii)
(b)	(i)	(iii)	(ii)	(iv)
(c)	(iv)	(iii)	(ii)	(i)
(d)	(iii)	(iv)	(ii)	(i)

27. Criminal Law (Amendment) Act, 2013 seems to have determined quantum of punishment proportionate to the severity of offence. Following are two sets of offences and punishment. Match the correct ones and give appropriate answer using the code.

Offences

A. Voluntarily causing grevious hurt by acid attack

B. Stalking
C. Gang rape
D. Sexual intercourse by husband upon his wife during separation

Maximum Punishment

(i) Life imprisonment (Remainder of the period of life)
(ii) 3 years
(iii) Life imprisonment and fine
(iv) 7 years and fine

Codes:	(A)	(B)	(C)	(D)
(a)	(ii)	(iii)	(i)	(iv)
(b)	(iii)	(ii)	(i)	(iv)
(c)	(i)	(ii)	(iii)	(iv)
(d)	(i)	(iii)	(ii)	(iv)

28. X a servant committed theft of Mobile phone of his master M and ran away from home. While travelling the said mobile phone was taken away by Y a co-traveller without the knowledge of X. Decide the liability of Y, choose correct one among the following:
(a) Criminal misappropriation as the phone was lying on the seat of X.
(b) Criminal Breach of Trust-as they were co-travellers
(c) Theft-as property in possession of X was taken without his consent
(d) Chealing as the method adopted was dubious

29. Certain factors are essential to get Extortion converted to Robbery. Following are a few given factors, Choose the one which is not required for the said conversion:
(a) Dishonesty
(b) Removal of property from the possession of another, by putting him in fear
(c) It is immaterial whether the person putting another in fear must be in the immediate presence or far away
(d) Such fear should result in the delivery of property

30. "There are two facets to the definition of dishonesty and it is sufficient to establish the existence of any one of them. There is no requirement in Law to establish both."
Choose the correct case among the following in which the above statement of Supreme Court has been laid down as ratio.
(a) Tulsi Ram v. State of Uttar Pradesh
(b) Hari Sao v. State of Bihar
(c) Gurdatta Mal v. State of Uttar Pradesh
(d) State of Bihar v. Nathu Pandey

31. Following are given some Provisions of Law (IPC). Choose the odd one out.
(a) Section 149 (b) Section 141
(c) Section 34 (d) Section 147

32. Which one of the following institutions gave suggestion for imposing environmental tax?
(a) Amnesty International
(b) World Water Institute
(c) UNESCO
(d) United Nations

33. Under the Environment (Protection) Act, the term 'environment' does not include :
(a) Water, air and land
(b) Inter-relationship which exists between water, air and land, and human beings
(c) Inter-relationship which exists between water, air and land, and plants
(d) Environment at work place

34. Match List-I with List-II and select the correct answer using the codes given below:

List-I

A. Power of Central Government to take measures to protect and improve environment

B. Constitution of central Pollution Control Board

C. Power of Central Government to make rules to regulate environmental pollution

D. Gaseous or liquid pollutants in the atmosphere injurious to human beings

List-II

(i) Section 6 of Environment (Protection) Act

(ii) Section 3 of Environment (Protection) Act

(iii) Section 6 of the Water (Prevention and control of Pollution) Act

(iv) Section 2(a) of the Air (Prevention and Control of Pollution) Act

Codes:	**(A)**	**(B)**	**(C)**	**(D)**
(a)	(i)	(iii)	(iv)	(ii)
(b)	(ii)	(iv)	(i)	(iii)
(c)	(ii)	(iii)	(i)	(iv)
(d)	(iii)	(iv)	(ii)	(i)

35. Match List-I with List-II and select the correct answer using the codes given below:

List-I

A. Rylands v. Fletcher

B. Indian Council for Environment Legal Action v. Union of India

C. Vellore Citizens Welfare Forum v. Union of India

D. M.C. Mehta v. Kamal Nath

List-II

(i) Principle of public trust for ecological protection

(ii) Precautionary Principle

(iii) Principle of Polluter pays

(iv) Principle of strict liability

Codes:	**(A)**	**(B)**	**(C)**	**(D)**
(a)	(iv)	(iii)	(ii)	(i)
(b)	(i)	(ii)	(iv)	(iii)
(c)	(ii)	(iv)	(iii)	(i)
(d)	(i)	(ii)	(iii)	(iv)

36. Which one of the following statements is incorrect?

(a) The Public Liability Insurance Act was enacted to provide immediate relief to the victims of an accident involving a hazardous substance

(b) The Public Liability Insurance Act imposes 'no fault' liability upon the owner of the hazardous substance and requires the owner to compensate the victims irrespective of any neglect or default on his part

(c) The Public Liability Insurance Act, does not provide for maximum compensation for injury or death of the victims

(d) The Public Liability Insurance Act obligates every owner to take out an insurance policy covering potential liability from an accident

37. Read Assertion (A) and Reason (R) and answer using codes given below:

Assertion (A): Polluter pays principle means polluters should internalise the costs of their pollution, control it at its source, and pay for its effects, including remedial or cleanup costs, rather than forcing other states or future generations to bear such costs.

Reasons (R): Vellore citizen's welfare forum Vs. Union of India decided so.

Codes:

(a) (A) is right but (R) is wrong

(b) Both (A) and (R) are right and (R) is the correct reason of (A)
(c) Both (A) and (R) are wrong
(d) Both (A) and (R) are right but (R) is not the correct reason of (A)

38. Match List-I with List-II and select the correct answer using the codes given below:

List-I

A. Rural Litigation and Entitlement Kendra, Dehradun v. State of Uttar Pradesh
B. Samatha v. State of Andhra Pradesh
C. K.V. Shanmugam vs. State of Tamil Nadu
D. State of Himachal Pradesh v. Ganesh Wood Products

List-II

(i) Grant of a lease of land or its renewal without the approval of the central government is void
(ii) Balancing environmental and ecological integrity against industrial demands on forest resources.
(iii) Renewal of lease on forest land is not a vested right
(iv) Forest-based industries donot have an absolute or an unrestricted right to operate their units where forest resources are scarce.

Codes:	**(A)**	**(B)**	**(C)**	**(D)**
(a)	(ii)	(iii)	(i)	(iv)
(b)	(i)	(iv)	(ii)	(iii)
(c)	(ii)	(iii)	(iv)	(i)
(d)	(i)	(ii)	(iii)	(iv)

39. Who of the following has remarked that International law is a "Living and Expanding Code"?

(a) Judge Alvarez
(b) Lord Chancellor Sankey
(c) J.G. Starke
(d) Prof. Lissitzyn

40. Which of the following statement/ statements is/are incorrect?

1. Long duration is an essential element for International Custom
2. The custom should he completely uniform and consistent to be an International custom
3. In an International custom, Universality of pratice is not necessary, the pratice should have been generally observed or repeated by numerous states.
4. *Opinio Juris* is present, that is to say, customary pratice to be a International Custom, must be recognised as being required by International law.

Codes:

(a) Only 1 is incorrect
(b) Only 1 and 2 are incorrect
(c) 2, 3 and 4 are incorrect
(d) 1, 2, 3, 4 all are incorrect

41. Match List-I with List-II and give the correct answer by using the codes given below the lists:

List-I (Topics)

A. Sources of International law
B. Recognition
C. Extradition
D. Asylum

List-II (Related Cases)

(i) Haya Dela Torra Case
(ii) Re Castioni Case
(iii) The Arantzazu Mendi Case
(iv) United States V. Schooner

Codes:	**(A)**	**(B)**	**(C)**	**(D)**
(a)	(iv)	(iii)	(ii)	(i)
(b)	(iii)	(ii)	(iv)	(i)

(c)	(iv)	(iii)	(i)	(ii)
(d)	(ii)	(iv)	(iii)	(i)

42. Which one of the following cases is not a case decided by permanent court of International Justice?
    (a) Movrommatis Palestine Concessions Case
    (b) S.S. Wimbledon Case
    (c) Anglo Norwegian Fisheries Case
    (d) Chorzow Factory (Indemnity) Case

43. Read both statements (A) and (R) and give the correct answer by using the codes given below:

    Assertion (A): By the term 'Asylum' we generally mean the shelter and active protection which is extended to a political refugee from another state, by a state which admits him on his request.

    Reason (R): Everyone has a right to seek and enjoy in other countries, an asylum from prosecution.

    Codes:
    (a) Both (A) and (R) are correct and (R) is the correct explanation of (A)
    (b) Both (A) and (R) are correct but (R) is not correct explanation of (A)
    (c) (A) is correct but (R) is wrong
    (d) (A) is wrong but (R) is correct

44. Which of the following is the only Principal organ of the UNO which consists of all the Members of United Nations?
    (a) Security Council
    (b) General Assembly
    (c) The Economic and Social Council
    (d) Trusteeship Council

45. Match List-I with List-II and give the correct answer by using the codes given below:

    List-I (Provisions)
    A. Suspension of Members
    B. Veto Power
    C. Appointment of Secretary General
    D. Composition of Trusteeship Council

    List-II (Articles of U.N. Charter)
    (i) Article 5 (ii) Article 97
    (iii) Article 27 (iv) Article 86

Codes:	**(A)**	**(B)**	**(C)**	**(D)**
(a)	(i)	(iii)	(ii)	(iv)
(b)	(iv)	(iii)	(ii)	(i)
(c)	(iii)	(ii)	(iv)	(i)
(d)	(ii)	(i)	(iii)	(iv)

46. Which is not the official language of the United Nations?
    (a) Russian (b) Japenese
    (c) Spanish (d) Arabic

47. The offence of bigamy is not committed under the Hindu Marriage Act, 1955 if a person marries during life time of his or her spouse provided:
    1. The first marriage is null and void
    2. The first marriage was performed without ceremonies
    3. The first marriage is voidable and decree annulling it has not been passed
    4. The first marriage is valid

    Codes:
    (a) 1 and 3 (b) 1 and 2
    (c) 2 and 3 (d) 2 and 4

48. A marriage under the Hindu Marriage Act, 1955 must be solemnised in accordance with the customary rites and ceremonies of:
    (a) The bridegroom.
    (b) The bride.
    (c) Either bride or bridegroom.
    (d) Both bride and bridegroom.

49. The absence of witnesses make a Muslim marriage:
   (a) Irregular under Sunni law, but void under Shia law.
   (b) Irregular under Sunni and Shia Law.
   (c) Valid under Sunni law but irregular under Shia law.
   (d) Valid under Shia law, but irregular under Sunni law.

50. Section 14 of the Hindu Marriage Act, 1955 enacts a 'fair trial' rule, according to which a person:
   (a) Can petition for divorce within one year of marriage
   (b) Cannot petition for divorce within one year of marriage except in exceptional cases
   (c) Cannot petition for judicial separation within one year of marriage
   (d) Can petition for restitution of Conjugal Rights within one year of marriage

51. With the help of codes given below mark the incorrect statement in the light of the Hindu Adoptions and Maintenance Act, 1956:
   1. Permission of the court is not necessary except when guardian gives the child in adoption.
   2. An adoption once made is revocable by natural parents only.
   3. Mother may give the child in adoption with the consent of father.
   4. Performance of 'datta homam' ceremony is essential for a valid adoption.

   Codes:
   (a) 3 and 4 (b) 4 and 2
   (c) 2 and 3 (d) 1 and 4

52. Abstinence from sexual intercourse for a period of not less than four months persuant to a vow is called:
   (a) Divorce in hasan form
   (b) Divorce in ahsan form
   (c) Divorce by Zihar
   (d) Divorce of Ila

53. In which of the following cases the Supreme Court of India has not addressed the issue of Uniform Civil Code:
   (a) Sarla Mudgal v. Union of India
   (b) John Vallamattom v. Union of India
   (c) Romesh Chander v. Savitri
   (d) John Deingdeh v. S.S. Chopra

54. Answer using the following codes:
   A Hindu wife is entitled to claim maintenance from her husband under the provisions of the Hindu Adoption and Maintenance Act, 1956 if:
   1. She is unchaste but living with her husband
   2. She is unchaste but not living with her husband
   3. She is living separate on any ground mentioned under section 18(2) of the Act.
   4. She has converted to Muslim religion

   Codes:
   (a) 1 and 3 (b) 1 and 2
   (c) 2 and 3 (d) 3 and 4

55. Which of the following statement is wrong? Answer using codes given below:
   1. Human Rights are essentially a product of bureaucracy.
   2. Human Rights are a reaction to tyranny
   3. Primitive man could move all over world, without any restriction
   4. All women are born free, but everywhere they are in chains.

   Codes:
   (a) 1 (b) 2
   (c) 3 (d) 4

56. Read Assertion (A) and Reason (R) and answer using codes given below:

Assertion (A): In the exercise of his rights and freedoms, no one shall be subjected only for such limitations as are determined by law solely for the purpose of securing due recognition and respect for the rights and freedoms of others, and of meeting the just requirements of morality, public order, and the general welfare in a democratic society.

Reason (R): Because Article 29(2) of the Universal Declaration of Human Rights states so.

Codes:

(a) Both (A) and (R) are right and (R) is correct reason of (A)
(b) (A) is right, but (R) is wrong
(c) (A) is wrong, but (R) is right
(d) Both (A) and (R) are wrong

57. Section 3 of the protection of Civil Rights Act, 1955 prescribes punishment for:

(a) Enforcing economic disabilities
(b) Civil disobedience
(c) Enforcing religions disabilities
(d) Enforcing political disabilities

58. Article 6 of the Universal Declaration of Human Rights provides for:

(a) Right to life
(b) Prohibition of slavery
(c) Right to be recognised as a person before law
(d) Equality before law

59. Match List-I with List-II in the light of Geneva Convention Relating to the Treatment of Prisoners of War, using codes given below:

List-I

A. Categories of Prisoners to be treated as prisoner of war
B. Prisoners of war to be humanly treated
C. No physical or mental torture
D. Escape of prisoner of war

List-II

(i) Article 13 (ii) Article 91
(iii) Article 4 (iv) Article 17

Codes:	**(A)**	**(B)**	**(C)**	**(D)**
(a)	(i)	(iii)	(ii)	(iv)
(b)	(i)	(iii)	(iv)	(ii)
(c)	(iii)	(i)	(ii)	(iv)
(d)	(iii)	(i)	(iv)	(ii)

60. Match List-I with List-II in the light of Human Rights under the constitution of India.

List-I (Case Law)

A. East Coast Railway v. Madhav Appa Rao
B. L.I.C. v. Professor Manubhai D. Shah
C. Vakil Prasad Singh v. State of Bihar
D. Aruna Roy v. Union of India

List-II (Principles)

(i) Freedom of expression
(ii) Equality
(iii) Religious instructions
(iv) Speedy trial

Codes:	**(A)**	**(B)**	**(C)**	**(D)**
(a)	(ii)	(i)	(iv)	(iii)
(b)	(i)	(ii)	(iv)	(iii)
(c)	(i)	(ii)	(iii)	(iv)
(d)	(ii)	(i)	(iii)	(iv)

61. State of Kerala v. N.M. Thomas is about:

(a) Religious minorities
(b) Linguistic minorities
(c) Area wise reservation
(d) Backward class

62. The main aims of law of tort are:

1. Punishment
2. Deterrence to wrong doers

3. Restoration of original position
4. Damages to victims

Codes:

(a) 1 and 3 (b) 3 and 2
(c) 2 and 4 (d) 3 and 4

63. The 'Absolute Liability' theory on the basis of pollution causing industrial injuries was propounded by:
(a) V.R. Krishna Iyer, J.
(b) P.N. Bhagwati, C.J.
(c) Kuldip Singh, J.
(d) M.N. Venkatachaliah, C.J.

64. Defence of absolute privilege in case of defamation is available in which of the following cases:
1. Parliamentary Proceedings
2. Publication of matters of Public interest
3. State of Communications
4. Judicial Proceedings

Codes:

(a) 1, 2 and 3 (b) 2, 3 and 4
(c) 1, 2 and 4 (d) 4, 3 and 1

65. The essential ingredients of the tort of negligence are:
1. One owes a duty of care towards the other
2. One commits a breach of that duty
3. The other person suffers damage as a consequence there of

Choose your correct answer with the help of codes given below:

Codes:

(a) Only the first is an essential ingredient
(b) None of them is an essential ingredient
(c) All of them are essential ingredients
(d) Even if the first is absent the tort of negligence is committed

66. Negligence is failure in duty of taking due care. The expression 'duty' means:
(a) A legal duty
(b) A legal as well as moral duty
(c) A legal as well as social duty
(d) A specific legal duty

67. There is no qualitative difference between a medical practitioner and an advocate,... from the point of view of his status, duties and regulatory control by a statutory body. Hence, there is no reason why the legal practitioner should be excluded from the purview of consumer protection Act.
From the following choose the correct decission in which it has been held:
(a) K. Vishnu v. National Consumer Dispute Redressal Commission and others
(b) Joshi v. Motor Industries Co.
(c) Charan Sing v. Healing Touch Hospital
(d) Arvind Mills Ltd. v. Associated Roadways

68. Read Assertion (A) and Reason (R) and answer using codes below:
Assertion (A): Consumer Act is made to simplify the procedure and avoid the complexity so that an oridinary citizen can file a complaint without a difficulty.
Reason (R): It intends to protect a large body of consumers from exploitation.

Codes:

(a) (A) and (R) are right and (R) is the right reason for (A)
(b) Both (A) and (R) are wrong
(c) (A) is right and (R) is wrong
(d) (R) is right and (A) is wrong

69. Which are essentials of sale of goods? Answer using codes given below:

1. Contractual capacity
2. Bilateral contract
3. Profit for seller
4. Mutual and free consent of parties to the contract of sale of goods

Codes:

(a) 1, 2, 3 (b) 1, 2, 4
(c) 2, 3, 4 (d) 1, 3, 4

70. Read Assertion (A) and Reason (R) and answer using codes given below:
Assertion (A): Every partner is an agent of the other partner.
Reason (R): Partnership is agency.

Codes:

(a) Both (A) and (R) are wrong
(b) (A) is right, but (R) is wrong
(c) (A) is wrong, but (R) is right
(d) Both (A) and (R) are right and (R) is correct reason of (A)

71. Match List-I with List-II and select the correct answer using the code given below:

List-I

A. Instalment Supply Ltd. v. STO
B. Gardiner v. Gray
C. Peter Darlington Partners Ltd. v. Gesho Co. Ltd.
D. Farquharson Bros v. King and Co.

List-II

(i) Conditions applied by trade usage
(ii) *Nemo dat quo non habet*
(iii) Sale by description
(iv) Difference between sale and agreement to sale

Codes:	(A)	(B)	(C)	(D)
(a)	(iii)	(iv)	(ii)	(i)
(b)	(iii)	(iv)	(i)	(ii)
(c)	(iv)	(iii)	(i)	(ii)
(d)	(iv)	(iii)	(ii)	(i)

72. Which one statement is correct from the following statements?
(a) A director of a company as a director is a servant of the company
(b) A director is an agent of his company
(c) A director is not a fiduciary person of his company
(d) A director is master of his company

73. Match List-I with List-II and select the correct answer using codes given below: Answer in context of the Negotiable Instruments Act.

List-I

A. Time and place for presentment
B. Cheques are payable in demand
C. Holder of a negotiable instrument
D. Fictitious drawer or payee

List-II

(i) Section 19 (ii) Section 8
(iii) Section 61 (iv) Section 42

Codes:	(A)	(B)	(C)	(D)
(a)	(i)	(iv)	(ii)	(iii)
(b)	(iii)	(ii)	(iv)	(i)
(c)	(ii)	(iii)	(iv)	(i)
(d)	(ii)	(iii)	(i)	(iv)

74. Which of the following statement is correct?
(a) Open cheques are those which cannot be directly presented to the drawee bank for payment across the counter
(b) A 16 year old girl can draw a cheque
(c) Indorsement is written on front of a cheque
(d) Indorsement cannot be made by the holder of a negotiable instrument

75. Which of the following statement(s) is/are incorrect? Answer using codes given below:
1. In Attorney General v. Great Eastern Railway Co. the House of Lords

observed that the doctrine of *ultra vires* as it was explained in the *Ashbury* case, should not be maintained.
2. Section 13 (i) (c) of the Companies Act provides incidental objects which need not be stated in the memorandum.
3. If incidental objects are not stated in the memorandum, they would not be allowed by the principle of reasonable construction.
4. The doctrine of indoor management operates to protect insiders against the company.

Codes:

(a) Only 1 and 2
(b) Only 2 and 3
(c) Only 1, 2 and 3
(d) 1, 2, 3 and 4

ANSWERS

1. (b)	2. (b)	3. (a)	4. (a)	5. (b)
6. (a)	7. (c)	8. (a)	9. (d)	10. (c)
11. (a)	12. (a)	13. (b)	14. (c)	15. (b)
16. (d)	17. (c)	18. (d)	19. (d)	20. (a)
21. (c)	22. (b)	23. (a)	24. (d)	25. (c)
26. (c)	27. (b)	28. (c)	29. (c)	30. (a)
31. (c)	32. (b)	33. (d)	34. (c)	35. (a)
36. (c)	37. (b)	38. (a)	39. (b)	40. (b)
41. (a)	42. (c)	43. (a)	44. (b)	45. (a)
46. (b)	47. (b)	48. (c)	49. (d)	50. (b)
51. (b)	52. (d)	53. (c)	54. (a)	55. (a)
56. (d)	57. (c)	58. (c)	59. (d)	60. (a)
61. (d)	62. (c)	63. (b)	64. (d)	65. (c)
66. (d)	67. (a)	68. (a)	69. (b)	70. (d)
71. (c)	72. (b)	73. (d)	74. (b)	75. (d)

PRACTICE PAPERS

MOCK TEST–1
PAPER–I

1. A teacher is called the leader of the class because
   (a) he is autocratic emperor of his class
   (b) he masters the art of oratory like a political leader
   (c) he is a maker of the future of his students
   (d) he belongs to a recognised teachers' union

2. The aim of introducing career courses in schools and colleges is to
   (a) increase G.K. in students
   (b) develop the ability to make the intelligent choice of jobs
   (c) provide professional knowledge to students
   (d) All of the above

3. The most effective attribute for a teacher is
   (a) Teaching skills (b) Knowledge
   (c) Feedback (d) Management

4. Those teachers are preferred most by students who
   (a) are themselves disciplined
   (b) give important questions before examination
   (c) dictate notes in the class
   (d) can clear their difficulties regarding subject-matter

5. The qualities of a teacher is/are:
   (i) He must not give any false promise
   (ii) He must not have any bad habits
   (iii) He should be mentally and physically fit
   (iv) He must not be superstitious about his class and students
   (a) Only (iii), (iv) and (ii)
   (b) Only (iv), (i) and (ii)
   (c) Only (i), (iii) and (iv)
   (d) All of the above

6. A teacher is more effective who can
   (a) motivate students to learn
   (b) control the class
   (c) correct the assignments carefully
   (d) give more information in less time

7. A teacher ought to know the problems prevalent in the field of education because
   (a) he can tell the government about it
   (b) with this knowledge, he can have information about education
   (c) he can tell about the same to another teacher
   (d) only he can do something about solving them

8. We can judge the quality of a research by the
   (a) experience of researcher
   (b) relevance of research
   (c) depth of the research
   (d) methodology followed in conducting the research

9. The theory or model developed through the fundamental research to the actual solution of the problems is applied in
   (a) educational research
   (b) action research

(c) applied research
(d) basic research

10. A write-up based on studies of the census data of a given area is called
(a) Research paper (b) Article
(c) Research report (d) Thesis

Direction: (11-16) Study the following passage and give answer to the questions based on it.

Knowledge creation in many cases requires creativity and idea generation. This is especially important in generating alternative decision support solutions. Some people believe that an individual's creative ability stems primarily from personality traits such as inventiveness, independence, individuality, enthusiasm, and flexibility. However, several studies have found that creativity is not so much a function of individual traits as was once believed, and that individual creativity can be learned and improved. This understanding has led innovative companies to recognise that the key to fostering creativity may be the development of an idea-nurturing work environment. Idea-generation methods and techniques, to be used by individuals or in groups, are consequently being developed. Manual methods for supporting idea generation, such as brainstorming in a group, can be very successful in certain situations. However, in other situations, such an approach is either not economically feasible or not possible. For example, manual methods in group creativity sessions will not work or will not be effective when: (a) there is no time to conduct a proper idea-generation session; (b) there is a poor facilitator (or no facilitator at all); (c) it is too expensive to conduct an idea-generation session; (d) the subject matter is too sensitive for a face-to-face session; or (e) there are not enough participants, the mix of participants is not optimal, or there is no climate for idea generation. In such cases, computerised idea-generation methods have been tried, with frequent success. Idea-generation software is designed to help stimulate a single user or a group to produce new ideas, options and choices. The user does all the work, but the software encourages and pushes, something like a personal trainer. Although idea-generation software is still relatively new, there are several packages on the market. Various approaches are used by idea-generating software to increase the flow of ideas to the user. Idea Fisher, for example, has an associate lexicon of the English language that cross-references words and phrases. These associative links, based on analogies and metaphors, make it easy for the user to be fed words related to a given theme. Some software packages use questions to prompt the user towards new, unexplored patterns of thought. This helps users to break out of cyclical thinking patterns, conquer mental blocks, or deal with bouts of procrastination.

11. The author, in this passage has focused on
(a) individual traits
(b) knowledge creation
(c) creativity
(d) idea-generation

12. Idea-generation software works as if it is a
(a) user-friendly trainer
(b) stimulant
(c) climate creator
(d) knowledge package

13. Which among the following personality traits is not believed to be a factor contributing to an individual's creative ability?
(a) Flexibility (b) Individuality
(c) Sophistication (d) Enthusiasm

14. In certain occasions, manual methods for the support of idea-generation
(a) can be less expensive
(b) do not need a facilitator

(c) require a mix of optimal participants
(d) are alternatively effective

15. Mental blocks, bouts of procrastination and cyclical thinking patterns can be won when
(a) idea-generation software prompts questions
(b) individuals acquire a neutral attitude towards the software
(c) manual methods are removed
(d) innovative companies employ electronic thinking methods

16. Fostering creativity needs an environment of
(a) decision support systems
(b) alternative individual factors
(c) idea-nurturing
(d) decision support solutions

17. For controlling noise in a classroom, the best method of communication is
(a) remaining calm and just looking at student
(b) saying 'don't talk'
(c) continue teaching without caring for noise
(d) raising one's voice above students voice

18. In India, Education TV was first introduced in the year
(a) 1978 (b) 1959
(c) 1987 (d) 1998

19. The failure of the teacher to communicate his ideas well to students may result into:
I. Classroom indiscipline.
II. Decrease in attendance in class.
III. Loss of student's interest in class.
(a) II only (b) III only
(c) I only (d) All of these

20. Visualisation in the instructional process cannot increase
(a) curiosity and concentration
(b) interest and motivation
(c) stress and boredom
(d) retention and adaptation

21. Communication helps in
(a) entertainment
(b) integration of country
(c) cultural promotion
(d) All of these

22. "Because you deserve to know" is the punchline used by
(a) *Hindustan Times*
(b) *The Telegraph*
(c) *The Times of India*
(d) *India Today*

23. Find the odd man out from the following groups of letters.
(a) UlmnE (b) AbcdE
(c) ApqrL (d) IfghO

24. The ambitious computerisation program of the Government of India aimed at connecting 60,000 government schools through Internet is known as
(a) Vidya Vahini (b) Gyan Vahini
(c) Kalpana project (d) Vidya Vani

25. Find the wrong number in the following sequence.
225, 336, 447, 557, 669, 771
(a) 669 (b) 557
(c) 336 (d) 771

26. In this question two words are given which have certain relationship followed by four paired lettered words. Select the paired words, that has the same relation as original pair.
ROOF : FOUNDATION
(a) Plateau : Valley
(b) Peak : Valley
(c) Mountain : Grassland
(d) Hill : Mountain

27. "Communication is a verbal process by which we understand each other and reduce uncertainty through the use of

symbol." Who is the author of this statement?
(a) David K. Barlo
(b) Dance
(c) P.S.K. Serichavenko
(d) K.J. Newman

28. Find out the missing number:
8 24 12 ? 18 54
(a) 28 (b) 32
(c) 36 (d) 38

29. A D C F
C F E H
O R ? ?
(a) JK (b) RN
(c) SU (d) QT

30. 3, 12, 27, 48, 75, ?, 147.
(a) 111 (b) 108
(c) 117 (d) 122

31. In this question four words have been given, out of which three are alike in some manner and the fourth one is different. Choose the odd one out.
(a) Epigraphy (b) Ecology
(c) Archaeology (d) Palaeontology

32. Which of the following figures will represent the right relationship between, societies, societies who run schools, DPS society.

(a) 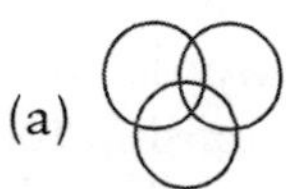 (b) 

(c) 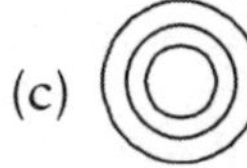 (d) 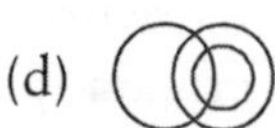

33. **Statements:**
I. All students are ambitious.
II. All ambitious persons are hard working.
Conclusions:
(i) All students are hard-working.
(ii) All hardly working people are not ambitious.
Which of the following is correct?
(a) (i) is correct
(b) (ii) is correct
(c) Both (i) and (ii) are correct
(d) Neither (i) nor (ii) is correct

34. In a certain code language:
'pit dit mit' means: 'Reena went to Delhi'.
'dit ket set' means: 'Delhi is closing'.
'mit set un' means: 'Reena' is educated.
Then what is the code for 'went'?
(a) dit (b) mit
(c) pit (d) None of these

35. EDITOR : MAGAZINE
Choose the pair from the answer choices that best expresses the relationship similar to that expressed by the question pair.
(a) Novel : Writer
(b) Director : Film
(c) Poem : Poet
(d) Chair : Carpenter

36. Should education in India be made free?
Arguments:
I. Yes, this is the only way to improve the level of literacy.
II. No, this would add already heavy burden on the exchequer.
(a) Argument I is strong
(b) Argument II is strong
(c) Both the arguments are strong
(d) None of these

Direction: (37-41) Study the table and answer the questions:

Export of Pulses and Import of Onion (in ₹ crores)

Year	Export of Pulses (in ₹ crores)	Import of Onion (in ₹ crores)
1998-99	44	58
1999-00	45	50
2000-01	60	54
2001-02	56	60

2002-03	92	68
2003-04	100	78
2004-05	68	60

37. During which year there was a maximum fall in export?
(a) 2004-05 (b) 2001-02
(c) 2003-04 (d) None of these

38. The percent of increase of imports in 2003-04 over 2002-03 is
(a) 14.9% (b) 14.7%
(c) 18.4% (d) 18.9%

39. In 1999-2000, the ratio of export to the import is
(a) 19:11 (b) 11:9
(c) 13:17 (d) 9:10

40. During which year there was maximum increase in import over its preceding year?
(a) 2003-04 (b) 2000-01
(c) 2001-02 (d) 2002-03

41. During which year there was minimum increase in import over its preceding year?
(a) 2003-04 (b) 2002-03
(c) 2001-02 (d) None of these

42. The sum of a positive number and its reciprocal is twice the difference of the number and its reciprocal. The number is:
(a) $\sqrt{3}$ (b) $\sqrt{2}$
(c) $\frac{1}{\sqrt{2}}$ (d) $\frac{1}{\sqrt{3}}$

43. Which one of the following states has the maximum number of Wildlife Sanctuaries (National Park and Sanctuaries)?
(a) Madhya Pradesh
(b) Rajasthan
(c) Uttar Pradesh
(d) West Bengal

Directions: (44-48) Answer the following questions based on the graph given below:

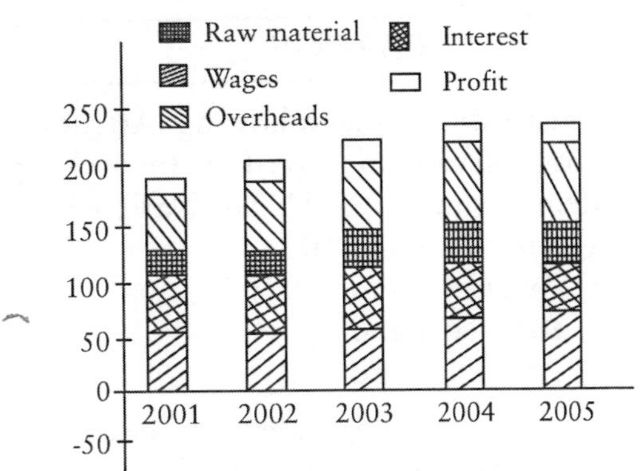

44. Which component of the cost of production has remained almost unchanged over the period 2001-05?
(a) Wages (b) Interest
(c) Raw material (d) Overheads

45. In which year was the increase in raw material maximum?
(a) 2004 (b) 2002
(c) 2003 (d) 2001

46. What percent of costs did the profits form over the period?
(a) 7% (b) 5%
(c) 2% (d) 1%

47. In which period was the change in profit maximum?
(a) 2002-03 (b) 2001-02
(c) 2004-05 (d) 2003-04

48. If the interest component is not included in the total cost calculation, which year would show the maximum profit per unit cost?
(a) 2001 (b) 2002
(c) 2003 (d) 2005

49. How many types of emergencies have been envisaged by the Constitution?
(a) One (b) Two
(c) Three (d) Four

50. Photocopying and other electrical equipments produce
(a) methane (b) ethane
(c) ozone (d) hydrogen dioxide

PAPER–II

1. Which set of the following Articles is most relevant in regard to the original Membership of the United Nations?
   (a) Articles 5 and 103
   (b) Articles 4 and 110
   (c) Articles 3 and 110
   (d) Articles 2 and 100

2. Read the following statements and choose the correct option given in Codes:
   Assertion (A): Unrecognised States have neither rights nor duties under Interntional Law.
   Reason (R): Recognition is in the formal acknowledgement through which established facts are accepted.
   Codes:
   (a) Both (A) and (R) are individually true and (R) is the correct explaination of (A)
   (b) Both (A) and (R) are individually true and (R) is not the correct explanation of (A)
   (c) (A) is true but (R) is false
   (d) (A) is false but (R) is true

3. Andhra Pradesh Reorganisation Act, 2014 provided for which of the following?
   (a) Inclusive developement of the state
   (b) Bifurcation of Andhra Pradesh into two states
   (c) Setting up a Disaster Management Committee
   (d) None of the above

4. An agreement between husband and the wife before the commencement of the Hindu Marriage Act, 1955
   (a) can take away the right of the wife under Section 13(2)(i)
   (b) cannot take away the right of the wife under Section 13(2)(i)
   (c) may or may not take away the right of the wife under section 13(2)(i) depending on the nature of compromise or agreement
   (d) Only (a) and not (b) or (c)

5. In the matter of appointment of High Court judges, the CJI is required to consult
   (a) Two seniormost judges of the concerned High Court
   (b) The Chief Justice of the concerned High Court
   (c) Governor of the State
   (d) Two seniormost judges of the Supreme Court

6. A owes ₹ 10,000 to B and promises to pay him on 10 Jan. 2002 along with interest. A offers ₹ 10,000 to B along with interest on 10 Jan. 2002, however A refuses to accept the same.
   (a) A is not discharged, however he will not be required to pay interest.
   (b) A is discharged from his liability to pay.
   (c) A is not discharged from his liability to pay.
   (d) A is required to pay the interest till the date B accepts money.

7. Under which Amendment Article 31 was amended and a new Article 31C was added?
   (a) Thirtieth
   (b) Twenty-fourth
   (c) Twenty-fifth
   (d) None of the above

8. The jurisdiction of the court rests on the consent of the parties. However,
   (a) consent can be express or tacit and can be deduced from one act or a series of successive acts
   (b) consent must be in an expressed form
   (c) (b) is true (a) is false
   (d) (a) is true (b) is false

9. Under which of the following Acts was a bid to bring about centralisation in legislative field made for the first time?
   (a) The Charter Act of 1833
   (b) Regulating Act 1773
   (c) The Government of India Act 1919
   (d) None of these

10. Consider the following judgements of the Supreme Court, which dealt with the appointment and transfer of Judges of the Supreme Court and High Courts.
    1. S.P. Gupta vs. Union of India
    2. Sankal Chand vs. Union of India
    3. In re special Reference No. 1 of 1998
    4. Supreme Court Advocate on Record Association vs. Union of India

    Which one of the following is correct chronological order in which the above judgements were delivered?

(a)	2	1	3	4
(b)	1	2	4	3
(c)	1	2	3	4
(d)	2	1	4	3

11. Which Amendment abolished the titles and special privileges of the former rulers of princely states?
    (a) 44th Amendment
    (b) 42nd Amendment
    (c) 26th Amendment
    (d) 24th Amendment

12. When was the Twenty-seventh Amendment passed?
    (a) 1973 (b) 1974
    (c) 1971 (d) 1972

13. Which of the following things accurately describes what a worker is entitled to upon return from maternity leave?
    (a) She should receive her job back, provided she completed her ten 'keeping in touch' days during her leave.
    (b) She should receive her old job back, with the same seniority as if she had not left, and with any general lock-step pay rises that were given to other employees in her job classification while she was on leave.
    (c) She will receive her job back at the same pay and seniority she enjoyed at the time her leave began.
    (d) She will receive her job back, or a similar job if the employer has found it necessary to replace her.

14. International law is
    (a) Body of rules and principles of action which are binding upon civilized states in their relation with each other.
    (b) Collection of legislations of various countries.
    (c) Collection of customs of various countries.
    (d) A legal instrument in service of domestic policy.

15. Match List I with List II and select the correct answer:

List I (Provisions)	List II (Sections of Cr.P.C.)
A. Arrest how made	1. Section 46
B. Search of place entered by person sought to be arrested	2. Section 47
C. Person arrested to be informed of grounds of arrest and of right to bail	3. Section 50
D. Search of arrested person	4. Section 51

Codes:	A	B	C	D
(a)	2	4	1	3
(b)	4	3	2	1
(c)	1	2	3	4
(d)	3	1	4	2

16. If a harm is caused by the escape of petroleum gas from one of the units situated in a residential area
    (a) the rule of M.C. Mehta Vs Union of India will apply

(b) the rule of Waghela Rajsanji Vs Shekh Masludin will apply
(c) the rule of Rylands Vs Fletcher does not meet the requirement
(d) the rule of Rylands Vs Fletcher will fully apply

17. Consider the following statements in regard to the difference between a contingent contract and a wagering agreement:
   1. A wagering agreement consists of reciprocal promises and the performance of promise by each party depends on the happening of an uncertain event.
   2. Every wagering agreement is of a contingent nature while every contingent contract is not of a wagering nature.
   3. In a wagering agreement, the future event is the sole determining factor while in a contingent contract, the future event is only collateral.
   4. A wagering agreement is valid while a contingent contract is absolutely void.

   Which of the above statements are correct?
   (a) 1, 3 and 4 (b) 1, 2 and 4
   (c) 2, 3 and 4 (d) 1, 2 and 3

18. Which of the following cannot sue in Torts?
   (a) Insolvent
   (b) Alien enemy
   (c) Both (a) and (b)
   (d) None of these

19. Section 56 deals with initial as well as subsequent impossibility. In this regard, which of the following statements is true?
   (a) In case of initial impossibility if the fact of impossibility was in knowledge of the promisor, promisee can ask for compensation.
   (b) Section 56 bars all kinds of compensation howsoever malafide parties have shown.
   (c) Impossibility implies absence of compensation in all cases.
   (d) All of the above.

20. To constitute fraud within the meaning of Section 12 of Hindu Marriage Act, 1955 the time which is relevant is
   (a) when the marriage is solemnised
   (b) when the parties consent to solemnise the marriage
   (c) Only (b) and not (a)
   (d) Both (a) and (b)

21. Which of the following statements are true?
   1. Finder is a bailee against the true owner.
   2. Finder is a bailee not only against the true owner but the whole world.
   3. Finder of the goods has right to sue the owner for compensation for trouble and expenses incurred by him.
   4. Where owner has offered certain reward for the lost goods, finder may retain the goods until he receives it.

   Codes:
   (a) 1, 2, 3 and 4 (b) 3 and 4
   (c) 1, 2 and 3 (d) 2, 3 and 4

22. The Supreme Court hears cases involving a substantial question of law as to the interpretation of the Constitution under its
   (a) Advisory Jurisdiction
   (b) Original Jurisdiction
   (c) Appellate Jurisdiction
   (d) None of these

23. In cases triable by the Sessions Court if the accused is poor and without any means of his own, he will be entitled to

(a) financial assistance
(b) fight his case
(c) free legal aid
(d) legal help

24. In case of frustration of contract,
(a) when promisor has knowledge that performance is impossible or unlawful, he must compensate promisee.
(b) promisor is not liable to compensate in any case.
(c) promisor should compensate promisee in all cases.
(d) None of the above.

25. The factories employing more than 1000 workers are required to submit their plan for approval to
(a) Deputy Chief Inspector of Factories
(b) Joint Chief Inspector of Factories
(c) Chief Inspector of Factories
(d) Additional Chief Inspector of Factories

26. For *Mahr,* the heirs of the deceased husband
(a) are not personally liable, but they are liable to the extent of the share of the inheritance which comes to their hands
(b) are not personally liable, but they are liable rateably to the extent of the share of the inheritance which comes to their hands
(c) are personally liable if the share of inheritance coming to their hands is not sufficient to liquidate the entire dower.
(d) are neither personally liable nor liable to any extent of the share of inheritance coming to their hand

27. Read the following statements and choose the correct option:
Assertion (A): It is the responsibility of the State to protect the rights of aliens in the same way as they protect the rights of their own citizens.
Reason (R): It is generally agreed that aliens living in a state should be given same rights which are given to the citizens of the state.
Codes:
(a) Both A and R are individually true and R is the correct explaination of A
(b) Both A and R are individually true and R is not the correct explaination of A
(c) A is true but R is false
(d) A is false but R is true

28. In which case the Supreme Court stated for the Preamble that "It is the key to open the mind of the constitution makers"?
(a) Berubari Union and Exchange of Enclave
(b) Golak Nath vs. State of Punjab
(c) Indira Gandhi vs. Raj Narain
(d) Keshavand vs. State of Kerala

29. The Parliament of India can legislate on the state subject,
1. when a matter becomes of national importance
2. if the state consents to such exercise
3. in case of emergency
4. when it becomes essential to give effect to an internation agreement.
Codes:
(a) 1, 2 (b) 1, 2, 3, 4
(c) 1, 2, 3 (d) 2, 3, 4

30. Read the following statements and choose the correct option:
Assertion (A): There is no liability for an attempt to commit an impossible theft.
Reason (R): No criminal liability can be incurred U/S 511 of IPC for an attempt to do an act which, if done will not be an offence.

(a) Both A and R are true but R is not the correct explanation of A
(b) Both A and R are true and R is the correct explanation of A
(c) A is false but R is true
(d) A is true but R is false

31. Hindu Marriage Act, 1955
(a) does not prescribe the ceremonies requisite for solemnization of marriage but leaves it to the parties to choose a form of ceremonial marriage which is in accordance with any custom or usage applicable to either party
(b) does not prescribe the ceremonies requisite, and does not leave it to the parties to choose
(c) does prescribe the ceremonies and at the same time leaves it to the parties to choose
(d) does prescribe the ceremonies and does not leave it to the parties to choose

32. The provision for cooling water during hotweather should be made by the organization if it employees _______ or more employees.
(a) 200 (b) 250
(c) 300 (d) 150

33. Read the following propositions:
1. A void marriage remains valid until a decree annulling it has been passed by a compe tent court.
2. A void marriage is never a valid marriage and there is no necessity of any decree annulling it.
3. A voidable marriage is regarded as a valid subsisting marriage until a decree annulling it has been passed by a competent court.

In respect of the aforesaid propositions which is correct?
(a) 2 and 3 are correct and 1 is incorrect
(b) 1 and 3 are correct and 2 is incorrect
(c) 1 and 3 are incorrect but 2 is correct
(d) 1, 2 and 3 all are correct

34. Which of the following statements is true?
(a) There is no difference between tort and crime
(b) Tort is a private wrong while crime is a public wrong
(c) Tort as well as crime is a public wrong
(d) Neither crime nor torts nor public wrongs are wrongs against the state

35. Match List I with List II and select the correct answer:

List I
A. A case relating to an offence punishable with death, imprisonment for life or imprisonment for a term exceeding two years
B. An offence for which a police officer has no authority to arrest without warrant
C. It includes 'inquiry' and 'trial' but not investigation
D. A proceeding which involves examination and determination of a cause by ajudicial tribunal which has jurisdiction over it

List II
1. Warrant case
2. Non-cognizable offense
3. Judicial proceeding
4. Trial

Codes:	A	B	C	D
(a)	2	4	1	3
(b)	4	3	2	1
(c)	3	1	4	2
(d)	1	2	3	4

36. Which one out of the following statements is not correct?
Salmond's definition of a tort consists of the following essentials?

(a) This wrong is different from breach of contract or breach of trust or other equitable obligations
(b) A tort is an infringement of right of a private individual
(c) Tort is a civil wrong
(d) This tort is redressible by an action for unliquidated damages

37. **Assertion (A):** Homicide is the killing of a human being by another human being.
Reason (R): Homicide is always unlawful.
Codes:
(a) (A) is true, but (R) is false.
(b) (A) is false, but (R) is true.
(c) Both (A) and (R) are true and (R) is the correct explanation of (A).
(d) Both (A) and (R) are true, but (R) is not correct explanation of (A).

38. Austin keeps international law under the heading
(a) Law of God
(b) Positive morality
(c) Positive law
(d) None of above

39. Auguste Comte's view that society is like an organism and it can progress when it is guided by scientific principle, is also known as
(a) Scientific outlook
(b) Scientific approach
(c) Scientific positives
(d) Law of metaphor

40. The Hindu Code was drafted by
(a) Rau Committee and was not referred to Select Committee of Constituent Assembly
(b) Rau Committee and was referred to Select Committee of the Constituent Assembly in 1948
(c) Hindu Code was drafted by Rau Committee
(d) Hindu Code was not drafted by Rau Committee

41. Read the following statements and choose the correct option:
Assertion (A): International Organisations also contribute to the development of customary International Law.
Reason (R): General Assembly of the United Nations where 191 member States are represented, the statements and the notes of the representatives on legal matters provide evidence of existing customary law.
Codes:
(a) Both (A) and (R) are individually true and R is the correct explanation of (A)
(b) Both (A) and (R) are individually true and R is not the correct explanation of (A)
(c) (A) is true but (R) is false
(d) (A) is false but (R) is true

42. "The Supreme Court shall be a Court of record and shall have all the powers of such court including the power to punish for contempt of itself." This has been mentioned under the article
(a) 129 (b) 125
(c) 102 (d) 128

43. Which of the following principles is meant when it is said that states are bound to fulfil in good faith the obligations assumed by them under treaties?
(a) Pacta sunt servanda
(b) Attentat
(c) Persona-non-grata
(d) Exequatur

44. The founder of Historical School of Law is
(a) Salmond (b) Harold Laski
(c) Austin (d) Savigny

45. Match List I with List II, and choose the correct option:

List I (Industry)
A. Cooperatives
B. Charitable Institution
C. Educational Institution run by a corporation
D. Chartered accountants

List II (Judicial decision)
1. Corporation of city of Nagpur case
2. Prabhudayal vs. Alwar Shakari Bhurni Vikas
3. Ramkrishna Iyyar Vaidyanathan vs. Fifth Industrial Tribunal
4. Bombay Pinjarapole case

Codes:	A	B	C	D
(a)	2	4	1	3
(b)	2	3	1	4
(c)	4	1	2	3
(d)	3	2	4	1

46. Duguit considers
 1. Sovereign as the supreme authority
 2. Sovereign can create law and has wide area of rights and duties
 3. States is under a duty to ensure "social solidarity"
 4. There is no distinction between private and public law

 Read the above statements and choose the correct option:
 Codes:
 (a) 1, 2, 4 (b) 1, 4
 (c) 3, 4 (d) 3, 2

47. The Twenty-sixth Amendment was passed in the year
 (a) 1975 (b) 1972
 (c) 1971 (d) 1970

48. The first attempt to regulate the affairs of the English East India Company was made by
 (a) Pitt's India Act of 1784
 (b) Dundas Bill of 1783
 (c) The Regulating Act of 1773
 (d) Charter Act of 1861

49. Read the following statements and choose the correct option:
 Assertion (A): Nothing is an offence which causes slight harm.
 Reason (R): Law does not take care of trivials.
 Codes:
 (a) Both (A) and (R) are true but (R) is not the correct explanation of (A)
 (b) Both (A) and (R) are true and (R) is the correct explanation of (A)
 (c) (A) is false but (R) is true
 (d) (A) is true but (R) is false

50. When was Twenty-fifth Amendment passed?
 (a) 1972 (b) 1973
 (c) 1970 (d) 1971

PAPER–III

1. Which of the following parts deals with special provisions relating to certain classes?
 (a) Part XVI (b) Part XI
 (c) Part XV (d) None of these

2. Wagering agreements are void but collateral transactions will be
 (a) valid, at the discretion of court
 (b) void
 (c) voidable
 (d) valid

3. In Islam, a person owning property
 (a) has the capacity to execute a will only in the absence of a legal heir
 (b) has the unqualified capacity to execute a will
 (c) has no capacity to execute a will
 (d) has the capacity to execute a will only when he has the legal heirs

4. "There shall be a Special Officer for the Scheduled Castes and Scheduled Tribes

to be appointed by the President", this has been stated under article

(a) 338 (b) 340
(c) 326 (d) 327

5. If a court gives a decision in ignorance of a decision of higher court
   (a) then higher court will look into the reasons and record it.
   (b) that decision will have no binding effect.
   (c) it will bind the parties, unless the point raised.
   (d) decision will have no binding force.

6. Dower in Muslim law is
   1. Dowry
   2. An obligation imposed upon husband as a mark of respect for wife
   3. Sale price of woman
   4. Consideration for marriage

   Select the correct answer by using the code given below:

   Codes:
   (a) 2 and 4 (b) 1 and 3
   (c) 1, 3 and 4 (d) 2 and 3

7. Which of the following is the correct statement?
   Vicarious liability means
   (a) Master's liability for the wrong of the servant
   (b) Damage which could not be prevented
   (c) Liability without fault
   (d) Servant's liability for the wrong of the master

8. Which one out of the following cases is not an instance of *Damnum Sine Injuria*
   (a) Ashby Vs White
   (b) Bradford Corporation Vs Pickles
   (c) Moghal Steamship Co. Vs Mcgregor Gow and Co.
   (d) Dickson Vs Reuters Telegraph Co.

9. Indian Constitution provides for
   (a) Double constituent authority
   (b) Single constituent authority
   (c) Double during peace single during emergency
   (d) None of the above

10. The cognizance is said to be taken by the court of the offence only when it first takes the judicial notice of the
    (a) police report (b) chargesheet
    (c) case (d) offence

11. Which of the following pairs of High Courts have held that notwithstanding the rule laid down in English cases, if the judgement against some of the promisors remains unsatisfied, there is no bar in India to subsequent actions against the other promisors?
    (a) Allahabad and Bombay High Courts
    (b) Calcutta and Madras High Courts
    (c) Allahabad and Madras High Courts
    (d) Calcutta and Bombay High Courts

12. Special provisions relating to Backward Classes and the Minority Communities have been made by the
    (a) Cabinet (b) President
    (c) Parliament (d) Constitution

13. In which of the following articles has the provision for reservation of seats for Scheduled Castes and Scheduled Tribes in the House of the People been made?
    (a) 333 (b) 332
    (c) 331 (d) 330

14. The Constitution of India vests the executive powers of the Union government in
    (a) the Prime Minister
    (b) the Council of Ministers
    (c) the President
    (d) the Parliament

15. The decision of High Courts are

(a) binding on all the subordinate court, who have given their consent.
(b) binding on all the subordinate courts within its jurisdiction.
(c) binding on all the courts in the territory of India.
(d) None of the above.

16. According to the decision in Rita Magov V.R. Mago, AIR 1977 Delhi 176, an order for interim maintenance and expenses under Section 24 of Hindu Marriage Act can be passed
(a) after the conclusion of trial and passing of the decree
(b) during the pendency of the proceedings only
(c) Either (a) or (b)
(d) Both (a) and (b) are correct

17. The provision for control of the Union over the administration of Scheduled Areas and the welfare of Scheduled Tribes has been made under article
(a) 350 (b) 370
(c) 239 (d) 33

18. A and B enter the house of C with avowedintention of stealing a jewel but unknown to having a small pistol concealed in his shirt, causes the death of C.
(a) C is liable but not B
(b) A and B are liable for causing death of C
(c) A and B are not liable for causing death of C
(d) A is liable but not B

19. Which of the following is not a category of work specified in the National Minimum Wage Act for the purpose of calculating hourly pay?
(a) 'Salaried hours work', i.e. where there are ascertainable basic hours in return for an annual salary, not varying with hours actually worked.
(b) 'Time work', i.e. work that is paid for by reference to the time worked.
(c) 'Overtime work', i.e. work in excess of the weekly hours required in the contract.
(d) 'Output work', i.e. work that is paid for wholly by reference to the number of pieces made or processed by the worker.

20. Special provisions with respect to educational grants; for the benefit of Anglo Indian community has been made under article
(a) 327 (b) 337
(c) 303 (d) 315

21. In which of the following articles has the provision for appointment of a Commission to investigate the conditions of Backward Classes been made?
(a) 340 (b) 360
(c) 140 (d) 240

22. Read the following statements and choose the correct option:

List I
A. Criminal Breach of Trust
B. Public Nuisance
C. Dacoity with murder
D. Assault with intention to outrage modesty of woman

List II
1. Section 396 2. Section 354
3. Section 405 4. Section 268

Codes:	A	B	C	D
(a)	4	3	2	1
(b)	3	4	1	2
(c)	1	2	3	4
(d)	2	1	4	3

23. If the husband or the wife dies during the period of *iddat* following upon the pronouncement of an irrevocable divorce
(a) neither of them can inherit from the other

(b) each is entitled to inherit from the other
(c) only the wife can inherit from the husband and not vice-versa
(d) only the husband can inherit from the wife and not vice-versa

24. The Provision for representation of the Anglo-Indian community in the House of the People has been made under article
(a) 331 (b) 390
(c) 370 (d) 330

25. Match List I with List II and select the correct answers:

List I (Provisions)	List II (Sections of Cr.P.C.)
A. Examination of Witnesses by Police	1. Section 161
B. Recording of confessions and Statements	2. Section 164
C. Search by Police Officer	3. Section 165
D. Procedure when Investigation cannot be completed in twenty-four hours	4. Section 167

Codes:	A	B	C	D
(a)	4	3	2	1
(b)	2	4	1	3
(c)	1	2	3	4
(d)	3	1	4	2

26. Which Amendment added a new article 363(A)?
(a) Twenty-sixth (b) Fifty-Second
(c) Thirtieth (d) Thirty-fifth

27. Under the Indian laws, husband
(a) is liable for the torts committed by his wife.
(b) is liable for the torts committed by his wife, in certain conditions.
(c) is not liable for the torts committed by his wife.
(d) None of these.

28. Which of the following is the soul of the Constitution of India?
(a) Preamble
(b) Fundamental rights
(c) Directive Principles of State Policy
(d) Fundamental duties

29. Match List I and List II (for Q. 29 to 31) and choose the correct option from the codes that follow:

List I
A. Claim for necessaries supplied to a person
B. Reimbursement of money paid due by another
C. Obligations of a person enjoying benefits of nongratutious act
D. Responsibility of finder of goods

List II
1. Section 70 2. Section 71
3. Section 69 4. Section 68

Codes:	A	B	C	D
(a)	2	1	3	4
(b)	4	3	1	2
(c)	1	2	3	4
(d)	4	3	2	1

30. Read the following statements and choose the correct option:

List I
A. Bhaurao Shankar Lokhande Vs. State of Maharashtra
B. Gul Mohammad Vs. Emperor
C. Pawan Kumar Vs. State of Haryana
D. Barendra Kumar Ghosh Vs. King Emperor

List II
1. Adultery 2. Cruelty
3. Joint Liability 4. Bigamy

Codes:	A	B	C	D
(a)	2	1	4	3
(b)	4	2	3	1
(c)	1	2	4	3
(d)	4	1	2	3

31. Match items in List I with items in List II using the code:

List I

A. Marriage during Iddat period is
B. Marriage with an impotent person is
C. Marriage below the age of 18 years is
D. Marriage with a person of unsound mind is

List II

(i) Voidable (ii) Valid
(iii) Voidable (iv) Voidable

Codes:	A	B	C	D
(a)	(i)	(iii)	(iv)	(ii)
(b)	(i)	(iii)	(ii)	(iv)
(c)	(iii)	(ii)	(i)	(iv)
(d)	(i)	(ii)	(iii)	(iv)

32. Legal right means
(a) right recognised and enforceable by society
(b) rights recognised by law and enforceable by society
(c) rights recognised by society and enforceable by law
(d) rights recognised and enforceable by law

33. Read the following statements and choose the correct option from the Codes:
Assertion (A): Some of the sources of International Law find mention in Article 38 of the statute of International Court of Justice.
Reason (R): International Court of Justice is not at all concerned with the sources of International Law.
Codes:
(a) Both (A) and (R) are individually true and (R) is the correct explaination of (A)
(b) Both (A) and (R) are individually true and (R) is not the correct explaination of (A)
(c) (A) is true but (R) is false
(d) (A) is false but (R) is true

34. Tort is the word of
(a) Chinese
(b) French language
(c) Japanese
(d) English language

35. Consider the following statements: States may be bound by the treaties only when they have given their consent. There are a number of ways in which a state may express its consent to a treaty. It may be given either by,
1. Signature;
2. Exchange of instruments;
3. Ratification;
4. Accession;

Which of these statements are correct?
(a) 2, 3 and 4 (b) 1, 2, 3 and 4
(c) 1, 2 and 3 (d) 1, 2 and 4

36. "The Directive Principles of State Policy are like a cheque on a bank payable at the convenience of the bank"—who said this in the Constituent Assembly?
(a) Pt. Jawaharlal Nehru
(b) K.T. Shah
(c) Dr. Rajendra Prasad
(d) Dr. B.R. Ambedkar

37. Representation of the Anglo-Indian community in the Legislative Assemblies of the States has been made under article
(a) 370 (b) 380
(c) 333 (d) 350

38. "Reservation of seats and special representation to cease after fifty years". This has been stated under article
(a) 334 (b) 333
(c) 331 (d) 330

39. Which of the following can be the parties in cases before the court?
1. All members of UN.
2. Non-UN members, who become parties to the statue on conditions to be determined in each case by

the General Assembly on the recommendations of the security council.

3. Non-UN members who wish to appear, before the court, without becoming parties to statue.
4. Any of the organs of the U.N.

Codes:

(a) 3, 4 (b) 1, 2, 3, 4
(c) 1, 2, 3 (d) 1, 2, 4

40. The Privy Purses of the Princes were abolished under
(a) Twenty-third Amendment
(b) Twenty-second Amendment
(c) Twenty-eighth Amendment
(d) Twenty-sixth Amendment

41. Consider the following statements:
1. To determine liability in tort it must be proved that the act done by the defendant was a wrongful act.
2. Violation of moral, social and religious duties does not come under the category of torts.
3. In tort, the plaintiff has to prove that his legal rights have been violated by the act of the defendant.
4. It is not the aim of the law of torts to protect harm being caused to the property or body, etc.

Which of the above statements are correct?

(a) 1, 3 and 4 (b) 1, 2 and 3
(c) 2, 3 and 4 (d) 1, 2 and 4

42. Which of the following is an essential ingredient to constitute torts?
1. violation of a legal right
2. wrongful act must result in legal damages
3. wrongful act must give rise to a legal remedy
4. actual damages must have accrued to the party

Codes:

(a) 3, 4 (b) 2, 3, 4
(c) 1, 2, 3 (d) 1, 2, 3, 4

43. In Deepa Vs Sub-Inspector of Police, the Kerala High Court has held that Sections 87 and 88 of IPC cannot be held to be applicable in cases where interest of the
(a) government is involved
(b) society is involved
(c) public is involved
(d) community is involved

44. To attract application of Section 34
(a) physical presence at the scene of occurrence is necessary
(b) participation is necessary in all cases
(c) physical presence at the scene of occurence is not necessary
(d) Both (a) and (b) are correct

45. Read the following statements and choose the correct option from the Codes

Assertion (A): Law of contract recently facing a problem due to frequent use of contract of adhesion.

Reason (R): One party to contract has no choice to negotiate but to accept it.

Codes:

(a) (A) is wrong but (R) is right
(b) (A) is right but (R) is wrong
(c) (A) and (R) both right but (R) is not the correct explanation of (A)
(d) (A) and (R) both right and (R) is the correct explanation of (A)

46. Reservation of seats for Scheduled Castes and Scheduled Tribes in the Legislative Assemblies of the States have been mentioned under article
(a) 333 (b) 332
(c) 331 (d) 330

47. Which of the following will not exclude a worker from the entitlement to daily rest breaks?

(a) Where the worker's activities involve the need for continuity of service or production.
(b) Where the worker's activities are such that his place of work and place of residence are distant from each other or his different places of work are distant from one another.
(c) Where the worker has signed an 'opt-out'.
(d) Where there is a foreseeable surge of activity, as may be the case in relation to agriculture.

48. The convention on the right of child came into being in the year
(a) 1990 (b) 1991
(c) 1988 (d) 1989

49. Match List-I with List-II in regard to contingent contracts and select the correct answer

List-I
A. Contract contingent on the future conduct of a living person
B. Contracts contingent on happening of specified event within fixed time
C. Contracts contingent on not happening of specified event within a fixed time
D. Agreements contingent on impossible event

List-II
1. Section 34 of the Indian Contract Act 1872
2. Section 35, Para 1 of the Indian Contract Act 1872
3. Section 35, Para 2 of the Indian Contract Act 1872
4. Section 36 of the Indian Contract Act 1872

Codes:	A	B	C	D
(a)	3	4	1	2
(b)	2	3	4	1
(c)	1	2	3	4
(d)	4	1	2	3

50. Which one of the following is a provision regarding the Scheduled Castes and Scheduled Tribes?
(a) Certain reservations have also been made for them in the appointments to services and posts of the Union and States
(b) A Special Officer for the Scheduled Castes and Scheduled Tribes is to be appointed by the President of India
(c) Seats for them have been reserved in both the Houses of Parliament as well as the State Legislatures
(d) All of the above

ANSWER SHEET
PAPER—I

1. (c)	2. (c)	3. (a)	4. (d)	5. (d)
6. (a)	7. (d)	8. (b)	9. (c)	10. (b)
11. (d)	12. (a)	13. (c)	14. (c)	15. (a)
16. (c)	17. (a)	18. (b)	19. (a)	20. (c)
21. (d)	22. (a)	23. (c)	24. (a)	25. (b)
26. (b)	27. (b)	28. (c)	29. (d)	30. (b)
31. (b)	32. (c)	33. (a)	34. (c)	35. (b)
36. (b)	37. (a)	38. (b)	39. (d)	40. (a)
41. (d)	42. (c)	43. (a)	44. (b)	45. (c)
46. (b)	47. (d)	48. (b)	49. (c)	50. (c)

PAPER—II

1. (a)	2. (a)	3. (b)	4. (a)	5. (d)
6. (a)	7. (a)	8. (a)	9. (b)	10. (d)
11. (c)	12. (d)	13. (d)	14. (c)	15. (b)

16. (b)	17. (d)	18. (a)	19. (c)	20. (b)
21. (a)	22. (b)	23. (a)	24. (a)	25. (c)
26. (a)	27. (c)	28. (a)	29. (b)	30. (d)
31. (d)	32. (d)	33. (c)	34. (b)	35. (b)
36. (b)	37. (c)	38. (a)	39. (c)	40. (d)
41. (b)	42. (c)	43. (b)	44. (d)	45. (d)
46. (b)	47. (c)	48. (d)	49. (c)	50. (d)

PAPER—III

1. (a)	2. (a)	3. (b)	4. (a)	5. (d)
6. (a)	7. (a)	8. (a)	9. (b)	10. (d)
11. (c)	12. (d)	13. (d)	14. (c)	15. (b)
16. (b)	17. (d)	18. (a)	19. (c)	20. (b)
21. (a)	22. (b)	23. (a)	24. (a)	25. (c)
26. (a)	27. (c)	28. (a)	29. (b)	30. (d)
31. (d)	32. (d)	33. (b)	34. (b)	35. (b)
36. (b)	37. (c)	38. (a)	39. (c)	40. (d)
41. (b)	42. (c)	43. (b)	44. (d)	45. (d)
46. (b)	47. (c)	48. (d)	49. (c)	50. (d)

MOCK TEST–2
PAPER–I

1. Minimum program of guidance includes
   (a) occupational information service
   (b) data collector service
   (c) counselling service
   (d) All of these
2. If majority of students in a class is weak, a teacher should
   (a) not care about intelligent students
   (b) keep his speed of teaching fast so that students' comprehension level may increase
   (c) keep his teaching slow which can also be helpful to bright students
   (d) keep his teaching slow along with some extra guidance to bright students
3. If the principal of your institution is not satisfied with your performance and charges you with the act of negligence of duties, how would you behave with him?
   (a) You would neglect him
   (b) You would take revenge by giving physical and mental agony to him
   (c) You would keep yourself alert and make his efforts unfruitful
   (d) You would take a tough stand against the charges
4. What makes people to undertake research?
   (a) Desire to get intellectual joy of doing some creative work
   (b) Desire to get a research degree along with its consequential benefits
   (c) Desire to face the challenge in solving the unsolved problems
   (d) All of these
5. Which of the following aims at probing into the phenomenon to formulate a more precise research problem or to develop a new hypothesis?
   (a) Descriptive research
   (b) Conclusive research
   (c) Diagnostic research
   (d) Exploratory research
6. Which of the following is not instructional material?
   (a) Transparency
   (b) Overhead projector
   (c) Printed material
   (d) Audio cassette
7. Of great importance in determining the amount of transference that occurs in the process of learning is the

(a) knowledge of the teacher
(b) IQ of the teacher
(c) presence of identical elements
(d) use of appropriate elements

8. The characteristic(s) of hypothesis is/are:
   I. It can be tested.
   II. It must consist of known facts.
   III. It must be objective and specific.
   (a) I and III (b) I and II
   (c) I only (d) All of these

9. The guide for the research requires which of the following qualities?
   (a) Interdisciplinary expertise
   (b) Subject matter expertise
   (c) Methodological expertise
   (d) All of these

10. Which of the following indicates evaluation?
   (a) Seema got 195 marks out of 200
   (b) Sapna got 72 percent marks in English
   (c) Asha got First Division in final examination
   (d) All of the above

Direction: (11-16) Study the following passage and give answer to the questions based on it.

Much of the theoretical literature of archeology in the 1980s devotes considerable energy to bashing the 1970s, and the target often turns out to be the so-called New or Processual Archeology. While many of the attacks come from recent theorists who are attempting to replace it with post-processual archeology, some criticism comes from within what was New Archeology even from the hand of its original champion, Lewis Binford. If scholars from both outside and inside the theoretical developments of the 1970s are rejecting the New Archeology, why am I defending its importance to us today? The answer is very simple...for better or worse, it is us! As Alison Whylie has recently said the New Archeology of the 1960s quickly became everybody's archeology in the 1970s. Most of today's faculty members and senior archeologists were the people who, in one way or another, adopted the teachings of New Archeology. Although most archeologists did not claim to agree with all aspects of New Archeology nor could more than two or three people agree on what it was, virtually one rejected it outright. Typically, each one presented her or his version, often using a New Archeology text as a starting point for pedagogical purposes. Few wanted to be left out of the exciting new theoretical movement of those years, and New Archeology was passed on to the succeeding generation of students who reached maturity in the 1980s and are today's young professionals.

Criticisms now leveled against the New Archeology of the seventies do have merit, but by discounting that era as misguided, critics have overlooked its crucial importance. New Archeology has an important historical role in the developments of the field we have today and it has continuing importance because it is still guiding archeology's trajectory into the future. Equally troubling is that some critics ask us to reject the basic tenets of New Archeology and to replace them with a system often called post processualist archeology. I believe this is rhetoric that not only misrepresents the achievements of the New Archeology of the seventies, but also does not successfully articulate the potential contributions of its own position.

To put the New Archeology of the seventies into perspective, it is important to review the decades leading up to its development. In the first years following World War II, archeology was still a small field, but by the fifties and the sixties, it was expanding rapidly and taking itself quite seriously. Since the launching of Sputnik in 1957 there had emerged a frenzy in the United States to make all disciplines more scientific. Great strides were made in bringing science into archeology through new dating techniques a multidisciplinary approach, early experiments with the use of statistics, and devoting substantial attention to increasing the precision of artifact classification. The sixties provided the nation with both the optimistic Kennedy years, with an emphasis on science and the conviction that we were capable of accomplishing wondrous; things, and the cynical Vietnam era. Coming on the heels of a decade of civil rights unrest, the widespread dissatisfaction with the Vietnam conflict in the late sixties molded a generation of young Americans who were distrustful of established authority. In academic life, there was an increasing emphasis on environment, other cultures, and people oriented disciplines. Anthropology and archeology grew markedly because of these trends. Archeologists were urged to become concerned with sociological issues—the people behind the artifacts.

It was during these decades of rapid change that many of the core concepts of the New Archeology entered the literature. However, they were not, at first, assembled into a program for action that attracted a solid following. Water Taylor advocated the conjuctive approach with little effect, while Leslie White's evolutionism and Julian Styeward's cultural ecology attracted some attention, but largely among cultural anthropologists. Albert Spaulding led a one-man campaign to bring science and statistics into archeology. But the individual whose work catalyzed the New Archeology movement was Lewis Binford, who incorporated these earlier lines of thinking together with an explicit concern for scientific methods and field research designs. Much of Binford's thinking probably crystallised while he was at the University of Michigan, but was during his relatively few years at the University of Chicago that he changed the direction of modern archeology.

11. New Archeology refers to
    (a) newer techniques used in Archeology
    (b) newer inventions used in Archeology
    (c) newer theoretical foundations in Archeology
    (d) None of these
12. The author defends the Archeology of the 1970s because
    (a) he has a nostalgic feeling about it
    (b) it has research value
    (c) it paved way for newer traditions
    (d) it has historical value
13. The author suggests that
    (a) We should respect new Archeology as a movement in Archeology
    (b) We should go back to the tenets of processual Archeology
    (c) We should treat tenets of new Archeology with respect
    (d) All of the above
14. The importance of Archeology arose from
    (a) the end of World War II
    (b) an increasing scientific outlook
    (c) the launch of Sputnik in 1957
    (d) All of these
15. Which one of the following is not an area of focus for archeologist?
    (a) Study the interaction of people of small group
    (b) Studying cultures of other people
    (c) Study the social structure of the past societies
    (d) Study the man-environment relationship in the past
16. An archeologist is concerned with
    (a) classification of artefacts
    (b) maintenance of museums
    (c) digging of ancient cities
    (d) All of these
17. Rhetorics means

(a) study of the technique and rules for using language effectively
(b) using language effectively to please or persuade
(c) excessive use of verbal ornamentation
(d) All of the above

18. If a receiver replying on 'hmm-mm' or 'Isee'. This type of reply is known as
(a) positive feedback
(b) ambiguous feedback
(c) negative feedback
(d) None of these

19. Which of the following FM radio stations is owned by the Times of India group?
(a) AIR
(b) Radio Rainbow
(c) Radio Mirchi
(d) Red FM

20. Find the next number in the following sequence:
9, 8, 25, 12, 49, 18, 121, 26, ?, ?
(a) 142, 36 (b) 169, 36
(c) 225, 36 (d) 196, 36

21. **Statement:** Should there be complete ban on pouched tobacco products (like Gutka) in India?
Arguments:
(i) Yes, it is the most important cause of mouth cancer and mouth ulcer in our country.
(ii) No, there are many people employed in this industry right from manufacturing to retailing. This ban will hamper their livelihood.
(a) Argument (i) is strong
(b) Argument (ii) is strong
(c) Both the arguments (i) and (ii) are strong
(d) Neither argument (i) nor (ii) is strong

22. The relationship between Animal, Cows, Dogs can be shown by

(a) 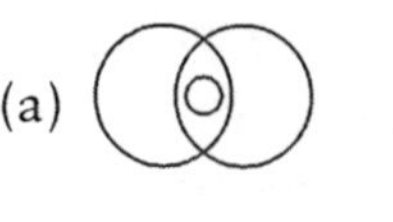 (b) 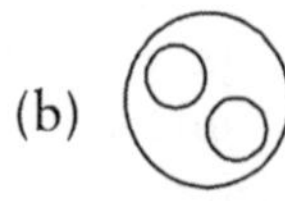

(c) 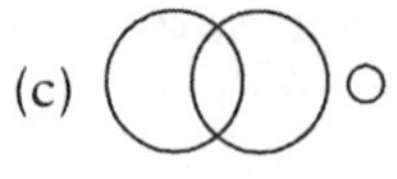 (d) 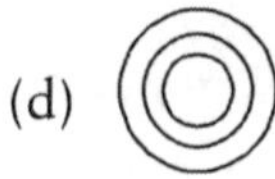

23. If in a certain code:
'nso prt kli chn' means 'sharma gets marriage gift'.
'pit lnm wop chn' means 'wife gives marriage gift'. 'tti wop nhi' means 'he gives nothing'. What would mean gives:
(a) kli (b) tti
(c) wop (d) lnm

24. Characteristics of all informal and formal communications are
(a) Same (b) Structured
(c) Different (d) None of these

25. Three of the following four are alike in a certain way and so form a group. Find the one which doesn't belong to that group?
(a) Dog (b) Tiger
(c) Horse (d) Lion

26. What is research design?
(a) The methods used in analysis and finding the final conclusion is known as research design
(b) A researcher needs to prepare a plan of action for his study which is known as research design
(c) The presentation of final data is known as research design
(d) None of these

27. Recording a television program on a Set Top Box is an example of
(a) content reference
(b) time-shifting
(c) media synchronisation
(d) mechanical clarity

28. Which of the following statements say the same thing?
    (i) "I am a teacher" (said by Arvind)
    (ii) "I am a teacher" (said by Binod)
    (iii) "My son is a teacher" (said by Binod's father)
    (iv) "My brother is a teacher" (said by Binod's sister)
    (v) "My brother is a teacher" (said by Binod's only sister)
    (vi) "My sole enemy is a teacher" (said by Binod's only enemy)

    Choose the correct answer from the codes given below:

    Codes:
    (a) (v) and (vi)
    (b) (i) and (ii)
    (c) (ii) and (vi)
    (d) (ii), (iii), (iv) and (v)

29. In this question there are two statements followed by four conclusions numbered I, II, III and IV.

    Statements:
    A. All books are trees.
    B. All trees are lions.

    Conclusions:
    I. All books are lions.
    II. All lions are books.
    III. All trees are books.
    IV. Some lions are books.

    Choose the correct answer.
    (a) I and IV follow
    (b) II and III follow
    (c) None of conclusions follow
    (d) All conclusions follow

Directions: (30-34) Answer the questions based on following table.

Machines X and Y can independently produce either product P or product Q. The time taken by machines X and Y (in minutes) to produce one unit of product P and Q are given in the table below. (Each machine works 8 hours per day.)

Product	X	Y
P	10	8
Q	6	6

30. If the number of units of P is to be three times that of Q, what is the maximum idle time to maximise total units manufactured?
    (a) 8 minutes (b) 0 minute
    (c) 12 minutes (d) None of these

31. If X works at half its normal efficiency, what is the maximum number of units produced, if at least one unit of each must be produced?
    (a) 119 (b) 135
    (c) 127 (d) 136

32. What is the maximum number of units that can be manufactured in one day?
    (a) 250 (b) 160
    (c) 270 (d) 195

33. If equal quantities of both are to be produced, then out of four choice given below the least efficient way would be
    (a) 59 of each with 8 min. idle
    (b) 71 of each with 9 min. idle
    (c) 53 of each with 10 min. idle
    (d) 48 of each with 4 min. idle

34. What is the least number of machine hours required to produce 30 pieces of P and 25 pieces of Q respectively?
    (a) 6 hr 30 min. (b) 9 hr 30 min.
    (c) 6 hr 40 min. (d) 8 hr 30 min.

35. Telematic is a combination of
    (a) Telecommunication and computer
    (b) Telecommunication and information
    (c) Television and computer
    (d) All of the above

36. Following is a part of balance sheet of Timas Pvt. Ltd. Study the table and give answer to the question given below:

(All values in ₹ crore)

Year	Expenditure	Income
1990	3400	4000
1995	3800	4500
2000	4500	5400
2005	6400	8000

Which of the following conclusions is not true?
(a) There has been a steady growth in % profit of the company
(b) There is around 90% increase in expenditure of the firm from 1990 to 2005
(c) Income of the company is doubled in 15 years
(d) Percentage profit in 2000 was 18%

37. If EFGHUK is coded as VUTSRQ then LIMIT can be coded as
(a) KNRNC (b) ORNRG
(c) JKOKG (d) RSTSG

38. The more is 'Resolution Power' of a printer better is its
(a) Speed (b) Colour
(c) Memory (d) Quality

39. Laterite soil develops due to
(a) deposits of alluvial
(b) deposition of loess
(c) leaching
(d) continued vegetation cover

40. Line access and avoidance of collision are the main functions of
(a) network protocols
(b) wide area networks
(c) the CPU
(d) the monitor

41. Communication satellites are placed in
(a) Geostationary Orbit
(b) Polar Orbit
(c) Both (a) and (b)
(d) None of these

42. DLL stands for
(a) Data Deriving Language
(b) Data Definition Language
(c) Data Design Language
(d) All of the above

43. Transistors were first used in
(a) 2nd generation computers
(b) 3rd generation computers
(c) 4th generation computers
(d) None of these

44. Which of the following is not provided in the constitution?
(a) Planning Commission
(b) Election Commission
(c) Finance Commission
(d) Public Service Commission

45. The 1st satellite launched in space was
(a) Early Bird (b) Sputnik-1
(c) Skylab (d) Aryabhatta-1

46. At what time between 5.30 and 6.00 will the hands of a clock be at right angles?
(a) 45 minutes past 5
(b) minutes past 5
(c) minutes past 5
(d) 40 minutes past 5

47. A person can be a member of Council of Ministers without being a member of Parliament for a maximum period of
(a) 45 days (b) 90 days
(c) 180 days (d) one year

48. Many engineers and architects use a different type of pen called a
(a) Pointer pen (b) Computer pen
(c) Light pen (d) Logical pen

49. Which of the following are wrongly matched?

Name of Volcano	Country
(a) Mt. Spur	USA
(b) Mt. Fuego	Guatemala
(c) Mt. Ag'ung	Indonesia
(d) Mt. Lascor	Equador

50. How many types of emergency can be declared by the President of India?
(a) 1 (b) 2
(c) 3 (d) 4

PAPER–II

1. Failure of the husband to provide for wife's maintenance is a ground for divorce under
(a) Section 2(iii) of the Dissolution of Muslim Marriage Act, 1939
(b) Section 2(ii) of the Dissolution of Muslim Marriages Act, 1939
(c) Section 2(vi) of the Dissolution of Muslim Marriages Act, 1939
(d) Section 2(i) of the Dissolution of Muslim Marriages Act, 1939

2. Which of the following could be said to be a requirement of the 'employee' definition, but not the 'worker' definition?
(a) Control
(b) Mutuality of obligations
(c) A contract
(d) Personal service

3. What should be the order of the use of material source of International Law?
1. Treaties and conventions
2. Customs
3. General principle of law recognised by civilised states
4. Judicial decisions and juristic opinion as subsidiary means for the determination of law

Codes:
(a) 2, 3, 1, 4 (b) 1, 2, 3, 4
(c) 4, 3, 2, 1 (d) 4, 2, 1, 3

4. During judicial separation the
(a) parties continue to be husband and wife and may suspend or may not suspend the marital rights and obligations
(b) parties continue to be husband and wife and the marital rights and obligations remain intact
(c) parties cease to be husband and wife
(d) parties continue to be husband and wife but marital rights and obligations are suspended

5. The wages under the Minimum Wages Act, 1948 shall include
(a) a basic rate of wages and dearness allowance variable according to cost of living.
(b) CTC.
(c) A consolidated amount decided by the employer.
(d) basic rate of wages, DA, HRA and CCA.

6. Which among the following is not a source of law?
(a) Veda or Smiriti
(b) Sadachar
(c) Self-satisfation
(d) Natural law

7. Section 93 of the Indian Evidence Act 1872 makes a specific provision regarding the
(a) ambiguous tender
(b) ambiguous contract
(c) ambiguous agreement
(d) ambiguous document

8. Which one of the following is not a provision for the Backward Classes?
(a) The Commission will make recommendations to improve the conditions of the Backward Classes
(b) President will place a copy of the Commission's report together with a mamorandum explaining the action

taken thereon to be laid before each House of Parliament
(c) The President may appoint a Commission to investigate the conditions of socially and educationally backward classes
(d) None of the above

9. Which of the following is true about the statement that conspiracy is an essential factor or abetment?
(a) There must be at least two persons
(b) They must engage in some conspiracy in the doing of an act
(c) An act or ommission must take place in pursuance of the conspiracy
(d) All of the above

10. The Governor nominates those persons who
(a) are famous politicians
(b) are having special knowledge or practical experience in respect to such matters as literature, science, art, cooperative movement and social service
(c) are recommended by the ministers
(d) are recommended by his friends.

11. Which of the following is not legal personality?
(a) Company
(b) Bench of judges
(c) Cabinet of ministers
(d) Both (b) and (c)

12. In India, a person who is stranger to the consideration
(a) Can sue the contract
(b) Cannot sue the contract
(c) Depends on the conditions
(d) None of the above

13. Which of the following provisions has been made for the Anglo-Indian Community?
(a) Certain special provisions have also been made regarding the educational grants for the benefit of Anglo-Indian Community
(b) Special provisions for the adequate representation of the community in the House of the People and the State Legislative Assemblies have been made
(c) The President of India can nominate two members belonging to the Anglo-Indian Community to Lok Sabha and the Governor of a State can nominate one member of Anglo-Indian Community to the Legislative Assembly
(d) All of the above

14. A servant is a person
(a) Who acts on behalf of other
(b) Who is employed by another
(c) Who voluntarily agrees to work under the control and command of another during the period of employment
(d) None of the above

15. Which one of the following provisions has been made regarding the protection of Linguistic Minorities?
(a) Provisions for adequate facilities for instruction in the mother tongue at the primary stage to the children of the minority groups have been made
(b) The President or India has been given the powers to issue directives to the States in this regard as well as to appoint a Special Officer for Linguistic Minorities
(c) Certain provisions for the protection of Linguistic Minorities were added by the Seventh Amendment Act of 1956
(d) All of the above

16. Act of God is also known by the name
(a) Damnum Fatale
(b) Vis major

(c) Vis major or Damnum Fatale
(d) None of the above

17. A Schedule is a
(a) Written supplementary, explanatory or expended documents. It is an apendix to a Bill or an act of Parliament
(b) Syllabus of a College
(c) Law
(d) None of the above

18. When one of the parties to the contract has performed its part of the promise which constitutes the consideration for the promise by the other side, it is known as
(a) Past consideration
(b) Executed consideration
(c) Executory consideration
(d) Future consideration

19. The failure of Security Council to fulfil its primary purpose for maintaining international peace and security has led to three developments.
1. Assumption by General Assembly, role of determining a breach of peace, an act of aggression and recommending action by members including armed forces.
2. The development of powerful regional security system or alliance outside U.N. such as NATO.
3. Lack of confidence in the efficacy of the general collective security system based on security council.
4. Development of peace keeping operation using limited military powers.

Read the above statements and choose the correct option.
Codes:
(a) 1, 2, 3, 4 (b) 3, 4
(c) 1, 2 (d) 1, 2, 3

20. Which Schedule details the territories of the States and Union territories?
(a) Schedule VII (b) Schedule VIII
(c) Schedule I (d) None of these

21. The principle *Ubijus ibi remedium* has been established for the first time in the case of
(a) Action Vs Blandell
(b) Ashby Vs White
(c) Chesmore Vs Richards
(d) Marzetti Vs Williams

22. The renewal application for a license submitted after December 31st of the every year shall pay the fine amount
(a) 10% of the license fee
(b) 20% of the license fee
(c) 30% of the license fee
(d) None of these

23. How many Schedules are there in the Indian Constitution?
(a) Eleven (b) Twelve
(c) Nine (d) Ten

24. In which one of the following cases Justice Chinnappa Reddy observed that "there can be no question that nations must march with the international community and municipal law must respect of rules oflnternational law"?
(a) Motilal Vs UP Government
(b) Nirmal Vs Union of India
(c) Gramophone Company of India Ltd. Vs Birendra Bahadur Pandey
(d) Maganbhai Vs Union of India

25. Match the following columns of Schedules and their contents:

A. Fourth	I. Allocation of seats in the Council of States
B. Second	II. Emoluments, allowances and service conditions of President
C. Seventh	III. Three Lists

D. Sixth IV. Provisions relating to administration of tribal areas

Select the correct answer using the codes below:

Codes:	A	B	C	D
(a)	I	II	III	IV
(b)	IV	III	I	II
(c)	I	III	II	IV
(d)	I	II	IV	III

26. Which of the following statements is not correct regarding Article 23 of the International Covenant on Civil and Political Rights?
   (a) Every child has the right to acquire a nationality
   (b) No marriage shall be entered into without the free and full consent of the intending spouses
   (c) The right of men and women of marriageable age to marry and to found a family shall be recognized
   (d) The family is the natural and fundamental group unit of society and is entitled to protection by society and the State

27. Which of the following schedules deals with the provisions as to the Administration and control of Scheduled Areas and Scheduled Tribes?
   (a) Fifth (b) Sixth
   (c) Seventh (d) Eighth

28. *Qui facit per alium fetch per se* establishes the
   (a) Vicarious liability
   (b) Liability under the Indian contract act
   (c) Liability under the law of torts
   (d) Liability under IPC

29. An interim government of 'Romalia' seeks control over certain funds belonging to the Republic of Romalia. Romalia is in a state of civil war. An application is filed before a UK Court by the interim government. The evidence before the court is that—the UK government has no dealings with the interim government. The court comes to the conclusion that there is no effective government of Romalia. The court
   (a) will not accept the application because the interim government is not in its determination—a sovereign government
   (b) will accept the application because the applicant is an interim government
   (c) will not accept the application because the government has not been recognized by UK
   (d) will not accept the application because it has no jurisdiction

30. Indicate the correct order in which the following decisions appeared
   1. Namibia case
   2. Naulilaa case
   3. Nauru vs. Australia
   4. Nicaragua vs. Honduras

   Codes:
   (a) 2 1 3 and 4 (b) 3 4 2 and 1
   (c) 1 3 4 and 2 (d) 4 3 2 and 3

31. Provisions as to the Judges of the Supreme Court and of the High Courts have been included under Schedule
   (a) Third (b) First
   (c) Second (d) None of these

32. Beribari Union Re, AIR 1960 SC 845; held,
   (a) Parliament has power to cede national territory in favour of a foreign state.
   (b) The power to amend constitution conferred on Parliament includes the power to amend Art.
   (c) Both of the above.
   (d) None of the above.

33. The Vienna school is also known as
   (a) Analytical school
   (b) Sociological school
   (c) Realist school
   (d) The pure theory of law

34. **List I**
   A. While evolving principle of reasonableness from Articles 14, 19, 21, the court said Directive Principles would serve as standard for testing reasonableness of a legislation.
   B. Court referred Article 43 of Directive Principles and upheld the validity of Minimum Wages Act, 1948.
   C. Court took into consideration Article 39 in upholding its view that the abolition of Zamindari was for a public purpose.
   D. In the light of Articles 45 and 41 the court held that every child/citizen of this country has a right to free education until he attains the age of 14 years.

   List II
   1. Unni Krishnan vs. State of A.P.
   2. Bijay Cotton Mills vs. State of Ajmer
   3. State of Bihar vs. Kameshwar Singh
   4. Kasturi Lal vs. State of J&K

Codes:	A	B	C	D
(a)	1	2	3	4
(b)	4	2	3	1
(c)	4	3	2	1
(d)	1	2	4	3

35. Ninth Schedule of the Indian Constitution is associated with which Article of the Indian Constitution?
   (a) 224 (b) 31B
   (c) 346 (d) 344

36. Which one of the following does not fall within the financial powers of the Indian Parliament?
   (a) No taxes can be levied without the consent of the Parliament
   (b) No expenditure can be incurred without the sanction of the Parliament
   (c) The Parliament can propose any tax
   (d) The Parliament List and Residual List

37. A grows poisonous trees on his own land and lets the projection of the branches of this tree on the B's land. B's cattle dies because of nibbling the poisonous leaves. In the light of these facts which of the following statements is true?
   (a) A is not liable because he is not acting negligently
   (b) A is not liable to B because B must have taken due care to control his cattle
   (c) A is not liable because trees are still on the A's land and there is no escape of dangerous thing
   (d) A is liable because projection of poisonous branches amount to escape of dangerous thing.

38. The Ninth Schedule
   (a) Was added to the Constitution by the First Amendment
   (b) Formed part of the original Constitution
   (c) Was added to the Constitution by the 42nd Amendment
   (d) Was added to the Constitution by the 24th Amendment

39. A consideration is
   (a) Doing or abstaining from doing something at the desire of the promisor
   (b) A reason for making a proposal
   (c) Regard for the condition of other party
   (d) None of the above

40. Provisions as to disqualification on ground of detection have been made under Schedule

(a) Sixth (b) Eighth
(c) Tenth (d) Seventh

41. Match List I with List II and choose the correct option using the codes given below

List I (Theory)	List II (Subject)
A. Retributive Theory	1. Legal right
B. Sociological Theory	2. Source of law
C. Theory of Precedent	3. Punishment
D. Theory of Property	4. Roscoe pound

Codes:	A	B	C	D
(a)	3	4	2	1
(b)	3	3	1	4
(c)	4	3	1	2
(d)	1	4	3	2

42. ________ absolves the employer's liability under the Maternity Benefit Act and Workmen's Compensation Act.
(a) Industrial Employment (Standing Order) Act
(b) Employees Provident Fund Act
(c) Industrial Disputes Act
(d) Employees State Insurance Act

43. Which one of the following is wrong?
(a) The Second Schedule contains the details regarding the salaries and allowances for the President, Governor, Prime Minister, Ministers, etc.
(b) The Third Schedule contains the forms of oaths and affirmations
(c) The First Schedule contains the names of the States ofthe Indian Union
(d) None of the above

44. In which one of the following cases the accused committed gruesome murder of two ladies without any reason by cutting their heads by an axe. There was evidence on record that earlier also he had sufferred from attacks of mental disorder. After the occurrence the accused was saying that he was haunted by God and hence had cut the heads of the two ladies. The Madhya Pradesh High Court accepted the plea of insanity and directed that the accused be kept in mental hospital until cured?
(a) Queen Emp Vs Latif Khan
(b) Niman Sha Vs State of Madhya Pradesh
(c) State Govt. M.P. Vs Rangaswamy
(d) Chirangi Vs State

45. The pure theory of law was propounded by
(a) Austin (b) Ehrlich
(c) Hans Kelsen (d) Comte

46. Which one of the following is correct?
(a) The Fifth Schedule gives provisions for the administration and control of the Scheduled Areas and Schedule Tribes
(b) The Sixth Schedule gives provisions for the administration of Tribal Areas in Assam
(c) The Fourth Schedule gives the allocation of seats in different Legislative Councils
(d) All of the above

47. A consideration must necessarily be
(a) Only in present
(b) Only in past
(c) Only in future
(d) Past present or future

48. Which one of the following Articles of the Vienna Convention on the Law of Treaties provides that treaty is an international agreement concluded between States in written form and governed by International Law, whether embodied in a single instrument or in two or more related instruments and whatever its particular designation?

(a) Article 4(1)(a) (b) Article 5(1)(a)
(c) Article 3(1)(a) (d) Article 2(1)(a)

49. Read the following statements and choose the correct option.

List I

A. Kent B. Holland
C. Hegal D. Savigny

List II

Possession must be protected because

1. man by taking possession has brought the object within the sphere of will.
2. in possession there is manifestation of individuals will.
3. every act of violence is unlawful.
4. it is essential for preservation of peace.

Codes:	A	B	C	D
(a)	1	2	3	4
(b)	3	2	4	1
(c)	1	4	2	3
(d)	2	4	3	1

50. A piece of delegated legislation
   1. will be ultra-vires if it goes beyond the basic policy underlying the parent act.
   2. will not be ultra-vires if it goes beyond the basic policy.
   3. If in rule making agency on whom rule making power has been conferred transcends its authority the rule will be invalid.
   4. Legislature can delegate its powers without laying down the policy.

   Which of the following statements is true?

   Codes:

   (a) 1, 4 (b) 1, 3
   (c) 1, 3, 4 (d) 2, 3, 4

PAPER–III

1. The defendant had invited two of friends A and B for sight seeing by car A driving the car and due to his negligent driving a person D was injured and subsequently died _______.
   (a) The defendant is liable, to the successor of the deceased D as the owner had retained his control of the vehicle
   (b) A is liable to the successors of the deceased D as he was the main culprit
   (c) The defendant and A both are liable as A was driving the car with the approval of the defendant
   (d) The defendant is not held liable to the successors of the deceased D as the owner had retained his control of the vehicle

2. Which one of the following is wrong?
   (a) The Eighth Schedule gives description of eighteen languages
   (b) The Ninth Schedule includes certain Acts regarding Land Ceiling and Abolition of Zamindari passed by the State Government which have been given protection under the Constitution
   (c) The Seventh Schedule gives three lists of subjects, the Union List, the State List, and Concurrent List
   (d) None of the above

3. An essential feature of consideration is that
   (a) It must be encashable
   (b) It must be given by the promise alone
   (c) It must be at the desire or request of the promisor
   (d) It must be guaranteed

4. Which one of the following has been wrongly listed as a recommendation of the Sarkaria Commission?
   (a) It has favoured formation of Inter-Governmental Council consisting of Prime Minister and Chief Ministers of states

(b) It has favoured liberal use of Article 356 of the Constitution in the interest of unity and integrity of the country
(c) It has turned down the demand for the abolition of the office of the Governor
(d) It has favoured implementation of the three language formula in the interest of unity and integrity of the country

5. The second wife in a case of bigamous marriage
(a) has a status of wife
(b) has no status of wife
(c) may have or may not have a status of wife
(d) Either (a) or (c)

6. Which amendment added the Tenth Schedule to the Constitution?
(a) 53rd (b) 48th
(c) 52nd (d) None of these

7. The Tenth Schedule contains
(a) Provision regarding disqualifications on grounds of defections
(b) Terms and conditions of the associate status of Sikkim
(c) Details regarding the territories of the newly created state of Mizoram and special provisions in respect of that state
(d) None of the above

8. Which one of the following is the act of God?
(a) Rainfall (b) Flood
(c) Storm (d) All of these

9. According to Chen, "Recognition is both a declaration of fact and an expression of intention to enter into political relations with the power recognised. As a declaration of fact, it is both irrevocable and incapable of being subject to conditions and as an expression of the intention to enter in to political relations, it is both revocable and capable of being subject to conditions."
Which theory of international law holds the above view?
(a) Consent Theory
(b) Natural Law Theory
(c) Constitutive Theory
(d) Evidentory Theory

10. The Inter-State Councils are appointed by the
(a) Vice-President
(b) Chief Justice of India
(c) Prime Minister
(d) President

11. Which one of the following is not a financial power of State Council of Ministers?
1. Formulating the budget proposals and presenting the same to the State Legislature for approval.
2. All proposals for taxation emanate from the State Council of Ministers.
3. Regulating the Contingency Fund of the State and advancing money out of it to meet the unforeseen contingencies.

Select the correct answer using the codes given below:
(a) 2 (b) 2 and 3
(c) 1 (d) 3

12. The provision for the establishment of the Inter-State Council has been made by the
(a) Constitution (b) Parliament
(c) Cabinet (d) None of these

13. Which of the following could be said to 'fail' the test of mutuality of obligation?
(a) The contract says that the employer will provide work when it chooses to and the employee can refuse that work any time, for any reason,

although in practice the employer offers work less often to workers who turn down offers of work.
(b) There is no express contractual requirement of the employer to provide work or of the worker to accept it, but the employer consistently provides the same amount of supplies each week and expects to pick up roughly the same number of completed products each week.
(c) The contract declares that the parties have no mutual obligations, but the worker will be disciplined for not coming in to work, and the employer has never failed to have work available.
(d) The contract denies that the employer has any obligation to provide work, and indicates that the worker can turn down work, but requires that the worker be available for possible work during specific periods of time.

14. India is known as a parliamentary democracy because
(a) The President is not a member of the Parliament
(b) The members of Parliament are directly elected by the people
(c) The executive is responsible to the Parliament
(d) The powers have been clearly distributed between the Centre and the States

15. An agreement in restraint of marriage is void, if restraint is
(a) Absolute or partial
(b) Absolute
(c) Partial
(d) None of above

16. When can the President establish an Inter-State Council?
(a) When the Governor of a State asks for it
(b) During an emergency
(c) At his sweet will
(d) If at any time it appears to the President: that the public interests would be served by the establishment of an Inter-State Council he can establish the same

17. The essentials of an act of state are
(a) The act is done by the representative of a state
(b) The act is injurious to some other state or its subjects
(c) The act may be either previously sanctioned or subsequently ratified by the state
(d) All of the above

18. Under which of the following Articles the provision for Inter-State Councils has been made?
(a) Article 163 (b) Article 170
(c) Article 263 (d) Article 363

19. A workman is employed in a salt mine. While returning home finishing his work has to go by a public path, then through a sandy area in the open public and finally across a creek through a ferry boat. The workman while crossing the creek in a public ferry boat
(a) can be said to be working in the course of employment
(b) cannot be said to be working in the course of employment
(c) is fully within the concept of course of employment
(d) can partly be said to be working in the course of employment

20. International Covenant on Civil and Political Rights was adopted by the General Assembly of the United Nations on

(a) 15 August 1965
(b) 16 December 1967
(c) 16 December 1966
(d) 14 June 1966

21. The States Reorganisation Act, 1956 divided the entire country into
(a) 22 States and 9 Union territories
(b) 14 States and 6 Union territories
(c) 17 States and 7 Union territories
(d) Four categories of states

22. Which one of the following is the function of an Inter-State Council?
(a) Investigating and discussing subjects in which some or all of the States or the Union and States have a common interest
(b) Making recommendations upon any subject and for the better co-ordination of the policy and action with respect to that subject
(c) Inquiring into and advising upon disputes which may have arisen between States
(d) All of the above

23. Western Zone consists of
(a) Maharashtra, Gujarat, Karnataka, Goa, Daman Diu, Dadra and Nagar Haveli
(b) Maharashtra, Gujarat, Karnataka, Goa and Nagar Haveli
(c) Maharashtra, Madhya Pradesh, Gujarat, Karnataka and Goa
(d) None of the above

24. Dismissal, removal or reduction in rank of persons employed in civil capacities under the Union of a State has been stated under Article
(a) 309 (b) 310
(c) 311 (d) 312

25. Which one of the following is not a function of the Zonal Councils?
(a) To remove evils of linguism, regionalism, etc.
(b) To establish common police force
(c) To promote the idea of mutual co-operation
(d) To promote the idea of co-ordination in the developmental projects in the region

26. In which one of the following cases the Supreme Court of India while considering the International Convention on Civil and Political Rights have said—The positive commitment of the State parties ignites legislative action at home but does not automatically make the covenant enforceable part of the *corpusjuris* of India?
(a) Luther Vs Sagor
(b) Jolly George Vs The Bank of Cochin
(c) Maghanbhai Ishwarbhai Patel Vs Union of India
(d) None of these

27. A finds B's purse and gives it back to him; B promises A to give ₹ 50. This is a/an
(a) Agreement (b) Contract
(c) Acceptance (d) Offer

28. Which of the following functions is performed by the Zonal Council?
(a) Can decide the mutual disputes in a peaceful and friendly atmosphere
(b) Can co-ordinate their activities regarding the establishment of law and order and to meet any threat to the region
(c) Work for the planned and co-ordinated economic development of the region by pooling their resources
(d) All of the above

29. Which of the following is represented in the Rajya Sabha?
(a) Andaman and Nicobar Islands
(b) Dadra and Nagar Haveli
(c) Arunachal Pradesh
(d) All of the above

30. Match List-I with List-II and select the correct owner from the given codes.

List I

A. Right against exploitation
B. Right to freedom of religion
C. Cultural and educational right
D. Right to constitutional remedies

List II

1. Arts. 23-24 2. Arts. 25-28
3. Arts. 29-30 4. Arts. 32-35

Codes:	A	B	C	D
(a)	2	3	1	4
(b)	1	2	3	4
(c)	4	3	2	1
(d)	2	3	4	1

31. Which one of the following is a leading recommendation of the Sarkaria Commission?
(a) Abolition of All India Services
(b) Activation of Zonal Councils
(c) Drastic changes in the present division of functions between the Finance Commission and Planning Commission
(d) Abolition of Zonal Councils

32. The rule of absolute liability was first laid down by
(a) Lord Atkin in 1635
(b) C.J. Holt in 1868
(c) Winfield in 1765
(d) J. Blackburn in 1868

33. When an agent commits a tort in the course of performance of his duty as an agent, the liability of the principal arises for such a wrongful act. In such a case, which is correct about the plaintiff?
(a) He can sue the agent
(b) He can sue the principal
(c) He can sue both of them
(d) All of the above

34. The following States were created after 1960. Arrange them in ascending chronological order of their formation
I. Haryana II. Sikkim
III. Nagaland IV. Meghalaya
Select the correct answer using the codes given below:
(a) II, III, IV and I
(b) III, I, IV and II
(c) I, II, III and IV
(d) II, IV, I and III

35. Which State enjoys the distinction of being the latest State of the Indian Union?
(a) Sikkim (b) Telangana
(c) Nagaland (d) Uttarakhand

36. Employers of independent contractors, unlike those employing servant are
(a) sometimes liable for the collateral negligence of their contractors
(b) very often liable for the collateral negligence of their contractors
(c) never liable for the collateral negligence of their contractors
(d) always liable for the collateral negligence of their contractors

37. Which section of Indian Contract Act defines consideration?
(a) Section 2(a) (b) Section 2(b)
(c) Section 2(c) (d) Section 2(d)

38. The first commission appointed by the government in 1948 to examine the case for the reorganisation of States on a linguistic basis was headed by
(a) Justice S.K. Dhar
(b) Justice Wanchoo
(c) Justice M.C. Mahajan
(d) None of the above

39. Under which of the following Acts was the Federal Public Service Commission created?
(a) Indian Councils Act, 1861
(b) Government of India Act, 1935
(c) Indian Councils Act, 1909
(d) None of these

40. Degrees of prohibited relationship include relationship by

(a) full blood
(b) adoption
(c) half or uterine blood
(d) All of the above

41. In Bridges vs. Hawkesworth, the finder was allowed to keep the goods on the ground that
(a) if given to the owner, it would amount to unjust enrichment
(b) the owner of the shop was not traceable
(c) the owner of the shop was not aware of the fact that the item was in his shop
(d) the item was found in an area where public is admitted and the finder was one among them

42. Which of the following States were initially given status of autonomous States and subsequently made full fledged States?
(a) Meghalaya and Sikkim
(b) Assam and Bihar
(c) Meghalaya and Jammu & Kashmir
(d) Nagaland and Assam

43. If a wrong is committed by a servant
(a) The liability of master and servant is joint
(b) The liability of master and servant is several
(c) The liability of master and servant is joint and several
(d) None of the above

44. The famous JVP Committee consisting of Jawaharlal Nehru, Vallabhbhai Patel and Pattabhi Sitaramayya was appointed by the Indian National Congress in December 1948 to
(a) Determine the compensation to be paid to rulers of Indian States consequent to the merger of their States with India
(b) Examine the case of establishment of secular polity in the country
(c) Examine the issue of reorganisation of States on linguistic basis
(d) None of the above

45. According to Hindu legal theory, origin of law is
(a) Dharma (b) Rita
(c) Divine (d) Shruti

46. Which one of the following is true about the defence of act of God?
(a) There must be working of natural forces.
(b) The occurrence must be extraordinary and not one which could be anticipated and reasonably guarded against.
(c) Both (a) and (b).
(d) None of these are correct.

47. A right which is protected by law but not enforceable is called
(a) Local right
(b) Imperfect right
(c) Unconstructive right
(d) Moral right

48. In India the relations between the Union and the States are regulated
(a) According to the provisions of the Constitution
(b) According to the parliamentary laws
(c) According to the directions of the President
(d) According to the well established conventions

49. Kelsen's theory is in some respects close to the theory of
(a) Bentham (b) Spencer
(c) Austin (d) Blackstone

50. Which of the following statements are not correct?

1. Res ipsa loquitur is used for the purpose of fixing liability based on strict liability.
2. Inference of negligence could properly be drawn in res ipsa loquitar.
3. Res ipsa loquitur dispenses with taking of evidence.
4. Res ipsa loquitur mostly favours defendant.

Codes:

(a) 1, 3, 4 (b) 1, 2, 4
(c) 1, 2, 3 (d) 2, 3, 4

ANSWER SHEET
PAPER—I

1. (d)	2. (d)	3. (c)	4. (d)	5. (d)
6. (a)	7. (b)	8. (d)	9. (d)	10. (d)
11. (d)	12. (c)	13. (c)	14. (b)	15. (a)
16. (d)	17. (d)	18. (b)	19. (c)	20. (b)
21. (a)	22. (b)	23. (c)	24. (c)	25. (c)
26. (b)	27. (b)	28. (c)	29. (b)	30. (b)
31. (a)	32. (b)	33. (c)	34. (a)	35. (b)
36. (d)	37. (b)	38. (d)	39. (c)	40. (a)
41. (a)	42. (b)	43. (a)	44. (a)	45. (b)
46. (c)	47. (c)	48. (c)	49. (d)	50. (c)

PAPER—II

1. (b)	2. (a)	3. (b)	4. (d)	5. (d)
6. (d)	7. (d)	8. (d)	9. (d)	10. (b)
11. (d)	12. (a)	13. (d)	14. (c)	15. (d)
16. (c)	17. (a)	18. (b)	19. (a)	20. (c)
21. (b)	22. (b)	23. (b)	24. (c)	25. (a)
26. (a)	27. (a)	28. (a)	29. (a)	30. (a)
31. (c)	32. (c)	33. (d)	34. (b)	35. (b)
36. (c)	37. (d)	38. (a)	39. (a)	40. (c)
41. (a)	42. (d)	43. (d)	44. (b)	45. (c)
46. (d)	47. (d)	48. (d)	49. (c)	50. (b)

PAPER—III

1. (a)	2. (d)	3. (c)	4. (b)	5. (b)
6. (c)	7. (a)	8. (d)	9. (b)	10. (c)
11. (d)	12. (a)	13. (a)	14. (c)	15. (a)
16. (d)	17. (d)	18. (c)	19. (b)	20. (c)
21. (b)	22. (d)	23. (a)	24. (c)	25. (b)
26. (b)	27. (b)	28. (d)	29. (c)	30. (b)
31. (b)	32. (d)	33. (d)	34. (b)	35. (d)
36. (c)	37. (d)	38. (a)	39. (b)	40. (d)
41. (c)	42. (a)	43. (c)	44. (c)	45. (c)
46. (c)	47. (b)	48. (b)	49. (c)	50. (d)

ATLANTIC TITLES FOR UGC-NET/SLET AND OTHER COMPETITIVE EXAMINATIONS

Commerce: For UGC-NET/SLET and Other Competitive Examinations (Objective Type Questions), *Atlantic Research Division*

Economics: For UGC-NET/SLET and other Competitive Examinations (Objective Type Questions), Third Revised and Enlarged Edition, *K.R. Gupta*

CAT Cracker: Quantitative Aptitude, *K.R. Gupta*

Education: For UGC-NET/SLET, (Objective Type Questions), 2nd ed., Revised, Updated and Enlarged, *Atlantic Research Division*

English: For UGC-NET/JRF/SLET (Paper II and III) and Other Competitive Examinations, (Objective Type Questions), Third Edition Revised, Updated & Enlarged, *R.S. Malik*

History: For UGC-NET/SLET and Other Competitive Examinations (Objective Type Questions), 2nd ed., & Enlarged Edition, *Atlantic Research Division*

Library and Information Science: For UGC-NET/SLET and other Competitive Examinations (Objective Type Questions), *D.K. Pandey*

Management: For UGC-NET/SLET and Other Competitive Examinations (Objective Type Questions), Second ed., Revised, Updated & Enlarged, *Atlantic Research Division*

Mass Communication and Journalism: For UGC-NET/SLET (Objective Type Questions), 2nd ed., Revised, Updated and Enlarged, *Atlantic Research Division*

Political Science: For UGC-NET/SLET (Objective Type Questions), *Atlantic Research Division*

Public Administration: For UGC-NET/SLET (Objective Type Questions), *Atlantic Research Division*

Sociology: For UGC-NET/SLET and Other Competitive Examinations (Objective Type), *Atlantic Research Division*

PREVIOUS YEARS' SOLVED PAPERS

Commerce: For UGC-NET/SLET/JRF Paper I, II, and III, Previous Years' Solved Papers, *Atlantic Research Division*

Education: For UGC-NET/SLET/JRF Paper I, II, and III, Previous Years' Solved Papers, *Atlantic Research Division*

English: For UGC-NET/SLET/JRF Paper I, II, and III, Previous Years' Solved Papers, *Atlantic Research Division*

Environmental Science: For UGC-NET/SLET/JRF Paper I, II, and III, Previous Years' Solved Papers, *Atlantic Research Division*

Geography: For UGC-NET/SLET/JRF Paper I, II, and III, Previous Years' Solved Papers, *Atlantic Research Division*

Graduate Aptitude Test in Engineering (GATE): Mathematics, Previous Years' Solved Papers, *K.R. Gupta*

Graduate Aptitude Test in Engineering (GATE): Physics, Previous Years' Solved Papers, *Atlantic Research Division*

History: For UGC-NET/SLET/JRF Paper I, II, and III, Previous Years' Solved Papers, *Atlantic Research Division*

Home Science: For UGC-NET/SLET/JRF Paper I, II, and III, Previous Years' Solved Papers, *Atlantic Research Division*

Library and Information Science: For UGC-NET/SLET/JRF Paper I, II, and III, Previous Years' Solved Papers, *Atlantic Research Division*

Management: For UGC-NET/SLET/JRF Paper I, II, and III, Previous Years' Solved Papers, *Atlantic Research Division*

Political Science: For UGC-NET/SLET/JRF Paper I, II, and III, Previous Years' Solved Papers, *Atlantic Research Division*

Public Administration: For UGC-NET/SLET/JRF Paper I, II, and III, Previous Years' Solved Papers, *Atlantic Research Division*

Sociology: For UGC-NET/SLET/JRF Paper I, II, and III, Previous Years' Solved Papers, *Atlantic Research Division*

Hindi: For UGC-NET/SLET/JRF, Paper I, II, and III, Previous Years' Solved Papers, *Atlantic Research Division*